T0305070

Business Risk and Simulation Modelling in Practice

For other titles in the Wiley Finance series
please see www.wiley.com/finance

Business Risk and Simulation Modelling in Practice

Using Excel, VBA and @RISK

MICHAEL REES

WILEY

This edition first published 2015

Registered office
John Wiley & Sons Ltd, The Atrium, Southern Gate, Chichester, West Sussex, PO19 8SQ, United Kingdom

For details of our global editorial offices, for customer services and for information about how to apply for permission to reuse the copyright material in this book please visit our website at www.wiley.com.

Library of Congress Cataloging-in-Publication Data

Rees, Michael, 1964–
Business risk and simulation modelling in practice : using Excel, VBA and @RISK / Michael Rees.
pages cm
Includes index.
ISBN 978-1-118-90405-3 (cloth)
1. Risk management–Computer simulation. 2. Risk management–Data processing. 3. Microsoft Excel (Computer file) I. Title.
HD61.R44 2015
658.15′50285554–dc23

2015019955

A catalogue record for this book is available from the British Library.

ISBN 978-1-118-90405-3 (hbk) ISBN 978-1-118-90403-9 (ebk)
ISBN 978-1-118-90404-6 (ebk) ISBN 978-1-118-90402-2 (ebk)

Cover Design: Wiley
Cover Image: ©iStock.com/Mordolff

Set in 10/12pt Times by Aptara Inc., New Delhi, India
Printed in Great Britain by TJ International Ltd, Padstow, Cornwall, UK

To my wife and children

Contents

Preface

This book aims to be a practical guide to help business risk managers, modelling analysts and general management to understand, conduct and use quantitative risk assessment and uncertainty modelling in their own situations. It is intended to provide a solid foundation in the most relevant aspects of quantitative modelling and the associated statistical concepts in a way that is accessible, intuitive, pragmatic and applicable to general business and corporate contexts. It also discusses the interfaces between quantitative risk modelling activities and the organisational context within which such activities take place. In particular, it covers links with general risk assessment processes and issues relating to organisational cultures, incentives and change management. Some knowledge of these issues is generally important in order to ensure the success of quantitative risk assessment approaches in practical organisational contexts.

The text is structured into three parts (containing 13 chapters in total):

- Part I provides an introduction to the topic of risk assessment in general terms.
- Part II covers the design and use of quantitative risk models.
- Part III provides an introduction to key ways to implement the repeated calculation steps that are required when conducting simulation, covering the use of VBA macros and that of the @RISK add-in.

The text has been written to be software independent as far as reasonably practical. Indeed (apart from an assumption that the reader wishes to use Excel to build any models), most of the text in Parts I and II would be identical whichever platform is used to actually perform the simulation process (i.e. whether it is VBA or @RISK). Thus, although some of the example files use Excel functionality only, and others use features of @RISK, essentially all could be readily built in either platform if necessary (there are a handful of exceptions): One would have to make a few simple formula changes in each case, with the tools presented in this text showing the reader how to do so. On the other hand, in the context of presenting data arising from probabilistic processes and simulation results, @RISK's graphical capabilities are generally more flexible (and quicker to implement) than those in Excel. Thus, for purposes of quality, consistency and convenience, many of the illustrations in the book use @RISK in order to show associated graphs, even where the model itself does not require @RISK *per se*. Thus, a reader is not required to have a copy of @RISK at that point in the text. Indeed, apart from when working with the examples in Chapter 13, there is no fundamental requirement for a reader to own a copy (or a trial version) of @RISK in order to gain value from the text. In fact, readers who wish to use other implementation platforms for the simulation itself may find many aspects of this text of relevance.

The choice to present both Excel/VBA and @RISK approaches serves a number of purposes:

- Whichever platform is used for the simulation, the core concepts, most of the modelling techniques and issues concerning process alignment and other organisational challenges are essentially the same. An integrated approach allows a reinforcement of some of the concepts from different perspectives, and provides a comparison between the possible implementation approaches whilst ensuring minimum repetition.
- Each platform has its own merits, so that in practice, some readers may need one approach whilst other readers would need another. In particular, not only is Excel essentially ubiquitous (and hence the implementation within Excel/VBA involves no additional cost), but also the range of possibilities to use Excel/VBA for risk modelling is larger than is often realised. For example, it is fairly straightforward to create random samples from over 20 probability distributions, and to correlate them. On the other hand, the use of @RISK can facilitate many aspects of the process associated with the building and communication of risk models and their results; in many organisation contexts, its use would be the most effective, flexible and transparent option, with the cost of the required licences generally being insignificant compared to the potential benefits and the investments being made (both in terms of participants' time and in terms of project investment budgets). The visual tools in @RISK also represent very powerful benefits from an organisational process perspective, where there is typically a large variety in the level of understanding of statistics and modelling within groups of participants.

The main content of each part and chapter is as follows:

- Part I introduces the need for risk assessment, its uses, the general process steps, possible approaches to risk quantification and the associated benefits and implementation challenges:
  - In Chapter 1, we discuss the use of risk assessment in many day-to-day situations as an informal activity that most people conduct naturally, albeit implicitly and informally. We also present some prominent examples of where risk management has failed in business-related contexts. We then discuss some general challenges to the implementation of formalised risk assessment processes, before presenting key drivers of the need for more structured, explicit and formal approaches in some contexts, especially in many business situations. Finally, we present the main uses and objectives of general risk assessment processes.
  - In Chapter 2, we cover general aspects of the risk assessment process, including tools to ensure that risk identification is appropriately thorough, the potential objectives and challenges in risk prioritisation, categories of risk mitigation actions, and some other selected process issues.
  - In Chapter 3, we present a variety of possible qualitative and quantitative approaches to risk assessment, including their core aspects and relative benefits. We discuss the more demanding requirements of quantitative aggregation or full risk modelling approaches, especially in terms of risk identification and risk mapping. We note the associated challenges when qualitative or non-aggregate approaches are used as a basis for the subsequent development of quantitative models.

  - In Chapter 4, we discuss the benefits of full risk modelling approaches, in relation both to risk register approaches to risk assessment and to traditional static (non-risk) modelling approaches to project evaluation and to general business analysis.
  - In Chapter 5, we discuss many challenges in implementing quantitative risk modelling, especially those that relate to issues of an organisational, incentive, cultural, process and communications nature. An awareness of these can be of great importance both to modelling analysts and to senior management who wish to implement risk-based decision-making processes and to install a more risk-aware culture within their organisations.
- Part II provides a detailed discussion of the design and building of risk models:
  - In Chapter 6, we present the key principles of simulation methods. We also cover the relationships between simulation and other numerical modelling techniques, such as sensitivity, scenario and optimisation analysis.
  - In Chapter 7, we discuss core aspects in the design of risk models. We highlight some important similarities between risk modelling and traditional static modelling, as well as covering some of the key differences. We also discuss issues that need to be addressed in order to align the modelling activities with those of a general risk assessment process, as well as issues faced when integrating risk assessment into existing models.
  - In Chapter 8, we cover statistical measures of risk and probability distributions, as well as the general topic of risk measurement using properties of distributions; this has general relevance for the use of distributions as inputs to risk models, and for the interpretation of simulation results.
  - In Chapter 9, we describe over 20 distributions and their uses; these are usually sufficient for most practical activities in business risk modelling, and are available both in @RISK and in Excel/VBA. We also discuss the approximation of distributions with each other, and the processes and possible frameworks to select an appropriate distribution to use.
  - In Chapter 10, we present methods to create random samples from the distributions discussed in Chapter 9; this is fundamental to readers wishing to use Excel/VBA approaches, whereas it is in-built as part of @RISK's distribution functions.
  - In Chapter 11, we discuss the modelling of dependency relationships that are specific to risk models, including techniques such as the use of conditional probabilities, parameter dependencies, scenarios, correlated sampling, time-series modelling and others.
- Part III presents practical methods to implement the repeated calculations of a model that is the hallmark of simulation methods. The advantages of presenting this topic at the end of the text include that the core concepts apply to whichever platform is used for the simulation, and that it allows readers to achieve a strong basis in the concepts and understand the possibilities that quantitative risk modelling may offer, without needing to necessarily become involved in the technical aspects of implementation. We initially focus on the "mechanical" aspects of each platform, which are presented in a step-by-step fashion within the context of a simple model. We aim for the early part of the discussion to be largely self-contained, focusing on the simulation process, rather than establishing a tight link into the subject of model design. This part of the text can be read essentially independently to the modelling techniques covered earlier. Nevertheless, in the later parts of the discussion, we do cover more general topics, and make links to the earlier text:
  - Chapter 12 presents the use of Excel/VBA. We discuss many aspects of simulation models that can be readily implemented in this approach, ranging from running basic

simulations to the creation of flexible ways to store and analyse results, generate correlated random numbers and increase simulation speed. A template model is provided, which contains the core functionality that would be needed in many cases; its use is explained with several example models. Although we show techniques that allow for the creation of reasonably sophisticated approaches to the design of risk models, the running of simulations and to results analysis, we do not attempt to replicate the functionality of an add-in, such as @RISK. Rather, where such functionality would be complex and time-consuming to implement in Excel/VBA, but is available within @RISK, we take the pragmatic view that for readers working in a business or organisational context (to whom this book is targeted), it would almost always be more effective to use @RISK in order to access this functionality, in order for them to be able to retain a focus on the core aspect of providing decision support.

- Chapter 13 covers the use of @RISK. By presenting it in the last chapter of the text, one can create a clearer comparison with Excel/VBA approaches, especially of its relative benefits. These include not only its sophisticated and flexible graphics capabilities, but also tools to rapidly build, experiment with and modify models, and to analyse the results. In addition, there is a larger set of distributions and parameters available, an ability to control many aspects of the simulation and random number selection, and to create dependency relationships. The chapter focuses on the core aspects of the software and on the features required to work with the models in this text, as well as being guided by the general modelling considerations that the author wishes to emphasise. Although it covers many topics, it does not intend to be a substitute or alternative to the software manual (which, at the time of writing, is approximately 1000 pages, as a pdf file). Nevertheless, in the latter part of the text, additional features that may be of importance in some specific practical situations are mentioned. These include functionality to fit distributions and time series to data, to conduct optimisation under uncertainty and to integrate Excel with Microsoft Project. The book was written when @RISK version 6.3 was the latest one available, so that new features may become available in the future (such as when version 7 is released). However, the fundamental concepts in risk assessment, risk model design and simulation modelling remain largely unchanged as such developments occur, and later software versions are generally fully backward compatible with prior ones, so that it is hoped that this text will nevertheless provide a useful guide to core functionality, even as future versions are released.

Readers who wish to review specific models that use @RISK may install a trial version (if they do not have, or do not wish to buy, a full version). Trial versions are fully functional but time limited, so that readers should ensure that the installation of any trial is appropriately timed. In particular, readers may choose to read (or skim) all of the text before installing the trial, and revisit relevant parts of the text afterwards. At the time of writing, trial versions are valid for 10 days and are available at www.palisade.com. Readers may contact Palisade Corporation directly who may – entirely at its discretion – be able to extend the duration of a trial. For the purposes of the models used in this text, it is sufficient to download @RISK Industrial; however, some features within this – whilst briefly mentioned in this text – are not required for the example files provided, so that the additional software associated with these features does not need to be acquired (in particular the SQL-related content used for the Library functionality, and Microsoft Project, are not required). Technical aspects of installation and licensing options for @RISK are not covered in this text. Please note that the author is totally independent of Palisade Corporation, and has no control over the availability (or not) of trial versions, so the above is (in theory) subject to change, although trial versions have been available for many years without issue.

As far as possible, we have aimed to present concepts in a logical and linear order, but also to remain practical and to introduce technical aspects only where they are genuinely needed, and not simply for their own sake. Due to the richness of the subject, this has not been possible to do perfectly. In particular, whereas the detailed discussion of simulation concepts and definitions of statistical terms is covered in Part II (Chapter 8), on occasion in Part I we make reference to some basic statistical concepts (such as averages or percentiles, or to probability in general), and also show some simulation results. It is hoped that readers will nevertheless be able to follow this earlier discussion; many will no doubt have some (at least limited) experience of such concepts that is sufficient to be able to follow it; if not, of course the option to read first (or selectively refer to) this later chapter is open to them.

About the Author

Michael Rees has a Doctorate in Mathematical Modelling and Numerical Algorithms, and a BA with First Class Honours in Mathematics, both from Oxford University. He has an MBA with Distinction from INSEAD in France. In addition, he studied for the Wilmott Certificate of Quantitative Finance, where he graduated in first place for course work and also received the Wilmott Award for the highest final exam mark.

Since 2002, he has worked as an independent expert in financial modelling, risk modelling and quantitative decision support, providing training, model building and advisory services to a wide range of corporations, consulting firms, private equity businesses and training companies. As part of his activities as an independent consultant, Michael worked closely with Palisade Corporation, the developers of the @RISK software, for which he is one of the world's most experienced instructors, having taught several thousand people in this area.

Prior to becoming independent, Michael was employed at J.P. Morgan, where he conducted valuation and research work, and prior to that he was a partner with strategy consultants Mercer Management Consulting (now Oliver Wyman), both in London, UK, and Munich, Germany. His earlier career was spent at Braxton Associates (a strategy consulting firm that became part of Deloitte and Touche), where he worked in London and as a founding member of the start-up team in Munich.

Michael is a dual UK/Canadian citizen. He is fluent in French and German, and has wide experience of working internationally and with clients with diverse cultural backgrounds. In addition to this text, he is the author of *Financial Modelling in Practice: A Concise Guide for Intermediate and Advanced Level* (John Wiley & Sons, 2008). He can be contacted at michael@michaelrees.co.uk or through the website www.michaelrees.co.uk.

About the Website

Please visit this book's companion website at www.wiley.com/go/reesbrsm for more information on the models discussed in this book.

To find the password, you'll need to answer the following question: what is the first word of the caption for Figure 8.8 in the book?

PART I

An Introduction to Risk Assessment – Its Uses, Processes, Approaches, Benefits and Challenges

CHAPTER 1

The Context and Uses of Risk Assessment

This chapter provides a general discussion about the uses of risk assessment. We start by describing some simple examples; these demonstrate that risk assessment is a natural process that is conducted by most people in day-to-day situations, albeit informally and often implicitly. We also present some prominent examples of risk management failures in business-related contexts. We then describe some contextual challenges in decision-making processes, including that of achieving an appropriate balance between rational considerations and intuition, as well as the presence of biases. In the latter part of the chapter, we present key drivers of the need for structured, explicit and formal approaches to risk assessment in some contexts, and present the main uses and objectives of such activities.

1.1 RISK ASSESSMENT EXAMPLES

This section presents some simple examples of the use of risk assessment in everyday situations. From these, we aim to draw some general conclusions, including that the conducting of risk assessment is quite natural to most of us (and not something unusual, in principle). Indeed, in situations that are fairly simple or that are encountered frequently, the process is usually implicit; our plans automatically incorporate some element of risk mitigation and contingency planning based on experience, without us being particularly aware of it. For situations faced less frequently (or where the situation does not closely fit a recognised pattern), the process is generally slightly more explicit.

We also aim to show that a risk assessment process – whether explicit or implicit – may result in modifications to original (base case) plans in several possible ways:

- It may result in no change to the underlying plan or project, but simply to the adaptation of targets or of objectives to make them more realistic or achievable, such as the addition of contingency, whether it be extra time, resources or budget.
- It may lead to moderate changes to the initial plan or project, by leading one to look for measures to respond to risks, such as mitigation or exploitation measures.

- It could result in more fundamental changes to the project, such as the requirement for it to be re-scoped or changed in a major way, or for completely new structural or contextual possibilities to be developed.

We also show that the results of the process often depend on personal judgement, rather than robust analysis and criteria. In particular, we typically make a number of judgements in ways that are neither explicit nor formalised, and these depend on our experiences, personal situations, preferences and biases. Although, in personal situations, we often have discretion as to which decision option or mitigation measure to implement, and the consequences are borne directly by us, in some cases, consultation and agreement with others may nevertheless be required.

1.1.1 Everyday Examples of Risk Management

The following describes some simple examples, each of which aims to demonstrate some of the above points.

When planning to cross a road, in normal circumstances, one first looks each way. This can be considered as risk mitigation behaviour that has been instilled in us since a young age, and has become a natural reflex: it is clear that the benefits of looking are significant when compared to the cost of doing so; the small investment in time and effort is easily outweighed by the reduction in the risk of having an accident. However, when the circumstances are a little different to normal (e.g. the road is particularly busy, or the traffic signals are broken), one tends to naturally take extra precautions: one may look more carefully than usual, or walk more cautiously. Under more unusual circumstances (e.g. if considering crossing a very busy multi-lane highway), one would tend to try to identify risks explicitly, and to reflect even more carefully on possible risk mitigation measures: if it had been foreseen in advance that one may face such a situation, one may already have put on sports shoes or a coloured reflecting jacket before setting out on the journey. If such precautions had not been taken, and time were available, one may return home in order to change into the appropriate shoes and jacket. One may even wish to be able to build a bridge, if only time and money would allow! However, if all of the possible mitigation approaches are judged insufficient, impractical, too costly or too time-consuming, one would consider whether to abandon the plan to cross, and thus to have to develop completely new options or to revise one's objectives and targets.

When planning a major business trip, one could simply book an air ticket for the dates concerned. On the other hand, one would often naturally consider (the risk) that the dates of the trip may need to be changed, and take this into account in some way. In particular, one may consider a range of possible options, each with different costs, benefits and risks:

- Buy (now) a non-flexible ticket: This would generally be the cheapest option but also would result in the whole investment being lost if the trip were rescheduled. As a variation, one may be able to buy trip-cancellation insurance (thus increasing the cost slightly): indeed, there may be a range of such insurance types available, at different prices, with different levels of reimbursement, and different general terms and conditions.
- Buy (now) a fully-flexible ticket: This would generally be a more expensive option than purchasing a non-flexible ticket, but at least trip-cancellation insurance would not be required, and the cost would have been fixed.

- Delay the purchase of the ticket until the dates are fixed with more certainty; at that future point, make a final decision as to whether to buy a fixed-date ticket at that point or to purchase one that is flexible, and possibly also with trip-cancellation insurance.
- One could think of an even wider set of decision options of a more structural nature that are fundamentally different to the originally planned actions, and which nevertheless aim to achieve the desired objectives; for example, one may conduct a series of video conferences coupled with electronic document sharing, instead of having an in-person meeting.

When planning a major building or renovation project (for example, of an old apartment that one has just bought), one may estimate a base budget for the works and then add some contingency to cover "unexpected" issues: these could include that materials or labour costs may be higher than expected, or that asbestos would be discovered in currently hidden (or inaccessible) wall or ceiling cavities, or that supporting structures would not be as solid as expected, and so on. This process would result in a revised figure that may be sufficient to cover the total project costs even when several of the risks materialise. If this revised budget is covered by available funds, one would presumably proceed with the project as originally conceived. However, if this revised budget exceeds the funds available, one may have to develop further decision options, such as:

- To continue the project as originally planned and "hope for the best" (whilst potentially looking for other possible mitigation measures, such as borrowing money from a family member if required, and taking in a lodger to repay the borrowings more quickly).
- To re-scope the project (e.g. use less expensive finishings).
- To restructure the project into phases (e.g. delay for several years the renovation of the spare bathroom until more funds are available).
- To cancel the project entirely.

When planning to travel from home to the airport, if one has already conducted such a journey many times, one would know from experience how much travel time to allow: this "base case" plan would implicitly already take into account to some extent that there may be unforeseen events that can materialise en route. In other words, the base plan would have some contingency (time) built in. On the other hand, where the journey is new (e.g. one has recently moved into the area), one may do some explicit research to estimate the base journey time, and then perhaps add some extra contingency time as well.

When planning a journey that will be undertaken with another person, each person's desired contingency time would typically be different to the other's: each will have different tolerances for risk, with both their perceived cost of excess waiting time (e.g. at the airport) and the implications to them of missing the plane being different.

Of course, in general, these informal processes can be very valuable; indeed they may often be sufficient to ensure than an adequate decision is taken. In other cases, they will be insufficient.

1.1.2 Prominent Risk Management Failures

Clearly, in both the public and private sectors there have been many projects in which significant unexpected delays or cost overruns occurred, most especially in the delivery of major infrastructure, transportation and construction projects. An example (chosen only as it appeared in the general press around the time of the writing of this text) was the project to deliver a tramway in Edinburgh (Scotland), which was due to cost around £400 million when announced in 2003, but rose to around £800 million by the date of project completion in 2014.

In fact, it is probably fair to say that most failures (and many successes) of risk management in business contexts are not publicly observable, for many reasons, including:

- They are of a size that does not impact the aggregate business performance in a meaningful way (even if the amounts concerned may be substantial by the standards of ordinary individuals), and the losses are absorbed within a general budget.
- They are not openly discussed, and the failure is not objectively investigated (nor the results made public).
- It is challenging to demonstrate that risks that did materialise could and should have been mitigated earlier: in other words to distinguish the "benefits of hindsight" from what should reasonably have been known earlier in the process.

However, occasionally there have been major cases that have been of sufficient size and public importance that their causes have been investigated in detail; some of these are briefly discussed below:

- The Financial Crisis. The financial crisis of the early 21st century led to the creation of a Financial Crisis Enquiry Commission, whose role was to establish the causes of the crisis in the United States. Although its report, published in January 2012, runs to hundreds of pages, some key conclusions were:
  - "… this financial crisis was avoidable … the result of human action and inaction, not of Mother Nature or computer models gone haywire. The captains of finance and the public stewards of our financial system ignored warnings, and failed to question, understand, and manage evolving risks."
  - "Despite the view of many … that the crisis could not have been foreseen … there were warning signs. The tragedy was that they were ignored or discounted."
  - "Dramatic failures of corporate governance and risk management at many systemically important financial institutions were a key cause of this crisis …"
- The Deepwater Horizon Oil Spill. In April 2010, the Macondo oil well being drilled in the Gulf of Mexico suffered a severe blowout, costing the lives of 12 men, and resulting in the spillage of millions of barrels of crude oil. This disrupted the region's economy, damaged fisheries and habitats, and led to BP's having to pay large sums in compensation and damages. A commission was set up by President Obama to investigate the disaster, its causes and effects, and recommend the actions necessary to minimise such risks in the future. The Report to the President, issued in January 2012, runs into several hundred pages. Some key conclusions include:
  - "The loss … could have been prevented."
  - "The immediate causes … a series of identifiable mistakes … that reveal … systematic failures in risk management."
  - "None of [the] decisions … in Figure 4.10 [Examples of Decisions that Increased Risk at Macondo while Potentially Saving Time] appear to have been subject to a comprehensive and systematic risk-analysis, peer-review, or management of change process."

- *Columbia* Space Shuttle. On 1 February 2003, space shuttle *Columbia* broke up as it returned to Earth, killing the seven astronauts on board. The Accident Investigation Board reported in August 2003, and showed that a large piece of foam fell from the shuttle's external tank on re-entry, which breached the spacecraft wing. The report also noted that:
  - The problem … was well known and had caused damage on prior flights; management considered it an acceptable risk.
  - "… the accident was probably not an anomalous, random event, but rather likely rooted … in NASA's history and … culture."
  - "Cultural traits and organizational practices detrimental to safety were allowed to develop, including … a reliance on past success as a substitute for sound engineering … [and] … organizational barriers that prevented effective communication and stifled professional differences of opinion."

1.2 GENERAL CHALLENGES IN DECISION-MAKING PROCESSES

This section covers some of the general or contextual challenges in decision-making processes, including that of achieving an appropriate balance between rational considerations and intuition, as well as the possibility of the presence of a variety of biases.

1.2.1 Balancing Intuition with Rationality

Most decisions are made based on a combination of intuition and rational considerations, with varying degrees of balance between them.

Intuitive approaches are typically characterised, driven or dominated by:

- Gut feel, experience and biases.
- Rapid decision-making with a bias to reinforce initial conclusions and reject counter-narratives.
- Ignoring or discounting items that are complex or not understood well.
- Little (formalised) thinking about risks, uncertainties and unknowns.
- Little (formalised) decision processes or governance procedures.
- Lack of transparency into decision criteria and the importance placed on various items.
- Seeking input from only a small set of people, rather than from a diverse group.

At its best, intuitive decision-making can be powerful and effective, e.g. low investment nevertheless resulting in a good decision (generally). Indeed, justification for such approaches can be made using the framework of "pattern recognition"; that is, the decision-maker (typically subconsciously) views the particular situation being faced as being similar (or identical for decision purposes) to other situations that have been experienced many times before. Thus, such approaches are most appropriate where a particular type of situation is faced frequently, or where the consequences of a poor decision are not significant (or can be reversed), or in emergency situations where a very rapid decision is required. Examples include:

- Planning at what time to leave to travel to work in the morning, which may be based on many years of (non-documented) experience of using the same route.
- An experienced driver who is not overtly conscious of conditions on a road that he drives frequently, but is nevertheless making constant implicit decisions.

Of course, intuitive-driven approaches can have their more extreme forms: an article in *The New York Times* of 20 October 2013 ("When C.E.O.'s Embrace the Occult") reports the widespread use of fortune tellers by South Korean executives facing important decisions.

Rational approaches can be contrasted with intuitive ones, and are characterised by:

- Non-reliance on personal biases.
- Strong reliance on analysis, models and frameworks.
- Objective, holistic and considered thinking.
- Self-critical: ongoing attempts to look for flaws and possible improvements in the process and the analysis.
- Openness to independent review and discussion.
- Formalised processes and decision governance.
- Setting objectives and creating higher levels of transparency into explicit decision criteria.
- A desire to consider all factors that may be relevant, to incorporate alternative viewpoints, the needs of different stakeholders, and to achieve diverse input from various sources.
- Explicitly searching out more information, a wide variety of diverse inputs and the collection of data or expert judgement.
- Openness to use alternative tools and techniques where they may be appropriate.
- Willingness to invest more in time, processes, tools and communication.
- Exposing, challenging, overcoming or minimising biases that are often present in situations where insufficient reflection or analysis has taken place.
- (Usually) with some quantification and prioritisation.
- (Ideally) with an appropriate consideration of factors that may lead to goals being compromised (risks and uncertainties).

Many decisions are made based on a combination of intuition and rational considerations; clearly formalised risk assessment is concerned in principle with increasing the rational input into such processes.

Intuitive approaches may be less reliable for decisions concerned with major investment or with very long-term implications; it would seem logical that no management team could genuinely have already had very significant experience with large numbers of very similar or identical projects over their full life cycle.

On the other hand, it is probably fair to say that intuition is generally the dominant force in terms of how decisions are made in practice:

- A course of action that "feels" wrong to a decision-maker (but is apparently supported by rational analysis) is unlikely to be accepted. Similarly, a course of action that "feels right" to a decision-maker will rarely be rejected, even if the analysis would recommend doing so; rather, in each case, invariably one would search for factors that have been incorrectly assessed (or omitted) from the rational approach. These may include important decision criteria that were overlooked, or other items that a team conducting the analysis was not aware of, but which were relevant from a decision-maker's perspective.

- In most business situations, there will almost always be some characteristics that are common from one project to another (otherwise the company may be straying from its core competence), and hence intuitive processes have some role. As a result, even where the use of rational approaches would seem appropriate (e.g. major investments, expansion or restructuring projects), such approaches may not receive the priority and attention that they deserve.
- The rational approaches are more complex to implement, requiring higher levels of discipline, extra time and potentially other investments; intuitive processes require less effort, and match many people's inherent personal preference for verbal communication and rapid action. In this context, some well-known quotes come to mind: "Opinion is the medium between knowledge and ignorance" (Plato), and "Too often we enjoy the comfort of opinion without the discomfort of thought" (John F. Kennedy).
- However much rational analysis has been conducted, management judgement (or intuition) will typically still need to play an important role in many decisions: very few situations can be understood perfectly, with all factors or risks identified and correctly captured. For example, some qualitative factors may not have been represented in the common terms required for a quantitative model (i.e. typically in financial terms). In addition, and as a minimum, there will always be some "unknown unknowns" that decision-makers need to be mindful of.

Thus, ideally a robust and objective rational analysis would help to develop and inform a decision-maker's intuition (especially in the earlier stages of a decision process), and also to support and reinforce it (in later stages). Where there is a mismatch between the intuition of a particular decision-maker and the results of a rational analysis, in the first instance, one may look for areas where the rational analysis is incomplete or based on incorrect assumptions: there could be factors that are important to a decision-maker that an analytic-driven team is not aware of; ideally these would be incorporated as far as possible in revised and more robust rational analysis. On the other hand, there may be cases where even once such factors are included, the rational and intuitive approaches diverge in their recommendations. This may lead one to be able to show that the original intuition was incorrect and also to the drivers of this; of course, generally in such cases, there may be extra rounds of communication that are required with a decision-maker to explain the relevant issues. In other words, genuinely rational and objective analysis should be aligned with intuition, and may serve to modify understanding and generate further intuition in parallel.

1.2.2 The Presence of Biases

The importance of intuitive decision-making, coupled with the presence of potential biases, will create yet more challenges to the implementation of rational and disciplined approaches to risk assessment. Biases may be thought of as those that are:

- Motivational or political. These are where one has some incentive to deliberately bias a process, a set of results or assumptions used.
- Cognitive. These are biases that are inherent to the human psyche, and often believed to have arisen for evolutionary reasons.
- Structural. These are situations where a particular type of approach inherently creates biases in the results, as a result of the methodology and tools used.

Motivational or political biases are common in many real-life decision situations, often resulting in optimistic scenarios being presented as a base case, or risks being ignored, for many reasons:

- The benefits and cost may not have unequal or asymmetric impacts on different entities or people. For example, project implementation may allow (or require) one department to expand significantly, but may require another to be restructured.
- "Ignorance is bliss." In some cases, there can be a lack of a willingness to even consider the existence of risks. There are certainly contexts in which this reluctance may be justified (in terms of serving a general good): this would most typically apply where the fundamental stability of a system depends on the confidence of others and credibility of actions, and especially where any lack of confidence can become detrimental or self-fulfilling. In such cases, the admission that certain risks are present can be taboo or not helpful. For example:
  - A banking regulator may be reluctant to disclose which institutions are most at risk from bankruptcy in the event of a severe economic downturn. The loss of confidence that may result could produce a run on the bank, in a self-fulfilling cycle (in which depositors withdraw their money due to perceived weakness, which then does weaken the institution in reality, and also may have a knock-on effect at other institutions).
  - A central bank (such as the European Central Bank) may be unwilling to publicly admit that certain risks even exist (for example, the risk of a currency break-up, or of one country leaving the eurozone).
  - Generally, some potential credit (or refinancing) events may be self-fulfilling. For example, a rumour (even if initially false) that a company has insufficient short-term funds to pay its suppliers may lead to an unwillingness on the part of banks to lend to that company, thus potentially turning the rumour into reality.
  - A pilot needing to conduct an emergency landing of an aeroplane will no doubt try to reassure the passengers and crew that this is a well-rehearsed procedure, and not focus on the risks of doing so. Any panic within the passengers could ultimately be detrimental and hinder the preparations for evacuation of the aircraft, for example.
- Accountability and incentives. In some cases, there may be a benefit (or perceived benefit) to a specific party of underestimating or ignoring risks. For example:
  - In negotiations (whether about contracts, mergers and acquisitions or with suppliers), the general increased information and transparency that is associated with admitting specific risks exist could be detrimental (to the party doing so).
  - Many publicly quoted companies are required to make a disclosure of risks in their filing with stock market regulators. Generally, companies are reluctant to provide the information in any more detail than is mandated, in order not to be perceived as having a business that is more risky than competitors; a first-mover in such disclosure may end up with a consequential drop in share price. Therefore, such disclosures most typically are made at a very high level, are rather legalistic in nature and generally do not allow external analysts to truly understand or model risks in the business in practice.
- "Don't worry, be happy" (or "We are too busy to (definitely) spend time considering things that may never happen!" or "You are always so pessimistic!"). In a similar way to the "ignorance is bliss" concept, since identified risks are only potential, and may never happen, there is often an incentive to deny that such risks exist, or that they are not material, or to insist that they can be dealt with on an *ad hoc* basis as they arise. In particular, due to implementation time and other factors, it is often the case that accountability is only

considered at much later points in time (perhaps several years); by which time the truly accountable person has generally moved to a different role, been promoted, or retired. In addition, defenders of such positions will be able to construct arguments that the adverse events could not have been foreseen, or were someone else's responsibility, or were due to non-controllable factors in the external environment, and so on. Thus, it is often perceived as being more beneficial to deny the existence of a problem, or claim that any issues would in any case be resolvable as they arise. For example:

- A senior manager or politician may insist that a project is still on track despite some indications to the contrary, although the reality of the poor outcome is only likely to be finally seen in several years or decades.
- A manager might not admit that there is a chance of longer-term targets being missed or objectives not being met (until such things happen).
- A project manager might not want to accept that there is a risk of a project being delivered late, or over budget, or not achieving its objectives (until the events that provoke it actually occur).
- Management might not want to state that due to a deterioration in business conditions there is a risk that employees will be made redundant (until it actually happens).
- A service company bidding for a contract against an established competitor may claim that they can provide a far superior level of service at a lower cost (implicitly ignoring the risks that this might not be achievable). Once the business has been secured, then "unexpected" items start to occur, by which time it is too late to reverse the contract award. Unless the negotiated contracts have clear service-level agreements and penalty clause elements that are adequate to compensate for non-delivery on promises, such deliberate "low balling" tactics by potential suppliers may be rational; on the other hand, if one bids low and is contractually obliged to keep to that figure, then a range of significant difficulties could arise, so that such tactics may not be sensible.
- Often clauses may exist in contracts that would only apply in exceptional circumstances (such as if consequential damages may be sued for if a party to the contract delivers a performance that is materially below expectations). During contract negotiations, one or other party to the contract may insist that the clause should stay in the contract, whilst maintaining that it would never be enforced, because such circumstances could not happen.

Specific examples that relate to some of the above points (and occurred during the time at which this book was in the early stages of its writing) could be observed in relation to the 2012 Olympic Games in London:

- The Games were delivered for an expenditure of approximately £9bn. The original cost estimate submitted to the International Olympic Committee was around £2bn, at a time when London and Paris were in competition to host the games. Shortly after the games were awarded to London in July 2005, the budget estimate was revised to closer to £10bn, resulting (after the Games) in many media reports stating that they were "delivered within budget". Some of the budget changes were stated as being due to heightened security needs following a major terrorist attack that occurred in London shortly after the bid was awarded (killing over 50 people). Of course, one can debate such reasons in the context of the above points. For example, the potential terrorist threat was already quite clear following the Madrid train bombings of 11 March 2004 (which killed nearly 200 people), the invasion of Iraq in 2003, and the attacks in the United States of 11 September 2001, to name a few examples; security had also been a highly visible concern during the 2004 Athens Olympics. An external observer may hypothesise that perhaps a combination of factors each played a role to some extent, including the potential that the original bid was biased downwards, or that the original cost budget had been estimated highly inaccurately. In any case, one can see the difficulty associated with assigning definitive responsibility in retrospect, and hence the challenge in ensuring that appropriate decisions are taken in the first place.

- A private company had been contracted by the UK government to provide the security staff for the Games; this required the recruitment and training of large numbers of staff. Despite apparently having provided repeated reassurances that the recruitment process for the staff was on track for many months, at the last minute (in the weeks and days before the Games) it was announced that there was a significant shortfall in the required staff, so that several thousand soldiers from the UK Armed Forces were required to step in. An external observer may hypothesise that the private company (implicitly by its actions) did not perceive a net benefit to accepting or communicating the existence of the risk of non-delivery until the problem became essentially unsolvable by normal means.

Cognitive biases are those that are often regarded as resulting from human beings' evolutionary instinct to classify situations into previously observed patterns, which provides a mechanism to make rapid decisions (mostly correctly) in complex or important situations. These include:

- Optimism. The trait of optimism is regarded by many experts as being an important human survival instinct, and generally inherent in many individual and group processes.
- Bias to action. Management rewards (both explicit and implicit) are often based on the ability to solve problems that arise; much rarer is to create rewards around lack of action, or for the taking of preventive measures. The bias to action rather than prevention (in many management cultures) can lead to lack of consideration of risks, which are, after all, only potential and not yet tangibly present.
- Influence and overconfidence. This refers to a belief that we have the ability to influence events that are actually beyond our control (i.e. that are essentially random). This can lead to an overestimation of one's ability to predict the future and explain the past, or to an insufficient consideration of the consequences and side effects. A poor outcome will be blamed on bad luck, whereas a favourable one will be attributed to skill:
  - A simple example would be when one shakes dice extra hard to try to achieve certain numbers.
  - People may make rapid decisions about apparently familiar situations, whereas in fact some aspect may be new and pose significant risks.
  - Arguably, humans are reasonable at assessing the effects of, and managing, individual risks, but much less effective at assessing the effects and combinations when there are multiple risks or interdependencies between them, or where the behaviour of a system (or model) output is of a non-linear nature as its input values are altered.
- Anchoring and confirmation. This means that the first piece of information given to someone (however misleading) tends to serve as a reference point, with future attitudes biased to that point. New information becomes selectively filtered to tend to try to reinforce

the anchor and is ignored or misinterpreted if the information does not match the pre-existing anchor. One may also surmise that many educational systems (especially in the earlier and middle years) emphasise the development of students' ability to create a hypothesis and then defend this with logic and facts, with at best only a secondary focus on developing an enquiring mind that asks why an analysis or hypothesis may be wrong. The bias of confirmation describes that there is typically more focus on finding data that confirm a view than in finding data to disprove or question it.

- Framing. This means the making of a different decision based on the same information, depending on how the situation is presented. Typically, there is a different behaviour when faced with a gain versus when faced with a loss (one is more often risk seeking when trying to avoid losses, and risk averse when concerned with possible gains):
  - A consumer is generally more likely to purchase an item that is reduced in price from $500 to $400 (that is, to "save" $100), than to purchase the same item if it had always been listed at $400.
  - An investor may decide to retain (rather than sell) some shares after a large fall in their value, hoping that the share price will recover. However, when given a separate choice as to whether to buy additional such shares, the investor would often not do so.
  - Faced with a decision whether to continue or abandon a risky project (after some significant investment has already been made), a different decision may result depending on whether the choice is presented as: "Let's continue to invest, with the possibility of having no payback" (which is more likely to result in the project being rejected) or "We must avoid getting into a situation where the original investment was wasted" (which is more likely to result in a decision to continue).
  - Framing effects also apply in relation to the units that are used to present a problem. For example, due to a tendency to think or negotiate in round terms, a different result may be achieved if one changes the currency or units of analysis (say from $ to £ or €, or from absolute numbers to percentages).
- Incompleteness. Historical data are inherently incomplete, as they reflect only one possible outcome of a range of possibilities that could have occurred. The consequence is that (having not observed the complete set of possible outcomes) one assumes that variability (or risk) is lower than it really is. A special case of this (sampling error) is survivorship bias (i.e. "winners" are observed but "losers" are not). For example:
  - For stock indices, where poorly performing stocks are removed from the index to be replaced by stocks that have performed well, the performance of the index is overstated compared to the true performance (which should use the original basket of stocks that made up the index, some of which may now be worthless).
  - Similarly, truly catastrophic events that could have wiped out humanity have not yet occurred. In general, there can be a failure to consider the possible extremes or situations that have never occurred (but could do so in reality), specifically those associated with low probability, large impact events. Having said that (as discussed in Chapter 2) the consideration and inclusion in analysis of truly rare events (especially those that are, in principle, present in any project context, such as an asteroid destroying life on the planet) are probably in general not relevant to include in project and business risk assessments, or for management decision-making.
- Group think. A well-functioning group should, in principle, be able to use its diversity of skills and experience to create a better outcome than most individuals would be able to. However, very often, the combination of dominant characters, hierarchical structures, an

unwillingness to create conflict, or a lack of incentive to dissent or raise objections, can instead lead to poorer outcomes than if decisions had been left to a reasonably competent individual. The fact that individual failure is often punished, whereas collective failure is typically not, provides a major incentive for individuals to "go with the pack" or resort to "safety in numbers" (some argue this provides part of the explanation for "bubbles" and over-/underpricing in financial markets, even over quite long time periods).

Structural biases are where particular types of approach inherently create bias in the results, independently of psychological or motivational factors. An important example is a static model populated with most likely values that will, in general, not show the most likely value of the true output range (the "fallacy of the most likely", as discussed in Chapter 4). Key driving factors for this include non-symmetric distributions of uncertainty, non-linear model logic or the presence of underlying event risks that are excluded from a base assumption. The existence of such biases is an especially important reason to use risk modelling; paraphrasing the words of Einstein, "a problem cannot be solved within the framework that created it", and indeed the use of probabilistic risk techniques is a key tool to overcoming some of these limitations.

1.3 KEY DRIVERS OF THE NEED FOR FORMALISED RISK ASSESSMENT IN BUSINESS CONTEXTS

Generally, risk assessment will be useful where there is a significant level of investment (i.e. non-reversible commitments in money, time, resources or reputation), and where there is inherent uncertainty (as there usually is in any future situation). More specifically, the key drivers of the need for formalised risk assessment in business contexts include:

- The complexity of typical projects.
- The size and scale of the decisions, in terms of financial and other resource commitments.
- To provide support to the procedures required to identify and authorise mitigation actions, or to change project structures, and to assign responsibilities for executing the required measures.
- Corporate governance requirements, both in a formal sense relating to specific guidelines or regulations, and in the sense of optimising executive management and decision-making, i.e. to make decisions that are the best ones that can be made, are not just adequate, and create some competitive advantage.
- The frequent need to support decisions with quantified analysis.
- The need to be able to reflect risk tolerances in decision-making and in business portfolio design, and to be able to compare projects of different risk profiles.

These are discussed individually below.

1.3.1 Complexity

Clearly, as projects become more complex, the potential increases as informal or intuitive risk assessment processes become inadequate, with risks overlooked or underestimated. On the other hand, in some cases, an intuitive awareness that one may be underestimating risks may – in the absence of a more formalised process – be overcompensated by planning with excessive contingency or pessimism; this can also be detrimental (discussed further in Chapters 4 and 5).

The notion of complexity may take several forms:

- Technical complexity, or the level of specialist knowledge required. A business project will often involve issues of a technical nature that cannot be fully understood, dealt with or mitigated without the involvement of experts.
- Organisational complexity. The cross-functional nature of many business projects means that one must rely on inputs from a wide variety of people of different expertise. In some cases, there may also be third-party resources, contractors, partners or government departments involved.
- Interactions. Even where individual risks are identified and managed reasonably well using informal approaches, the possible effects of a large number of risks on the key aggregate metrics of project success (cost, time, quality, etc.) are hard to estimate by purely intuitive methods; this is even more the case when there are interdependencies between them, such as the knock-on effects on other project tasks if one particular activity is delayed. Such interactions can easily be overlooked, but – even where identified – their existence can make it more challenging to develop an understanding of the aggregate impacts of risks, and to correctly assess the value of various mitigation measures. Formal processes and the appropriate tools can help to address such issues in a more robust and transparent manner.
- Lack of previous experience with certain key elements. The more experience with similar situations one already has, the less is the level of complexity: if all elements of a project were essentially identical to those in many other already-implemented projects, then prior experience should be invaluable in designing projects and optimising their risk profile. On the other hand, where a project has non-standard components (e.g. in terms of technical, product, geographic, legal, regulatory, environment, team resources, or the requirement for the involvement for a wider than usual set of organisational departments), then there is a higher likelihood that it contains risks that may be overlooked or underestimated. Even where previous experience exists, an excessive reliance on it can have pitfalls because:
  - The time and place are different, and contextual circumstances are likely to have changed in some way.
  - The fact that risks did not materialise in earlier projects does not mean that they (the same or similar items) cannot happen in similar current projects.
  - It is easy to underestimate new factors that may be involved, unless proper consideration is given to trying to identify them. For example, a company may have successfully launched a new product in one European country and then finds that its launch in another country fails due to cultural, legal or local regulatory requirements that could have been anticipated and mitigated with a more formal assessment, including research and information gathering.

1.3.2 Scale

In practice, larger projects are typically more complex (or risky) than smaller ones, although this does not need to be the case, at least in theory. In addition, where a project is large (even if it is apparently "simple", such as the undertaking of a major construction project using a prefabricated template), then the consequences of the materialisation of an unforeseen risk may be too large to be absorbed within the available budget, whereas similar risks in smaller projects could be absorbed without undue attention. In this sense, of course, the concept of scale is a relative one, depending on the context and organisation concerned.

1.3.3 Authority and Responsibility to Identify and Execute Risk-Response Measures

Measures to respond to risk can include changes to project scope, structures, deliverables, timelines, budgets, targets and objectives. In many personal situations, the individual concerned can make decisions related to such topics without reference to others. In contrast, in organisations and businesses (and in some personal situations) such actions would almost always require authorisation from others, typically from more senior management. In addition, project collaborators within the organisation, as well as third parties (external agencies, contractors, etc.), may also be impacted by any changes. Therefore, significant communication, negotiation and coordination are often required. Indeed, even fairly simple or common-sense risk measures may require significant analysis in order to prepare the groundwork for formal authorisation processes. The particular contexts in which this is mostly likely include:

- If the benefits of risk-response actions are "external" or highly asymmetric, such as where the costs of risk mitigation are borne by one department, but the benefits may accrue to another department or project.
- If changes are required to organisational processes, budgets, targets, timelines, quality or other performance indicators, or to contractual or other relationships with third parties.
- If the identification of risks may potentially expose issues of a political or motivational nature, for example if problems are uncovered that should have already been addressed within normal work, or if a lack of expertise capability or competence would be highlighted.

In such contexts, formalised risk assessment processes will support the activities of a project team by creating robustness in the analysis, in the assessment of the cost–benefit trade-offs, and will increase objectivity and transparency.

1.3.4 Corporate Governance Guidelines

There is an increasing requirement for decisions within businesses to be supported by formal governance processes, particularly in publicly-quoted (listed) companies, where management is ultimately responsible to shareholders, and not to themselves. One may think of governance issues in two categories:

- Mandated governance requirements and guidelines.
- Processes that enhance general organisational effectiveness and competitive advantage (see later).

A complete description of published governance guidelines is beyond the scope of this text: their focus is typically on structured frameworks and processes to manage risk (especially operational risk) and less on the details of modelling issues and associated challenges. Here, we simply highlight a few examples from various contexts; the interested reader can no doubt easily find others by general internet or other searches:

- The UK Combined Code on Corporate Governance. This sets out standards of good practice in relation to Board leadership and effectiveness, remuneration, accountability and relations with shareholders. Certain listed companies are required to explain in their annual report and accounts how they have applied the Code. The Code includes the following (June 2010 edition):
  - "Every company should be headed by an effective Board, which is collectively responsible for the success of the company ... The Board's role is to provide entrepreneurial leadership within a framework of prudent and effective controls which enables risk to be assessed and managed ..."
  - "The Board should be supplied in a timely manner with information in the form and of a quality appropriate to enable it to discharge its duties. All directors should ... regularly update and refresh their skills and knowledge."
  - "The Board is responsible for determining the nature and extent of the significant risks it is willing to take in achieving its strategic objectives. The Board should maintain sound risk management and internal control systems."
- The Corporate Governance Council of the Australian Stock Exchange publishes Corporate Governance Principles and Recommendations (or Principles), of which Principle 7 concerns recognising and managing risk. Selected sections (2nd edition, 2010) state:
  - "Risk management is the culture, processes and structures that are directed towards taking advantage of potential opportunities while managing potential adverse effects."
  - "Companies should establish policies for the oversight and management of material business risks and disclose a summary of those policies."
  - "The Board should require management to design and implement the risk management and internal control system to manage the company's material business risks and report to it on whether those risks are being managed effectively. The Board should disclose that management has reported ... the effectiveness of the company's management of its material business risks."
- The Sarbanes–Oxley Act (2002) requires management to certify the accuracy of financial information of companies listed on US exchanges. The guidelines cover issues relating to risk assessment and internal controls, rather than management decision-making.
- A number of other organisations have provided guidelines, recommendations and standards relating to risk assessment and its methods. A few examples include:
  - The International Organization for Standardization (ISO) has published ISO 31000 Risk Management – Principles and Guidelines and 31010 Risk Management – Risk Assessment Techniques. The British Standards Institution (BSI) has published BS 31200:2012 Risk Management: Code of practice and guidance for the implementation of BS ISO 31000, and other works.
  - The Institute of Risk Management (IRM), the Association of Insurance and Risk Managers (AIRMIC), Alarm (the Public Risk Management Association) the Federation of European Risk Management Associates (FERMA) and the Committee of Sponsoring Organizations (COSO) each regularly publishes documents, such as COSO Enterprise Risk Management – Integrated Framework. Each provides guidance on risk

management processes and controls for management. The PRMIA (Professional Risk Managers' International Association) also publishes on a number of similar topics.

1.3.5 General Organisational Effectiveness and the Creation of Competitive Advantage

Of course, organisations will not succeed simply by following mandated guidelines: of utmost importance is the ability to create, identify and exploit opportunities that are aligned with strategy, create value and have some competitive differentiation. According to financial theory, in efficient markets, higher risks should be associated with higher returns only where such risks cannot be reduced economically efficiently or diversified away: the taking of risk *per se* is not rewarded. In contrast to many personal situations (for which the making of an "adequately good" decision is usually sufficient) organisations exposed to high levels of competition will need to perform to a superior standard, and to create opportunities, structure projects and make decisions that are (close to) the best possible ones available.

Formalised risk assessment can support effectiveness in these areas in several ways:

- Supporting the consideration of a full range of decision options.
- Helping to ensure that the opportunities being considered are value-creative and structured optimally.
- Ensuring that decisions are supported by robust rational analysis and data, and are appropriately transparent.
- Ensuring more transparent trade-offs and appropriate risk tolerances in decision-making.
- Reducing biases in analysis and in decision-making.
- Ensuring that project execution risks are appropriately considered within decision evaluation processes, as well as within the detailed implementation projects.

1.3.6 Quantification Requirements

Businesses almost always require that important decisions are supported with fairly detailed quantitative analysis. Risk assessment can be used to support this in many ways:

- Reflecting the reality that the situation inherently contains risk and uncertainty.
- Providing a structured process to ensure that all relevant factors are included in the analysis and quantitative model.
- Understanding the range of possible outcomes, and generating an understanding of how likely a particular (e.g. "base") case is to be achieved, and what modifications are required (e.g. to targets, inclusion of contingencies, implementation of risk-response measures, or development of new structural options).
- Enhancing the ability to compare projects with different risk profiles, and to support the development of optimal business portfolios.
- Allowing risk tolerances to be made explicit, reflected in decision-making and to be done in a way that is aligned with organisational objectives (see below for further discussion).
- Increasing transparency, reducing biases and supporting the achievement of the appropriate balance between intuition and rationality in decision-making.

1.3.7 Reflecting Risk Tolerances in Decisions and in Business Design

Robust decision-making in business contexts requires a consideration of risk tolerances:

- Corporate governance. Shareholder demands for appropriate risk taking (to create rewards for equity investors by taking appropriate risk) need to be reflected in decision-making and in project selection: in theory (and practice), some companies should be more risk seeking than others, but it would seem difficult for a company to appropriately manage its risk profile without knowing and measuring (quantitatively) how much risk is being taken. Instead, very often, such processes remain intuitive, non-transparent and elusive, and are likely to be suboptimal.
- Consistency. Without a formal consideration of risk tolerances, a decision that would be authorised on one occasion may not be authorised on another. Thus, in one instance a project that is high risk/high reward may be favoured over a lower risk/lower reward one, whereas in similar circumstances on another occasion the reverse would be the case. This may be due to the presentation or framing of the decision, or to short-term inconsistencies and fluctuating optimism or pessimism that occur in day-to-day behaviours when formal processes are not put in place.
- Business portfolio optimisation. Most businesses can be considered as portfolios of components (e.g. customers, geographies, projects or products). As such, there is an optimisation aspect to the appropriate business design and strategic choices, with an optimal portfolio consisting of a combination of components with different profiles, so that some elements balance out against others.

Given these drivers, the application of a formalised risk analysis process in many business situations is likely to create significant benefits in terms of the quality of the final decision.

1.4 THE OBJECTIVES AND USES OF GENERAL RISK ASSESSMENT

Risk assessment processes and tools are already widely used in some business contexts. Typical applications include general planning and forecasting (e.g. revenue and capital expenditure, financing needs), cost estimation and contingency planning, project schedule uncertainty, portfolio structuring and optimisation, valuation of the flexibilities associated with being able to respond to uncertain outcomes or of gaining additional information (such as real option analysis), and general decision-making under uncertainty. Such applications apply to essentially any sector; key examples include oil, gas, energy, resources, construction, pharmaceuticals, insurance, reinsurance and finance.

Of course, formalised risk assessment is much more than simply "expecting the unexpected" by identifying possible risk factors in advance. Ultimately, the overall objective is to enhance organisational performance through superior project design, selection, decision-making and management. In particular, the essential role of risk assessment is to support the development and choice of the optimal context in which to operate (operating within the best structural context, and mitigating and responding to risks within it in the best way), and to support the evaluation of a final decision within that context by taking into account the residual uncertainty and risk tolerances of the decision-maker. This may be achieved through more specific objectives, which are generally of several forms:

- Adapting and improving the design and structure of plans by managing, mitigating or exploiting uncertainties.
- Achieving optimal project structures and economically efficient risk mitigation.
- Enhancing decision-making concerning project evaluation, objectives and target setting, contingency planning and the reflection of risk tolerances within the decision-making processes.
- Managing project execution and implementation effectively.
- Constructing, selecting and optimising business portfolios.
- Supporting the creation of strategic options and corporate planning.

1.4.1 Adapt and Improve the Design and Structure of Plans and Projects

Perhaps the main role of risk assessment is to enhance a particular set of (original) plans to include risk mitigation, management or response measures:

- The identification of risks, and the generation of an understanding of their interactions, dependencies and likely significance, drives the identification and development of possible response actions.
- In this way, plans are improved, both reducing adverse risks and exploiting upsides (such as operational or strategic flexibilities), with such actions, and their effects, costs and benefits, being included in a revised plan.

Much benefit can often be achieved even when such processes are only of a qualitative nature, because key individual risks would nevertheless typically be identified, and some consideration of possible risk-response actions would be undertaken. However, quantitative approaches will provide a much larger set of benefits, as discussed later in the text.

1.4.2 Achieve Optimal Risk Mitigation within Revised Plans

When considering the structure of a project or plan, there are generally many possible risk-response measures available. Some risk items are more controllable (or exploitable) than others, and the cost of doing so will be different for each. For example, the variation in oil prices may be essentially uncontrollable (there may be possibilities to hedge or engage in forward contracts in the short term, but in the medium term the impact on a business is typically largely uncontrollable).

In general, one may prioritise and implement measures in some order driven by a cost–benefit analysis of each one, and after implementing some of them, one would arrive at a point where the use of further measures is not economically efficient. For example, the risk of having an accident when crossing the road is rapidly reduced when low-cost measures are implemented (such as looking each way, or perhaps wearing running shoes or reflective clothing) but in many cases it would not be economically efficient, or practical, to eliminate the risk entirely (by having a bridge built): the marginal risk reduction that would be achieved by such a measure cannot be justified by the marginal cost increase that would be needed to implement it.

There may also be interaction between any such measures, so that there may be some measures that would make (economic) sense in isolation, but would not make sense within the wider context of a set of measures. Indeed, whether a particular measure makes sense may depend on which other measures are implemented first.

Further, in practice, risk-response actions may also affect multiple metrics (or line items in a model), so that the making of the appropriate trade-off between them may be non-trivial.

Thus, although the choice of measures to implement could be considered as a quantitative optimisation problem, the use of such approaches in these contexts is usually limited by practical considerations; a mixture of judgement, pragmatic considerations and some basic quantitative analysis is usually sufficient to find a mix of measures that is (close to) optimal.

1.4.3 Evaluate Projects, Set Targets and Reflect Risk Tolerances in Decision-Making

Once the "risk-optimised" structure has been found, there is still generally residual risk; some risks will not be economically effective to eliminate, even where doing so would be possible. One is still exposed to potentially adverse outcomes, so that the ultimate outcome may not be satisfactory (of course, the chance of a satisfactory outcome should increase as a result of the risk assessment activities).

Nevertheless, it is still of fundamental relevance to understand the extent of residual (or non-controllable) risk that remains after all worthwhile measures (or decisions) have been implemented: the range of possible outcomes will help to establish whether to proceed or not with a particular decision, or to inform the process of modifying targets and setting contingencies. For example, before a decision is made, one may typically wish to know the average outcome, as well as the best or worst 10% of cases for key metrics (such as sales, cost, cash flow). Risk tolerances therefore come into play when the final decision is being made: one person may reject a decision that has a 10% chance of a significantly bad outcome (even if all other outcomes would be highly favourable), whereas another person may choose to proceed, in order to generally benefit from the mostly positive outcomes.

1.4.4 Manage Projects Effectively

Risk assessment also has a key role to play in project management and execution. For example, one may wish to analyse potential risks relating to the schedule, potential delays, specific cost items or on-specification delivery. To some extent, such activities are a continuation of those that may have been initiated at project design and conception: risk considerations relating to project execution should ideally be reflected in the earlier stages of conception and basic design; projects that are expected to be more complex to execute than others should be evaluated less favourably.

However, in practice it is not possible to fully take into account all project execution risks at the earlier stages of project conception:

- Very often, following authorisation, a much more detailed planning procedure is undertaken prior to (or as part of) the implementation: items such as detailed technical planning, obtaining quotes from several suppliers for all outsourced items, conducting contractor

negotiations, planning internal resources and making resource trade-off decisions can really only be conducted once decisions to proceed have been finally made.
- In the time period between the authorisation and the implementation of a decision, the external environment may have altered (such as a change in regulations issued by the government, or other risk events materialize, which alter the best possible future course of action). There may often be some change to the scope, or other changes that may have occurred.
- The project may inherently contain phases (or decision gates), where future activities within the project may need to be adapted as the project proceeds; examples include exploration, appraisal and development projects in the oil, gas and resource sectors, as well as in pharmaceutical development.

1.4.5 Construct, Select and Optimise Business and Project Portfolios

Most businesses are portfolios of activities or other elements in some way. For example, sales revenues are the sum of those of different product lines, regions, business units, customers, geographies, projects or assets. In general, the constituent components typically have different characteristics in terms of their implications for key business metrics, such as growth rates, capital investment requirements, project delivery timeframe, cost, cash flow, return on capital, etc. (as well as for their associated risks):

- Mature projects (or products that may be generating a fairly dependable stream of revenues or cash flow) may require little ongoing investment or development activity.
- Projects currently in the implementation phase may require significant amounts of cash investment: whilst not yet producing revenues, these may nevertheless be of medium risk, in the sense that future revenues and cash flow may be uncertain, subject to uncontrollable factors, or to overruns in capital expenditure, or to implementation delays.
- Projects in research or early-stage development may currently require fairly small investments, but their success or failure (and associated timeframe) may be crucial to the medium-term performance or to the long-term survival of the business; in that sense, these projects may be considered highly risky.
- There may also be existing joint ventures, potential acquisition possibilities, and so on; each will have its own specific risk profile for key metrics.

In addition, there will be some issues that are important at a corporate (or aggregate) level, even though such issues may be less relevant at the level of individual projects. For example:

- Generally, issues concerning corporate cash flow, financing, debt and equity structures, treasury and tax have to be dealt with at the corporate level, even though the aggregate corporate position is driven by individual projects.
- Although individual projects within a set of investment projects may appear to make sense on a stand-alone basis (for example, each may have a highly positive net present value, resulting from some initial investment and then a series of positive cash flows), in aggregate, the investment requirements for the full set of projects may be too high to allow them all to be implemented simultaneously. There could also be non-financial

constraints to their simultaneous implementation, such as technical expertise or material resources.

- Holding a portfolio of "high risk/high return" projects may be acceptable, even if – when viewed in isolation – each individual project would likely be judged as too risky. For example, a project with a 30% chance of success (creating a net gain of \$100m), and a 70% chance of failure (creating a net loss of \$10m), will have a positive (weighted) average net gain of \$23m (i.e. 0.3 × 100–0.7 × 10). On a stand-alone basis, one may wish to avoid the possibility of a \$10m loss; however, as part of a portfolio, the project may be acceptable:
  - As part of a mixed portfolio of stable cash-generative projects (whose cash flow could be used to cover the investment of the newer projects, or of any additional costs resulting from unexpected events), the single project may also be acceptable.
  - If the project were shared with partners, in order to reduce the effective investment and exposure to losses, one could still partly benefit from the average positive nature of the project whilst reducing the downside losses proportionally.
  - A large portfolio of similar but independent projects would be profitable not only on average, but also in almost all cases. For example, given 100 such projects, it is very likely that outcomes close to the average would be observed in most cases, i.e. close to 30 successes and 70 failures. Since the benefits of success easily outweigh the cost of failure, such a portfolio would be attractive in general, as success at the portfolio level is almost guaranteed (providing that there is financing available to cover early failures). Figure 1.1 shows the distribution of the number of successful projects, such as that in 77% of cases the number of successes is between 25 and 35 inclusive (the details of such analyses are discussed later in the text).

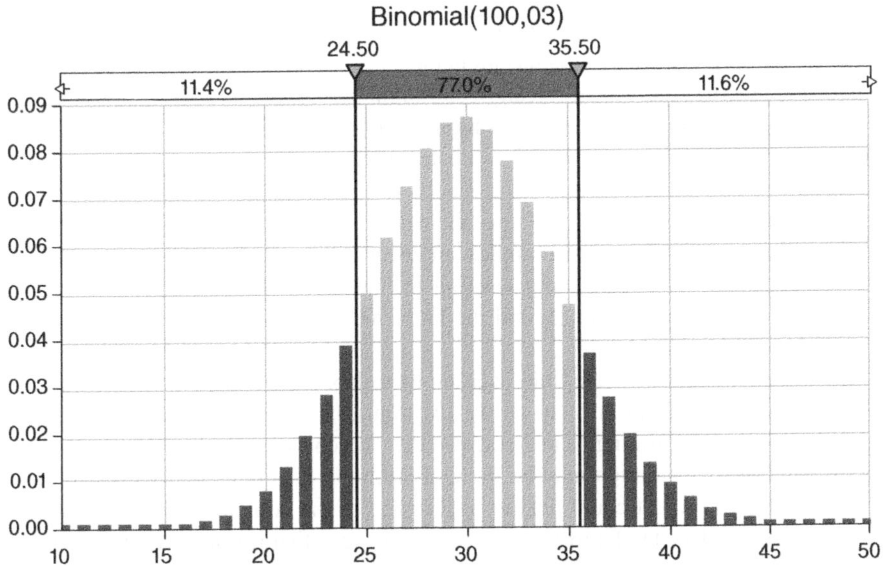

FIGURE 1.1 Number of Successful Projects out of 100, Each with Probability of Success Equal to 30%

Risk assessment (and uncertainty analysis) can have a number of applications in the construction, adaptation and optimisation of project portfolios, to help to ensure that business growth or other objectives are met:

- Identify, for any assumed portfolio, how likely it is that corporate objectives and targets would be achieved with that portfolio:
  - Identify whether new projects or different activities are required; this is related to the development of strategic options, which is covered separately below.
  - Understand the level of "natural diversification" within it: for example, where cash-producing projects can cover the financing of key investments, so that new calls to financing are not required at the corporate level.
  - Understand the level of residual uncertainty within the portfolio, to ensure it is appropriate and in line with risk tolerances. For example, equity investors generally expect that the business will take some level of risk, but one that is appropriate for its strategic positioning and which is in line with reasonable expectations for a business of that nature.
- Ensure that commonalities across portfolio elements are correctly evaluated:
  - Common risks could be related to technology, exchange rates, regulatory regimes, price levels, input costs, and so on. A risk that is common to all projects or business units may be important at the corporate level but may only appear to be of medium importance at the project or business unit level.
  - In general, dependencies between the portfolio elements need to be captured correctly in order to avoid either excess or insufficient diversification of the portfolio.
- Optimise project contingencies within a corporate context:
  - Individual project contingencies, when added up at the corporate level, could be significantly too high (or significantly too low), depending on the contingency level planned for each component (see Chapter 4).
  - The issue of balancing the amount of contingency to hold at the level of an individual item versus at an aggregate organisational level is perhaps one of the most challenging issues in practice, and has implications for organisation design (e.g. issues of centralisation and decentralisation), authorisation processes and project management.
- Have a framework to compare and evaluate projects with different risk profiles. For example:
  - It is clearly more risky to drill for oil in the sea bed of a new unexploited area, where the water is deep and complex engineering and technology is required, than to do so in shallow water using existing technologies: the first may be higher risk with potentially higher reward, and the latter may have lower risk with lower likely reward.
  - One decision could be preferable over another, depending on the context and criteria used: a higher risk option may sit well within a large portfolio of mature projects, where one may be aiming to use new projects to achieve growth objectives. A lower cost and lower risk option may be more appropriate if failure of a larger (potentially higher reward) project could lead to bankruptcy of the company, or if the company's (or its shareholders') risk profile or tolerance are such that it is not willing to take such risks for other reasons.
  - A risk assessment provides a framework to estimate the impact of each decision option and its possible outcomes, so that one can make a more informed and appropriate

judgement about which option is best (rather than perhaps relying mainly on gut feel, intuition or suboptimal simplifications).

As agents of shareholders, management should understand the corporate risk profile and behave in alignment with it: thus, residual risk exposure, shareholders' risk expectations and corporate risk tolerances should all be considered within the process of project evaluation, selection and portfolio construction. A project should be evaluated based not only on its individual merit, but also on its fit within the business portfolio, and on its contribution and effect on aggregate risk at the corporate level.

1.4.6 Support the Creation of Strategic Options and Corporate Planning

Generally speaking, the processes of strategy development and the creation of strategic options typically need to be addressed using open and creative approaches. The "changes of context" required to proactively conceive, generate or identify new structural or strategic options is typically of a different nature to the more reactive processes of risk assessment (in which generally the frame of consideration has been narrowed to some extent).

Nevertheless, risk assessment has some valuable uses in strategy development and corporate planning:

- To assess the range of possible outcomes (aggregate risk) in a portfolio of business projects.
- To set corporate and business unit targets and assess the likelihood of achieving them.
- To ensure, before selecting a final strategic option, that each has been risk optimised for its own context. For example, some options may have inherent flexibilities that are not present in others, and hence a fair comparison between the strategic options would need to properly take into account the value associated with these flexibilities (this is the topic of real options analysis, for which examples are provided later in the text).
- To assess the likelihood that current business and already-planned strategic initiatives will be sufficient (or not) to meet the company's objectives. This may identify whether further strategic, high-level or structural projects may be required to increase the likelihood of objectives being achieved.

As an example of the latter point, when using base case assumptions on project success rates, a base plan to grow revenues in the medium term through the development of new products may seem sufficient to meet the growth objectives. However, if the risk of failure or of potential delays in new product development processes is properly considered, then the base plan may, in fact, be shown to be inadequate in most cases. Thus, a company may be drawn to consider adding additional products to its portfolio, or adding new projects that are more likely to be able to be delivered in the shorter term, or to pursue acquisition, partnership or other opportunities. The consideration of such possibilities through quantitative modelling can, in fact, be fairly simple to implement at a high level (e.g. using summary figures for each key element of the portfolio, such as cash flow) whilst having major implications for the appropriate business structure and corporate planning activities.

As a specific numerical example, assuming that a company needs six successful projects to meet its business targets, where each has a 60% chance of success, then the initial plan may

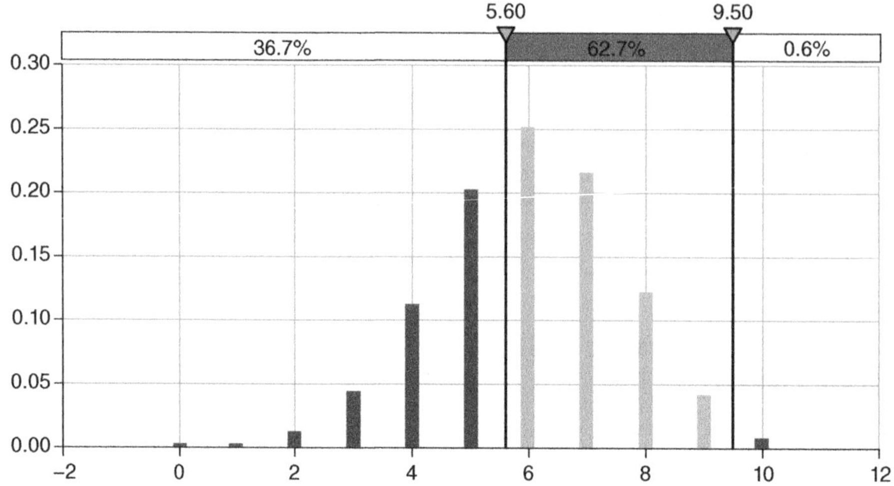

FIGURE 1.2 Number of Successful Projects out of 10, Each with Probability of Success Equal to 60%

be to conduct 10 projects (6/60%). This may appear to be a logical basis on which to base resource plans and make forecasts of future performance. However, such a portfolio would only be successful on average. Figure 1.2 shows the distribution of the number of successful projects; in particular, there is a 36.7% chance of five or fewer successes, i.e. that the targets would not be met.

If one wished instead for the chance of meeting the target (of six successes or more) to be 90% (10% chance of failure), then the number of projects would need to increase to around 13. This can be seen from the bottom table in Figure 1.3,which shows a sensitivity analysis of

	A	B	C	D
1				
2		**Initial Plan**		
3		No. Successes Required	6	
4		P(Success)	60%	
5		Estimated Number of Projects	10	=ROUNDUP(C3/C4,0)
6		Prob (Number of successes is less than required)	36.7%	=BINOMDIST(C$3-1,C5,C$4,1)
7				
8		**Revised Plan**		
9		Number of Projects	10	
10		Prob (Number of successes is less than required)	36.7%	=BINOMDIST(C$3-1,C9,C$4,1)
11		Prob (Number of successes is sufficient)	63.3%	=1-C10
12				
13		P(Six or More i.e. Success) Sensitivity Analysis to Number of Projects	**63.3%**	
14		10	63.3%	
15		11	75.3%	
16		12	84.2%	
17		13	90.2%	
18		14	94.2%	
19		15	96.6%	
20				

FIGURE 1.3 Number of Projects Required to have Six Successes, where Each has a 60% Probability of Success

the probability of having six or more successes depending on the number of projects engaged (once again, the detailed statistical concepts are covered later in the text).

The file Ch1.ProjectNumbers.xlsx contains the calculations in Figure 1.3, for the interested reader to explore further. Note that the assumption that each project would have the same probability of success may not be realistic in many practical cases; this provides one reason to use simulation methods to perform analogous calculations, as exact analytic solutions become harder to find in cases of unequal probabilities.

CHAPTER 2

Key Stages of the General Risk Assessment Process

In this chapter, we describe the stages of the risk assessment process, which apply whether qualitative or quantitative approaches are used. In particular, we describe some ways to bring structure into the risk identification process, criteria to consider at the prioritisation stage and the iterative nature of the process.

In Chapter 3, we discuss the implications of specific qualitative or quantitative approaches on this general process, and in Chapter 7 we discuss issues associated with the alignment of the process with risk modelling activities.

2.1 OVERVIEW OF THE PROCESS STAGES

The general stages of a risk assessment process are:

- Identification. This involves the identification and analysis of the key risks and uncertainties. A core aspect is that all main risks are identified, and are defined with the precision necessary to perform any further activities.
- Mapping. The mapping of risks involves describing risks and their impacts in a way that allows them to be reflected in quantitative models. It is a process step that is essentially not required when using qualitative approaches to risk assessment. It may be considered to be part of risk identification, in that – in order to generate a list of risks that are defined with sufficient accuracy to be included in a quantitative model – one may first have to map the nature of the risks in detail.
- Prioritisation. Some risks may need to be prioritised in order to highlight the required decisions, to facilitate general communication, to reflect cost–benefit trade-offs of risk-mitigation measures, or due to resource constraints (amongst other reasons). Prioritisation can be considered as being part of risk identification; the finalisation of the set of identified risks may require some prioritisation to have taken place, such as excluding risks that are deemed not worthy of further consideration.
- Mitigation and response. This involves adapting an original plan(s) to manage, mitigate and/or exploit risks. Generally, the activities will result in a set of risk-response actions, but they may also result in targets being reset or modified. There may also be new risks or

side-effects that result from the initial mitigation or response actions. It may also highlight the need for alternative structural (contextually distinct) decision options; in other words, for a major change in the context in which one is choosing to act, so that the full range of strategic and decision options is considered. The prioritisation of such actions is also a key area that needs consideration at this stage.

- Decision selection. The selection for implementation of a final modified plan or decision option would typically involve an analysis of the risks and uncertainties remaining (i.e. the residual risks that either cannot be managed or that cannot be done in a way that is economically efficient). The final selected option(s) should have a profile of residual risks that is in line with the risk tolerances of the decision-makers.
- Monitoring, management and controlling of project execution (and the risks therein). This will generally include the updating of risk assessment on an ongoing basis, or as appropriate to the context.

2.2 PROCESS ITERATIONS

In practice, risk assessment is not a fully "linear" process, but is an iterative one. In other words, one cannot simply move directly from one stage to the other without returning to stages that may be considered to be complete. The iterative nature of the process is due to several factors.

First, there may be inherent interactions between the process steps:

- Identification and mitigation. Generally, one would mitigate risks only after explicitly identifying them. However, many base plans have common-sense mitigation actions implicitly built into them, even before any formal risk identification has taken place. In addition, mitigation actions or risk-response measures may create new risks or uncertainties, due to side effects that need to be assessed, identified and possibly mitigated: for example, a measure to switch to an alternative technology or to involve additional third parties may create new risks.
- Identification and prioritisation. Generally, one can only prioritise risks after they have been explicitly identified. On the other hand, the final list of identified risks that would be used for general communication and project planning may exclude some very low probability items, or items that are contextual and common to all projects. Thus, risk identification can only be completed with some notion of prioritisation having taken place.
- Prioritisation and mitigation. Generally, one may develop mitigation actions according to risks that are deemed to be most important. On the other hand, a key approach to risk prioritisation is based on the effectiveness of their mitigation actions, rather than risks as such. Thus, one may have to develop mitigation actions before the prioritisation stage.

Second, the process itself typically requires that several ideas need to be considered in parallel, and is often more creative, and less mechanical or tightly prescribed, than some may initially believe or desire:

- The nature of the risks and uncertainties may be complex, requiring particular technical expertise or cross-functional inputs to identify and respond to. Additionally, a cross-functional risk assessment team may neither have the budget, nor other relevant authorisations to implement risk-response measures, so that the risk analysis process may be required in order to surface issues for escalation to a higher level.

- A separate data-gathering and analysis exercise may be required to assess the nature and impact of the risks, their extent and their interdependencies. For example, a range of products may have prices or costs that are linked to some common factors (such as the oil price); analysis of actual historic data would be needed to properly calibrate the risk model with valid data.

Third, once results are presented, invariably new insights are developed or questions raised about specific items; these may result in additional assessments often needing to be undertaken:

- The residual risks associated with the base plan may not be in line with the risk tolerance of decision-makers, who may have a view on what is acceptable that is different to the view of the individual or group that conducted the analysis (decision-makers may also have different risk tolerances to each other, sometimes with more senior management willing to take more risk).
- There may be a need to rethink fundamental objectives or reset targets, so that originally planned actions may need to be revised (e.g. the conducting of an acquisition instead of using organic methods to achieve growth objectives).

Clearly, in the context of supporting any particular decision at a fixed point in time, the risk management process cannot go on forever, and will stop when the point has been reached where any further risk mitigation is not economically effective. Generically, at each process iteration one should arrive closer to a final decision, which would be taken based on the evaluation of the decision and the residual risks:

- At the very early stages, the overall objectives and "frame" should be set, with the aim of developing a full set of possible options to achieve these objectives. Risk assessment may help to develop some of the strategic options at this stage, and to understand the risk within each.
- Once a basic decision is selected, risk assessment can help with the detailed design options, including risk-response measures (some of which may be in a base plan, whilst others result from a formal process and may require specific authorisation). During iterations of this step, one may need to analyse in more depth (perhaps quantitatively) which risk mitigation measures are worth implementing, and so on.

Finally, an analysis of the potential impact of the risks that remain after all sensible measures have been taken (i.e. of a "risk-optimised plan") should support the taking of a final decision. In theory, the process may need to be reset at this point (for example, if it turns out that, after all considerations and mitigation actions, the planned course of action is, in fact, too risky or not appropriate in some way).

2.3 RISK IDENTIFICATION

At its most basic, the objective of a risk identification process is straightforward, aimed at answering the question: "What factors would cause the outcome of the situation to vary (or to be different to a base plan)?"

2.3.1 The Importance of a Robust Risk Identification Step

The identification of risks is the foundation of any form of risk analysis (whether qualitative or quantitative): it is clear that the omission of an important risk would significantly diminish the value of any assessment. Therefore, the identification process should be conducted in a way that is thorough, and is as objective and accurate as possible.

The involvement of a wide set of experts is usually required, with the extent of such involvement being broader in risk assessment processes than when traditional sensitivity analysis thought processes are used: whereas sensitivity-related thinking poses a "What if?" question, risk assessment also asks "Why?" The factors that cause variation in a particular quantity (such as in the assumed sales price or the volume of production) may be very diverse; their identification may require detailed input from marketing staff, technical specialists, operations experts, human resource representatives, macro economists, and so on.

Cross-functional activities will also often uncover aspects of a situation that either have not been thought of, or have not been given sufficient priority; they are also more likely to identify commonality, underlying drivers and dependencies between the risks. For example, a delay in a project, or a change in the exchange rate, may affect a number of different items that may not be major risks within each area (and hence overlooked or deprioritised by individual risk assessments), but could be significant when considered collectively. Such activities may also help to make explicit those areas where people may be making different assumptions, and will generally create an improved understanding of a situation, aid communication and consensus building, as well as identify additional action steps that may need to be taken.

Nevertheless, group discussions require significant investment in time and are not always as creative or productive as one may wish. Some issues that inhibit the effective functioning of groups include the domination of a small number of participants, sensitivities to airing some issues in public and a lack of patience of groups to deal with issues that require detailed explanation or difficulties in discussing competing hypotheses within a group setting. Therefore, a productive process usually requires a range of one-to-one discussions (even if these are with a set of experts from different functions), as well as group work. Thus, participants may be involved in using a variety of formats, including:

- One-to-one discussions and communications.
- Workshops devoted to specific issues.
- Workshops devoted to enterprise, holistic and cross-functional issues, and to interdependencies or change processes required to implement mitigation and response measures.

2.3.2 Bringing Structure into the Process

In addition to the use of a variety of formats, it is often beneficial to have some structure and discipline within the process itself. Specifically, in order to ensure that the process is as complete as possible, it is often helpful to have a range of questions that can be discussed (typically starting with ones of a fairly open nature, and then reverting to more specific forms of lists or approaches), such as:

- General questions, for example:
  - What factors would cause the outcome to be different to what was expected?
  - What scenarios are possible?
  - What is the worst (and best) case, and what factors lead to these occurring?
  - Can central cases result from some factors having low values and some having high values? Which factors are these?
  - What factors or drivers might have been forgotten in the base case analysis?
  - Why might our assumptions be wrong ... or why might this analysis still be insufficient or have not yet identified the relevant risks?
  - Can no one think of any other reason why the outcome may be different ... or where things could be better or worse than expected?
- Checklists, for example:
  - What strategic, financial and operational risks are there?
  - What uncertainties are there?
  - What are the risks affecting revenues, costs, investment, cash flow or financing requirements (such as those relating to prices, volumes, individual cost items, etc.)?
  - What commercial, product/service, operational or competitive risks are there?
  - What are the legal, technical, regulatory, reputational and environmental risks?
  - What risks are there in management capabilities, ethics, partners, processes, resources and suppliers?
  - Has an initial financial model been built? Which line items within it are uncertain or risky? (This process may highlight risks that have implicitly been considered by a modeller, but not explicitly by a formal process, and provide information on how the model may need to be adapted in order to include the identified risks.)
- Working from specifics to general principles and back to specifics. In other words, an identified risk may be associated with a category of risks, so that other risks may exist within that which may not yet have been identified at the current process stage. For example, the potential unavailability of the internet at a particular hotel could be considered as part of a category of "interrupted communications", which may lead on to identify other items that had not been considered. These thought processes can lead to further risks, dependencies and mitigation actions being identified and implemented. Their repeated use, starting with different items or categories, can often generate a large list of risks, which may be considered individually or perhaps grouped into risk categories for the purposes of further analysis, and to avoid double-counting.
- Reward-driven approaches. After other approaches have been exhausted, one can spend a few minutes (working individually or in subgroups) to identify at least, say, three to five new ideas as to why outcomes could be different. A small prize could be offered to the person or group that generates the best idea (in terms of overall importance or general contribution to the discussion, or as judged by the full group).
- Case studies and other external sources. These involve looking either at direct learnings or more general analogies that can be drawn from previous projects, standards or published public examples of businesses or projects that have been subject to extensive risk analysis or where major issues arose.

- Formal creativity techniques. If conducted thoroughly, the above steps are generally adequate to ensure that risk identification has been sufficiently complete. In very important cases, or where there is a belief that the process is not complete for some reason, one could employ formal brainstorming or creativity-enhancement techniques, or engage specialist external consultants to facilitate the process and its contents.

2.3.3 Distinguishing Variability from Decision Risks

Risk identification processes often act as a "catch-all" repository for a variety of areas of concern within a business, and in particular they often identify items that are "decision risks", i.e. within the control of the overall organisation, but where a working group feels that there is a chance that an incorrect decision may be taken: a typical example is "there is a risk that the management may not authorise the recommended technical solution". These are not traditional risks (which have an associated variability even if no decision about them is taken), and their inclusion in a process can cause ambiguity or controversy; they are of potential high importance to the overall success of a project, yet fully controllable by the organisation.

The challenge in such situations is:

- To ensure that such items are not overlooked. The structured forum of a cross-functional risk assessment team may be the only forum in which such issues can be identified and surfaced within the organisation; if they are ignored in that forum, then they may not be considered at all, despite their importance. The natural focus on risk issues (within a risk assessment process) must not be to the detriment of the overall decision process.
- To find a mechanism to compare with traditional risk items, where there is an uncertainty or variability component.

From a modelling perspective, the need to make the distinction between controllable and non-controllable items arises to some degree in both traditional static modelling and risk modelling. However, there is added importance in risk modelling contexts, because the tools required to deal with each issue are different (see Chapters 6 and 7).

2.3.4 Distinguishing Business Issues from Risks

In a similar way to controllable variables or decision risks, there is also frequent ambiguity around items that are business issues, but surface within risk identification processes: typically, a risk relates to the idea that a business issue may not be fully successfully addressed or resolved, rather than to the existence of the issue *per se*.

As an example, a strategy review for a project-based firm may identify that a "key business risk" is that "the conversion rate is too low" (i.e. the percentage of deals closed relative to the number of bids submitted; so that much work is being conducted in submitting bids that are not successful). Several initiatives may be developed to address this, for example to provide additional training to new sales representatives, to implement a more systematic process to track competitor activities, and so on. Thus, the conversion rate being too low is a business issue, whilst the risk is that these initiatives may be insufficient to improve the conversion rate to the required level (with risk drivers being the success or not of each individual initiative, for example).

As for decision risks, it is important that business issues are not overlooked or ignored by a risk identification process (as they may be valid considerations that need to be addressed, perhaps even as part of the overall situation of which the risk assessment is one supporting element). It is also important that there is clarity within the process (both for modelling and for communication purposes) about which aspects are being referred to; it is easy for confusion to arise.

2.3.5 Risk Identification in Quantitative Approaches: Additional Considerations

The above activities are usually sufficient to identify a set of risks that is adequate for a qualitative risk assessment. When quantitative approaches are used, one is almost always required to enhance such activities to take into account a range of additional specific issues (as discussed in Chapter 3).

2.4 RISK MAPPING

Risk mapping involves describing the nature of the risks or uncertainties in a way that allows their inclusion within a quantitative model. As such, it is a core foundation of quantitative risk modelling. This section provides an overview of its key objectives and of some of the challenges; the discussion of more detailed aspects and issues appears later in the text.

2.4.1 Key Objectives

Risk mapping is generally the most challenging part of the risk modelling process, as it requires an integration of many building blocks, such as:

- Establishing the nature of risks and their impacts (e.g. whether risk events or general variability or uncertainty, as well as the timeframe of its occurrence or duration), including that dependencies are understood and appropriately captured.
- Ensuring that risks and impacts are precisely defined, expressed in common terms and with double-counting and overlaps eliminated.
- Adapting the models to reflect the impacts of the risks, perhaps requiring additional line items, creating formulae that are dynamic and flexible and capturing dependencies between risks and between impacts.
- Using distributions and data that are appropriate, with suitable approximations or estimates made where necessary.
- Aligning the risk modelling activities with the general risk assessment and decision process.

These issues are addressed in detail later in the text, especially in Chapters 7, 9 and 11.

2.4.2 Challenges

Despite its importance in quantitative modelling, risk mapping is a process step that is often conducted inadequately:

- For qualitative assessment, the step is essentially not required; therefore it may not be well understood, or given sufficient attention, especially when qualitative processes are used as a first step in an overall process that subsequently uses quantitative techniques.
- Risk mapping is often overlooked (or barely mentioned) in many standard frameworks, which tend to focus on risk management issues (such as risk identification and mitigation) and tend be of a qualitative (or semi-quantitative) nature, rather than having a focus on risk aggregation or full risk modelling. Thus, many process participants (even those who are experienced and well read in operational risk management) will not be familiar with the much richer range of concepts and specific processes and requirements associated with risk mapping and quantitative modelling.
- An overly simplistic risk mapping process can lead to one being inadvertently drawn into frameworks that are too narrow to capture the true nature of the uncertainty. For example, the mapping implicit in many frameworks is one that treats all items as event-type or operational risks (e.g. with a probability-of-occurrence and an impact-on-occurrence), and which have no (or limited) interaction with other variables, or a time component. Such assumptions may not have a strong basis in reality for many items that have general uncertainty (such as price or volume fluctuations), so that models built on such bases may represent the true situation quite poorly; indeed, a modeller may find the building of such models to be rather unsatisfactory and frustrating, as they try to "force square pegs into round holes".
- The required information is of a more detailed nature than for qualitative assessments; it can be challenging to retain the attention of a group of participants, to explain additional concepts and to ensure that the appropriate deliverables result from group processes.

2.5 RISK PRIORITISATION AND ITS POTENTIAL CRITERIA

The prioritisation of risk is more subtle than is commonly considered. On the one hand, as in many forms of activity, it would seem common sense to prioritise items. On the other hand, one can question the reason(s) for needing to do so. For example, it would not seem sensible to ignore a risk that can easily be mitigated simply because it is "small". Similarly, risks that are easy to deal with should generally be responded to, even if detailed communication about such items has not taken place with management. More fundamentally, it is arguably not possible (or even sensible) to prioritise risks; rather it is the mitigation (or response) measures that require prioritisation.

Thus, the choice and implementation of appropriate prioritisation criteria can be more challenging than may first appear, and will often depend on the context and objectives, with one risk perhaps being more important (or having higher priority) according to one criteria, but being of lower importance according to another.

In this section we discuss the potential approaches, objectives and criteria that may be used in risk prioritisation, as well as areas where potential pitfalls or misunderstandings can arise.

2.5.1 Inclusion/Exclusion

To some extent, one can argue that risks should not be prioritised at all; each risk should simply be dealt with in the way appropriate for that item. In principle, the exclusion of any risks cannot be considered to be good practice. First, it will result in an understatement of the risk. Second, if a potential risk-response measure is available and would be beneficial (after taking into account its cost), then it would seem sensible to implement it, however small the underlying risk is judged to be. These arguments would favour the principle of not excluding risks that have been identified.

On the other hand, because it is important to identify all relevant risks as thoroughly as possible, the process to do so may be most effective when conducted in a non-judgemental manner: especially in the early stages, the making of an immediate judgement about the importance of the ideas being generated may stifle both the willingness of participants to surface potential issues (and provide a recognised forum for such items to be quashed), which will generally hinder the overall creative nature of the processes that is often required at this stage. Thus, if ideas are noted (but not judged) as they are initially generated, then it is highly likely that some post-processing of these initial results would be required. Such post-processing activities may involve grouping risks into categories with common underlying drivers, or eliminating double-counting and overlaps, and so on. This implicitly means that some initially identified risks are no longer pursued as separate explicit items (however, this is not the same as excluding them).

2.5.2 Communications Focus

Some items may need to be emphasised (or de-emphasised) in order to focus communication with management and with other staff, with such emphasis (and the level of detail) being adapted according to the audience:

- The implementation of risk-response measures requires authorisation, especially where there are implications for budgets, project scope, deliverables, timelines or implications for other organisational units, third parties or renegotiation of certain items if needed.
- To communicate about items that have already been mitigated or where plans are already in place to do so, as well as about remaining items.
- To communicate about the risks that will cause the most variation in the outcome, whether or not such risks are controllable through risk mitigation measures.
- To refocus attention away from items that may naturally draw attention, but which may not be relevant to a particular discussion. For example, one may wish to de-emphasise an item that is large but where its range of possible variation is small (including cases where further mitigation possibilities are limited); one may wish to focus on items that are larger contributors to the overall risk profile or which can be influenced, and on the required decisions associated with such actions.

Of course, risks that are not regarded as priority items from a communication perspective cannot be ignored: a project team should still plan to respond to individual risk items, even for risks for which wider communication activities are not appropriate.

The use of risk categories is an important approach in this respect (both in the context of communication of process outputs, and with quantitative risk models). For example, risks that are regarded as low priority for communication purposes could be assigned to a specific category, with risks being shown by category. In this way, the impacts of all risks are still captured, even where they are not emphasised. Examples of the use of risk categories are shown later in the text.

2.5.3 Commonality and Comparison

There are generally some contextual (or "macro") risks, which are common to any project that a company would conduct. In such cases, it would be inappropriate to penalise a project that included such risks in its evaluation compared to a project that did not do so. Hence, it may be decided to standardise certain aspects of the methodology for project analysis and evaluation, in order to make clear the nature of items that should be included or excluded within individual projects. Examples of items that may be considered for exclusion on a standard basis could be:

- Events that could cause mass extinction on the planet or change fundamentally the global context: asteroid strikes, major pandemics of incurable diseases, global nuclear or cyber wars, global environmental catastrophes or volcanic super eruptions are some examples! (Apparently, volcanic super eruptions occur, on average, approximately every 50,000 years – a 0.002% annual probability.)
- The risk of a war in the region of the company's operations, or of a global nuclear war.
- Changes in the political or governmental environment; if a company operates in only one country, these risks may be common to all projects.

Of course, such approaches to standardisation are valid only if the likelihood of occurrence and proportional impact of such risks is similar across all potential projects: one needs to be careful not to ignore important risk factors, especially where they would disproportionally affect one project when compared to others. Possible examples of where such pitfalls may arise include:

- A company may have different business units that use the same (or highly related) raw materials, such as oil-derived products or some chemicals, or alternatively it may manufacture end products that are similar or sell into related markets. In such a context, one may consider excluding the risk of cost or price variation from all projects. On the other hand, it could be that the variation in such prices may create an unacceptable "worst case" situation for one project, but not for another (where such variation could be absorbed in its generally better economics, such as if it has much lower fixed costs).
- An oil company that produces a variety of grades of oil, but which has only very small associated commercial gas production, may decide to standardise the price assumptions used for gas in business cases, whilst nevertheless using different oil prices to reflect the price of different grades (quality) of oil. However, if the company starts to consider investing in gas-dominated assets, this standardisation of gas prices would no longer be appropriate.

Clearly, the use of standardised risk definitions (which are used in the evaluation of all projects) would appear to be the most suitable approach in theory; in practice, it can be hard to implement in some organisations. A number of other options to handle the standardisation of risk may be considered: these include the creation of standard scenarios for relevant risk items (e.g. for future oil prices), or the creation of standardised full risk profiles for these items (e.g. an agreed set of parameters and processes that determine the fluctuation in future oil prices), which are to be used in all business cases.

2.5.4 Modelling Reasons

It is important to keep models "as simple as possible, but no simpler" (Einstein). However, if models are designed (and laid out) according to best practice principles, and other options are considered (such as the grouping of risks into categories), the exclusion of risks simply because they are "small" (or not material) is generally not necessary from a modelling perspective.

On the other hand, in practice, it may be that some risks cannot readily be represented in a quantitative model:

- The true nature of some risks or their impacts may indeed be very complex to implement within a quantitative model. For example, a risk profile may follow a complex behaviour driven by a distribution of outcomes that cannot be captured analytically (and which is not available in any associated software being used), whilst being considered as a relatively immaterial item. In such cases, one may instead search for simpler approximations concerning the nature of the risk and its impact, so that some indicative, albeit imperfect, analysis can be performed. In some cases, one may consider excluding immaterial items from a modelling process where reasonable approximations cannot be found.
- Risks associated with "softer" issues, such as those relating to quality, environment or political or governmental relations, and so on, may not be able to be captured in a quantitative model. However, of course, their exclusion from a model should not mean that they are forgotten or overlooked when presenting and reporting the overall results of a project risk assessment.

2.5.5 General Size of Risks, Their Impact and Likelihood

It is natural to want to prioritise or emphasise items that are larger than others. This can be more challenging than it may at first appear. In principle, rather than its size as such, what is generally relevant is the impact if an item is changed. For example, the profitability of a project may critically depend on one item whose cost is very high compared to that of others. However, if this item is fixed and cannot be changed (either through management action or as a result of general uncertainty or risk), then arguably the item should no longer be considered important (as a simple example, the item may have already been purchased). Attention should then be switched to other items over which one has more control.

In general, the impact of a risk item is often hard to assess without a full quantitative model. For example, the effect of a volume reduction on a company's post-tax cash flow may be hard to establish without a full model that calculates the effect on revenues, variable costs and other items. Some risks may only have an indirect monetary impact (such as a time delay to a project task), some risks will affect multiple line items and others develop over time (such as exchange rates, price levels of inputs and of end products, and so on). Therefore, the impact of particular risks may be very hard to assess in the absence of a full quantitative model.

On the other hand, it is inconvenient to have to build a full quantitative model simply to find out which items are perhaps not significant. Indeed, once a model has been built with a particular risk included, there would seem little point in excluding this risk even if it were shown by the model to be unimportant.

Therefore, sometimes one aims to use simple framework or proxy (substitute) models or measures to assess the size of each risk. The use of "probability-impact" matrices (or the multiplication of probabilities with impacts) is one such tool that is sometimes used in order to create a risk prioritisation framework. Whilst such approaches may appear simple, and apply to some situations, they also have significant disadvantages including:

- The probability and impacts may be irrelevant, as by themselves they do not give an indication of whether such items can be changed, or the extent of mitigation possible (unless one implicitly assumes that all items can be fully mitigated or that the extent of mitigation actions will be in proportion to the size of the risks, neither of which is generally valid).
- The framework is problematic for capturing general uncertainties, which do not map into it, so that probability-impact estimates are hard to truly establish.
- The focus tends to be on prioritising with respect to an average figure (e.g. probability-weighted impact), which can be misleading for general uncertainties: for example, the average potential price variation may be zero, whereas the variability it creates on both the up and down side may be very important for decision-making; measures of spread (e.g. risks that affect the worst 10% of cases) are typically important in risk assessment, not only averages.
- There may be important interactions, dependencies or common underlying drivers of the risks, which could change the true extent of an impact (or the effect of a single mitigation measure).

Thus, the prioritisation of risks based on their "size" may often be difficult, or inaccurate, but also potentially misleading and irrelevant.

2.5.6 Influence: Mitigation and Response Measures, and Management Actions

Arguably, the main objective of risk prioritisation should be to focus on items that one can influence, in other words items that require decisions to be made about taking specific courses of action. These could concern:

- Decisions as to which risk-mitigation (or response) measures to implement. An example would be a measure that, at some cost, would reduce the probability-of-occurrence of a risk, and so a decision would need to be taken as to whether the benefit is worth the investment required.
- Decisions that change the context or structure of a project, but that may not be explicitly related to risk. An example would be where the selection of a different technical solution could reduce the cost of an item from a higher value to a lower one (with such low or high values being fixed within each specific context, i.e. not subject to any variability or other influences within each).

For the purpose of prioritisation, the latter category may be thought of as "decision risks"; these may initially appear to be not comparable to those of traditional risks (i.e. those that have a variability associated with them even where no decisions relating to them are taken). For example, it would not seem sensible to attach a "probability-of-occurrence" to a decision risk, as the outcome is entirely controllable by the organisation by way of a decision. The commonality between them is that the prioritisation of risks is based not on the contribution of any item to the variability of the output, but rather on the relative effectiveness of the action that could be taken (whether a risk-response measure or a decision). In other words, this approach prioritises items according to the effectiveness of the associated decisions relating to them.

This has (potentially major) implications for risk modelling activities, and for the analysis and display of outputs:

- Very often, risk models are built to capture the variability associated with risk items, and display results that show how the output variability relates to input variability (such as some types of tornado graphs), rather than explicitly to capture the relevant possible decisions and the post-decision values for the items in the model (e.g. pre- and post-mitigation ranges for risks and modified base values for other decision items).
- Whereas some risk models do capture the effects of some decisions (such as pre- and post-mitigation parameters), very often models include only a subset of the full possibilities for the decisions that truly influence project success; the most important factors could easily be overlooked if they are decision risks, rather than traditional risks.

The existence of any such decisions (whether they are risk mitigation or more general management decisions) cannot be identified from a model, but only through processes that are exogenous to it. Thus, a model that captures the risks and their effects cannot itself identify what mitigation actions or other decisions are available, nor their impact: such inputs must come from a process that is separate to the modelling process. In Chapter 7, we provide a specific example of how such issues may be treated within a modelling context.

2.5.7 Optimising Resource Deployment and Implementation Constraints

At its most basic, a working group may decide to prioritise risks simply because the group has limited working time (and limited group patience) to spend time (as a group) working on items that seem of little significance.

More generally, risk-response measures and other decisions will have an impact on resources, budgets and timeframes so that some prioritisation of activities is necessary. In some cases, the analysis of such constraints, and the generation of alternative options to overcome or to accept them, may be complex, as items may:

- Compete for resources (including staff time, project expertise as well as financial resources).
- Interact or have joint impacts that mean that other constraints or project issues need further consideration (e.g. the elapsed time to deliver several mitigation measures would be too long, so that only some measures can be considered).
- Interact in a way that means that the effectiveness of particular actions is reduced after measures have been implemented. Thus, actions that make sense in isolation may not make sense when considered within a full set of possible actions. Thus, some prioritisation of actions will be needed, with perhaps some actions that were considered effective on a stand-alone basis having a reduced priority when considered holistically.

2.6 RISK RESPONSE: MITIGATION AND EXPLOITATION

The range of possible mitigation and exploitation actions is, of course, very diverse. Nevertheless, most actions usually fall into one or more – often overlapping – areas, as discussed below.

2.6.1 Reduction

Risk reduction aims to reduce the probability or impact of adverse risks. Simple examples include:

- Looking carefully before crossing the road instead of crossing directly or only listening for traffic.
- Ensuring the family car is well maintained to reduce the chance of accidents or breakdowns.
- Gathering quotes from suppliers before undertaking a building project.
- Checking the train timetable so that one can walk to the station just in time to catch the train, instead of just turning up at the station without prior planning and catching the next train that arrives.
- Many day-to-day planning activities may be thought of as measures that reduce risk, at least compared to the situation that would apply if actions were implemented with little planning or analysis.

2.6.2 Exploitation

Risk exploitation actions explicitly seek to create advantage from the uncertainty, usually by adding a response (or optionality) component, which reflects the ability to make a subsequent decision or to modify behaviour after a risk has materialised:

- Building flexibility into the design of a manufacturing facility, so that production volumes (and/or product mix) can be altered according to changes in market demand, i.e. to create the ability to expand production if actual demand exceeds initial planned estimates or to cut production (or reconfigure the facility to make an alternative product) if the initial plans are not met or if the market alters in some way.
- The structuring of projects into phases, so that a subsequent phase proceeds only if the prior one is successful. This is using the inherent uncertainty to create additional value, rather than simply proceeding immediately with a full investment that might fail. This can also be seen as a risk reduction measure, or as a research and information gathering one.
- Creating a clause in a supply contract to the effect that the unit cost of items purchased from the supplier is lower if the (uncertain) volumes to be purchased are high, but is capped to a fixed amount when volumes are low.

2.6.3 Transfer

This involves transferring some of the responsibility for absorbing the impact of risks when they occur. This is typically a risk reduction measure that requires some payment to be made, although it could involve receiving a payment if some exploitable risk (i.e. a potential benefit) is transferred. Examples include:

- Outsourcing some activities, with services paid for only on delivery of defined goals; the risk of non-delivery may have been partially passed to the outsourcing company, compared to the situation in which there is a fixed cost of employees (whose productivity may be uncertain).
- Purchasing an insurance contract.
- Purchasing an option to hedge the risk associated with a financial asset or portfolio.

2.6.4 Research and Information Gathering

A natural instinct when faced with uncertainty is to gather more information before making a final decision, or to delay a decision (perhaps implicitly hoping that the additional time will provide more information). Such information is typically ultimately used to reduce or to exploit risk. Examples include:

- Checking the weather forecast before making a decision as to whether to take the bicycle or the car for a short journey.
- The conducting of a blood test (or other tests) by a doctor before making a final diagnosis about a treatment regime, rather than prescribing drugs or recommending an operation based only on some initial indicators.
- An oil company conducting further geological tests, rather than immediately drilling for oil. In the case that the test indicates that oil is likely to be present, a full drilling programme can be conducted, otherwise the project can be abandoned (so that drilling is not conducted unnecessarily, and the cost of potentially doing so is saved). This can also be seen as a risk reduction or risk exploitation measure.
- When facing a decision about who to promote between someone who is quieter versus one who appears to be more outgoing, one may search for more information about the true leadership potential of each, such as examples of actual leadership roles conducted and their outcomes, the integrity, the work ethic of each, and so on, rather than making a decision based on gut feeling or more limited information.

2.6.5 Diversification

Diversification seeks to use the statistical properties of random processes to create a more acceptable risk profile. It contrasts with other typical risk-response measures in that it does not seek to intervene in the operational nature or definition of projects. Examples include:

- An oil company may choose to own 50% of each of two (independent but essentially similar) oil fields, rather than owning 100% of a single field. In this way, there will be less variation in the level of oil production: instead of (simplistically speaking) only a low or a high outcome being possible (as it is with one field), the portfolio of two fields also allows for "middle" cases, in which the production in one field is a high amount whilst the other is low. Such combinatorial effects are explored more generally in Chapter 6, as well as through many of the examples in the rest of the text.

- In general, if two projects are perfectly related, diversification would have no benefit (e.g. both would be successes or both would be failures). On the other hand, a fully negative relationship between projects (e.g. one fails whenever the other succeeds and vice versa), would create the possibility to essentially eliminate risk (a portfolio of two projects would have one guaranteed success and one guaranteed failure, so its outcome would be known for sure). In many practical business cases, the best one can generally hope to achieve is independence between the projects. In practice, businesses remaining within their core competence are likely to have some relationship between the outcomes of projects, due to underlying factors that are common across projects (e.g. commodity prices, staff resources or technical solutions used).

2.7 PROJECT MANAGEMENT AND MONITORING

The role of risk assessment in project management and execution was discussed in Chapter 1, so this is not addressed further here in detail. Briefly, its use is both an independent objective (i.e. to improve project management through the early identification of risks) and a process stage: it can be used as an ongoing activity as a project moves through the stages of conception, design, evaluation and implementation.

CHAPTER 3

Approaches to Risk Assessment and Quantification

This chapter discusses a variety of approaches that may be taken to risk assessment activities, ranging from those that are informal and unstructured, to those that are structured but purely qualitative, to those that are highly quantitative. We discuss the content, benefits, challenges and requirements of each, and in particular we emphasise some key issues to be aware of when the focus of activities changes from qualitative to quantitative, as may often happen in the later stages of an analysis.

The discussion of various approaches is presented according to the following categories:

- Informal or intuitive approaches.
- Risk registers, capturing individual risks but without aggregation:
  - Qualitative approaches for each risk.
  - Quantitative approaches for each risk.
- Risk registers, focusing – for a particular key variable (such as cost) – on the aggregate impact of all risks on that variable. These approaches are inherently quantitative, and include:
  - Aggregation of impacts of static risk (or average) values.
  - Aggregation of impacts of risk-driven occurrences (using either static or uncertain values of the impact on occurrence).
- Full (integrated) risk modelling: these capture each risk, its impact and dependencies on all variables of a full quantitative model (e.g. revenue, cost, the time profile of cash flow, etc.); such approaches are the counterpart, or extension, of traditional (static, non-risk) modelling approaches.

Of course, there are some possible variations of these, such as the extension of risk register approaches to capture the impact of each risk on several model variables. However, the explicit treatment of such variations would not provide additional insight into the core of the discussion at this point.

Clearly, the appropriate choice of approach will depend on the circumstances: informal or qualitative approaches may be sufficient when faced with a fairly simple decision, whereas more formalised processes and quantitative approaches are likely to be appropriate for many large or complex ones. In principle, quantitative approaches should be able to deliver more benefits, but they are also more complex to implement correctly. Therefore, in any given situation, it may make sense to start with a simple approach (for example, purely qualitative) and then add more sophistication if it is later judged necessary. On the other hand, in some respects, the approaches do not form a continuum, so that if one wishes to move from one approach to the next, additional work may be required in areas that may have been considered complete. For example, in qualitative risk assessment, overlaps between risk items (or even a repetition of an item) may be relatively unimportant. However, such double-counting would be much more serious in quantitative aggregation approaches. Thus, a set of risks that may have been (adequately) identified for the purposes of general (essentially qualitative) risk management may be inappropriate (without significant rework of risk definitions) if used as a basis for risk quantification. These points are discussed in more detail at specific places in the chapter.

3.1 INFORMAL OR INTUITIVE APPROACHES

The most basic risk assessment approach is one in which there is no explicit or formalised process, as often applied naturally and intuitively to some everyday situations (as described in Chapter 1). There is often an implicit recognition of some risks, and an adaptation of a plan or of targets to some extent.

In some business situations, such informal assessments could, of course, also be appropriate: this may apply where the decision is of fairly small consequence, where all relevant mitigating actions are known from much prior experience, and where such actions lie within the authority of the project analyst or planner, then one is faced with a day-to-day situation that may require little analysis; rather, appropriate actions may be able to be directly implemented without further ado.

Generally, of course, most business situations are subject to complexity and other issues, resulting in a need for more formalised and rigorous approaches.

3.2 RISK REGISTERS WITHOUT AGGREGATION

This section discusses the use of "risk registers", which are essentially a list (or structured database) of risks that have been identified. In this section, we cover both qualitative and quantitative approaches to such registers, in the specific context in which each risk is treated as a separate item and in which there is no attempt to assess the aggregate impact of the set of risks.

3.2.1 Qualitative Approaches

The qualitative "risk register" is characterised by:

- A focus on identification, mitigation and management of individual risks. It will generally include a description of each risk and its impact, and will typically be a resource that is in continual development, acting as a "living repository" of identified risks, mitigation measures, responsibilities, timelines, and so on.

	Risk Item	Action	Delivery Date	Responsible
3	Project delay			
4	Volume lower than expected			
5	Price fluctuation			
6	Competitor enters market			
7	Exchange rate risk			
8	Project manager becomes ill			
9	Insurance cost not defined			
10	Staff turnover			
11	Cost variation			
12	Site management problems			
13	Change of law			
14	Low availability of construction materials			
15	Contractors working inefficiently			
16	High Rainfall			
17	Steelwork Supply to site			
18	Quality of fabricated steel			
19	Mechanical Equipment List Changes			
20	Basis of mechanical equipment estimate			
21	Piping Design Schedule			
22	Low availalbility of electrical cabling			
23	Demand Inflation			
24	Late delivery of power line			
25	Higher than expected cost for power line			
26	Contractors camp delivery			
27	Inaccurate escalation allowance			
28	Change in forex rate or hedging cost			
29	Increased requirements on outside consultants			
30	Change in cost of staff housing			
31				

FIGURE 3.1 Example of a Generic Qualitative Risk Register

- Limited, if any, quantification; risk impacts, risk prioritisation or the effect of mitigation measures are not quantified in this approach.

Such registers can be stored in an Excel workbook, and structured as a database, but of course other applications or methods can be used to keep a track of such items. Figure 3.1 shows a generic example of a register (stored in Excel) in a (fictitious and non-specified) project context.

There are several benefits to using such approaches:

- They are, to some extent, a step that is in any case required in any risk assessment process, even ones that ultimately aim to build full quantitative risk models.
- They can be applied very quickly and with little investment (in time), but may nevertheless generate further insights and improve the basic planned design of a project. They are especially important in early phases of a potential project:

  - They are likely to help to identify many of the key risks and mitigation or response actions, especially for major issues that can be considered "clearly" important without any significant or formalised reflection.
  - The underlying business situation or structural aspects of a project's design may not yet be clear at this stage, so that more detailed analysis, quantification or modelling is not yet possible or practical. Of course, at some point, major projects should generally not be authorised unless a sufficient level of basic understanding has been achieved, and so the more integrated quantitative modelling approaches discussed later will often be more appropriate before a final decision is made about a project.
  - They do not require detailed or precise definitions of risks, or for a risk-mapping process to be conducted, and thus are quick to perform.
- Some estimate of the comparative importance of each risk may be (try to be) assessed using qualitative proxies, such as high/medium/low categories, even if this would be far from perfect.
- They are often quite effective at facilitating the workings of groups (such as cross-functional teams) and in supporting communication to management and other stakeholders.
- They are fairly robust, in the sense that the final actions taken may be quite insensitive to imprecisions in the process, such as poor descriptions or definitions of risks, or overlapping impacts:
  - The potential inclusion of a risk (or its impact) twice is not typically of particular consequence: it is generally unlikely in practice that the same mitigation measure would be implemented twice (e.g. purchase of insurance policy, delay in a particular start date of a project), because the overlap at the risk mitigation stage would almost inevitably be quite clear (and hence not undertaken) due to the very concrete nature of the action. This is in contrast with the more conceptual nature of the risks, which are more likely to result in a particular risk being included twice, for example if a similar risk is described with two different linguistic formulations.
  - The dependencies and interactions between risks (or their impacts) need not generally be defined in detail, as long as the risks are identified and managed effectively.
  - Risks need not be expressed in common terms. Thus, mitigation actions can be developed even if one risk has a direct monetary impact, whereas another's impact is on project delivery time or on quality.

The disadvantages of this approach are, of course, that the benefits of quantitative aggregation and full modelling approaches are not available: these benefits are covered in the later discussion of each approach, so are not presented here.

3.2.2 Quantitative Approaches

A natural extension of the qualitative risk register is one where the individual risks are quantified. Note that we are not considering the case where the risk impacts are added up (aggregated) or interact with each other in any way; such cases are the subject of a later discussion.

In the simplest form, each risk is characterised by a probability-of-occurrence and an impact-on-occurrence (or a consequence or severity). More generally (as the term "probability" would tend to suggest a one-off potential occurrence), one may wish to allow risks to happen multiple times within the timeframe under consideration, so that a frequency-of-occurrence (per unit time) is used in place of a probability.

The main advantages of this approach (over the qualitative risk register) are:

- In principle, quantitative approaches still address all issues that would be covered by qualitative ones (e.g. risk identification and response measures); hence all the benefits of qualitative approaches should be generated in any case.
- The definitions of risks will be more precise and rigorous. For example, when quantifying the occurrence, one may be led to a discussion of the time impact of the risk, dependencies with other risk occurrences, and so on. Similarly, to quantify the impact, one is essentially obliged to consider the nature of that impact (e.g. whether on revenue, cost, quality or time, or on several items). These reflections will add rigour, generate a better understanding about the risks and result in the consideration of a wider range of possible response actions.
- This approach begins to provide a basis on which to evaluate and prioritise the effectiveness of any risk-response actions. For example, one can begin to compare the cost of implementing a risk mitigation action with the benefits in terms of risk reduction (or exploitation). For risks that have a direct economic impact, the benefits and costs of risk mitigation are easier to evaluate (for example, a probability-of-occurrence multiplied by an impact-on-occurrence would provide a measure of the average impact). For risks with only an indirect impact (such as time delay to a project), although the true economic effect could be significant, in the absence of a full model to assess the impact, the cost-effectiveness of a measure would often need to be established more heuristically or by using common sense judgement.

Once again, the disadvantages are not covered in detail here, as they are dealt with implicitly when the benefits of the later approaches are discussed. For the moment, we simply note that some potential major drawbacks are:

- They implicitly assume that the risks are of an operational nature (i.e. essentially event risks with a particular impact-on-occurrence, such as an extra cost arising); as such they are not suitable in general, where the nature of the risks and uncertainty is of a richer nature.
- It is often extremely hard to estimate reliably the quantitative impact of some items. For example, the effect of a project delay may require a very precise assessment (or a full risk model) to be able to be expressed in quantitative terms (especially if monetary impacts are required, not just the time impact). Other items (e.g. quality or environment impacts) may need to be left out of a quantitative assessment, and although they can still be included in an overall presentation of the risk assessment in principle, there is a risk that they would be overlooked as focus is shifted to quantitative analysis.
- The benefits of aggregation and modelling are not achieved, including understanding the impacts of risks at the project level, such as the implications for a range of key project metrics.

Figure 3.2 shows a (fictitious) example of such a display (note that, since we are currently discussing non-aggregate approaches, there is no total displayed in row 31).

Risk Item	Probabilty	Impact ($)	Prob*Impact	Action	Delivery Date	Responsible
Project delay	40%	1000000	400000			
Volume lower than expected	20%	670000	134000			
Price fluctuation	40%	250000	100000			
Competitor enters market	20%	880000	176000			
Exchange rate risk	20%	100000	20000			
Project manager becomes ill	30%	150000	45000			
Insurance cost not defined	70%	530000	371000			
Staff turnover	30%	310000	93000			
Cost variation	40%	500000	200000			
Site management problems	30%	3500000	1050000			
Change of law	10%	780000	78000			
Low availability of construction materials	30%	1200000	360000			
Contractors working inefficiently	20%	350000	70000			
High Rainfall	10%	500000	50000			
Steelwork Supply to site	20%	610000	122000			
Quality of fabricated steel	20%	950000	190000			
Mechanical Equipment List Changes	40%	370000	148000			
Basis of mechanical equipment estimate	10%	200000	20000			
Piping Design Schedule	10%	240000	24000			
Low availalbility of electrical cabling	20%	360000	72000			
Demand Inflation	20%	200000	40000			
Late delivery of power line	40%	500000	200000			
Higher than expected cost for power line	30%	200000	60000			
Contractors camp delivery	30%	810000	243000			
Inaccurate escalation allowance	10%	930000	93000			
Change in forex rate or hedging cost	30%	780000	234000			
Increased requirements on outside consultants	20%	370000	74000			
Change in cost of staff housing	20%	230000	46000			

FIGURE 3.2 Example of a Generic Quantitative Risk Register Without Aggregation

3.3 RISK REGISTER WITH AGGREGATION (QUANTITATIVE)

Risk aggregation approaches aim to assess the total risk profile resulting from a set of risks, and focus not just on individual risks. Of course, it is the individual risks that drive the aggregate profile, and so these should not be ignored or de-emphasised; rather, one is conducting an assessment both at the individual level and at the aggregate (or "project") level.

3.3.1 The Benefits of Aggregation

Although the consideration only of individual risk items can play an important part in risk management, there are many situations in which measures of aggregate risk are (or should be) indispensable:

- To avoid cases where individual risks are being managed effectively, but within a poor overall situation (or project) that is essentially destined to fail ("rearranging deckchairs on the *Titanic*"):
  - A process that focuses only on managing individual risk items (even where quantified) may be insufficient, or severely limiting, when used as a process to evaluate and select projects.
  - In other words, a business model that involves applying world-class risk management to projects that are fundamentally poor (or poorly designed and selected) would likely not be successful.

- To prioritise risks for mitigation action. Given resource constraints, it is the overall aggregate impact of mitigation measures that would be most relevant when considering risk prioritisation issues:
  - In the initial stages of a project, the selection of mitigation actions may be clear, but as the detail of the project structure evolves and becomes more optimised due to the inclusion of these actions, one needs to start making more complex trade-offs in terms of benefits and costs of potential risk mitigation actions.
  - A proper quantified aggregation process is generally necessary if one wishes to optimise the portfolio of risk mitigation measures in any rigorous and robust way.
  - Organisational processes and individuals are, arguably, typically fairly effective at managing individual risks, but much less so at generating insight into the aggregate risk profile; formal processes and tools can help to overcome this.
- To have a measure of the possible impact of risks on project-level metrics:
  - To assess the overall value of a project, including whether to proceed with it or not.
  - To assess contingency requirements (extra budget, time or resources). For example, one approach sometimes used is to calculate contingency requirements for a cost budget as the sum of the average cost impact of each risk (we discuss other approaches later).
  - To set objectives and targets at a project level, such as for revenue, cost, capex or delivery time.
- To support interfaces with external parties who are involved at a project (or subproject) level:
  - To assess a project's (or an organisation's) financing requirements, and to support the raising of debt or equity finance, for example.
  - To assist in discussions and negotiations about partnerships or contractual arrangements.

Note that the quantitative risk register approach typically provides an "overlay", i.e. the results are ultimately added to those of a base case static model, and thus the approach is essentially a proxy (or substitute) for a full risk model. An overlay model will, however, usually focus only on the effect of the risks on certain key variables (most often just one, such as cost or revenue); to calculate the effect on many model variables would generally require a full risk model.

When using risk registers for aggregation, there are two core approaches, which are discussed in the remainder of this section:

- Aggregation of static values (typically the product of probability and impact).
- Aggregation of impacts-on-occurrence, where the occurrence is modelled as a risk event, and the impact may either be a static value or an uncertain one.

3.3.2 Aggregation of Static Values

Figure 3.3 shows the aggregation of static risk values for our fictitious example. The impacts-on-occurrence are multiplied by the probability-of-occurrence to give an "average" impact (cell E31).

	Risk Item	Probabilty	Impact ($)	Prob*Impact	Action	Delivery Date	Responsible
3	Project delay	40%	1000000	400000			
4	Volume lower than expected	20%	670000	134000			
5	Price fluctuation	40%	250000	100000			
6	Competitor enters market	20%	880000	176000			
7	Exchange rate risk	20%	100000	20000			
8	Project manager becomes ill	30%	150000	45000			
9	Insurance cost not defined	70%	530000	371000			
10	Staff turnover	30%	310000	93000			
11	Cost variation	40%	500000	200000			
12	Site management problems	30%	3500000	1050000			
13	Change of law	10%	780000	78000			
14	Low availability of construction materials	30%	1200000	360000			
15	Contractors working inefficiently	20%	350000	70000			
16	High Rainfall	10%	500000	50000			
17	Steelwork Supply to site	20%	610000	122000			
18	Quality of fabricated steel	20%	950000	190000			
19	Mechanical Equipment List Changes	40%	370000	148000			
20	Basis of mechanical equipment estimate	10%	200000	20000			
21	Piping Design Schedule	10%	240000	24000			
22	Low availability of electrical cabling	20%	360000	72000			
23	Demand Inflation	20%	200000	40000			
24	Late delivery of power line	40%	500000	200000			
25	Higher than expected cost for power line	30%	200000	60000			
26	Contractors camp delivery	30%	810000	243000			
27	Inaccurate escalation allowance	10%	930000	93000			
28	Change in forex rate or hedging cost	30%	780000	234000			
29	Increased requirements on outside consultants	20%	370000	74000			
30	Change in cost of staff housing	20%	230000	46000			
31	TOTAL			4713000			

FIGURE 3.3 Example of a Generic Quantitative Risk Register with Aggregation of Static Values

Note also (as discussed in Chapter 7) that risks may often be able to be assigned to categories (for example, geography, department, or related to a specific risk driver), so that they may be aggregated and presented by category, as well as in total.

3.3.3 Aggregation of Risk-Driven Occurrences and Their Impacts

In this approach, the underlying nature of each risk is captured, i.e. whether the risk happens or not. In general, simulation techniques would typically be required to capture the various combinations that may materialise, and in such cases, whilst capturing the random risk occurrence, one may also wish to reflect that the impact of each item could be an uncertain figure drawn from a range (or distribution) of possible values. The implementation of such simulation models is, of course, the main topic of this text, so the details are discussed later. Here we simply illustrate such a model, in which both the occurrence of the risk event and the impact of each is uncertain (we have assumed that the impact uncertainty range is from –10% to +20% around the original base value). Figure 3.4 shows one sample of the model and Figure 3.5 shows the distributions of outcomes after generating 10,000 such samples using @RISK.

The additional benefits of using risk-driven occurrences compared to the static aggregation include:

- It more accurately reflects the underlying nature of the situation, as it captures many scenarios, all of which can occur (the average value calculated in the static method may not even be a possible outcome, just as a coin is unlikely to land on its side when tossed).

Risk Item	Probabilty	Occurrence	Impact Min ($	Impact ML ($	Impact Max ($)	Occur*Impact ($)
Project delay	40%	1	900000	1000000	1200000	1025889
Volume lower than expected	20%	1	603000	670000	804000	712756
Price fluctuation	40%	0	225000	250000	300000	0
Competitor enters market	20%	0	792000	880000	1056000	0
Exchange rate risk	20%	0	90000	100000	120000	0
Project manager becomes ill	30%	1	135000	150000	180000	162452
Insurance cost not defined	70%	1	477000	530000	636000	601135
Staff turnover	30%	0	279000	310000	372000	0
Cost variation	40%	0	450000	500000	600000	0
Site management problems	30%	1	3150000	3500000	4200000	3636939
Change of law	10%	0	702000	780000	936000	0
Low availability of construction materials	30%	0	1080000	1200000	1440000	0
Contractors working inefficiently	20%	0	315000	350000	420000	0
High Rainfall	10%	0	450000	500000	600000	0
Steelwork Supply to site	20%	0	549000	610000	732000	0
Quality of fabricated steel	20%	0	855000	950000	1140000	0
Mechanical Equipment List Changes	40%	0	333000	370000	444000	0
Basis of mechanical equipment estimate	10%	0	180000	200000	240000	0
Piping Design Schedule	10%	0	216000	240000	288000	0
Low availalbility of electrical cabling	20%	0	324000	360000	432000	0
Demand Inflation	20%	0	180000	200000	240000	0
Late delivery of power line	40%	0	450000	500000	600000	0
Higher than expected cost for power line	30%	1	180000	200000	240000	198701
Contractors camp delivery	30%	0	729000	810000	972000	0
Inaccurate escalation allowance	10%	0	837000	930000	1116000	0
Change in forex rate or hedging cost	30%	0	702000	780000	936000	0
Increased requirements on outside consultants	20%	0	333000	370000	444000	0
Change in cost of staff housing	20%	0	207000	230000	276000	0
TOTAL						6337872

FIGURE 3.4 Example of a Generic Quantitative Risk Register with Aggregation of Uncertain Values

- One assesses the range of possible outcomes, not just average values. The range is important for many reasons:
  - To establish how likely it is that any particular case (such as a base case) would be achieved.

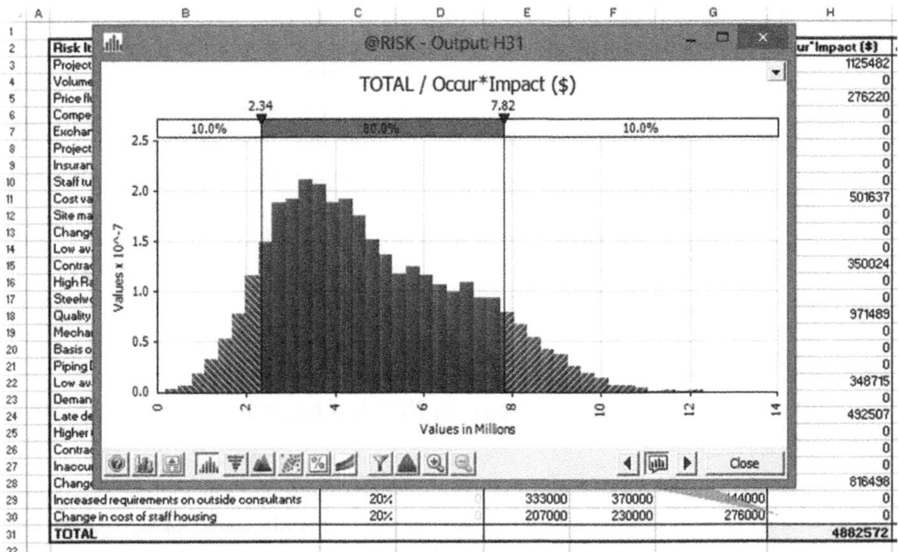

FIGURE 3.5 Distribution of Outcome for Quantitative Risk Register with Aggregation of Uncertain Values

  - To establish levels of contingency and reserves; for example, a level that is sufficient to cover 90% of possible outcomes.
  - To enable risk tolerances to be incorporated into decision-making processes (most management teams would not want to undertake a project that has only a 50/50 chance of success, for example).
  - It is often insufficient to use the average value to assess the impact (or importance or priority) of a risk: for example, if prices can fluctuate in an upwards and downwards direction (with an average of zero), then such fluctuations could still cause a company to suffer severe profit falls or cash flow problems (even if no such problems would arise in the case that prices were fixed at the average level).
- It can correctly assess the average, as the figures used for risk impacts in the static approach may not, in fact, be the real averages of their ranges:
  - The range of the impact (i.e. the impact distribution) may not be symmetric; whereas the (best estimate) assessment of the base value may be at its most likely value, this will not generally be the same as the average. For example, if the impact followed a triangular distribution whose minimum, most likely and maximum values are $80, $100 and $150, the average impact is $110 (the precise statistical terms are covered in Chapter 8, and properties of specific distributions is the subject of Chapter 9).
  - The probability and impact parameters are often misinterpreted, often with the probability (provided as an estimate by an expert or experienced person) corresponding to a percentile of the impact distribution. For example, an initial qualitative assessment may state that "there is a risk that prices will be different to those planned". Each risk may be initially placed in a qualitative probability-impact framework (e.g. using low-medium-high categories for each axis), following which some quantitative estimates of probability and impact are made. At this point, a statement may arise such as "there is a probability of 40% of an incremental cost impact of $10m due to input price deviation" (with an average impact of $4m). However, the reality of the situation may be that prices will always deviate in either a favourable or an unfavourable sense from the base assumption (so that the probability of deviation is 100%); the $10m may really be the impact figure that would be exceeded in 40% of cases. In such cases, the true average is likely to be quite different to the one resulting from the incorrect approach (and could be more or less). These issues are discussed in detail in Chapter 9, where more specific examples are provided.
  - The aggregate figure that arises when several items are added, each of which is moderately different to the individual average, may be significantly different to the true average of the aggregate. This is explored in Chapter 4.

3.3.4 Requirements and Differences to Non-Aggregation Approaches

Despite the apparent simplicity and potential value-added of aggregation approaches, there are important differences between aggregation approaches and the individual risk item approaches. In particular, a frequent mistake is to directly add the impacts of risks that have been quantified at the line item level (as we did in the above examples). This will often simply be invalid. In particular, the risk (and impact) definitions may need to be significantly modified compared to quantitative line item (i.e. non-aggregate) approaches, and generally also made more precise:

- Risk impacts need to be expressed in common terms. For example, some risks may have a monetary impact, whereas others may have a time or quality impact; these would have to be re-expressed in a common way, such as translating the impact of a time delay into monetary terms, which will often require a full model.
- Risks need to be identified and defined in a way that avoids double-counting or overlaps. Any significant double-counting could result in a decision to abandon a (good) project that is apparently too risky. In practice, it is easy to overlook that some identified risks could essentially represent the same (or a similar) item. Similarly, close inspection of the set of risks identified in a line item approach will often lead to a realisation that there is some overlap (partial double-counting) between the defined risks or their impacts. For example:
  - The risks of "price fluctuation" and "exchange rate risk" could essentially be really only a single risk if one item is driven by another (e.g. only an exchange rate risk if price fluctuations are determined by a key foreign exchange rate).
  - Overlaps tend to arise most frequently where several participants describe similar or related risks in different ways. For example, both "site management problems" and "contractors working inefficiently" could cause a delay, but in reality there may be some relationship between them; one could cause or increase the likelihood of the other, or the risk impacts may occur in parallel, so that only the larger of the two effects should be counted.
  - Even where the occurrence of two event risks is independent, their impacts may not be. For example, if the risks of "competitor entry" and "volume lower than expected" (or of "production disruption") materialise at the same time, the aggregate impact on sales volume would typically be less than the sum of the individual impacts (for example, the full volume cannot be lost twice).
- Dependencies and interactions between risks or their impacts need to be captured: if this is not done, then the aggregate risk may be either over- or understated, depending on the situation. For example:
  - The risks of "price fluctuation" and "cost variation" may both be driven by a single factor (such as variability in raw material input prices or exchange rates). Although both would still be needed as line items, their values would each be calculated with reference to the value of this (uncertain) underlying driver, with profit calculated as the difference between them; their inclusion as two independently varying items would overstate the potential variability in the profit.
  - The simultaneous occurrence of a price risk and that of a volume risk would have a revenue effect that is less than the sum of the two effects. In a traditional risk register approach, the revenue effect of each risk would be calculated separately and added, so that the impact would be overstated. There would even be a potential for negative revenues, especially if the effects of other risks (such as a delay to the start of a project) were treated additively. Of course, where the aggregate revenue impact is calculated directly as the product of price and volume, and if the model correctly captures the effect of start-up delays (as would be the case in a full risk model), then this issue would not arise.

In other words, the simple act of adding up line item risks may be trivial, yet the underlying conditions that need to hold for this to be valid are not so. Thus, the transition from a line item-focused approach to an aggregation one represents a more significant step than is often realised, even where line item risks are already individually quantified: in particular, the outputs of a risk identification that has been completed for a line item-focused assessment may need to be revisited when the intention is to develop an aggregate assessment. In practice, such revisiting of process stages that may have been regarded as complete (especially risk identification and the associated definitions) can be an organisational and process challenge. Thus, the introduction of full quantitative assessments at a later stage in a process that had previously been mostly of a qualitative nature will be a challenge; risks and their definitions may already have been communicated widely within an organisation, yet may have been established in a way that does not allow them to be used as the basis for accurate quantitative modelling. At the same time, the revisiting of the identification process or the conducting of major changes to the risk definitions would not be practically possible, and would potentially undermine the appearance of robustness of the process.

Thus, it is important to establish – as early in the process as possible – which approach will ultimately be used: if it is known that the final risk assessment should be at an aggregate level (or indeed require a full model), then extra care with definitions can be taken earlier in the process to minimise rework.

3.4 FULL RISK MODELLING

Full risk models are complete models that incorporate effects of risks and uncertainties on all variables that are relevant to a situation (e.g. prices, volume, revenues, costs, cash flow, tax, etc.), rather than only one or two performance metrics (such as cost) that are captured in risk register approaches. Such models are in many ways simply natural extensions of traditional static models.

Full risk models are a type of "aggregation" approach, but clearly are much richer in terms of their possibilities than the approaches discussed in this chapter, and have a number of benefits over them.

The design and creation of such models is, of course, the main subject of this text (in particular, it is the whole focus of Part II); therefore we do not discuss the specific content in detail here. Rather, in Chapter 4, we cover the main characteristics of models, and discuss their benefits in detail.

3.4.1 Quantitative Aggregate Risk Registers as a First Step to Full Models

Despite the many benefits of full risk models (see Chapter 4), there may be circumstances where a risk register approach may have some advantages compared to full risk modelling ones:

- In the early stages of a project, its fundamental structure and design may not yet have been decided upon. For example, basic decisions about the geographic location of a production facility, its size and design, or the products to be produced may still need analysing before they can be finalised. In such cases, the building of a full risk model in the early stages may not be effective, and a full (even qualitative) risk assessment may not yet even be possible.

- Very often, a base static model may already exist at the time that a formal risk analysis starts. The static approaches can help to give useful "ball park" estimates and comparison of the various structural choices available. In other cases, a template from another project may have been used to quickly assess the broad viability of a project. Thus, it may be deemed to be too complex or inefficient to modify the base model to incorporate risk calculations. In other words – although ideal from a pure modelling perspective – the building of a risk model right from very earliest stages may be inefficient in terms of resource and time usage.
- In practice, as risk assessments are often conducted in the later stages of project evaluations, given the time and resources available, sometimes the risk register approach, although unsatisfactory in many ways, may be deemed to be the only practical one available, with there being insufficient time and resources to build a full risk model.
- As an overlay model, it can be built and maintained by a separate organisational unit. For example, a base model may be "owned" by a finance or a technical function, whereas a project team may be responsible for conducting and "owning" the risk assessment and keeping the risk register and associated model up to date as project planning activities proceed.

On the other hand, although it may be appealing to pursue the use of aggregate (quantitative) risk register approaches beyond fairly early stages of a project, it can be challenging to introduce a full risk modelling approach that is ultimately often required (for example, to evaluate a range of project metrics and their development over time): it is highly likely that (quantitative) inconsistencies in the risk assessment of the same project will arise when one introduces a second (more detailed and sophisticated) approach later on in the process. Therefore, once again, it is important to have clarity of objectives and approach as early in the overall process as possible, as well as to have support from top management throughout the lifetime of the process.

CHAPTER 4

Full Integrated Risk Modelling: Decision-Support Benefits

In this chapter, we discuss the uses and benefits of full (integrated) risk models. We start with a discussion of their main characteristics, in particular highlighting their differences and benefits compared to risk register approaches, and then provide a detailed discussion of their benefits when compared to traditional static (non-risk) modelling approaches.

(We refer to traditional Excel modelling approaches as "static". This is not intended to imply that the input values of such models cannot be changed; rather only to indicate that such approaches do not incorporate risk elements as a fundamental part of their conception"; some people prefer the term "deterministic".)

4.1 KEY CHARACTERISTICS OF FULL MODELS

Full risk models are complete models that incorporate the effects of risks and uncertainties on all variables (e.g. prices, volume, revenues, costs, cash flow, tax, etc.); they are simply the counterpart (or extension) of traditional static models, but in which risk and uncertainty are incorporated.

Full risk models contrast with aggregate risk register approaches in several ways:

- The effect on all model variables and on multiple metrics is captured.
- The true nature of the risk is reflected, and time components and dependencies are incorporated.

These points are discussed in more detail below.

In many cases, knowledge of the effect of risks on a range of variables, metrics and performance indicators is fundamental in order to meet the needs of multiple stakeholders. For example:

- A project team may wish to better understand the effect of a delay on resource requirements and on subcontractor arrangements.

- A sales department may be mostly interested in revenue risk, but the manufacturing team may need to focus on the effect of potential breakdowns on volume (which also affects revenue).
- A treasury or finance department may need information on the cash flow, tax or financing profile, or aspects relating to discussion with potential lenders or sources of finance.
- The strategy or business development department may wish to know items that have implications for potential business partnerships.
- Senior management may wish to know about all of the above items (in an integrated, not piece-by-piece or fragmented, analysis), as well as about general project economics and value creation.

Full risk models can also support the development of more enhanced capabilities in areas such as optimisation (or optimised decision-making), as they allow the effect of multi-variable trade-offs to be established. Their use may also be the only way to accurately prioritise risk mitigation actions and general decisions. Similarly, they allow an exploration of issues concerning the structure of individual projects and of business or project portfolios, as in general there will be interactions between the items that need a full risk model in order to be captured.

The true nature of many items is too rich to be captured in risk register approaches, whereas doing so in full models is generally straightforward. For example:

- Items that are best described with simple uncertainty ranges do not fit into operational risk frameworks. For example, the variation in price or sales volume of a product, or the cost of a particular raw material, or a piece of machinery follows general uncertainty profiles (in continuous ranges), and does not usually fit well into a probability-impact framework.
- An explicit time axis is often required, for example:
  - In order to calculate items such as net present value (NPV) and internal rate-of-return (IRR), to model cash flow and financial requirements, and to capture project schedules and resource planning issues.
  - The time-series development of some items is fundamental to their nature; they may fluctuate around a long-term trend, or have mean-reversion properties, or be subject to multiple random shocks and impacts that are persistent. Some risks may materialise or be active at different points in time (e.g. have an earliest start date, or have a duration), such as for the breakdown of a facility, the entry of a new competitor into the market, a strike by the workforce, the introduction of new technologies, and so on.
  - Without an explicit time axis, even basic issues, such as distinguishing between probability-of-occurrences within a period from those over the course of the project, are often overlooked (see Chapter 9 for more discussion of this).
  - In general, the use of a single figure to estimate the aggregate time impact would often be inappropriate (as would be done in a risk register approach).
- Dependency relationships between items can be captured in a way that is not possible with risk register approaches. For example:
  - A project delay drives investment, production volumes, revenues and some operating costs, with a knock-on effect on profit, taxes and cash flows, and so on.
  - The fluctuation in sales prices may be driven by commodity prices, and hence also affect variable costs, with a knock-on effect on margin and subsequent model variables.

- Generally, in models with multiple variables or line items, some are impacted directly by risks whereas others are calculated from other items, which themselves depend on risk impacts. In a standard risk register, impacts are treated as independent, which can lead to incorrect calculations, such as when risks that impact price, volume and launch date aggregate (independently) to result in a negative figure for revenues (in a risk register that aggregates the revenue impact of each risk, for example).

Full models may generally be integrated with a base case model, if one exists (in some cases, only a risk model has been built and no base case has been defined). Often, it is possible to build a switch that governs whether the model's inputs are set to the base values or to the risk values (examples are shown in Chapter 7). Models that are integrated in this way are more likely to be accurate and updated appropriately as the general risk assessment process proceeds.

Risk registers are generally "overlays" that are held separately to a base model, and may be discussed by different groups of people. This separation can lead to base models not being updated even as risk mitigation measures are planned for, and as a project structure changes. For example, plans may be made that require a different product mix, a delayed start time, extra risk-mitigation costs or a different manufacturing location or technology, but these may simply not be reflected in the base model. As a result, it may not reflect the true final structure of a project, and be an inappropriate basis to make decisions; indeed, when used as a reference point for final project authorisation, budget allocations and business planning, the model would be inadequate.

Clearly, the activities associated with building full models are more demanding than those associated with risk register approaches, due to the richness, potential complexity and flexibility requirements that are usually present.

4.2 OVERVIEW OF THE BENEFITS OF FULL RISK MODELLING

The remainder of the chapter focuses on the benefits of using full risk modelling approaches compared to traditional static ones. The following provides an overview of the main points that are discussed in detail:

- It supports the creation of more accurate models:
  - Reflects the uncertainty that is present in the real situation.
  - Uses a structured and rigorous process to identify all key risk drivers.
  - Allows event risks to be included explicitly and unambiguously.
  - Allows for risk-response or mitigation measures, their costs and impacts to be embedded within the base case model.
  - Captures the simultaneous occurrence of multiple risks or uncertainties.
  - Allows one to assess the outcomes for models whose behaviour is non-linear as the inputs change, or where there is a complex interaction between items in a situation.
  - Allows one to capture accurately the value that is inherent in flexibilities and embedded decisions.
  - Allows the use of forms of dependency that do not exist in traditional static approaches.
- It enables the reflection of the possible range of outcomes in decision-making:

  - Establishes where any planned (or base) case fits within the true possible range of outcomes, and hence the likelihood of such a case being achieved.
  - Helps to overcome the structural bias of the "trap of the most likely" (in which static models populated with the mostly likely values of their inputs are often assumed to show the most likely outcome, whereas in fact they may show an output value that is quite different to this).
  - Supports the understanding of the implications of other possible base case assumptions on model outputs, as well as the exploration of alternative, or more precise, modelling possibilities of the base case.
  - Establishes metrics that are relevant in general decision-making processes, including the economic evaluation of projects and the reflection of risk tolerances, as well as providing a framework to compare projects with different risk profiles, and thus to support the development of business portfolios and strategy.
  - Allows for a robust and transparent process to plan contingencies, to revise objectives or modify targets.
- It facilitates the use of more transparent assumptions and fewer biases:
  - Allows the base case assumptions (on the value of inputs) to be held separately and to be explicitly compared with the range of their possible values, thus creating transparency and helping to reduce motivational or political biases.
  - Supports the balancing and alignment of intuition and rationality in decision-making processes.
  - Facilitates the creation of shared accountability for decision-making.
- It facilitates the processes of group work and communication:
  - Provides a framework for more rigorous and precise group discussions.
  - May allow (apparently) conflicting views on values for assumptions or likely outcomes to be reconciled.

4.3 CREATING MORE ACCURATE AND REALISTIC MODELS

This section discusses in detail how the use of risk modelling allows the creation of more accurate and realistic models, as summarized through the key points mentioned above.

4.3.1 Reality is Uncertain: Models Should Reflect This

It is probably fair to say that static models do potentially have a valid role to play in some circumstances, most especially in the earlier stage of considering a new project:

- It is a quick way to explore the basic aspects of a specific situation, and may lead to some valuable insights. For example, an estimate of the order of magnitude of the potential benefits and costs of a project can help to establish whether it needs to be changed in some major structural way, or fundamentally re-scoped, or cancelled.
- Initial attempts to build quantitative relationships between variables will help to drive a thought process about key factors, their interactions and hypotheses that need to be tested, and will generally help to identify whether further research and data gathering is required, and the nature of the information needed.

- It may support the testing of key sensitivities. (However, especially at the early stages of a project, one needs to be mindful of the potential for circular reasoning. The sensitivities shown by the model are a result of the assumptions used and logic of the model, so may be misleading if one concludes that a variable is unimportant in its contribution to risk simply because one has initially incorrectly assumed [due to lack of information at that point] that its possible range of variation is narrow.)

On the other hand, almost any future situation contains risks or uncertainties, and to conduct decision-support analysis that does not reflect this would not seem sensible. In particular, once a basic project concept is considered more seriously (and cannot be ruled out by simple calculations or "back of the envelope" analysis), then it would seem logical to include risks in the analysis: risk modelling "simply" aims to reflect the reality that uncertainties and risks are present, and that an appropriate basis for decision-making should capture their nature and effects, including the potential for their simultaneous occurrence.

4.3.2 Structured Process to Include All Relevant Factors

A formal risk assessment aimed at building a quantitative model has a number of benefits in terms of identifying all relevant factors and includes:

- A high level of rigour and precision in order to correctly identify risks, understand their nature and that of their impacts, avoid double-counting and capture dependencies.
- A focus on the drivers of risk (rather than sensitivity) that will often result in a more accurate and precise capturing of the variation than would a process that is focused only on sensitivity analysis.

4.3.3 Unambiguous Approach to Capturing Event Risks

Risk models can capture explicitly the presence of event risks in a way that is unambiguous. On the other hand, where event risks are present in a situation, the appropriate way to treat them within traditional (static) Excel models is not clear, and is therefore done in a variety of "proxy" ways, resulting in ambiguity, potential confusion or misleading conclusions. In some cases, event risks may not be included at all in a quantitative model: generally speaking, the most likely outcome for any individual risk is its non-occurrence (i.e. the probability of occurrence is less than 50%), so that populating a model with each of its inputs at the most likely value would be equivalent to the risk not happening, so it may as well be left out of the model. On the other hand, if a situation contains multiple such event risks, then from an aggregate perspective, the most likely outcome would be that one or more of them do occur; therefore an approach that ignores them is unrealistic and potentially misleading. Similarly, where a sequence of events is required to happen for an overall outcome to be achieved (such as each of various phases of a drug development needing to succeed for the drug to be brought to market), the most likely case (at each process step) could be for a successful outcome, but in aggregate the success may, in fact, be quite unlikely (see later in this section for an example). As a result of such issues, approaches that are sometimes used involve:

- Including event risks in the model at a fixed value equal to their average probability (or frequency) of occurrence. (This approximation to the average impact may be a reasonable

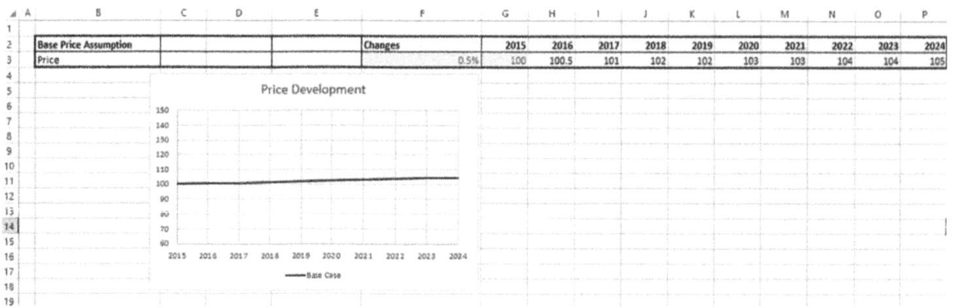

FIGURE 4.1 Original Model of Price Development

starting point, but as discussed in Chapter 3 may be misleading or inappropriate in many cases, and of course still only provides a static figure. In addition, a model's formulae may require that an input assumption is either one or the other of the valid values, such as if it contains an **IF** function whose logic is activated one way or the other according to the outcome of the event risk.)

- From a set of possible events, assuming that some will occur and some will not.
- Excluding them from the base model (and the presentation of its results) but listing them separately (e.g. in an appendix of supporting documents), with a brief note under the "model assumptions" that the base case excludes these risks. Thus, in fact, the base case may be extremely unlikely to ever be observed, but this will be hard for decision-makers to assess, and so they are likely to anchor the base case in their minds as if it were a realistic case (which may be acceptable to proceed with as a project), whereas almost all realistic cases may, in fact, be unacceptable if the analysis were correctly conducted.

Thus, in general, when in reality there are event risks in a situation (which is very common), decision-makers are placed in a difficult position to be able to judge the true risks of that situation, unless they are explicitly modelled and their effects captured.

The file Ch4.PriceUpgradePaths.xlsx contains an illustration of an example of such a situation. The context is that a company is facing a rapidly changing market in which any particular product is under price pressure, with an annual reduction in market prices of 5% p.a. expected. However, there are a number of grades of the product that can be sold into the market, with the higher grades achieving higher market prices (at any point in time), but also suffering annual price reductions. The company currently produces only the base grade product, but has plans to invest in research and development in order to develop the (non-public) technology that is required in order to produce the higher grades.

Figure 4.1 shows the company's original plan (contained in the worksheet Original), in which the modelling analyst has not explicitly modelled every process step, but has tried (by using a price increase of 0.5% p.a.) to balance the pressure of the price reduction against the possibility to sell the higher price products; the modest annual increase may be presented as "conservative" if one considers that the higher graded products sell for at least 20% more than the base plan.

On the other hand, it may make sense to build a model in which one can test the effect of the success of each of the product upgrade processes. The worksheet named Sens (within the same file) contains the calculations in which the price development of each product is

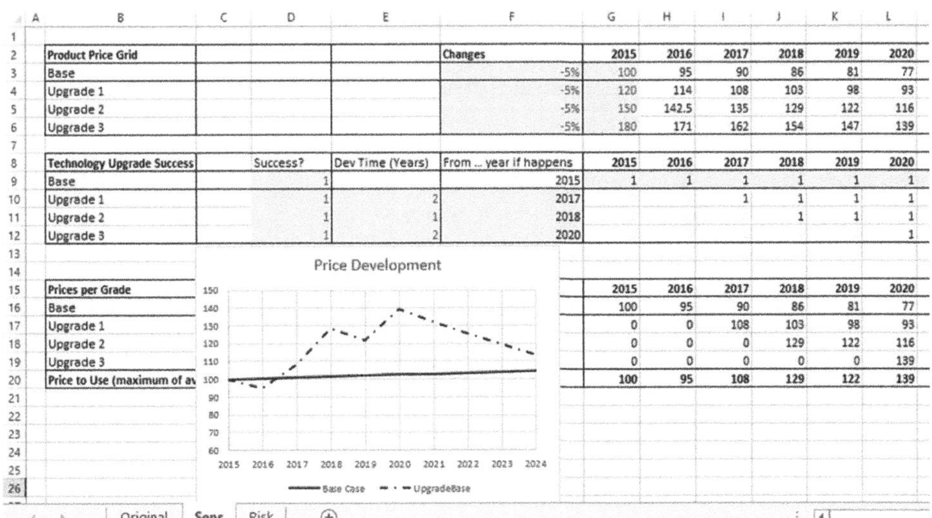

Product Price Grid	Changes	2015	2016	2017	2018	2019	2020
Base	-5%	100	95	90	86	81	77
Upgrade 1	-5%	120	114	108	103	98	93
Upgrade 2	-5%	150	142.5	135	129	122	116
Upgrade 3	-5%	180	171	162	154	147	139

Technology Upgrade Success	Success?	Dev Time (Years)	From ... year if happens	2015	2016	2017	2018	2019	2020
Base	1		2015	1	1	1	1	1	1
Upgrade 1	1	2	2017			1	1	1	1
Upgrade 2	1	1	2018				1	1	1
Upgrade 3	1	2	2020						1

Prices per Grade	2015	2016	2017	2018	2019	2020
Base	100	95	90	86	81	77
Upgrade 1	0	0	108	103	98	93
Upgrade 2	0	0	0	129	122	116
Upgrade 3	0	0	0	0	0	139
Price to Use (maximum of av	100	95	108	129	122	139

FIGURE 4.2 Revised Plan for Price Development Assuming Successful Upgrade at Each Step

explicitly shown. The switches in cells D10:D12 can be used to set whether a particular product upgrade process is successful or not. If a particular upgrade process is successful, the company immediately produces the grade that sells for the higher price.

After consulting internal experts, the modeller is informed that the likelihood of success for the first upgrade is 90%. The second upgrade process can start only if the first one is successful, in which case its probability of success is estimated at 75%, and similarly the third process would have a probability of 60% of success, but can be engaged in only if the second is successful. Not having any risk-modelling tools at his or her disposition, the modeller judges that since the most likely case for each upgrade process is that it will (as an individual process) be successful, it would be inappropriate to assume that some of them are not successful. Indeed, a choice by the modeller to assume that a particular process step would fail will not endear him/her to the organisation or to the particular people responsible for that step, and may not be defensible (since the most likely outcome for that step is its success). Therefore, the revised base case is presented on the assumption that all product upgrade processes are successful, and is shown in Figure 4.2.

Clearly, the revised (more detailed) base calculations seem to suggest that there is significant upside to the business case, compared to the original plan in which prices were increasing only 0.5% p.a. However, of course, the issue here is that the uncertainty in the upgrade processes has not been taken into account. The worksheet Risk (in the same file) has the upgraded processes represented as risk events, which are either successful or not (with the given probability, and using the **RAND**() function to capture this), and captures that a future upgrade process can only be engaged in if the prior one has succeeded. Figure 4.3 shows the results of running a simulation of this in which many scenarios are captured. The graph shows the average price development over these scenarios, as well as the development in the worst 10% of cases.

With respect to the issue of event risks, this model aims to demonstrate the ambiguity that can be present if one does not engage in explicit risk modelling, and the different, possibly misleading, results that can arise in such cases.

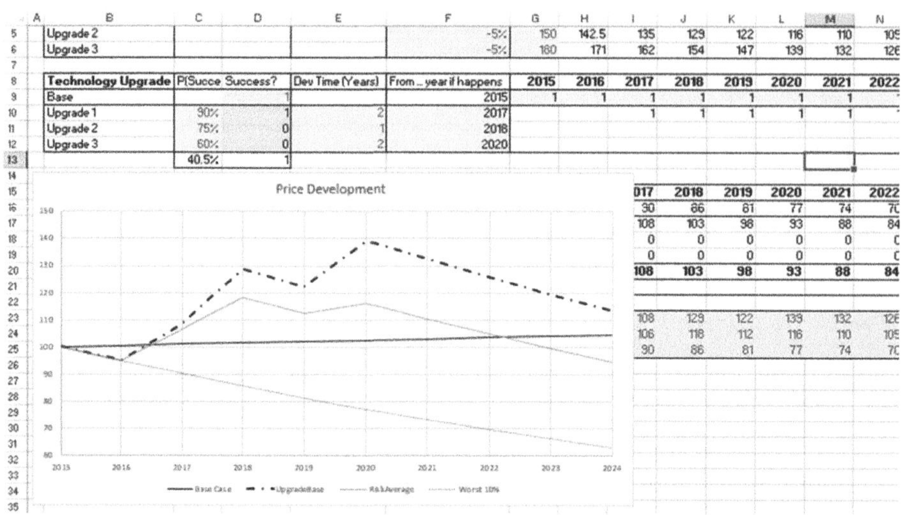

FIGURE 4.3 Revised Plan for Price Development Assuming Uncertainty of the Success of the Upgrade at Each Step

4.3.4 Inclusion of Risk Mitigation and Response Factors

The process of risk assessment clearly results in adapting plans in order to respond to or mitigate potential uncertainties and risks. By explicitly including these risk-response measures (including their costs and their impact on the risk items, such as a reduction in uncertainty), one achieves a more accurate model of the reality of the project structure.

Without a formal risk modelling process, it is surprising how often project activity plans are adapted by project teams to respond to risk, but without the base static model being adapted to reflect the cost and effect of these activities. Such a situation is particularly likely to occur due to:

- Lack of awareness. The modeller may be in a different part of the organisation (such as finance), and is not part of the day-to-day workings of the project team.
- Inappropriate base model structure. If the base static model has not been designed to reflect the risk structure of a project (which it almost certainly will not have been without a formal process), then there will simply not be a specific or explicit line item to capture the risk or the effect of the response measures. Thus, the mechanism required to update the model to include the effect of risks and the mitigation measures is not present.

A formal risk assessment process will help to ensure sufficient shared awareness, and support the correct design of a model, so that the effect of response measures can be reflected efficiently.

4.3.5 Simultaneous Occurrence of Uncertainties and Risks

Risk-based simulation captures the effect of the simultaneous variation in all uncertain variables and risks, and in a way that is consistent with their true behaviour. This contrasts with

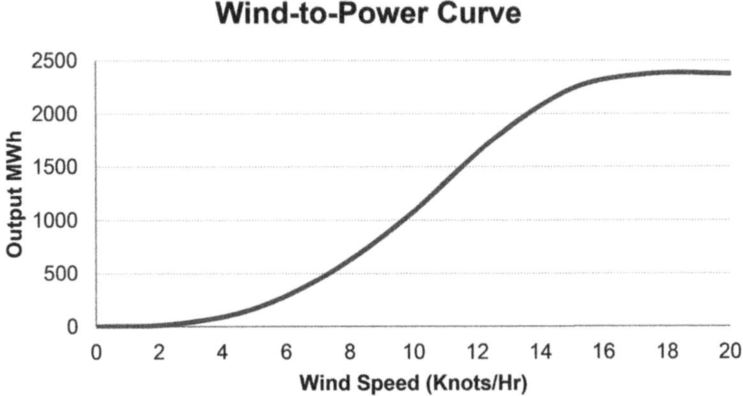

FIGURE 4.4 Translation of Wind Speed into Power Output

sensitivity and scenario analysis, in which only a limited number of cases are shown, and whose likelihood is not clearly defined or known, as discussed in detail in Chapter 6.

4.3.6 Assessing Outcomes in Non-Linear Situations

Where the output of a model varies in a non-linear way with its inputs, it can be particularly difficult to assess the true output behaviour by using traditional static models or sensitivity analysis. A simple example would be if one were assessing the power output of a wind turbine, which is determined by the wind speed, with (for example) a wind-to-power response curve as illustrated in Figure 4.4.

As this is a non-linear curve, if the wind speed is uncertain, it would be challenging to assess the true power output (such as the average) unless many scenarios were run (and their probabilities known). For this reason, simulation techniques are suited to calculate the distribution of possible power output, with each sampled wind speed translating into a particular power output during the simulation.

Figure 4.5 shows the assumed distribution of wind speed in Knots/Hr (a Weibull (2,8) distribution is often used here; see Chapter 9 for details of this distribution), and Figure 4.6 shows the distribution of possible power outputs. (In practice, such a calculation would need to be done for many specific time intervals within the day, e.g. for intervals of 15 minutes, with the Weibull process representing the average wind speed within that interval.)

4.3.7 Reflecting Operational Flexibility and Real Options

Some modelling situations require an explicit consideration of variability for them to be sufficiently accurate or even meaningful. This is especially the case in situations in which there are embedded flexibilities (or decisions that may be taken), but where the particular actions that would be taken depend on the scenario. In general, this is a special case of the non-linear behaviour of models discussed above, in which the uncertainty profile causes a decision to switch results from an interaction of uncertain factors. In such cases, a static model may have very limited relevance, as the values shown in a single case (or in a small set of cases

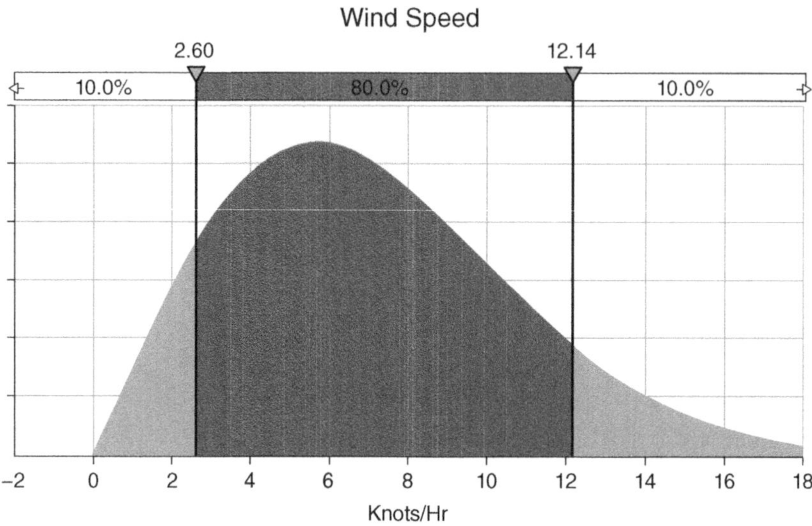

FIGURE 4.5 Assumed Distribution of Wind Speed

using sensitivity or scenario analysis) will not provide a sufficient basis to accurately evaluate the situation. The general application areas are those that involve contingent claims, liabilities or penalties, as well as real options (i.e. the valuation of flexibility and contingent benefits), such as:

- Government guarantees. A government wishing to encourage private sector investment in a particular industry might provide a guaranteed floor to the minimum prices that the private sector would receive or be able to charge (or a ceiling to the costs that the private

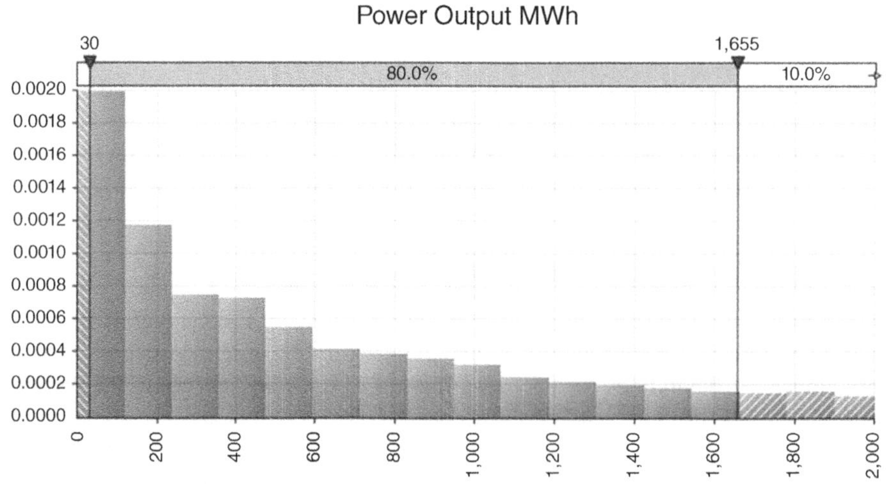

FIGURE 4.6 Simulated Distribution of Power Output

sector may face). An example was announced on 21 October 2013 by the UK government, which offered some long-term price guarantees to potential French and Chinese investors in the nuclear energy production sector. In general, in such cases:

  - If market prices were always above the guaranteed price level, then the guarantee would turn out not to have any direct value, whereas if market prices were below the guaranteed level, then the government's liability could be large.
  - In reality, market prices (or other relevant factors) will develop in an uncertain fashion over a multi-year timeframe, so that they may be below the guarantee level in some periods and above it in others.
  - Therefore, the consideration of any single scenario (or even a few selected ones) will not reflect the reality of the situation, and would likely underestimate the benefit to one party and overestimate the costs to the other, or vice versa. To assess the value embedded in such guarantees it would be necessary to capture the payoffs and costs to each party under a wide range of scenarios, as well as to take the likelihood of each scenario into account. For a multi-period situation, and with additional complexities (such as the guaranteed level inflating over time), such a calculation would only be practical with a full risk model.
- Comparing the value in building a mixed-use facility with a dedicated-use one:
  - It would generally be more expensive to design, build and operate a production facility that can use a variety of inputs (according to the one that is cheapest) than to do so for a facility that is required to use a single type of input. For example, it would be more expensive to implement the ability to switch to the cheapest in a range of chemical feedstocks (or to different energy types, such as oil, gas or electricity). However, the flexible facility will have lower overall production costs, due to being able to always use the cheapest input. Just as in the above example, the valuation of the benefit achieved by (potentially frequently) switching to the currently cheapest input (and hence to compare this to the operating costs saved) would require the consideration of the full range of scenarios that may happen. In particular, the value of this flexibility will be more in a situation of high variability (volatility) in input prices (especially so if correlations between the price development paths are lower), and the longer the timeframe of consideration. (This "real option" has many analogies to financial market options in terms of the drivers of its value.)
  - Similar arguments apply to situations where the end product can be adapted (or optimised) according to market conditions, such as the flexibility to produce different end products for sale (such as a range of chemicals, or a range of vehicles if one has the ability to retool a car manufacturing plant).
- These concepts hold for other types of payoff that depend on the level of an uncertain process or processes, such as profit share agreements, and contracts relating to insurance, reinsurance and general penalty clauses (for example, in service-level agreements).

The file Ch4.OpFlexRealOptions.TripleFuel.xlsx contains an example in which, when designing a manufacturing facility, one has the choice as to which fuel source should be planned to be used: oil, gas or electricity. (To keep the example focused for the purposes of the text at this point, the numbers are only illustrative and are not intended to represent a genuine forecast; we have not considered total expenditure based on volume forecasts, nor do we concern ourselves here with any discounting issues.)

	A	B	C	D	E	F	G	H	I	J	K	L	M	N	O	P	Q
1		Choosing a Single Fuel Source															
2																	
3						0	1	2	3	4	5	6	7	8	9	10	
4		Values, $/unit	Total $/unit														
5		Oil	1,249			100	104	108	112	117	122	127	132	137	142	148	=O5*(1+P10)
6		Gas	1,331			90	96	103	110	118	126	135	145	155	165	177	=O6*(1+P11)
7		Electricity	1,453			110	116	121	127	134	140	147	155	163	171	179	=O7*(1+P12)
8																	
9		% Changes			Change												
10		Oil			4.0%		4.0%	4.0%	4.0%	4.0%	4.0%	4.0%	4.0%	4.0%	4.0%	4.0%	=$E10
11		Gas			7.0%		7.0%	7.0%	7.0%	7.0%	7.0%	7.0%	7.0%	7.0%	7.0%	7.0%	=$E11
12		Electricity			5.0%		5.0%	5.0%	5.0%	5.0%	5.0%	5.0%	5.0%	5.0%	5.0%	5.0%	=$E12

FIGURE 4.7 Ten-year Forecast of Total Expenditure for Each Fuel Type, Using Static Growth Assumptions

In principle, one could construct a multi-year forecast that calculates the total energy consumption according to each choice, compare the three cases and choose the one for which the costs are lowest. The worksheet Static contains a model in which there are three fuel types whose price development is forecast over a 10-year period. Figure 4.7 shows the calculations, and in particular that the lowest cost choice over the 10-year period would be to use oil (resulting in a total expenditure of $1249 per unit of fuel used, shown in cell C5). In this specific context, we assume that this choice is permanently fixed once it has been evaluated at the beginning of the 10-year period.

On the other hand, one may have the possibility to build a (more expensive) facility that can be run on any fuel source, so that the fuel used would change each period to that which is cheapest. The worksheet RStaticWSwitch in the same file contains the calculations in which an extra line is added, showing the value of the minimum fuel source in each period, which would correspond to the expenditure in the case that one can switch to that source. This is shown in Figure 4.8. One can see that the best course of action would be to select to use gas for three periods before switching to oil at the beginning of the fourth period and then to always use oil thereafter. In this case, the expenditure over 10 years would be $1234 per unit, or a saving of $15 compared to having no switching possibility (cell C8).

However, the model does not yet fully capture the effect of uncertainty, because the number of switching possibilities is limited to at most two (as the price change assumptions apply for the full model timeframe); if price changes are uncertain within each period, then there are many more switching scenarios. The worksheet RiskWSwitch includes a forecast in which the uncertain development of each is taken into account (this uses a normal distribution, discussed in detail in Chapters 8, 9 and 10). By pressing **F9** to recalculate the model, one sees

	A	B	C	D	E	F	G	H	I	J	K	L	M	N	O	P	Q
1		Valuing a Switching option															
2																	
3						0	1	2	3	4	5	6	7	8	9	10	
4		Values, $/unit	Total $/unit														
5		Oil	1,249			100	104	108	112	117	122	127	132	137	142	148	=O5*(1+P10)
6		Gas	1,331			90	96	103	110	118	126	135	145	155	165	177	=O6*(1+P11)
7		Electricity	1,453			110	116	121	127	134	140	147	155	163	171	179	=O7*(1+P12)
8		Expenditure with a switching option	1,234			90	96	103	110	117	122	127	132	137	142	148	=MIN(P5:P7)
9		% Changes			Change												
10		Oil			4.0%		4.0%	4.0%	4.0%	4.0%	4.0%	4.0%	4.0%	4.0%	4.0%	4.0%	=$E10
11		Gas			7.0%		7.0%	7.0%	7.0%	7.0%	7.0%	7.0%	7.0%	7.0%	7.0%	7.0%	=$E11
12		Electricity			5.0%		5.0%	5.0%	5.0%	5.0%	5.0%	5.0%	5.0%	5.0%	5.0%	5.0%	=$E12

FIGURE 4.8 Ten-year Forecast of Total Expenditure for each Fuel Type, Using Static Growth Assumptions and Including a Switching Option

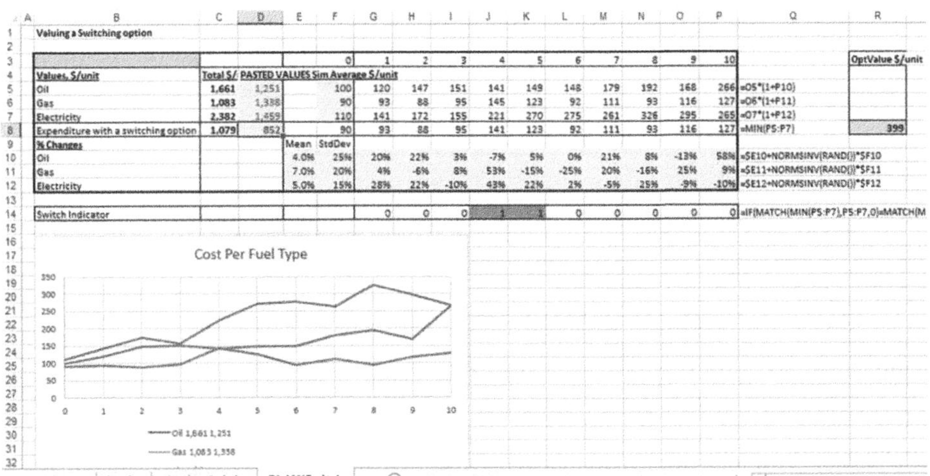

	B	C	D	E	F	G	H	I	J	K	L	M	N	O	P	Q	R
1	Valuing a Switching option																
2																	
3					0	1	2	3	4	5	6	7	8	9	10		OptValue $/unit
4	Values, $/unit	Total $/	PASTED VALUES Sim Average $/unit														
5	Oil	1,661	1,251		100	120	147	151	141	149	148	179	192	168	266	=O5*(1+P10)	
6	Gas	1,083	1,338		90	93	88	95	145	123	92	111	93	116	127	=O6*(1+P11)	
7	Electricity	2,382	1,459		110	141	172	155	221	270	275	261	326	295	265	=O7*(1+P12)	
8	Expenditure with a switching option	1,079	852		90	93	88	95	141	123	92	111	93	116	127	=MIN(P5:P7)	399
9	% Changes			Mean	StdDev												
10	Oil			4.0%	25%	20%	22%	3%	-7%	5%	0%	21%	8%	-13%	58%	=$E10+NORMSINV(RAND())*$F10	
11	Gas			7.0%	20%	4%	-6%	8%	53%	-15%	-25%	20%	-16%	25%	9%	=$E11+NORMSINV(RAND())*$F11	
12	Electricity			5.0%	15%	28%	22%	-10%	43%	22%	2%	-5%	25%	-9%	-10%	=$E12+NORMSINV(RAND())*$F12	
13																	
14	Switch Indicator					0	0	0	1	1	0	0	0	0	0	=IF(MATCH(MIN(P5:P7),P5:P7,0)=MATCH(M	

FIGURE 4.9 Ten-year Forecast of Total Expenditure for each Fuel Type, Using Uncertain Growth Assumptions and Including A Switching Option

many different scenarios: in some cases, the source that is initially cheapest may remain so, whereas in others, there may be frequent switching, so that the savings would be higher. A simulation can be run to capture the average saving over many scenarios. Figure 4.9 shows the results of having done so. The results suggest an average expenditure of approximately $850 per unit (cell D8), or a saving of approximately $400 per unit compared to the original case in which there was no switching possibility; cell R8 contains the calculation of the savings made by the use of the switching approach compared to the next best possibility.

The example shows once again that (although the core aspect of the model design is the creation of the extra line item to incorporate the switching possibility) it is the presence of uncertainty that creates most of the value in the real-world situation. On the other hand, without any consideration of the uncertainty, both the possibility to consider the switching option and the utility of pursuing this as an option to be analysed could have been overlooked, with the result that the potential benefits of the operational flexibility would not have been considered or exploited.

4.3.8 Assessing Outcomes with Other Complex Dependencies

In general, when a model's logic is not simple (even the presence of **IF** or **MAX** functions, or other non-linear behaviours is sufficient), and especially when certain calculation paths are only activated by a change in the value of multiple items, it can be challenging to use intuitive methods to assess the sensitivity of output to input values. In such contexts, the use of uncertainty modelling can be extremely valuable. Examples include:

- Where there are operational flexibilities that need to be captured in the evaluation of a project (as shown above).

	A	B	C	D	E	F	G	H	I	J	K
1											
2		TASK		Duration (Days)	Uncertainty Case			Samples		Case To Use	
3				Base Case	Min	Max	Prob Occu	Duration	Occur	1	=RiskSwitchDuration
4		Series 1								37.0	=SUM(J5:J7)
5		Task 1.1		10	8	15		9.8		10.0	=CHOOSE(RiskSwitchDuration,D5,H5)
6		Task 1.2		15	12	18		14.2		15.0	=CHOOSE(RiskSwitchDuration,D6,H6)
7		Task 1.3		12	10	15		11.4		12.0	=CHOOSE(RiskSwitchDuration,D7,H7)
8		Series 2								32.0	=SUM(J9:J11)
9		Task 2.1		18	15	21		20.3		18.0	=CHOOSE(RiskSwitchDuration,D9,H9)
10		Task 2.2		8	5	10		7.3		8.0	=CHOOSE(RiskSwitchDuration,D10,H10)
11		Task 2.3		6	4	8		4.1		6.0	=CHOOSE(RiskSwitchDuration,D11,H11)
12		Series 3 (Project Risks)								0.0	=SUM(J13:J15)
13		Task 3.1		0	20	60	40%	42.1	1	0.0	=CHOOSE(RiskSwitchDuration,D13,H13*I13)
14		Task 3.2		0	15	30	30%	15.3	0	0.0	=CHOOSE(RiskSwitchDuration,D14,H14*I14)
15		Task 3.3		0	10	25	20%	21.7	0	0.0	=CHOOSE(RiskSwitchDuration,D15,H15*I15)
16											
17				Project Duration = max(series totals)						37.0	=MAX(J4,J8,J12)

FIGURE 4.10 Model of Project Duration (Base Case View)

- Where only the joint occurrence of a number of items would cause a product to fall below a safety limit, one would need to capture this by checking this condition in the model. In a simple sensitivity approach, in which only one or two factors would be altered (e.g. switch variables to turn a risk on or off), such scenarios may never materialise, potentially resulting in a modeller overlooking the need to check whether failure can occur at all.
- In project schedule analysis, an increase in the length of a task that is not on the critical path may have no effect on the project's duration, whereas an increase in the duration of activities that are on the critical path would increase the project's duration. For some tasks, an increase in its duration may have only a partial effect (for example, if the path on which the task lies becomes the critical one only after the task length has increased by a certain amount). Additionally, when there are multiple variables (or items that affect task durations) that may change at the same time, establishing the overall effect of these on the project's duration is difficult, unless an uncertainty modelling approach is used.

For fairly simple situations, schedule models can be built in Excel. In particular, where a project consists of a simple series of tasks (in which each always has the same predecessor and successor), and where task series occur in parallel with no interaction between them, then Excel can be used to determine project schedules: the duration of a series of tasks is the sum of their durations (including the duration of planned stoppages and other non-working time), and the duration of task series conducted in parallel is the maximum of such series. One advantage of using the Excel platform in such cases is that cost estimation can be linked to the schedule.

The file Ch4.ProjectSchedule.xlsx contains an example; Figure 4.10 shows a screen clip. There are three main task series, each consisting of three tasks. Within each series, the tasks are performed in sequence, so that the series duration is the sum of the duration of its tasks (e.g. cell J4), but the task series are in parallel, so that the total project duration is the maximum of these sums (cell J17). There is also a switch cell to choose between the risk case and the static case; in the case shown, the model is shown at its base values (in column J). Column G shows the probabilities for the third task series, which consists of event risks, whose occurrence is captured in column I (since the model is shown at the base case, these event risks are not active within the calculations in column J).

Note that since the model is built in Excel, it is relatively straightforward to add a cost component, in which costs are determined from durations, as well as having their own variability. Figure 4.11 shows the cost component of the model, in which total costs for each

M	N	O	P	Q	R
Cost/Day				Case To Use	TOTALCOST
Base	Min	Max	Sample	1	
25000	20000	37500	21228	25000	250000
18750	15000	22500	17383	18750	281250
15000	12500	18750	13129	15000	180000
22500	18750	26250	20517	22500	405000
10000	6250	12500	9324	10000	80000
7500	5000	10000	7469	7500	45000
27000	18000	40000	21390	27000	0
18000	15000	25000	16299	18000	0
6500	5000	15000	5862	6500	0
Total Cost = Sum					1241250

FIGURE 4.11 Model of Project Cost (Base Case View)

activity are calculated as the product of the duration (in days) and the cost per day. The cost per day also has a switch to be able to use either fixed values or base case static values.

A simulation can be run to calculate the distribution of the duration, and of the costs, of the project; see Figures 4.12 and 4.13, respectively (once again the simulation is run using @RISK in order to use its graphics features, but the reader may use the tools of Chapter 12 instead in order to do so purely in Excel/VBA).

Finally, a scatter plot can be produced showing the cost range for each possible duration; see Figure 4.14.

As a final note with respect to this area of application, the more general challenge in such project schedule analysis is where the critical path changes in more complex ways as task durations vary, so that the formula that defines its duration is too complex to capture in Excel. This is one of the reasons for using the MSProject tool within @RISK (see Chapter 13).

4.3.9 Capturing Correlations, Partial Dependencies and Common Causalities

Risk models can capture relationships between input variables that are not possible in traditional models:

- In a traditional model, as soon as one input is made to depend on another – such as volume decreasing as price increases – then this second variable (volume) is no longer a true input: it becomes a calculated quantity, with the inputs becoming price and the scaling factors that are required to calculate volume from any given price.
- In a simulation model, there can be relationships between input variables (distributions), such as conditional probabilities, partial dependencies, correlations (correlated sampling), copulas and others. This provides for a richer set of possible relationships that generally enable one to more accurately capture the reality of a situation (see Chapter 11).

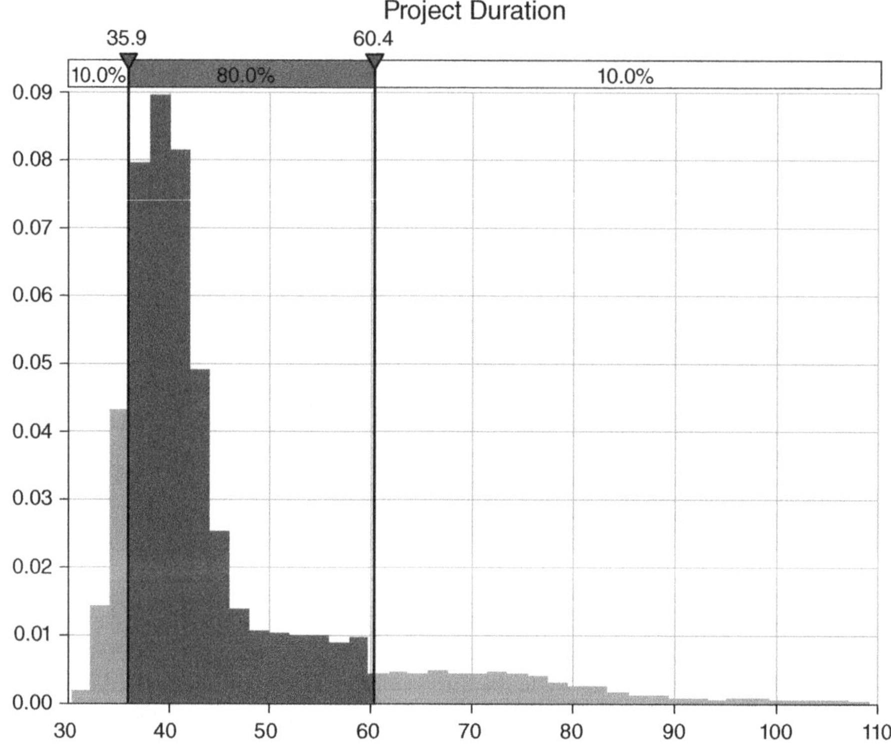

FIGURE 4.12 Simulated Distribution of Project Duration

- In addition, the risk assessment process will also help to identify common dependencies that are often overlooked if one uses a sensitivity analysis approach (see Chapter 7).

4.4 USING THE RANGE OF POSSIBLE OUTCOMES TO ENHANCE DECISION-MAKING

The use of risk modelling (including the simultaneous variation of multiple risks) provides one with an estimation of the distribution of possible outcomes. From this, one can find the likelihood that any particular case could be achieved (for example, that costs will be within budget, or revenues less than expected, and so on). In addition, the variability of the outcome is also relevant for real-life decision-making since risk tolerances (preferences or aversion) need to be able to be reflected; we may not, in reality, wish to continue with a project that has only a 50% chance of success, or that will go over budget in 50% of cases.

Generally, of course, one implicitly assumes that if a static model uses "reasonable" assumptions for input values then the output will also show reasonable values. Indeed, the phrase "garbage in, garbage out" is often used to express the importance of using reasonable estimates of input values, and of course it is important to pay attention to the selection of base case values (e.g. perhaps using "best estimates"). On the other hand, statements such as the following are either assumed or implicitly believed:

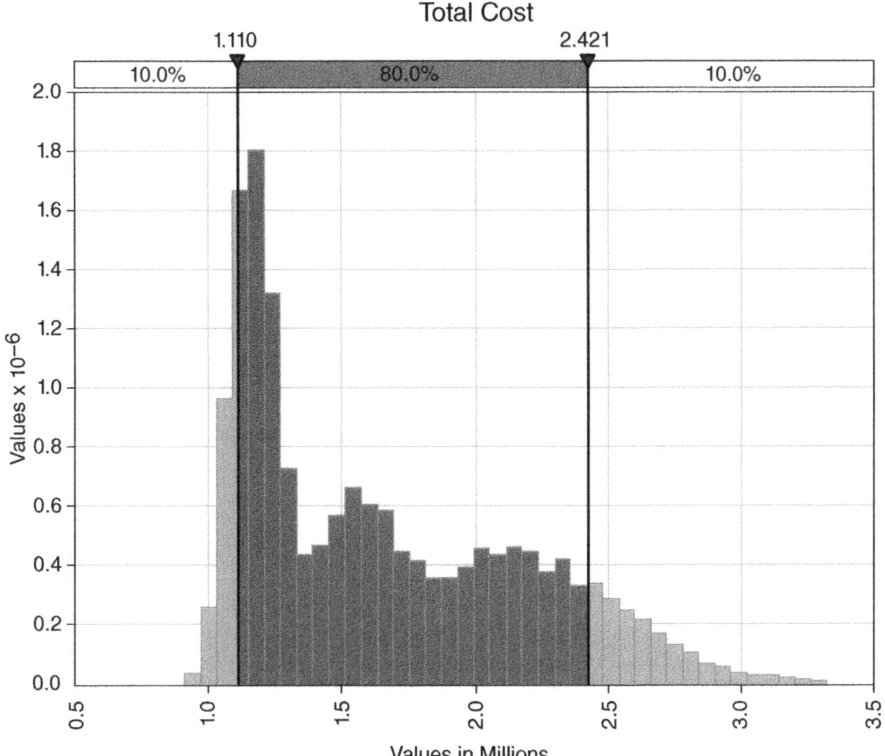

FIGURE 4.13 Simulated Distribution of Project Cost

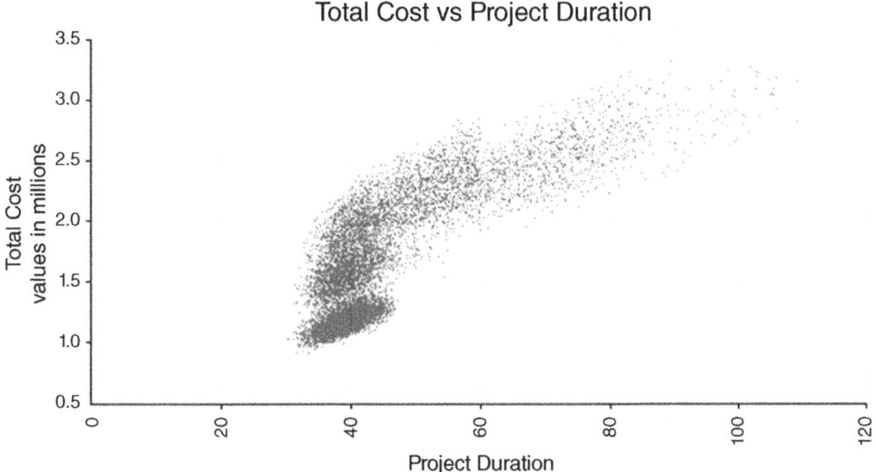

FIGURE 4.14 Simulated Distribution of Project Duration Against Cost

- "There is essentially a 50/50 chance of deviating either side of the base case."
- "If a model's inputs are at their most likely values, then the model's output is also its most likely value."
- "If a model's inputs are set to be their average (or mean) values, then the model's output also shows its average (or mean) value."
- "As long as the inputs are not too optimistic/pessimistic, then the output will be a reasonable representation of reality."
- "Any optimism and pessimism in the input assumptions will more or less offset each other."

In reality, none of these statements is generally true, although they may each be true in specific circumstances, depending on both the nature of the uncertainty and the logic contained within the model. In general, the output case shown by a model will not be aligned with the input case definitions (in terms of definitions or the placement of each value within its own range). This potential non-alignment is driven by:

- Non-symmetry of uncertainty. The driving forces that can cause random processes to be non-symmetric in practice are discussed later in the text.
- Non-linear model logic. Once models contain even relatively simple non-linear behaviours, such as **IF** statements, then it becomes very difficult to make any general assertion about the position of a single scenario with the full range of outcomes.
- Event risks. For some individual event risks, the most likely outcome may be that they do not occur (for probabilities less than 50%), whereas when there are several such risks within a model, the most likely outcome is generally that at least one would occur.

(Thus, alignment is to be found in special cases, such as models that are linear and additive. In such a model, the average or mean values for the inputs translate into the output's average, and absolute best and worst cases are also each aligned.)

Whilst it may be intuitively clear that if base case values are slightly biased or imperfect, then the output will be so, what is much less clear is the strength of the effect, which can be very significant in the presence of multiple uncertain variables. In effect, these are structural issues (or biases) that are often overlooked, and provide a compelling argument to use risk modelling techniques and conduction simulation: Einstein's comment that "a problem cannot be solved within the framework that created it" is pertinent here.

These issues are examined further in this section.

4.4.1 Avoiding "The Trap of the Most Likely" or Structural Biases

Where each input value of a traditional (static) Excel model is chosen to be the most likely value of its underlying distribution (a "best guess"), it is often believed that the base case is "non-biased"; when required to select only a single figure as a fixed estimate of the outcome of an uncertain process, this figure would seem appropriate (as any other figure is less likely to occur). However, in such cases, the output that is displayed in the base case may, in fact, be quite different to its true most likely value; indeed, the likelihood of its being achieved could be very low (or very high).

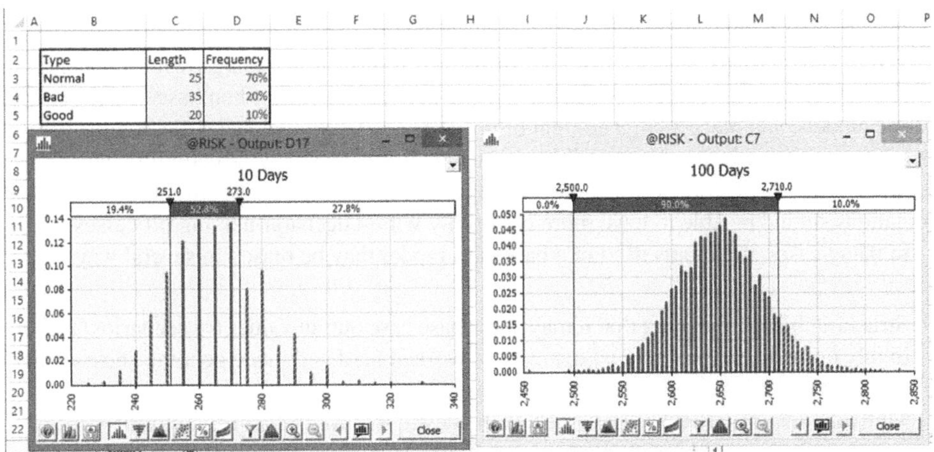

FIGURE 4.15 Simulated Total Travel Time for 10 Days and 100 Days

As a simple example, assume that one regularly takes a journey which, based on experience, takes 25 minutes in 70% of cases (the most likely case), but which is sometimes longer (35 minutes in 20% of cases), and sometimes shorter (20 minutes in 10% of cases). If one is planning how much time will be spent travelling over the next 10 days (perhaps one reads during the journey and wishes to plan one's reading schedule), then one could add up 10 sets of 25 minutes, giving 250 minutes. This corresponds to building an Excel model, with a row for each of the 10 days, and populating each row (day) with its most likely value. However, it is intuitively clear that the average (and perhaps the most likely) total time will be more than the base figure of 250 minutes, since the journey lasts 10 minutes longer in 20% of cases, but only 5 minutes less in 10% of cases; these do not offset each other. Figure 4.15 shows the results of running a simulation model using @RISK to generate many scenarios, from which one sees that the base case of 250 minutes is exceeded with a frequency of approximately 80%; indeed, in around 25% of cases, the total journey time is more than 275 minutes (so that over the course of 10 days, one has used the equivalent of an extra 25-minute journey). Moreover, over the course of 100 days (shown in the graphic on the right), there is essentially no realistic chance that the total journey time would be 2500 minutes or less, and that the most likely journey time is approximately 2650 minutes, not 2500.

Of course, the same principle would hold when applied to other situations that are logically similar, such as estimating the costs for a project by adding up the individual components; if each component is uncertain and with a balance of risk to the upside, for example, then the likelihood of the final outcome being below or at the sum of the base values is low.

Thus, the "trap (or fallacy) of the most likely" refers to the fact that models calculated using the most likely values of the inputs will often not show the most likely value of the output (although it is often implicitly believed that they do). Thus, it is clear that decision-makers may often be given misleading information; the base cases referred to for decision-making purposes may, in fact, represent scenarios that are quite unlikely.

(The issue as to whether the most likely case of the output is a relevant decision-making metric is discussed in Chapter 8.)

4.4.2 Finding the Likelihood of Achieving a Base Case

In a sense, it is perhaps unsurprising that decision-makers have often grown sceptical as to how much weight to give to the numerical side of decision-making when based on the output of static models, and place a large amount of importance on intuitive, heuristic or judgemental processes: the process used to provide them with information is structurally flawed. On the other hand, if these biases and misleading results could be overcome, then numerical calculations should be able to have more credibility within decision-making processes.

In many cases, the inputs used in a base case model may be biased in several ways:

- Structural biases, meaning that it may show base case output values (or scenarios) that are highly unlikely, even as project teams have worked hard and made genuine "best efforts" to populate the assumptions with "non-biased" inputs.
- Motivational or political biases, such as the desire to have the project authorised.

The cumulative effect of several "small biases" (or "white lies") may be stronger than one's natural intuition would expect, so that establishing the likelihood of achieving a particular base case is perhaps the single most important benefit of quantitative risk modelling in many situations.

(Note that we are assuming that a static base case exists, which is generally the situation. In principle, one could argue that base cases should not be needed once inputs are represented by distributions. For example, after simulating a risk model, one may decide that the P75 of the output should be considered to be the base. However, in practice, input base values are required for line items that correspond to those against which plans are made, or resources or budgets committed to. For a given output figure, such as a P75, there is no one single input combination that will produce such a figure, and hence some form of base case is usually required.)

One can explore (using simulation) the issue of how a particular selection of base case affects the position of that case within the range of the true output. Figure 4.16 shows an example of a cost budget with 10 items, each of which has a possible range (for the sake

Symmetric Case	Min	ML	Max	P40
Materials	8000	10000	12000	9785
Labour	8000	10000	12000	9785
Plumbing	8000	10000	12000	9785
Electrical	8000	10000	12000	9785
Decorating	8000	10000	12000	9785
Kitchen Cabinet	8000	10000	12000	9785
Tiling	8000	10000	12000	9785
Legal and Architecture Fees	8000	10000	12000	9785
Cost 9	8000	10000	12000	9785
Cost 10	8000	10000	12000	9785
Total				97850

FIGURE 4.16 Cost Budget with Each Base Case Value Equal to the P40 of its Distribution

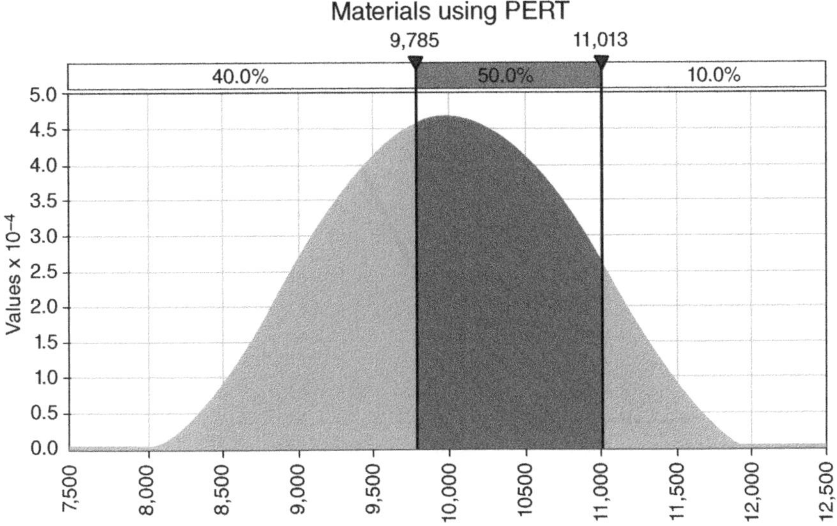

FIGURE 4.17 Assumed Cost Distribution for Each Item

of presentation only, we assume that their parameter values are all the same). For simplicity here, we assume that the ranges are symmetric, and that each range is described by a PERT distribution (relevant details are covered in Part II; here we are concerned only with the concept), as shown in Figure 4.17. Thus, if the base case for each input were assumed to be slightly optimistic (i.e. lower than average cost), for example its P40 value (9785), then the sum of these values shown in the base model would be 97,850 (as shown in Figure 4.16).

On the other hand, Figure 4.18 shows the result of running a simulation to work out the distribution of total cost, from which one sees that the figure 97,850 is approximately equal to the P20 of the distribution, and hence is even more optimistic.

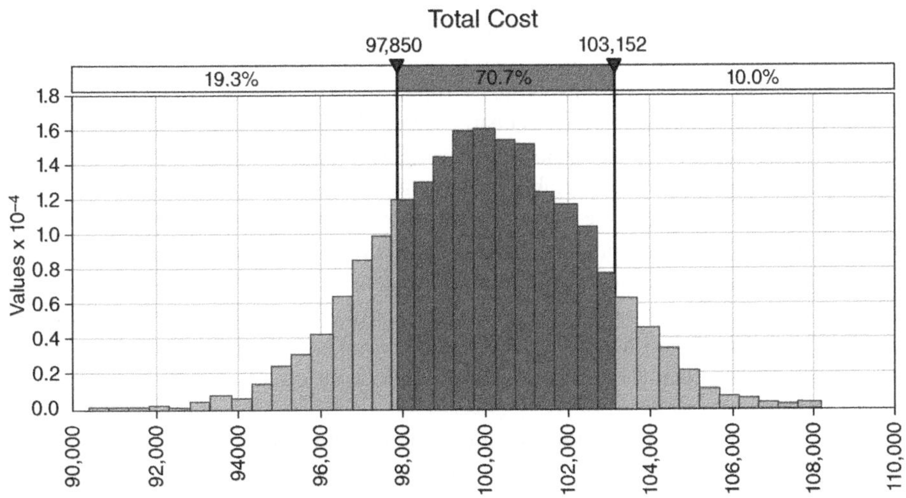

FIGURE 4.18 Simulated Distribution of Total Cost

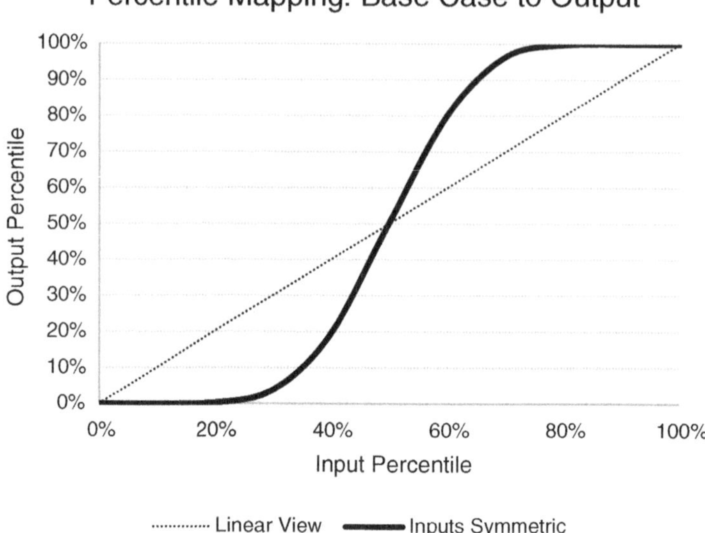

FIGURE 4.19 Mapping of Base Case Percentiles to Output Percentiles for 10 Symmetric Inputs

More generally, one can compare cases for how various input assumptions would map to various outputs. Figure 4.19 shows how particular assumptions for base values (as percentiles of their distributions) would map to the percentile of the output. One can see that P50 inputs map to P50 outputs (as we have assumed symmetric distributions), but that optimistic input percentiles (below P50) map to lower percentiles of the output (and hence the output is even more optimistic than is the input), whereas pessimistic inputs (above the P50) create even more pessimistic cases in the output.

When the input distributions are non-symmetric, the same basic principles apply; however, the cut-off (or equilibrium) point (which is, in fact, the average) has a different percentile; for a positively skewed distribution, a P50 input would be optimistic (and lead to an even lower percentile for the output than in the symmetric case). This is shown in Figure 4.20, in the case where the maxima of the distributions in the examples were 15,000, rather than 12,000.

Clearly, the precise outputs shown in charts such as Figures 4.19 and 4.20 depend on the nature of the model and on that of the uncertainties. For example, the diagonal line effectively corresponds to a model with one variable, so that there is a direct correspondence between the input and output. Thus, the line becomes narrower and steeper if more cost elements are added to the model (all other things being equal). Figure 4.21 shows this as the number of items in the model changes (for one, two, five and 20 items). For models with more variables, since the curve is steeper, for base cases toward the middle of the range (i.e. ones that could be considered "reasonable" or not excessively biased), even a small change in the chosen case described by (all) the input values would have a significant effect on the percentile of the output.

The basic principle at work in this situation is that of diversification. For example, with reference to the case in which there are only two uncertain items, and for which the base case for each input is defined as its P90 (so that it would be exceeded in 10% of cases), then for the sum of the two uncertain processes to exceed the sum of these two figures, at least one of

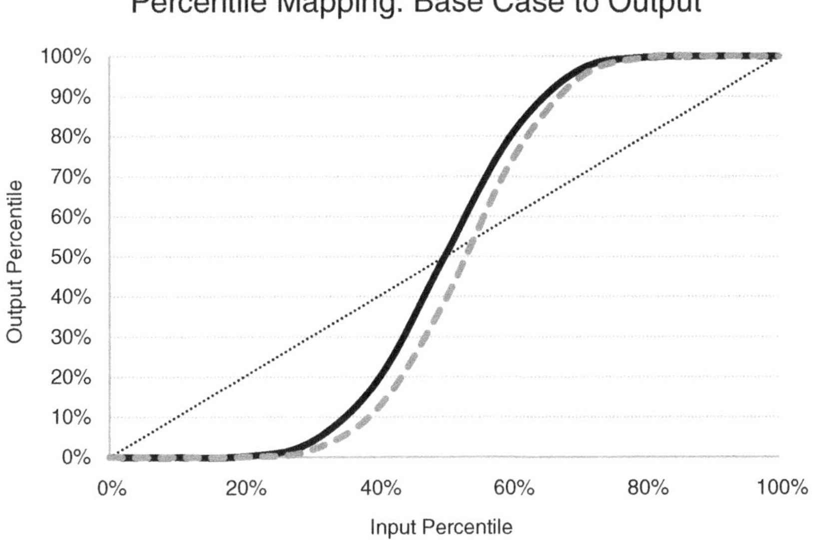

FIGURE 4.20 Mapping of Base Case Percentiles to Output Percentiles for 10 Symmetric and Non-symmetric Inputs

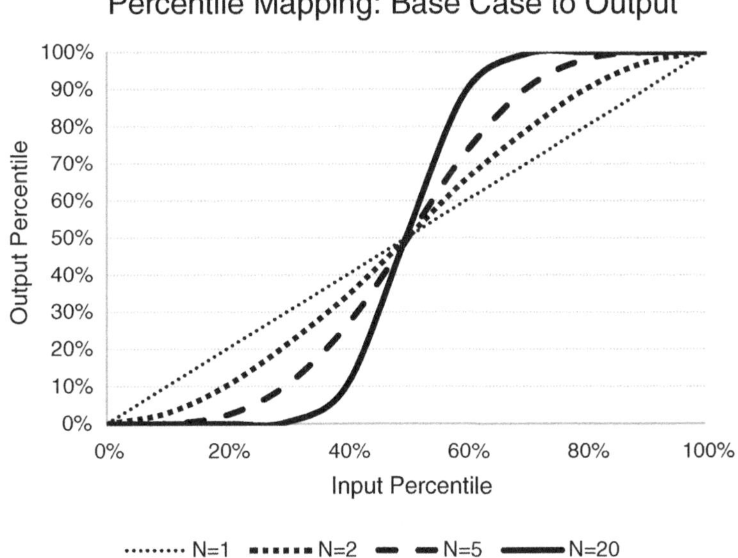

FIGURE 4.21 Mapping of Base Case Percentiles to Output Percentiles for Various Numbers of Symmetric Inputs

the uncertain values has to be at least equal to its P90 value (which happens only 10% of the time); in the majority of such cases, the second variable will not be sufficiently high for the sum of the two to exceed the required figure (because in 90% of cases, the value of the second one will be below its own base figure). Roughly speaking, the base case (sum of the P90s) may be thought of as being the P99 of the sum; in fact the percentage would be lower (in Figure 4.21, it is approximately 97%) because there will be cases where one process is above its own P90 by a reasonable margin, whilst the other is only slightly below its own P90, so that the sum of the two is nevertheless above the sum of the individual P90 figures.

A number of other points are worthy of note here:

- The notions of optimism and pessimism mentioned above depend on whether a higher percentile is good or bad from one's perspective. For example, whereas in cost contexts, an assumption of low cost would be optimistic, in a profit context it would be pessimistic. Thus, in the case of the estimation of uncertainty of oil and gas reserves, where P50 estimates for individual assets may be used as a base, and where the distribution of reserves is often regarded as lognormal (and therefore skewed to the right; see later), the sum of a set of P50 values will be less than the true P50 of the sum. Thus, a simple aggregation of base figures would underestimate the true extent of reserves, and thus is a pessimistic estimate (so that on average, in reality, there will be more reserves than originally expected, even without further technical advances or new enhanced recovery procedures). Similarly, the summation of the P90s (or P10s) of the reserves estimated for different assets does not provide the P90 or P10 of the total reserves.
- In general, the set of values used in a base case will be some mixture of items: some may be the most likely values, some may be optimistic and some pessimistic. Simulation techniques can be used to assess the consequences of these various assumptions in terms of how the shown base case output relates to its position within the true output range. Indeed, such an assessment may help one to avoid undertaking activities that in fact have little chance of success, even where the "base case" seems to suggest a reasonable outcome.

4.4.3 Economic Evaluation and Reflecting Risk Tolerances

The knowledge of the distribution of outcomes can assist in many ways in project evaluation and associated activities:

- The average outcome is the core reference point for economic valuation (such as the average of the net discounted cash flow), as explained in detail in Chapter 8.
- In some practical cases, the average will not be so relevant, but other properties of the distribution of outcomes are required in order to reflect risk preferences (corporate and personal) in the decision. This applies, for example, to the economic evaluation of projects that are large and cannot be regarded as repetitive decisions, or where failure could result in bankruptcy of the business or a loss of status for the decision-maker. In addition, in non-financial contexts, such as schedule analysis, the average (e.g. time to delivery of a project) is often not as relevant as other aspects:
  - Often, very senior management may be willing to take more risk to achieve corporate objectives, as long as this risk is well managed and the risk exposure understood.

  - More junior management will typically be more risk averse, and may consider that the occurrence of a loss would not be acceptable to his or her career prospects, and hence would tend to reject the same project.
  - These differences in risk preference may lead to apparently inconsistent decision-making according to which level of an organisation is involved, but this can partly be offset by a transparent approach to risk evaluation and the setting of more explicit risk tolerances that quantitative assessment allows.
- To compare projects with different risk profiles. A project with a more positive base case but also higher chance of a severe failure than another (i.e. higher risk reward) may be favoured (or not) depending on the context and its potential role within a portfolio of other (perhaps low risk) projects.
- To identify early on projects that may be unsuitable due to their risk profile. In particular, the early elimination of potential "zombie" projects is a key objective. These are projects that in reality have little prospect of success, but become embedded in the organisation if not stopped early; vested interests start to grow, including those of the original project sponsors who may find it difficult (and career limiting) to change their position on the benefits of a project. The pursuit of such projects can require much investment in organisational resources, time and money before (perhaps) being stopped at a very late stage and with great controversy (e.g. at the final authorisation gate or only when the main project sponsor leaves the company).
- Incorporate risk assessment into the consideration of the available project options, such as in the design of multi-use facilities and the evaluation of operational flexibilities, as discussed earlier.

4.4.4 Setting Contingencies, Targets and Objectives

The setting of contingencies, targets and objectives is closely linked to the consideration of the distribution of possible outcomes. Once the distribution is known, one could decide to base the budget (say) on the P75 of costs (or schedule), meaning that the plan should be achieved in 75% of cases (costs or time-to-delivery being less than or equal to the plan in such cases). This is essentially also the same as the setting of targets or revising objectives; for example, a "stretch" target for revenue may be set at (say) a P75 or P90 value of the possible revenue distribution.

In general, the choice of the appropriate target will depend on the risk tolerances of decision-makers, and be context dependent. For example:

- A company with many similar projects may generally set the contingency for each one to be less than would a company with fewer projects.
- Similarly, where the consequences of failure to deliver within the revised target are severe (e.g. company bankruptcy, serious environmental issues, etc.) then contingencies would generally be set higher.

The choice of the target is essentially the counterpart to the definition of contingency (or safety margin). Contingency can be broken into two components, which separate the risk tolerance from the underlying economic view. For example, if the project plan is based on a P75, then compared to the original base or static case:

- Contingency = P75 − Base = (P75 − Mean) + (Mean − Base), where the brackets are used for emphasis only.
- The first term (P75 − Mean) is directly related to risk tolerances, whereas the second (Mean − Base) is related to biases in the base case, whether they be structural, political or motivational.

In general, one wishes to find a balance between having too much or too little contingency:

- Excess contingency (excess pessimism) at the level of individual projects would generally result in a total contingency figure that is far in excess of what is truly needed when viewed from a portfolio perspective:
  - In a resource (or capital) constrained environment, this "resource hoarding" can lead to a company not investing in other potential projects, in other words launching too few new projects, and not achieving its growth objectives.
  - A simple day-to-day analogy would be if one were to plan a multi-stage journey so that there is extra time built into each stage, resulting in the actual journey time taking much less than the time that has been allowed for (even if one or two risks do materialise en route): this would not be desirable if the resulting free time could not be used, or if one had turned down other important commitments in order to undertake the journey.
- Insufficient contingency (excess optimism) would mean that insufficient consideration was given to the consequences of some of the unfavourable possible outcomes:
  - In business contexts, this can have serious consequences, such as project or business failure, or delays to projects whilst new funds and resources are found, or to the forced sales of business units or other assets, to bankruptcy, or to forced debt/equity raises, and so on.
  - A day-to-day example would be to go on vacation with not enough funds to cover emergencies.

With reference to the earlier example, Figure 4.21 showed that the correspondence between the values used for the input and the (true) case shown is not linear for multi-variable models. In other words, a small excess of contingency at the level of each individual item may lead to a significant excess at the project level, and vice versa. Thus, it can be very challenging to really know the implications at the aggregate level of the individual (and contingency) plans, unless one uses a risk quantification tool to do so.

Fortunately, basic yet value-added aggregation models are extremely easy to build (and more sophisticated extensions are possible in which one attempts to formally optimise the process), so that the implications of various contingency levels can be explored.

4.5 SUPPORTING TRANSPARENT ASSUMPTIONS AND REDUCING BIASES

This section discusses that the use of risk modelling can help to ensure that the assumptions used are more transparent (than in traditional static modelling) and how this can support the reduction in biases.

4.5.1 Using Base Cases that are Separate to Risk Distributions

The highlighting of the true position of the base case within the possible range (both of inputs and of outputs) can help to reduce and expose biases:

- Many motivational, political and other potential biases (e.g. optimism/pessimism) will become clearer, simply by seeing where the base case is in relation to the true range.
- The potential for other structural biases may be important, such as the "trap of the most likely" discussed earlier.

In order to ensure that biases are not hidden by a risk assessment, in practical terms, the ranges used for the risk assessment should not be derived from the base case, but should be defined or estimated separately. For example, if one creates a "process standard" in which all participants must assume by default that the risk range for any variable is a fixed percentage variation around a base value (e.g. ±20%), then risk ranges are anchored to the base case; thus, any motivational bias in the base case assessment will also be present in the risk assessment. Whilst hard to achieve in some group processes, it is fundamental to estimate the range totally separately to the base case: ideally, one should estimate possible ranges before fixing a base, as part of the process to reduce anchoring. Tools to help to do so include: having separate people estimate the ranges (including external participants or third party consultants), as well as looking at comparative situations and considering worst and best case scenarios. The checklist of questions covered in Section 2.3 in Chapter 2 provides some additional tools in this respect.

4.5.2 General Reduction in Biases

Important general techniques to reduce biases include:

- Awareness that they might be occurring.
- Reflect on what their source and nature might be.
- Use of a robust risk identification process should also expose (and thus help to reduce) biases:
  - The appropriate use of cross-functional input and expert resources will highlight many potential biases.
  - The seeking and supporting of dissension or alternative opinions is part of the philosophy of formalised risk assessment methods.
  - Look for data to support objective assumptions.
  - Cross-check answers with questions that are phrased both positively and negatively.

4.5.3 Reinforcing Shared Accountability

The embedding of risk assessment approaches within management decision-making creates a measure of transfer of accountability for bad outcomes to decision-makers that would have been less clear when using static models.

The forecasts from static models will essentially never match the actual outcome, so that the potential will always exist for decision-makers to blame a poor outcome on a poor forecast. On the other hand, a risk model resulting from a robust risk assessment process will show a range in which the actual outcome will generally lie (unless truly unforeseeable events happen), and to the extent that a poor outcome was foreseen as a possibility, such an allocation of responsibility is less credible: it becomes more difficult to transfer responsibility when one has been provided with correct information than when one has been given incorrect information.

The potential creation of a higher level of shared accountability (between modellers, project teams and decision-makers) is a benefit in that it bridges the separation between analyst and decision-maker to some extent; at the same time, it is a challenge, as discussed in Chapter 5.

4.6 FACILITATING GROUP WORK AND COMMUNICATION

This section discusses how risk assessment processes can facilitate group work and communication and in some cases allow the reconciliation of apparently conflicting views.

4.6.1 A Framework for Rigorous and Precise Work

The risk assessment process, both in general and when considering the specific aspects associated with quantitative modelling, requires a more structured and rigorous discussion, and provides a set of tools and objectives to support this. This will create a better, and shared, understanding of a situation, its important driving factors and required actions.

4.6.2 Reconcile Some Conflicting Views

Risk assessment may, in some cases, allow views that are apparently conflicting to be reconciled:

- In particular, since static models are based on essentially arbitrary base cases (and are generally inherently biased), it is common for people to have different views on what a "base case" value should be.
- To a large extent, as long as the ranges used (distribution parameters) are correctly selected (and done so independently of the base case, as discussed earlier), then such differences become less relevant.

CHAPTER 5

Organisational Challenges Relating to Risk Modelling

In Chapter 1, we discussed some general contextual challenges in the implementation of robust decision-making processes, including:

- The presence of motivational, political, cognitive or structural biases.
- Challenges in achieving an appropriate balance of rationality and intuition.

This chapter discusses some additional challenges in the implementation of full risk modelling activities, focusing especially on issues relating to organisational structure, processes and culture. These include:

- Beliefs that sufficient risk assessment is already being done.
- The approaches may have been tried previously but were not found to be useful.
- Beliefs that results of the models will not be useful, or that implementing the processes and models will create too much extra work.
- Issues relating to the integration and alignment with existing processes, incentive systems, culture, decision accountability, organisational structures, level of centralisation and general change management issues.

5.1 "WE ARE DOING IT ALREADY"

Risk assessment and management is already widely used in many organisations, at least to some extent. For example:

- Many base plans often include some consideration of risks and mitigation measures, especially when projects have some aspects that are well understood from similar previous cases.
- Cross-functional teams are often brought together to identify risks, develop and assess mitigation actions, and assign responsibilities for further actions, especially for major projects.

- Many larger companies have a risk management department, or an enterprise-wide risk management ("ERM") group.

Thus, it can easily be believed that existing procedures are already sufficient, and that further formalisation or development is not necessary. There may indeed be organisations for which this is true, although it is a rare one that genuinely has all the elements in place. This section covers specific challenges in this respect.

5.1.1 "Our ERM Department Deals with Those Issues"

In principle, staff functions (such as ERM) should not be the "owners" of risk assessments of projects that relate to specific business unit activity or projects:

- Such staff will not have the required technical knowledge about the business.
- The business will not be properly incentivised to adapt and optimise its projects.
- The independence of the oversight function will be lost.

Certainly, the working procedures between business units (or departments) and corporate ERM functions should not, in general, arrive at a point where business units are asking ERM questions such as: "What are the key risks to my project?" or "What are you doing to manage the risk within my project?", although such cases do nevertheless arise in practice!

Thus, the existence of such staff functions is, in general, not sufficient to ensure that business project risks are adequately addressed.

Such staff functions do, of course, have important and valid roles, generally around:

- Acting as facilitators of processes, and providing objectivity and challenge.
- Acting as a centre of expertise for tools, techniques and methodologies, so that new and up-to-date processes and best practices are shared and implemented widely.
- Providing a mechanism to identify and escalate risks that are common to different business units.
- Providing independent objective evaluation of projects, or acting in a risk-auditing capacity.

5.1.2 "Everybody Should Just Do Their Job Anyway!"

Although the use of risk assessment principles should generally be integrated into day-to-day activities, and led by the project's business owners, doing so would nevertheless be insufficient: there may be important items that may be outside the scope or capability of an individual or small team or department, and there are many areas where there are significant challenges relating to organisation culture, processes and biases, which may be insurmountable for an individual or small group to overcome. Thus, even if one is "doing one's job", it would still be necessary to formalise the process in some cases, especially where:

- The projects are complex and of significant scale (meaning that risks can easily be overlooked and that input from a wide range of experts and functions is generally required).
- Potential risk-response actions need to be escalated, agreed, authorised or communicated more widely, as their implementation is within neither the scope nor the authority of the staff performing the risk assessment.

5.1.3 "We Have Risk Registers for All Major Projects"

The use of risk registers is often a valuable step in the overall risk management process. However, risk registers are insufficient in some cases, so that full risk models are necessary. The reader is referred to the discussion at the beginning of Chapter 4 in this respect.

5.1.4 "We Run Sensitivities and Scenarios: Why Do More?"

Sensitivity and scenario analyses, and their implementation, are no doubt familiar to most readers. They are indeed a powerful tool in some contexts. These techniques, their relationship to risk and simulation, and their Excel implementation are described in detail in Chapter 6. Here, we simply note some of their key limitations:

- A model designed around using traditional sensitivity or scenario methods (or thought processes) will typically not be able to capture the genuine risk profile (or risk scenarios) that one may be exposed to. Whilst it may be able to address some "What if?" questions, such questions are generally not able to be addressed for specific risk factors unless the model has been designed in a way that is aligned with the nature of the underlying risks; this is discussed in Chapter 7 in detail.
- There is no explicit attempt to calculate the likelihood associated with output values or the full range of possible values (which would require multiple inputs being varied simultaneously and probabilities being attached to these variations). Thus, the decision-making basis is potentially inadequate:
  - The average outcome is not known.
  - The likelihood that a base case (or other assumed) plan can be achieved is not known.
  - It is not possible to reflect risk tolerances (nor contingency requirements) adequately in the decision.
  - It is not easy to compare one project with another.
- They do not show a representative set of cases. For example, a base case that consists of most likely values will, in fact, typically not show the most likely value of the output; indeed the base case may be quite far from any central point of the possible range, as discussed in Chapter 4.
- They do not distinguish between variables that are uncertain and those to be optimised, and hence may fail to highlight important decision possibilities.

5.2 "WE ALREADY TRIED IT, AND IT SHOWED UNREALISTIC RESULTS"

Simulation techniques have been applied to business applications for several decades. Unfortunately, some experiences were not as value-added as they perhaps should have been; thus, one sometimes encounters scepticism as to their benefits. In this section, we discuss some of the issues that most frequently arise in this respect. Generally, one reason for risk models to lose credibility with senior decision-makers is when the results presented are plainly wrong, unintuitive or fail to pass the "common sense" test.

5.2.1 "All Cases Were Profitable"

It is (perhaps surprisingly) quite common for the results of risk-based simulation models to show that all possible outcomes are profitable or reasonably favourable. For example, one may have a simulation of the total discounted cash flow in a project (or of its net present value), in which all values in the possible outcome range are positive. Such results are generally unrealistic: it is unlikely in practical business situations that a project would still succeed even in the "worst case" scenario. One would be very fortunate to be involved in such a business! (Of course, the future values of a project may be positive in all cases if historic investment is not included in the calculations; here we are referring to the entire scope of a project.)

Nevertheless, when faced with such a case, one could perform a mental exercise (or group discussion) to identify what could happen in a worst case scenario (or a set of possible near-worst case or bad scenarios): if one cannot even conceive of a single scenario in which the project fails, then either one's thinking may be too narrow (i.e. not all costs or other variables, and/or risks and uncertainties have been taken into account), or it would be so intuitively clear that the project is a "no brainer" proposition and that no analysis on it should be needed at all!

In fact, almost always (with some genuinely well-intentioned and disciplined thinking), one can readily conceive of outcomes in which a project would fail (when the full set of costs are included), but it is "simply" that the model does not capture the correct behaviour of the situation.

One of the challenges (also mentioned later) is therefore an education and communication process in which higher levels of management should *expect* to see a range of possible outcomes in which in some cases the project is not particularly successful or even fails.

5.2.2 "The Range of Outcomes Was Too Narrow"

Another frequent observation about the output of some risk models is that the ranges generated were too narrow compared to one's intuition or historic data. Where this is the case, the credibility of the risk modelling process can be drawn into question.

There is much commonality between drivers of this and the above issue (in which a model shows that all cases are profitable):

- The values used to populate the input risk ranges may be unrealistically narrow. In particular, the use of preset default ranges of variation (such as ±25%), rather than considering (or using) data to estimate what the true range might be, is a potential risk. For example, some cost budgets exceed their base figure by factors of five (+400%), even at the aggregate level; the possible range for individual line items may often be even wider than this. In addition, the derivation of parameters of the ranges with reference to a base case figure, rather than by separate estimation, will mean that any biases in the base figures are also reflected in the risk model.
- Event risks may have been ignored or excluded, such as those that may only occur in 20% of cases; their inclusion would often result in "tail risk" and wider ranges.
- Dependencies were not reflected correctly in the model; for example, if risks or their impacts in reality generally occur together or take (say) high values together, then if this is not also reflected in the model, the range for the output will be incorrectly captured (it may be too narrow or too wide depending on what is calculated and the nature of the true dependencies). Similarly, if a model is excessively detailed, then it can be challenging to

capture all relevant dependencies between the items, resulting in an incorrectly estimated range (this is often a result of overlooking common underlying drivers of risk, as discussed further in Chapter 7).

- The non-symmetry of processes is not captured, e.g. one uses a ±10% range (as is often typical in sensitivity analysis), whereas the true possible range may be from –10% to +50%.

5.3 "THE MODELS WILL NOT BE USEFUL!"

Although there are some modelling challenges in risk contexts, in many cases, models can be built that are simple yet powerful and value-added. Of course, no model is perfect, and some are better or more useful than others (see Chapter 7 for further discussion). Nevertheless, any model can be criticised or challenged in principle, as discussed below.

5.3.1 "We Should Avoid Complicated Black Boxes!"

It is sometimes claimed that risk modelling using simulation involves creating models that are too complex for most people to understand, and that they become non-transparent "black boxes" that only the model builder (at best) can understand, with the result that the models are not reliable and cannot be reviewed or questioned by others.

It is true that risk models are in some ways more complex than static models:

- There may be additional areas of knowledge or capability that are necessary to learn, such as statistical and probabilistic concepts, their application and interpretation, as well as (perhaps) modelling techniques, e.g. more advanced use of Excel lookup functions or VBA coding, in order to be able to capture the dynamic logic that is often (ideally) required in risk models. The nature and extent of the required knowledge will, of course, depend on one's role in the process (modelling analyst, technical expert or decision-maker).
- The input area is usually larger than for the corresponding static model; it will generally contain the parameters for the distributions or ranges, as well as a base case. In addition, it may need to reflect all items and parameters associated with the relevant decisions (risk mitigation and response decisions, and general project decisions).

On the other hand, both the process of identifying risk and of reflecting these in a model should create more transparency, not less: for example, the cross-functional inputs, more formal processes and separation of risk ranges from base cases are steps that all shed light on potential incorrect logic or biases.

5.3.2 "All Models Are Wrong, Especially Risk Models!"

Any form of modelling (whether risk modelling or static modelling) has some inherent ambiguity to it: models are simplifications of reality (and hence always "wrong", otherwise known as "model error"), and are effectively statements of hypothesis about the nature of reality. Thus, in order to build a model with reasonable accuracy, one has to understand a situation to some degree (key drivers, interactions, etc.); on the other hand, where a situation is understood perfectly, a model would not be necessary. There is an important exploratory component to model building that is often underestimated or overlooked: the process of building a model can generate new insight and intuition, and thus help to achieve a balanced (and aligned) rationality and intuition in a decision process.

Of course, there are cases where the output of models is relied on too much, with insufficient consideration given to factors that cannot generally be included explicitly within models: typically every model is valid only with an assumed context, usually implicitly, and non-documented. For example, most financial models implicitly assume that liquidity traps do not happen, and that refinancing will always exist as a possibility. Some major financial failures are arguably linked to such issues (such as the 2008 Financial Crisis, or the failure in 1998 of the hedge fund Long Term Capital Management).

In principle, there is generally no real difference between building either a useful risk model or a useful traditional static model, and there will be situations in practice in which useful risk models cannot be built. This issue is explored in Chapter 7 in more detail.

5.3.3 "Can You Prove that It Even Works?"

The identification of appropriate risk-response measures is a fairly tangible benefit of a risk assessment process. On the other hand, some of the benefits of such processes are less tangible: it is not easy to "prove" that any particular decision is correct or not (except in extreme cases, for example, where all outcomes are not desirable ones). Indeed, one may make a rationally-based decision, with an optimal risk profile, but still find that the occurrence of residual risks leads to an unfavourable outcome. Thus, a major challenge is to distinguish a good decision from a good outcome (and similarly a poor decision from a poor outcome).

Despite the fact that many organisations have introduced risk analysis into their decision processes and have more confidence in their decisions, finding robust evidence that the decisions are better (or that such organisations even perform better) is not easy:

- It would be insufficient to compare the performance of organisations that use risk assessment methods with that of organisations that do not. The real test is whether a specific organisation becomes "more effective and successful" than it otherwise would have been: thus, one would have to compare the performance of the same organisation with itself (in the cases where risk assessment was and was not used), which in practice cannot really be done.
- One can think of an analogy in which one aims to assess whether people receiving health care treatment are in better health than those who are not currently receiving any: at the (macro) level of the population, people who receive treatment are likely to be *less* healthy than people who are not receiving treatment (there will be some exceptions at the individual level, of course). However, at a micro level, an individual receiving treatment is generally in better health after the treatment than beforehand. Thus, the effectiveness of the treatment can only be observed by micro studies (e.g. clinical trials with many patients in the stages of drug development, and then specific patient studies once a treatment is on the market). However, the analogous studies are much harder to do in real-life business contexts.

5.3.4 "Why Bother to Plan Things that Might Not Even Happen?"

One objection that is sometimes made about risk assessment is that one is "planning to lose": a risk (especially an event risk) may not even occur, whereas the cost of mitigation (e.g. of reducing their likelihood or their impact) is a definite cost if the measure is implemented:

- An attitude can exist that it may be better not to spend time and resources discussing, identifying and mitigating items that may not even happen, but rather to simply wait for them to (perhaps) happen and then deal with the consequences: why incur additional cost to deal with an issue that might not even arise?
- Such an attitude is often reinforced by accountability-related issues: when a risk does materialise, one may argue that "it could not have been foreseen" or "we were just unlucky" or that "someone (else) didn't do their job", or the "external environment changed unexpectedly".

Thus, it may be organisationally more credible not to spend money on risk mitigation (or delay a project until more information is available) than it would be to spend money to reduce the probability of something that may not happen anyway. Hence, someone opposed to the implementation of risk assessment or mitigation measures may be able to position themselves as acting in the interests of the organisation (keeping costs low, implementing projects quickly, etc.). If such risks do occur, they may also be able not only to shield themselves from any blame but also to capitalise on the occurrence by, at that point, taking a leading role in dealing with the consequences, and thus being perceived as a person of action.

5.4 WORKING EFFECTIVELY WITH ENHANCED PROCESSES AND PROCEDURES

In general, the implementation of a formal risk assessment process requires additional work, for example as a minimum:

- The more precise requirements concerning risk definitions that are needed for quantitative approaches mean that some additional iterations of process stages are typically required.
- It may lead to the identification of areas where additional information or research is needed, or where supplementary data or external expertise are required, or raise issues that need further internal communication or authorisation.
- One will generally be required to seek input from a wider set of staff (such as cross-functional teams) to identify risks and assess mitigation actions.

5.4.1 Selecting the Right Projects, Approach and Decision Stage

Clearly, it is important that any effort put into the process has a payback in terms of the value generated: just as it would not make sense to perform an elaborate risk assessment on a simple situation, so it would be unwise not to do so for large, complex projects. In fact, for many projects, the incremental effort and investment would represent a very small proportion of the total project investment, especially if the process is organised efficiently. Thus, the more significant the need for a risk assessment, the more formalised and sophisticated should be the approach chosen.

In practice, any particular organisation would likely need to develop criteria (such as project size limits) in order to decide which approach to risk assessment is most suitable for a particular project. Such criteria may be able to be aligned to some extent with those used within existing processes (such as those that define when a project needs Board-level approval).

Most large organisations have "gating" systems for authorising projects, with projects required to pass through a series of gates (or hurdles) before definitive approval is granted, and in which investments and other resources are committed:

- The early steps (prior to the passing of a project through the gating system) will typically be a non-formalised process involving a range of discussions and plans concerning a potential project and the approximate benefits and costs of doing so. Different options and strategic alternatives may be discussed and compared at this stage.
- Once a project appears to become more appropriate for further pursuit, the gating system may be entered into (the precise criteria and level of detail required to pass from one gate to the next will depend on the specific organisation and business context):
  - The formal passing of a project into the gating system will be a signal (and perhaps a requirement) that a wider set of staff should become involved.
  - A budget may need to be authorised to cover the costs of more detailed planning processes, and some resources may need to be formally committed to analysing the project in more detail.
  - As the project moves through the gates, increased research, work and general planning will be required, for example in areas such as market research, product development, engineering designs, production and manufacturing planning, relationships with partners, preliminary coordination with third parties, government agencies, infrastructure planning, design and construction planning activities, and so on.

The challenge in this respect is that there are competing forces at work in terms of finding the right balance between using risk assessment too early and too late in the process (and in what form to use it at each stage).

Reasons in favour of using the techniques earlier in the process include:

- It has an important role to play in optimising the design and structure of projects, and the setting of appropriate objectives, targets and contingencies for them.
- To do so conforms to the established management practice of aiming to "work smarter" in the earlier (upstream) stages of multi-stage projects and decision processes.
- To take an extreme case, clearly for a large and complex project it would not make sense to consider risks only after a project has been authorised (or even at the last stage prior to authorisation), which may result in having to reject projects after much development work, time and cost have been invested.

One reason to use the techniques only at later stages is that a full and detailed quantitative model on every project option from the very earliest stages of the consideration of these options would not be practical: this creates extra work, and could disrupt and damage some of the more creative and flexible processes that are required at the earlier stages, such as ensuring that a complete and varied set of decision options is being considered.

5.4.2 Managing Participant Expectations

The implementation of risk assessment will typically involve the participation of multiple stakeholders and experts, including cross-functional resources. It is generally important that expectations are set early on about the process and time commitments that are likely to be required. If not, the situation can arise where process participants may feel that their contribution to the cross-functional risk assessment is complete once risks have been identified, and mitigation plans put in place. In fact, their input is likely to be needed at later stages, especially in quantitative approaches; thus, participants may become frustrated (or are unwilling to cooperate to the fullest extent of their capabilities), as they are asked to provide input on aspects that they feel have already been completed, and an impression of a lack of direction or organisation can result. Specifically, it is important to be clear that:

- Risk assessment should be an inherent part of all project activities.
- The process is, by nature, iterative.
- As the project develops, additional deliverables are needed:
  - The various stages of an informal and formal gating system will have different requirements.
  - The approaches used, and the precision required concerning risk definitions, will likely change; especially as one moves from qualitative line item risk management to full risk modelling.
  - Objectives may change, even if they have been clearly defined at the beginning. For example, once some results of a risk assessment have been seen by senior management, it may awaken a desire to demand more, such as creating full risk models. This can mean that the revisiting of process stages becomes necessary, despite best efforts to have clarified the objectives early on.
- Participants are very likely to have to provide additional inputs and make additional assumptions as the process progresses and results become available.

5.4.3 Standardisation of Processes and Models

One key challenge is to decide which parts of the process should be standardised and which should be left more open. This is especially relevant to risk quantification and the building of models:

- In principle, one needs to allow for flexibility and creativity in the analysis, in order to be able to reflect the true risk structure of the situation at hand, which may be one that is complex and will typically change from project to project. The challenge in this respect is to ensure that those participants who are tasked to build the associated quantitative models indeed have the right skills and capabilities to do so.
- On the other hand, especially when the introduction of risk assessment is in its early stages, it may be more effective to work to standard templates (especially for those participants who are less familiar with the concepts), whilst the creation of common

understandings, formats and tools is being generated. The challenge here is to avoid "box-ticking" exercises, or work that is of low value-added.

Certainly, once risk assessment is deeply embedded within an organisation, its processes and culture, the scope for more creative approaches should be readily available; on the other hand, to reach this stage, one must not oversimplify to the point that there is little perceived value-added.

5.5 MANAGEMENT PROCESSES, CULTURE AND CHANGE MANAGEMENT

Perhaps the biggest (but often overlooked) challenge in achieving successful implementation of formalised risk assessment processes (especially ones that use aggregation and full modelling approaches) is the need for a change in management practices at many levels. Some of these are explored in this section.

5.5.1 Integration with Decision Processes

It is probably fair to say that some risk assessment activities already take place within many existing business projects, but where results are not communicated explicitly to higher levels of management:

- Where an individual or project team uses a risk assessment as a tool to support project design (as discussed in Chapters 1 and 2), then the results may be directly and implicitly reflected in modified base projects. The explicit details of the assessment may never be discussed with higher management in detail.
- By necessity, upward communication is of a summarised nature, focusing on key points, and if risks are considered unimportant in a particular project, then this may not be an area of focus.
- In many organisations, there is a strong cultural norm that it is almost always best only to communicate positive messages upwards; as such, risks are not usually near the top of the discussion list (one may nevertheless on occasion be able to frame a discussion of risks in positive terms).

However, in general, the use of risk assessment will not achieve its full benefit unless there is more explicit communication with management, with the results used as a core basis for decision-making:

- To achieve fair comparability between projects, the cost and benefits of risk-response actions would need to be included in all projects (to avoid favouring projects that ignore or understate some or all of their key risks).
- Typically, the authorisation and implementation of many key risk-response measures would require higher-level management involvement:
  - Additional budget or cross-functional activities may be required, or modifications to targets such as project completion dates may need to be considered.

- A final decision on project authorisation needs to reflect the cost and benefit of such measures, and so may need to occur later than the time at which the measures were authorised.
- In order to reflect risk tolerances in decision-making in a structured way, at least some communication of the likely range of output will be needed.

5.5.2 Ensuring Alignment of Risk Assessment and Modelling Processes

In general, there will be some form of specialisation of activities within a risk assessment project; that is, a variety of technical and project specialists will be involved in one-on-one and group discussions, as well as in other cross-functional activities (as discussed in Chapter 2); there may also be a team member assigned specifically to the modelling activities.

It is clear that the building of a model without proper knowledge of the risks will likely lead to one that is inappropriate to address the needs of a project team and of decision-makers. It is highly unlikely that a model built without appropriate alignment with the general risk assessment process would contain the right variables, be built at the right level of detail, or have formulae that are flexible enough to include the effect of risks or their impacts within them, or to allow additional risks to be readily incorporated within them.

On the other hand, it can be challenging for a modelling analyst to receive the required inputs from a general risk assessment team:

- There are many activities within a general risk assessment process that do not require any specific inputs from quantitative risk modelling activities. In particular, many aspects of risk identification and mitigation planning may not require any input from modelling or quantification activities.
- Many established risk management practices do not require specific modelling or aggregation activities (see Chapter 3), so that even experienced risk assessment practitioners may have a lack of exposure to the issues required to be addressed in risk modelling contexts.
- The modelling analyst will often be perceived as an addition to the team, rather than a core part of it, and is likely also to be junior to many of the process participants in terms of organisational hierarchy and authority.

Thus, it is often the case that a general process team (that is focused on risk mitigation management) may have less perceived need or incentive to alter the nature of its activities to accommodate the needs of modelling activities.

There is, therefore, the possibility that activities that are undertaken within a general risk assessment process are not properly reflected in the modelling activities, due to lack of communication or of joint incentives (or responsibility) for the overall output of the process.

This is not to say that teams conducting general risk assessment activities have no incentive to interact appropriately with modelling activities. However, such incentives are inherently much weaker than is the incentive of the modelling analyst to have appropriate input from the general process. Indeed, a general risk assessment team would have some incentives in this respect because it is also the case that a process that is conducted in isolation of the modelling activities will also be conducted inefficiently to some extent:

- There would generally not be a correspondence between the outputs of the general risk assessment process (such as identified risks) and the quantitative model, which can act to reduce the credibility of both processes.
- A project team that plans activities and mitigation measures, but whose required budget and resource requirements are not reflected in the model, may find that such measures are not available for implementation once a project has been authorised (or the project expenditure will then exceed the planned amount, without risks even materialising, as the base planned figure would be lower).
- There is likely to be the need for significant process rework if decision-makers wish to see a clear linkage between the output of a model and the general risk assessment process. For example, as discussed in Chapter 3, the risk assessment process will not be conducted with clear objectives as to the requirements for risk definitions (e.g. to avoid double-counting, overlaps, capture dependencies, etc.), and so many fundamental process steps may need to be revisited in order to identify risks in the appropriate way.

Thus, where a quantitative risk model is required as an output of the general process, then the success of each will be determined by a close coordination and alignment between the processes. Nevertheless, the (typically more senior) general process participants generally have a much weaker inherent need for such alignment of activities than does a modelling analyst.

Thus, it is incumbent on process leaders and senior management to define the approach that is to be used with respect to risk quantification, and to ensure that all participants in the process are appropriately engaged and have clear objectives as to the role of, and need for, quantified risk modelling.

5.5.3 Implement from the Bottom Up or the Top Down?

Of course, any successful implementation needs to have significant genuine "bottom-up" support. In addition, it is probably fair to say that management's role must be much more proactive than just supporting any bottom-up initiatives; senior management needs to drive the implementation to make it happen. With the multitude of challenges that relate to organisational processes and culture, a strong "top-down" implementation is almost always necessary (if the use and acceptance of risk modelling is to extend widely into the organisation, and not be conducted only by a few specific individuals). Many of the challenges would otherwise be insurmountable for individuals or small groups of like-minded people, and others would create additional difficulties that in their totality may also be too challenging to overcome.

Examples of ways in which implementation can be driven top down include:

- Ensuring that the objectives of each risk assessment project are made clear. In particular, where quantitative modelling activities are desired, process participants will need to provide additional (or modified) inputs into the process, as discussed earlier.
- Laying out (compulsory) guidelines as to what outputs of risk models are required at each stage of a gating system or decision process.
- Including risk-based metrics in required medium- and long-term plans, and in some key performance indicators or incentives.

- "Walking the talk": providing budgets, human resources and training to enable participants to implement the extra work and new techniques that are generally required, and allowing time for such analysis within planning timeframes.
- Rewarding proactive bottom-up initiatives (and being seen to do so). Staff who proactively drive these processes can be given rewards in one form or another; this can range from informal "prize-giving" to formalised recognition (with incentive, career development and promotion systems), as well as the granting of leeway to allow for some mistake-driven learning.

5.5.4 Encouraging Issues to Be Escalated: Don't Shoot the Messenger!

Where cultural norms mean that lower-level staff generally prefer to present an optimistic story to higher level management, it is easy for issues to become hidden until they are critical (or too late), and for assumptions to be too optimistic.

Indeed, attitudes from management such as "bring me solutions, not problems" are common:

- Such attitudes may be justified, for example where management feels that the lower-level staff have not given enough genuine thought to the situation, and wish them to redouble their efforts.
- In other cases, where a project team has done all within its power to develop risk-response measures and need more senior-level authorisation for them to be implemented, such attitudes are not generally justified.

Whilst it may be advisable for lower-level staff (as far as possible) to make an effort to frame their communication in positive terms (e.g. "uncertainty" may be less negative than "risk" and "opportunities to improve project performance" are the flip side of risk-mitigation or risk-response measures), there is a responsibility on all layers of management to achieve appropriate levels of delegation for project responsibility, whilst being open to risks being escalated. For example, management may communicate that they *expect* to see a range of possible outcomes in which in some cases the project is not as successful as desired or fails, and to see the causal factors of this. Additionally, management must be willing to "roll up one's sleeves" to support the appropriate risk-responses, and not "shoot the messenger".

5.5.5 Sharing Accountability for Poor Decisions

Most organisations (apart from perhaps the smallest) have decision-makers who are separate from other key process participants. Specifically, there is very often a separation between senior management and those who provide the information on which management make decisions, as well as shareholders and other important stakeholders.

This separation can hinder the creation of a desire to base decisions using objective methods, such as robust quantitative risk assessment, and rather to rely on their own knowledge, judgements, intuition and biases. In particular, one can surmise that as long as the costs of poor outcomes are borne disproportionately by others, and that any particular decision-making basis is widely accepted as being appropriate (so that its use is not regarded as a weakness), then the accuracy or validity of that basis is largely irrelevant. The incentives for decision-makers to make the genuinely right decision can be outweighed by other factors. Cases such as the widespread acceptance of "static" forecasts (as well as the Financial Crisis of the early 21st century) are perhaps driven by such issues.

In particular, the use of static forecasting methodology (which provides a forecast that is essentially always wrong, despite being widely accepted as a methodology) may be preferred by decision-makers and also create a justification for the use of biases, intuition and personal preferences in the decision process: if the project in question is implemented, then two cases will arise:

- The project goes well (in the sense that the aggregate risk occurrence is not particularly unfavourable); everyone is content, and the favourable outcome will be attributed to good decision-making, skill and competent project delivery.
- The project goes badly. In this case, the outcome can be blamed on a poor forecast (amongst other factors), as a static forecast would not have generally reflected such a case.

On the other hand, if a full and robust risk assessment had been conducted prior to the project, then this risk assessment would have shown a mix of outcomes, some positive and some negative. If an unfavourable outcome occurs (due to a risk scenario that was represented in the model), then the attribution to a poor forecast would not really be possible.

Thus, to some extent, the embedding of risk assessment approaches within management decision-making creates a measure of transfer of accountability for bad outcomes to decision-makers in a way that would have been less clear without it; this can create both a challenge and a benefit.

5.5.6 Ensuring Alignment with Incentives and Incentive Systems

One of the key organisational challenges in implementing risk-based planning processes is to ensure that the conflict with incentive systems is minimised.

Most situations involving risk contain a mixture of controllable and non-controllable items: the identification and implementation of risk-response measures is controllable, whereas – once such measures are implemented – the actual occurrence or extent of impact of a risk or uncertainty is not. In other words, the response measure will (for example) alter the likelihood or the impact of a risk or uncertainty, but not change the fundamental situation as to whether (or with what impact) a risk or uncertainty will arise.

Implicit in setting (appropriate) incentives is that one has some control over the aspect of the situation that is being incentivised. Indeed, if incentives were set in a situation in which there were truly no control, the effect of doing so may have a negative consequence; it could lead to feelings of unfairness when some staff are awarded bonuses whilst others (perhaps more capable or who worked harder) were not.

Broadly speaking, one may distinguish between two categories of incentives:

- Process- (or activity-) based incentives are not related to achieving some target objective, but to the processes that are judged important to doing so. For example, a sales manager may be awarded a bonus for making more than a specified number of new customer contacts (irrespective of the actual level of sales achieved in the short term); of course, there may be a long-term strategy behind such thinking. The outcome, even if bad (but within the originally predicated range), would then not influence incentive awards as long as all relevant process and decision stages were correctly followed: if a thorough risk assessment showed that most (but not all) possible outcomes for a future project were good, but on implementation a poor outcome arises due to "non-controllable" factors that had been identified within the risk assessment, then the decision to proceed was not necessarily a poor one.

- Outcome-based incentives, which are based around an outcome being achieved, i.e. a decision is judged by its outcome, not by whether it was fundamentally a good one. For example, a sales manager may be awarded a bonus if he or she achieves some specified sales target.

Many managers have a (deep-seated) intuition to prefer outcome-driven incentives. This is probably driven by the fact that many situations are so complex that it is not possible to define all the scenarios that might happen. For example, the market may be changing so quickly with many possible new product innovations or competitor entries (within the timeframe applicable to the incentive system) that a process-based system may track activities that are not generating benefit. On the other hand, an outcome-based incentive could encourage the staff to respond dynamically in an appropriate way, as they find innovative ways to reach their targets, even if the nature of such adaptations cannot be foreseen in advance.

One can argue that in the presence of risk, a process-based incentive has some role, because some elements of the outcome are simply beyond the control of participants, even if they act in the best conceivable manner; it would be unfair to punish genuine bad luck (or to reward genuine good luck). Part of a process-based incentive scheme could therefore simply be to ensure that risk analysis is being used at the appropriate time by the appropriate staff.

One may be drawn to the conclusion that both approaches are necessary in general, with some form of weighting towards one or the other.

5.5.7 Allocation and Ownership of Contingency Budgets

One of the most important applications of aggregate risk assessment is the calculation of the required contingency to include in a plan, as discussed in Chapter 4. In principle, with an appropriate risk model, the calculation of a contingency amount at the aggregate project level is straightforward. For example, one may budget with reference to the P75 of a project's costs (with contingency being the difference between this figure and a base case).

In practice, once contingency amounts are determined, the issue often arises as to whether (or how) to allocate this budget to the underlying individual components. In other words, the total figure is calculated by reflecting the uncertainty within each subproject or project task (or department, geographical area, business unit, project phase, time period, etc.) and aggregating these together, so that one may expect that this resulting contingency be allocated back to them.

The challenge in doing so relates directly to the discussion in Chapter 4, in which we showed (e.g. Figure 4.19) that in general (due to the diversification effect) there is not a linear mapping between the aggregate percentile and that of the individual components. Thus, for example, in the case of the model with five items (Figure 4.21), the P75 of the output resulted in a case when inputs were set at (approximately) their P60 values. Hence, the allocation of an aggregate P75 budget (so that each component has its "fair" proportion of it) would result in a situation where each component would exceed its budget in 40% of cases (whereas the aggregate project would only do so in 25% of cases). Such an amount may be regarded as insufficient by the staff responsible for that particular component; they may each desire a P75 budget for their component, which would lead to the total budget being around its P95 point.

Thus, there is an inherent conflict, with the possibility of resource hoarding and excess contingency (as discussed in Chapter 4). There is no perfect solution to this, as it is inherent in the nature of the diversification and combinatorial effect associated with uncertainty; thus, it is an organisational challenge.

One may consider centralising budgets at an aggregate project level, with a variety of degrees of strictness:

- Hold all budgets centrally.
- Give each component its base budget (with no contingency); any overspend would have to be authorised centrally, and perhaps only if the reasons for needed overspend relate to the materialisation of a previously-identified risk (in order to ensure sufficient incentive for adequately accurate planning at the component level).
- Give each component some contingency, whilst also maintaining some centrally. This may be preferable from a general management perspective, in order to give the task managers some freedom of action, and to reduce the transaction costs of the frequent communication with central contingency functions that would be required, even for small amounts of overspend.

Clearly, such choices may have profound implications for organisational responsibilities, structures, authorisation and other processes, and generally for the fundamental relationship of power and control within organisations, and thus present potentially significant challenges.

5.5.8 Developing Risk Cultures and Other Change Management Challenges

The issues discussed in this chapter clearly show a multitude of challenges that need to be addressed in order to successfully achieve the benefits of risk assessment processes, especially those associated with full risk modelling. These typically involve changes to many areas, including:

- Management decision processes, attitudes and leadership.
- Responsibilities, incentive systems, structure and authorisation processes.
- Communication and training (e.g. on quantitative risk modelling and process modifications).

One may aim to install a more risk-aware culture, with characteristics such as:

- The embedding of risk analysis results in decision-making processes (for example, creating a cultural non-acceptance of the presentation of static forecasts, or of ones in which high quality risk assessments are not conducted).
- A general desire at all levels for openness, transparency and rigour, and objectivity in discussions, plans and decision-making processes.
- High levels of competence, good corporate governance and leadership.

- Encouragement of open debate to question and challenge ingrained thinking, and an acceptance of a diversity of opinion.
- Room for curiosity, creativity and problem-solving, a desire to innovate, to make mistakes, to learn and to improve.
- A feeling of shared responsibility and accountability, nurtured by management example, behaviour, leadership and the appropriate structure to incentive systems.

In principle, change management frameworks and tools can support this process. Indeed, the well-known Kübler–Ross model (for stages of grief) may be adapted as if it were to apply to the general change processes associated with the implementation of risk assessment:

- Denial: "We don't need this/it is not happening/it won't create any benefit."
- Anger: "Why have we let ourselves into this situation? Who is to blame?"
- Bargaining: "OK, how are we going to move forward? What do we need to do/what investments are to be made/what trade-offs might there be?"
- Depression: "This is harder than we thought. We are not getting anywhere."
- Acceptance: "We have made a breakthrough, we can see the benefits. We need to keep pushing ahead, to accept that it will take time and we'll make some mistakes."

As the framework shows, there are typically different phases, and these require patience, management of the fear of failure (and of failure itself), encouragement and leadership. Therefore, an important element of achieving success (in terms of widespread implementation and cultural change) is to have a strong top-down implementation, which acts as a catalyst to bottom-up activities.

The use of simulation tools (especially if they are user-friendly) such as @RISK can often provide fairly simple ways to demonstrate the benefits, create some practical results and generally support the process of cultural change. Of course, they are only a small part of the overall process, and are not a "silver bullet", nor a substitute for the myriad of other changes required for a truly successful implementation.

PART II

The Design of Risk Models – Principles, Processes and Methodology

CHAPTER 6

Principles of Simulation Methods

This chapter provides an overview of simulation methods, their role in risk quantification and their relationship to sensitivity, scenario, optimisation and other techniques. We aim to introduce the basic principles in an intuitive and non-technical way, leaving the more technical aspects and implementation methods to later in the text.

6.1 CORE ASPECTS OF SIMULATION: A DESCRIPTIVE EXAMPLE

For the purpose of describing the fundamental principles of simulation methods, we shall consider a simple model in which:

- There are 10 inputs that are added together to form a total (the model's output).
- Each of the 10 inputs can take one of three possible values:
  - A "base" value.
  - A "low" value (e.g. 10% below the base).
  - A "high" value (e.g. 10% above the base).

Of course, despite its simplicity, such a model (with small adaptations) has applications to many other situations, such as:

- Forecasting total revenues based on those of individual products or business units.
- Estimating the total cost of a project that is made up of various items (materials, labour, etc.).
- Forecasting the duration of a project whose completion requires several tasks to be conducted in sequence, so that the total duration is the sum of those of the individual tasks.

6.1.1 The Combinatorial Effects of Multiple Inputs and Distribution of Outputs

With some reflection, it is clear that there are 3^{10} (or 59,049) possible combinations of input values: the first input can take any of three values, for each of which, the second can take

	Cumulative number of combinations
Item 1	3
Item 2	9
Item 3	27
Item 4	81
Item 5	243
Item 6	729
Item 7	2187
Item 8	6561
Item 9	19683
Item 10	59049

FIGURE 6.1 Number of Possible Combinations of Values for Various Numbers of Inputs, where Each Input can Take One of Three Values

any of three values, giving nine possible ways to combine the first two inputs. Once the third input is considered, there would be 27 possibilities, as each of the nine from the first two is combined with the values of the third, and so on. This sequence is shown in Figure 6.1 as the number of inputs increases.

The implicit assumption here is that the input values are independent of each other, so that one having a specific value (e.g. at, above or below its base) has no effect on the values that the others take; the consequence when there is dependence is discussed later. Additionally, we implicitly assume that each of the 10 base values is different to one another (in a way that each possible choice of input combination creates a unique value for the output), and is of a similar order of magnitude.

In general (and also as specifically assumed above), each input combination will result in a unique value for the output, so that the number of possible output values is the same as the number of input combinations, i.e. 3^{10} or 59,049.

The question then arises as to how the output values are spread (distributed) across their possible range. For example, since each individual input varies equally ($\pm10\%$) around its base, one might at first glance expect a more or less even spread. In fact, one can see that there are only a few ways to achieve the more extreme outcomes (i.e. where the output values are at the very high or low end of the possible range). For example:

- Only one combination of inputs results in the absolute lowest (or highest) possible value of the output, i.e. that combination in which each input takes its low (or high) value.
- There are only 10 ways for output values to be near to the absolute lowest (or highest) value, i.e. those combinations in which one input takes its base value, whilst all others take their low (or high) values.

There are many ways in which output values could be in the "central" part of the possible range (even if the precise values are slightly different to each other, and even though there is only one combination in which each input takes exactly its base value). For example, we can see that:

Number of Low Inputs \ Number of High Inputs	0	1	2	3	4	5	6	7	8	9	10
0	1	10	45	120	210	252	210	120	45	10	1
1	10	90	360	840	1260	1260	840	360	90	10	
2	45	360	1260	2520	3150	2520	1260	360	45		
3	120	840	2520	4200	4200	2520	840	120			
4	210	1260	3150	4200	3150	1260	210				
5	252	1260	2520	2520	1260	252					
6	210	840	1260	840	210						
7	120	360	360	120							
8	45	90	45								
9	10	10									
10	1										

FIGURE 6.2 Number of Combinations Involving Inputs Taking a Particular Number of High or Low Values

- There are 10 ways in which one input can take its high value, whilst all others take their base values. Similarly there are 10 ways in which one input takes its low value, whilst the others all take their base values. These 20 cases would result in output cases close to the central value, as only a single value deviates from its base.
- There are 90 ways in which one input takes its high value, one takes its low value and all remaining eight take their base values; these would result in output cases (very) close to the central value, due to the two deviating inputs acting in offsetting senses.
- There are many other fairly central combinations, such as two inputs taking high values, whilst two or three are low, and so on. Although the number of possibilities for such cases becomes harder to evaluate by mental arithmetic, it is nevertheless easy to calculate: it is given by the multinomial formula $10!/(L!H!B!)$, where L, H and B are the number of assumed low, high and base values (with $L + H + B = 10$), and ! is the factorial of the respective number (i.e. the product of all integers from one up to this number).

Figure 6.2 shows (calculated using this multinomial formula) the number of ways in which any number of inputs can take their low value whilst another number can take its high value (with the remaining inputs taking their base values). The highlighted areas indicate fairly central regions, in which the number of inputs that take their high value is the same as, or differs by at most one from, the number that take their low value. From this, one can see:

- The simpler cases discussed above (one, 10 and 90 combinations) are shown in the top left, top right and bottom left of the table.
- The more complex cases can be seen by close inspection: for example, there are 2520 possibilities in which three inputs take low values whilst two take high values, with (implicitly) the other five inputs at their base case, resulting in a fairly central case for the output.

When considered in percentage terms (of the total 59,049), we see in Figure 6.3 that:

- In 15.1% of cases, the number of high and low cases is the same (i.e. the sum of the diagonal of the table).

		Number of High Inputs										
	59049	0	1	2	3	4	5	6	7	8	9	10
Number of Low Inputs	0	0.0%	0.0%	0.1%	0.2%	0.4%	0.4%	0.4%	0.2%	0.1%	0.0%	0.0%
	1	0.0%	0.2%	0.6%	1.4%	2.1%	2.1%	1.4%	0.6%	0.2%	0.0%	
	2	0.1%	0.6%	2.1%	4.3%	5.3%	4.3%	2.1%	0.6%	0.1%		
	3	0.2%	1.4%	4.3%	7.1%	7.1%	4.3%	1.4%	0.2%			
	4	0.4%	2.1%	5.3%	7.1%	5.3%	2.1%	0.4%				
	5	0.4%	2.1%	4.3%	4.3%	2.1%	0.4%					
	6	0.4%	1.4%	2.1%	1.4%	0.4%						
	7	0.2%	0.6%	0.6%	0.2%							
	8	0.1%	0.2%	0.1%								
	9	0.0%	0.0%									
	10	0.0%										

FIGURE 6.3 Percentages of Combinations Involving Inputs Taking a Particular Number of High or Low Values

- In 28.4% of cases, the number of high and low cases differs by exactly one (i.e. the sum of the items immediately below and immediately above the diagonal).
- Thus, over 40% of cases are central ones in the sense that, with the exception of at most one input, the high and low values work to offset each other.

In other words, the use of frequency distributions to describe the range and likelihood of possible output values is an inevitable result of the combinatorial effect arising due to the simultaneous variation of several inputs.

In a more general situation, some or all of the inputs may be able to take any value within a continuous range. The same thought process leads one to see that values within the central area would still be more frequent than those towards the ends of the range: for example, where the values for each input are equally likely within a continuous range (between a low and a high value), there are very few combinations in which the inputs are all toward their low values (or all toward their high ones), whereas there are many more ways in which some can be fairly low and others fairly high. Of course, due to the presence of continuous ranges in such a case, there would be infinitely many possible values (for each input, and in total).

6.1.2 Using Simulation to Sample Many Diverse Scenarios

The number of possible output values for a model is determined by the number of inputs and the number of possible values for each input. Generally speaking, in practice, not all possible output values can be explicitly calculated, either because their number is finite but large, or because it is infinite (such as when an input value can take any value within an infinite set of discrete values, or can be any value in a continuous range).

Simulation methods are essentially ways to calculate many possible combinations by automating several activities:

- The generation of input combinations.
- The recalculation of the model to reflect the new input values.
- The storage of results (i.e. of key model calculations or outputs) at each recalculation.
- The repetition of the above steps (typically, a large number of times).

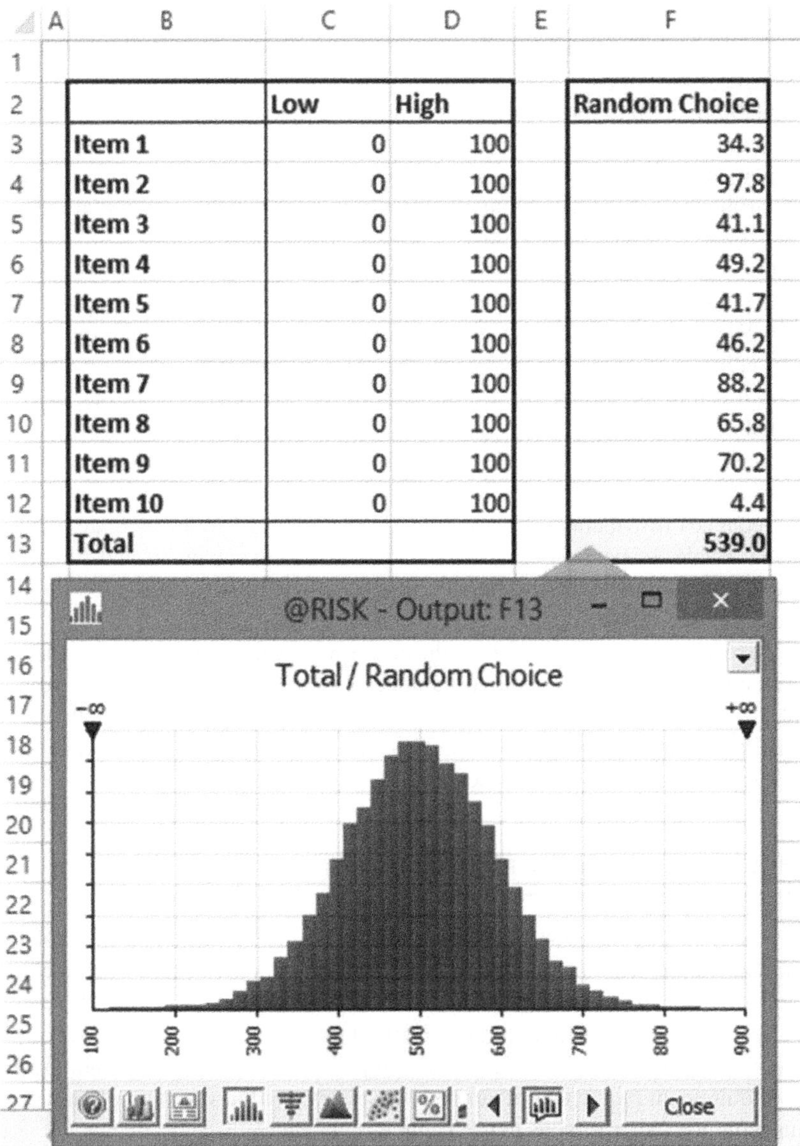

	Low	High		Random Choice
Item 1	0	100		34.3
Item 2	0	100		97.8
Item 3	0	100		41.1
Item 4	0	100		49.2
Item 5	0	100		41.7
Item 6	0	100		46.2
Item 7	0	100		88.2
Item 8	0	100		65.8
Item 9	0	100		70.2
Item 10	0	100		4.4
Total				539.0

FIGURE 6.4 Simulated Distribution of Output Values for Uniform Continuous Inputs

For example, Figure 6.4 shows the simulated distribution of output values that results for the above 10-item model on the assumption that each input is drawn randomly from a range between zero and 100, in such a way that every input value would have equal likelihood.

A key aspect of simulation methods is that the generation of the input values is achieved by creating them using random sampling from a range (or distribution) of possible values. In other words, (Monte Carlo) simulation can be succinctly described as "the automated recalculation of a model as its inputs are simultaneously randomly sampled from probability distributions".

This contrasts with traditional sensitivity or scenario techniques, for which the input values used are explicitly predefined, and usually – by necessity – represent a small set of the possible combinations that may occur.

Note that the creation of randomness *per se* is not an objective of Monte Carlo simulation; rather, it is an implementation method to ensure that a representative set of scenarios is produced when the automated process is implemented.

Note the following about the output resulting from such repeated recalculations:

- The output is a finite set of data points (calculated by repeated recalculation of the model).
- The data points are a sample (subset) of the "true" distribution of the output, but are not a distribution function *per se*. Nevertheless, one often refers to a simulation as providing a "distribution of the output"; this is usually done for simplicity of presentation, but on occasion it can be important not to lose sight of the fact that the core output is a set of individual data points.
- The data set allows one to estimate properties of this true distribution, such as its average or the value in the worst 10% of cases, or to plot output graphically (such as a histogram of the frequency distribution of the points). It also allows one to calculate relationships between variables (especially correlation coefficients between inputs and an output), and to generate *X–Y* scatter plots of the values of variables (providing the relevant data are saved at each recalculation).
- The more recalculations one performs, the closer will be the estimated properties to those of the true distribution. The required number of recalculations needs to be sufficient to provide the necessary basis for decision support; in particular, it should ensure the validity and stability of any resulting decision. This will itself depend on the context, decision metrics used and accuracy requirements.

6.2 SIMULATION AS A RISK MODELLING TOOL

Simulation and risk modelling are often thought of as equivalent, since in most business contexts the application of simulation methods is almost always to risk assessment; conversely, quantitative risk assessment often requires the use of simulation. However, there are some differences between the two: simulation is a method used to establish a large set of possible outcomes by automating the process of generating input combinations, using random sampling. There is no requirement *per se* that the underlying reason for the variation of an input is due to risk or uncertainty. Other reasons to use simulation include:

- Optimisation. The variation of input values could be a choice that is entirely controllable (rather than risky or uncertain), with the output data used as a basis to search for the input combination that gives the most desirable value. In general, however, simulation is often not a computationally efficient way to find optimal input combinations, especially in situations in which there are constraints to be respected. Nevertheless, simulation may be required in some cases.
- As a tool to conduct numerical integration. The first major use of simulation techniques was in the 1940s by scientists working on nuclear weapons projects at the Los Alamos National Laboratory in the USA: The value of the integral $\int_0^1 f(x)\,dx$ is equal to the average value of $f(x)$ over the range 0 to 1. Hence, by calculating $f(x)$ for a set of x-values

(drawn randomly and uniformly) between 0 and 1, and taking their average, one can estimate the integral. The scientists considered that the method resembled gambling, and coined the term "Monte Carlo simulation". This numerical integration method is simple to implement, and is especially powerful where the function $f(x)$ can be readily evaluated for any value of x, but where the function is complex (or impossible) to integrate analytically.

In addition to these uses of simulation for non-risk purposes, there are also methods to perform risk quantification that do not use simulation, such as "analytic" methods and "closed-form" solutions; these are briefly discussed later in this chapter.

6.2.1 Distributions of Input Values and Their Role

From the above discussion, we see that probability distributions arise in two ways:

- Distributions of output values arise inevitably due to combinatorial effects, typically with more extreme cases being less frequent, as fewer input combinations can produce them.
- Distributions of inputs are used deliberately in order to automate the generation of a wide set of input combinations (rather than having to explicitly predefine each input combination or scenario). In such contexts, there is no requirement that the underlying reason that inputs vary is due to risk, uncertainty or general randomness:
  - Where the purpose of the analysis is to assess all possible output values (as it may be in the above-mentioned cases of optimisation or numerical integration), it would generally be sufficient to assume that the possible values of any input are equally likely (i.e. are uniformly distributed). Only in special cases may it be necessary to use other profiles.
  - Where the intention is explicitly for risk modelling, it is necessary (or preferable for accuracy purposes) to use input distributions that match the true nature of the underlying randomness (risk, variability or uncertain variation) in each process as closely as possible: it is clear that the use of different input distributions (in place of a uniform one) would affect the properties of the output distribution. For example, if an input distribution has highly likely central values, the frequency of more central values for the output will be increased.

On the other hand, in a risk modelling context, it is important to be aware of the (seemingly obvious) point that the use of a distribution is to represent the non-controllable aspect of the process, at least within the very particular context being modelled. This point is more subtle than it may appear at first: the context may be controllable, even where the process within that context is not. For example:

- When crossing a road, one can choose how many times to look, whether to put running shoes on, and so on; once a choice is made, the actual outcome (whether one arrives safely or not on the other side) is subject to non-controllable uncertainty.
- In the early phases of evaluating a potential construction project, the range for the cost of purchasing materials may be represented by a distribution of uncertainty. As more information becomes available (e.g. quotes are received or the project progresses), the range may narrow. Each stage represents a change of context, but at any particular stage, a distribution can be used to represent the uncertainty at that point.

Thus, an important aim is to find the optimal context in which to operate; one cannot simply use a distribution to capture that there is a wide possible range and abdicate responsibility to optimise the chosen context of operation! Indeed, one of the criticisms sometimes levelled at risk modelling activities is that they may interfere with the incentive systems. Indeed, if one misunderstands or incorrectly interprets the role of distributions, then the likelihood that such issues may arise is significant.

6.2.2 The Effect of Dependencies between Inputs

The use of probability distributions also facilitates the process of capturing possible dependencies between input processes. There are various types of possible relationship, which are discussed in detail later in the text. Here we simply note the main types:

- Those of a directional, or causal, nature (e.g. the occurrence of one event increasing the likelihood of another).
- Those that impact the way that samples from distributions are drawn jointly, but without directionality or causality between them. Correlation (or "correlated sampling") is one key example, and copula relationships are another.

At this point, we simply note that any dependencies between the inputs would change the likelihood profile of the possible outcomes. For example (referring to the simple model used earlier), if a dependency relationship were such that a low value of the first input would mean that all other inputs took their low values (and similarly for the base and high values), then – since this one item fully determines the others – there would only be three possible outcomes in total (all low, all base or all high).

6.2.3 Key Questions Addressable using Risk-Based Simulation

The model outputs that one chooses to capture through a simulation will, of course, need to be the values of the key metrics (performance indicators), such as cost, profit, cash flow, financing needs, resource requirements, project schedule, and so on. In particular, specific statistical properties of such metrics will be of importance, such as:

- The centre of the range of possible outcomes:
  - What is the average outcome?
  - What is the most likely outcome?
  - What value is the half-way point, i.e. where we are equally likely to do better or worse?
- The spread of the range of possible outcomes:
  - What are the worst and best cases that are realistically possible?
  - Is the risk equally balanced on each side of a central point?
  - Is there a single measure that we can use to summarise the risk?
- The likelihood of a particular base or planned case being achieved:
  - How likely is it that the planned case will be achieved (or not)?
  - Should we proceed with the decision as it is, or should we iterate through a risk-mitigation and risk-response process to further modify and optimise the decision?

- Questions relating to the sources of risk, and the effect and benefits of risk mitigation, e.g.:
  - Which sources of risk (or categories of risk) are the most significant?
  - How would the risk profile be changed by the implementation of a risk-mitigation measure?
  - What is the optimal strategy for risk mitigation?

6.2.4 Random Numbers and the Required Number of Recalculations or Iterations

Of course, all other things being equal, a more accurate result will be achieved if a simulation is run many times. Clearly, this also depends on the quality of the random number generation method. For example, since a computer is a finite instrument, it cannot contain every possible number, so that at some point any random number generation method would repeat itself (at least in theory); a poor method would have a short cycle, whereas superior methods would have very long cycles. Similarly, is it important that random numbers are generated in a way that this is representative and is not biased, so that (given enough samples) all combinations would be generated with their true frequency?

In general, for most reasonable random number algorithms, an "inverse square root law" is at work: on average, the error is halved as the number of recalculations (iterations) is quadrupled. An increase from 25 to 1600 recalculations corresponds to quadrupling the original figure three times (i.e. 1600 = 25.4.4.4); the result of this would be for the error to be halved three times over (i.e. to be about 1/8th of the original value). In this context, "error" refers to the difference between a statistic produced in the simulation and that of the true figure. However, such a true figure is rarely known – that is the main reason to use simulation in the first place! Nevertheless, on occasion, there are some situations where the true figure is known; these can be used to test the error embedded within the methods and speed of convergence. An example is given in Chapter 13, in the context of the calculation of π (3.14159...).

Although truly accurate results are only achievable with very large numbers of iterations (which at first sight may seem to be a major disadvantage of simulation methods), there are a number of points to bear in mind in this respect:

- Although many iterations (recalculations) may be required to improve the relative *error* significantly, the actual calculated values are usually quite close to the true figures, even for small numbers of iterations; in other words, the starting point for the application of an inverse-square-root law is one in which the error (or numerator) is generally quite low.
- The number of iterations required may ultimately depend on the model's objectives: estimating the mean or the values of other central figures usually requires far fewer iterations than estimating a P99 value, for example. Even figures such as a P90 are often reasonably accurate with small numbers of iterations.
- The error will (generally) never be zero, however many iterations are run.
- Usually it is the stability and validity of the decision that is the most important source of value-added, not the extremely precise calculation of a particular numerical figure. Thus, running "sufficient" iterations may be more important than trying to run many more (the use of a fixed seed for the random number algorithm in order to be able to repeat the simulation exactly is also a powerful technique in this respect, so that one can always work with the same [reasonably accurate] estimate).

- In business contexts, the models are not likely to be highly accurate, due to an imperfect understanding of the processes and the various estimates that are likely to be required. In addition, one is generally more interested in central values (in which we include the P90) than in unlikely cases.
- When one is building models, testing them, exploring hypotheses and drawing initial directional conclusions, the most effective working method can be to run relatively few iterations (typically several hundred or a few thousand). When final results are needed, the numbers of iterations can be increased (and perhaps the random number seed can be fixed, in order to allow repetition of the simulation).
- The reliance on graphical displays to communicate outputs (instead of on statistics) will generally require more iterations to be run; when it is intuitively clear that the underlying situation is a smooth, continuous process, participants will expect to see this reflected in graphical outputs. In particular, histograms for probability density curves that are created by counting the number of output data points in each of a set of predefined "bins" may not look smooth unless large numbers of samples are used (due to randomness, a point may be allocated to a neighbouring bin by a close margin). The use of cumulative curves and statistics can partially overcome this, but graphical displays in general will be apparently less stable than statistical measures.

6.3 SENSITIVITY AND SCENARIO ANALYSIS: RELATIONSHIP TO SIMULATION

Sensitivity and scenario techniques are no doubt familiar to most readers to a greater or lesser extent. We briefly describe these here for the purposes of comparison with simulation.

6.3.1 Sensitivity Analysis

Sensitivity analysis is the observation of the effects on particular model outputs as input values are varied. It can be used to answer many important ("What if?") questions treated within a financial model, so long as the model has an input variable which corresponds to the desired sensitivity, and has a logical structure that is valid when the input value is changed.

The file Ch6.Time.Price.NoShift.xlsx (shown in Figure 6.5) contains an example of a simple business plan in which one has a forecast of cash flows over time, based on assumptions

	A	B	C	D	E	F	G	H	I
1									
2		Data and Assumptions	Growth/Time Assumptions	2016	2017	2018	2019	2020	
3		Contribution Margin based on Market Prices: $/Unit		10.0	10.0	10.0	10.0	10.0	
4		Fixed Cost of Site $m p.a	2.0%	-10.0	-10.2	-10.4	-10.6	-10.8	
5		Capital Expenditure		-100	-75.0	-25.0	0.0	0.0	
6		Volume Produced	5.0%	6.0	6.3	6.6	6.9	7.3	
7									
8		Summary Cash Flow		2016	2017	2018	2019	2020	
9		Margin $m		60.0	63.0	66.2	69.5	72.9	
10		Fixed Cost of Site $m p.a		-10.0	-10.2	-10.4	-10.6	-10.8	
11		Capex $m		-100.0	-75.0	-25.0	0.0	0.0	
12		Cash Flow $m		-50.0	-22.2	30.7	58.8	62.1	
13		10-year NPV $m	10.0%	208.5					

FIGURE 6.5 Generic Business Plan with Static Inputs

NPV for volume growth rates	208.5
1.0%	144.8
2.0%	159.6
3.0%	175.1
4.0%	191.4
5.0%	208.5
6.0%	226.4

FIGURE 6.6 Sensitivity Analysis of NPV to Growth Rate in Volume

for margin, volume, capital expenditure and fixed cost. The net present value (NPV) of the first 10 years of these cash flows is $208.5m (shown in cell D13).

One could then ask what effect a reduction in the growth rate of the volume produced (cell C6) would have on the output (cell D13). Of course, this could be established by simply manually changing the value of the input cell (say from 5% to 2%). However, in order to see the effect of multiple changes in an input value, and in a way that is still live-linked into the model (i.e. would change if other assumptions were reset), Excel's **DataTable** feature is useful (under **Data/What-If Analysis**). Figure 6.6 shows an example of how to display NPV for several growth rate assumptions.

On the other hand, one can only run sensitivities for items for which the model has been designed. For example, if a model does not allow delaying the start date of the project, then a sensitivity analysis to such a situation cannot be performed. Therefore, the model may have to be modified to enable the start date to be altered; in an ideal world, one would have established (before building the model) the sensitivities required, and use this information to design the model in the right way from the beginning; the core principles of risk model design are discussed in detail in Chapter 7.

The file Ch6.Time.Price.Flex.xlsx (shown in Figure 6.7) contains formulae that allow for the start year of a project to be altered: these use a lookup function to map a profile of volume

	A	B	C	D	E	F	G	H	I
1									
2		Generic schedule	Growth/Time Assumptions	1	2	3	4	5	
3		Capital Expenditure		-100	-75.0	-25.0	0.0	0.0	
4		Volume Produced (m units)	5.0%	6.0	6.3	6.6	6.9	7.3	
5									
6		Specific dates		2016	2017	2018	2019	2020	20
7		Contribution Margin based on Market Prices: $/Unit		10.0	10.0	10.0	10.0	10.0	1
8		Fixed Cost of Site $m p.a	2.0%	-10.0	-10.2	-10.4	-10.6	-10.8	-1
9									
10		Project Start date (year 1)	2017	2016	2017	2018	2019	2020	20
11		Capital Expenditure		0.0	-100.0	-75.0	-25.0	0.0	
12		Volume Produced		0.0	6.0	6.3	6.6	6.9	
13									
14		Summary Cash Flow		2016	2017	2018	2019	2020	20
15		Margin $m		0.0	60.0	63.0	66.2	69.5	7
16		Fixed Cost of Site $m p.a		-10.0	-10.2	-10.4	-10.6	-10.8	-1
17		Capex $m		0.0	-100.0	-75.0	-25.0	0.0	
18		Cash Flow $m		-10.0	-50.2	-22.4	30.5	58.6	6
19		10-year NPV $m	10.0%	150.9					
20									

FIGURE 6.7 Business Plan with Flexible Start Date for Capital Expenditure and Production Volume

Launch Year	
2016	208.5
2017	150.9
2018	100.1
2019	55.3
2020	16.1
2021	-18.2

FIGURE 6.8 Sensitivity Analysis of NPV to Start Dates

and capital expenditure from a generic time axis (i.e. years from launch) on to specific dates, which are then used in the model's calculations. One can see that the effect of a delay in the start date to 2017 is a reduction in NPV from $208.5m to $150.9m.

Similarly, Figure 6.8 shows a **DataTable** of NPV for various start dates.

One can also create **DataTables** in which two inputs are varied simultaneously. Figure 6.9 shows NPV as both initial volume and start dates are changed.

In relation to risk-based simulation methods, one can make the following observations:

- A core element of sensitivity and simulation modelling (and modelling more generally) is that models are designed so that they allow the relevant inputs to be changed; very often, inadequate attention is paid at the model design stage to the consideration of the sensitivity analysis that will be required, which needs to be done as it impacts the design of the (correct) model.
- For risk modelling, the inputs and model structure need to reflect the drivers of risk, and to capture the nature of that risk. For example, in a risk model it may be important for the project delay (after the planned launch in 2016) to be any figure, not just a whole number (such as if the delay were drawn randomly from a continuous range).
- Simulation modelling will change multiple inputs simultaneously (rather than a maximum of two when using a **DataTable**).
- In some cases (especially where other procedures are required to be run after any change in the value of an input), then – in place of a **DataTable** – it would generally be necessary

	1.0%	2.0%	3.0%	4.0%	5.0%	6.0%
2016	144.8	159.6	175.1	191.4	208.5	226.4
2017	102.6	113.9	125.7	138.0	150.9	164.3
2018	64.5	72.9	81.6	90.7	100.1	109.8
2019	30.1	36.1	42.3	48.7	55.3	62.2
2020	-1.0	3.1	7.3	11.7	16.1	20.7
2021	-29.0	-26.4	-23.7	-21.0	-18.2	-15.4

FIGURE 6.9 Sensitivity Analysis of NPV to Start Dates and Growth Rate in Volume

to embed such procedures within a VBA macro that implements the sensitivity analysis by running through the various values to be tried.

These topics are addressed in detail in Chapter 7.

6.3.2 Scenario Analysis

Scenario analysis involves assessing the effect on the output of a model as several inputs (typically more than two) are changed at the same time, and in a way that is explicitly predefined. For example, there may be three scenarios, including a base case, a worst case and a best case. Each scenario captures a change in the value of several variables compared to their base values, and is defined with a logically consistent set of data. For example, when looking at profit scenarios, a worst case could include one where prices achieved are low, volumes sold are low and input costs are high.

Scenario analysis is a powerful planning tool with many applications, including:

- When it is considered that there are distinct cases possible for the value of a particular variable, rather than a continuous range.
- To begin to explore the effect on the model's calculations where several input variables change simultaneously. This can be used either as a first step towards a full simulation, or as an optimisation method that looks for the best scenario. In particular, it can be useful to generate a better understanding of a complex situation: by first thinking of specific scenarios, and the interactions and consequences that would apply for each, one can gradually consolidate ideas and create a more comprehensive understanding.
- As a proxy tool to capture dependencies between variables, especially where a relationship is known to exist, but where expressing it through explicit formulae is not possible or too complex. For example:
  - In the context of the relationship between the volume sold and the price charged for a product, it may be difficult to create a valid formula for the volume that would apply for any assumed price. However, it may be possible to estimate (through judgement, expert estimates or market research) what the volume would be at some specific price points. In other words, although it may not be possible to capture the whole demand curve in a parameterised fashion, individual price–volume combinations can be treated as discrete scenarios, so that the dependency is captured implicitly when one changes scenario.
  - The relationship between the numbers of sales people and the productivity of each, or that of employee morale with productivity.
  - In macro-economic forecasting, one may wish to make assumptions for the values taken by a number of variables (perhaps as measured from cases that arose in historic data), but without having to define explicit parameterised relationships between them, which may be hard to do in a defensible manner.

Scenarios are generally best implemented in Excel by combining the use of lookup functions (e.g. **CHOOSE** or **INDEX**) with a **DataTable**: each scenario is characterised by an integer, which is used to drive a lookup function that returns the model input values that apply for the scenario. The **DataTable** is then used to conduct a sensitivity analysis as the scenario number is changed. (As for sensitivity analysis, and as also discussed in Chapter 7, where a

	A	B	C	D	E	F	G	H	I	J
1										
2		3	Scenario To use	1	2	3	4	5		
3		Volume Produced (m units)	5.0%	5.0%	2.0%	5.0%	5.0%	2.0%		
4		Project Start date (year 1)	2017	2016	2016	2017	2017	2017		
5		Discount rate for 10 year-NPV calculation	10.0%	10.0%	10.0%	10.0%	12.0%	12.0%		
6										
7		Generic schedule	Growth/Time Assumptions	1	2	3	4	5	6	7
8		Capital Expenditure		-100	-75.0	-25.0	0.0	0.0	0.0	0.0
9		Volume Produced (m units)	5.0%	6.0	6.3	6.6	6.9	7.3	7.7	8.0
10										
11		Specific dates		2016	2017	2018	2019	2020	2021	2022
12		Contribution Margin based on Market Prices: $/Unit		10.0	10.0	10.0	10.0	10.0	10.0	10.0
13		Fixed Cost of Site $m p.a	2.0%	-10.0	-10.2	-10.4	-10.6	-10.8	-11.0	-11.3
14										
15		Project Start date (year 1)	2017	2016	2017	2018	2019	2020	2021	2022
16		Capital Expenditure		0.0	-100.0	-75.0	-25.0	0.0	0.0	0.0
17		Volume Produced		0.0	6.0	6.3	6.6	6.9	7.3	7.7
18										
19		Summary Cash Flow		2016	2017	2018	2019	2020	2021	2022
20		Margin $m		0.0	60.0	63.0	66.2	69.5	72.9	76.6
21		Fixed Cost of Site $m p.a		-10.0	-10.2	-10.4	-10.6	-10.8	-11.0	-11.3
22		Capex $m		0.0	-100.0	-75.0	-25.0	0.0	0.0	0.0
23		Cash Flow $m		-10.0	-50.2	-22.4	30.5	58.6	61.9	65.3
24		10-year NPV $m	10.0%	150.9						

FIGURE 6.10 Business Plan Model Adapted to Include Input Scenarios

model requires some procedure to be run after any change in a model input, then the scenario analysis would need to be implemented with a macro in place of the **DataTable**.)

The file Ch6.Time.Price.Scen.xlsx has been adapted to allow five scenarios of three input assumptions to be run (volume growth, start date and discount rates), with the original input values overwritten by a lookup function that picks out the values that apply in each scenario (the scenario number that drives the lookup function is in cell B2). Figure 6.10 shows the main model, and Figure 6.11 shows a **DataTable** of NPV for each scenario.

Limitations of traditional sensitivity and scenario approaches include:

- They show only a small set of explicitly predefined cases.
- They do not show a representative set of cases. For example, a base case that consists of most likely values will, in fact, typically not show the most likely value of the output (see earlier in the text).
- They do not explicitly drive a thought process that explores true risk drivers and risk mitigation actions (unlike a full risk assessment), and hence may not be based on genuine risk scenarios that one may be exposed to. Nor do they distinguish between variables that are risky or uncertain from those that are to be optimised (chosen optimally).

NPV by Scenario	
1	208.5
2	159.6
3	150.9
4	127.4
5	95.1

FIGURE 6.11 Sensitivity Analysis of NPV to Scenario

- There is also no explicit attempt to calculate the likelihood associated with output values, nor the full range of possible values. To do so would require multiple inputs being varied simultaneously and probabilities being attached to these variations. Thus, the decision-making basis is potentially inadequate:
  - The average outcome is not known.
  - The likelihood of any outcome is not known, such as that of a base plan being achieved.
  - It is not easy to reflect risk tolerances (nor contingency requirements) adequately in the decision, or to set appropriate targets or appropriate objectives.
  - It is not easy to compare one project with another.

6.3.3 Simulation using DataTables

As an aside, basic "simulations" can be done using a **DataTable** to generate a set of values that would arise if a model containing **RAND()** functions were repeatedly recalculated. Since the recalculation does not require anything in the model to be changed (apart from the value of the **RAND()** functions, which is done in any case at every recalculation), one could create a one-way **DataTable**, whose output(s) is the model output(s) and the inputs to be varied is a list of integers, each corresponding to a recalculation indexation number (i.e. the number one for the first recalculation, the number two for the second, etc.). The column input cell that would then be varied to take these integer values would simply be a blank cell in the sheet (such as the empty top-left corner of the **DataTable**). This approach would avoid any need for VBA.

In practice, this would generally be unsatisfactory for several reasons:

- The results would change each time the model recalculated, so that there would not be a permanent store of results that could be used to calculate statistics, create graphs and reports, and so on. One would need to manually copy the values to a separate range for this purpose.
- It would be inconvenient when working with the main part of the model, as to recalculate it when any change is made would require a full "simulation", which would slow down the general working process, compared to running a simulation only when it was needed.
- It particular, it would be bad modelling practice to run a sensitivity analysis to a blank cell (in case some content were put into that cell, for example).
- It would be inflexible if changes needed to be made to the number of recalculations required, or to where results were placed, and so on.

This approach is generally not to be considered seriously for many practical situations, as the VBA code to run a basic simulation is very simple (although one may add more sophisticated functionality if desired); see Chapter 12.

6.3.4 GoalSeek

The Excel **GoalSeek** procedure (under **Data/What-If Analysis**) searches (iteratively) to find the value of a single model input that would lead to the output having a particular value that the user specifies.

For example, one may ask what volume growth would be required (with all other assumptions at their base value), so that NPV was $220m. From Figure 6.6, one can see that the figure

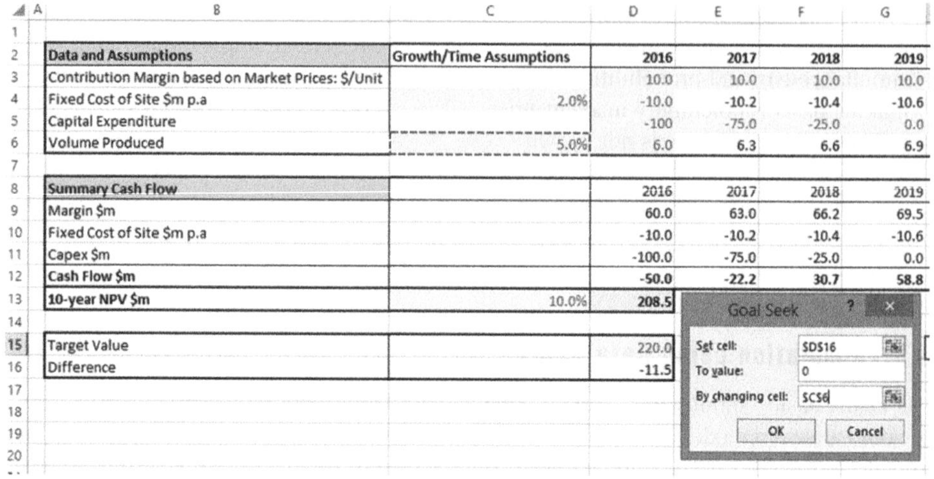

	A	B	C	D	E	F	G
1							
2		Data and Assumptions	Growth/Time Assumptions	2016	2017	2018	2019
3		Contribution Margin based on Market Prices: $/Unit		10.0	10.0	10.0	10.0
4		Fixed Cost of Site $m p.a	2.0%	-10.0	-10.2	-10.4	-10.6
5		Capital Expenditure		-100	-75.0	-25.0	0.0
6		Volume Produced	5.0%	6.0	6.3	6.6	6.9
7							
8		Summary Cash Flow		2016	2017	2018	2019
9		Margin $m		60.0	63.0	66.2	69.5
10		Fixed Cost of Site $m p.a		-10.0	-10.2	-10.4	-10.6
11		Capex $m		-100.0	-75.0	-25.0	0.0
12		Cash Flow $m		-50.0	-22.2	30.7	58.8
13		10-year NPV $m	10.0%	208.5			
14							
15		Target Value		220.0			
16		Difference		-11.5			

Goal Seek
Set cell: $D$16
To value: 0
By changing cell: $C$6
OK Cancel

FIGURE 6.12 Finding the Required Growth Rate to Achieve a Target NPV

is between 5% and 6%; to answer this question precisely using sensitivity techniques would require many iterations and generally not be very efficient.

The file Ch6.Time.Price.GoalSeek.xlsx (shown in Figure 6.12) has been adapted by placing the desired value for NPV in a cell of the model and calculating the difference, so that the target value is zero; this approach is generally more transparent and flexible (for example, the target value is explicit and recorded within the sheet, and it also allows for easier automation using macros).

(Once the OK button is clicked in the procedure shown above, the value in cell C6 will iterate until a value of approximately 5.65% is found.)

Note that it is generally not a valid question to ask what combination of inputs (i.e. what scenario) will lead to a specific outcome; in general there would be many.

6.4 OPTIMISATION ANALYSIS AND MODELLING: RELATIONSHIP TO SIMULATION

This section discusses the relationship between simulation and optimisation analysis and modelling.

6.4.1 Uncertainty versus Choice

When conducting sensitivity and scenario analysis, it is not necessary to make a distinction between whether the input variable being tested is one whose value can be fully controlled or not. Where the value of an input variable can be fully controlled, then its value is a choice, so that the question arises as to which choice is best (from the point of view of the analyst or relevant decision-maker). Thus, in general, as indicated in Figure 6.13, there are two generic subcategories of sensitivity analysis:

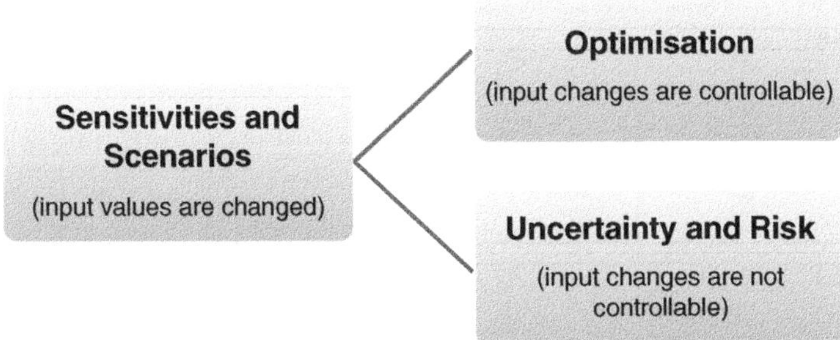

FIGURE 6.13 Relationship Between Sensitivities, Uncertainty and Optimisation

- Risk or uncertainty context or focus, where the inputs are not controllable within any specific modelled context (and their possible values may be represented by distributions).
- Optimisation context or focus, where the input values are fully controllable within that context, and should be chosen optimally.

The distinction between whether one is faced with an uncertain situation or an optimisation one may depend on the perspective from which one is looking: one person's choice may be another's uncertainty and vice versa. For example:

- It may be an individual's choice as to what time to plan to get up in the morning. On a particular day, one may plan to rise at a time that takes into account the possibility that heavy rain may create travel disruptions, or that other unforeseen events may happen. These reflections may result in a precise (optimal) time that one chooses to rise. However, from the perspective of someone else who has insufficient information about the details of the other person's objectives for the day, travel processes and risk tolerances, the time at which the other person rises may be considered to be uncertain.
- It is a company's choice where to build a factory, with each possible location having a set of risks associated with it, as well as other structural differences between them. Once the analysis is complete, the location will be chosen by the company's management according to their criteria. However, an outsider lacks sufficient information about the management decision criteria and processes, and may regard the selection of the location as a process with an uncertain outcome.
- In some situations a company may be a price-taker (accepting the prevailing market prices), and hence exposed to the potential future uncertainty of prices (the same would apply if one's product sold at a premium or discount to such market prices). In other contexts, the company may be a price-maker (where it decides the price level to sell at); a modest increase in price may lead to sales increasing (if volume stays more or less constant), whereas a very high price would likely cause a catastrophic fall in sales volume, which leads to reduced sales in total. In such contexts, there would be an optimal price point.

The file Ch6.TimeFlex.Risk.Opt.xlsx (shown in Figure 6.14) contains an example portfolio of 10 projects, with the cash flow profile of each shown on a generic time axis (i.e. an investment

	A	B	C	D	E	F	G	H	I	J	K	L	M
1													
2		**Generic schedule**		1	2	3	4	5	6	7	8	9	10
3		Project 1	$m	-250	67	67	67	60	54	49	44	40	36
4		Project 2	$m	-300	87	87	87	87	78	70	63	57	51
5		Project 3	$m	-160	43	43	43	43	43	39	35	32	28
6		Project 4	$m	-120	46	46	46	41	37	34	30	27	24
7		Project 5	$m	-240	97	97	97	97	87	79	71	64	57
8		Project 6	$m	-300	80	80	80	80	80	72	65	58	52
9		Project 7	$m	-160	44	44	44	40	36	32	29	26	24
10		Project 8	$m	-200	77	77	77	77	70	63	56	51	46
11		Project 9	$m	-180	72	72	72	72	72	65	58	53	47
12		Project 10	$m	-360	95	95	95	85	77	69	62	56	50
13													
14		**Specific dates**	Start date (year 1)	2016	2017	2018	2019	2020	2021	2022	2023	2024	2025
15		Project 1	2016	(250)	67	67	67	60	54	49	44	40	36
16		Project 2	2016	(300)	87	87	87	87	78	70	63	57	51
17		Project 3	2016	(160)	43	43	43	43	43	39	35	32	28
18		Project 4	2016	(120)	46	46	46	41	37	34	30	27	24
19		Project 5	2016	(240)	97	97	97	97	87	79	71	64	57
20		Project 6	2016	(300)	80	80	80	80	80	72	65	58	52
21		Project 7	2016	(160)	44	44	44	40	36	32	29	26	24
22		Project 8	2016	(200)	77	77	77	77	70	63	56	51	46
23		Project 9	2016	(180)	72	72	72	72	72	65	58	53	47
24		Project 10	2016	(360)	95	95	95	85	77	69	62	56	50
25		**Cash Flow**		**-2270**	**709**	**709**	**709**	**684**	**635**	**571**	**514**	**463**	**417**
26													
27		**Disc Cash flow yrs 1-10**	1212	$m									
28		**Min CF years 1-5**	-2270	$m									
29		**Min acceptable**	-500	$m									
30													

FIGURE 6.14 Project Portfolio with Mapping from Generic Time Axis to Specific Dates

followed by a positive cash flow from the date that each project is launched). Underneath the grid of generic profiles, another grid shows the effect when each project is given a specific start date (which can be changed to be any year number). In the case shown, all projects launch in 2016, resulting in a total financing requirement of $2270 in 2016 (cell D25).

However, the role of the various launch dates of the projects could depend on the situation:

- Risk or uncertainty context. Each project may be subject to some uncertainty on its timing, so that the future cash flow and financing profile would be uncertain. In this case, the modeller could replace the launch dates with values drawn from an appropriate distribution (one that samples future year numbers as integers), and a simulation could be run in order to establish the possible time profiles.
- Optimisation context. Where the choice of the set of dates is entirely within the discretion and control of the decision-maker. In this case, some sets of launch dates would be preferable to others. For example, one may wish to maximise the NPV of cash flow over the first 10 years, whilst not investing more than a specified amount in each individual year. Whereas launching of all projects simultaneously may exceed available funds, delaying some projects would reduce the investment requirement, but would also reduce NPV (due to the delay in the future cash flows). Thus, generically, a middle ground (optimal set of dates) may be sought, the precise values of which would depend on the objectives and specific constraints.

In this example (as shown in cell C29) the desired constraint may be one in which the minimum cash flow in any of the first five years should not fall below –$500m. Therefore, the case shown in Figure 6.14 would not be considered an acceptable set of launch dates.

The file Ch6.TimeFlex.Risk.Opt.Solver.xlsx (see Figure 6.15) contains an alternative set of launch dates, in which some projects start later than 2016. This is an acceptable set of dates, as the value in cell C28 is larger than that in C29. It is possible that this set of

	A	B	C	D	E	F	G	H	I	J	K	L	M
1													
2		**Generic schedule**		1	2	3	4	5	6	7	8	9	10
3		Project 1	$m	-250	67	67	67	60	54	49	44	40	36
4		Project 2	$m	-300	87	87	87	87	78	70	63	57	51
5		Project 3	$m	-160	43	43	43	43	43	39	35	32	28
6		Project 4	$m	-120	46	46	46	41	37	34	30	27	24
7		Project 5	$m	-240	97	97	97	97	87	79	71	64	57
8		Project 6	$m	-300	80	80	80	80	80	72	65	58	52
9		Project 7	$m	-160	44	44	44	40	36	32	29	26	24
10		Project 8	$m	-200	77	77	77	77	70	63	56	51	46
11		Project 9	$m	-180	72	72	72	72	72	65	58	53	47
12		Project 10	$m	-360	95	95	95	85	77	69	62	56	50
13													
14		**Specific dates**	Start date (year 1)	2016	2017	2018	2019	2020	2021	2022	2023	2024	2025
15		Project 1	2019	0	0	0	(250)	67	67	67	60	54	49
16		Project 2	2016	(300)	87	87	87	87	78	70	63	57	51
17		Project 3	2016	(160)	43	43	43	43	43	39	35	32	28
18		Project 4	2017	0	(120)	46	46	46	41	37	34	30	27
19		Project 5	2017	0	(240)	97	97	97	97	87	79	71	64
20		Project 6	2019	0	0	0	(300)	80	80	80	80	80	72
21		Project 7	2017	0	(160)	44	44	44	40	36	32	29	26
22		Project 8	2018	0	0	(200)	77	77	77	77	70	63	56
23		Project 9	2018	0	0	(180)	72	72	72	72	72	65	58
24		Project 10	2018	0	0	(360)	95	95	95	85	77	69	62
25		**Cash Flow**		**-460**	**-390**	**-422**	**12**	**709**	**691**	**652**	**602**	**550**	**495**
26													
27		**Disc Cash flow yrs 1-10**	**820**	$m									
28		**Min CF years 1-5**	**-460**	$m									
29		**Min acceptable**	**-500**	$m									

FIGURE 6.15 Delayed Launch Dates to Some Projects may Create an Acceptable or Optimal Solution

dates is the best one that could be achieved, but there may be an even better solution if one were to look further. (Note that in a continuous linear optimisation problem, an optimal solution would meet the constraints exactly, whereas in this case the input values are discrete integers.)

This example demonstrates the close relationship between simulation and core aspects of optimisation: in both cases, there is generally a combinatorial issue, i.e. there are many possible combinations of input and output values. Given this link, one may think that the appropriate techniques used to deal with each situation would be the same. For example, one may (try to) find optimal solutions by using simulation to calculate many (or all) possible model values as the inputs are varied simultaneously, and simply choose the best one; alternatively, one may try a number of predefined scenarios for the assumed start dates to see the effect of various combinations. In some cases, trial and error (applied with some common sense) may lead one to an acceptable (but perhaps not the truly optimal) solution.

Although such approaches may have their uses in some circumstances, they are not generally very efficient ways of solving optimisation problems. First, in some cases, properties implicit within the constraints can be used to reduce the number of possible input combinations that are worth considering. Second, by adapting the set of trial values based on the outcomes of previous trials, one may be able to search more quickly (i.e. by refining already established good or near-optimal solutions, rather than searching for completely new possibilities).

Therefore, in practice, tools and techniques specifically created for optimisation situations are usually more effective: Excel's **Solver** or Palisade's **Evolver** can be considered as possible tools. (The latter is part of the **DecisionTools Suite**, of which @RISK is also a key component.) For very large optimisation problems, one may need to use other tools or work outside the Excel platform (these are beyond the scope of this text).

Figure 6.16 shows the **Solver** dialog box that was used (**Solver** is a free component (add-in) to Excel that generally needs to be installed under **Excel Options/Add-Ins**, and will then appear on the **Data** tab; the dialog box is fairly self-explanatory).

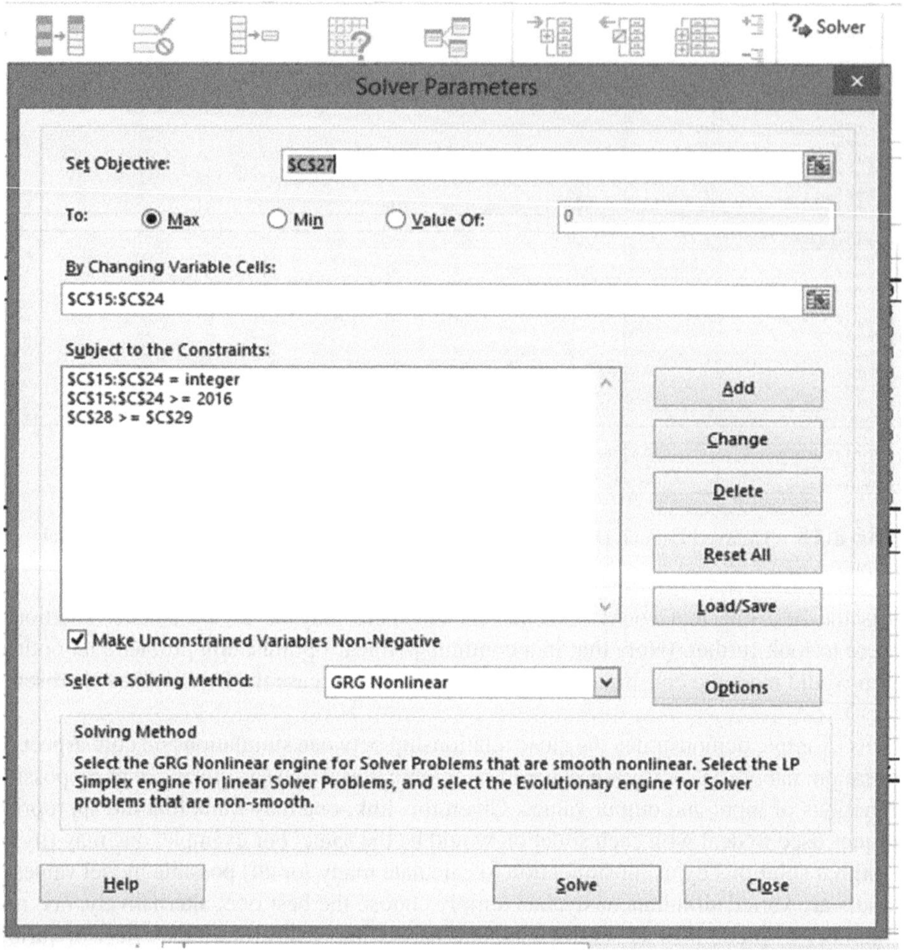

FIGURE 6.16 The Solver Dialog Box

It is important in practice to note that most optimisation tools allow for only one objective (e.g. maximise profits or minimise cost). Thus, qualitative definitions of objectives such as "maximising revenues whilst minimising cost" cannot typically be used as inputs into optimisation tools without further modification. Generally, all but one of the initial (multiple) objectives must be re-expressed as constraints, so that there is only one remaining objective and multiple constraints, such as "maximise profit whilst keeping costs below $10m and delivering the project within 3 years".

Optimisation problems also arise when the number of possible options is low, but each option relates to a quite different situation. This can be thought of as "structural" optimisation, in which a decision must be taken whose consequence fundamentally changes the basic structure of the future, with the aim being to choose the best decision. For example:

- The choice as to whether to go on a luxury vacation or to buy a new car:
  - If one goes on vacation and does not buy the car, one will thereafter have a very onerous journey to work each day (for example, a long walk to a bus stop on a narrow road, a

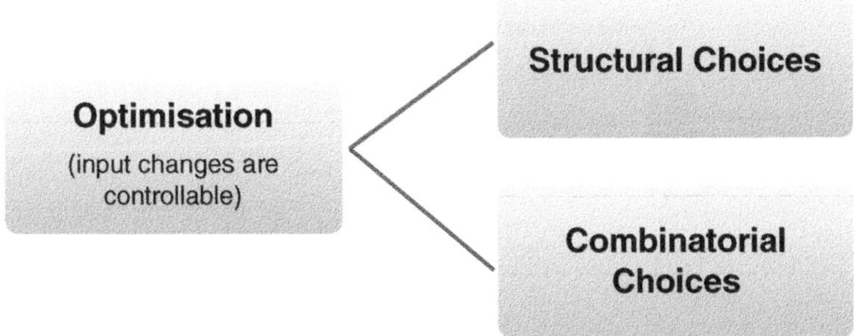

FIGURE 6.17 Categories of Optimisation Situations

bus journey to the train station, then a train journey, followed by another bus ride, and so on).
    - If one buys the car, one will have a relatively easy drive to work in future, but not having had the benefits of the vacation one may become unhappy and quit the job!
- The choice as to whether a business should expand organically, through an acquisition or a joint venture, is a decision with only a few combinations (choices), but where each is of a fundamentally different (structural) nature.
- The choice as to whether to proceed or not with a project whose scope could be redefined (e.g. abandoned, expanded or modified) after some initial information has been gained in its early stages (such as the results of a test which provides an imperfect indicator of the likely future success of the project).

Figure 6.17 shows these two categories of optimisation situations.

Decision-tree methods are often used when faced with structural choices. In the following, we make some brief remarks about their benefits, beyond the purely visual aspect; however, a detailed treatment of them is beyond the scope of this text.

Figure 6.18 shows a simple example of a case in which the decisions to be taken are shown in a sequence: first, whether to go on vacation or buy a new car and second, the type of car that one buys in the case that the decision to buy a car is taken.

Note that when there are no further items appearing between the decisions that are in sequence (i.e. those concerned with the potential car purchase), then the tree shown in Figure 6.18 is the same as that shown in Figure 6.19 in terms of the ultimate available decisions, even though the sequencing is less visually explicit.

Figures 6.18 and 6.19 were produced using Palisade's **PrecisionTree** software (which is part of the **DecisionTools Suite**). The quantitative (rather than the visual) benefit of such a tool is that it implements a backward calculation path that would be required if uncertainties occurred in between decisions within a decision sequence (by default, using the average outcome of each decision option). For example, whereas the tree shown in Figure 6.20 recommends that one stays in bed, the tree in Figure 6.21 recommends that one gets up. In each case, the average branch value (taking into account the probabilities shown by the branch percentages above the chance nodes, and the values shown below the branches) is calculated. However, whereas in Figure 6.20 this calculation can be done either from left to right or from right to left, in the structure of Figure 6.21 it can only be done from right to left (i.e. "backwards").

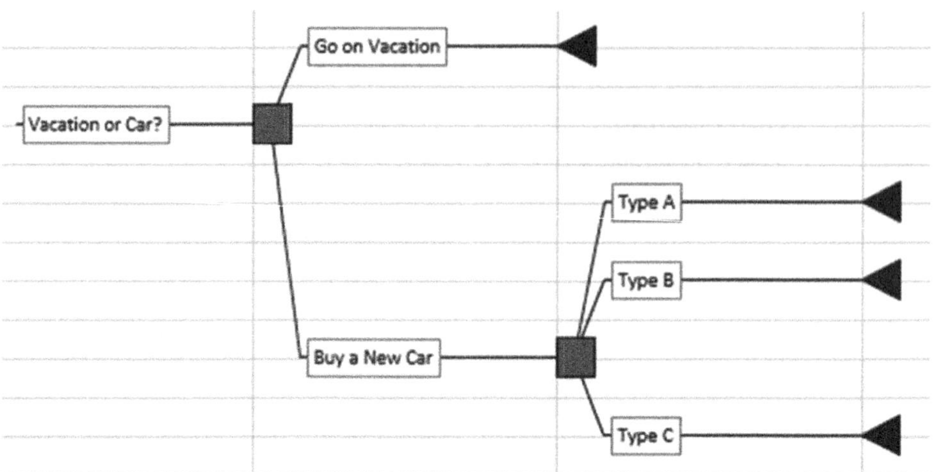

FIGURE 6.18 Simple Example of a Decision Structure

The tree in Figure 6.21 shows a higher value than that in Figure 6.20; the difference (of 0.6) can be thought of as the "real options" value (value of flexibility) of having the choice (option) as to whether to go home or go to the cinema when one is having a bad day (as opposed to having no choices at all): to evaluate the basic decision as to whether to get up or not, one needs to know that this future potential possible behaviour has some value; hence the need for the backward process, which is not required in the pure "decision-making under uncertainty" context (as long as decisions are made using average future outcomes); Figure 6.20. Thus, there is a tight link between the topics of optimisation, real options and decision trees.

The backward calculation aspect within the software is perhaps its most important aspect, as the equivalent implementation in Excel can be quite cumbersome (and often overlooked as a required process), as shown in Figure 6.22.

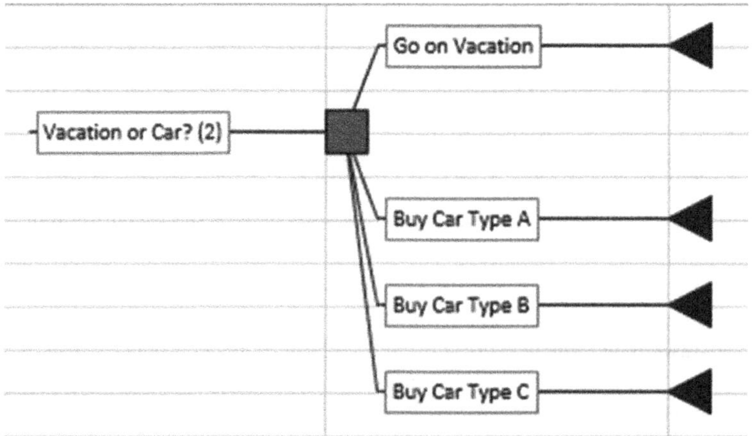

FIGURE 6.19 Sequential Decisions Presented as a Single Full Decision Set

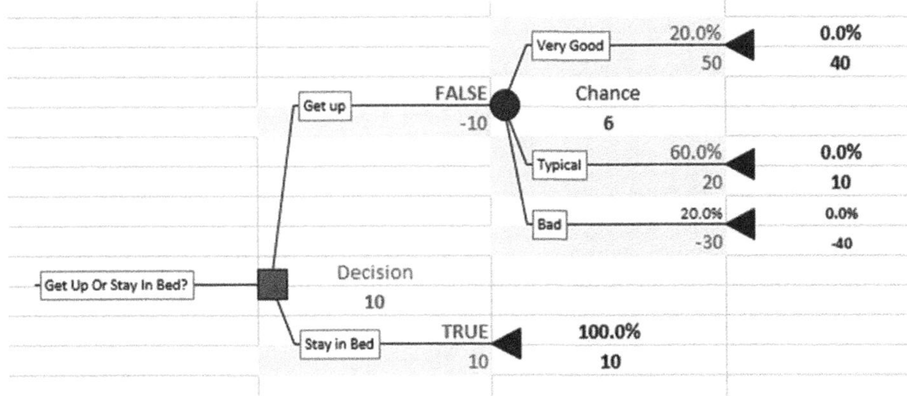

FIGURE 6.20 Simple Example of Decision Tree with Future Uncertainty

6.4.2 Optimisation in the Presence of Risk and Uncertainty

Uncertainty may also be present in optimisation situations. Whereas the discussion associated with Figure 6.13 may seem to suggest that situations involving optimisation and those containing risk (or uncertainty) are mutually exclusive, there is, in fact, a more complex interaction between them: simply speaking, when a situation contains risk (or uncertainty), one is confronted with the question as to how to respond to that risk in an optimal way.

The optimal response to risk involves choosing optimally the context in which to act, which involves taking into account the risk or uncertainty within each context (as well as other decision factors). For example, it may be under our control as to whether we decide to make a journey by bus, bicycle or on foot. Each choice results in a base case (say average or expected) travel time that is different, and each has different costs. In addition, there is uncertainty within each option, which may affect the decision. Thus, it is possible that one may choose to walk on a particular day, in order to have a travel time that is more predictable than the other methods even if it may take longer on average.

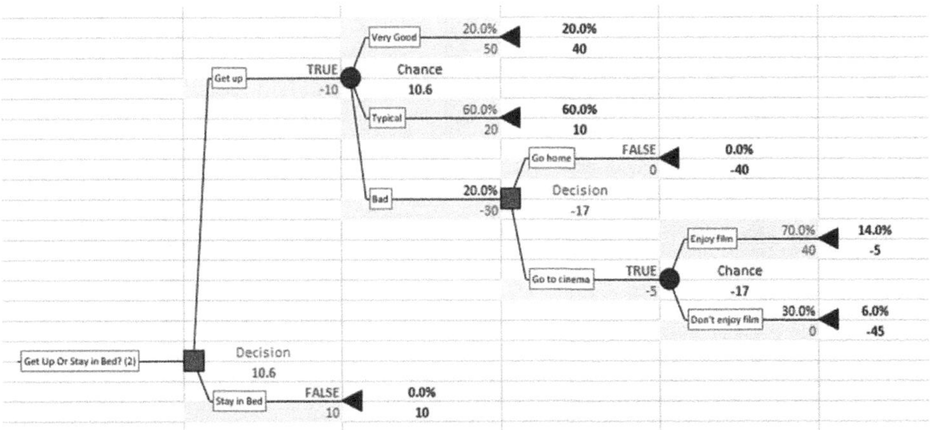

FIGURE 6.21 Decision Tree with Decisions Taken Following an Uncertain Outcome

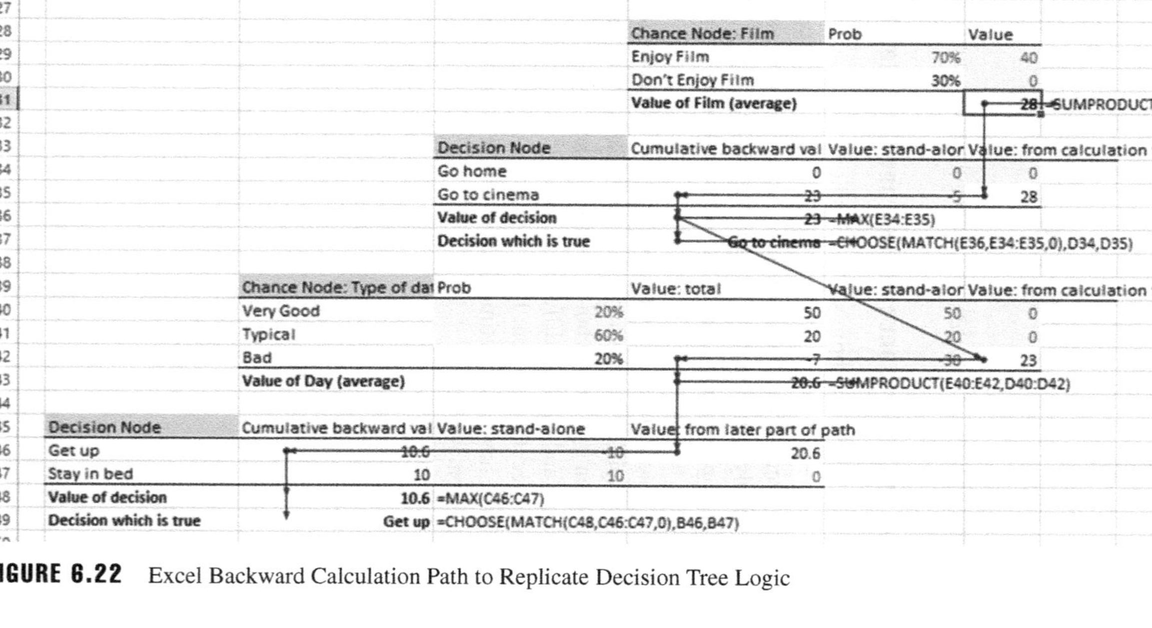

Excel version with Backward Calculation
Chance Node: Film
Prob
Value
Enjoy Film
70%
40
Don't Enjoy Film
30%
0
Value of Film (average)
28
=SUMPRODUCT(G29:G30,F29:F30)
Decision Node
Cumulative backward val
Value: stand-alor
Value: from calculation for later part of path
Go home
0
0
0
Go to cinema
23
-5
28
Value of decision
23
=MAX(E34:E35)
Decision which is true
Go to cinema
=CHOOSE(MATCH(E36,E34:E35,0),D34,D35)
Chance Node: Type of dat
Prob
Value: total
Value: stand-alor
Value: from calculation for later part of path
Very Good
20%
50
50
0
Typical
60%
20
20
0
Bad
20%
-7
-30
23
Value of Day (average)
20.6
=SUMPRODUCT(E40:E42,D40:D42)
Decision Node
Cumulative backward val
Value: stand-alone
Value: from later part of path
Get up
10.6
-10
20.6
Stay in bed
10
10
0
Value of decision
10.6
=MAX(C46:C47)
Decision which is true
Get up
=CHOOSE(MATCH(C48,C46:C47,0),B46,B47)

FIGURE 6.22 Excel Backward Calculation Path to Replicate Decision Tree Logic

An optimal risk mitigation (or response) strategy may have elements both of structural and combinatorial optimisation: structural optimisation about which context in which to operate, and combinatorial optimisation to find the best set of risk mitigation measures within that context.

Indeed, as discussed in Chapter 1, the essential role of risk assessment is to support the development and choice of the optimal context in which to operate (operating within the best structural context, mitigation and responding to risks within it), and to support the evaluation of a final decision taking into account the residual uncertainty and risk tolerances of the decision-maker.

6.4.3 Modelling Aspects of Optimisation Situations

As discussed above, optimisation and risk situations are inherently related, and many aspects of the underlying modelling issues are also similar. Nevertheless, there are some specific aspects that are worth summarising and emphasising at this point.

First, generally speaking, one needs to consider early on in the process what the correct tool and overall approach is, specifically whether tree, combinatorial, heuristic, mathematical or other approaches are the most suitable; this will also affect the basic platform (e.g. Excel or other) and tools (e.g. add-ins or other software) that should be used. Some optimisation situations can be challenging and complex: in particular, where the decision criteria are not based on future average outcomes but on other statistical measures, and where there is a sequence of decisions, then the optimal choice of decisions is harder; these stochastic optimisation situations are beyond the scope of this text.

Second, an explicit distinction between choice variables and uncertain ones needs to be made when using risk-based simulation or optimisation approaches (unlike when performing traditional sensitivity analysis, for example):

- In general, the inputs to Excel models are made up of numbers that are choice variables (to be optimised), uncertain variables (to be randomly sampled in a simulation) and other parameters that are fixed for the purposes of the model (e.g. scaling factors, etc.). In the general case, a single model may have items of each nature. For example, in the model shown in Figure 6.14, the generic cash flow profiles from the date of project launch could be uncertain, whilst the set of launch dates is to be optimised.
- Whereas in some specific application areas the uncertainty can be dealt with analytically, in general, simulation is required. This means that for every possible set of dates tried as a solution of the optimisation, a whole simulation would need to be run to see the uncertainty profile within that situation.
- Where a full simulation is required for each trial of a potential optimal solution, it is often worth considering whether the presence of the uncertainty would change the actual optimum solution in any significant way. The potential time involved in running many simulations can be significant, whereas it may not generate any different solutions. For example, in practice, the optimal route to travel across a large city may (in many cases) be the same irrespective of whether one considers the travel time for each individual potential segment of the journey to be uncertain or whether one considers it to be fixed. (There can be exceptions in situations where the uncertainty is highly non-symmetric, or due to the decision-maker's risk tolerances; in order to have more predictability of the total journey

time, one may choose to walk one route rather than take the bus on a different route, even if walking is longer on average.)

- The **RiskOptimizer** tool (part of the Industrial version of @RISK), allows for a simulation to be run within each optimisation trial (which is powerful, but can be time consuming).

Third, from a process perspective, most optimisation algorithms allow for only one objective, whereas most business situations involve multiple objectives (and stakeholders with their own objectives). Thus, one typically needs to reformulate all but one of these objectives as constraints. Whilst in theory the optimal solution is found to be the same in each, in practice process participants would often be (or feel themselves to be) at an advantage if their own objective is the one taken as the single objective for the optimisation, and at a disadvantage if their objective is one that is translated into one of many constraints:

- Psychologically, an objective has positive overtones, whereas a constraint sounds more negative: an objective is something that one should strive to achieve; a constraint should be overcome.
- Whereas an objective is something that one is often reluctant to change, constraints are more likely to be de-emphasised, or to be regarded as items that can be modified or negotiated.
- When one's objective becomes expressed as only one item within a set of constraints, a focus on it is likely to be lost.

Fourth, models that are intended to be used for optimisation purposes sometimes have more demanding requirements on their internal logic than those that are to be used for simple "what-if" analysis. For example:

- Generically, the objective function of an optimisation model should follow a U-shaped (or inverted U-shaped) profile as the value of an input (choice) variable changes. The main exception is where the optimisation arises only as a result of constraints.
- A model that calculates sales revenues by multiplying price by volume may be sufficient for some simple purposes of sensitivity analysis, but if used to find the optimal price, then it would be meaningless unless volume is made to depend on price (with higher prices leading to lower volumes); otherwise an infinite price would be the best one to charge, which in practice would lead to sales being zero. As mentioned earlier, scenario approaches are often used if such dependencies are hard to accurately capture through parameterised relationships.

Finally, although optimisation situations often have a unique solution, there will often be many other possible sets of trial values that provide a close-to-optimal solution. This will be the case due to the U-shaped nature of the curve (which is flat at the optimal point, unless such a point is determined only by constraints). This feature of optimisation problems is part of the reason why heuristic or pragmatic methods can be so effective, as one may be able to find a very good solution with some trial and error and common sense. It can also explain why such techniques are hard to apply in practical organisational contexts; many similar variants of a close-to-optimal project will give a similar result, whereas some may be more favourable than others to specific process participants.

6.5 ANALYTIC AND OTHER NUMERICAL METHODS

This section provides an overview of analytic methods that are sometimes used in the context of financial and risk modelling activities. This provides some basis for comparison with simulation methods, and the applicability of each.

6.5.1 Analytic Methods and Closed-Form Solutions

In some cases, the distribution of a quantity (or of selected statistical properties of it) can be represented in an equation derived by mathematical manipulation of underlying assumptions (sometimes termed "analytic" techniques or "closed-form" solutions). Examples include:

- The Black–Scholes formula for the valuation of a European option (see below).
- The Huang–Litzenberger formulae for the calculation of the optimal composition of a financial portfolio, i.e. of the portfolio that has the minimum risk for any given expected return (also known as the Markowitz [efficient] frontier). The formula applies to the case where there is no constraint on the amount of each asset that may be held (such as no restrictions on short-selling or borrowing).
- In credit, insurance and reinsurance modelling, many analytic formulae exist in various areas, such as to calculate the distribution (or statistics thereof) of maxima (or extreme values) of random processes; this is the topic of extreme value theory (see Chapter 9 for more details).

An example of the first point above is the following: a European option is traded prior to an expiry date, and at expiration, the holder of a call option may buy an underlying asset, whereas the holder of a put option can sell it (each would be exercised at expiry if the asset price at expiry was above or below the exercise price respectively). The Black–Scholes formula gives the value of such options. It contains six variables: S (the current price of the underlying asset), E (the future exercise price at expiry of the option), τ (the time to expiry, or $T-t$ where t is the current time and T the time of expiry), σ (the volatility of the return of the asset), r (the risk-free interest rate) and D (the constant dividend yield). The Black–Scholes formulae for call (C) and put (P) option values are:

$$C = Se^{-D\tau}N\left(d_1\right) - Ee^{-r\tau}N\left(d_2\right)$$
$$P = -Se^{-D\tau}N\left(-d_1\right) + Ee^{-r\tau}N\left(-d_2\right)$$

where:

$$d_1 = \frac{\left(LN\left(\frac{S}{E}\right) + \left(r - D + \frac{\sigma^2}{2}\right)\tau\right)}{\sigma\sqrt{\tau}}$$

$$d_2 = \frac{\left(LN\left(\frac{S}{E}\right) + \left(r - D - \frac{\sigma^2}{2}\right)\tau\right)}{\sigma\sqrt{\tau}}$$

and $N(x)$ is the cumulative probability to point x for the standard normal distribution.

Formulae also exist for the valuation of derivatives that are more complex than simple (vanilla) European options, and in some cases for where the underlying assumptions are generalised (e.g. where volatility may not be constant).

Closed-form (analytic) solutions are typically powerful to use when they are available. However, they also suffer from a number of potential drawbacks:

- Additional assumptions are generally required in order to be able to conduct the necessary mathematical manipulations to derive them. Thus, the "analytic" formulae are therefore still approximations to reality, so "model error" is nevertheless present (i.e. the conceptualised specification is not a perfect representation of reality). For example, in applications relating to financial options, derivatives and portfolios, it is often assumed that there are no transaction costs, or taxes, that certain processes are assumed to follow a normal (or lognormal) distribution and that some parameter values (such as volatility) are constant over time.
- The actual calculation of a specific result for a closed-form solution may be so complex that numerical approximations (such as simulation) are, in any case, required; as mentioned earlier, the origin of Monte Carlo methods was in the scientific arena, as a numerical tool to approximate the value of integrals.
- Even where possible to treat analytically, the models typically require a high degree of mathematical skill to understand and work with; as such they are often not practically applicable in business decision-making contexts, even where they may theoretically be so.
- In addition, in most practical applications relating to real-life business projects, closed-form solutions are generally not possible to derive:
  - The processes that determine the inputs to a model, and the process by which inputs lead to outputs, are only partially understood and require judgement.
  - There may be a lack of data to justify some assumptions with sufficient rigour.
  - Even where the processes are understood and data are available, the mathematical manipulations are generally too complex. Even an apparently relatively simple set of calculations in an Excel spreadsheet (such as taking the maximum of two values, where each value itself results from other calculations that are derived from several inputs) would be difficult to evaluate in a closed-form sense, especially where the inputs may be themselves uncertain or have a distribution of possible values.

Where closed-form solutions are not appropriate or available, other numerical techniques sometimes exist for risk quantification, optimisation modelling and related areas. Examples include:

- Finite difference methods or finite element methods (part of the category of "grid-based" numerical techniques). These numerical approaches are widely used in scientific areas as well as in the financial area to solve partial differential equations. Binomial trees are another example of grid techniques.
- Linear, non-linear, dynamic programming and other optimisation techniques.

Once again, in practical business applications most of these techniques apply to specialised areas (e.g. optimisation of production schedules and product mixes), rather than being readily applicable to almost any situation.

The interested reader can find more details about these and further examples through simple internet or general literature searches.

6.5.2 Combining Simulation Methods with Exact Solutions

Simulation methods can sometimes be used in combination with exact solutions for specific purposes, including:

- Testing the accuracy of random number processes. For example (as discussed in detail in Chapter 13), one can establish an estimate of the value of π (3.14159...) using simulation. This could be used to test the accuracy of random number sampling methods, for example.
- Exploring the effect of uncertainty in values of the parameters used in exact analytic formulae (which typically assume that the parameter values are fixed). The volume of a cube is the product of its three dimensions, but what may the volume be if the measurement of each dimension is uncertain? This has applications to the modelling of uncertainty in oil reserves and mineral or resource volumes. Similarly, one may test the effect in the above options value formula of some of the parameters being uncertain (although often other mathematical approaches are also used to do that).

6.6 THE APPLICABILITY OF SIMULATION METHODS

Simulation techniques have already found wide use in many applications. The reasons for this include:

- They can be used in almost any model, irrespective of the application or sector.
- They are conceptually quite straightforward, involving essentially the repeated recalculation to generate many representative scenarios.
- They are generally easy to implement, requiring only an understanding of fairly basic aspects of statistics and probability distributions, dependency relationships and (on occasion) some additional modelling techniques; the required level of mathematical knowledge is quite focused.
- They generally provide a surprisingly accurate estimate of the properties of the output distribution, even when only relatively few recalculations have been conducted (see earlier).
- They can be a useful complement to analytic or closed-form approaches; especially in more complex cases, simulation can be used to create intuition about the nature and the behaviour of the underlying processes and of the associated mathematics.

Thus, in many practical situations, simulation is the most appropriate tool, and indeed may be either the only, or by far the simplest, method available. Its use can often produce a high level of insight and value-added with fairly little effort or investment in time or money.

CHAPTER 7

Core Principles of Risk Model Design

In this chapter, we highlight some core principles in the design of risk models. Many of these are similar to those in traditional static modelling, but there are, of course, some differences.

The extent of similarity is often overlooked, resulting in modellers who are competent in traditional static approaches being apprehensive to engage in potential risk modelling, or overwhelmed when initially trying to do so. Key similarities include:

- The importance of planning the model and its decision-support role, bearing in mind the context, overall objectives, organisational processes and management culture.
- The importance of keeping things as simple as possible, yet insightful, useful, but not simplistic.
- The importance of distinguishing the effect of controllable items (i.e. decisions) from that of non-controllable variables, both in terms of model building and in results presentation.
- The use of sensitivity thought processes as a model design tool.
- The need to build formulae that contain logic that is flexible enough to capture the nature of the sensitivity or uncertainty.
- The use of switches to control the running of different cases or scenarios.
- The need to capture general dependency relationships, both between inputs and calculations, and between calculated items.
- Very often, from the perspective of the formulae required in a model, it is often irrelevant whether the process to vary an input value is a manual one, or one that uses sensitivity techniques, or one that uses random sampling.

There are, of course, some differences between risk model design and that of traditional static models, including:

- The focus is on specific drivers of risk, rather than on general sensitivities.
- The structure and formulae in the model typically need adapting so that risks can be mapped into it. In particular, the impact of each risk must have a corresponding line item.
- The formulae may need to be more flexible or more general, for example to allow variations of values drawn from a continuous range, rather than from a finite set of discrete values.
- The model needs to be closely aligned with any general risk assessment process that is typically happening in parallel.

- The model needs to capture any dependencies between sources of risk, in addition to the general dependencies mentioned above; this topic is covered in detail in Chapter 11.

7.1 MODEL PLANNING AND COMMUNICATION

This section covers key aspects of the activities associated with the overall planning of a model and ensures that it is designed in a way that takes the likely communication issues into account.

7.1.1 Decision-Support Role

In any modelling context, it is clearly vital to remain focused on the overall objectives. In particular, the ultimate aim is usually to provide information to support a decision process in some way.

In a risk context, such decisions relate to:

- The implementation of actions to respond to risks and uncertainties.
- Decisions related to project design, structure and scope (these may not be traditional risks, but the potential to make a poor decision in respect of some particular issue is sometimes classified as a "decision risk").
- The making of a final go/no-go decision on a project, based on the risk profile that results in the optimal context, i.e. where all other decisions have been considered, and the resulting risk profile is a residual.

A common shortfall in risk assessment activities in general is that so much attention is paid to the (less familiar) concepts of uncertainty and risk, that the necessary focus on the possible decision options is lost. This is generally due to the extra potential complexity involved in quantitative risk assessment activities, coupled with the fact that many participants are likely to have insufficient understanding of the real purpose and uses of the outputs.

7.1.2 Planning the Approach and Communicating the Output

A number of core points are vital about planning the overall approach to the modelling activities and to the presentation of results:

- Ensuring that a model is appropriately adapted to be able to reflect the key business issues. In particular, the ability to show the effect of decisions, not only uncertainties or risk, can be an important consideration (see later for an example).
- Adapting the model to reflect other likely communication needs. For example, when presenting results, one may desire to show items in categories, rather than as individual risks. If these items have not been considered in the model planning stage, significant rework of the model may be required later (often, this will be needed at the precise point in the project when there is no time to do so, i.e. shortly before results are presented).
- Planning communications around decision-makers' preferred media. Some decision-makers will prefer a more visual approach (such as graphs of distributions) and others may prefer more numerical approaches (such as key statistics). Similarly, some will wish to

know the details of the methodology and assumptions, and others will be more interested in the overall message and recommendations.

- In general, there is a risk of excess information being shown, as the overall process is much richer than one based on static analysis: there is more information to be communicated about organisational processes and decision options, and there are more data and many more graphical possibilities.
- It is important not to overlook at what stage of the risk management process one is. For example, in the earlier stages, the focus may be on the effectiveness of risk-response measures or project-related decisions, and on the gaining of authorisation for them. In the later stages (once the effect of all sensible measures and decisions has been included), the focus may switch to a decision concerning the final project evaluation, i.e. whether to implement the project or not, given the revised economic structure and residual risks within the redesigned (optimised) project.

7.1.3 Using Switches to Control the Cases and Scenarios

Generally, one may need to use switches to control which set of assumptions is being used for the input values. There are many possible applications of this in risk modelling contexts:

- To be able to show the values of the base case static model (perhaps as the first scenario), as well as of additional static scenarios (if required).
- To show the effect of project-related decisions ("decision risks").
- To show the effect of risk-related decisions, such as values that apply in a pre- and post-mitigation case.

Of course, the use of a switch is generally predicated on the model having the same structure for each scenario (or value) that the switch may take. The creation of a suitable common structure can often be achieved by making small modifications, in particular the use of items whose values are zero in the base case and non-zero in other cases. For example, line items could be added to represent the cost of various risk mitigation activities, and these included in the base model at a value of zero.

Note that there are various ways that switches may be used and implemented:

- A single (global) switch may change the values of all input variables.
- Multiple switches allow items to be activated or deactivated independently to others. In many cases, each decision may have its own switch, whereas switches for risk items would apply globally, at a category/group level or individually.
- One may wish to automate the process of ensuring that "risk" values are always used when a simulation is run, whereas base values are used once this is finished. This can be achieved by use of simple macros; an example is given later in the chapter.
- Where there are only two scenarios for each item (e.g. base case and risk case), one could use an **IF** function to implement the switch. More generally, there may be several scenarios, in which case another lookup function is usually preferable, especially the **CHOOSE** function.

An example of this latter point was provided in the discussion of scenarios in Chapter 6 (for example, see Figures 6.10 and 6.11).

	A	B	C	D
1				
2		Model Switch (1=use base, 2=use risk samples)	2	
3				
4		Volume % lost due to trade sanctions (%)		
5		Base	0%	
6		Min	0%	
7		Max	10%	
8		Random Sample	0.6%	=C6+(C7-C6)*RAND()
9				
10		Model		
11		Price ($/unit)	100	
12		Volume (000 units): total	1000	
13		Volume % lost due to trade sanctions (%)	0.6%	=CHOOSE(RiskSwitch,C5,C8)
14		Volume lost due to trade sanctions (000 units)	5.9	=C13*C12
15		Volume sold	994.1	=C12*(1-C13)
16		Sales	99409	=C11*C15
17				

FIGURE 7.1 Use of Model Switch to Use Either a Base or a Risk Case Within the Model

The file Ch7.BaseSwitch.xlsx contains another simple example of a switch, shown in Figure 7.1. In this model, the percentage of sales volume that is lost to trade sanctions is considered to be zero in the base case, but is to be drawn from a uniform continuous distribution in the risk case (as discussed in more detail later in the text, the **RAND**() function will produce a uniform random number between zero and one, which is rescaled by the desired minimum and maximum, so that in this case, the result is a random value between zero and 10%).

7.1.4 Showing the Effect of Decisions versus Those of Uncertainties

The ability to distinguish the effect of decisions from those of uncertainties is a fundamental aspect of appropriate decision support.

Models can be used to show the effects of decisions by using multiple scenarios governed by model switches: for each decision, one defines "paired" scenarios that capture the effect of that decision being taken or not. In a static model, the values of the input variables would be altered as each decision scenario is run. In a risk model, the parameters of the input distributions may change as each decision is run.

One of the challenges in practice is to find the appropriate visual display for analysis, which involves both controllable decisions and uncertain factors:

- A focus on displaying the effect of decisions may help to support the appropriate selection of which decisions to implement (i.e. to find heuristically the optimal decision combination). Bespoke tornado diagrams (i.e. bar charts) may show the effect of each decision on some specific measure of the output (e.g. on the base, or on the simulated average or other measures), but they do not capture the uncertainty profile within each decision.

	A	B	C	D	E	F	G	H	I	J	K	L	M
1													
2			Ass/Start	1	2	3	4	5	6	7	8	9	10
3		Price	100	103.0	106.1	109.3	112.6	115.9	119.4	123.0	126.7	130.5	134.4
4		Price Growth Rate (% p.a.)	3.0%	3.0%	3.0%	3.0%	3.0%	3.0%	3.0%	3.0%	3.0%	3.0%	3.0%
5													
6		Volume	1000	1000	1000	1000	1000	1000	1000	1000	1000	1000	1000
7		Volume Growth Rate (% p.a.)	0.0%	0.0%	0.0%	0.0%	0.0%	0.0%	0.0%	0.0%	0.0%	0.0%	0.0%
8													
9		Location Selection Charge	0	0	0	0	0	0	0	0	0	0	0
10		Location Charge Growth Rate (% p.a	2.0%	2.0%	2.0%	2.0%	2.0%	2.0%	2.0%	2.0%	2.0%	2.0%	2.0%
11													
12		Fixed Cost	25000	25250.0	25502.5	25757.5	26015.1	26275.3	26538.0	26803.4	27071.4	27342.1	27615.6
13		Fixed Cost Growth Rate (% p.a.)	1.0%	1.0%	1.0%	1.0%	1.0%	1.0%	1.0%	1.0%	1.0%	1.0%	1.0%
14													
15		**Revenue**		**103000**	**106090**	**109273**	**112551**	**115927**	**119405**	**122987**	**126677**	**130477**	**134392**
16													
17		Variable Cost (% of revenues and tota	40%	41200	42436	43709	45020	46371	47762	49195	50671	52191	53757
18													
19		**Cash Flow**		**36550**	**38152**	**39806**	**41515**	**43281**	**45105**	**46989**	**48935**	**50944**	**53019**
20		**Net Present Value @ 10.0%**	**264343**										

FIGURE 7.2 Calculation of NPV for a Simple Project

- Classical tornado diagrams (in simulation software such as @RISK) typically show the sensitivities in the output that are driven by the uncertainty of a variable within a specific decision context, but do not typically show the effect of decisions that may be taken. Thus, they are arguably mostly relevant in order to provide information about the key sources of uncertainty in a specific context (such as at the end of an assessment process to highlight the sources of risk that drive the residual, in principle non-controllable, uncertainty within the optimal context), rather than indicating which decisions are appropriate or have the most effect.

The file Ch7.DecisionsandRisks.Displays.xlsx contains an example of a bespoke "decision tornado" versus a "risk tornado". Figure 7.2 shows a base model (contained in the worksheet BaseModel), which calculates the net present value (NPV) for a project. The worksheet BaseModelDecisions shows the input values that would apply for three possible decision scenarios for the project:

- The base project as currently planned.
- Moving the project to an alternative location (for example, closer to the end-user market), where it is estimated that volumes would be higher. However, there would also be higher fixed costs as well as an additional location charge (for example, local taxation) that would apply, and which is listed separately to the fixed costs.
- Remaining at the base location but using an alternative technology. The prices would be higher, and the variable cost percentage lower (i.e. a higher quality product with lower raw material waste), but the volumes would also be lower.

Figure 7.3 shows the specific input data for each scenario, as well as a **DataTable** that calculates NPV for each scenario (this uses the techniques discussed earlier, in which the scenario number drives a **CHOOSE** function).

The differences displayed in the bottom row of the table can be expressed in "tornado-like" form (a form of bar chart), as in Figure 7.4.

Assuming that one settles on the decision to use the alternative technology, one may conduct a risk assessment to establish key uncertainty drivers within this scenario. The worksheet RiskWithinScenario3 of the same file shows a simple case in which all inputs are assumed to

	Base	Alternative Location	Alternative Technology
Price	100	100	105
Price Growth Rate (% p.a.)	3.0%	3.0%	3.0%
Volume	1000	1100	950
Volume Growth Rate (% p.a.)	0.0%	2.0%	1.0%
Location Selection Charge	0	10000	0
Location Charge Growth Rate (% p.a.)	2.0%	2.0%	2.0%
Fixed Cost	25000	40000	30000
Fixed Cost Growth Rate (% p.a.)	1.0%	1.0%	1.0%
Revenue			
Variable Cost (% of revenues and total)	40%	40%	35%
NPV/Scenario	**1**	**2**	**3**
264343	**264343**	**191795**	**289886**
Difference to Base	**0**	**-72548**	**25543**

FIGURE 7.3 NPV for Three Decision Options

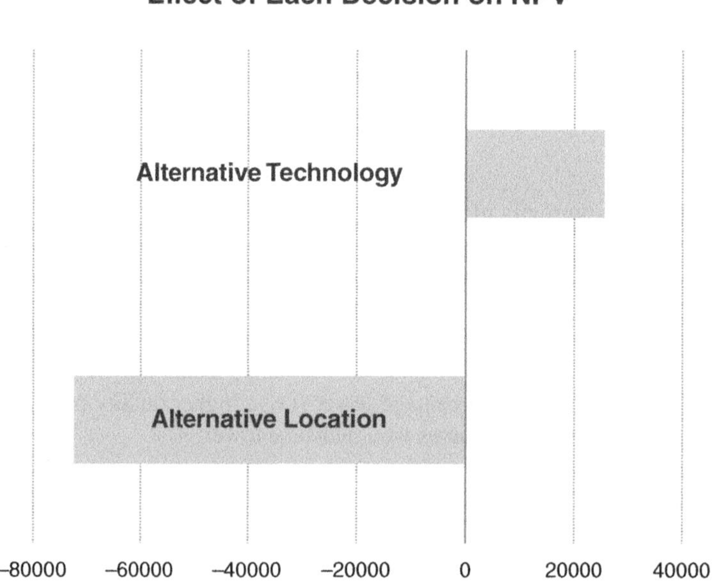

FIGURE 7.4 Tornado Chart for Decision Options

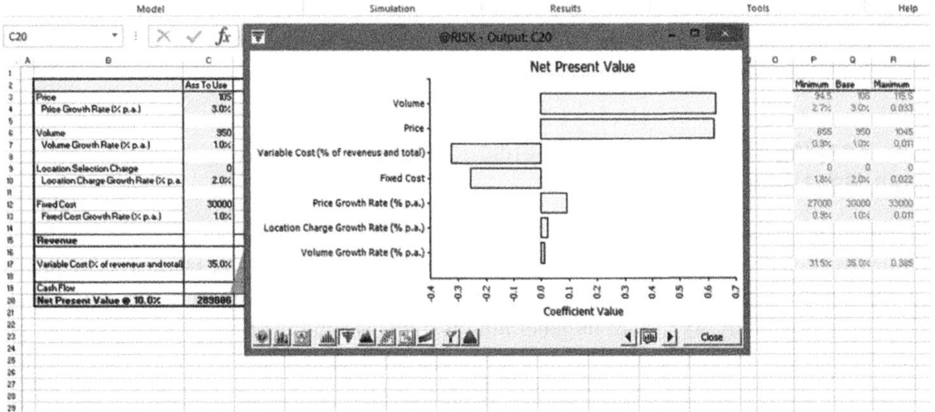

FIGURE 7.5 Tornado Chart for Uncertainties Within a Decision Option

vary in a ±10% range. The @RISK tool is used to run a simulation and to display a classical (correlation-coefficient) tornado chart, as shown in Figure 7.5.

Despite the importance of this issue, which was also partly addressed in the previous discussions concerning optimisation (Chapter 6) and risk prioritisation (Chapter 2), this distinction (between decisions and risks) is often overlooked in both static and risk contexts:

- Traditional sensitivity analysis or scenario analysis is often conducted without asking whether the items are controllable (choice or decision) variables.
- Models are very frequently built to show the effect of sensitivities, but not that of the available possible decisions. In particular, in group and organisational processes, the analysis of risks and uncertainties can dominate attention, resulting in a lack of sufficient explicit focus on the relevant decision possibilities.
- Even where the effect of some decisions is explicitly captured, very often the decisions that are available to be analysed within the model are not the full set of relevant decisions. For example, in some risk models, one may be able to compare the distribution of outcomes in the pre- and post-mitigation cases, but not to see the effect of other decisions that are not directly associated with risk (such as the effect of a decision to change the location at which a factory will be built, or the technical solution that will be employed).

Note also that the existence of any such decisions cannot be identified from a model, but only through processes that are exogenous (or separate) to the pure modelling activities.

In theory, there is a tight link between these issues and that of optimisation under uncertainty: in principle, if one could calculate the uncertainty profile of the outcome that would result for each combination of possible decisions, then the optimal combination could be chosen (by taking into account its overall effect and its uncertainty profile; it may increase average cost, whilst mitigating the worst possible outcomes, for example). In practice, a fully quantitative approach to such optimisation is often not possible or is excessively complex: one would need to have a model that captured the outcome and uncertainty profile for every decision combination, and that reflected the interactions between the decisions (for example, the effect of any particular decision may generally depend on which other decisions or mitigation options have been implemented). Thus, as discussed in Chapter 6, heuristic (pragmatic) methods are often sufficient to at least find close-to-optimal solutions.

7.1.5 Keeping It Simple, but not Simplistic: New Insights versus Modelling Errors

Whilst some spreadsheet models are built purely for calculation purposes, in many cases the modelling process has an important exploratory component. Whereas in later process stages there may be more emphasis on the calculated values, in earlier project stages the exploratory aspect can be especially important in generating insights around the project and its economic drivers.

Indeed, a model is implicitly a set of statements (hypotheses) about variables that affect an outcome, and of the relationships between them: the overlooking or underestimation of the exploratory component is one of the main inefficiencies in many modelling processes, which are often delegated to junior staff who are competent in "doing the numbers", but who may not have the experience, or lack sufficient project exposure, or lack appropriate authority (or credibility) within the organisation, so that many possible insights are never generated or are lost.

The output of a model is a reflection of the assumptions and logic (which may or may not tell one anything useful about the situation); the modelling process is often inherently ambiguous (both in traditional static and in risk contexts):

- If one truly understood every facet of a situation completely, a model would be unnecessary.
- One must understand the situation reasonably well in order to be able to build a model that corresponds to it appropriately.
- To capture the reality of a situation, a model will need to have some level of complexity.
- Models can be made too complex, for example through the use of the wrong fundamental design, or being built in ways that use unnecessarily complex formulae, or by being too detailed, or simply by being presented in a confusing or non-transparent manner.
- Insight is usually generated when models have an appropriate balance between simplicity and complexity.

In this context, the following well-known quotes come to mind:

- "Every model is wrong, some are useful" (Box).
- "Perfection is the enemy of the good" (Voltaire).
- "Everything should be made as simple as possible, but no simpler" (Einstein).

Where a model produces results that are not readily explained intuitively, there are two generic cases:

- It is oversimplified, highly inaccurate or wrong in some major way. For example, key variables may have been left out, or dependencies not correctly captured, so that sensitivity analysis may produce ranges that are far too narrow (or too wide). Alternatively, the assumptions used for the values of key variables may be wrong, mistyped or poorly estimated. Of course, in such a situation, in the first instance one must correct any obvious mistakes.

- It is essentially correct in terms of the variables used, their relationships, data and input assumptions, but provides results that are not intuitive. In a sense, this is an ideal situation to face (especially in the earlier stages of a project); the subsequent process can be used to adapt, explore and generate new insights and intuition, so that ultimately both the intuition and the model's outputs are aligned. This can be a value-added process, particularly if it shows where one's initial intuition may be lagging, so that a better understanding is ultimately created.

In fact, there may be situations where useful models cannot be built:

- Where the objectives are not defined in a meaningful way. For example, doing one's best to "build a model of the moon" might not result in anything useful, at least without further clarification.
- Where basic structural elements or other key factors that drive the behaviour of the situation are not known or have not been decided upon. For example, it could prove to be a challenge to try to model the costs of building a new manufacturing facility in a new but unknown country, which will produce new products that still need to be defined and developed in accordance with regulations that have not yet been released, using technology that has not yet been specified.
- Where there are no data, no way to create expert estimates, or use judgements, and no proxy measures available. (Even in some such cases models that capture behaviours and interactions can be built, and used with generic numbers to structure the thought process and identify where more understanding, data or research is required.) In a risk modelling situation, with disciplined thinking, one can usually estimate reasonable risk ranges, although one needs to be conscious of potential biases, especially of anchoring and overconfidence (see Chapter 1).

In general, such barriers are only temporary and decrease as more information becomes available and project decisions are taken, and other objectives or structural elements are clarified. In principle, there is no real difference between static and risk models in this respect.

On the other hand, there can be differences between static and risk models in some areas:

- Risk models are often more detailed than static ones:
  - There may be more line items required in order to capture the impacts of the risks (in some cases, such line items are used in aggregation calculations before the uncertainty is reflected in the model, such as when using the risk category approach discussed later).
  - The input area will generally be larger. A single original input value that is subsequently treated as uncertain will have additional values associated with it, such as probability-of-occurrence and parameters for the impact range. In addition, there may be pre- and post-mitigation values of each of these parameters, as well as the cost of mitigation.
- The building of a useful risk model may only be able to happen at a slightly later stage than the building of an initial static model:

- Basic static models can be useful early in a process to "get a feel" about a particular project (for example, to support a hypothesis that a project may be unrealistic in its current form and should not be continued, or to help structure the process of identifying the nature of the further information and data requirements).
- The application of a full quantitative risk assessment at a very early process stage would generally not be an effective use of resources. Nevertheless, even basic qualitative statements of risk factors (perhaps with some selected basic quantification) can either reinforce the case for rejecting a project or help to define the flexibility requirements of any static model that is to be built to conduct further analysis.
- A well-structured risk model usually cannot be completed in its entirety before a general risk assessment process is complete, whereas a static model may typically be able to be completed earlier.

7.2 SENSITIVITY-DRIVEN THINKING AS A MODEL DESIGN TOOL

Since simulation is effectively the recalculation of a model many times, one core requirement is that any model is robust enough to allow the calculation of the many scenarios that are automatically generated through random sampling. In many respects, this requirement is the same as when one is conducting explicitly generated scenarios or traditional sensitivity analysis: the basic principle is that the logic and formulae in a model should be designed in a way that allows such sensitivities and scenarios to be run. These issues are discussed in more detail in this section.

Modelling can often be thought of as a process in which one starts with the objective or ultimate model output (such as profit), and asks what drives or determines this output (e.g. profit is equal to revenue minus cost), and building the corresponding calculations (i.e. with revenue and cost as inputs and profit as a calculated quantity). This process can be repeated (e.g. with the revenue determined as the sum of the revenues of each product group, each of which is itself the price multiplied by the volume for that product, and so on). Once completed, the model inputs are those items that are not calculated.

This "backward calculation" approach by itself is not sufficient to build an appropriate model. First, it is not clear at what point to stop, i.e. at what level of detail to work with. Second, there are typically many ways of breaking down an item into subcomponents. For example:

- Total sales could be broken down as:
  - The sum of the sales for products (or product groups).
  - The sum of the sales by customer (or by region).
  - The number of products multiplied by the average sales figure for each.
  - Etc.
- The cost of construction may be made up of:
  - The cost of each type or category (e.g. materials, labour, energy), or that of more detailed categories (e.g. materials split into concrete, steel, wood, cabling, etc.).
  - The cost by phase (e.g. planning, design and various build phases).
  - The cost by component (e.g. office area, factory area, public areas).

- The cost by month of construction.
- As an aggregate base figure multiplied by cost escalation factors that change over time, and so on.

The use of "sensitivity analysis thinking" is a key technique to ensure that this backward calculation approach delivers an appropriate model: in practical terms, this means that when designing models, one should define as early as possible the specific sensitivity questions that will need to be addressed once the model has been completed. For model design purposes, such a thought process can be a qualitative one; there is no need to actually perform such sensitivities at this stage.

The definition of the sensitivities will result in many aspects of the model being defined as a consequence, and helping to ensure that:

- An appropriate choice is made for the variables used (i.e. the correct approach to break down items into possible subcomponents), and the necessary level of detail (i.e. where in the backward calculation process one should stop).
- Any required sensitivities can be run when the model is complete, and that drivers of variability that are common to several items are captured.

Note that if a (static) model has been built sufficiently robustly to allow any input to be varied, then (generally speaking):

- The nature of the process used to vary an input is not of significance: whether it is done manually, by an automated sensitivity tool (such as a **DataTable**) or by the random sampling of a distribution is essentially irrelevant (from the perspective of the formulae and calculations).
- Whether a change is made to a single input value or to multiple input values simultaneously will typically not affect the integrity of the model's calculations (there may be exceptional cases where this is not so). The sensitivity-thought process helps to retain the integrity of the calculations even as multiple input combinations are selected. Where "scenario thinking" is used to augment the core sensitivity thought processes, the model should be even more robust, as it should ensure that simultaneous variation of multiple input values is possible (as is required in simulation and combinatorial optimisation contexts).

The file Ch7.HRPlan.DataFixedSensRisk.xlsx provides a simple example that covers many of the issues above. Figure 7.6 shows a screen clip from the worksheet Data. This contains what is essentially a data set showing the expected number of people needed to be employed by a company for each year in a 5-year period. The only calculation is that of the total requirement over the 5-year period, which is 284 (cell H8).

If one wished to explore the situation in more detail, one could then start to consider the factors that drive sensitivity of the number of people needed each year. One may conclude that this depends on the volume (i.e. on the work required), as well as on the productivity of the people. Thus, one may build a model as contained in the worksheet Orig, shown in Figure 7.7. In this model, additional assumptions are required for each of these driving factors. It may be the case that once best estimates of these factors are made, then the estimate of the number of people needed changes (as it is now a calculated quantity); in this case, the revised figure for the 5-year period is 275.

Base Data	1	2	3	4	5	Total
No. of people needed	50	54	58	60	62	284

FIGURE 7.6 Simple Resource Plan

Base Model	1	2	3	4	5	Total
Volume of business (units)	100	105	110	115	120	550
Productivity (units/per person)	2.0	2.0	2.0	2.0	2.0	
No. of people needed	50	52.5	55	57.5	60	275

FIGURE 7.7 Resource Plan with First Approach to Calculations

Base Model	1	2	3	4	5	Total
Volume of business (units)	100	105	110	114	118	547
% change in volume		5.0%	4.5%	4.0%	3.5%	
Productivity (units/per person)	2.0	2.0	2.0	2.1	2.1	
% change in productivity		1.0%	1.0%	1.0%	1.0%	
No. of people needed	50	52	54	55	57	268

FIGURE 7.8 Resource Plan with Second Approach to Calculations

Similarly, one may continue the process in which the volume of business depends on a periodic growth rate, and the productivity depends on productivity changes or improvements. Thus, as shown in Figure 7.8, and contained in the worksheet OrigSens, a revised model may show some changes to the values, as each of the volume and productivity figures (from year 2 onwards) is calculated from estimates of their driving factors; in this case, the new total is 268.

Of course, the process could continue if that were judged appropriate. On the other hand, one may decide that no further detail is required, but that a risk assessment of the base figure (268) could be appropriate.

	A	B	C	D	E	F	G	H	I
1									
2		Base Model	1	2	3	4	5	Total	
3									
4		Volume of business (units)	100	105	110	114	118	547	
5	1	% change in volume		5.0%	4.5%	4.0%	3.5%		=CHOOSE(RiskSwitchVol,F11,F12)
6		Productivity (units/per person)	2.0	2.0	2.0	2.1	2.1		
7	1	% change in productivity		1.0%	1.0%	1.0%	1.0%		=CHOOSE(RiskSwitchProd,F16,F17)
8		No. of people needed	50	52	54	55	57	268	
9									
10		Volume Changes %							
11		Base (static value)		5.0%	4.5%	4.0%	3.5%		
12		Distribution Sample		4.5%	5.5%	5.6%	7.7%	=G13+(G14-G13)*RAND()	
13		Min		-2.0%	-2.0%	-2.0%	-2.0%		
14		Max		8.0%	8.0%	8.0%	8.0%		
15		Productivity Changes %							
16		Base (static value)		1.0%	1.0%	1.0%	1.0%		
17		Distribution Sample		-0.1%	2.2%	1.0%	1.2%	=G18+(G19-G18)*RAND()	
18		Min		-1.0%	-1.0%	-1.0%	-1.0%		
19		Max		3.0%	3.0%	3.0%	3.0%		

FIGURE 7.9 Resource Plan with Uncertainty Ranges

As mentioned earlier, if a model is constructed to allow the running of the appropriate sensitivities (in this case, by varying the figure for the change in volume or productivity), then the process used to implement such variation is essentially of no significance from the perspective of the model's formulae and logic. The worksheet RiskView shows the implementation of this. Two switches have been created, one to show either base or risk values for the volume, and one to show those for the productivity (see Figure 7.9). Once again, for illustration purposes, the **RAND**() function has been used to create the ranges; this is not to suggest the appropriateness or not of the distribution in this context, rather to illustrate that the process used to vary an input is essentially irrelevant.

For completeness, Figure 7.10 shows the results of running a simulation, in terms of the distribution of the total number of people needed; the change from a "data set" to a traditional

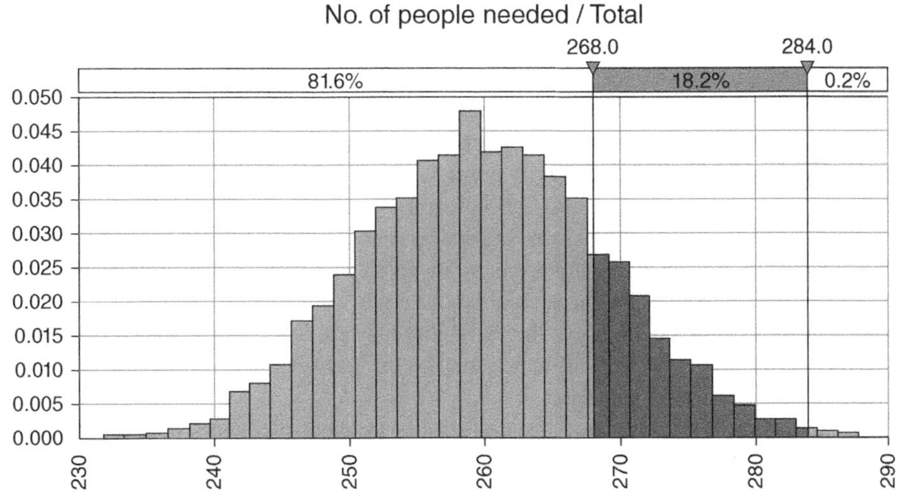

FIGURE 7.10 Distribution of Total Resource Requirements

static model with sensitivity capability led to a modification of the estimated number of people required from 284 to 268, with the risk model showing that the required number would be less than 268 in approximately 80% of cases, and that a figure of 260 would be the average requirement.

7.2.1 Enhancing Sensitivity Processes for Risk Modelling

Although the importance of using sensitivity-driven thought processes represents a commonality in the design of static models and risk models, some additional considerations and modifications are usually necessary in risk modelling contexts.

In particular, whereas sensitivity (and scenario) processes focus on "What if?" questions, in risk assessment one also asks "Why?", i.e. one aims to identify the factors that may cause variation in the item concerned (i.e. the "risk drivers"), whereas sensitivity analysis does not have this focus.

In practice, this would often lead to differences in the models that would be built.

First, the fact that one can conduct a sensitivity analysis in a traditional static model by changing the value of individual inputs does not mean that such changes actually reflect the true nature of the risk associated with that item; to do so may require that new line items are added or other modifications made to the model. Typical issues that arise in this respect include:

- A risk may affect only a portion of a line item. For example:
  - A potential trade barrier (or import duties) may apply to only part of the volume, and this may also have an effect on part of the revenues and part of the cost, so that major modifications to many aspects of a model would be required if this risk were initially overlooked. Note that the model in Figure 7.1 provides an example of how each core component of a model may be structured in such a case. For the purposes of the discussion here (although the issue may appear trivial when reviewing the completed model in retrospect), if the starting point for the modelling process had been a model that simply calculated revenues by simply multiplying volume by price, then the later inclusion of the risk impact into the model would have required significant modification.
  - Similarly, an exchange rate risk may affect only the export portion of the revenues, and a disruption to the supply of a specific raw material may partially affect production volume, or have an effect on highly specific parts of the cost structure, and so on.
- Risk assessment approaches are more likely to identify common drivers of variability that may be overlooked in pure sensitivity approaches. For example, one may be able to test the sensitivity of construction costs of a project by varying the daily rate for the cost of manual labour. However, the risk driver may be whether a new law concerning minimum wages would be passed by the government, in which case many other model items would be affected (not just the specific manual labour cost).
- The consideration of the drivers of the variability may guide the appropriate level of detail that the model should be built at, which may be different in the case that risk drivers are properly considered. For example:
  - When dealing with a revenue forecast, the assessment of factors that could cause a variation in the price may include: whether a competitor enters the market, the nature of the promotional activity undertaken by the company, exchange rates, the overall macro-economic situation, and so on.

  - The possible variation in production volume could be driven by: whether the overall product development project is delayed, whether the production facility breaks down, possible delays to material supplies or other problems with the supply chain, whether workers go on strike, whether there is a delay or failure in a process to have a patent awarded, whether to develop certain specialised technologies, and so on.
  - The uncertainty in total labour cost may depend on the uncertainty in the number of labourers required, their cost per day and the number of days required. Once again, these would often not be required or done in a sensitivity-driven approach that only asks a "What if?" question about the effect of changes to the labour cost.
- A static model may not capture event risks (or may overlook them), particularly where their probability is less than 50% (so that the most likely case for each risk is that it would not occur). The use of risk techniques allows for event risks to be formally identified and included in a model in an unambiguous fashion (as discussed in Chapter 4).

Thus, the line items (or variables) within a risk model need to be defined at a level of granularity that allows the risks and their impacts to be captured. In other words, there is a "matching" between model items and the underlying identified risks (with each risk impact having a corresponding line item), and the impact of a risk will generally affect or interact with other model variables.

Second, a sensitivity-driven approach may not identify all of the key flexibilities required of a risk model, as in principle these relate directly to the identified risks and their nature. For example:

- In a sensitivity ("What if?") approach, one may have built a model that allows for the on-stream date of a production facility to be delayed (for example, by whole periods within the Excel model, such as months, quarters or years). However, the nature of the delay uncertainty may be a continuous process, corresponding to partial model periods.
- A static model may include lookup functions that always return a valid value within the range of sensitivities that are run (for example, the effect of a 2-year delay to a project). However, the true nature of the possible delay may be something that can exceed the range of the lookup functions, and require structural adjustments or modifications to model formulae.

Thus, in a model designed using traditional sensitivity methods, from a mechanical perspective, one can often overwrite the inputs with random samples from distributions without causing numerical errors (although the continuous granularity of the time delay is an exception to this). However, the results produced by doing so are not likely to reflect the true nature of the risk or uncertainty in this situation: the inputs being varied may not correspond to the risks in the situation, the model may not have the right line items to reflect such risks and dependencies between risks and impacts may not have been appropriately reflected in the formulae (or variables) of the original static model.

7.2.2 Creating Dynamic Formulae

It is clear from the above discussion that a core modelling principle (for static and risk approaches) is to ensure that the logic and formulae within the model have the appropriate flexibility. However, it is frequently the case that this is not so. For example:

- Many models calculate tax charges using formulae that are valid only when taxable profit is positive, and do not account for cases where profit is negative (this may require capturing the accumulation and use of tax-loss carry-forwards, which would have an important cash flow effect compared to a direct tax rebate). Indeed, the consideration of the possibility of a tax loss may never arise when a static model is being built using sensitivity techniques, as the occurrence of a loss may arise only if multiple adverse events occur, and not through the occurrence of only one or two events, as would be detected in traditional sensitivity analysis.
- Some models use direct formula links, whereas indirect or lookup processes would allow for more flexibility. For example, when working out the value in local currency of an item expressed in a foreign currency, rather than creating a formula link between the item and a particular exchange rate, one could use the currency of each variable as a model input, with a lookup process used to find the relevant exchange rate; in this way, more items or currencies could easily be added to the model.
- Many models implicitly assume that the timing aspect of a project is fixed, for example that the production of a new manufacturing facility will begin on a specific date. In fact, there may be a risk relating to the on-time completion of the facility. In principle, there is no reason why such delays should not be considered as part of a sensitivity analysis in traditional modelling contexts. However, in many practical cases the "risk of a delay" is an item that often first appears only once a formal risk identification process has been conducted. At that point, a base model has often been completed, and there is insufficient time to adapt the model, because such a delay may affect many model items in different ways, so that many new formulae and linkages would need to be built, meaning that aligning the model with the actual risk assessment process would become challenging or impossible:
  - Volume produced and sold may be fully shifted in time.
  - The price level achieved per unit may not be shifted, as it may follow a separate time process related to market prices.
  - Variable costs may be shifted in time.
  - Some fixed overhead costs may remain even during the pre-start-up period, whereas others may be able to be delayed in line with the production volume.

The lack of sufficient flexibility in formulae arises most often in practice due to a combination of:

- A lack of consideration of the required sensitivities that decision-makers would like to see. (In a risk modelling context, this would also encompass cases where there has been a lack of consideration of the risks and their impacts.)
- A lack of consideration of how variations in multiple line items may interact.
- A lack of capability to implement the formulae required within Excel.

The creation of more flexible and advanced models revolves around removing hard-coded or structural assumptions and replacing them with values that can be altered as part of a sensitivity analysis (in which the original, structurally fixed case is one possible sensitivity or scenario); an example is given in the following.

7.2.3 Example: Time Shifting for Partial Periods

As an example of the difference between the formulae that are required in the case that a potential delay is discrete (as might suffice for sensitivity analysis) versus those that are required if potential delays are from a continuous range (as may be required for a risk model, especially if the delay is calculated as the result of other processes or is to be input as an expert estimate), we consider the following cases:

- Whole period delays.
- Partial period delays of less than one time grid within the Excel model.
- Partial period delays of any length.

Figure 6.14 (and the associated discussion and example file provided in Chapter 6) demonstrated the use of lookup functions to implement a capability to shift project start dates so that they are any year (expressed as a whole number). The reader can inspect the formulae used in the model, which are not discussed in more detail here; in the following, we present the more general case where the time shift could be any partial period.

The file Ch7.TimeShift.Various.xlsx contains an example in which an initial planned production volume can be delayed by various amounts, as shown in Figure 7.11. The formulae for both whole and short partial delays are relatively straightforward (two options are shown for the whole period delay, one using the **INDEX** function and the other using **OFFSET**). However, the formula that covers the case of any delay amount is more complex, and not shown fully in the screen clip due to its size; the reader can inspect the file. (As an aside, due to the complexity of this formula, and in particular the fact that it uses the same input cell in several places, it could be more robust and transparent to implement it as a VBA user-defined function; this is not done here for reasons of presentational transparency.)

Of course, although the above example has the delay amount as an input, in many cases, it would be a calculated quantity that results from the impact of other risk factors. For example, a plan to launch a major new product that requires the construction of a production facility could be subject to delays such as those relating to:

- Building permissions required.
- An overrun of the construction project.
- Licences required for use of a particular technology.
- The development process for future products and technologies.
- Etc.

	A	B	C	D	E	F	G	H	I	J
1										
2		Period Number		1	2	3	4	5	6	
3		Volume: without shift		100	110	115	120	125	125	
4										
5		Methods to shift in time through a single delay amount i.e. spread across two future periods								
6										
7				1	2	3	4	5	6	
8		Delay in periods: whole numbers	2	0	0	100	110	115	120	=IF(AND(I$7-$C8>=1,I$7-$C8<=10),INDEX($D$3:$I$3,1,I$7-$C8),0)
9		Delay in periods: whole numbers	2	0	0	100	110	115	120	=IF(I2<=$C9,0,OFFSET(I3,0,-$C9))
10		Delay is anything less than 1	0.3	70	107	114	119	124	125	=H3*$C10+I3*(1-$C10)
11		Delay is any number	1.6	0	40	104	112	117	122	=IF(I$2<(ROUNDDOWN($C11,0)+1),0,OFFSET(I$3,0,-(ROUNDDOWN($C11,0)+1))*($C11-INT($C11))

FIGURE 7.11 Various Approaches to Implementing Time Shifting in Excel

	A	B	C	D	E	F	G	H	I	J	K	L	M
1													
2		Risk Items	To Use	Time Delay in Months									
3			2	Base Valu	Risk Figures	Prob	Min	Max					
4		Overrun of the construction project	0.0	0	0.0	30%	0	8					
5		Licences required for use of a particular technology	5.4	0	5.4	50%	0	12					
6		Delay in achieving on spec production grade	0.0	0	0.0	30%	0	6					
7		Delay	5.4	0.0	5.4								
8													
9				1	2	3	4	5	6	7	8	9	10
10		Volume: without delay (Units)		100	110	115	120	125	125	125	125	125	125
11		Volume: without delay (Units)	5.4	0	0	0	0	0	62	106	113	118	123
12													

FIGURE 7.12 Calculations of Aggregate Delay As an Uncertain Amount

The file Ch7.ScheduleShift.xlsx contains an example in which there are three delay risks, each of which may happen with a given probability, and with an uncertain extent (in terms of monthly periods) that is described with minimum and maximum values. The aggregate delay is calculated as the maxima of the delay of each task (as the tasks are assumed to occur in parallel). This aggregate delay drives the updated production volume profile, using a calculation as shown in Figure 7.11. This structure is shown in Figure 7.12. One can also see that the model has been built with a switch, so that the base case (zero delay for each item) can also be shown.

7.3 RISK MAPPING AND PROCESS ALIGNMENT

Risk mapping involves describing the nature of the risks or uncertainties in a way that allows their inclusion within a quantitative model. As such, it is a core foundation of quantitative risk modelling. As mentioned in Chapter 2, it can be the most challenging part of the risk modelling process, as it requires an integration of many building blocks of risk quantification, such as:

- Ensuring that risks and impacts are precisely defined.
- Establishing the nature of risks and their impacts.
- Adapting the models to reflect the impacts of the risks, perhaps requiring additional line items, creating formulae that are dynamic and flexible (as discussed earlier in this chapter).
- Capturing dependencies between risks and between impacts (see later in this chapter and Chapter 11).
- Using distributions and data that are appropriate, with suitable approximations or estimates made where necessary (see Chapter 9).
- Aligning the risk modelling activities with the general risk assessment and decision process.

In this section, we highlight some key aspects concerning the nature of risks and their impacts, and the alignment with the general risk assessment process.

7.3.1 The Nature of Risks and Their Impacts

Clearly, a key aspect of being able to reflect the effect of a risk or uncertainty within a model is to establish its nature, including that of its impact.

Typical issues that one needs to consider include:

- Ensuring that the risk identification activities make an adequate distinction between business issues, controllable (decision) variables and risks or uncertainties.
- Ensuring that risks are described in a way that is appropriate for the approach taken. In particular, for risk aggregation and full risk models, one will need to find a way to express items in common terms (such as translating the effect of time delays into financial impacts, perhaps through volume or sales delays), and to avoid double-counting and overlaps of impacts.
- The core drivers or nature of the process: whether it is a risk event, a discrete process (such as having various possible distinct scenarios), a continuous process or a compound process (i.e. a mixture of discrete and continuous processes, such as a set of scenarios where a continuous range of values is possible within each scenario). It can also be helpful to consider whether the process is bounded or unbounded, as this may aid in the general understanding of the risk and in the selection of distributions.
- The time behaviour of the process (in a multi-period model), for example:
  - Whether it can occur only once in total, or once during each period, or multiple times within each period.
  - Whether there is a random fluctuation within each period around a long-term trend, or other aspects related to time-series modelling.
  - Whether there is first a possible start time and a duration; if so, whether these also are uncertain.
  - Whether the impact changes over time, such as fading.
- What is the nature of the impact? For example:
  - Which model items are directly impacted (and which are only indirectly impacted through other calculations)?
  - Are there interrelationships or overlaps between impacts of other risks?
- What other linkages are there with other risks and processes? For example:
  - Are there common risk drivers or risk categories that should be reflected in the model?
  - Do other general dependency relationships need to be captured as a result of the inclusion of the risk in a model, such as those between risk impacts or other core aspects?
  - What dependency relationships exist between sources of risk, such as parameter dependencies or correlation? As discussed in Chapter 11, parameter dependencies require more intervention in a model than do sampling dependencies, which have less consequence for the formulae.
- What insights are provided by the above questions in terms of selecting the appropriate distributions to use for risks and/or their impacts (see Chapter 9 for a more detailed discussion)?
- What other relevant aspects need to be captured, so that the model is adaptable and its output is suitable for communication purposes? For example:
  - Are categories required for communication purposes as well as risk purposes?
  - How can the base case and the effect of decisions, as well as risk profiles, best be captured in the model?

7.3.2 Creating Alignment between Modelling and the General Risk Assessment Process

It is important to ensure that modelling activities are appropriately aligned with general risk assessment processes. This section covers the nature of such alignment activities; many of the points have been touched upon at various places in the text, so that the discussion here partly serves a consolidation purpose, and is therefore fairly brief, despite its importance.

Risk aggregation approaches require that risks and uncertainties are defined in a way that allows them to be expressed in common terms, and avoid overlaps or double-counting, both for any risk-occurrence events and for their impacts (as discussed in Chapter 3):

- This represents a modification in the information and data requirements compared to pure risk management approaches. Indeed, such topics may appear unnecessary or uninteresting to participants whose focus is on operational risk management.
- The capturing of the nature of the risks with sufficient detail and precision can be a challenge; even experienced risk management practitioners may not have had sufficient exposure to this specific area. The thought processes or concepts that are required in order to provide the appropriate information can be challenging to some participants. It can also be difficult to retain the attention of a group of participants, to explain additional concepts and to ensure that the appropriate deliverables result from group processes.
- An adequate distinction must be made between business issues, decision variables (controllable processes) and uncertainty variables, and the role of the general risk assessment (and modelling) process to treat these. For example, a "risk model" may, in fact, have a focus that is more of a decision-support nature, with the captured risks ultimately reflecting residual uncertainties.

Thus, there may be many aspects of the general risk assessment process that need adapting in order to be able to adequately build a full risk model:

- The modelling assumptions and inputs needed to design, build and use the results of models in fact (should) require a significant proactive role in specifying the nature of the required outputs from general risk assessment activities. It is important to reflect these directly in the process as far as possible, because if they are ignored, modelling analysts will ultimately need to make assumptions related to these points, even where such assumptions have not been debated within the wider project team. Thus, once initiated, an ongoing interaction between a general risk assessment process and the modelling activities linked to it is essential.
- There may be (real or perceived) differences in the requirements that participants in a general risk assessment process may have compared to the requirements of modelling analysts, and the alignment between their objectives will often ultimately need to be driven by top management.

It is important to gain agreement from senior management on the approach to be used to risk quantification, and ensuring that the consequences of this are communicated and implemented within the overall risk assessment activities. Clearly, the embedding of additional elements into the process can create a challenge, especially if expectations are not properly managed and communications are not sufficiently clear.

7.3.3 Results Interpretation within the Context of Process Stages

In practice, one usually passes through many stages of a process. The message and items to communicate may differ at each stage, or at least have a different focus:

- Core risk assessment and modelling stage. This is where the model is adapted to ensure that all relevant risks are captured, and their impacts and interdependencies reflected in the model. As discussed elsewhere, it will often also require that the more general risk assessment process is adapted to provide the correct inputs into a model. At this stage the focus will be on ensuring that:
  - The model is free from errors.
  - The risks are captured in a way that reflects their true nature and underlying properties (e.g. that risks that develop over time are captured appropriately and that no event risk is treated as being of an event or operational risk nature).
  - The impact of each risk on the aggregate model's output makes sense and aligns with intuition (or alters that intuition and understanding of a situation).
  - The risks can be presented in appropriate categories, and that base cases can be captured separately, and perhaps pre- and post-mitigation scenarios can be shown.
  - The model will be adapted iteratively as the complete set of risks is identified and as the risk definition is made more precise, so that their impacts can be captured correctly in the model.
- Interim results presentation. Once a basic model is more or less complete, there could be a number of possible results and uses:
  - It may immediately become clear that the project is too risky and should be cancelled.
  - More generally, some risk-response measures and mitigation actions may be built into the project plans at little or no cost, whereas others may require specific escalation and authorisation (for the reasons discussed in Chapter 1, for example).
  - This process stage may be iterative, as discussed earlier.
- Final results and decision stage. At this stage, the effect of all proposed and appropriate response and mitigation actions will have been included in the model and a final decision about a project's viability will need to be made, reflecting, for example, the average benefits as well as the exposure to potential adverse outcomes.

Note that as this process proceeds, one can generally state that:

- In the earlier stages, one may use a wide variety of measures and tools to analyse the model and its outputs, but one will typically not need to focus very precisely on the presentational aspects of individual activities. For example, one may look to a range of statistical measures, look at density and cumulative distributions, at ascending and descending forms, consider tornado graphs and scatter plots, experiment with the effect of different numbers of recalculations (iterations), and so on.
- In the later stages, or for senior management reporting, one may focus on a much more limited set of measures and wish to be able to present specific graph types in the way that management may desire. This may involve specific steps that may not be so relevant in the earlier stages (e.g. to be able to place and display risks within categories, or to be able to repeat a simulation exactly, or to show before/after-type analysis, and so on).

Questions about the output distribution are most relevant when the risk-response process (and the implementation of other project-related decisions) is complete. The resulting uncertainty profile is then one associated with residual risk in the optimal project structure, and is required for making a final decision that reflects the risk tolerances of the decision-maker (or of the organisation).

7.4 GENERAL DEPENDENCY RELATIONSHIPS

The capturing of dependencies between variables is one of the key foundations of modelling: Indeed, a model is, in essence, only a statement of such relationships, which one uses to perform calculations, test hypotheses or generate a better understanding of a situation; this contrasts with data sets (or databases), which contain lists of items but without relationships between them.

Of course, the nature and effect of any relationships within a model can be observed and tested with sensitivity analysis. Whereas the values shown in a model's base case may appear reasonable, if relationships are not captured correctly, then the model's calculations may either be fundamentally incorrect or will not reflect the true level of variation in the output when input values are altered. For example:

- Where the total cost of a project is estimated as the sum of several items, if such items in fact have a common driver, then a model that does not capture this would show sensitivities to the costs of individual items that are too low; in reality, a change in the cost of one item would be possible only if the cost of the others also changed, thus creating a wider range.
- Where the margin achieved by selling a product is calculated as the difference between the sales price and its input costs, then a model that does not reflect that both are closely related to the market price of an input raw material would show sensitivities to sales prices or input costs that are too high and not realistic (for example, it would show cases where the sales price is high but input cost is low).

In this text, we cover the aspect of the modelling of dependency relationships in two main areas:

- In Chapter 11, we cover relationships between sources of risk (or distributions of uncertainty). These are where an input is modelled as a distribution and has a specific consequence on the way that the model's formulae or logic should be built, and as such is only relevant in risk modelling. Examples include where there are relationships between samples and distribution parameters (such as conditional probability-of-occurrence), or between the sampling processes of several distributions (such as correlated sampling).
- In this chapter, we discuss general model relationships. These are ones where formulae in the model depend (directly or indirectly) on a model input item, but where such formulae are essentially the same irrespective of whether the final process to change the input values is a manual one or one that is done through random sampling.

In the following, we provide examples of many common forms of dependency, with a particular emphasis on showing approaches that are required in any modelling situation. These include the capturing of:

- Common drivers of variability.
- Scenarios.
- Categories of drivers of variability or risk-related categories.
- The impact of items that fade over time (as a risk impact may).

We also address some more subtle situations, in which the formulae to assess the aggregate impact of several variables may be more complex than simple arithmetic operations. For example:

- In some cases, the impact of risks or other items in a list (or risk register) should not be added, but have more complex relationships between them, resulting from interactions when more than one occurs; even if the occurrences of the items are independent, the formula to determine the impact is not a simple addition. For example:
  - Where several detrimental events happen, only the maximum of their impacts may be relevant.
  - A set of business improvement initiatives may have an aggregate effect that is less than the sum of the individual initiatives.
- In other cases, the logic of a situation is such that certain calculation paths are only activated by a change in the value of multiple items. Such occurrences may never materialise in a basic sensitivity approach (or thought process) and may be overlooked by them. Such cases may arise, for example:
  - Where only the joint occurrence of a number of items would cause a product to fall below a safety limit, one would need to check in the model whether this condition has been met.
  - Where tax losses would arise only where several detrimental events or processes occur, and not if only one or two risks materialise.
  - Where there are operational flexibilities that need to be captured in the evaluation of a project (an example of this was provided in Chapter 4, so it is not discussed further here).
  - Where tasks in a project schedule may interact in different ways depending on which of them is on the critical path (an example of this was provided in Chapter 4, so it is not discussed further here).

Thus, although the correct capturing of dependency relationships is important in all types of models, the fact that multiple inputs vary simultaneously in most risk models means that there are potentially extra dependencies and richness required in the formulae in order to reflect interactions between risks or their impact. Although such situations should (in theory) be captured through a robust sensitivity- or scenario-driven model design process, they can easily be overlooked in sensitivity approaches.

7.4.1 Example: Commonality of Drivers of Variability

When a particular model item is driven by common underlying factors, this needs to be captured in both traditional models (for sensitivity analysis purposes) and in risk models. However, this may only become apparent when one conducts a risk assessment and asks what the underlying risk drivers of variation are.

	A	B	C	D
1				
2				
3				
4		Description	Cost	
5		Remove old kitchen	5000	
6		Redo electrics	5000	
7		New plumbing	5000	
8		Plaster	5000	
9		Paint and decorate	5000	
10		New floor	5000	
11		Buy kitchen cupboards	5000	
12		Buy other appliances	5000	
13		Install security system	5000	
14		Legal and architectural fees	5000	
15		Total	**50000**	=SUM(C5:C14)

FIGURE 7.13 Cost Budget with Independent Items

The file Ch7.MultiItem.Drivers.xlsx contains a simple example. In the worksheet Indep (shown in Figure 7.13), one sees a cost budget in which there are 10 (numerical) input assumptions, cells C5:C14. (For simplicity all items are deemed to be the same size.) Clearly, it would be possible to change any of the 10 input values and see the effect on the total cost; thus, one could run a more formal sensitivity analysis (for example, using a **DataTable**). On the other hand, a consideration of the true drivers of sensitivity (or the risk drivers) may lead one to conclude that there is only one (or a small set of) underlying driver(s) that affect all (or some of) the items (as examples, this could be the hourly cost of labour, or an exchange rate, or general inflation). In such situations, a sensitivity analysis in which only one item is changed would be invalid, as it would not represent a genuine situation that could happen.

The worksheet OneSource shows a modified model in which there is a common driver for all items; the model's formulae are adjusted appropriately to reflect this (see Figure 7.14).

Note that the values in the range C5:C14 are still inputs to the model, and may now be able to be changed independently to reflect uncertainties in each that are not driven through the common factor.

7.4.2 Example: Scenario-Driven Variability

In Chapter 6, we mentioned that one use of general scenario approaches is to capture dependencies between items, and in particular to act as a proxy tool to capture dependencies that are difficult to express through explicit formulae (such as price–volume demand curves).

The file Ch7.PriceScenarios1.xlsx contains an example in which there are four possible scenarios for the future development of prices, each with its own periodic growth rate and starting value. Figure 7.15 shows the model in which a standard growth formula is applied to calculate the future time profile, but where the parameters for the growth formula (in cells D10

	A	B	C	D	E
1					
2		Unit labour cost	10		
3					
4		Description	Cost/unit	Cost	
5		Remove old kitchen	500	5000	=C5*$C$2
6		Redo electrics	500	5000	=C6*$C$2
7		New plumbing	500	5000	=C7*$C$2
8		Plaster	500	5000	=C8*$C$2
9		Paint and decorate	500	5000	=C9*$C$2
10		New floor	500	5000	=C10*$C$2
11		Buy kitchen cupboards	500	5000	=C11*$C$2
12		Buy other appliances	500	5000	=C12*$C$2
13		Install security system	500	5000	=C13*$C$2
14		Legal and architectural fees	500	5000	=C14*$C$2
15		Total		50000	=SUM(D5:D14)

FIGURE 7.14 Cost Budget with a Common Driver

	A	B	C	D	E	F	G	H	I	J	K	L	M	N	O
1															
2						1	2	3	4	5	6	7	8	9	10
3															
4		Price Scenarios		Growth Rate	Starting Value										
5		Base	1	2.0%	100										
6		Scenario A	2	5.0%	80										
7		Scenario B	3	-5.0%	80										
8		Scenario C	4	10.0%	60										
9															
10		To Use	2	5.0%	80	84	88	93	97	102	107	113	118	124	130
11															

FIGURE 7.15 Scenarios for Price Development

DataTable		84	88	93	97	102	107	113	118	124	130
	1	102	104	106	108	110	113	115	117	120	122
	2	84	88	93	97	102	107	113	118	124	130
	3	76	72	69	65	62	59	56	53	50	48
	4	66	73	80	88	97	106	117	129	141	156

FIGURE 7.16 Price Development in Each Scenario, Using Sensitivity Analysis

and E10) are established by using the **CHOOSE** function to pick out the appropriate values from the table of scenario data (cells D5:D8), based on the scenario number selected in cell C10.

In terms of the similarity between static modelling and risk modelling, it is of no relevance (from the perspective of the formulae required in the model) if the scenario number (cell C10) is set manually or by using a discrete probability distribution that returns a random integer between one and four. Figure 7.16 shows a multi-output **DataTable**, which contains the full price profile for each scenario (which is also contained in the example file). If the scenario numbers were chosen randomly, then the profile of price development would simply be a randomly varying selection between the four profiles.

7.4.3 Example: Category-Driven Variability

The assignment of items to categories can be an invaluable tool when building and communicating models.

From a modelling perspective, the use of categories may be relevant in several types of situations:

- It provides a more general way to capture sources of common variation (rather than a single one used in the above example). In other words, several risk items may be affected by one particular underlying risk driver, and other items by another, and so on.
- It can help to capture relationships between risk impacts (even where the occurrences are independent). For example, there may be a set of risks whose individual occurrence affects the volume produced (or sold) by a company of a particular product (and/or in a particular region), but where the total impact is only that of the largest one that has occurred. The use of categories allows Excel functions (such as **SUMIFS** or other conditional calculations) to capture the impact.
- As a method to group smaller item risks, so that those that are individually of little significance are not simply ignored.

From a communication and results presentation perspective, the use of categories can be an important tool: one may often wish to communicate results at a higher (more aggregate) level than the one that a project team is working at within its day-to-day risk assessment activities.

The file Ch7.Cost.HouseRenovation.Categories.xlsx contains an example. A detailed list of cost items for a renovation project is shown in the worksheet ListofCostItems; see Figure 7.17.

These items could be categorised by the area (room) of the house, and by the nature of the activity, as shown in the worksheet AggCategories of the same file; see Figure 7.18.

The data are effectively structured as a database that can be presented in summary form in different ways for reporting and communication purposes. Figure 7.19 shows the summary presentation by area (room) and by item (activity); in the example file, this is shown immediately below the table.

It is important to note that the categories used for sensitivity and modelling calculations should correspond to the drivers of sensitivity or risk. Therefore, the choice of such categories is much more limited than it is for categories that may be desired for communication or presentation purposes (e.g. geographical region, department, responsible person, process stage, subtask, etc.).

The worksheet SensCategories of the same file (partly shown in Figure 7.20) contains a supposed categorisation for sensitivity and risk purposes, in which there are four categories (perhaps associated with the structure of the contractor relationships, for example); a summary of the cost structure by sensitivity group (risk drivers) is shown in Figure 7.21.

One can then conduct a sensitivity analysis of the total cost by varying the ranges that apply for the different sensitivity categories or risk drivers: these calculations are contained in the worksheet SensCategoriesRanges; see Figure 7.22.

	A	B	C
1			
2		**DETAILED ITEMS**	
3		**Area**	**$ Expected**
4		Removal of asbestos in roof in the Kitchen	5000
5		Rebuild roof in the Kitchen	3000
6		Redo electrics in the Kitchen	2500
7		New floor in the Kitchen	2000
8		Repaint the Kitchen	500
9		Redo electrics in the Dining room	2000
10		New floor in the Dining room	3000
11		Repaint the Dining room	500
12		Redo electrics in the Reception Room	2000
13		New floor in the Reception Room	3000
14		Repaint the Reception Room	500
15		Redo electrics in Bedroom 1	1000
16		New floor in Bedroom 1	1000
17		Repaint in Bedroom 1	500
18		Redo electrics in Bedroom 2	1000
19		New floor in Bedroom 2	1000
20		Repaint in Bedroom 2	500
21		Redo electrics in Bedroom 3	1000
22		New floor in Bedroom 3	1500
23		Repaint in Bedroom 3	500
24		Redo electrics in Bedroom 4	1000
25		New floor in Bedroom 4	1500
26		Repaint in Bedroom 4	500
27		Rebuild wall in the Garden	1500
28		Paint outside area in the Garden	2500
29		Relay paving stones in the Garden	1000
30		**Total**	**40000**

FIGURE 7.17 Detailed Cost Budget Without Categories

Note that the mechanism by which any subsequent variation is implemented (e.g. traditional sensitivities or random sampling) is essentially irrelevant from a modelling perspective. Figure 7.23 shows a **DataTable** as the sensitivity factors for the drivers A and B are varied.

Of course, the use of categories of risk drivers means that there is a smaller set of underlying risk drivers than if risks were treated as individual items; each category is implicitly a set of risks that vary together (or are jointly dependent). Clearly, this will affect the extent of variability at the aggregate level when a simulation is run.

The file Ch7.Cost.HouseRenovation.Categories.Comparison.xlsx contains an example in which two separate modelling approaches are implemented: in the first, the risks are independent items, and in the second, each risk is driven by a risk category. Figure 7.24 shows a screen clip of the two approaches, with Figure 7.25 showing an overlay of the simulated results. Clearly, the approach that uses categories has a wider range for the possible outputs; in the first case, it is more likely that some of the items offset each other (due to combinatorial effects), so that the range is narrower.

	A	B	C	D
1				
2		DETAILED ITEMS		
3		Area	Item	$ Expected
4		Kitchen	Removal of asbestos in roof	5000
5		Kitchen	Rebuild roof	3000
6		Kitchen	Redo electrics	2500
7		Kitchen	New floor	2000
8		Kitchen	Repaint	500
9		Dining room	Redo electrics	2000
10		Dining room	New floor	3000
11		Dining room	Repaint	500
12		Reception Room	Redo electrics	2000
13		Reception Room	New floor	3000
14		Reception Room	Repaint	500
15		Bedroom 1	Redo electrics	1000
16		Bedroom 1	New floor	1000
17		Bedroom 1	Repaint	500
18		Bedroom 2	Redo electrics	1000
19		Bedroom 2	New floor	1000
20		Bedroom 2	Repaint	500
21		Bedroom 3	Redo electrics	1000
22		Bedroom 3	New floor	1500
23		Bedroom 3	Repaint	500
24		Bedroom 4	Redo electrics	1000
25		Bedroom 4	New floor	1500
26		Bedroom 4	Repaint	500
27		Garden	Rebuild wall	1500
28		Garden	Paint outside area	2500
29		Garden	Relay paving stones	1000
30		**Total**		**40000**

FIGURE 7.18 Detailed Cost Budget with two Types of Category

Thus, although the use of great detail at the line item level can be important to capture all factors when working with static models, such detailed approaches may not be directly applicable to the creation of risk models; often, items need to be grouped into categories, with any variation driven at the category level (thus, involving the creation of intermediate calculations compared to the case where risks are treated as individual items only). In general, as a model becomes more detailed, there are more potential dependency relationships, because any item can theoretically interact with any other. Therefore, one of the modelling challenges is to build the risk drivers into the model at the appropriate level of detail.

Although the categories used for sensitivity and risk modelling purposes should correspond to the drivers of risk, one may wish to communicate the results of models according to other categories. In this example, this has been done by aggregating the results by risk driver (cells H35:H38) to create scaling factors by communication category (cells J35:J38); these show the amount by which the item in each category varies from its base case (in a particular sample or recalculation of the model). These factors are then applied to the detailed model (cells J4:K29), using lookup functions to find the scaling factors that apply for each individual

	A	B	C	D	E
32					
33			**AGGREGATE SUMMARY 1**		
34			**Item**	**$ Expected**	
35			Removal of asbestos in roof	5000	=SUMIFS(D$4:D$29,$C$4:$C$29,$C35)
36			Rebuild roof	3000	=SUMIFS(D$4:D$29,$C$4:$C$29,$C36)
37			Redo electrics	10500	=SUMIFS(D$4:D$29,$C$4:$C$29,$C37)
38			New floor	13000	=SUMIFS(D$4:D$29,$C$4:$C$29,$C38)
39			Repaint	3500	=SUMIFS(D$4:D$29,$C$4:$C$29,$C39)
40			Rebuild wall	1500	=SUMIFS(D$4:D$29,$C$4:$C$29,$C40)
41			Paint outside area	2500	=SUMIFS(D$4:D$29,$C$4:$C$29,$C41)
42			Relay paving stones	1000	=SUMIFS(D$4:D$29,$C$4:$C$29,$C42)
43			**Total**	**40000**	=SUM(D35:D42)
44					
45			**AGGREGATE SUMMARY 2**		
46			**Item**	**$ Expected**	
47			Kitchen	13000	=SUMIFS(D$4:D$29,$B$4:$B$29,$C47)
48			Dining room	5500	=SUMIFS(D$4:D$29,$B$4:$B$29,$C48)
49			Reception Room	5500	=SUMIFS(D$4:D$29,$B$4:$B$29,$C49)
50			Bedroom 1	2500	=SUMIFS(D$4:D$29,$B$4:$B$29,$C50)
51			Bedroom 2	2500	=SUMIFS(D$4:D$29,$B$4:$B$29,$C51)
52			Bedroom 3	3000	=SUMIFS(D$4:D$29,$B$4:$B$29,$C52)
53			Bedroom 4	3000	=SUMIFS(D$4:D$29,$B$4:$B$29,$C53)
54			Garden	5000	=SUMIFS(D$4:D$29,$B$4:$B$29,$C54)
55			**Total**	**40000**	=SUM(D47:D54)
56					

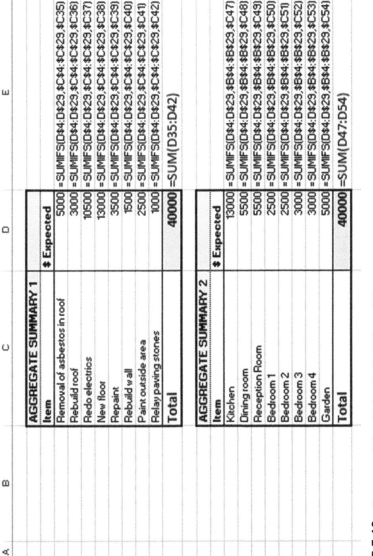

FIGURE 7.19 Summary of Cost Budget by Each Type of Category

	A	B	C	D	E
1					
2		**DETAILED ITEMS**			
3		**Area**	**Item**	**Risk Driver Categor**	**$ Expected**
4		Kitchen	Removal of asbestos in roof	A	5000
5		Kitchen	Rebuild roof	A	3000
6		Kitchen	Redo electrics	B	2500
7		Kitchen	New floor	C	2000
8		Kitchen	Repaint	C	500
9		Dining room	Redo electrics	B	2000
10		Dining room	New floor	C	3000
11		Dining room	Repaint	C	500
12		Reception Room	Redo electrics	B	2000
13		Reception Room	New floor	C	3000
14		Reception Room	Repaint	C	500
15		Bedroom 1	Redo electrics	B	1000
16		Bedroom 1	New floor	C	1000
17		Bedroom 1	Repaint	C	500
18		Bedroom 2	Redo electrics	B	1000
19		Bedroom 2	New floor	C	1000
20		Bedroom 2	Repaint	C	500
21		Bedroom 3	Redo electrics	B	1000
22		Bedroom 3	New floor	C	1500
23		Bedroom 3	Repaint	C	500
24		Bedroom 4	Redo electrics	B	1000
25		Bedroom 4	New floor	C	1500
26		Bedroom 4	Repaint	C	500
27		Garden	Rebuild wall	D	1500
28		Garden	Paint outside area	D	2500
29		Garden	Relay paving stones	D	1000
30		**Total**			**40000**

FIGURE 7.20 Detailed Cost Budget with Risk Categories

item based on its category. The individual items are then summed by communication category (cells H44:H51), and these would also form a simulation output, if a simulation were done. (This approach is numerically equivalent to one in which the model was built by sampling the percentage scaling factor for each risk category and then applying that to the items within that category, before summing the figures according to communication category).

Figure 7.26 shows a screen clip of this, with the distribution of costs for the kitchen-related items. (The simulation is done using @RISK, in order to easily display the output graphically; a reader working with the model can run the simulation using the tools and template of Chapter 13, if desired, as the model formulae are created without using @RISK.)

AGGREGATE SUMMARY 3		
Item	**$ Expected**	
A	8000	=SUMIFS(E$4:E$29,$D$4:$D$29,$C59)
B	10500	=SUMIFS(E$4:E$29,$D$4:$D$29,$C60)
C	16500	=SUMIFS(E$4:E$29,$D$4:$D$29,$C61)
D	5000	=SUMIFS(E$4:E$29,$D$4:$D$29,$C62)
Total	**40000**	=SUM(E59:E62)

FIGURE 7.21 Summary of Cost Budget by Risk Category

AGGREGATE SUMMARY 3		Sensitivity Factors		
Item	$ Expected	(Change to Base)	$ Final	
A	8000	0%	8000	=E35*(1+F35)
B	10500	0%	10500	=E36*(1+F36)
C	16500	0%	16500	=E37*(1+F37)
D	5000	0%	5000	=E38*(1+F38)
Total	40000		40000	=SUM(G35:G38)

FIGURE 7.22 Sensitivity Analysis of Cost Budget by Risk Category

		A	A	A
	40000	-20%	0%	20%
B	-20%	36300	37900	39500
B	0%	38400	40000	41600
B	20%	40500	42100	43700

FIGURE 7.23 Sensitivity Analysis of Cost Budget for Two Risk Categories

DETAILED ITEMS				Low	High	
Area	Item	Risk Dri	$ Expected	-25%	25%	Sample
Kitchen	Removal of asbestos in roof	A	5000	3750	6250	5240
Kitchen	Rebuild roof	A	3000	2250	3750	3712
Kitchen	Redo electrics	B	2500	1875	3125	2631
Kitchen	New floor	C	2000	1500	2500	2474
Kitchen	Repaint	C	500	375	625	584
Dining room	Redo electrics	B	2000	1500	2500	1639
Dining room	New floor	C	3000	2250	3750	3027
Dining room	Repaint	C	500	375	625	383
Reception Room	Redo electrics	B	2000	1500	2500	1651
Reception Room	New floor	C	3000	2250	3750	3171
Reception Room	Repaint	C	500	375	625	546
Bedroom 1	Redo electrics	B	1000	750	1250	916
Bedroom 1	New floor	C	1000	750	1250	789
Bedroom 1	Repaint	C	500	375	625	595
Bedroom 2	Redo electrics	B	1000	750	1250	1174
Bedroom 2	New floor	C	1000	750	1250	1023
Bedroom 2	Repaint	C	500	375	625	393
Bedroom 3	Redo electrics	B	1000	750	1250	930
Bedroom 3	New floor	C	1500	1125	1875	1328
Bedroom 3	Repaint	C	500	375	625	562
Bedroom 4	Redo electrics	B	1000	750	1250	977
Bedroom 4	New floor	C	1500	1125	1875	1571
Bedroom 4	Repaint	C	500	375	625	503
Garden	Rebuild wall	D	1500	1125	1875	1688
Garden	Paint outside area	D	2500	1875	3125	2063
Garden	Relay paving stones	D	1000	750	1250	1194
Total			40000			40766

AGGREGATE SUMMARY 3		Low	High	
Item	$ Expected	-25%	25%	Sample
A	8000	6000	10000	3777
B	10500	7875	13125	8801
C	16500	12375	20625	14419
D	5000	3750	6250	3820
Total	40000			36817

FIGURE 7.24 Uncertainty Model of Cost Budget by Risk Category

This example also shows that, in order to present the results of risk models in a particular way (i.e. in this case, by the category associated with the room type), additional work may be necessary to build the appropriate formulae; such issues should be taken into account as early in the process as possible, because the conducting of such rework only once results are being presented can lead to time shortages and errors, which can severely detract from the credibility

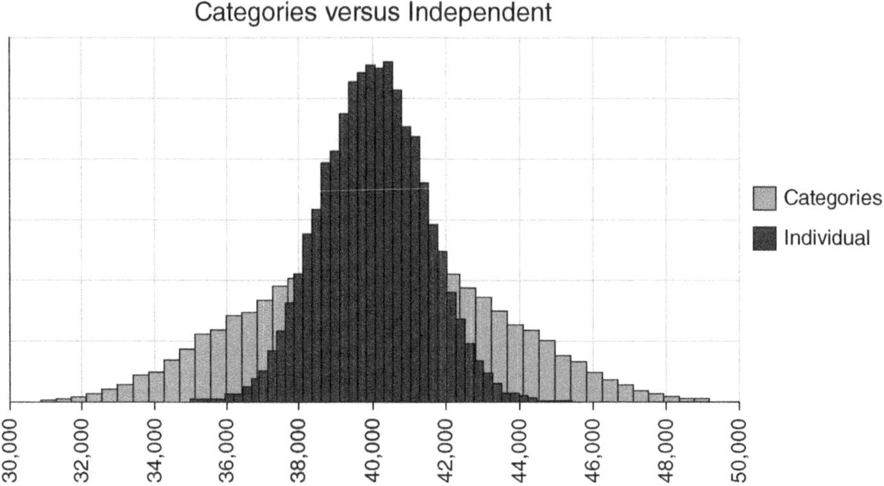

FIGURE 7.25 Simulated Distribution of Total Costs, Comparing Individual Independent Items Versus the Use of Risk Categories

of the results (and provide reinforcement to those who are sceptical about the benefits of such approaches).

7.4.4 Example: Fading Impacts

When considering the risks associated with the start-up phase of a new production facility, there may be a risk that it cannot immediately be operated at planned capacity, perhaps due to a lack of experience that a company has in producing identical products. More generally,

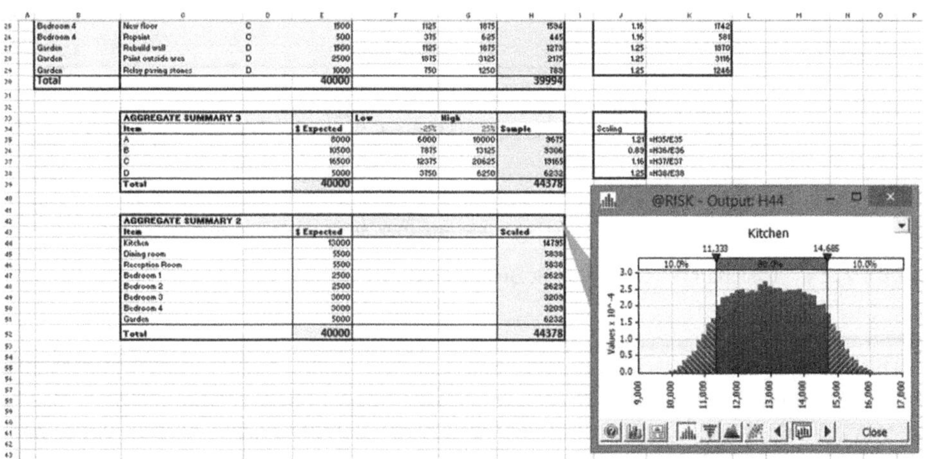

FIGURE 7.26 Simulated Distribution of Costs by Presentation Category

the impact of a risk (if it materialises) may reduce over some period (which itself may be uncertain).

Note that the risk is in relation to a planned figure (i.e. a deviation from it), so that other planned items would, as a general rule, be part of the base plan and not considered as genuine risks, at least relative to a reasonable base plan. For example, there may be a ramp-up phase in which planned production starts below full capacity but then increases over time to full capacity, or that sales prices may initially be lower in order to attract new customers; the fact that the initial values are expected to be below their long-term equilibrium is not a risk as such.

The file Ch7.FadeFormulae.xslx contains some examples of possible implementations of the calculations for the loss of capacity (expressed as a percentage of the total), which decreases over time. A screen clip is shown in Figure 7.27.

- In Model 1, the figures are hard coded.
- In Model 2, there is a constant improvement per year, which is determined by the assumed starting and ending values over a fixed period of time (i.e. between period 1 and period 5 in this case).
- In Model 3, the end period to which improvements apply can be changed, with constant improvement per year, so that an additional check is built into the formulae to prevent values becoming negative in some cases.
- In Model 4, the end period can also be changed, but the improvements are applied in a relative sense, so that the loss of capacity is calculated in a multiplicative fashion from the prior period figure, until the end period is reached.

Of course, the advantage of Model 1 is that any figures can be used for the time profile (simply by typing in the desired figures); the other approaches have the advantages that the number of inputs is reduced, and that the conducting of sensitivity analysis is more straightforward.

Since the inputs to the formulae can be changed, such changes may either be sensitivity related or risk driven. For example, in Model 4, the percentage that applies in the first period could be replaced by a sample from an appropriate uncertainty distribution, as could the ending year and the annual relative change. The calculated capacity loss may also be used to represent the impact of a risk on its occurrence, and combined with the outcome of a sample from a "yes/no" (Bernoulli) process (see Chapter 9) by simple multiplication.

Similar approaches can be used if there are several potential risks that may interact. For example, in each period there may be a risk of a shock event to market prices. Where the

	B	C	D	E	F	G	H	I	J	K	L	M	N
1													
2	**Loss of Capacity (on occurrence of item), as %**												
3													
4	**Model 1: Hard-Coded Figures**				1	2	3	4	5	6	7	8	
5	Percentage Loss in Capacity				10.0%	7.0%	5.0%	3.0%	1.0%	0.0%	0.0%	0.0%	
6													
7	**Model 2: Parameterised Formula: Linear**	Year 1	Year 5	Change (absolute)	1	2	3	4	5	6	7	8	
8	Percentage Loss in Capacity	10.0%	1.0%	2.3%	10.0%	7.8%	5.5%	3.3%	1.0%	0.0%	0.0%	0.0%	=IF(M7<=5,L8-$E8,0)
9													
10	**Model 3: Parameterised Formula: Linear Flex End Year**	Year 1	End Year	Change (absolute)	1	2	3	4	5	6	7	8	
11	Percentage Loss in Capacity	10.0%	6	3.0%	10.0%	7.0%	4.0%	1.0%	0.0%	0.0%	0.0%	0.0%	=MAX(IF(M10<=$D11,L11-$E11,0),0)
12													
13	**Model 4: Parameterised Formula: Relative Flex End Year**	Year 1	End Year	Change (relative)	1	2	3	4	5	6	7	8	
14	Percentage Loss in Capacity	10.0%	8	30%	10.0%	7.0%	4.9%	3.4%	2.4%	1.7%	1.2%	0.8%	=IF(M13<=$D14,L14*(1-$E14),0)

FIGURE 7.27 Various Possible Implementations of Fade Formulae

impact of each shock may persist over several periods, then within each period, one would need to calculate the impact of all prior shocks whose effect is still applicable at that point. Such calculations would be similar to some of those shown in the next section.

7.4.5 Example: Partial Impact Aggregation by Category in a Risk Register

Relationships that are more subtle or complex than those discussed above can often arise. For example, one can envisage a situation in which a company has identified some initiatives to improve the efficacy of its sales processes, such as:

- Improved screening of customers, so that low potential leads are not followed.
- The reuse of bid documents, so that quotes can be provided at lower cost.
- Enhanced training of new sales representatives.
- The development of new products.
- A more systematic process to track competitor activities.

From a qualitative perspective, these initiatives would seem sensible and could presumably be authorised for implementation. On the other hand, it would be natural to ask whether these initiatives would be sufficient for the company to achieve its improvement targets; thus, some quantitative analysis would be required.

One could consider various quantitative approaches to this:

- Using a static approach, assess the impact of each initiative quantitatively (as a fixed improvement percentage) and add up these static figures.
- Using a static approach, attempt to reflect that the effect of subsequent initiatives is reduced (compared to its stand-alone value) as other initiatives take effect. One could think of a number of possibilities (described in more detail in the example model):
  - A multiplicative diminishing effect.
  - A weighting effect, in which the largest initiative is fully effective, the second one is less effective, and so on.
  - A risk approach, in which the success of each initiative (and more generally its impact) is uncertain.

The file Ch7.ImprovInit.Effect.xlsx contains various worksheets that show possible calculations for each case. It aims to demonstrate that the core challenge is to identify and build the appropriate aggregation formulae. Once this has been done, the mechanism by which input assumptions are changed (sensitivity analysis or random sampling) is not of significance for the formulae. Figure 7.28 shows the static case, where the effect of the initiatives is added up (shown in the worksheet Additive).

Figure 7.29 shows the situation where it is believed that there is a diminishing cumulative multiplicative effect (shown in the worksheet Multiplicative).

Figure 7.30 shows the case where the initiative with the largest effect has its effect included with a 100% weighting, the second with a 50% weighting (of its base stand-alone value), and so on; in order for the model to be dynamic as the input values for the base improvement percentages are changed, the **LARGE** function is used to order the values of the effects of the initiatives (shown in the worksheet SortedWeighted).

	A	B	C	D	E
1		**Productivity Improvement**			
2					
3		Initiative	% Improvement	Calc	Formulae
4		Improved screening of customers so that low potential leads are not followed	5.0%	5.0%	=C4
5		Re-use bid documents so that quotes can be provided at lower cost	2.0%	2.0%	=C5
6		Enhance training of new sales representatives	3.0%	3.0%	=C6
7		The development of new products	4.0%	4.0%	=C7
8		A more systematic process to track competitor activities	1.0%	1.0%	=C8
9		**Aggregate**		**15.0%**	=SUM(D4:D8)

FIGURE 7.28 Approaches to Aggregating the Effect of Improvement Initiatives: Addition of Static Values

	A	B	C	D	E
1		**Productivity Improvement**			
2					
3		Initiative	% Improvement	Calc	Formulae
4		Improved screening of customers so that low potential leads are not followed	5.0%	5.0%	=1-(1-C4)
5		Re-use bid documents so that quotes can be provided at lower cost	2.0%	6.9%	=1-(1-C5)*(1-D4)
6		Enhance training of new sales representatives	3.0%	9.7%	=1-(1-C6)*(1-D5)
7		The development of new products	4.0%	13.3%	=1-(1-C7)*(1-D6)
8		A more systematic process to track competitor activities	1.0%	14.2%	=1-(1-C8)*(1-D7)
9		**Aggregate**		**14.2%**	=D8

FIGURE 7.29 Approaches to Aggregating the Effect of Improvement Initiatives: Multiplication of Static Values

	A	B	C	D	E	F	G	H	I	J	K	L
1		**Productivity Improvement**										
2												
3		Initiative	% Improvement		Rank	Value	Weighting	Calc		Formulae		
4		Improved screening of customers so that low potential leads are not followed	5.0%		1	5.0%	1.000	5.0%		=LARGE($C$4:$C$8,E4)	#N/A	=F4*G4
5		Re-use bid documents so that quotes can be provided at lower cost	2.0%		2	4.0%	0.500	2.0%		=LARGE($C$4:$C$8,E5)	=G4/2	=F5*G5
6		Enhance training of new sales representatives	3.0%		3	3.0%	0.250	0.8%		=LARGE($C$4:$C$8,E6)	=G5/2	=F6*G6
7		The development of new products	4.0%		4	2.0%	0.125	0.3%		=LARGE($C$4:$C$8,E7)	=G6/2	=F7*G7
8		A more systematic process to track competitor activities	1.0%		5	1.0%	0.063	0.1%		=LARGE($C$4:$C$8,E8)	=G7/2	=F8*G8
9		**Aggregate**						**8.1%**				=SUM(H4:H8)

FIGURE 7.30 Approaches to Aggregating the Effect of Improvement Initiatives: Weighting Factors of Static Values

Note that whichever of the three approaches is deemed appropriate (the reader may be able to think of others), the final step – of adding risk or uncertainty for the percentage improvement figures – is straightforward. The worksheet SortedWeightedRiskRAND (Figure 7.31) contains the case where each initiative has a probability of success (using the **RAND()** function within an **IF** statement), and the worksheet SortedWeightedRiskAtRisk (Figure 7.32) shows the equivalent using the **RiskBernoulli** distribution in @RISK, as well as a graphic (using @RISK) of the simulated distribution of improvement percentage.

7.4.6 Example: More Complex Impacts within a Category

When working with categories, one may need to be able to find the minimum or maximum value within a category. Whereas Excel contains functions such as **SUMIF**, **SUMIFS**, **AVERAGEIF**, **AVERAGEIFS,** and so on, it does not (at the time of writing) have a **MAXIFS** or **MINIFS** function. Whereas **SUMIF** or **SUMIFS** can be replicated using array functions, the analogous formulae for maxima and minima would not work in general. The **AGGREGATE** function can be used instead (although it is available only in later versions of Excel). The key

Productivity Improvement

Initiative	P(Success)	Success?	% Improvement on	% Improvement		Rank	Value	Weighting	Calc
Improved screening of customers so that low potential leads are not followed	60%	1	5.0%	5.0%		1	5.0%	1.000	5.0%
Re-use bid documents so that quotes can be provided at lower cost	80%	0	2.0%	0.0%		2	4.0%	0.500	2.0%
Enhance training of new sales representatives	50%	1	3.0%	3.0%		3	3.0%	0.250	0.8%
The development of new products	30%	1	4.0%	4.0%		4	0.0%	0.125	0.0%
A more systematic process to track competitor activities	60%	0	1.0%	0.0%		5	0.0%	0.063	0.0%
Aggregate									7.8%
		=IF(RAND()<=C4,1,0)		=D4*E4			=LARGE($F$4:$F$8,H4)	#N/A	=I4*J4
		=IF(RAND()<=C5,1,0)		=D5*E5			=LARGE($F$4:$F$8,H5)	=J4/2	=I5*J5
		=IF(RAND()<=C6,1,0)		=D6*E6			=LARGE($F$4:$F$8,H6)	=J5/2	=I6*J6
		=IF(RAND()<=C7,1,0)		=D7*E7			=LARGE($F$4:$F$8,H7)	=J6/2	=I7*J7
		=IF(RAND()<=C8,1,0)		=D8*E8			=LARGE($F$4:$F$8,H8)	=J7/2	=I8*J8
									=SUM(K4:K8)

FIGURE 7.31 Approaches to Aggregating the Effect of Improvement Initiatives: Uncertainty Ranges Around the Selected Static Approach (Excel)

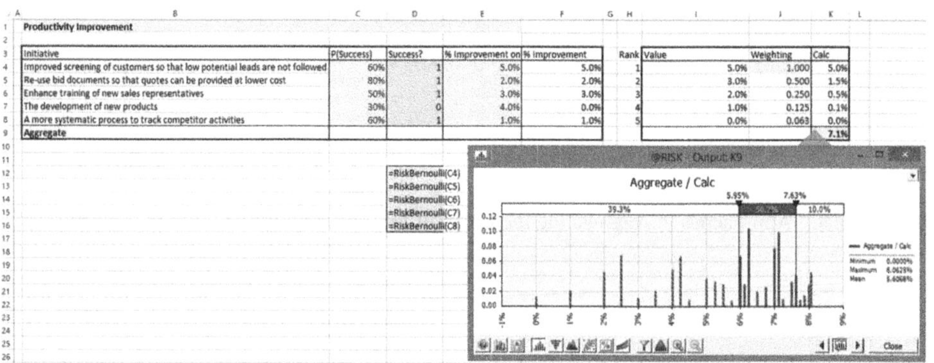

Productivity Improvement

Initiative	P(Success)	Success?	% Improvement on	% Improvement		Rank	Value	Weighting	Calc
Improved screening of customers so that low potential leads are not followed	60%	1	5.0%	5.0%		1	5.0%	1.000	5.0%
Re-use bid documents so that quotes can be provided at lower cost	80%	1	2.0%	2.0%		2	3.0%	0.500	1.5%
Enhance training of new sales representatives	50%	1	3.0%	3.0%		3	2.0%	0.250	0.5%
The development of new products	30%	0	4.0%	0.0%		4	1.0%	0.125	0.1%
A more systematic process to track competitor activities	60%	1	1.0%	1.0%		5	0.0%	0.063	0.0%
Aggregate									7.1%
		=RiskBernoulli(C4)							
		=RiskBernoulli(C5)							
		=RiskBernoulli(C6)							
		=RiskBernoulli(C7)							
		=RiskBernoulli(C8)							

FIGURE 7.32 Approaches to Aggregating the Effect of Improvement Initiatives: Uncertainty Ranges Around the Selected Static Approach (@RISK)

CustomerId	Country	Revenue	Cost
2314	Germany	505	-423
5635	France	405	-328
9864	Italy	435	-364
6338	Germany	890	-731
6418	France	962	-655
2985	Italy	727	-474
2153	France	908	-738
2423	Italy	634	-459
1649	Germany	72	-48
5007	Germany	61	-50
587	France	567	-458
5660	Italy	447	-346
4536	France	303	-234
1278	Germany	598	-503
3903	France	299	-220
934	Italy	722	-491

	MAXIFS as array function		Using AGGREGATE, where criteria creates an error, which are ignored due to function's setting option 6		
	Revenues	Cost	Revenues	Cost: Maximum	Cost: Minimum
Germany	890	0	890	-48	-731
France	962	0	962	-220	-738
Italy	727	0	727	-346	-491

{=MAX((D$3:D$18)*($C$3:$C$18=$G4))}

{=AGGREGATE(15,6,((E$3:E$18)/($C$3:$C$18=$G4)),1)}

FIGURE 7.33 Working with Only the Maximum Impact Within a Category

is to use the **function** option, which ignores errors (i.e. with its **Options** parameter set to the value 6), and to calculate it as an array function in a way that its elements create errors when a criterion is not met, so that only items meeting the criteria are included within the calculation.

The file Ch7.MaxIfs.Aggregate.Array.xlsx contains an example; a screen clip is shown in Figure 7.33. Whereas the maximum of the (positive) revenues can be calculated using an array form of the **MAX** function (e.g. using the formula

{=**MAX**((D$3:D$18)*($C$3:$C$18=$G4))}), such a formula would not work for the (negative) cost field (see columns H and I, respectively). However, by using the **AGGREGATE** function in an analogous way (using division to create an error if the criteria are not met, and ignoring this error through the function's option 6), one can create a formula that could find the maximum or minimum of any set of numbers, whether positive or negative, as shown in columns J, K and L.

7.5 WORKING WITH EXISTING MODELS

When building a risk model in practice, very often one has an existing model, populated with base case numbers, as well as perhaps some sensitivity or scenario analysis that has been conducted. A frequent issue is therefore whether, and how, such models can be used as the basis for the creation of risk models. Indeed, a project team may sometimes be charged with the task of "adding risk" to the existing model.

In this section, we discuss the issue of the design of risk-based simulation in such circumstances. This section is not intended to be complete by itself, as the building of models requires techniques and processes that are mostly covered earlier. The discussion here highlights only selected key points. Indeed, some issues are not covered again at all below, such as the use of model switches to be able to capture the effect of key project decisions and mitigation actions.

7.5.1 Ensuring an Appropriate Risk Identification and Mapping

From the earlier discussion, it is clear that one can, in principle, take (almost) any well-built existing static model and replace the fixed input assumptions with distributions, thus creating an uncertainty model that can be repeatedly recalculated. On the other hand, such an approach is unlikely to result in a risk model that is genuinely appropriate, due to issues mentioned earlier:

- The line items are unlikely to match the risks; significant model restructuring would generally be necessary, both to provide the granularity required and to include the impact of event risks or other items.
- The formulae are likely to be insufficiently flexible, especially concerning delay-type risks, which are rarely built into static models (unless detailed thought was given to model requirements early in the process).
- Dependencies between items may have been overlooked, especially common drivers of risk, or relationships may only take effect in more complex scenarios of multiple input variation.

Of course, with sufficient restructuring, any existing model can be adapted (or essentially completely rebuilt) to include the risks and their impacts. However, as a general rule, the effort required to do so (correctly) is often extensive. Indeed, the potential complexity in restructuring an existing model is one of the reasons why "overlay" models, such as risk registers, are frequently used.

Of course, such restructuring activities will be minimised if one can consider the risk issues early in the model design process: thus, as well as considering "What-if?" sensitivities at this stage, one would ideally also begin to consider the likely key risks and their impact for model design. A frequently observed case is essentially the extreme opposite, where an analyst spends perhaps several weeks or months building a detailed static model, without considering risks, and then finds that the effort required to modify the model to incorporate the results of a risk assessment is so extensive that it is never undertaken.

7.5.2 Existing Models using Manual Processes or Embedded Procedures

There may be cases where an existing static model is believed to be appropriately structured to be suitable directly for risk modelling purposes, in the sense that simple replacement of its input values with the appropriate probability distribution would lead to a model with a valid risk mapping (and not simply to a model that produces no calculatory errors, but whose scenarios shown are not realistic cases, with, for example, inappropriate line items, as discussed earlier).

In some cases, models require other (non-simulation) procedures to be run, some of which may (for a static model) be run manually, and others may involve automated (macro) procedures. Examples include:

- Before and after a simulation, to ensure that model switches are automatically set to their appropriate values; so that the model's presentation (when a simulation is not running) is always of the base case, with the "risk case" used automatically whenever a simulation is run.
- Before a simulation, to ensure that Excel **Data Filters** are cleared on databases, so that the integrity of the calculations (and of the filtered display) is maintained.
- Before a simulation, to refresh the input data by updating some values taken from an external data source of worksheet (or similarly to write simulation results to an external database at the end of a simulation).
- Before or after a simulation, a **GoalSeek** or **Solver** procedure might be used to find or optimise the values of other model inputs.
- During a simulation, some procedures may need to be run at each iteration (recalculation) of it. This may include:
  - **GoalSeek** or **Solver**. For example, for every sample of an exchange rate, one may wish to know what the target sales price should be to achieve breakeven, or to find an optimal selling price. These would be items that would be determined if that specific case arose in the real-life situation, and so need to be reflected within the simulation.
  - Circular references. These are usually resolved by iterative means (where they have not arisen by mistake, or can be eliminated by algebraic manipulation or model reformulation). There are two main iterative approaches used: first, Excel's iterations option (using the **Enable iterative calculation** within the **Excel Options/Formulas**) and second, the creation of a "broken" calculation path within Excel, so that (for a particular variable on the circular path) its prior calculated values are contained in one set of cells, and its updated values are contained in another adjacent set. The updated values are pure values (not formulae), which feed all model calculations (including the calculations of the prior values), but there is no formula link from the prior value to the updated ones; rather a macro is used to iteratively assign (copy) the values from the (calculated) prior field into the (pure) values of the updated field until the difference between the two is close to zero.

- A model may contain **DataTables** that, by default, update automatically at each iteration, but whose values are only relevant in the static (base view).
- A bespoke macro or other procedure may be required whenever inputs change. For example, once the geographic area to be focused on is decided, then a database (or another workbook) needs to be consulted in order to find the model values that apply for that geography.

The principles of dealing with such cases are as follows.

First, for procedures that are required only before or after a simulation, these can be either:

- Run manually at the appropriate time, as they would have been if working with the model without running a simulation; or
- Encoded within a macro that is embedded within the overall simulation (i.e. automatically run either at its start or at its end).

Second, procedures that need to be run each time that input values change (i.e. at each iteration or recalculation of the simulation) must be encoded within a macro that is embedded within the simulation. The key points in this respect are:

- The core challenge is to ensure the integrity of the calculations; many procedures (including some formatting operations) would cause Excel to recalculate as the procedure is running, so that distributions are resampled. This would create not only a slower simulation but also a potential lack of integrity of the calculations: the initially recorded values of input distributions may not correspond to the actual values used in the final calculation, or iterative procedures may never find a solution, as their target value changes as the procedure is being run.
- The solution is to ensure that the distribution samples are "frozen" whilst such procedures are running (at each recalculation or iteration of the main simulation loop). The implementation of such "freezing" procedures is different in Excel/VBA than it is in @RISK, and also varies according to the version of @RISK used. Therefore, the details of the discussion are contained within the individual chapters devoted to each topic (i.e. Chapters 12 and 13).

The remainder of this chapter provides a number of examples of encoding macros to turn manual procedures into automatic ones; these apply to procedures that need to be run before and/or after a simulation, but not during it. (The examples, of course, all use macros; Chapter 12 provides an introduction to macros for readers who have little experience of the subject.)

7.5.3 Controlling a Model Switch with a Macro at the Start and End of a Simulation

The file Ch7.BaseSwitch.Macro.xlsm contains an example in which macros are used to switch between the base and risk cases, by clicking on the corresponding button (i.e. a text box, with the associated macro assigned to it). This is shown in Figure 7.34. In practice, the macros could be run automatically (rather than manually using the button) by calling the MRSwitchtoRisk macro immediately before the start of a simulation, and then calling MRSwitchtoBase at the end.

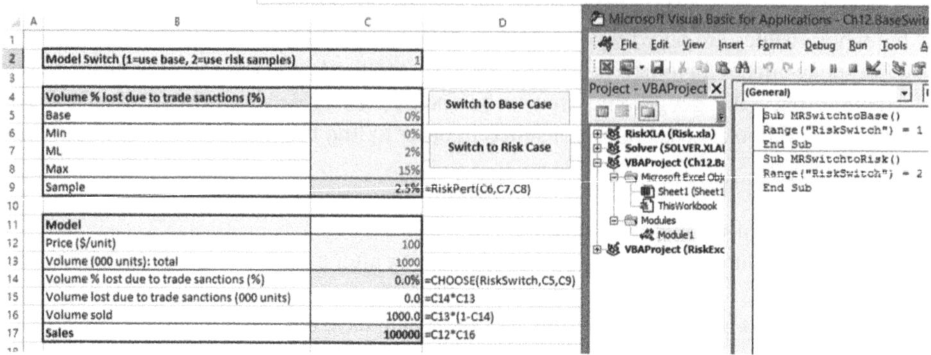

FIGURE 7.34 Controlling a Model Switch with a VBA Macro

The macros are contained within a new code module that was inserted in the VBA Window, and the code for each is:

```
Sub MRSwitchtoBase()
Range("RiskSwitch") = 1
End Sub
and
Sub MRSwitchtoRisk()
Range("RiskSwitch") = 2
End Sub
```

Note that (as covered in more detail in Chapter 12), it is more robust to refer to Excel cells from VBA using named ranges rather than cell references, which is why cell C2 has been given the name RiskSwitch within the Excel worksheet.

7.5.4 Automatically Removing Data Filters at the Start of a Simulation

Whereas the above macros were very simple to write directly, in other cases one may need to record the process steps in order to create a macro. This is typically the case when procedures that are more complex than just changing the value in a single cell are required.

An important case is to ensure that any **Data/Filters** in Excel are not in operation when a simulation is run. Some models (especially for cost budgets and portfolios of projects) are structured as data sets, and the use of filters is highly convenient to display subcategories of items using a drop-down menu. On the other hand, the values shown by the filters or the calculations can be incorrect or unexpected if the filters are active as risk values are updating. Thus, one should generally remove filters before a simulation is run. To ensure that this is not overlooked, one may encode their removal in a macro that is embedded within the simulation, so that it is run automatically immediately before the main recalculation loop of any simulation.

One can record a macro of the steps of removing a filter (by using **Developer/Record Macro**, removing the filter, and then using **Developer/Stop Recording**). When removing the

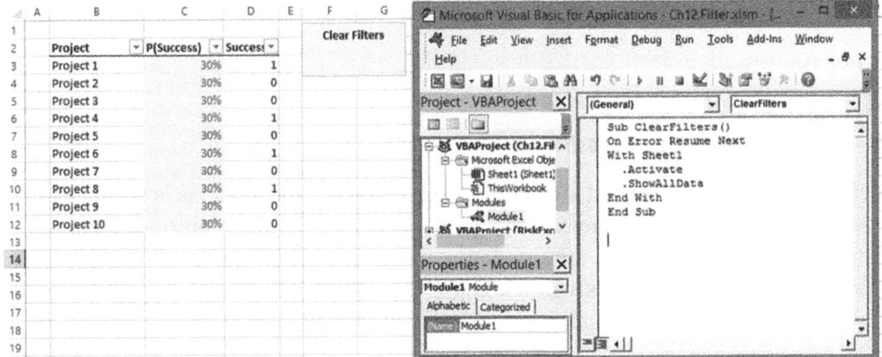

FIGURE 7.35 Clearing Filters with a VBA Macro

filter, the Excel toolbar or the short-cut **Alt+D+F+S** can be used. After doing so, the code would have been inserted into a new module within the VBE:

```
Sub ClearAllFilters
ActiveSheet.ShowAllData
End Sub
```

One may generalise the code in certain ways, such as to use On Error Resume Next so that the code runs without stopping if no filters are active. For example, slightly more general code would be:

```
Sub ClearFilters()
On Error Resume Next
With SheetContainingtheFilters
  .Activate
  .ShowAllData
End With
End Sub
```

Further generalisation could include the case where there are filters on multiple worksheets of the workbook, in which case one can apply the above procedure to each worksheet by working through all worksheets in a workbook using a For Each…In loop that is also used in Chapter 12.

The file Ch7.Filter.xlsm contains an example, as shown in Figure 7.35.

The principles of recording code (before perhaps adapting it) would also apply when other more complex syntax would be necessary, such as when using **GoalSeek** or **Solver**. In essence, one would again need to record the step of running the code once. One subtlety is that when using code that results from recording a run of **Solver**, a True statement needs to be added in order for the macro to completely run to the end. Thus, one may record code such as:

```
SolverOk SetCell:="$G$3", MaxMinVal:=1, ValueOf:="0",
ByChange:="$D$5:$F$5"
    SolverSolve
```

whereas the required code would need to end with:

```
SolverSolve True.
```

7.5.5 Models with DataTables

In general, **DataTables** are almost always only required when the model is in the static or base case view. On the other hand, they will be recalculated at each iteration (recalculation) of a simulation, and hence slow down the simulation (switching off the automatic recalculation of **DataTables** using **Excel/Options** will not change this, as the simulation forces a workbook recalculation). There are a number of options available to deal with this:

- Deletion or clearing. In some cases, the use of **DataTables** is a first step in a process of sensitivity analysis, which ends in a decision to build a full simulation model; in such cases the tables may no longer be relevant. As a variation, one may instead clear out only the content of the ranges containing array formulae within the **DataTables**, in order to retain their basic structure and formatting, allowing them to be reimplemented quickly if needed.
- Placement in another worksheet whose recalculation is turned off during the simulation run, so that the **DataTables** will not be unnecessarily recalculated. The procedure to switch off the recalculation of a worksheet requires VBA code that is explained in Chapter 12. In a sense, this approach is the most robust and transparent, as it ensures user control of the calculation process. The main complexity is that a **DataTable** can only vary input values that are in the same worksheet, so the base values would need to be in such a worksheet.
- Using macros to create a replacement for a **DataTable**. In this approach, a macro is used to sequentially assign (from a predefined list) the values to be used for a model's input and each time a new value is assigned, the model is recalculated and the results recorded. This "sensitivity" macro could therefore be run separately to the simulation, and is shown in the following example.

The file Ch7.RevSensitivity.xlsm provides an example of the use of a macro to replace a **DataTable**, and is shown in Figure 7.36. The macro sequentially places the values for revenue growth (from the cells below the header I12) into the cell corresponding to the relevant model input (cell E4) and recalculates the model before recording the result (contained in the cell J9) in the corresponding cell (below the header J12).

The appropriate cells that are involved in the operations (or serve as reference points for finding the input values to use and to store the results) have been given named ranges in Excel. The code is:

```
Sub MRRunSens()
N = Range("RevGrowthTrial").CurrentRegion.Rows.Count
For i = 1 To N - 1
 Range("RevGrowth") = Range("RevGrowthTrial").Offset(i, 0)
 Application.Calculate
 Range("OutputHeader").Offset(i, 0) = Range("vOutput")
Next i
End Sub
```

Income Statement	2014	2015	2016	2017	2018	2019	2020	
Revenues	537	577	612	649	688	729	773	
% growth		7.5%	6.0%	6.0%	6.0%	6.0%	6.0%	
Variable Costs	193	202	208	221	234	248	263	
% revenues		35.0%	34.0%	34.0%	34.0%	34.0%	34.0%	
Fixed Costs (incl. depreciation)	79	81	83	86	89	91	94	
% Growth		3.0%	3.0%	3.0%	3.0%	3.0%	3.0%	
EBIT	265	294	320	342	365	390	416	1,833

Named Range	Cell Reference
OutputHeader	=Model!$J$12
RevGrowth	=Model!$E$4
RevGrowthTrial	=Model!$I$12
vOutput	=Model!$J$9

Run Sensitivities to Revenue Growth

RevGrowth	5 Year EBIT
-2.0%	1,351
-1.0%	1,405
0.0%	1,462
1.0%	1,520
2.0%	1,579
3.0%	1,640
4.0%	1,703
5.0%	1,767
6.0%	1,833

FIGURE 7.36 Running Sensitivities with a VBA Macro

Note that in the context of a simulation model, in which the actual input cell to the model is a **CHOOSE** function that selects either a base value or a risk value, the above code would be used to place the desired input values into the cells originally containing the base value (which then feeds into the model via the **CHOOSE** function if the model switch is set to show the base case). In more general cases, the macro would work through a set of integers, which drives a lookup function to replace several model inputs at the same time, as discussed in the scenario approach in Chapter 6.

CHAPTER 8

Measuring Risk using Statistics of Distributions

This chapter introduces some key terms and core aspects of risk measurement, focusing on principles and concepts that apply both to general risk measurement and to properties of simulation inputs and outputs. We aim to use an intuitive and practical approach; much of the chapter will be supported by visual displays, mostly using @RISK's graphical features.

8.1 DEFINING RISK MORE PRECISELY

Precise measures of risk are necessary for many reasons, not least because a statement such as "one situation is more risky than another" may be either true or false according to the criteria used. For example, the implementation of risk-mitigation actions that require additional investment may increase the average cost, whilst reducing the variability in a project's outcomes.

8.1.1 General Definition

Risk can be described fairly simply as "the possibility of deviation from a desired, expected or planned outcome". Note that this allows the deviation to be driven either by event-type or discrete risks, as well as by fluctuations due to uncertainty or general variability.

8.1.2 Context-Specific Risk Measurement

Risk often needs to be described at various stages of a process, such as pre- and post-mitigation. More generally, as noted earlier in this text, one usually has a choice of context in which to operate, and a fundamental role of risk assessment is to support this choice.

Thus, risk represents the idea of non-controllability within any specific context, so that a more precise definition may be "the possibility, within a specific context, of deviation from a particular outcome that is due to factors that are non-controllable within that context".

When making quantitative statements about risk, it is often overlooked to state or specify explicitly which context is being assumed. However, such information is, of course, very important for any quantitative measure to be meaningful. For example, the risk involved in crossing the road, when measured quantitatively (such as by the probability of having an accident), will be different according to whether, and how carefully, one has looked before crossing, or whether one is wearing running shoes or a coloured jacket.

By default (in the absence of other information), it would seem that any measurement of risk for a situation should be the one that applies in the optimal context. For example, it would not make sense to measure the risk in crossing the road as that associated with not looking before crossing (unless this was explicitly stated and done for particular reasons). In the optimal context, the risk is the residual after all economically efficient mitigation and response measures have been implemented, and is essentially non-controllable, in that it no longer makes sense to alter the context (i.e. to one other than that which is optimal).

Thus, when measuring risk, one either needs to state the context, or one should be aware that a "true" measure of risk in a situation is that which relates to the non-controllable (residual) element within the optimal context.

8.1.3 Distinguishing Risk, Variability and Uncertainty

In the text so far, we have not made a specific distinction between the terms "risk", "uncertainty" and "variability", and have generally simply used the term "risk". In some cases, a more precise and formal distinction may be made:

- In natural language, "risk" is often used to indicate the potential occurrence of an event, whose impact is typically adverse. One often uses the word "chance" in place of "risk", especially where the impact may have a benefit: thus, "there is a risk that we might miss the train", but "there is a chance that we might catch it".
- Uncertainty is used to refer to a lack of knowledge (e.g. the current price of a cup of coffee in the local coffee shop, or whether a geological area contains oil, or at what time the train is due to depart). Uncertainty can often be dealt with (mitigated) by acquiring additional information, but often such information is imperfect or excessively expensive to acquire, so that a decision will need to be taken without perfect information. For example:
  - To find out (with certainty) if oil is present or not in a geological prospect, one could simply drill a well. However, if in the particular context the chance of finding oil is low, then it may be better first to conduct further testing (e.g. seismic assessments) and to abandon the project if the chance of oil truly being present is indicated as low. Conversely, one would drill for oil if the test indicates its presence is likely. In aggregate, the cost incurred in conducting any worthwhile testing procedure should be more than offset by the savings made by not drilling when oil is unlikely to be present, so that drilling (or other expensive) activities are focused only on the most promising prospects.
  - One may first conduct additional market research about the likely success of a potential new product, rather than launching the product directly; a direct launch would give perfect information, but the cost of doing so would be wasted if the product did not appeal to customers.
  - In general, in the presence of uncertainty, one often naturally proceeds with activities and decisions in a stepwise or phased fashion, so that further information is acquired before any final decision is made at any point in the sequence.
- Variability is used to refer to the random (or stochastic) nature of a process (e.g. the tossing of a coin producing one of two outcomes, or whether a soccer player scores

during a penalty shoot-out). Philosophically, there is arguably no difference between uncertainty and variability: for example, once a coin has been tossed, whether it lands heads or tails is not random, but is fully determined by the laws of physics, with the outcome simply being unknown to the observer, and therefore uncertain from his/her perspective.

In many practical cases, the specific terminology used to describe the causes of deviation in a process (e.g. whether it is a risk or an uncertainty) is not particularly helpful or necessary. However, there can be cases where such distinctions can be useful, as discussed in the following.

The use of the terms "uncertainty" or "variability" (rather than "risk") may help to ensure that the frame being considered is not too narrow. In particular, it can help to avoid inadvertently (implicitly) assuming that every risk item is of an event-type or operational ("yes/no") nature; such a framework is not appropriate for many forms of general variation, as discussed earlier in the text. Especially where a set of risks that has initially been described qualitatively is used as a starting point for risk modelling, the use of these terms can ensure a wider focus on the true nature of the items. Similarly, the term "risk" often invokes negative connotations in natural language, whereas risk analysis makes no assumption on whether the various outcomes in a situation are good or bad; indeed, the variability under consideration may be a source of potential value creation, such as when considering the benefits that may be achievable by exploiting operational flexibilities. Thus, once again, the use of terms such as uncertainty or variability can be preferable in many cases.

In Bayesian analysis and other formal statistical settings, a distinction between uncertainty and variability can be helpful in the choice of distributions and their parameters.

In principle, in this text, we shall continue not to make a formal distinction between these terms, unless we feel it necessary in specific areas: we shall mostly use the term "risk" as a general term to cover all cases. However, sometimes we will use "risk or uncertainty" (or similar combinations of terms) to reinforce that in that particular context we are referring to the more general case, and not only to event-type or operational risks.

8.1.4 The Use of Statistical Measures

The discussion in Chapter 6 showed that distributions of outcomes arise naturally due to the effect of varying multiple inputs simultaneously. We also noted that, generally, an individual outcome within the set of outputs is simply one of many possibilities, which in most cases does not require a specific focus to be placed on it. Rather, key questions about the situation are addressed with reference to specific statistical measures of the appropriate distribution(s) of outcome(s), such as:

- The position of the "central" point(s) of the possible range of outcomes (e.g. average, mid-point, most likely).
- The spread of the possible outcome range (e.g. best and worst 10% of cases).
- The likelihood of a particular case being achieved (e.g. a base or planned case).
- The main sources of risk, and the effect and benefits of risk mitigation.

8.2 RANDOM PROCESSES AND THEIR VISUAL REPRESENTATION

The use of frequency (probability) distributions is essentially a way of summarising the full set of possible values by showing the relative likelihood (or weighting) of each.

In the following, we make reference to a simple illustrative example. We assume that the cost of a project to renovate an apartment can be described as a distribution of possible values, with a minimum value of £10,000, a most likely value of £15,000 and a maximum value of £25,000 (although it is not of particular relevance at this point, we use a PERT distribution [see Chapter 9] to reflect the weighting of each outcome within the range).

8.2.1 Density and Cumulative Forms

The distribution of cost may be expressed in a compact way using one of two core visual displays:

- As a density curve, where the *y*-value represents the relative likelihood of each particular *x*-value (see Figure 8.1). The advantage of this display is that key properties of the distribution (e.g. the mean, standard deviation and skew) can be more or less seen visually. The disadvantage is that the visual estimation, for any *x*-value, of the probability of being below or above that value is harder.
- As a cumulative curve, where the *y*-value represents the probability of being less than or equal to the corresponding *x*-value (see Figure 8.2). The advantage of this display is that the probability of being less (or more) than a particular *x*-value can be read from the *y*-axis (as can the probability of being between two values, or within a range). The

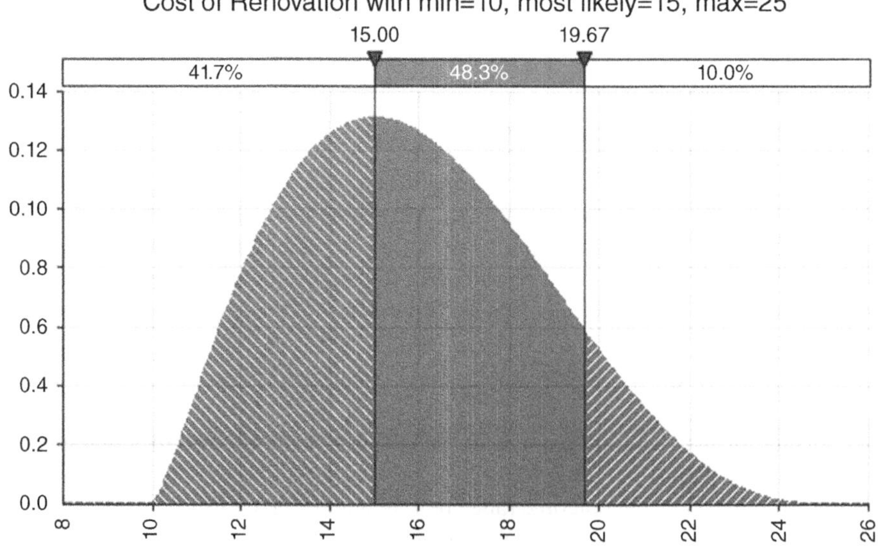

FIGURE 8.1 Example of a Probability Density Curve for a Continuous Process

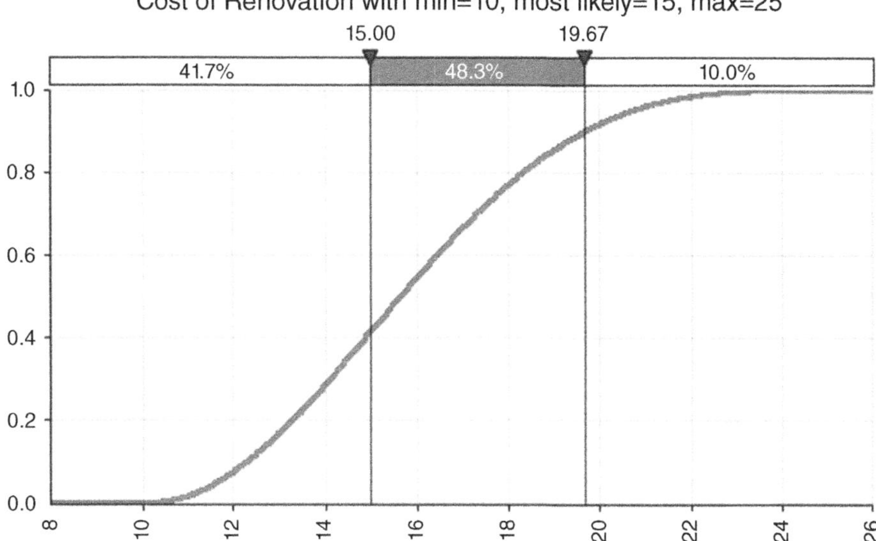

FIGURE 8.2 Example of a Cumulative Curve for a Continuous Process

disadvantage is that some potentially important properties are harder to notice without careful inspection; for example, whether the range is symmetric, or is made up of discrete scenarios.

The cumulative curve itself may also be expressed in the descending form rather than in the (traditional) ascending one, as shown in Figure 8.3.

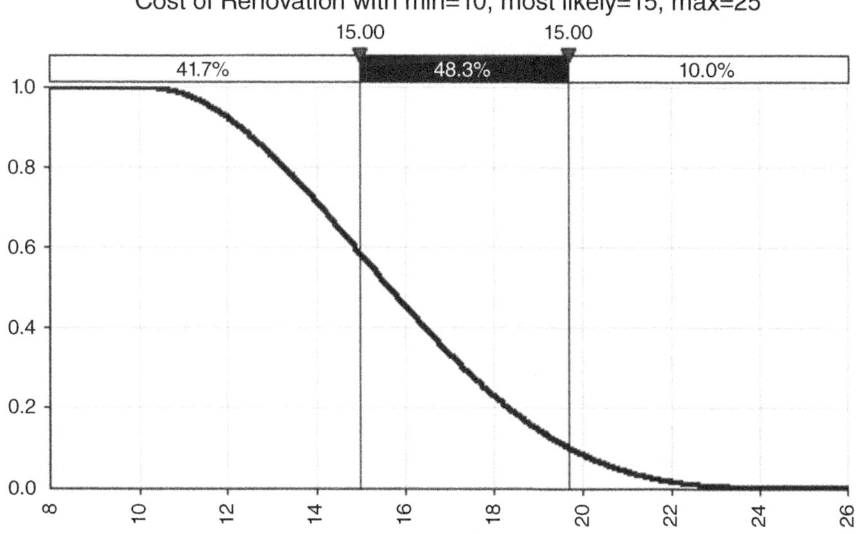

FIGURE 8.3 Example of a Descending Cumulative Curve for a Continuous Process

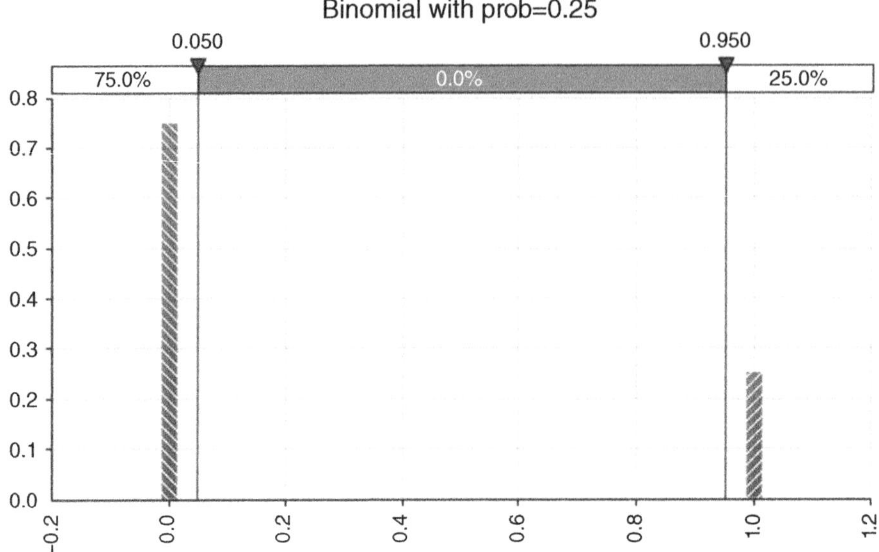

FIGURE 8.4 Example of Distribution for an Event Risk (Bernoulli or Binomial)

8.2.2 Discrete, Continuous and Compound Processes

Distributions, whether they are used for model inputs or as a result of model outputs, can broadly be classified into three categories:

- Discrete. These describe quantities that occur as separate (non-continuous) outcomes. For example:
  - The occurrence or not of an event (see Figure 8.4 for an example).
  - The number of goals in a soccer match.
  - The outcome of tossing a coin or rolling a die.
  - Where there are distinct scenarios that may arise.
- Continuous. These represent processes that can take any value within a single range. There are an infinite number of possible outcomes, although the distribution may still be bounded or unbounded on one or both sides. For example:
  - Many processes that involve money, time or space are usually thought of as continuous. Even where a quantity is not truly infinitely divisible (such as money, which has a minimum unit of one cent, for example), for practical purposes it is often perfectly adequate to assume that it is divisible (for example, one may still be able to own half of such a project). Hence, financial items such as revenues, costs, cash flows and values of a business project are usually considered as being continuous.
  - The duration of a project (or a journey) would have a bounded minimum, but the values of longer durations could be potentially unbounded. For example, although in practice one may return home if one encounters a large snow storm shortly after leaving, the underlying process associated with completing the journey irrespective of the conditions could have a very long duration in some extreme cases.

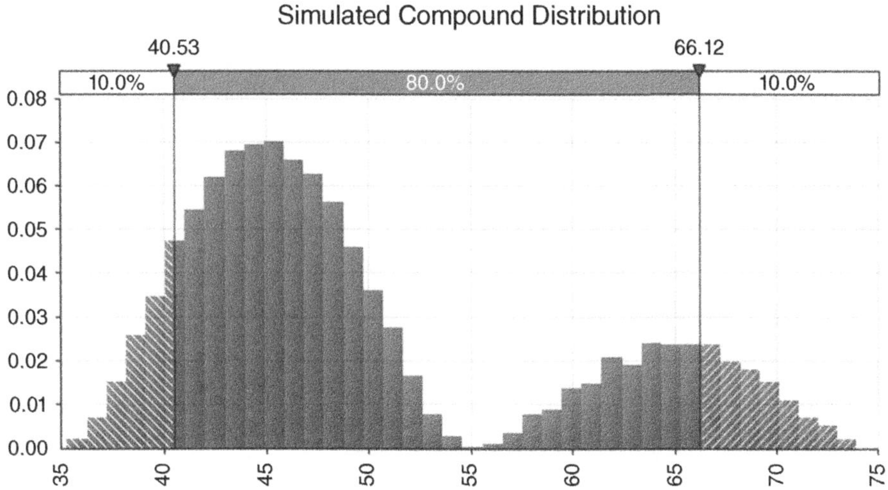

FIGURE 8.5 Example of a Compound Distribution: Density Curve

- Compound. These typically arise where there are multiple discrete scenarios that are possible, and where within one (or more) of these scenarios another process can take a continuous range (see Figures 8.5 and 8.6 for an example of the density and ascending cumulative curve). This would result in a discrete–continuous compound distribution (the second process could also be discrete, resulting in a discrete–discrete situation). For example:
  - There may be three discrete scenarios for the weather, and within each there may be a continuous range of possible travel times for a journey undertaken within each weather scenario.
  - There may be several possible macro-economic (or geo-political) contexts; within each the price of a particular commodity (such as oil) may take a range of values.
  - Very often the reality of a situation (as well as management's expression and thought processes) is that there are compound processes at work; when informally discussing the minimum, most likely and maximum values, one may, in fact, be referring to distinct cases or scenarios. It may be that each of these points is (for example) the central or most likely point of three separate discrete scenarios.

Note that the interpretation of the y-axis as the relative likelihood of each outcome is always valid. However, for a discrete distribution, this relative likelihood also represents the actual probability of occurrence, whereas for a continuous distribution, a probability can be associated only with a range of outcomes.

8.3 PERCENTILES

A percentile (sometimes called a centile) shows – for any assumed percentage – the x-value below which that percentage of outcomes lies. For example, the 10th percentile (or P10) is the value below which 10% of the outcomes lie, and the P90 would be the value below which

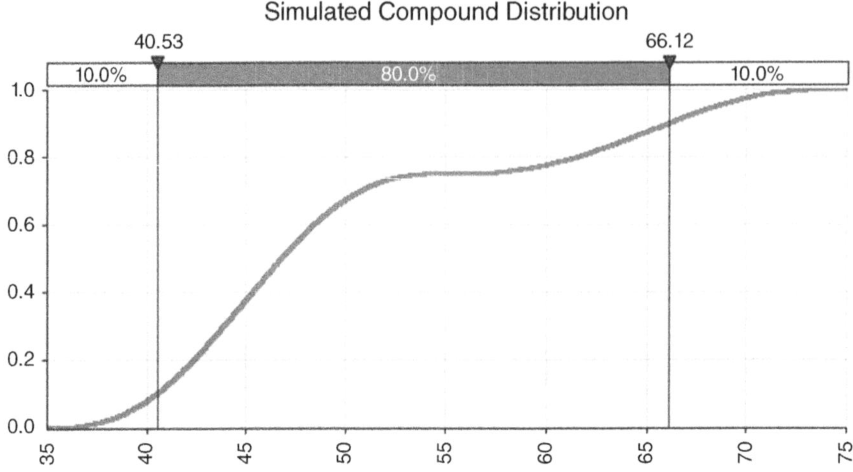

FIGURE 8.6 Example of a Compound Distribution: Cumulative Curve

90% of occurrences lie. Typical questions that are answered by percentiles of a distribution include:

- What is the probability that a particular case will be achieved (such as the base case)? The answer is found by looking for the percentile that is equal to the value of the particular case, and reading its associated probability.
- What budget is required so that the project has a 90% chance of success of being delivered within this budget?

We can see that in the illustrative example (with reference to Figure 8.1 or Figure 8.2), the value of £15,000 corresponds to (approximately) the P42, so that the budget will be less than that in approximately 42% of cases. The P90 of the project (approximately £19,670) would provide the figure corresponding to that for which the project would be delivered in 90% of cases. The difference between these (£4670) is the contingency required for a 90% chance of success.

In Excel, functions such as **PERCENTILE, PERCENTILE.INC** and **PERCENTILE.EXC** can be used to calculate percentiles of data sets, depending on the Excel version used.

8.3.1 Ascending and Descending Percentiles

The above definition is more accurately called an ascending percentile, because the value of the variable is increasing as the associated percentage increases (for example, in the simple example, the P90 is larger than the P42). Sometimes it can be more convenient to work with descending percentiles, which show – for a given assumed percentage – the value of a variable *above* which that percentage of outcomes lies. That is, the ascending P90 would be the same figure as a descending P10 (or P10D). Descending percentiles are often used when referring to a “desirable” quantity. For example, the P10D of profit would be the figure that would be exceeded in 10% of cases.

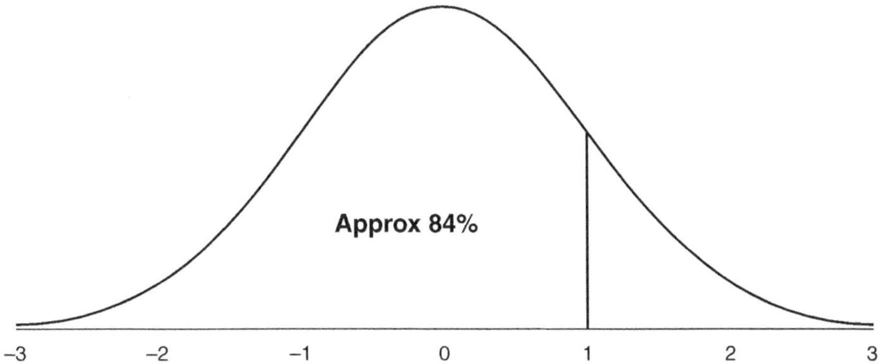

FIGURE 8.7 Standard Normal Distribution, Containing Approximately 84% of Occurrences in the Range from Infinity to One Standard Deviation Above the Mean

8.3.2 Inversion and Random Sampling

In visual terms, the mapping of a percentage figure into a percentile value (such as 10% leading to the P10) is equivalent to selecting a point on the y-axis of the cumulative distribution (10%), and reading across to meet the curve and then downwards to find the corresponding x-value. In mathematical terms, this is equivalent to the "inversion" of the cumulative distribution function. In other words, the regular (non-inverse) function provides a cumulated probability for any x-value, whereas the inverse function provides an x-value for any cumulated probability.

As an example, Figure 8.7 shows the density curve for a standard normal distribution (i.e. with a mean of zero and a standard deviation of one), for which approximately 84% of outcomes are less than the value one. Figure 8.8 shows the cumulative normal distribution, showing the inversion process, i.e. that when starting with approximately 84%, the inverted value is one.

This inversion process is of fundamental importance for the implementation of simulation methods because:

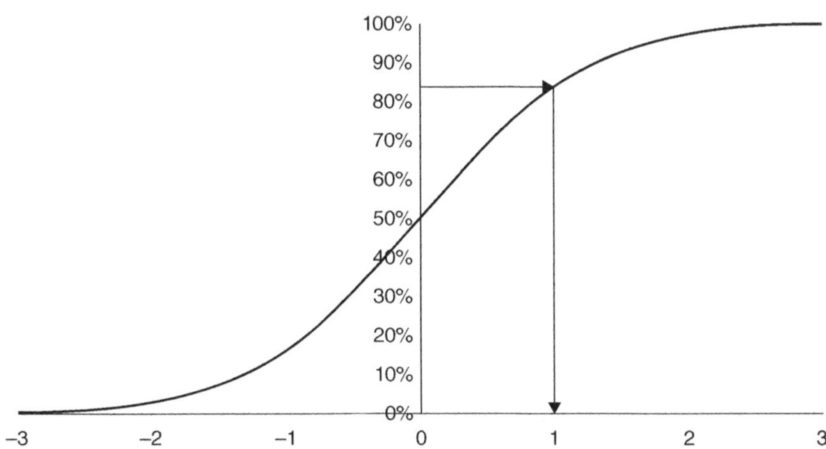

FIGURE 8.8 Inversion of the Standard Normal Distribution: Finding the Point Below which Approximately 84% of Outcomes Arise

- If the particular probability that drives the inversion is chosen randomly, the calculated percentile is a random sample from the distribution. If the probabilities are created in a repeated fashion as random samples from a uniform continuous (UC) distribution (between 0 and 1, or 0% and 100%), then the calculated percentiles form a set of random samples from the distribution. For example, samples (from the UC) for the probability between 0% and 10% will create samples between the P0 and P10 of the inverted distribution. Similarly, 10% of (UC) sample values will be between 30% and 40%, and hence 10% of inverted (percentile) values will lie between the P30 and P40 of the distribution.
- Where the distribution to be sampled (and its cumulative form) is a mathematical function described by parameters (such as a minimum, most likely or maximum), which – for any given x-value – returns a probability (P), the inverse function will be a mathematical function of the same parameters. In other words, it will – for any given probability (P) – return the x-value (percentile) corresponding to this probability, taking into account the functional form of the inversion calculation, which will depend on the parameters of the distribution. Thus, if an explicit formula can be found for the inversion process (i.e. one that takes the parameter values and a given probability value as inputs and returns the corresponding x-value as the output), then one can readily create samples from the distribution. This process is required when creating simulation models using Excel/VBA, and is discussed in detail in Chapter 10. On the other hand, when using @RISK, the sampling procedure is taken care of automatically as an in-built feature, as also discussed later.
- The quality of the UC sampling process will determine the quality of the samples for the inverted distribution (assuming that the inversion is an exact process).
- Any relationship between the processes used to sample two UC distributions will be reflected in the samples of their corresponding inverted distributions. For example, if the processes that sampled the two UC distributions were "linked", such that high values for one occurred when the other also had high values, then the percentiles of the sampled distributions would also be such that higher values would tend to occur together. In particular, for simulation methods, if the UC sampling processes are correlated, then a correlation will arise in the sampled distributions. (As discussed later, in the special cases that the uniform processes are correlated according to a rank correlation, then this same value of the rank correlation would result between the distribution samples.)

8.4 MEASURES OF THE CENTRAL POINT

This section discusses various ways to measure central outcomes within a possible range.

8.4.1 Mode

The mode is the value that occurs with highest frequency, i.e. the most likely value:

- The mode may be thought of as a "best estimate", or indeed as the value that one might "expect" to occur: to expect anything else would be to expect something that is less likely.
- The mode is not the same as the mathematical or statistical definition of "expected value", which is the mean or average.

The mode is often the value that would be chosen to be used as the base case value for a model input, especially where such values are set using judgement or expert estimates. Such a choice would often be implicit, and may be made even where no explicit consideration has been given to the subject of probability distributions. Of course, other choices of model input values may be used, but modal values to some extent represent "non-biased" choices.

Despite this, the calculation of a mode can pose challenges: for some processes, a single mode may not exist; these include the toss of a coin, or the throw of a die. More generally, in a set of real-life observations of a continuous process, typically no mode exists (generally, every value will appear exactly once, so that each is equally likely). One could try to overcome this by looking for clusters of points within the observations (in order to find the most densely packed cluster), but this could easily lead to a wrong or unstable conclusion simply depending on the placement of the points within the range, on the size of the cluster or on random variation; two random data points may be close to each other even though the true mode is in a different part of the range.

In Excel, functions such as **MODE** and **MODE.SNGL** can be used to calculate the statistic, depending on the Excel version used, and on the assumption that the data set does contain a single mode (the function returns error messages for data sets of individual distinct values, as would be expected).

8.4.2 Mean or Average

The mean (μ) of a distribution is simply its average, and is also known as:

- The weighted average, or probability weighted average. Just as the average of a data set is easy to calculate by summing up all the values and dividing by the number of points, the "weighted" average is effectively the same calculation, but in which values that are more frequent than others are mentioned explicitly only once, but at a weighting that corresponds to their frequency of occurrence; this is equivalent to using a full data set of individual values but where values are repeated a number of times, according to their frequency. Thus, for many practical purposes of communication, it is often simplest just to use the term "average", which covers all cases.
- The "expected value" ("EV"). This is a mathematical or statistical expectation, rather than a pragmatic one (which is the mode). The EV may not even be a possible outcome of discrete processes (e.g. the EV for a die roll is 3.5, and in practice a coin will not land on its side). However, for processes that are continuous in a single range, the average will be within the range and will be a valid possibility.
- The "centre of gravity". The mean is the x-value at which the distribution balances if considered visually; this can be a useful way to estimate the mean, when a visual display for a distribution is available.

From a mathematical viewpoint, the definition is therefore:

$$\mu = \sum p_i x_i = E(x)$$

where the ps are the relative probability for the corresponding x-values, and E denotes the mathematical expectation. This formula applies for a discrete process; for a continuous one, the summation would be replaced by an integral.

In economics and finance, the mean is a key reference point (especially when analysing the outputs of models); it plays a fundamental role in the definition of "value" in processes whose payoff is uncertain. It is the payoff that would be achieved from a large portfolio of similar (but independent) projects, as some would perform well whilst others would not, with the aggregate result being the average (or very close to it depending on the number of projects). Similarly, it represents the payoff if many similar independent projects were conducted repeatedly in time, rather than in a large portfolio at a single point in time. For a single project that could be shared or diversified (i.e. by owning only a small fraction of any project), in a portfolio of many such projects, the outcome that would arise would be (very close to) the average. Specific examples of the role of the mean in economics and finance include:

- The economic value of a game that has two equally likely payoffs of zero or 10 is usually regarded as being equal to five.
- In corporate finance, the net present value of a series of cash flows is the mean (average) of the discounted cash flows, with the discount rate used to reflect both the risk and timing of the cash flows when using the Capital Asset Pricing Model.
- In the valuation of options and derivatives, the value of an instrument is the mean (average) of its payoff after appropriate (usually risk-free) discounting.

Underlying the use of the mean (average) in economics and finance is the implicit assumption of the "linearity" of financial quantities: in simple terms, that two extra dollars are worth twice as much as one, and that the loss of a dollar on one occasion is offset if one is gained shortly thereafter.

The mean is therefore typically not relevant when the variable under consideration is not of a linear nature in terms of its true consequence: i.e. where a deviation in one direction does not offset a deviation in the other. For this reason, the mean (average) is often not so relevant in many non-financial contexts, for example:

- When regularly undertaking a train journey, arriving early on some days will not generally compensate for being late on others. Similarly, arriving on time for work on average might be inappropriate if there is an important coordination meeting at the start of each day.
- If a food product contains low levels of toxins that are safe on average, it is nevertheless important for any individual sample to also be within safety limits, and not that some have levels well below the safety threshold and a few have levels that are above it. Similar remarks can be made in general about many quality control or safety situations.

In terms of modelling, where a model's logic is linear and additive (such as the simple example discussed in Chapter 6), if the input values are set at their average values, then the output value shown will directly be the true average of the output: in other words, there would be no need to run a simulation in order to find the average. The average is also easy to measure from a set of data. Thus, when building static models, the setting of model inputs to be their average values is often considered. However, such a choice may not be suitable in many cases:

- Average (mean) values may not be valid outcomes of the input process, especially for discrete ones (and hence inappropriate to use). Examples include "yes/no" event-risk processes (such as whether there will be oil in a prospect), or the roll of a die (where the average is 3.5). Similarly, a model that contains **IF** or lookup functions may return errors or misleading figures if invalid values are used, such as if integer inputs are required.

- Average values will often not be equal to the most likely ones, and hence may be regarded as inappropriate. Especially in group processes (or multi-stage "sign-off" processes) this can result in a circular process happening in which one cycles between mean and most likely values (from one meeting to the next), with resulting confusion!
- Where a model has a non-linearity in its logic (e.g. it uses **IF**, **MAX** or **MIN** functions), then the value shown for the output when the inputs are their average values will not generally be the same as the true average; generally, one would have to rely on the results of a simulation to know what the average was. (Thus, generally speaking, the mean value of the output of a financial model may only be able to be calculated (estimated) using simulation techniques.)

In Excel, functions such as **AVERAGE** and **SUMPRODUCT** are most relevant to calculating the mean of a data set. In some cases, such as using **SUM** and **COUNT**, other functions may be useful, as may **AVERAGEIFS**, **SUMIFS** or **COUNTIFS** if one is working with categories or subsets of a full list.

8.4.3 Median

The median is simply the 50th percentile point (P50); that is, the value at which half of the possible outcomes are below and half are above it. It can measure the "central view" in situations where large or extreme values are (believed or required to be) of no more significance than less extreme ones. For example:

- To measure the "typical" income of individuals, when a government is considering how to define poverty, or is setting income thresholds for other policy purposes. If one used the average income level, then the reference figure would be increased by the data of individuals with very large incomes. Thus, a reasonably well-off person (who has an income larger than most but less than this "distorted" average) would be considered as having a "below average" income; in other words, a more appropriate measure may be one that is of a relative nature.
- To measure the "average person's" opinion about some topic, such as a political matter.

In Excel, either the **PERCENTILE**-type functions or the **MEDIAN** function can be used to calculate the statistic, depending on the Excel version used.

8.4.4 Comparisons of Mode, Mean and Median

The above statistical measures of the central points of a distribution are identical in some special cases (i.e. for processes that are symmetric and have a single modal value, such as the normal distribution). However, there are a number of potential differences between them:

- In the case of non-symmetric processes, the values may be different to each other. For example, in the hypothesised distribution of costs used earlier, the modal value is £15,000, whereas the median and means are approximately £15,637 and £15,833, respectively; these latter two values are shown in Figure 8.9 by means of the two delimiter lines.

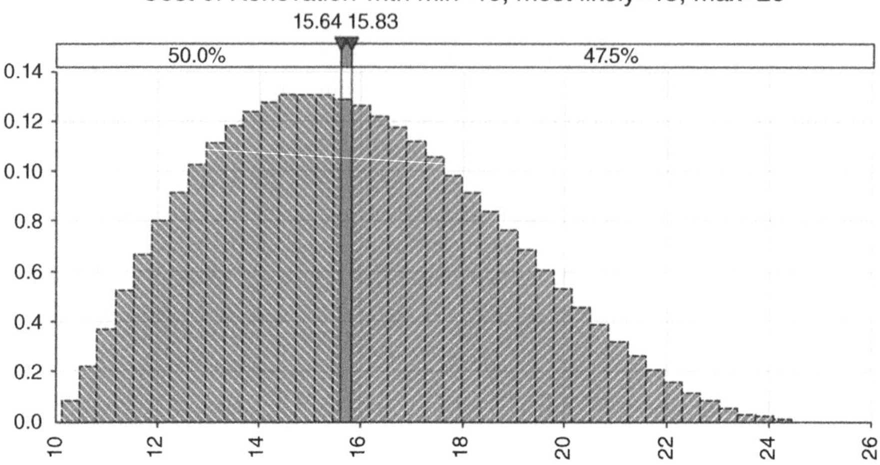

FIGURE 8.9 Hypothesised Input Distribution for Cost Example

- For discrete distributions, the median and mean may not represent outcomes that can actually occur (e.g. the toss of a coin or roll of a die). However, the mode (even if there are several) is always a valid outcome, as it is the most likely one.
- Whereas independent processes have the (additive) property that the sum of their means is the same as the mean of the sum of the processes (so simulation is not required in order to know the mean of the sum), this does not hold for modal and median values (unless they happen to be equal to mean values due to symmetry or other reasons). Thus, there is generally no "alignment" between the input case used and the output case shown, when modal or median (or indeed most other) input cases are used as inputs even in a simple additive model. The modal (most likely) case is especially important because it may correspond to a model's base case.

8.5 MEASURES OF RANGE

It is clear that measuring risk is very closely related to measuring the extent of variability, or the size of a range. In this section, we discuss a number of possible such measures.

8.5.1 Worst and Best Cases, and Difference between Percentiles

The worst and best cases are essentially the 0th and 100th percentiles. In general, the occurrence of either is highly unlikely, and so not likely to be observed. For example, some ranges may be unbounded (e.g. in the direction of large values), so that any observed (high) value is nevertheless an understatement of the true maximum, which is infinite. As discussed in Chapter 6, even for bounded ranges for individual variables, there are generally very few combinations of multiple variables that lead to extreme values when compared to the number of combinations that create values toward more central elements of a range. (The main exception is discrete distributions, where the theoretical worst and best cases may have some significant probability of occurrence, and, if these are dominant in a situation, then values closer to the extremes will typically become more likely. Similarly, if there are strong [reinforcing] dependencies between variables, values close to extreme ones are more likely to be observed.)

Thus, the worst (or best) cases, as observed either in actual situations or in simulation results, are likely to be underestimates (in their respective directions) of the true values. For this reason, it is often better to work with less extreme percentiles. Thus, the difference between two percentiles (such as the P90 and P10) can often be a useful indicator of the range of outcomes that would be observed (in 80% of cases).

Of course, these are non-standardised measures, because one still has to choose which percentiles to work with, such as P10 to P90, P5 to P95 or P25 to P75, and so on.

8.5.2 Standard Deviation

The standard deviation (σ) provides a standardised measure of the range or spread that applies to all data sets or distributions. In a sense it measures the "average" deviation around the mean. All other things being equal, a distribution with a standard deviation that is larger than another is more spread and is "more risky" in a general sense.

The standard deviation is calculated as the square root of the variance (V):

$$V(x) = \sum p_i \left(x_i - \mu\right)^2$$

and:

$$\sigma = \sqrt{V} = \sqrt{\sum p_i \left(x_i - \mu\right)^2}$$

There are several points worthy of note:

- Strictly speaking, the standard deviation measures the square root of the average of the squared distances from the mean: this is not exactly the same as the average deviation of the (non-squared) distances; the squaring procedure emphasises values that are further from the mean than does the absolute deviation.
- The standard deviation has the same unit of measurement as the quantity under consideration (e.g. dollar or monetary values, time, space, etc.), and so is often straightforward to interpret in a physical or intuitive sense; the variance does not have this property (e.g. in a monetary context, its unit would be dollar squared).
- As well as being a measure of risk, the standard deviation is one of the mathematical parameters that define the normal and lognormal distributions, the other parameter being the mean:
  - These two parameters therefore provide full information about each distribution, from which all of their properties can be determined (such as the P10 or P90, and so on).
  - These are important and frequently occurring distributions, as in many contexts it is often assumed, believed or can be demonstrated statistically (to within reasonable accuracy in many cases) that the underlying processes are distributed in this way. In such contexts (such as in financial markets), the standard deviation is often thought of as the core measure of risk, and is often called volatility.

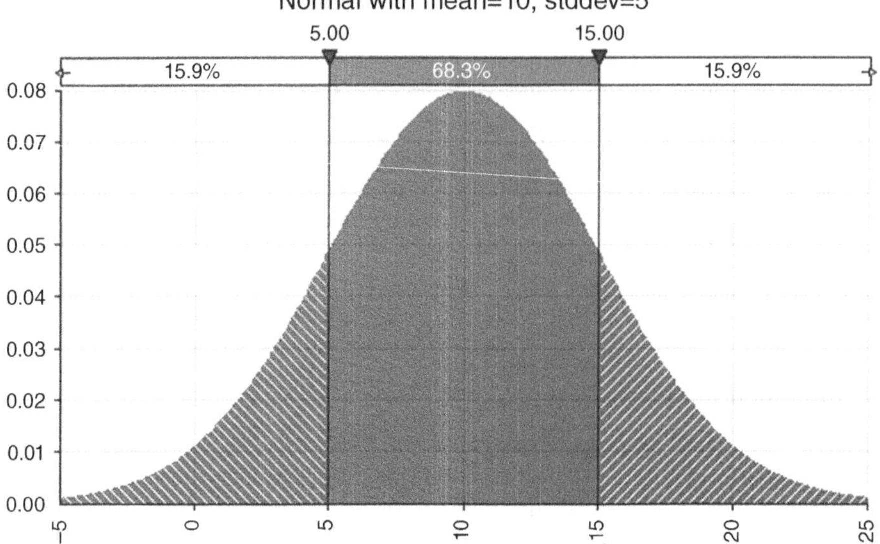

FIGURE 8.10 Normal Distribution with Average of 10 and Standard Deviation of 5; Approximately 68% of Outcomes are within the Range that is One Standard Deviation Either Side of the Mean

- A useful rule of thumb is that the one standard deviation band around either side of the mean contains about two-thirds of the outcomes. For a normal distribution, the band contains around 68.3% of the outcomes, as shown in Figure 8.10. For the cost distribution used earlier (which is a PERT, not normal distribution), Figure 8.11 shows that the one standard deviation band around the mean contains approximately 65% of the area (i.e. approximately the range from £13,069 to £18,597, as the mean is £15,833 and the standard deviation is approximately £2764); this percentage figure would alter slightly as the parameter values are changed but would typically be approximately about two-thirds. The two standard deviation band on either side of the mean contains around 95.4% of the outcomes for a normal distribution, as shown in Figure 8.12; once again this figure would be approximately the same for other single-moded continuous processes.
- This two-thirds rule of thumb applies with reasonable accuracy to continuous processes with a single mode, but not to discrete processes. For example, for the binomial distribution (representing a single possible event risk), the mean is equal to p, and the standard deviation is equal to $\sqrt{p(1-p)}$. So, when $p < 0.5$, the standard deviation is larger than the mean and hence the lower part of the band around the mean contains the entire outcome of non-occurrence (which has probability $1 - p$, which will approach 100% for small values of p); similarly for large values of p, the entire outcome of occurrence (which has probability p) will be within the upper part of the band. Figure 8.13 shows an example in which (with a probability of occurrence of 25%) the non-occurrence outcome (represented by zero) has a 75% probability and is entirely contained within the one standard deviation band around the mean, as the mean is 0.25 and the standard deviation is approximately 0.43.

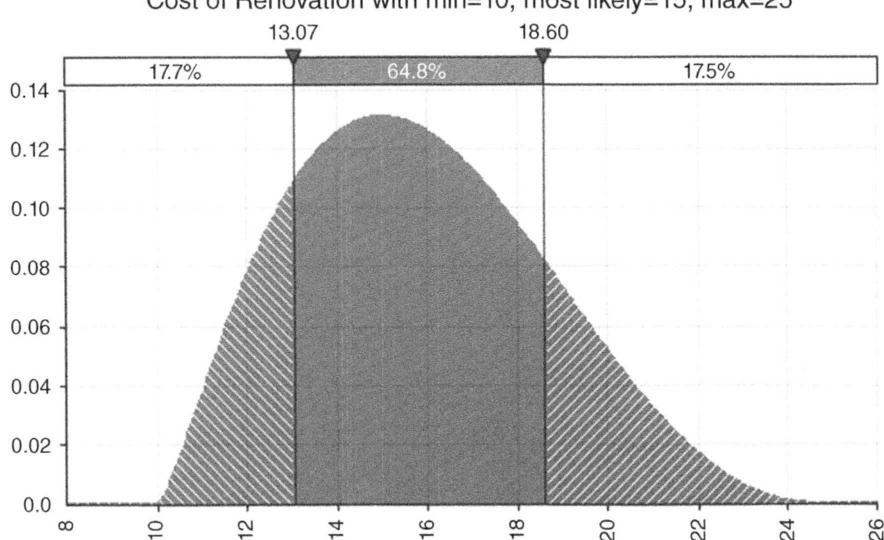

FIGURE 8.11 The One Standard Deviation Bands for the Hypothesised Cost Distribution

Note that by expanding the term in square brackets (and using the fact that $\sum_i^p = 1$), the formula for the variance can be written as:

$$V(x) = \sigma^2 = \sum\nolimits_i^p x_i^2 - \mu^2$$

or:

$$\sigma^2 = E\left(x^2\right) - (E(x))^2$$

The following observations result from this:

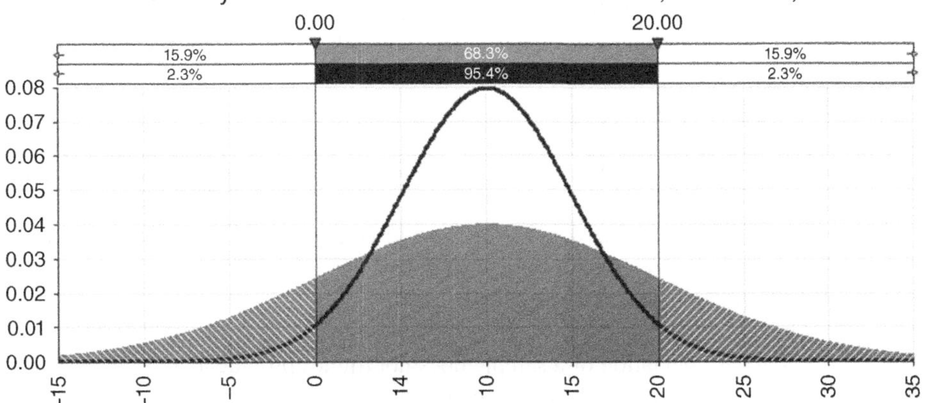

FIGURE 8.12 Comparison of Normal Distributions with Various Standard Deviations

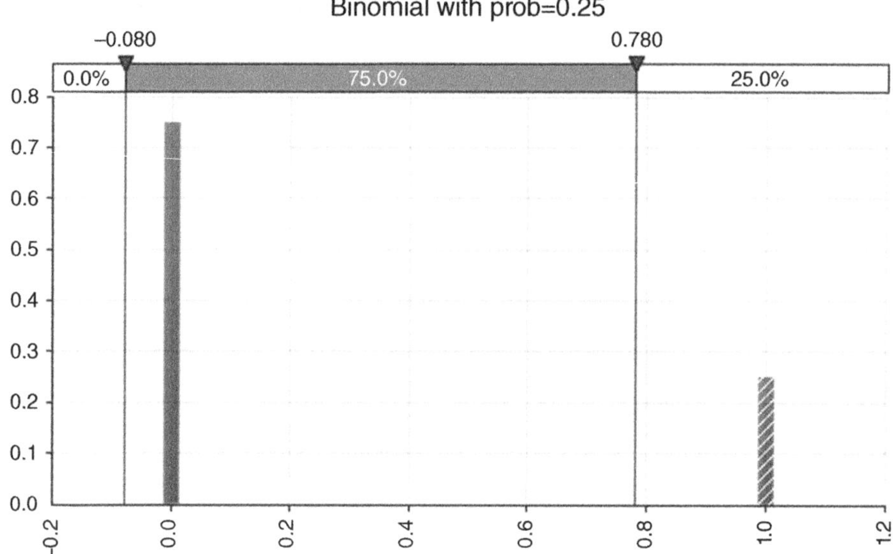

FIGURE 8.13 The One Standard Deviation for the Bernoulli (Binomial) Distribution Contains the Bar with the Larger Probability

- The formula gives a more computationally efficient way to calculate the standard deviation: fewer steps are required to square the x-values, take the average of these figures and then subtract the square of the average of the original values, than (as would be done with the original formulae) to deduct the mean from each value, square these differences and then take the average of the squared figures.
- Since the variance is a sum of squared values, it is always greater than zero (for any process with more than one outcome). Therefore, the right-hand side of the formula shows that the average value of the square of a random process is greater than the square of the average of the original process.

Note that the above formulae assume that the data represent the whole population for which the standard deviation is to be calculated. If one were dealing with only a sample (i.e. a subset) of all possible values, then one may need to address the issue as to whether the formula accurately represents the actual standard deviation of the population from which the sample was drawn. In this regard, one may state:

- Any statistical measure of the sample can be considered an estimate of that of the underlying population.
- There is a possibility that the data in the sample could have been produced by other underlying (population) processes, which each have slightly different parameters (such as slightly different means or standard deviations).

In fact, the standard deviation of a sample does not (quite) provide a "best guess" (non-biased estimate) of the population's standard deviation, and requires multiplication by a correction factor of $\sqrt{\frac{n}{n-1}}$, where n is the number of points in the sample. The application of this factor will avoid systematic underestimation of the population parameter, although its effect is really of much practical relevance only for small samples: where $n = 5$ this results in a correction of approximately 10%, which when $n = 100$, 1000 and 5000 reduces to approximately 0.5%, 0.05% and 0.01%, respectively. (Such correction factors are not required for the calculation of the average, where the sampled average is a non-biased estimate of that of the population.) In Excel (depending on the version), the functions **STDEV** or **STDEV.S** can be used to calculate the estimated population standard deviation from sample data; these functions have the correction factors automatically built in. The functions **STDEVP** and **STDEV.P** can be used to calculate the population standard deviation from the full population data. Note that the @RISK statistics functions for simulation outputs (e.g. **RiskStdDev**) do not have these correction factors built in, so samples are treated as if they were the full population.

Even after the application of appropriate correction factors, one is, in fact, provided with a non-biased estimate of the value of the population's parameter. However, since (slightly different) parameters could have nevertheless produced the same sample, this figure provides only an estimate of the central (average) value of this parameter, and its true possible values could be different. Typically, if desired, one can measure a confidence interval in which the parameter lies (with the interval being wider if one needs to have more confidence). Of course, as the sample size increases, the required width of the confidence interval (for any desired level of confidence, such as 95%) decreases, so that this issue becomes less important for large sample sizes. This topic is explored further in Chapter 9 in order to retain here a focus on the core principles.

8.6 SKEWNESS AND NON-SYMMETRY

Skewness (or skew) is a measure of the non-symmetry (or asymmetry), defined as:

$$\text{Coefficient of skewness} = \frac{\sum_i^p (x_i - \mu)^3}{\sigma^3}$$

The numerator represents the average of the "cube of the distance from the mean", and the denominator is the cube of the standard deviation, so that the skewness is a non-dimensional quantity (i.e. a numerical value with a unit such as dollars, time or space). As for the calculation of standard deviation, a sample will underestimate the skewness of the population, so that the above formula would be multiplied by $\frac{n^2}{(n-1)(n-2)}$ in order to give a non-biased estimate of the population's skewness parameter, with the standard deviation figure used as the estimate of that of the population, i.e. the non-biased corrected figure calculated from the sample. In Excel, the **SKEW** function has this correction factor built in; later versions include the **SKEW.P** function, which does not have the correction factor, and so can be used for population data.

Although there are some general rules of thumb to interpret skew, a precise and general interpretation is difficult because there can be exceptions in some cases. General principles include:

- A symmetric distribution will have a skewness of zero. This is always true, as each value that is larger than the mean will have an exactly offsetting value below the mean; their

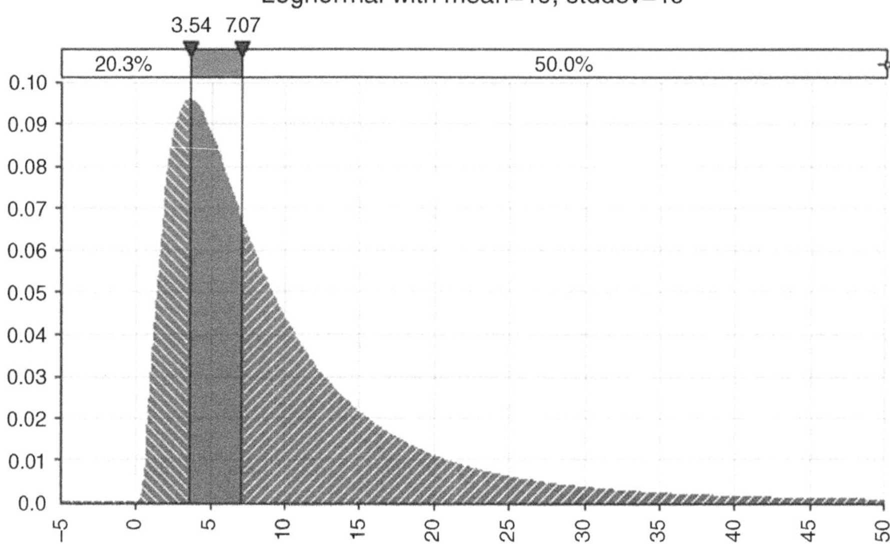

FIGURE 8.14 Example of a Lognormal Distribution

deviations around the mean will cancel out when raised to any odd power, such as when cubing them.

- A positive skew indicates that the tail is to the right-hand side. Broadly speaking, when the skew is above about 0.3, the non-symmetry of the distribution is visually evident.

Figure 8.14 shows an example of a lognormal distribution with a mean and standard deviation of 10, a mode of approximately 3.54, a median of approximately 7.07 and a coefficient of skewness of 4.0.

On the other hand, in special cases, the properties of distributions and their relationship to skew may not be as one might expect:

- A zero skew will not necessarily imply symmetry; some special cases of non-symmetric distributions will have zero skew, as shown by the example in Figure 8.15.
- For positively skewed distributions, typically the mean is larger than the median, which itself is typically larger than the mode: intuitively, the mean would be larger than the median (P50 point), because the 50% of outcomes that are to the right of the median are typically more to the right of the median than are the corresponding points to the left. However, this ordering of the mode, median and mean values does not hold for all distributions:
  - Figure 8.16 shows an example of a positively skewed distribution in which the mean (approximately 1.64) is less than the mode (2.0).
  - Figure 8.17 shows an example of a positively skewed distribution where the modal, median and mean values are all identical (and equal to zero).

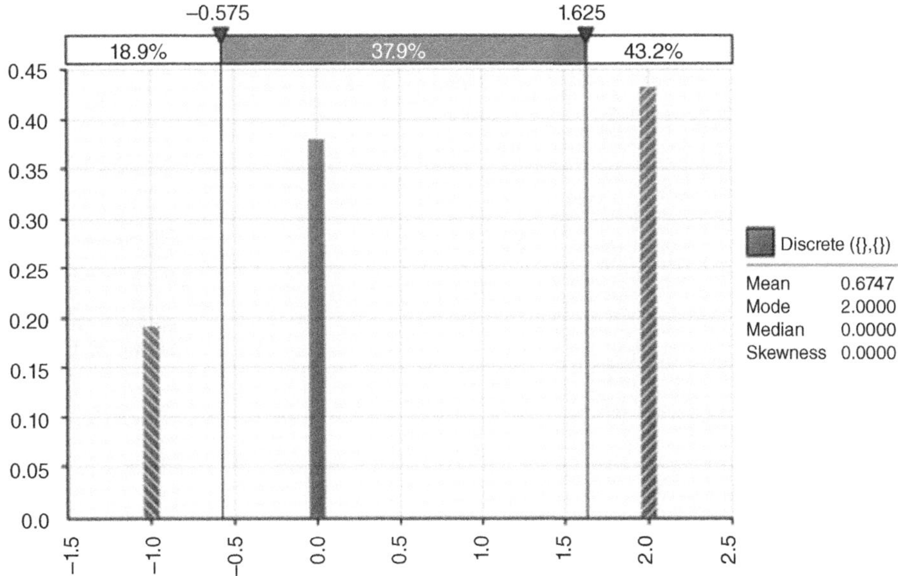

FIGURE 8.15 A Special Case of a Distribution with Zero Skewness

8.6.1 The Effect and Importance of Non-Symmetry

Although the issue of non-symmetry is not precisely identical to that of skewness, or to that of whether a distribution has the same modal and mean values, in most practical applications there will be a very close relationship between these topics (the counter-examples shown

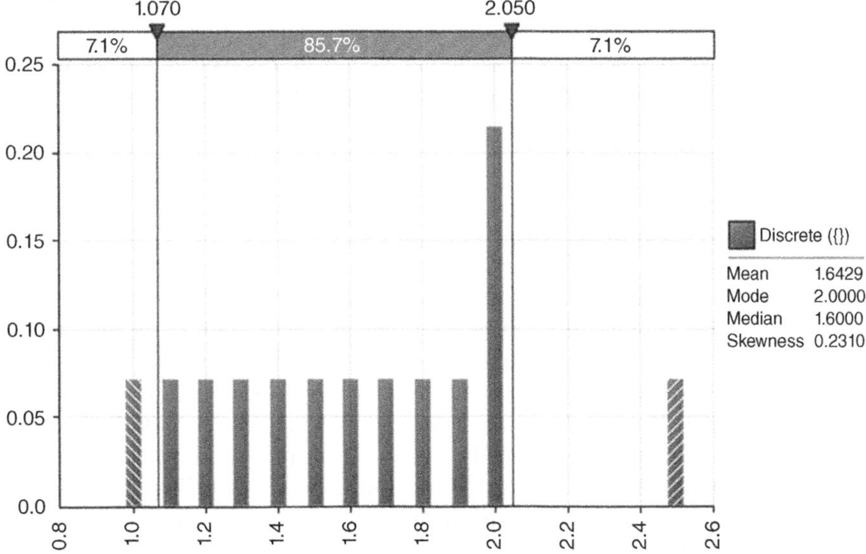

FIGURE 8.16 A Special Case of a Positively Skewed Distribution Whose Mean is Less than its Mode

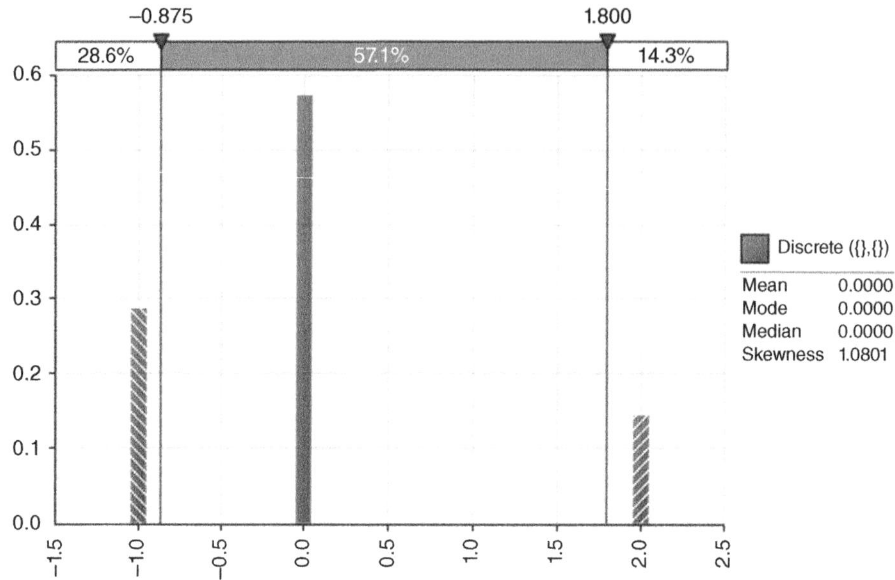

FIGURE 8.17 A Special Case of a Positively Skewed Distribution with Identical Mean, Median and Mode

to demonstrate possible exceptions were specially constructed in a rather artificial manner, using discrete distributions). Thus, non-symmetry is a loose proxy for situations in which the mode and mean values are different to each other (and also generally different to the median).

In practice, as mentioned earlier, where the modal and mean (and median) values of an input distribution are not equal, then even for simple linear additive models, the output case shown in the base case may not correspond to the input case. For example, if the inputs are set at their most likely values, then the output calculation will often not show the true most likely value of the output. Thus, a simulation technique may be required even to assess which outcome the base case is showing.

8.6.2 Sources of Non-Symmetry

There are a number of areas where non-symmetry can arise. For the discussion of these, it is important to bear in mind that, in general, model inputs could typically be further broken down so that they become outputs of more detailed calculations (i.e. of explicitly modelled processes). For example, an initial assumption about the level of sales could be broken down into volume and unit price assumptions, and the volume further broken down into volume by product or by month, and so on. In practice, however, this process of "backward derivation" cannot continue forever, and is chosen (usually implicitly) to stop at some appropriate point at which model inputs become represented either as numbers or as distributions (even where there is a more fundamental nature that is not explicitly captured).

Some of the key reasons for the existence of non-symmetric processes in practice include:

- Multiplicative processes. Generically speaking, multiplying two small positive numbers together will give a small number, whereas multiplying two large numbers together will give a very large number. As a practical example, the cost of a particular type of item within a budget could be that of the product of the (uncertain) number of units with the (uncertain) price per unit. However, where such a cost type is a direct model input (rather than being explicitly calculated), a non-symmetric process may be used as a proxy. This is discussed in more detail in Chapter 9 especially in relation to the lognormal distribution.
- The presence of event risks (or some other discrete processes). When used as a model input, an event risk may create non-symmetry in the output. On the other hand, non-symmetric continuous processes are sometimes used as model inputs, with the non-symmetry used as a proxy to implicitly capture the effect of underlying events. For example, one may use a skewed triangular process to capture the risk that the journey time (or the cost) of an item may be well above expectations.
- Non-linear processes. Processes that result from applying **IF** or **MAX** statements (amongst other examples) will usually have non-symmetry within them. For example, the event of being late for work may really be a test applied as to whether the uncertain travel time is more than that required to arrive on time. This applies also to outputs of calculations, but non-symmetric inputs can be a proxy for non-explicitly modelled non-linearities.
- Small sample sizes. Where one aims to estimate a probability of occurrence from small sample sizes of actual data, there is, in fact, typically a range of possible values for such a probability. For example, if one has observed five occurrences in 20 trials, then one may consider the probability to be 25% (or 5/20). However, any probability between 0% and 100% (exclusive) could have produced the five outcomes, with 25% being the most likely value. As discussed in Chapter 9, the true distribution of possible values for the true probability is, in fact, a beta distribution, which, in this example, would have a mean value of around 27% (3/12).
- Optimism bias. This is one of several biases that can occur in practice (see Chapter 1). Such biases are not, in fact, a source of non-symmetry of the underlying distribution, but rather reflect the place of the chosen (base) case within it. For example, a journey may have a duration that is 20 minutes on average and with a standard deviation of 5 minutes. However, if one makes an assumption (for base case planning purposes) that the journey will be undertaken in 18 minutes, then the nature of the journey does not change as a result of this assumption; rather, the likelihood of achieving the base plan is affected.

8.7 OTHER MEASURES OF RISK

The above ways to describe and measure risk are usually sufficient for most business contexts. In some specific circumstances, notably in financial markets and insurance, additional measures are often referred to. Some of these are briefly discussed in this section.

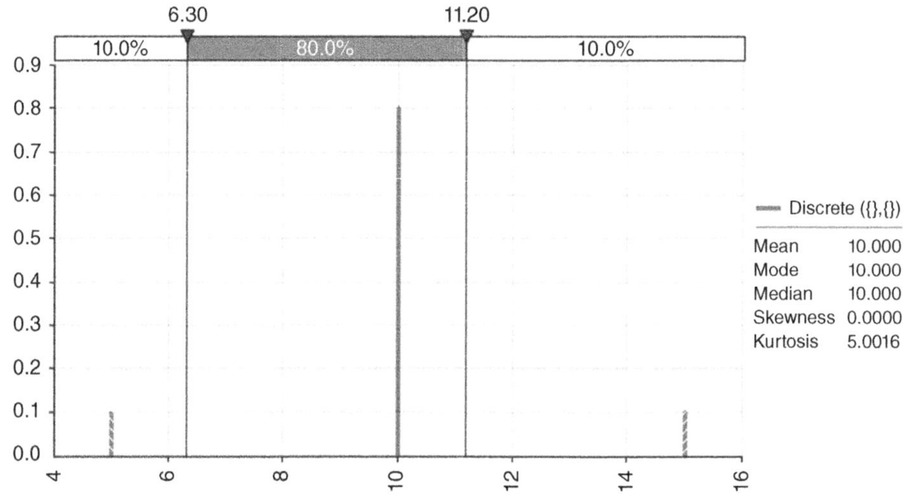

FIGURE 8.18 The Kurtosis of a Discrete Process may Decrease as Tail Events Become Less Likely

8.7.1 Kurtosis

Kurtosis is calculated as the average fourth power of the distances from the mean (divided by the fourth power of the standard deviation, resulting in a non-dimensional quantity):

$$\text{Kurtosis} = \frac{\sum_i^p (x_i - \mu)^4}{\sigma^4}$$

A normal distribution has a kurtosis of three. Distributions are known as mesokurtic, leptokurtic or platykurtic, depending on whether their kurtosis is equal to, greater than or less than three.

The Excel **KURT** function (and some other pre-built calculations) deducts three from the standard calculation in order to show only "excess" kurtosis (whereas in @RISK, the stated kurtosis is the raw figure):

$$\text{Excess kurtosis} = \frac{\sum_i^p (x_i - \mu)^4}{\sigma^4} - 3$$

As for the standard deviation and the skewness, corrections are available to estimate population kurtosis from a sample kurtosis in a non-biased way; however, these are not built into the Excel formulae (or into @RISK) at the time of writing.

Kurtosis can be difficult to interpret, but in a sense provides a test of the extent to which a distribution is peaked in the central area, whilst simultaneously having relatively fat tails. One situation in which the kurtosis is high is in the presence of discrete or event risks, particularly where the probability of occurrence is low but the impact is large (relative to other items). Figure 8.18 shows a discrete distribution with a central value that has 80% probability, and two tail events each having 10% probability; the total kurtosis is five. The kurtosis would

Data	Squared deviation		
1	9		
2	4		
3	1		
4	0		
5	0		
6	0		
7	0		
Mean	Sum()	Count>0	Semi-dev Calc
4	14.00	3	2.160

FIGURE 8.19 Simple Example of the Calculation of the Semi-Deviation of a Data Set

increase if the probability of the tail events were reduced (with the residual probability being added to the central value's probability); hence, the use of kurtosis to measure "tail risk" is not straightforward to interpret in practice.

8.7.2 Semi-Deviation

The semi-deviation is a measure of average deviation from the mean, but in which only those data points that represent adverse outcomes (relative to the mean) are included in the calculation (i.e. it represents "undesirable" deviation from the mean). For example, the semi-deviation of a distribution of profit would include only those outcomes that are below the mean; for a cost, it would count only those points above the mean.

For example, for the data set {1,2,3,4,5,6,7}, whose average is 4, assuming that larger values are undesirable, the semi-deviation would be calculated by considering only points 5, 6 and 7. The sum of the squared deviations (from 4) of these points is 14 (i.e. 1 + 4 + 9). So the average squared deviation of these points is 14/3, and the semi-deviation is the square root of this, i.e. approximately 2.16; see Figure 8.19.

At the time of writing, there is no Excel (or @RISK) function to directly calculate the semi-deviation of a data set. In this context, a VBA user-defined function can avoid having to explicitly create tables of calculation formulae in the Excel sheet, and allows a direct reference from the data set to the associated statistic.

For readers who intend to implement simulation techniques using Excel/VBA, user-defined functions are generally important; they allow flexible ways to create distribution samples and to correlate them (see Chapters 10 and 11). An introduction to basic aspects of the implementation of user-defined functions is given in Chapter 12. Here, we simply provide code that would calculate the semi-deviation of a data set, including the possibility of using an optional argument (iType) to define whether it is the values below or above the mean that one wishes to use for the measurement.

```
Function MRSemiDev(Data, Optional iType As Integer)
'Semi-deviation of items
'iType is an optional argument
'iType =1 is semi-deviation below the mean, and is the default
```

```
'iType =2 is semi-deviation above the mean
Dim n As Long, ncount As Long, i As Long
Dim sum As Single, mean As Single
ncount = 0
mean = 0
sum = 0
n = Data.Count
mean = Application.WorksheetFunction.Average(Data)
'Determine which form of function to use
 If IsMissing(iType) Then
  iType = 1
  Else
  iType = iType
 End If
'Calculate semi-deviation
If iType = 1 Then
 For i = 1 To n
  If Data(i) < mean Then
  ncount = ncount + 1
  sum = sum + (Data(i) - mean) ^ 2
  Else
  End If
 Next i
Else
 For i = 1 To n
  If Data(i) > mean Then
  ncount = ncount + 1
  sum = sum + (Data(i) - mean) ^ 2
  Else
  End If
  Next i
End If
MRSemiDev = Sqr(sum / ncount)
End Function
```

8.7.3 Tail Losses, Expected Tail Losses and Value-at-Risk

In a sense, the standard deviation represents all deviation, and the semi-deviation only the undesirable deviation. A related idea is to consider only the more extreme cases (which could be either double-sided, as for a standard deviation, or single-sided, as for a semi-deviation). Thus, a range of risk measures can be designed to reflect "realistic worst cases", for example:

- What is the loss in the worst 1% of cases?
  - The P99 of the distribution of losses (or the P1 using descending percentiles) would provide an answer to this.
  - The average loss for all cases that are above the P99 figure; this (conditional) mean or "expected tail loss" would be larger than or equal to the P99 itself.

- What is the value-at-risk (VaR)?
  - This is similar in principle to the above, but the percentage under consideration is usually converted into the corresponding number of standard deviations from the mean, rather than directly into a percentile figure; the implicit assumption is that the distribution is close to a normal one, so that each approach is effectively equivalent. Additionally, the standard deviation is used as a measure of volatility, so that the VaR is often calculated with respect to a quoted volatility. Finally, VaR is typically used as a short-term measure of risk (in percentage terms of asset price movements), so that the average would typically be low (and often ignored), with the dominant effect being that of volatility. For example, since a normal distribution has about 4.6% of the area that is more than two standard deviations from the mean (about 2.3% on each of the downside and upside), the VaR at the 2.3% level would be equal to two standard deviations in movement. Thus, for a portfolio valued at $1000, with a daily volatility of 1%, the daily VaR at the 2.3% level would be $1000*2*1%, or $20.
  - "Conditional value at risk" is a measure of the average loss when the outcome is within the tail of the distribution, i.e. the average loss when the outcome is at least as bad as the particular individual VaR point.

Note that for many practical business examples, rather than the use of the VaR, a simple statement of, say, a P95 (or other relevant percentile) is usually sufficient for the purposes at hand, even if the use of such a measure would be very close in concept to that of VaR.

8.8 MEASURING DEPENDENCIES

When implementing risk models, it is important to capture any dependency relationships between risks, their impacts and other model variables. When historic data or experience suggest a particular strength or type of dependency, it would, of course, be important for these to be captured within a model as far as possible. In this section, we provide a brief description of some core measures; many of these topics are covered in more depth in Chapter 11.

8.8.1 Joint Occurrence

At the most basic and intuitive level, dependency between risk items can be considered from the perspective of joint occurrence: risks that occur together (or do not do so) display some explicit or implicit dependence between them.

For example, if the probability of occurrence of each of two events were known, as were the frequency with which they both occur together (or both do not occur together), then one could calculate the frequency of all combinations and the conditional probabilities. Figure 8.20 shows an example of the initial data on individual probabilities and joint occurrence, and Figure 8.21 shows the completed matrix with the frequency of all combinations, derived in this simple case by simply filling in the numbers so that row and column totals add up to the applicable totals.

From the completed matrix, one can calculate the conditional probabilities, for example:

- P(B occurs given that A has occurred) = 24%/40%, i.e. 60%.
- P(B occurs given that A has not occurred) = 6%/60%, i.e. 10%.

		Not A	A
		60%	40%
Not B	70%	54%	
B	30%		

FIGURE 8.20 Initial Given Data on Probabilities

		Not A	A
		60%	40%
Not B	70%	54%	16%
B	30%	6%	24%

FIGURE 8.21 Completed Data on Probabilities

		Not A	A
		60%	40%
Not B	70%	42%	28%
B	30%	18%	12%

FIGURE 8.22 Data on Probabilities that would Apply for Independent Processes

Note that if the variables were independent, then the conditional probabilities would be the same as the underlying probabilities for each event separately (i.e. 30% probability of B whether A occurs or not), which would give the matrix shown in Figure 8.22.

Despite the apparent simplicity of this approach to considering dependencies between risks (and the use of conditional probabilities in some of the example models shown later), there are also drawbacks:

- It requires multiple parameters to define the dependency: in the above example, with only two variables, three pieces of data are required to define the dependency (the probability of each as well as that of joint occurrence). When there are several variables, the number of parameters required and the complexity of the calculations increases significantly.
- The extension of the methodology to cover the cases where the outcomes are in a continuous range, rather than having discrete values, is less intuitive.

8.8.2 Correlation Coefficients

The correlation coefficient (ρ) provides a single measure of the extent to which two processes vary together. For two data sets from the processes, X and Y, each containing the same number of points, it is calculated as:

$$\rho = \frac{\sum(x-\bar{x})(y-\bar{y})}{\sqrt{\sum(x-\bar{x})^2\sum(y-\bar{y})^2}}$$

where x and y represent the individual values of the respective data set, and $\bar{x}$ represents the average of the data set X (and similarly $\bar{y}$ is the average of the Y data set).

From the formula, we can see that:

- The correlation between any two data sets can be calculated as long as each set has the same number of points (at least one). Thus, a correlation coefficient can always be observed between any two data sets of the same size, although it may be statistically insignificant, especially if the sample sizes are small.
- The coefficient is usually expressed as a percentage, and it lies between −100% and 100%. This can be seen in a manner similar to the earlier discussion about the calculation of variance (in which the sum of the squares of numbers is at least as large as the square of the sum of those numbers, so that the denominator is at least as large as the numerator).
- Correlation refers to the idea that each variable moves relative to its own mean in a common way. By considering the numerator in the above formula, it is clear that a single value, x, and its counterpart, y, will contribute positively to the correlation calculation when the two values are either both above or both below their respective means (so that the numerator is positive, being either the product of two positive or of two negative figures). Thus, the values in one of the data sets could have a constant number added to each item, or each item could be multiplied by a constant factor, without changing the correlation coefficient. This has an important consequence when correlation methods are used to create relationships between distributions in risk models; for example, the values sampled for the Y process need not change, even as the nature of the X process is changed, and thus a correlation relationship is of a rather weak nature, and does not imply a causality relationship between the items (see Chapter 11).

From a modelling perspective, the existence of a (statistically significant) correlation coefficient does not imply any direct dependency between the items (in the sense of a directionality or causality of one to the other). Rather, the variation in each item may be driven by the value of some other variable that is itself not explicit or known, but which causes each item to vary, so that they appear to vary together. For example, the change in the market value of two oil-derived commodity or chemical products will typically show a correlation; each is largely driven by the oil price, as well as possibly having some other independent or specific variation. Similarly, the height above the seafloor of each of two boats in a harbour may largely be driven by the tidal cycle, although each height would also be driven by shorter-term aspects, such as the wind and wave pattern within the harbour. On the other hand, when a direct dependency between two items does exist, then generally speaking there will be a measured correlation coefficient that is statistically significant (there can always be exceptions, such as U-shaped relationships, but generally these are artificially created rather than frequently occurring in practical business applications).

There are, in fact, a number of ways to measure correlation coefficients. For the purposes of general risk analysis and simulation modelling, the two key methods are:

- The product or Pearson method. This uses the measure in the above formula directly. It is sometimes also called "linear" correlation.
- The rank or Spearman method (sometimes called "non-linear" correlation). In this case, the (product) correlation coefficient of transformed data sets is calculated. The transformed data sets are those in which each value in the X and Y set is replaced by sets of an integer that corresponds to the rank of each point within its own data set. The rank of a data point is simply its position if the data were sorted according to size. For example, if an x-value is the 20th largest point in the X data set, then its rank is 20.

Another measure of rank correlation is the Kendall tau coefficient; this uses the ranks of the data points, but is calculated as the number of pair rankings that are concordant (i.e. two pairs of x–y points are concordant if the difference in rank of their x-values is of the same sign as the difference in rank of their corresponding y-values). It is also more computationally intense to calculate, as each pair needs to be compared to each other pair; thus, whereas Pearson or rank correlation requires a number of calculations proportional to the number of data points, the calculations for the tau method are proportional to the square of that number. This method is generally not required for our discussion of simulation techniques (however, there is some relationship between this measure and the use of copula functions that are briefly discussed later in this text).

An example of the calculation of the Pearson and Spearman coefficients is given in the next section.

8.8.3 Correlation Matrices

Given several data sets (of the same size), one can calculate the correlation between any two of them, and show the result as a correlation matrix. It is intuitively clear (and directly visible from the formula that defines the correlation coefficient of any two data sets) that:

- The diagonal elements are equal to one (or 100%); each item is perfectly correlated with itself.
- The matrix is symmetric: the X and Y data sets have the same role and can be interchanged with each other without changing the calculated coefficient.

The file Ch8.CorrelCalcs.xlsx contains an example of the calculation of each type of coefficient, as shown in Figure 8.23. The calculation of the Spearman rank correlation first uses the **RANK** function (to calculate the rank [or ordered position] of each point within its own data set), before applying the **CORREL** function to the data set of ranks. (At the time of writing Excel does not contain a function to work out the rank correlation directly from the raw underlying data; another way to achieve this compactly is to create a VBA user-defined function directly with the intermediate set of the calculation of ranks being done "behind the scenes" in the VBA code).

	B	D	E	F	G	H	I	K	L	M	N	O	P
1													
2		Correlation Matrix of Raw Data						Correlation Matrix of Rank Data					
3			Asset 1	Asset 2	Asset 3	Asset 4			Asset 1	Asset 2	Asset 3	Asset 4	
4		Asset 1	100%	63%	62%	58%	=CORREL(E11:E210,H11:H210)	Asset 1	100%	81%	80%	80%	=CORREL(L11:L210,O11:O210)
5		Asset 2	63%	100%	73%	62%		Asset 2	81%	100%	90%	77%	
6		Asset 3	62%	73%	100%	58%		Asset 3	80%	90%	100%	78%	
7		Asset 4	58%	62%	58%	100%		Asset 4	80%	77%	78%	100%	
8													
9	DATE FIELDS		RETURNS DATA FOR THAT WEEK						RANK OF RETURNS DATA				
10	Week Number		Asset 1	Asset 2	Asset 3	Asset 4			Asset 1	Asset 2	Asset 3	Asset 4	
11	1		5.4%	2.9%	3.0%	1.2%			2	14	14	72	=RANK(H11,H11:H210,0)
12	2		-8.2%	-1.1%	-0.5%	0.6%			199	180	163	108	
13	3		-2.4%	-1.2%	-2.0%	-1.6%			189	181	194	185	
14	4		-1.0%	2.0%	3.5%	0.0%			175	32	6	144	
15	5		2.1%	1.6%	1.9%	1.7%			37	54	46	48	
16	6		0.8%	0.8%	0.6%	0.2%			103	108	125	131	
17	7		0.2%	-0.7%	-0.6%	-0.4%			136	170	167	157	
18	8		1.5%	0.3%	0.3%	2.1%			64	141	133	33	
19	9		1.2%	1.2%	1.2%	0.1%			78	86	80	132	

FIGURE 8.23 Calculation of Pearson and of Rank Correlation

Note that, for a fixed number of data points, as the data values themselves are altered, one could create infinitely many possible values for the Pearson correlation coefficient. However, for the rank correlation coefficient, as the basis for calculation is simply some combination of all the integers from one up to the number of data points, there would only be a finite number of possible values. In other words, if the value of a data point is modified anywhere in the range defined by the values of the two closest points (i.e. those that are immediately below it and above it), the rank of that point within its own data set is unaltered, and the rank correlation statistic is unchanged. This property partly explains the importance of rank correlation in simulation methods, because for any desired correlation coefficient it allows flexibility in how the points are chosen.

8.8.4 Scatter Plots (*X–Y* Charts)

In a traditional Excel model, a chart that shows (as the x-axis) the values of a model input and (on the y-axis) the values of an output as that input varies would form a line: as an input is varied individually (with all other items fixed), any other quantity in the model (such as an output) would vary in accordance with the logical structure of the model. For example, if there is a change in the production volume, then revenues may increase in proportion to that change, whereas fixed cost may be unaffected. Such a line would be horizontal if the input had no effect on the output (volume not affecting fixed cost) but would very often be a straight or perhaps curved line in many typical cases.

In a simulation model, the corresponding input–output graphs will generally be an X–Y scatter plot, rather than a line: for any particular fixed value of an input (i.e. if one were to fix the value of a particular random process or risk at one particular value), there would be a range of possible values for the model's output, driven by the variability of the other risk items. These charts can provide additional insight into the structure of a model or a situation in general.

The slope of a (traditional, least-squares) regression line that is derived from the data in a scatter plot is closely related to the correlation coefficient between the X and Y values, and the standard deviations of each:

$$\textbf{Slope} = \frac{\rho_{xy}\sigma_y}{\sigma_x}$$

Of course, the slope of a line also describes the amount by which the y-value would move if the x-value changed by one unit. Therefore, the above equation shows that if the x-value is changed by σ_x then the y-value would change by an amount equal to $\rho_{xy}\sigma_y$.

The file Ch8.ScatterPlot.xlsx contains an example with a data set of X–Y points, and the calculations of slope directly using the Excel **SLOPE** function and indirectly through the calculation of the correlation coefficients and standard deviations. A screenshot is shown in Figure 8.24.

8.8.5 Classical and Bespoke Tornado Diagrams

In relation to the above equation regarding the slope of an X–Y scatter plot, we noted that if the x-value was changed by σ_x then the y-value would change by $\rho_{xy}\sigma_y$. Thus, if the Y-variable is the output of a model, and has standard deviation σ_y, the multiplication of this by the coefficient

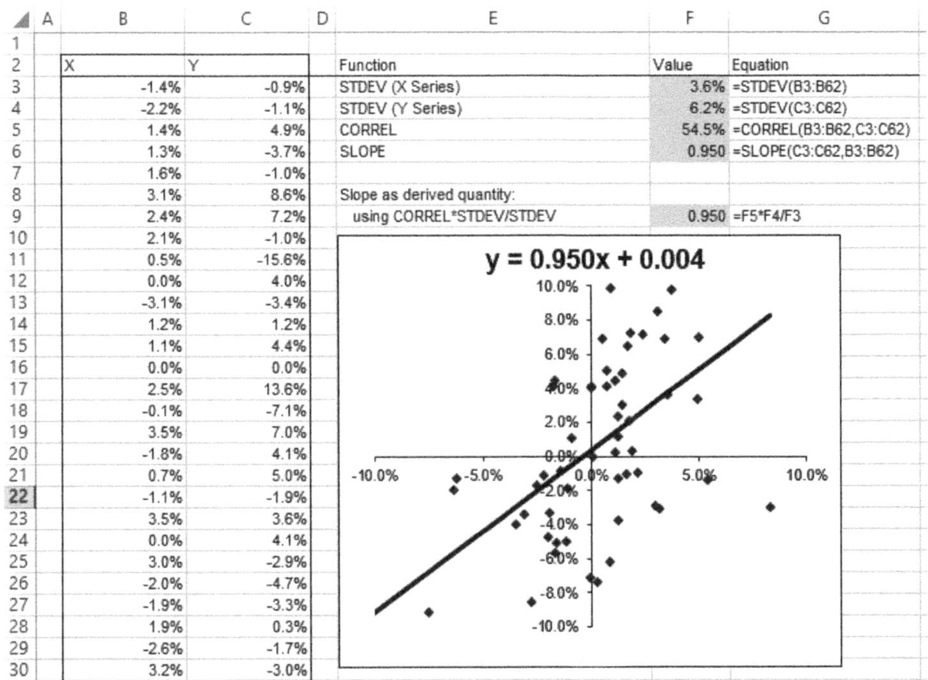

	A	B	C	D	E	F	G
1							
2		X	Y		Function	Value	Equation
3		-1.4%	-0.9%		STDEV (X Series)	3.6%	=STDEV(B3:B62)
4		-2.2%	-1.1%		STDEV (Y Series)	6.2%	=STDEV(C3:C62)
5		1.4%	4.9%		CORREL	54.5%	=CORREL(B3:B62,C3:C62)
6		1.3%	-3.7%		SLOPE	0.950	=SLOPE(C3:C62,B3:B62)
7		1.6%	-1.0%				
8		3.1%	8.6%		Slope as derived quantity:		
9		2.4%	7.2%		using CORREL*STDEV/STDEV	0.950	=F5*F4/F3
10		2.1%	-1.0%				
11		0.5%	-15.6%				
12		0.0%	4.0%				
13		-3.1%	-3.4%				
14		1.2%	1.2%				
15		1.1%	4.4%				
16		0.0%	0.0%				
17		2.5%	13.6%				
18		-0.1%	-7.1%				
19		3.5%	7.0%				
20		-1.8%	4.1%				
21		0.7%	5.0%				
22		-1.1%	-1.9%				
23		3.5%	3.6%				
24		0.0%	4.1%				
25		3.0%	-2.9%				
26		-2.0%	-4.7%				
27		-1.9%	-3.3%				
28		1.9%	0.3%				
29		-2.6%	-1.7%				
30		3.2%	-3.0%				

FIGURE 8.24 A Scatter Plot and its Associated Regression Line

of correlation with any individual input would provide the change in the Y-variable that would occur on average if the particular input was changed by its own standard deviation (σ_x).

In this sense, for each input variable, the correlation coefficient ρ_{xy} provides a (non-dimensional) measure of the extent to which the Y-variable would change as the X-variable was changed, bearing in mind that the range of change considered for each input is its own standard deviation, and thus different for each variable, with the dimensional (or equivalent absolute) values formed by taking the standard deviations (or extent of variability) into account.

Note that the presentation (in bar chart form) of either the correlation coefficients or of the scaled values is often called a "tornado diagram". This can be produced in both Excel/VBA and @RISK. However, as discussed in Chapter 7, in practice one may need to use bespoke tornado displays that show the effect of decisions, rather than the effect of risks within a specific assumed context.

CHAPTER 9

The Selection of Distributions for Use in Risk Models

This chapter describes key distributions that are required to capture the uncertainty profile of input variables in risk models. We describe their occurrence, some of their practical uses, methods to approximate one with another, as well as the topic of distribution selection.

Chapter 10 covers the specific calculation processes required to create random (percentile-value) samples from these distributions using inversion of their cumulative distribution functions, a process that is essential for those wishing to implement risk modelling using Excel/VBA. Chapter 11 covers the creation of relationships that involve dependency between distribution samples, which is relevant for users of both Excel/VBA and @RISK.

In this chapter, we describe over 20 distributions. These are generally sufficient for the large majority of practical applications in business risk modelling, and all are available in both Excel/VBA and @RISK (which also has more). Much of the subject can be adequately understood by focusing on their visual and basic statistical properties. However, some mathematics is necessary in places, in particular to be able to compare and approximate distributions, and to create inverse cumulative distribution functions when using Excel/VBA approaches.

The graphical displays in this chapter use both Excel and @RISK, and some results of simulations are shown. Most (but not all) of the calculations used to produce the figures are contained in the Excel files that accompany this text; all are simple to replicate in either Excel/VBA or @RISK (using the tools in Chapters 10 and 12, or those in Chapter 13 to perform the repeated calculations and analyse the results).

9.1 DESCRIPTIONS OF INDIVIDUAL DISTRIBUTIONS

Note that there is a distinction between a distribution function (which describes the probability of a particular value), and a value that is sampled from that distribution (which results from finding the value associated with a given probability). For example, Excel functions such as **NORM.DIST** (**NORMDIST** in versions prior to Excel 2010) provide probability values, whereas the creation of samples requires the use of inverse functions (such as **NORM.INV** or **NORMINV**).

TABLE 9.1 List of distributions covered in Chapters 9 and 10

	Continuous	Discrete
1	Uniform	
2		Bernoulli
3		Binomial
4	Triangular	
5	Normal	
6	Lognormal	
7	Beta, beta general	
8	PERT	
9		Poisson
10		Geometric
11		Negative binomial
12	Exponential	
13	Weibull	
14	Gamma	
15		General discrete
16		Integer uniform
17		Hypergeometric
18	Pareto	
19	Extreme value (max and min)	
20	Logistic, log-logistic	
21	*t* (Student), chi-squared, *F*	

This distinction is fundamental not only from a conceptual point of view, but also for the implementation of random sampling using Excel/VBA, but is often overlooked. In @RISK, a distribution function (such as **RiskNormal**) not only produces a random sample, but can also be used to calculate cumulative probability values and to display distribution functions graphically.

Table 9.1 shows the distributions that are discussed in this chapter (in the order in which they are presented). Broadly speaking, the order of presentation is chosen with the purpose of describing first the more fundamental ones, whilst reflecting that some are closely related to others, so that these should ideally be presented in close proximity to each other as far as possible.

9.1.1 The Uniform Continuous Distribution

The (general) uniform continuous distribution represents a situation in which all outcomes in a range are equally likely, with the bounds described by the minimum and maximum possible values.

The most basic case is the (standard) uniform continuous distribution, for which the minimum and maximum values are zero and one (or 0% and 100%), respectively. This is the most fundamental distribution in simulation and risk modelling, not least because samples from it are required as input into the inversion process that is generally used to generate samples of others. In particular, as already used in several places in the text, the **RAND()** function generates a sample of the distribution, which may then be used:

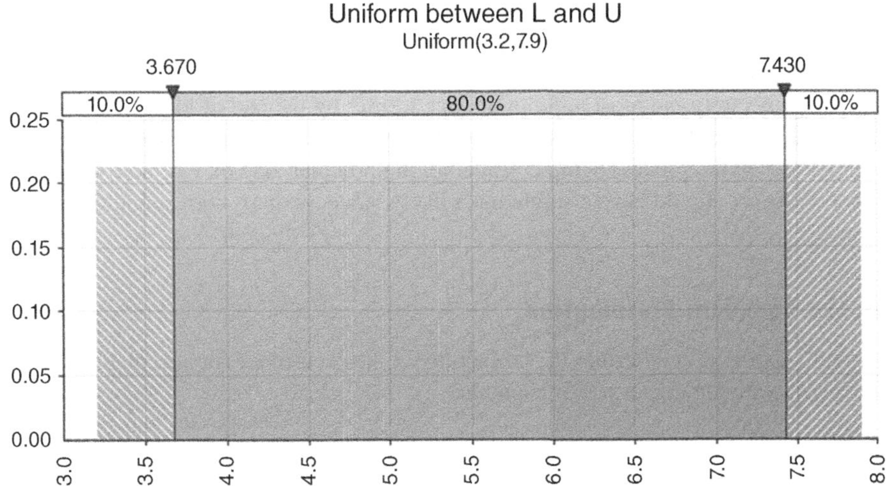

FIGURE 9.1 An Example of a Uniform Continuous Distribution

- Within an **IF** statement to generate samples for the occurrence or not of an event risk.
- To generate samples from a (general) uniform continuous distribution, by scaling (multiplying by the width of the range and adding the minimum). Note that, at the time of writing, the **RANDBETWEEN** function provides only a sample of integer values, not continuous ranges, and hence such a scaling process is necessary when working in Excel.

Figure 9.1 shows an example of the distribution, in the case that the minimum is 3.2 and the maximum is 7.9.

Beyond the creation of an input into other random sampling processes, the main use of the distribution is to capture uncertainty where there is little information, other than knowledge of fixed possible bounds:

- The position (in any particular dimension) of a specific air molecule in a room (e.g. if the doors and windows are closed and the air has been well mixed).
- The point on a car tyre where a puncture may next occur (measured in degrees between 0 and 360).
- The number of seconds past the minute at the current time (if one does not have a watch that indicates the time to this degree of accuracy).
- The length of time that one may have to wait for a train in an underground network (if one knows that trains leave precisely every 5 minutes, but one does not know when the last train left), and one has no other indicators (e.g. sound, wind) of when the next one is due to arrive.
- The position of the oil–water contact point in a potential oil exploration prospect (before further information is available, such as that which may arise through further testing or seismic studies).

The distribution is often called the "no knowledge" distribution. This term should not be used to avoid more disciplined thought and logical processes when selecting a distribution.

Although we have used the distribution fairly frequently in this text so far, those uses were in contexts that aimed to make general points about other key concepts in risk modelling, and did not make a genuine attempt to describe the specific nature of the uncertainty. In practice, the distribution is rarely the most appropriate one to use; by the use of logic and reasonable estimates (and without further research as such), it is typically readily possible to establish further properties of the process being considered. In particular, one may be able to reason as to whether a process should have a single most likely value, perhaps corresponding to a base case estimate.

9.1.2 The Bernoulli Distribution

The Bernoulli distribution describes the probability of the occurrence (or not) of an event-type ("yes/no") risk, with parameter p. For example:

- Whether a drug development process succeeds or not.
- Whether there will be commercially recoverable quantities of oil in a prospect that is being tested or drilled.
- Whether, during the course of a major renovation project on a house, asbestos will be discovered.
- Whether an employee wins a law suit about working conditions.
- The outcome of the toss of a coin.

The distribution is also used as a proxy (or pragmatic approximation) for cases where, in theory, an event could happen more than once (in a specific unit of time), but where such multiple occurrences are regarded as unlikely, with the only outcome worthy of practical consideration being an occurrence or not. For example:

- Whether – within the next 3 months – there is major industrial action, or a key employee becomes ill, or a major breakdown in the production facilities.
- Whether – within the next year – an important aspect of the regulatory environment will change (over a multi-year period, multiple aspects may change).
- Whether – within the next year – a competitor launches a major new product, with a corresponding detrimental impact on revenue (it may be unlikely that two major new products would be launched within the year; however, over a multi-year timeframe, such a possibility cannot generally be ignored).

Figure 9.2 shows an example in which the probability-of-occurrence is 30%.

In Excel, a sample of a Bernoulli distribution (which produces a 1 with frequency p, and 0 with frequency $1 - p$) can be created by using a formula such as:

$$= \mathbf{IF}\,(P \leq p, 1, 0)$$

or:

$$= \mathbf{IF}(P > 1 - p, 1, 0)$$

where P is a random sample generated using the **RAND**() function, i.e. $P =$ **RAND**().

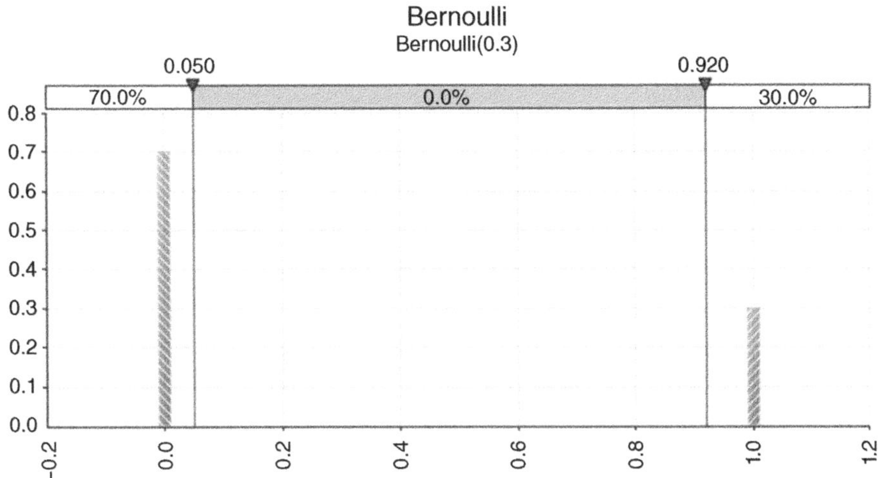

FIGURE 9.2 An Example of a Bernoulli Distribution

A Bernoulli distribution is also a special case of the binomial distribution (discussed below) and so may also be generated in that way.

9.1.3 The Binomial Distribution

The binomial distribution represents the probability for each number of possible occurrences (or successes, or failures) when a given number, n, of trials of a process are conducted, where each trial is independent and has the same probability, p. For example:

- With $n = 5$ and $p = 30\%$, the outcome would represent the probability for each possible number of discoveries of oil in a portfolio of five prospects, where each has a 30% chance of having oil present.
- When $p = 50\%$, it represents the probability for each possible number of heads (or tails) that would arise when tossing n coins.
- An important special case is where $n = 1$. In practical modelling situations, it is fairly rare that each possible event (or risk) has the same probability, so that each may need a separate distribution. This special case is called a Bernoulli distribution, which has a single parameter (p).

The density function gives the probability of i occurrences within the n trials:

$$f(i) = C(n, i)\, p^i (1 - p)^{n-i}$$

where $C(n, i)$ is the number of ways of choosing i items from n items.

The file Ch9.BinomDist.xlsx contains an example set of calculations (for $n = 5, p = 30\%$), as shown in Figure 9.3. It uses both the above formula explicitly (in which the function C is calculated using the Excel function **COMBIN**) and the direct approach (using the Excel function **BINOM.DIST**, or **BINOMDIST** in earlier versions; the cumulative probability

	A	B	C	D	E	F	G
1							
2		Trials	5				
3		Prob(Occur)	30%				
4							
5		**USING COMBIN ROUTE**					
6							
7		Occurrences	Number of Combinations		Probabilty Per Combination	**Total Probability**	
8		0	1	=COMBIN(C$2,B8)	16.8%	**16.8%**	=C8*E8
9		1	5	=COMBIN(C$2,B9)	7.2%	**36.0%**	=C9*E9
10		2	10	=COMBIN(C$2,B10)	3.1%	**30.9%**	=C10*E10
11		3	10	=COMBIN(C$2,B11)	1.3%	**13.2%**	=C11*E11
12		4	5	=COMBIN(C$2,B12)	0.6%	**2.8%**	=C12*E12
13		5	1	=COMBIN(C$2,B13)	0.2%	**0.2%**	=C13*E13
14						100.0%	=SUM(F8:F13)
15							
16		**USING DISTRIBUTION FUNCTION**					
17							
18		Occurrences	**Probabilty**				
19		0	**16.8%**	=BINOM.DIST(B19,C$2,C$3,0)			
20		1	**36.0%**	=BINOM.DIST(B20,C$2,C$3,0)			
21		2	**30.9%**	=BINOM.DIST(B21,C$2,C$3,0)			
22		3	**13.2%**	=BINOM.DIST(B22,C$2,C$3,0)			
23		4	**2.8%**	=BINOM.DIST(B23,C$2,C$3,0)			
24		5	**0.2%**	=BINOM.DIST(B24,C$2,C$3,0)			
25			100.0%	=SUM(C19:C24)			

FIGURE 9.3 Binomial Distribution Calculations in Excel

function can be calculated by switching the value of the last (optional) parameter from zero to one).

The values could be used to create a graph in Excel; alternatively @RISK's graphics capabilities could be applied directly to the **RiskBinomial** function, as shown in Figure 9.4.

9.1.4 The Triangular Distribution

The triangular distribution is a natural starting point to represent continuous uncertainty in a pragmatic way, as (unlike the uniform continuous distribution) it has a single most likely

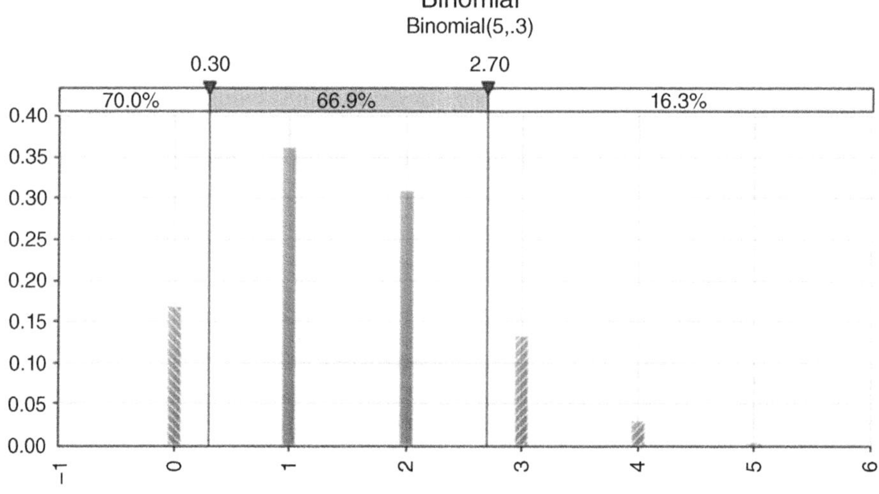

FIGURE 9.4 An Example of a Binomial Distribution

value, which may often correspond to a base case. (The parameters minimum, most likely and maximum are generally abbreviated as Min, ML and Max in the text.)

The distribution is simple in concept, and it can be useful as a communication tool, especially if one is explaining general concepts in uncertainty to those who have little experience with the subject.

In theory, the distribution arises as the sum (or difference) between two uniform continuous processes; thus, if revenue and cost were each distributed in that way, their difference (profit) would be a triangular distribution.

Even as a practical distribution, it does have some potential disadvantages:

- It will not generally fully match many real-life processes (and only be an approximation to them), since the underlying processes (such as revenue and cost) are themselves generally not distributed as uniform continuous processes.
- It is bounded on both sides, whereas many real-life processes are bounded on one side, but unbounded on the other (e.g. the travel time to work, the level of the stock market, the possible oil price, etc.).
- When the parameters are such that the distribution is highly skewed, it may overemphasise the outcomes in the direction of the skew. This is due to the straight-line nature of the function. For example, as the maximum is increased (whilst holding the minimum and most likely values fixed), the relative likelihood of the modal value must reduce (in order to keep the area under the density function at 100%); the consequence is that the probability of outcomes below the base case reduces significantly, and that of outcomes above the most likely value increases (see below for a mathematical explanation). This point is arguably the most important in many pragmatic contexts, and is one reason why a PERT distribution (see later) is often used as an alternative.

Figure 9.5 shows a triangular distribution with a minimum of 80, a most likely of 100 and a maximum of 200.

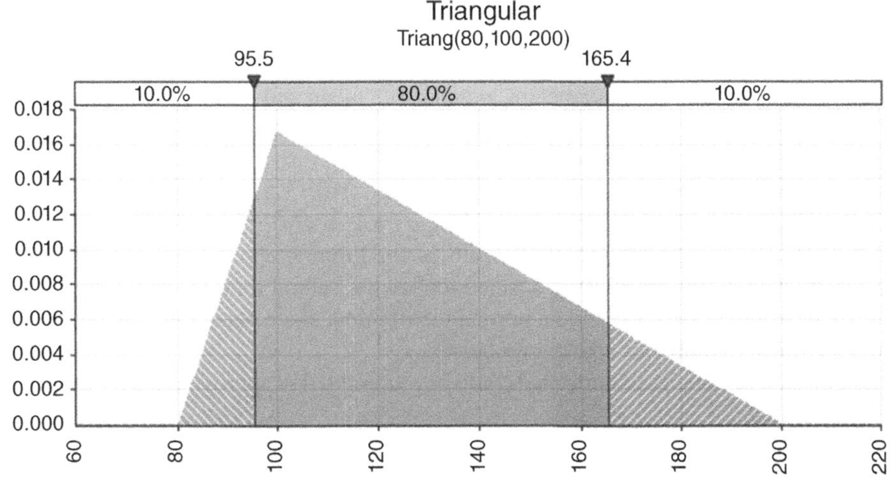

FIGURE 9.5 An Example of a Triangular Distribution

At the time of writing, there are no direct Excel functions associated with this distribution. However, since the density curve is made up of two straight-line segments on each side of the most likely value, it is easy to derive the formulae for it:

$$f(x) = \frac{2(x - \text{Min})}{D} \text{ if Min} \leq x \leq \text{ML}$$

$$f(x) = \frac{2(\text{Max} - x)}{D} \text{ if ML} \leq x \leq \text{Max}$$

where:

$$D = \frac{1}{(\text{Max} - \text{Min})(\text{ML} - \text{Min})}$$

(These are straightforward to derive if one recalls that the area of a triangle is half of the product of its base and height, and that the area under the triangle must be 100%.)

One can also establish that the cumulative probability at the most likely value (i.e. the area of the half-triangle up to that point) is:

$$P_{\text{ML}} = (\text{ML} - \text{Min}) / (\text{Max} - \text{Min})$$

From this equation, one can see that as the skewness increases (by increasing Max with other parameters fixed), the area (cumulative probability) to the left of the most likely value decreases, approaching zero when Max is very large compared to the other parameters.

Note also that the average (mean) of the distribution is calculated as the sum of the three parameters divided by three (i.e. as the simple average); this is the same as the average (mean) of a general discrete distribution that is formed with the same values and equal probabilities, but of course does not imply that the minimum and maximum values of the triangular distribution have the same likelihood as the most likely value!

9.1.5 The Normal Distribution

The normal distribution is a symmetric continuous distribution, which is unbounded on both sides, and is described by two parameters, μ and σ (its mean and standard deviation). Some basic properties and a visual display of the distribution were discussed in Chapter 8, so these specific points are not repeated here. The (standard) normal distribution is one for which the mean is zero and the standard deviation is one, denoted $N(0,1)$. The normal distribution can be shifted without changing its shape, so that $N(\mu, \sigma) = \mu + \sigma N(0,1)$.

In theoretical terms, the distribution results as the limiting case when (infinitely) many identical and independent processes are added (called the central limit theorem). In practice, the outputs of many models resemble a normal distribution, since many modelling situations contain a significant number of additive processes.

Some possible examples of items that could be represented or approximated by the normal distribution include:

- The total time spent travelling to work in the course of a year (adding up the uncertain, but essentially independent, duration of each day's journey).

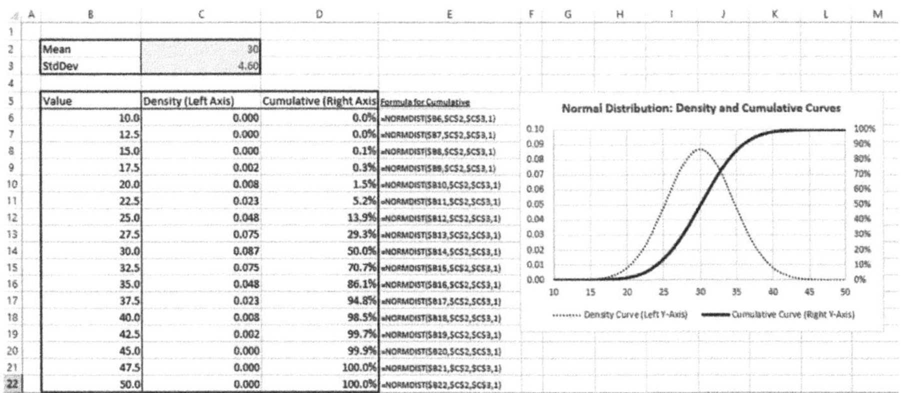

Mean	30
StdDev	4.60

Value	Density (Left Axis)	Cumulative (Right Axis	Formula for Cumulative
10.0	0.000	0.0%	=NORMDIST($B6,$C$2,$C$3,1)
12.5	0.000	0.0%	=NORMDIST($B7,$C$2,$C$3,1)
15.0	0.000	0.1%	=NORMDIST($B8,$C$2,$C$3,1)
17.5	0.002	0.3%	=NORMDIST($B9,$C$2,$C$3,1)
20.0	0.008	1.5%	=NORMDIST($B10,$C$2,$C$3,1)
22.5	0.023	5.2%	=NORMDIST($B11,$C$2,$C$3,1)
25.0	0.048	13.9%	=NORMDIST($B12,$C$2,$C$3,1)
27.5	0.075	29.3%	=NORMDIST($B13,$C$2,$C$3,1)
30.0	0.087	50.0%	=NORMDIST($B14,$C$2,$C$3,1)
32.5	0.075	70.7%	=NORMDIST($B15,$C$2,$C$3,1)
35.0	0.048	86.1%	=NORMDIST($B16,$C$2,$C$3,1)
37.5	0.023	94.8%	=NORMDIST($B17,$C$2,$C$3,1)
40.0	0.008	98.5%	=NORMDIST($B18,$C$2,$C$3,1)
42.5	0.002	99.7%	=NORMDIST($B19,$C$2,$C$3,1)
45.0	0.000	99.9%	=NORMDIST($B20,$C$2,$C$3,1)
47.5	0.000	100.0%	=NORMDIST($B21,$C$2,$C$3,1)
50.0	0.000	100.0%	=NORMDIST($B22,$C$2,$C$3,1)

FIGURE 9.6 Normal Distribution Calculations in Excel

- The electricity usage by a residential part of a town at a particular point in time during the day (adding up the amount used by each house or apartment).
- The amount of oil in the world, assuming that there are many reservoirs of approximately equal size, each containing an uncertain amount of oil.
- The discounted cash flow in a long-term forecast, consisting of summing the discounted cash flows of the individual years.

As an input to a model, it may make sense to use the normal distribution where it is believed that the input is itself the result of many similar random processes acting together in an additive manner (and where it is not efficient, or practical to model these detailed driving factors individually).

Although the normal distribution represents a variable whose value is continuous, it can be used to approximate some discrete processes where the number of possible outcomes is large (with appropriate rounding to give an integer outcome). For example, the total goals scored in a soccer season by all the teams in a league would be approximately normally distributed (as the sum of the number of goals in each game, which is itself approximately Poisson distributed, as described later).

The file Ch9.NormalDist.xlsx contains calculations of the density and cumulative curve using the Excel **NORMDIST** function; see Figure 9.6 (the corresponding function in @RISK is **RiskNormal**).

Some intuition into the drivers that cause the addition of many identical independent distributions to result in a symmetric process can be seen from the following: considering 100 possible independent events, each of probability 30%, on average 30 will occur. The actual number may be different to that of course (i.e. it could be any integer between zero and 100 inclusive); however, the possible range is, in fact, almost symmetric, as shown in Figure 9.7 (as a binomial distribution). One can begin to see that the likelihood of small deviations from either side of the average is symmetric by considering two examples:

- In order for only 29 to occur, one of the 30 occurrences would need to change to a non-occurrence, with each having a 70% probability of doing so: thus, there are 30 possible ways of doing so, each with probability 70%.

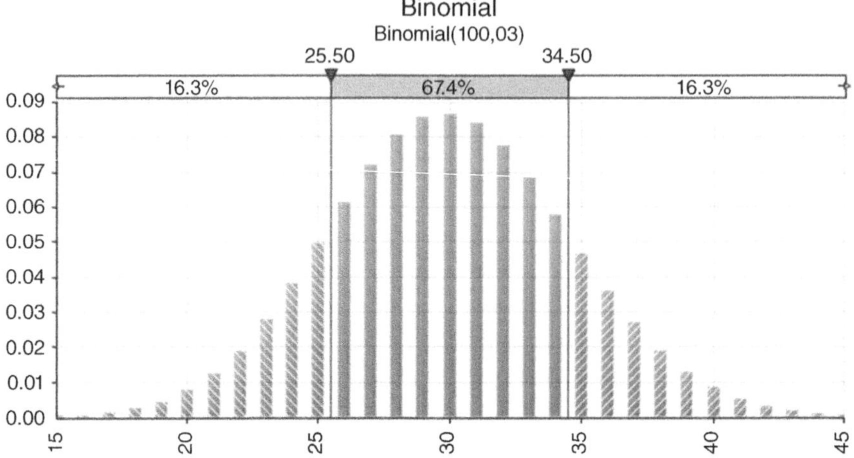

FIGURE 9.7 An Example of a Binomial Distribution for 100 Events

- In order for 31 to occur, one of the 70 non-occurrences would need to change to an occurrence, with each having 30% probability of doing so: thus, there are 70 possible ways of doing so, each with probability 30%.

Note that the non-symmetry present in the individual process affects the position of the mean (and the standard deviation), but not the symmetry of the resulting process (when the number of individual processes is sufficiently large).

Even for continuous processes, the assumption of a normal distribution is, of course, generally an approximation. For example, the distribution has a range of $-\infty$ to ∞, whereas many real-life processes cannot be negative. On the other hand, where the mean of a process is much larger than its standard deviation (e.g. four times or more) then the use of a normal distribution would result in a negative sampled value occurring only rarely (about three in 100,000 times), which is usually an acceptable approximation.

Generally speaking, all symmetric, single-moded, continuous distributions can provide a reasonable approximation to each other (providing the parameter values are chosen appropriately). For example, a normal distribution could be approximated by a triangular distribution, as shown in Figure 9.8. This approximation was derived in a purely pragmatic (visual) manner by overlaying the distribution graphs (using @RISK) and adjusting the parameters of the triangular distribution accordingly. The figure shows the case where its minimum and maximum are set to be equal to the P1 and P99 of the normal distribution.

A more rigorous approach would be to search for the required parameters of the triangular distribution so that it has the same mean and standard deviation as the normal distribution. Due to the symmetry of the normal distribution, it is clear that one would wish for the triangular distribution also to be symmetric. Thus, if we use the symbol λ to denote the half-width of the distribution (i.e. its width in each direction around the central most likely value):

$$\lambda = \text{ML} - \text{Min} = \text{Max} - \text{ML}$$

then we simply need to find the value λ so that the triangular distribution has a standard deviation of σ (and we would use $\text{ML} = \mu$ directly).

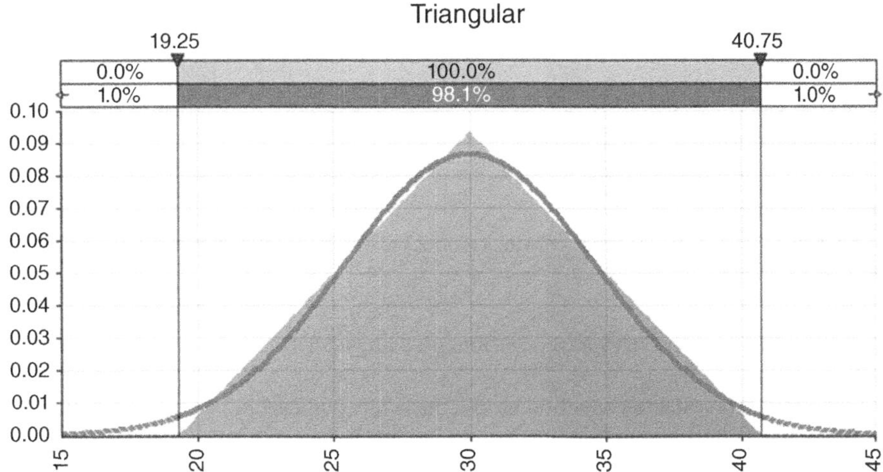

FIGURE 9.8 Overlay of a Triangular Approximating Distribution with the Underlying Normal Distribution

It is, in fact, easy to show (by manipulating the formulae for the triangular distribution) that its standard deviation can be written in terms of its half-width:

$$\text{StdDev} = \frac{\lambda}{\sqrt{6}}$$

Therefore, given a normal distribution with parameters μ and σ, the corresponding triangular distribution would be defined by:

$$\begin{aligned} \text{Min} &= \mu - \sigma\sqrt{6} \\ \text{ML} &= \mu \\ \text{Max} &= \mu + \sigma\sqrt{6} \end{aligned}$$

The resulting triangular distribution therefore has its minimum and maximum that are approximately two-and-a-half standard deviations to the side of its mean ($\sqrt{6} \approx 2.45$); these correspond to the percentiles with associated probability of approximately 0.7% and 99.3%, i.e. roughly to the P1 and P99 that were created using pragmatic visual methods.

When approximating more complex distributions with each other, a corresponding mathematical manipulation may not be possible. In such cases, the **GoalSeek** (or **Solver**) method may be used, combined with other approaches to calculating the appropriate properties of the distribution. In particular, when using @RISK, such a procedure could be implemented by using the **RiskTheo** functions, whose principles we demonstrate with the same example (but would need to be adapted for other distribution contexts):

- Enter the distribution to be approximated (i.e. the normal) as an @RISK function.
- Place the trial values for the parameters of the approximating distribution into Excel cells, and create any linkages between them that are known from the context. In the above example, there is, in fact, only the single parameter λ that is the relevant adjustable factor.

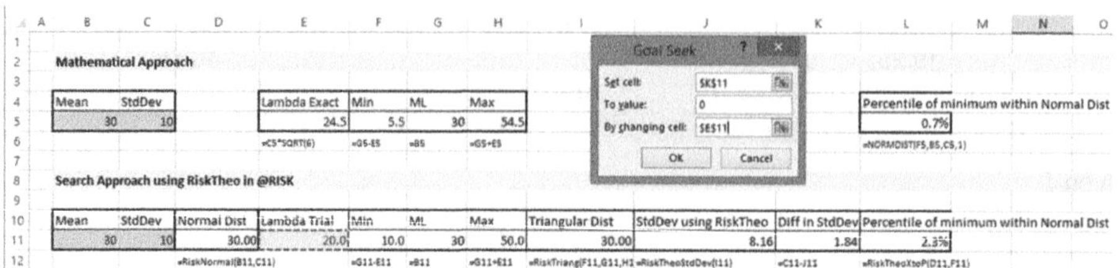

FIGURE 9.9 Calculations to Approximate a Normal with a Triangular Distribution

- Create a trial of the approximating distribution using an @RISK distribution function that references these cells.
- Use the **RiskTheoStddev** function to calculate the standard deviation of the (trial) triangular distribution (in general, one would use the required functions in this category to calculate, for both distributions, the parameters that one wishes to match).
- Use **GoalSeek** (or **Solver**) to find the value of λ that would result in the distributions having the same standard deviation (generally it is easier to calculate the difference between the two standard deviations, aiming for this to be equal to zero).

The file Ch9.NormalDist.TrigApprox.xlsx contains the implementation of each of these approaches; see Figure 9.9. The analytic procedure is implemented on row 5, whereas row 11 shows the search-based procedure. The figure shows **GoalSeek** as it is being implemented (but before the final result is derived and placed in cell E11), assuming an initial trial value of 20 is entered for the half-width in the cell E11.

9.1.6 The Lognormal Distribution

The lognormal distribution is a continuous distribution with a minimum of zero and which is unbounded in the positive direction (as a result, it is positively symmetric). It is described by two parameters, its mean and standard deviation.

It is related to the normal distribution in the sense that it results from forming the exponent of a set of x-values drawn from a normal distribution:

$$\text{Lognormal} = e^{\text{Normal}}$$

For example, the x-value of $-\infty$ (i.e. the minimum of the normal distribution) would map to the value of zero (the minimum of the lognormal distribution), and the P50 figure zero (for the normal distribution) would map to the value of one. When using such a mapping, if m and s are the mean and standard deviation of the underlying normal distribution, then the mean and standard deviation (μ, σ) of the resulting lognormal distribution are given by:

$$\mu = e^{m+\frac{s^2}{2}}$$

$$\sigma = \sqrt{\left(e^{2m+s^2}\right)\left(e^{s^2}-1\right)}$$

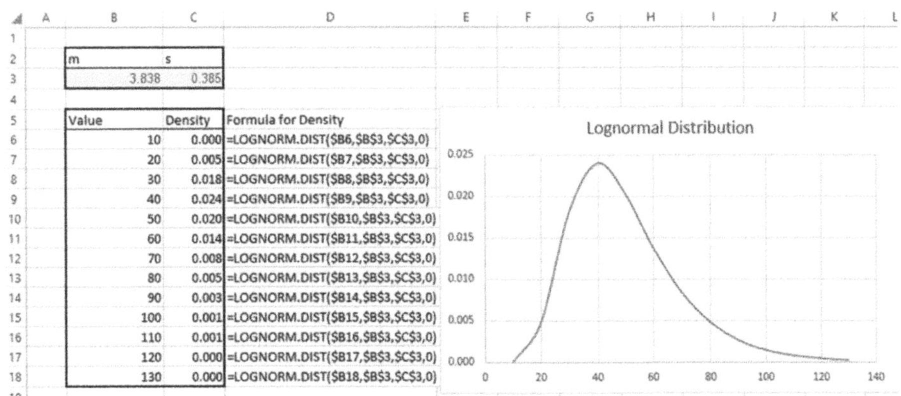

m	s
3.838	0.385

Value	Density	Formula for Density
10	0.000	=LOGNORM.DIST($B6,$B$3,$C$3,0)
20	0.005	=LOGNORM.DIST($B7,$B$3,$C$3,0)
30	0.018	=LOGNORM.DIST($B8,$B$3,$C$3,0)
40	0.024	=LOGNORM.DIST($B9,$B$3,$C$3,0)
50	0.020	=LOGNORM.DIST($B10,$B$3,$C$3,0)
60	0.014	=LOGNORM.DIST($B11,$B$3,$C$3,0)
70	0.008	=LOGNORM.DIST($B12,$B$3,$C$3,0)
80	0.005	=LOGNORM.DIST($B13,$B$3,$C$3,0)
90	0.003	=LOGNORM.DIST($B14,$B$3,$C$3,0)
100	0.001	=LOGNORM.DIST($B15,$B$3,$C$3,0)
110	0.001	=LOGNORM.DIST($B16,$B$3,$C$3,0)
120	0.000	=LOGNORM.DIST($B17,$B$3,$C$3,0)
130	0.000	=LOGNORM.DIST($B18,$B$3,$C$3,0)

FIGURE 9.10 Excel Calculations of a Lognormal Distribution

In this sense, μ and σ can be considered to be the natural (or true) values for the mean and standard deviation of the lognormal process, and m and s are its logarithmic parameters.

When using Excel's functions related to the distribution (such as **LOGNORM.DIST**, **LOGNORMDIST**, **LOGNORM.INV** and **LOGINV**), the input parameters required are not the actual mean values (i.e. not μ, σ), but the logarithmic ones (i.e. m, s).

Therefore, if one wishes to use the natural values as input to the Excel functions, one will need to conduct an intermediate step to derive the logarithmic parameters:

$$m = LN\left(\mu^2 \big/ \sqrt{\mu^2 + \sigma^2}\right)$$

$$s = \sqrt{LN\left(1 + \left(\sigma/\mu\right)^2\right)}$$

When used as inputs to the Excel functions, these create a distribution function whose true mean and standard deviation are the desired μ, σ.

The file Ch9.LogNormDist.xlsx contains an example of these calculations, in which $\mu = 50$, $\sigma = 20$, and m and s are (approximately) 3.838 and 0.385, respectively; see Figure 9.10. The **LOGNORM.DIST** function is used to calculate the density curve (the older **LOGNORMDIST** function calculates only the cumulative curve). From the graph, one can broadly see that, with the above input values of m and s, the actual values have an average of 50 (this can be seen by recalling that the average (mean) value is the centre of gravity or "balancing" point of the distribution).

In business applications, it is often preferable to work directly with the natural values, so that such transformations will often be necessary when working with Excel/VBA approaches.

When working with @RISK, the function **RiskLognorm2** also uses the logarithmic parameter form (i.e. using m, s), whereas one can work directly with the natural parameters by using the **RiskLognorm** function. Figure 9.11 shows an example, in which the natural (or true) mean and standard deviation (of 50 and 20, respectively) are used directly as the distribution's input parameters.

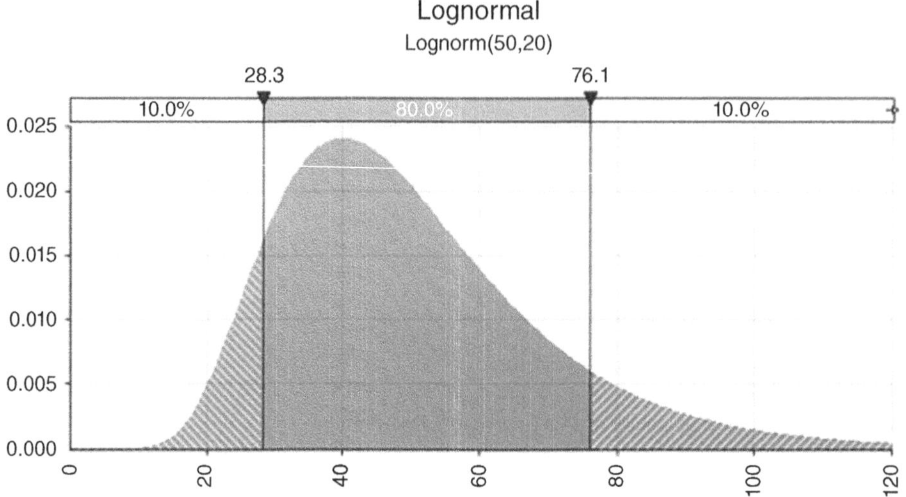

FIGURE 9.11 An Example of a Lognormal Distribution

When one has a data set of historic data available, the calculation of the required parameters (whether m, s or μ, σ) is straightforward. On the other hand, if the distribution is used in a pragmatic context in which parameter estimates are needed, it may be convenient to use the mode of the distribution as an input parameter. The mode is related to the required parameters through the formula:

$$\text{Mode} = \frac{\mu^4}{\left(\mu^2 + \sigma^2\right)^{\frac{3}{2}}}$$

or, using logarithmic parameters:

$$\text{Mode} = e^{m-s^2}$$

The lognormal distribution arises in theory as a result of multiplicative processes: just as a normal distribution results from adding many identical independent processes, so would a lognormal distribution result from multiplying them. Indeed, since:

$$\text{Log}(A.B.C\ldots) = \text{Log}(A) + \text{Log}(B) + \text{Log}(C) + \ldots$$

for any numbers A, B and C, then it would also be true if A, B and C were values from random processes. Thus, for independent, identical random processes, the right-hand side would be normally distributed, so that the product $A.B.C\ldots$ would be lognormal.

From an intuitive point of view, one can also see that multiplicative processes tend to generate positive non-symmetry. For example, if one were to take two identical independent processes (such as tossing two coins), where each has two equally likely outcomes (50% probability in each case), with values 0.1 and 10, then the results of multiplying these together would be: 0.01 in 25% of cases (both coins land on 0.1), 1 in 50% of cases (one coin lands on 0.1 and the other on 10, or vice versa) and 100 in 25% of cases (both coins land on 10). If one were to generalise the possible range so that the input processes were uniform continuous distributions between 0.1 and 10, then any value within a continuous range from 0.01 to 100 would be possible. If more processes were included in the multiplication (for example, five), the minimum would become a small positive number (0.00001), and the maximum a large number (10,000), whilst the modal value would still be fairly small.

Although the distribution may appear to be of a rather theoretical nature, there are many practical applications, because it has a number of properties that are also found in real-world processes:

- It has positive values and its range is unbounded (as would be the ranges for journey times, or the duration or cost of a project, and many other processes).
- Many items (whose uncertainty one may wish to represent as an input distribution) may, in reality, result from multiplicative processes that one may not wish to model explicitly (due to a lack of data at that level of detail, or for other reasons). For example:
  - The total cost of a particular item in a cost budget may be the product of price per unit per day, the number of units and the number of days. When used in such pragmatic contexts, there would nevertheless be a (partial) theoretical justification for its choice.
  - Similarly, in the modelling of oil, resources or mineral reserves, the amount of oil (or reserves) is a result of the multiplication (with certain adjustments) of the uncertain values of the spatial dimensions of the field, the porosity and water saturation, a formation factor and the recovery rate. Of course, this is an approximation, because the amount of oil in any particular field is finite (and certainly limited by the size of the planet).
- Time-based processes. The distribution can directly represent the future value of an asset, whose value develops over time such that its percentage change in each period is uncertain, and independent from one period to the next (but with the same parameters in each period); the value at a future time is calculated as the product of many changes. For example, an apartment may be valued initially at $100,000, with its value assumed to either increase or decrease each year by 10%. After 1 year the value would be either $120,000 or $90,000, after 2 years the possible range would be from $81,000 to $121,000 and after 3 years from $72,900 to $133,100. In other words, the range becomes non-symmetric and would be lognormal when modelled as a continuous-time process. Related applications include the future level of stocks, commodity and property prices, the size of an economy (GDP) or perhaps that of a company's revenues.
- It has a fairly flexible shape. When σ is small compared to μ, its skew is small and it resembles a normal distribution. When σ is large compared to μ, it has a high level of kurtosis, so it can capture processes with fairly heavy tails.

The effect of multiplicative processes can, of course, be explored by simulation. In the following, we show several examples that illustrate some of the above points.

Concerning the idea that multiplicative processes create skewness in the results, Figure 9.12 shows an example (using @RISK), in which we have run a simulation to assess the uncertainty range for the total hours of work required on a project, calculated as the product of the hours per person per day, the number of people and the number of days. Although the input ranges are assumed to be symmetric, the results show a skewness (in the distribution of possible total hours worked) of approximately 0.23. Figure 9.13 shows an extension of this in which the total cost is calculated by the multiplication of a symmetric distribution for the cost

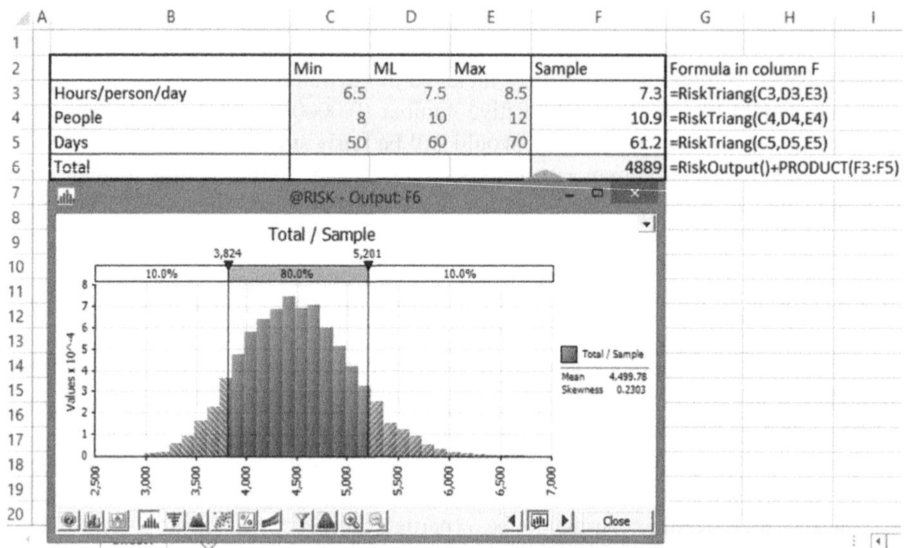

	Min	ML	Max	Sample	Formula in column F
Hours/person/day	6.5	7.5	8.5	7.3	=RiskTriang(C3,D3,E3)
People	8	10	12	10.9	=RiskTriang(C4,D4,E4)
Days	50	60	70	61.2	=RiskTriang(C5,D5,E5)
Total				4889	=RiskOutput()+PRODUCT(F3:F5)

FIGURE 9.12 Example of Skewness Arising from Multiplicative Processes

per hour by the hours worked. The inclusion of the extra process leads to the skewness of the results increasing to about 0.3 (which is a rule-of-thumb value for skewness to be visible from a distribution density curve).

Concerning the occurrence of lognormal processes within time series, Figure 9.14 shows an example (also using @RISK) in which one assumes that, in each period, the percentage change in the value of an asset is normally distributed; the distribution for the future value

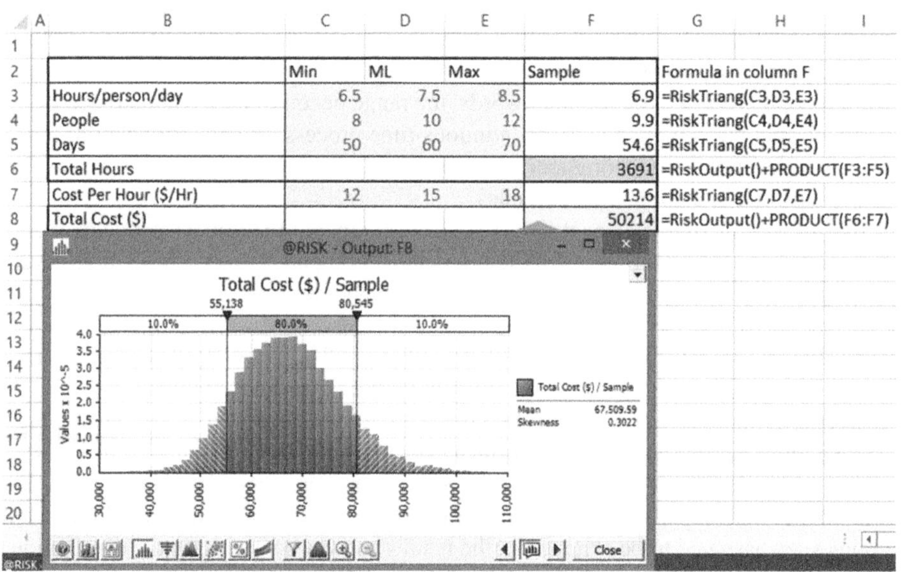

	Min	ML	Max	Sample	Formula in column F
Hours/person/day	6.5	7.5	8.5	6.9	=RiskTriang(C3,D3,E3)
People	8	10	12	9.9	=RiskTriang(C4,D4,E4)
Days	50	60	70	54.6	=RiskTriang(C5,D5,E5)
Total Hours				3691	=RiskOutput()+PRODUCT(F3:F5)
Cost Per Hour ($/Hr)	12	15	18	13.6	=RiskTriang(C7,D7,E7)
Total Cost ($)				50214	=RiskOutput()+PRODUCT(F6:F7)

FIGURE 9.13 Further Example of Skewness Arising from Multiplicative Processes

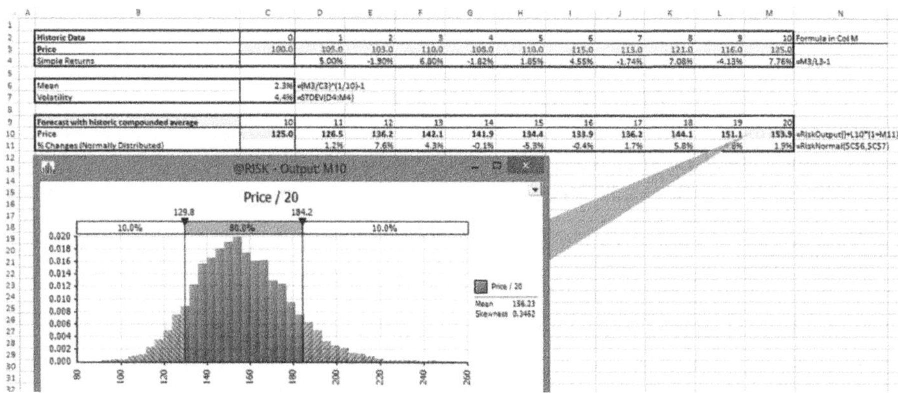

FIGURE 9.14 Multiplicative Processes Implicit within some Time Series

arises by the compound effect of multiplying several random changes together. One can see a skewness of the values in period 10 of approximately 0.34.

The lognormal distribution also provides an interesting case in studying how the statistical properties of random processes may behave in ways that are not always intuitive (which is part of the reason for using simulation and risk modelling to support decision-making, instead of relying on a traditional static model and on intuitive judgement of the risk component). As an example, one may explore whether the reciprocal of a positively skewed distribution would be negatively skewed or not. Whilst one might expect this to be the case, it is not so for the lognormal distribution: the reciprocal of the product of several numbers is equal to the product of the reciprocals, therefore the reciprocal of a lognormal distribution is also lognormal. Whether that is the case for triangular distributions could, of course, be explored further through mathematical manipulations, many of which are not trivial. However, such issues are easy to (start to) explore with simulation techniques. Figure 9.15 shows the key statistics that result from conducting a simulation of the reciprocals of a lognormal distribution and of two triangular distributions (one of which is negatively skewed and the other is positively skewed); in this case, all output distributions are positively skewed. In fact, unlike for the lognormal distribution, whether the reciprocals of a triangular distribution (or of many other processes) are positively or negatively skewed depends on the distribution and its parameters (such as whether values close to zero or negative values are possible); the interested reader can easily experiment further with such issues for different distributions and parameter values.

	Parameters			Skewness	
				Distribution	Reciprocal by Simulation
	Mean	StdDev			
Lognormal	20	5		0.77	0.82
	Min	ML	Max		
Triangular 1	5	10	12	-0.38	1.11
Triangular 2	5	10	25	0.42	0.89

FIGURE 9.15 Comparison of Skewness of Input and Reciprocal Distributions

9.1.7 The Beta and Beta General Distributions

The (standard) beta distribution describes the probability for a process whose outcome is between zero and one. It has two parameters α and β (also known as shape parameters; the distribution is symmetric when they have the same value).

From a theoretical perspective, it describes the likelihood that any particular value is the true probability of a Bernoulli process, based on observations (analogous to a confidence interval).

For example:

- One may have recently started a job at a new location, and recorded that on five out of 20 occasions, there was a significant delay in the journey to work. Is the probability of delay exactly 25%, or could there be some uncertainty around that?
- One may have a given number of total prospects of finding oil in areas with similar geology; after having conducted several tests (such as drilling) to determine if oil is present, one may deduce a probability range for subsequent drilling activities.
- If, within a set of food samples, several were found to be infected with specific bacteria, one may deduce the range of probabilities for further samples to be infected.
- If one estimates a probability that (within a year) a particular security would default, based on the fact that in the last year there was one default from a set of 100 similar securities, then one may wish to consider the uncertainty range for the probability of default.

In the above example concerning the journey, whilst the use of an assumed probability-of-occurrence of 25% (or 5/20) may be adequate for many purposes, it is simply the most likely value. Indeed, any probability between 0% and 100% could have produced the observed outcome, with the likelihood that a particular probability is the true one reducing as one considers values other than 25% (and decreasing to zero for true probabilities of 0% and 100%). It is also clear that (in general) the range of possible probabilities is non-symmetric: for example, by considering the absolute range of values that is ±25% around the most likely figure of 25% (i.e. by considering the range of probabilities from 0% to 50%), it is clear that the 0% case could not have produced five occurrences, whereas a 50% probability could have (as could have 60%, for example).

Figure 9.16 shows the beta distribution that corresponds to the above situation: the x-axis represents the true (but unknown) probability and the y-axis is the relative likelihood that such a probability would produce the observed outcomes.

In general, the uncertainty range for the possible values of the true probability is one in which the parameters are chosen as:

$$\alpha = \text{Number of occurrences} + 1$$

$$\beta = \text{Number of non-occurrences} + 1$$

The formula for the density function of a beta distribution can be derived by recalling that the binomial distribution density function describes the probability, for each i, of observing i occurrences in n trials, when the probability-of-occurrence per trial is p:

$$f(n, p, i) = C(n, i)\, p^i (1 - p)^{n-i}$$

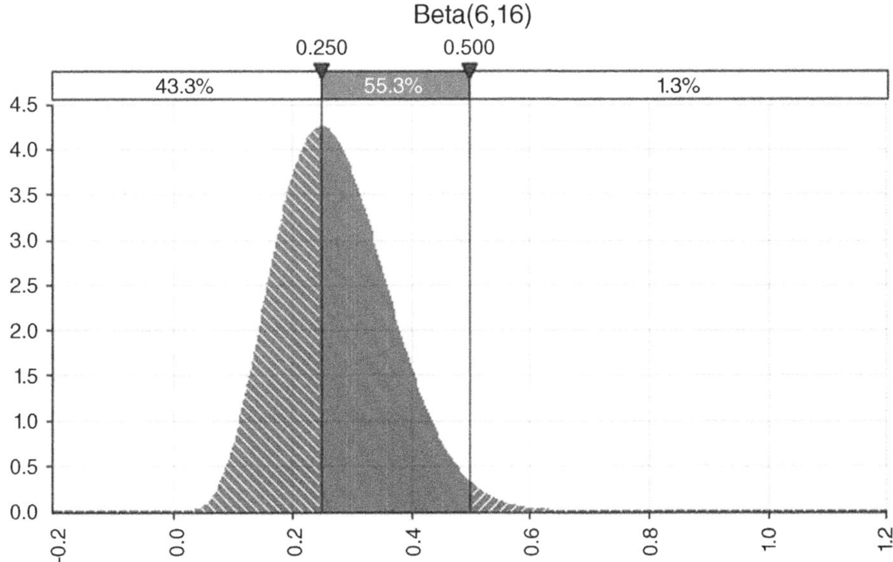

FIGURE 9.16 An Example of a Beta Distribution

Thus, in reverse, if i and n are both known, but p is not, we could treat the above equation as describing a density function for p, i.e. in which p is the uncertain variable. Thus, by defining:

$$\alpha = i + 1$$
$$\beta = n - i + 1$$

this equation could be written as:

$$\text{Beta}(\alpha, \beta, p) = \frac{p^{\alpha-1}(1-p)^{\beta-1}}{B(\alpha, \beta)}$$

where $B(\alpha, \beta)$ is a scaling factor to ensure that the total area under the density curve is 100%.

Although it is not directly clear from the above equations, the distribution is positively skewed where the number of occurrences is small compared to the number of observations. Similarly, it is negatively skewed if the number of non-occurrences is relatively small, and is symmetric when $i = n/2$. Thus, the most likely value is an underestimation of the mean when $i < n/2$, and an overestimation when $i > n/2$. We see from Figure 9.16 that the mean probability of a delay is around 27% (3/12). Thus, estimates that are based on most likely values may significantly underestimate the average probability-of-occurrence for rare events. Figure 9.17 shows the distribution of probability for an event that occurred only once in 100 observations, with a mean value of just under 2% (rather than the most likely case of 1%).

In general, when modelling with a Bernoulli (or binomial process), one could use the beta distribution to represent the uncertainty distribution of the probability. For example, at each recalculation (or iteration) of a simulation, one could first randomly sample a probability from a beta distribution, and use this as an input to the sampling of

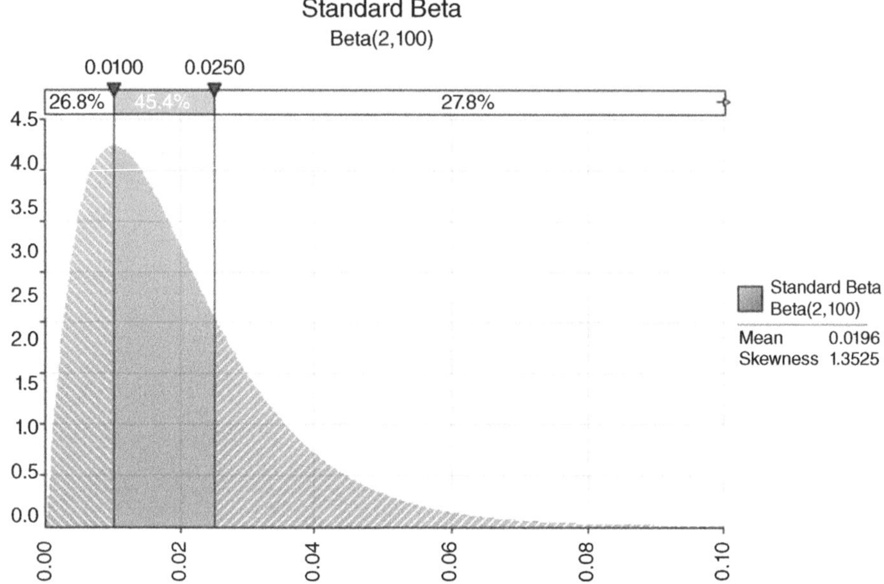

FIGURE 9.17 A Further Example of a Beta Distribution

the Bernoulli or binomial process. This would result in a beta-Bernoulli or beta-binomial process.

The Excel functions relating to the beta distribution (such as **BETA.DIST**) include additional (optional) parameters (A and B) that allow the distribution's x-values to take any value between A (the minimum) and B (the maximum); this is equivalent to manually scaling the standard distribution (i.e. multiplying the values by B–A and then adding A to the result). Such a scaling would, of course, not apply in the case of probability estimates, but is applicable when the distribution is used as a pragmatic one in other contexts (in particular, to create a PERT distribution; see later).

When using @RISK, the **RiskBeta** function has only two parameters (called $\alpha 1$, $\alpha 2$), i.e. it corresponds to the (standard) beta distribution. Although this could be scaled (as above) to create values in other ranges, one can instead use **RiskBetaGeneral** distribution (which has the parameters $\alpha 1$, $\alpha 2$, Minimum, Maximum). @RISK also has the **RiskBetaSubjective** distribution as a variation; this requires four parameters: the minimum, most likely, mean and maximum. In theory, this is very appealing, as the most likely value may correspond to one view of a base case, and the mean value to another. However, in practice, it may happen that the distribution cannot be formed with specific values that are desired to be used, especially if such parameters are derived from calculations or taken from estimates.

9.1.8 The PERT Distribution

The PERT (Program Evaluation and Review Technique) distribution is a special case of a (scaled) beta distribution. It is governed by three parameters: the minimum, most likely and maximum (denoted by Min, ML and Max below), which are, of course, the same parameters as a triangular distribution. The distribution can be created from a (scaled) beta distribution by setting the parameters of the beta distribution from the desired Min, ML and Max as:

$$A = \text{Min}, B = \text{Max}$$
$$\mu = (\text{Min} + 4\text{ML} + \text{Max})/6$$
$$\alpha = 6(\mu - \text{Min})/(\text{Max} - \text{Min})$$
$$\beta = 6(\text{Max} - \mu)/(\text{Max} - \text{Min})$$

Such a procedure would be necessary when using Excel/VBA approaches; when using @RISK, the **RiskPERT** function can be used directly.

The main use of the PERT is as a pragmatic alternative to the triangular and (explicit) beta distributions:

- It generally can be considered to create a more accurate representation (than a triangular distribution) of processes: it is a smooth curve, and for non-symmetric parameters, it will tend to have a smaller proportion of values in its tails.
- The physical interpretation of the parameters α, β of the beta distribution is not intuitive, and so choosing them appropriately to fit to a desired case can be difficult to achieve in practice, whereas the PERT's parameters are easier to interpret.

Figure 9.18 shows an overlay of each, in the case of a minimum value of 8, a most likely value of 10 and a maximum value of 15.

Of course, the PERT distribution is bounded on both sides; where it is important to capture the unbounded nature of the process, other distributions may be required. However, this limitation is often either not relevant, or the approximation of an unbounded process with a bounded one may be regarded as sufficient in many practical cases.

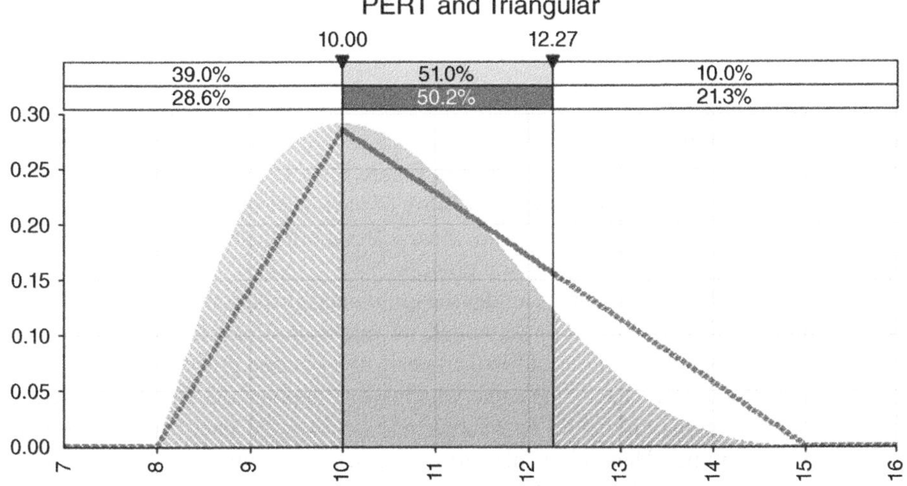

FIGURE 9.18 An Example of PERT and Triangular Distributions

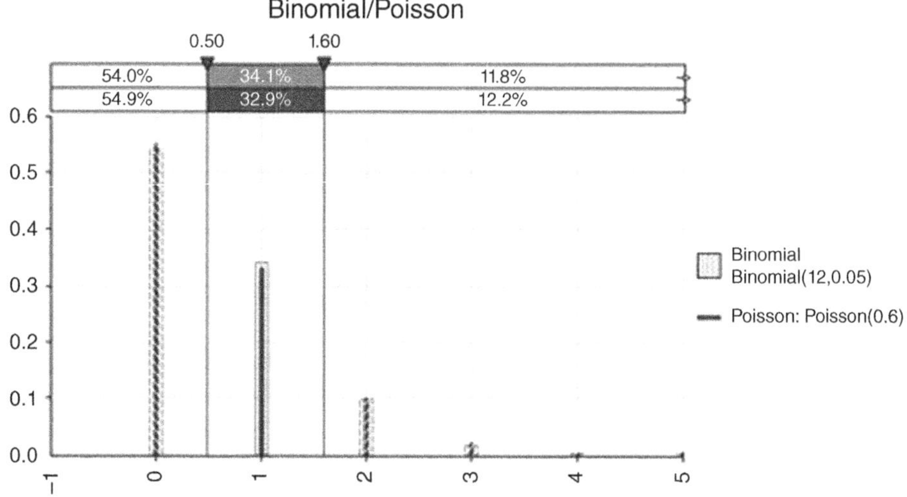

FIGURE 9.19 Binomial and Poisson Distributions

9.1.9 The Poisson Distribution

The Poisson distribution describes the probability that a specific (discrete) number of events occurs within a given (continuous) time period, where the average number of events per unit time is constant. It has a single parameter λ, which is the intensity of the process, equal to the average number of events per unit time.

The distribution is the continuous-time counterpart to a binomial distribution: for example, one may capture the number of times that a car breaks down in a year as binomial (12, 5%), corresponding to a 5% chance of a single breakdown each month, and an average of 0.6. Alternatively, a Poisson distribution (with its intensity of 0.6) would capture the annual number, and may be unbounded, although higher numbers are less likely. Figure 9.19 shows a comparison of the two.

The visual properties of the distribution change as λ increases:

- When λ is small (so that two or more events are unlikely to be observed), the distribution is approximately a Bernoulli one, as shown in Figure 9.20. Practically speaking, when λ is less than (approximately) 0.15, the probability of having more than one occurrence of the process is less than 1% per unit time; thus, a Bernoulli distribution is a reasonable approximation to a low-intensity Poisson process.
- When λ is larger, the distribution resembles the binomial distribution, and for large values will resemble a normal distribution (although its values are discrete); see Figure 9.21. Such a behaviour is a result of the additive property of a Poisson process: the distribution of the number of occurrences is the same whether one doubles the length of time over which the observations are made, or whether one doubles the intensity of occurrence for a fixed timeframe. Thus, high intensity processes are equivalent to adding many individual processes together, and thus will be approximately normally distributed. This fact is also important for creating samples of the distribution in practice; for large λ it is

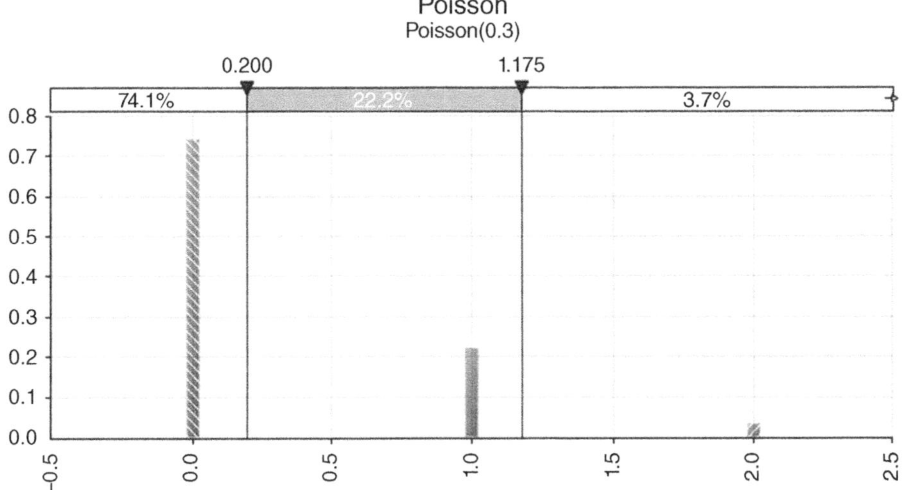

FIGURE 9.20 A Low Intensity Poisson Process

more computationally efficient to sample a normal distribution in place of using the true Poisson formulae.

The distribution is often used to represent the probability of outcomes for situations such as:

- The number of people arriving in a queue per minute.
- Number of traffic accidents in a town per day.
- The number of stock market crashes per decade.

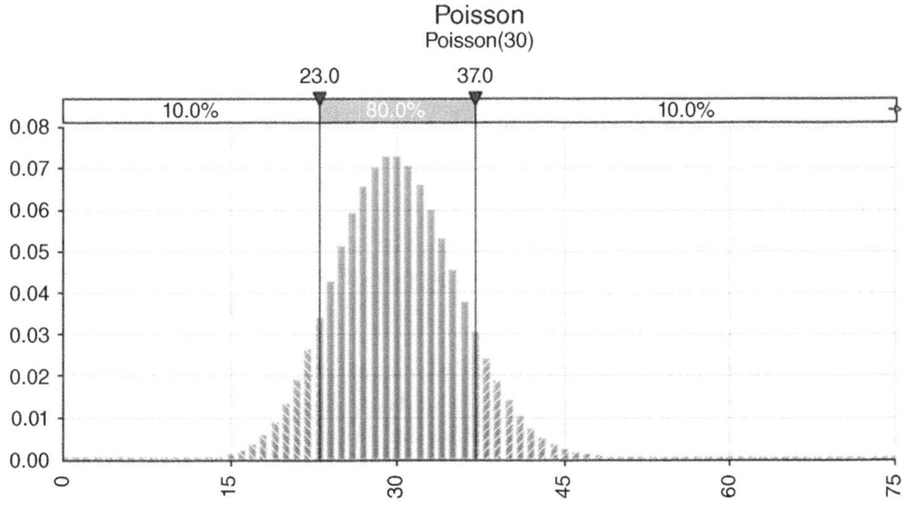

FIGURE 9.21 A High Intensity Poisson Process

- Operational and resources issues, such as the number of e-mails received per hour during the course of the working day, or the number of interruptions when making a presentation.
- The number of goals in a soccer game.

It can be applied to domains other than time (such as space) if the intensity of occurrence is constant: for example, it may capture the number of fish in a particular stretch of a river if the average density of fish (per metre length of the river) is constant.

The density function is given by:

$$f(i) = e^{-\lambda}\lambda^{i}/i!$$

and the cumulative function by:

$$F(i) = e^{-\lambda}\sum_{j=0}^{j=i}\frac{\lambda^{j}}{j!}$$

When using Excel/VBA, the density and cumulative functions can be evaluated using the functions **POISSON.DIST** (or **POISSON** in earlier versions): **POISSON.DIST**(i, λ, 0) provides the density function and **POISSON.DIST**(i, λ, 1) the cumulative function for each possible value, i.

The mean and the variance are both equal to λ (so that its standard deviation is $\sqrt{\lambda}$); its skewness is $\frac{1}{\sqrt{\lambda}}$. For large λ, the distribution becomes symmetric and the term $e^{-\lambda}$ becomes so small that it may be difficult to evaluate computationally; hence, a normal distribution is usually used as a proxy in such cases (see Chapter 11).

9.1.10 The Geometric Distribution

The geometric distribution describes the probability for the number of non-occurrences of a Bernoulli process before the first occurrence. Such non-occurrences may be described in different terms according to the context: the number of failures before a success, or the number of successes before a failure, or the number of periods or trials before the occurrence of an event. Note that the distribution of "waiting time", i.e. the total number of periods (or trials) until the first success has happened, is calculated by adding one to the (sampled) value of the distribution.

Examples of its use include:

- The number of periods before an event risk happens. This could also represent a positive outcome, such as the number of periods until a project is authorised, or until a development plan has succeeded, and so on.
- The number of periods before a breakdown of a manufacturing facility or of a car.
- The number of times a coin is tossed before a head is produced, or the number of sequential bets that one needs to make on roulette before the chosen number occurs.

The distribution has a single parameter, p, the probability of occurrence at each period (or trial), with the probability of non-occurrence of course being $1 - p$.

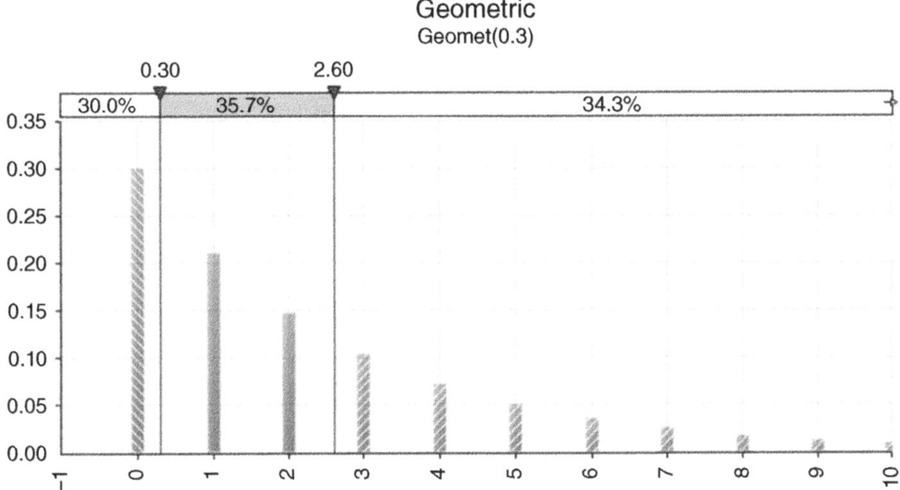

FIGURE 9.22 An Example of a Geometric Distribution

The density function is:

$$f(i) = p(1-p)^i$$

The cumulative function is:

$$F(i) = 1 - (1-p)^{i+1}$$

Figure 9.22 shows the distribution for $p = 30\%$.

There is, of course, a probability, p, that the event occurs on the first trial (i.e. zero failures before the first success). It may be counterintuitive that the most likely single outcome is that of an occurrence on the first trial; the reason is that the distribution measures only the first occurrence, so that subsequent trials take place less often than does the first.

The distribution is sometimes thought of as describing both beginner's luck and gambler's ruin; there is generally a probability of approximately two-thirds that the event will occur at, or before, it is intuitively expected to do so (so the gambler will perceive themselves to be ahead), but the long tail of the distribution means that there will be some cases where the gambler is repeatedly losing their money, and over time the likely initial winnings will be lost.

When used for issues such as maintenance modelling, there can be some limitations to the distribution:

- It is discrete, not continuous, in time.
- One may wish for the probability-of-occurrence to increase (or decrease) over time, so that something is more likely to break down as it gets older.
- It measures only the time-to-first-occurrence; in some cases, the second or third occurrences of an issue may be more relevant (one may have a policy of buying a new car whenever the existing one has broken down three times).

9.1.11 The Negative Binomial Distribution

The negative binomial distribution describes the probability for the number of non-occurrences (periods or trials) until several occurrences of a Bernoulli process (having probability-of-occurrence p) have happened. It has two parameters, s and p, with s being an integer that represents the number of occurrences sought, and p the probability-of-occurrence at each period (trial). The geometric distribution is a special case, corresponding to $s = 1$. When used as the distribution of "waiting time" (or the total number of periods (or trials) until s successes have occurred), the value s would need to be added to a distribution's sampled value to give the total number of trials until s has occurred.

Its main uses are:

- As for the geometric distribution, but where it is the repeated occurrences of an issue that are relevant (e.g. a structure may fail only after four occurrences of an event, not after the first one).
- As a distribution of the number of items that occur in a given time period, and in similar contexts to (or as a replacement of) the Poisson distribution.

The density function is:

$$f(i) = C(s + i - 1, i)\,p^s\,(1 - p)^i$$

where i is the number of trials and (as for the binomial distribution) $C(n, i)$ is the number of ways of choosing i items from n (as described earlier in this chapter).

The Excel distribution function **NEGBINOM.DIST** can be used to evaluate the density and cumulative curves (the earlier **NEGBINOMDIST** provides only the density curve, so would have to explicitly cumulate the distribution by repeated use of this density curve at its individual values).

Figure 9.23 shows an example where $s = 2$ and $p = 30\%$.

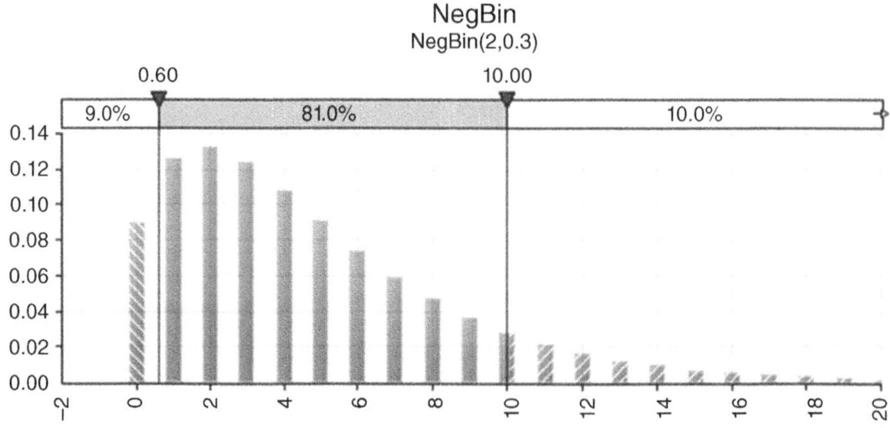

FIGURE 9.23 An Example of a Negative Binomial Distribution

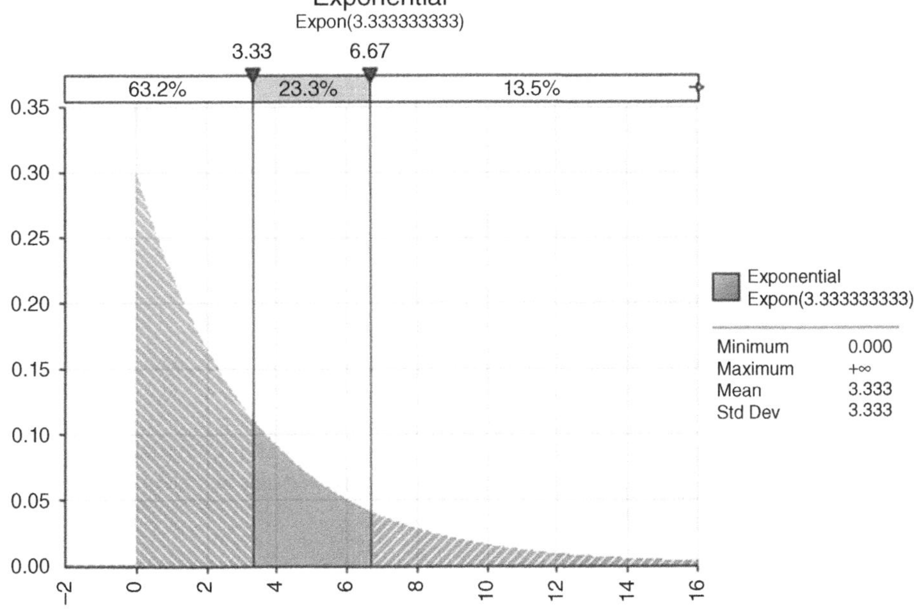

FIGURE 9.24 An Example of an Exponential Distribution

9.1.12 The Exponential Distribution

The exponential distribution is a continuous function describing the probability for the possible time-to-occurrence (or time between occurrences) of a process whose intensity is constant (i.e. of a Poisson process). It is the continuous-time counterpart to the (discrete-time) geometric distribution. It has the same parameter as the Poisson distribution (λ, a scale parameter, meaning that the x-values are scaled with it, so that a change of λ is equivalent to a rescaling of the x-axis).

The density function (for $x \geq 0$) is:

$$f(x) = \lambda e^{-\lambda x}$$

The cumulative curve is:

$$F(x) = 1 - e^{-\lambda x}$$

The mean of the distribution is $\frac{1}{\lambda}$, which is also equal to its standard deviation.

These can be evaluated in Excel with the functions **EXPON.DIST** or **EXPONDIST**. In @RISK the corresponding function (**RiskExpon**) uses the parameter β, where $\beta = \frac{1}{\lambda}$, so that β is the mean of the distribution. Figure 9.24 shows a graph of the distribution in the case $\lambda = 0.3$ ($\beta = 1/0.3$ or $3.33\ldots$).

9.1.13 The Weibull Distribution

The Weibull distribution is most often used to describe probability for the time to (first) occurrence of a process in continuous time, where the intensity of occurrence may not be constant. It has two parameters, α, β, with β acting as a scale parameter.

The density function is (for $x \geq 0$):

$$f(x) = \frac{\alpha x^{\alpha-1}}{\beta^{\alpha}} e^{-\left(\frac{x}{\beta}\right)^{\alpha}}$$

and the cumulative function is:

$$F(x) = 1 - e^{-\left(\frac{x}{\beta}\right)^{\alpha}}$$

In fact, in principle, any continuous distribution can be used to represent the time-to-first-occurrence of some process: the implied intensity-of-occurrence can be calculated from any density and cumulative function as:

$$I(x) = \frac{f(x)}{1 - F(x)}$$

This formula simply states that the instantaneous occurrence rate is the current relative frequency of occurrence relative to the subset of possible outcomes that have not yet happened.

For the Weibull distribution this gives:

$$I(x) = \frac{\alpha x^{\alpha-1}}{\beta^{\alpha}}$$

When $\alpha = 1$, the distribution is the same as the exponential distribution, and its intensity is constant ($\frac{1}{\beta}$). When $\alpha < 1$, the process has decreasing intensity (as x is a time variable in general), and when $\alpha > 1$, the intensity is increasing. Thus, many cases in maintenance or lifetime modelling would use α>1 to represent that the older something is, the more likely it is to fail.

Figure 9.25 shows an example of the distribution in the case that $\alpha = 2$, $\beta = 8$.

Since the density function for the distribution contains both a power term and an exponential term, its shape is quite flexible, and it is often used in contexts other than time-to-occurrence modelling. For example, it is sometimes used to capture the range for the possible speed of wind, as used in the example in Chapter 4.

9.1.14 The Gamma Distribution

The gamma distribution is the continuous-time equivalent of the negative binomial distribution. It has two parameters, α and β (α is a shape parameter, β is a scale parameter). When $\alpha = 1$, the process is the same as an exponential and Weibull distribution. In general, when α is an integer, it represents the time required for α events of a constant intensity process to occur. (In this case, it is also called an Erlang distribution, which is not covered further in this text.)

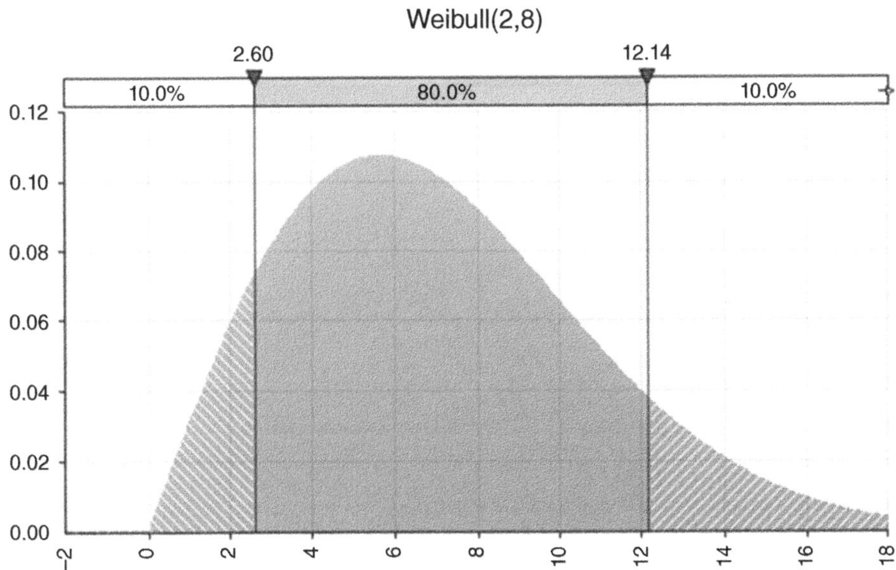

FIGURE 9.25 An Example of a Weibull Distribution

Its density function (for $x \geq 0$) is:

$$f(x) = \frac{1}{\beta\Gamma(\alpha)}\left(\frac{x}{\beta}\right)^{\alpha-1} e^{-\left(\frac{x}{\beta}\right)}$$

(Γ is a function required to ensure that the cumulative probability is 100%, called the gamma function.)

Although the cumulative function does not exist as an analytic (closed-form) expression, the Excel function **GAMMA.DIST** (**GAMMADIST**) can be used to evaluate both the density and cumulative functions (if one wished to evaluate the density function explicitly, using the above formula, the function **GAMMA** could be used to perform the required scaling).

Figure 9.26 shows a gamma distribution with $\alpha = 2$ overlaid with one for which $\alpha = 1$ (in both cases, the scaling factor β is set equal to 1).

The distribution also represents the uncertainty range associated with the parameter of a Poisson process when actual experimental observations are available, but the intensity is unknown. One can see this by using an approach similar to one used earlier: that is, we use the formula for the density function for a Poisson distribution with parameter λ at a particular outcome, i, but instead consider it as a function of λ, rather than of i:

$$f(i, \lambda) \sim e^{-\lambda}\lambda^{i}/i!$$

As a function of λ, and with $\alpha = i + 1$, this is a gamma distribution; a scaling factor dependent on i (or on α) needs to be included to ensure that the cumulative distribution is 100%; this is the role of $\Gamma(\alpha)$.

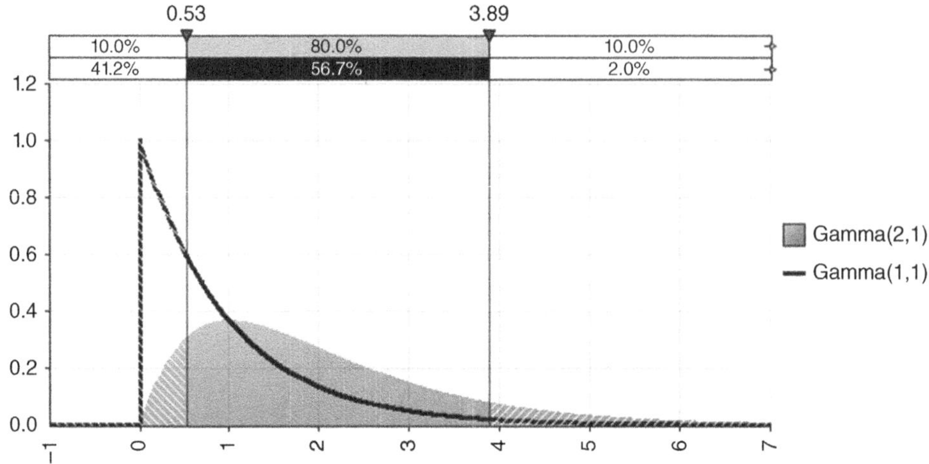

FIGURE 9.26 Examples of the Gamma Distribution

Thus, one could – at each iteration of a simulation – first randomly sample a gamma distribution and then use this as the (λ) parameter for the sampling of a Poisson distribution. If treated as a single process, this is called a Pólya process or distribution.

9.1.15 The General Discrete Distribution

The general discrete distribution explicitly defines the probabilities associated with each outcome of a finite set of possible values. It would generally be used:

- To model scenarios and other situations with only a few outcomes (e.g. low, medium, high).
- To approximate other distributions, including continuous ones.
- To replicate other discrete distributions where there are only a finite set of outcomes, such as the Bernoulli or binomial.

The distribution is defined through a table, which shows the value and probabilities of each possible outcome, such as that shown in Figure 9.27.

Clearly, to replicate other finite discrete processes (such as a binomial), one would need to list all the possible outcomes and their probabilities. When using @RISK, the distribution can be created using the **RiskDiscrete** function.

In @RISK, additional functions related to this are the continuous functions **RiskGeneral** and **RiskCumul**, with parameters minimum, maximum and {X1,X2,...,Xn},{p1,p2,...,pn}. In the first case, the p-values are the relative probabilities of a set of x-values, and in the second case they are the cumulative probabilities (expressed in ascending order). The functions generate distribution curves that are linearly interpolated between the points (so that for the **RiskCumul** function, the corresponding density curve would be uniform between each set of points, but with different relative probabilities in each range).

X-Values	Probabilities
10	25%
15	45%
25	55%

FIGURE 9.27 Example Table of Values and Probabilities for the General Discrete Distribution

Note also that the maximum discrete value that is used in such functions could itself also be a distribution, such as an (unbounded) lognormal distribution; in this way, the right-hand tail can be extended if needed.

9.1.16 The Integer Uniform Distribution

The integer uniform distribution represents a case where each integer in a range of possible outcomes (between a minimum [Min] and maximum [Max], both assumed to be integers) is equally likely. For example, the roll of a die has the possible outcomes 1, 2, 3, 4, 5, 6.

The density function (for integers i between Min and Max) is:

$$f(i) = \frac{1}{\text{Max} - \text{Min} + 1}$$

The cumulative function is:

$$F(i) = \frac{i - \text{Min} + 1}{\text{Max} - \text{Min} + 1}$$

The @RISK function **RiskIntUniform** provides this distribution.

An important application in practice is to resampling methods, an example of which is provided in Chapter 11.

9.1.17 The Hypergeometric Distribution

The hypergeometric distribution is a discrete distribution that describes, for each (feasible) integer outcome i, the probability that i items within a sample will be "tagged" items. The context is that there is a population of size M, within which D items are "tagged" (meaning that they are marked or special in some identifiable way), and that a sample of size n is drawn (i.e. where each item is not replaced if taken). The main application is to testing methods: for example, if it is known that 20 items out of a batch of 200 are contaminated, then a sample of 12 items could contain anything from zero to 12 contaminated items, with probabilities described by the distribution.

The distribution has three integer parameters n, D, M. The minimum number of feasible integer outcomes is given by max $(0, n + D - M)$, whereas the maximum number is min (n, D).

The Excel function **HYPGEO.DIST** can be used to calculate the density and cumulative curve (**HYPGEODIST** can be used for the density curve only); in @RISK the corresponding function is **RiskHypergeo**.

9.1.18 The Pareto Distribution

The Pareto distribution is a continuous distribution with two parameters, θ and a. It was used originally to represent the distribution of people's incomes, but has now found many applications where "fat-tailed" distributions are desired, such as in some insurance and financial applications.

The density function is (for $x \geq a$, $\theta > 0$, $a > 0$):

$$f(x) = \frac{\theta a^{\theta}}{x^{\theta+1}}$$

and the cumulative function is:

$$F(x) = 1 - \left(\frac{a}{x}\right)^{\theta}$$

It is considered a "fat-tailed" distribution, since the density declines as a power of x (rather than with an exponential decline term); small values of θ will have a fatter tail.

The minimum and the mode are equal to a. The mean is given by:

$$\mu = \frac{\theta a}{\theta - 1}$$

For θ slightly greater than 1, the mean is very large (and the mean no longer exists when $\theta \leq 1$). Similarly, the standard deviation exists only when $\theta > 2$, and becomes unboundedly large as θ is reduced towards two from above.

The distribution can be evaluated explicitly in Excel/VBA using the above formulae: in @RISK, one can use **RiskPareto** and **RiskPareto2**; the latter is simply a shifted version of the former, so that the minimum and modal values are zero, rather than a.

Figure 9.28 shows an example of the distribution in the case where $\theta = 3$, $a = 5$.

9.1.19 The Extreme Value Distributions

The use of the distribution of extreme values has wide application, such as in insurance, financial and environmental situations. For example, if one were to measure the maximum height reached each day by a river, then one may wish to understand the distribution of these maxima (such as what the largest or near-largest values may be).

One can determine some properties of extreme value processes using mathematics. For example, if $F(x)$ represents the cumulative distribution function for a single process, then the probability that the maximum of n such processes is less than x would be given by:

$$\emptyset(x) = (F(x))^{n}$$

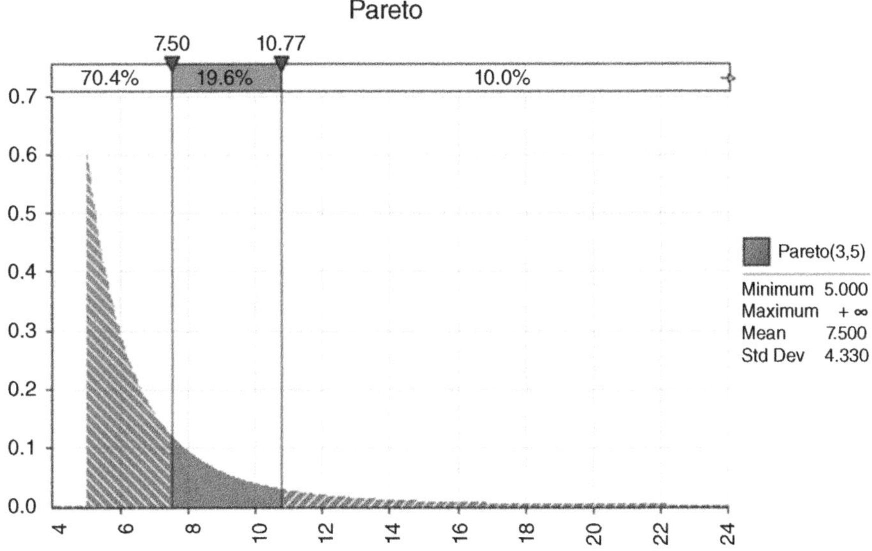

FIGURE 9.28 An Example of a Pareto Distribution

(The repeated multiplication of the probability $F(x)$ implied in the above formula is because each individual process needs to be less than x in order for their maximum to be so, and there is an assumption that the occurrences are independent of each other.)

In other words, $\emptyset(x)$ is the cumulative distribution function for the maximum, and the density function is the derivative of this:

$$\emptyset(x) = n\,(F(x))^{n-1} f(x)$$

where $f(x)$ is the density function for a single process.

Thus, an exact formula for the distribution function for the maximum of n underlying processes can be derived from that of the underlying process. There are various types of extreme value distributions, depending on the nature of the underlying process. The most common form is where the underlying distributions are of exponential nature (i.e. their tails decrease at an exponential rate), and n becomes large. In such cases, the distribution of extreme values has two parameters a and b, with a being the mode and b a scaling factor.

The density function is:

$$f(x) = \left(\frac{1}{b}\right) z e^{-z}$$

and the cumulative function:

$$F(x) = e^{-z}$$

where:

$$z = e^{-\frac{(x-a)}{b}}$$

The mean and variance are given by:

$$\mu = a + \gamma b$$
$$\sigma = \frac{b\pi}{\sqrt{6}}$$

Where γ is Euler's constant (approximately 0.5772156649).

It is positively skewed (with a constant value of approximately 1.14) and has kurtosis of 5.4.

These can be evaluated explicitly in Excel/VBA or using @RISK's **RiskExtValue** function.

In the particular case where the underlying distribution is the (pure) exponential distribution with parameter β, then:

$$a = \beta \mathbf{LN}(n)$$
$$b = \beta$$

In parallel with mathematical approaches (and to reinforce the understanding of them), simulation is one way to calculate the distribution of such extremes: for example, one may use a distribution to represent the outcome on each day, and calculate the maximum set of these at each iteration of the simulation (using the **MAX** function).

The file Ch9.ExtValue.ExponentialAsymptote.xlsx contains an example implemented using @RISK (a reader could choose to use Excel/VBA instead using the tools of Chapters 10 and 13). The file simulates the maxima of a set of exponential distributions (so that the simulation results show the distribution of such maxima); see Figure 9.29. The theoretical values for a and b (i.e. $a = \beta \mathbf{LN}(n)$, and $b = \beta$) are calculated directly (cells G4:G5) from the model's input assumptions (cells C4:C5). The results of the simulation are used to calculate estimates of these parameters (cells G10:G11), using:

$$b_{\text{Est}} = \frac{\sigma\sqrt{6}}{\pi}$$
$$a_{\text{Est}} = \mu - \gamma b_{\text{Est}}$$

where μ, σ are the mean and standard deviation derived through simulation. One can see from the values shown in column G that the simulated distribution has implied parameter values that broadly match those from the theory.

The extreme value distribution clearly has applications to areas such as engineering (i.e. construction of structures to withstand extreme winds, floods, and so on), but it can also be used in other areas, such as parameter estimation. For example, to estimate the upper bound, θ, of a range whose minimum is zero, where data are provided by a set of points drawn uniformly from that range, one may consider two possible approaches to the estimate.

The first approach could be:

$$\theta_1 = 2\mu$$

where μ is the calculated mean of the data set.

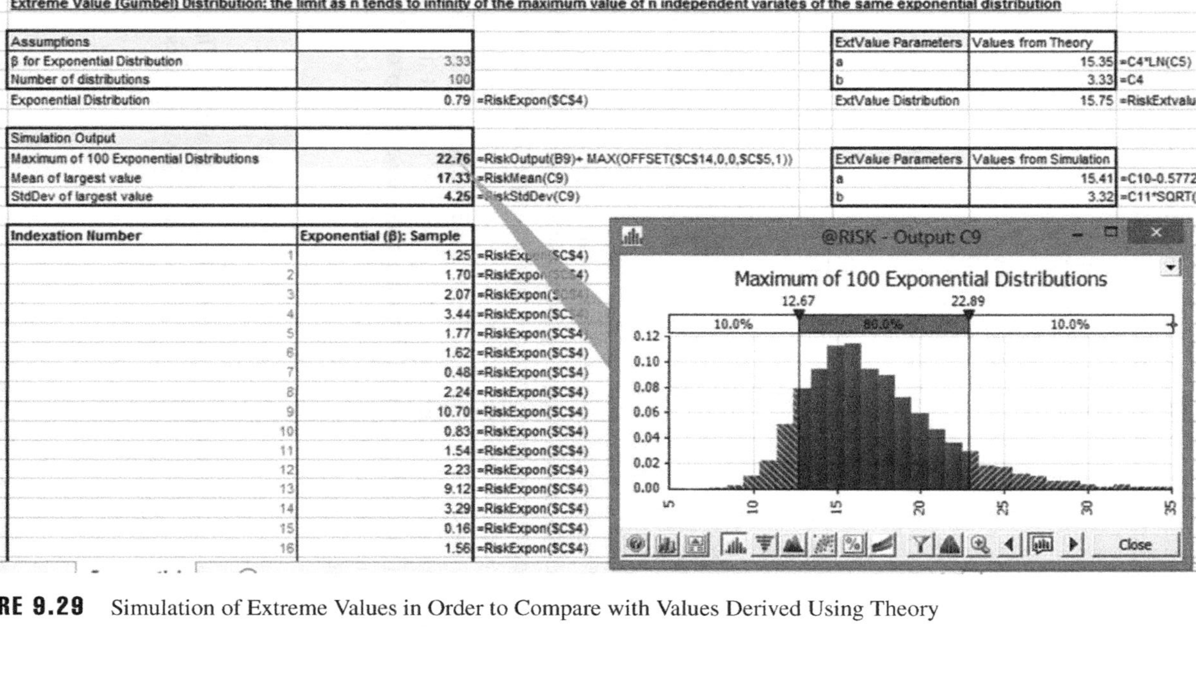

FIGURE 9.29 Simulation of Extreme Values in Order to Compare with Values Derived Using Theory

The second approach is:

$$\theta_2 = \frac{n+1}{n} x_n$$

where x_n is the largest of the n values in the data set.

In fact, it is possible to show that the second estimate is generally better; by considering the single underlying process as a uniform one between zero and θ, i.e.

$$f(x) = \frac{1}{\theta}$$

$$F(x) = \frac{x}{\theta}$$

and performing some further manipulations of the above equations for the extreme value, one can show:

$$E\left(x_n\right) = \frac{n\theta}{\theta + 1}$$

and:

$$V\left(x_n\right) = \frac{n\theta^2}{(n+2)(n+1)^2}$$

Therefore, the variance decreases in proportion to the square of n, so that its standard deviation decreases linearly; this contrasts with parameter estimation using standard sampling methods (see the later discussion regarding the t-distribution, for example), where error estimates of the mean decrease as the square root of the sample size. Thus, the second approach is the more accurate one as n becomes larger.

Other generalisations of its use include finding the minimum (rather than the maximum) of a set of random processes, or indeed the values of any ordered item within a set (such as the distribution of the P50 of a set of random processes), and so on. For example, when considering the minima of a set of values, analogous calculations can be performed, where the corresponding starting point is:

$$1 - \phi(x) = (1 - F(x))^n$$

This results in a distribution that is negatively skewed (with coefficient approximately –1.14), but with the same standard deviation and kurtosis as when considering the maximum values. Its mean is given by:

$$\mu = a - \gamma b$$

9.1.20 The Logistic Distribution

The logistic distribution is a continuous distribution with parameters α and β. α is equal to the mean and β is a scaling factor, which is a multiple of its standard deviation. It is symmetric, and (as one parameter is equal to the mean and the other relates to the standard deviation) is,

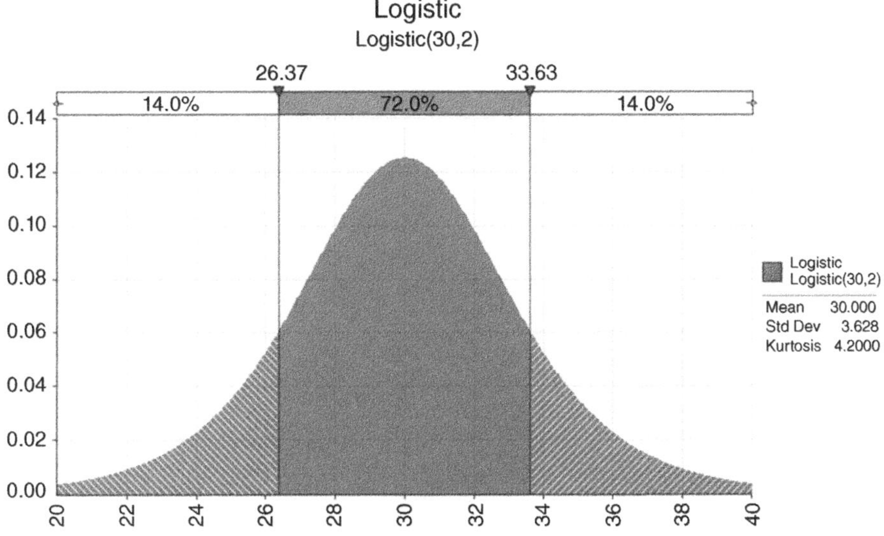

FIGURE 9.30 An Example of a Logistic Distribution

in many ways, similar to a normal distribution. However, it has a kurtosis of 4.2 (i.e. an excess kurtosis of 1.2), and so is sometimes used as a replacement for a normal distribution if one wishes to capture processes with slightly higher kurtosis.

The density function is:

$$f(x) = \left(\frac{z}{\beta(1+z)^2}\right)$$

and the cumulative function:

$$F(x) = \frac{1}{1+z}$$

where:

$$z = e^{-\frac{(x-\alpha)}{\beta}}$$

The mean and standard deviation are given by:

$$\mu = \alpha$$

$$\sigma = \frac{\beta\pi}{\sqrt{3}}$$

An example is shown in Figure 9.30, where α and β are 30 and 2, respectively.

9.1.21 The Log-Logistic Distribution

The log-logistic distribution is one in which the logarithm of the variable follows a logistic distribution (just as the logarithm of the values of the lognormal distribution are normally

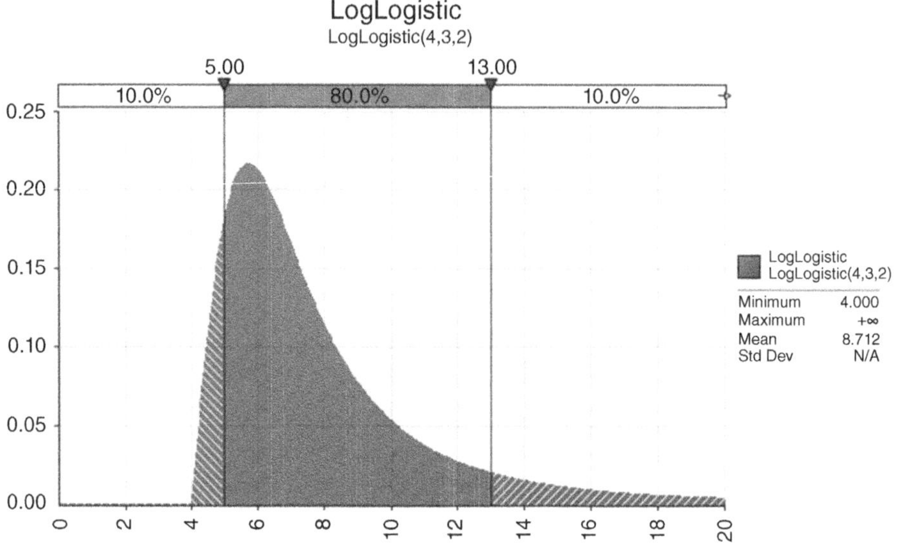

FIGURE 9.31 An Example of a Log-logistic Distribution

distributed). Just as the logistic distribution is sometimes used in place of a normal one, so the log-logistic is sometimes used in place of a lognormal one.

In principle, the distribution requires parameters similar to those of a logistic distribution (i.e. α and β). However, although the density and cumulative functions can easily be explicitly evaluated, at the time of writing, Excel does not contain in-built functions to calculate them. Therefore, in the following we will parameterise the function as it is given in @RISK; this includes an additional factor γ, which is the minimum possible value (i.e. it represents a location parameter).

The density function is:

$$f(x) = \frac{\alpha t^{\alpha-1}}{\beta(1+t^{\alpha})^2}$$

and the cumulative function is:

$$F(x) = \frac{t^{\alpha}}{1+t^{\alpha}}$$

where:

$$t = \frac{x-\gamma}{\beta}$$

Figure 9.31 shows an example.

9.1.22 The Student (*t*), Chi-Squared and *F*-Distributions

These distributions are usually used for statistical purposes, although there is a close link to risk modelling.

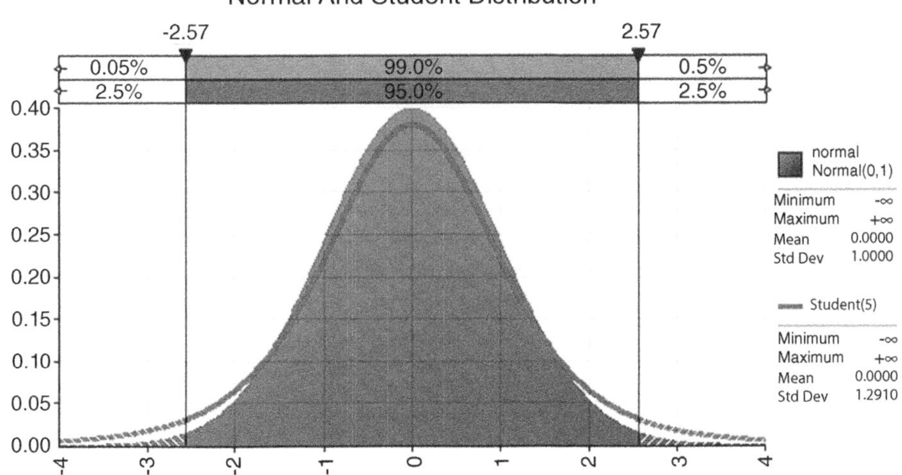

FIGURE 9.32 Comparison of (*t*) Student and Normal Distributions

In Chapter 8, we noted that the average of a data set provides an estimate of the true (but unknown) average of the distribution that generated the data (in other words, to the distribution of the whole population), but that the same data set could, in theory, have been generated by a different process. For example, it is possible that the sampling of another distribution with a similar average could have generated the data. It is also possible that a distribution with a significantly different average also could have done so, although this would be less likely, especially with large sample sizes.

The mean of a sample, in fact, provides a non-biased central (most likely) estimate of the true mean, but the possible values of the mean follow a *t* (or Student) distribution around that.

The *t*-distribution has a single parameter, ν, known as the number of degrees of freedom (in this case, equal to the sample size less one). In many ways, it is rather like a standard normal distribution:

- The mean is zero and it is symmetric (the mode is also zero).
- The standard deviation is $\sqrt{\frac{\nu}{\nu-2}}$, and hence is larger than one. When ν is large, the standard deviation becomes close to one, so that the distribution resembles a standard normal distribution, $N(0,1)$. Thus, for large sample sizes, the normal distribution is often used in place of the *t*-distribution.

Figure 9.32 shows a *t*-distribution with five degrees of freedom and compares this with a normal distribution.

The *t*-distribution represents a non-dimensional quantity, so that the distribution of the possible values of the mean around its central point (i.e. around the mean of the sample) needs to have a scaling factor applied to it. This is known as the standard error of the mean, and is equal to $\frac{\sigma_s}{\sqrt{n}}$, where σ_s is the unbiased (corrected) standard deviation as measured from the sample.

	A	B	C	D
1				
2		Sample Data		
3		Mean of Sample	30.0	
4		StdDev of Sample	5.0	
5		Number of Data Points	1000	
6		Standard error of mean	0.16	=C$4/SQRT(C$5)
7		Degrees of Freedom	999	=C5-1
8				
9		Mean		
10				
11		Confidence Interval	95%	
12		Probability outside either tail	2.5%	=(1-C11)/2
13		t-value	1.96	=-T.INV(C$12,C$7)
14				
15		Lower Band Around Sample Statistic	-0.31	=-C$13*C$6
16		Upper Band Around Sample Statistic	0.31	=+C$13*C$6
17		Lower estimate	29.69	=C$3+C15
18		Upper estimate	30.31	=C$3+C16
19				
20		StdDev		
21				
22		Confidence Interval	95%	
23		Probability outside either tail	2.5%	=(1-C22)/2
24				
25		Lower Band Scaling	0.96	=SQRT(C$7/CHIINV(C$23,C$7))
26		Upper Band Scaling	1.05	=SQRT(C$7/CHIINV(1-C$23,C$7))
27		Lower estimate	4.79	=C$4*C25
28		Upper estimate	5.23	=C$4*C26

FIGURE 9.33 Excel Calculations of Confidence Intervals

Thus, the distribution of the true mean around the sample can be estimated as an appropriately scaled *t*-distribution. Usually, although one can be (100%) sure that the true mean is between $-\infty$ and ∞, and with a most likely value equal to the sample mean, one specifies a confidence level (usually 95%). This is used to determine the width of the range around the sample mean that one wishes to consider as the feasible range for population means. In other words, for 95% confidence, one would determine the half-width of the corresponding *t*-distribution so that 95% of the area is either side of the mid-point (or 2.5% in each tail).

The confidence interval for the mean around the sample mean is then:

$$\mu_s \pm t\frac{\sigma_s}{\sqrt{n}}$$

The file Ch9.ConfInterval.MeanAndStdDev.xlsx contains the required calculations for the mean, using the summary statistics of the data set, and the required confidence level as inputs; see Figure 9.34.

Figure 9.33 also shows the analogous calculations for the confidence interval for the standard deviation, which requires the use of a chi-squared distribution. In this case, this has

Degrees of freedom	30

Cumulated Probabilty	T.INV(p)	TINV(p)	-TINV(2p)	RiskStudent
5%	-1.697	2.042	-1.697	-1.697
10%	-1.310	1.697	-1.310	-1.310
15%	-1.055	1.477	-1.055	-1.055
20%	-0.854	1.310	-0.854	-0.854
25%	-0.683	1.173	-0.683	-0.683
30%	-0.530	1.055	-0.530	-0.530
35%	-0.389	0.949	-0.389	-0.389
40%	-0.256	0.854	-0.256	-0.256
45%	-0.127	0.765	-0.127	-0.127
50%	0.000	0.683	0.000	0.000
55%	0.127	0.605	0.127	0.127
60%	0.256	0.530	0.256	0.256
65%	0.389	0.458	0.389	0.389
70%	0.530	0.389	0.530	0.530
75%	0.683	0.322	0.683	0.683
80%	0.854	0.256	0.854	0.854
85%	1.055	0.191	1.055	1.055
90%	1.310	0.127	1.310	1.310
95%	1.697	0.063	1.697	1.697

FIGURE 9.34 Comparisons of Various Implementations of the *t* (Student) Distribution

the same parameter and degrees of freedom as the *t*-distribution. However, it is a positively skewed distribution that becomes more symmetric as v increases; thus, the confidence interval for the standard deviation is also positively skewed, unlike that for the mean.

Note that the values of the individual data points are irrelevant for the calculations, only the summary data and the confidence percentage are required. From this information, the required percentiles are calculated using the inverse functions for the *t*- and chi-squared distributions, and these (non-dimensional figures) are then scaled appropriately in each case, as shown by the formulae in Figure 9.33.

The interested reader could also use simulation techniques in order to cross-check and provide further intuition into these formulae. By assuming that the mean and standard deviation of a population are known, one could generate a set of samples from this distribution, conduct the above confidence interval calculations based on the sample and check whether the true mean (or standard deviation) is within the interval: this check, conducted at each iteration (or recalculation), would be set to return either the number one or zero, depending on whether the true population mean was within the confidence interval determined from the sample. Its mean value over the course of the simulation should be equal to the confidence level (if the simulation is run sufficiently many times).

Note that when using Excel functions for the *t*-distribution, one needs to take care which Excel version is being used: whereas **T.INV** returns the *t*-value associated with the cumulated probability up to that point (i.e. up to 2.5% in the above example, so that the total confidence interval would exclude 2.5% of outcomes on each side, giving a 5% exclusion in total), if using **TINV**, the input probability required would be 5%, as the function calculates the width required to exclude 5% in total, as does the **T.INV.2T** function. Also, there is a reversal of signs between the distributions.

The file Ch9.TDist.xlsx contains calculations that compare various functions in this respect. As shown in Figure 9.34, the calculations compare the percentiles of various *t*-distributions in Excel and also @RISK's **RiskStudent** function. It shows that to use these consistently, when using **TINV**, one would need to reverse the sign for the function and double the probability value used (so that the initial values in column D are converted to those in column E, which are the same as those in columns C and F).

The *F*-distribution is used in statistics to compare the variance between two data sets to determine commonality in the underlying populations, and is generally less relevant in business risk modelling applications, so is not covered further here.

From the perspective of simulation and risk modelling, there are a number of other issues relating to the above that may need to be borne in mind:

- Much of the underlying statistical theory behind the above depends on the assumption that the data samples are drawn from a normal distribution; this is often not the case in practice. It also assumes that the random numbers are independent, whereas algorithms to generate sequences of numbers will not necessarily generate such items (as this may not be the most efficient way to generate representative samples).
- Analogous calculations can be made for other confidence intervals around other statistics – either of input data or of simulation results (for example, finding the confidence interval around the P90 of a simulation), including for the purposes of estimating required sample sizes, and so on.
- For multi-variable processes, one can explore issues such as the possible uncertainty range for (true) correlation coefficients between two processes given a set of data about each process. This can be relevant in a risk and simulation context for estimating the stability of correlation coefficients.

9.2 A FRAMEWORK FOR DISTRIBUTION SELECTION AND USE

The choice of distributions is clearly a key aspect of quantitative modelling: in principle, one would wish to use a distribution that best describes the uncertainty profile of the input variable under consideration.

Of course, one can only select from distributions that are available (or can be created) within the modelling platform that one is using. Although this chapter covers a wide set of distributions that can be created in Excel, there may be occasions when the use of an add-in is necessary in order to have access to a wider set. For example, as discussed in Chapter 13, @RISK has a number of distribution-fitting tools which, for a given set of data, find the best matching distribution and its associated parameters. In addition, the availability of compound processes (in which multiple independent samples are taken and added together) can be useful on occasion. Nevertheless, for many purposes, the distributions covered earlier in the chapter are sufficient, and the issue becomes how to select these appropriately, and to use them to the greatest effect.

Beyond the availability of distributions, the further general approaches to distribution selection involve the consideration of:

- The science of distributions.
- The availability of data.
- Industry standards.
- Pragmatic approaches.

9.2.1 Scientific and Conceptual Approaches

The scientific (or conceptual) approach to distribution selection is based on combining some knowledge (or assumed behaviour) of the underlying process with an understanding of how such a process would result in a particular type of distribution according to the theory (as outlined in this chapter, for example).

In principle, it is the key logical starting point for the choice of distributions: it may be argued that such an approach is the most accurate method. Many of the key points were covered earlier in the chapter, for example:

- A variable that results from the addition of many independent and identical random processes will follow a distribution that is approximately normal. This suggests the use of the normal distribution whenever the process in the real world results in the additive effect of many (non-modelled) random processes.
- A variable that results from the multiplication of many independent and identical random processes will follow a distribution that is approximately lognormal.
- The number of events that occurs over a continuous domain (usually considered to be a period of time) follows a Poisson distribution, whenever the likelihood (intensity) of occurrence is constant. For low intensity processes, this approximates a Bernoulli distribution, and for high intensity ones, it approximates a normal distribution.
- The uncertainty of single parameters of distributions (such as binomial/Bernoulli and Poisson processes) can generally be reflected if data are available (e.g. using beta and gamma distributions).
- The time-to-occurrences between events tends to follow distributions such as geometric, exponential, negative binomial, Weibull or gamma.

Although, in some contexts, one does need to find a theoretical or conceptual model for how an uncertain process behaves in order to justify the choice of distribution and validate the model, in many others this is not necessary. In practical business contexts, the use of such approaches may pose many challenges, both in terms of whether such a correspondence actually exists or can be found, and in terms of communication (where mathematical approaches may be more challenging to implement, with the extra accuracy potentially gained by doing so being outweighed by other practical factors).

9.2.2 Data-Driven Approaches

The use of historic data to select distributions or their parameters can be applied in several ways:

- Calculation of parameters for an assumed distribution. For example, the average and standard deviation (as required for a normal distribution) are easy to calculate given some data. However, when based on data, the calculation of a most likely value (as required for PERT and triangular distributions) can be challenging (even as such estimates are fairly easy to take from experts). Thus, it may be easier to use percentile parameters instead (e.g. a P10, P50 or P90). This is simple to do in @RISK, but when using Excel/VBA one may need to solve equations for the parameters of the distribution.
- Distribution fitting is part of the @RISK software (Chapter 13), and provides one way to select a distribution if data are available. Fitting methods, in fact, provide the best set of parameters for each distribution, and then compare the best-fitting distribution of each type. When using a fitting approach (in isolation) to select a distribution, one would, in principle, always use the top fitting distribution. However, in practice one may wish to combine the approaches and choose a well-fitting distribution (even if not the top fitting) if there are further reasons to do so. One can also use fitting simply to determine the best parameters for an assumed distribution (without comparing the fit with other distributions) if desired; this is useful as for some distributions the parameters may not have an easy direct statistical calculation procedure (unlike for the mean and standard deviation of a normal distribution, which can be easily calculated directly from data).
- Resampling the data. This was mentioned earlier; an example model is provided in Chapter 11.

Note that even large data sets of historic data may have limitations:

- Processes may not be stable over time, so that data are not comparable, even though they measure what is apparently the same process (e.g. quality, frequency of breakdowns, and so on). For example, a company may have improved its underlying efficiency, or restructured its contractual terms, or the macroeconomic environment may have changed.
- Data may need to be transformed, processed or other judgements about it made: For example:
  - When considering a set of data on the prices of stocks or commodities (e.g. oil) over time, the prices during 2015 are not from the same process as those from the 1980s. Rather, one would need to transform the data (such as to calculate the periodic percentage changes in the prices) to create a new data set whose items can be considered to come from the same process. Such a transformation may be quite complex to do in some cases: for example, although the periodic change in the price of a stock or commodity may be considered to arise from the same process (e.g. the probability of a 1% daily change in the price being the same in the 1980s or in the 2010s), such an assumption would not be valid for interest rates (which tend to follow mean-reverting processes; see Chapter 11).
  - If data are measured that concern a compound process or multiple processes (such as an event risk with an uncertain occurrence-on-impact) then one would need to isolate

each process separately. This can require criteria to be developed (or judgements to be made) concerning which items fall into which categories, which may be non-trivial to do.

9.2.3 Industry Standards

Some industries (especially finance, insurance and oil and gas) have adopted their own standardised distributions for certain variables; these have arisen typically from consideration of some combination of the data-driven and scientific approaches. For example, the normal, lognormal and Poisson distributions occur frequently in financial market and insurance applications; the Pareto distribution is also frequently used in the insurance industry to model severity of loss. The oil, gas and mining sectors tend to use the lognormal distribution for the uncertainty in the amount of reserves or deposits.

9.2.4 Pragmatic Approaches: Distributions, Parameters and Expert Input

Pragmatic approaches rely on using distributions whose main properties would seem to match those of real-life processes fairly well, and that are easy to parameterise and communicate.

In a sense, pragmatic approaches can be considered as a last option when scientific or data-driven approaches are unavailable (one may broadly consider a flow chart approach, which moves through the possibilities and on to the next only if the current consideration is not appropriate). On the other hand, in business contexts, it may be that one very quickly determines that a pragmatic approach is the most appropriate, or only available, method in practice.

When using pragmatic approaches, one would typically consider issues such as:

- Core nature and behaviour. Is it a risk event, a discrete process or a continuous one? Could it be a compound process, such as a set of scenarios where a continuous range of values is possible within each scenario? Can it occur only once in total, or once during each period, or multiple times within each period?
- Bounds. Is the process unbounded or bounded? Is it bounded on only one side (such as having a minimum possible value, but no maximum)? For an unbounded process, how closely would a bounded distribution approximate it?
- Accuracy. What requirements for high levels of accuracy are there, given the context of the analysis and the associated decision? What sort of approximations would be reasonable, and which would be unacceptable or unrealistic?

Distributions that in the first instance can be considered as pragmatic ones include:

- Uniform continuous, triangular and PERT. Each of these has simple parameters. In terms of choosing between them, the PERT is often a good default choice, for reasons discussed earlier:
  - The triangular and PERT distributions each have a single most likely value.
  - The PERT distribution is often preferable when a process is (or may be) non-symmetric.
- The Bernoulli, binomial and general discrete distributions often provide adequate pragmatic reflection of processes.

Other distributions are nevertheless often required, in particular:

- For discrete processes, the Poisson or geometric distribution is useful to capture the periods-to-occurrence of a Bernoulli process, or that multiple occurrences may be possible.
- To capture the unbounded nature of continuous processes, one may find that the normal, lognormal or Weibull distributions can be used. These are reasonably pragmatic:
  - The parameters of the normal and lognormal distribution (mean and standard deviation) are fairly easy to interpret in a physical sense. They can easily be calculated from data sets, and are fairly easy to estimate from experts (with the appropriate presentation, rules of thumb and visual tools).
  - The parameters of a Weibull distribution are harder to physically interpret, but they can be inferred instead by using (expert) estimates or data concerning their percentiles (see below).

For the Weibull distribution, the cumulative distribution function (for any x-value, in terms of its parameters α, β) is:

$$F(x) = 1 - e^{-\left(\frac{x}{\beta}\right)^{\alpha}}$$

Therefore, given its P_{10} and P_{90}, one could solve (for α, β):

$$0.1 = 1 - e^{-\left(\frac{P_{10}}{\beta}\right)^{\alpha}}$$

$$0.9 = 1 - e^{-\left(\frac{P_{90}}{\beta}\right)^{\alpha}}$$

which have the solution:

$$\alpha = \frac{\mathbf{LN}\left(\frac{\mathbf{LN}(0.1)}{\mathbf{LN}(0.9)}\right)}{\mathbf{LN}\left(\frac{P_{90}}{P_{10}}\right)}$$

and:

$$\beta = \frac{P_{90}}{\left(\mathbf{LN}\left(\frac{1}{0.1}\right)\right)^{\frac{1}{\alpha}}}$$

More generally, with the percentiles associated with the cumulative percentages P_l and P_h, being denoted X_l and X_h, the corresponding equations have the solution:

$$\alpha = \frac{\mathbf{LN}\left(\frac{\mathbf{LN}(1-P_h)}{\mathbf{LN}(1-P_l)}\right)}{\mathbf{LN}\left(\frac{X_h}{X_l}\right)}$$

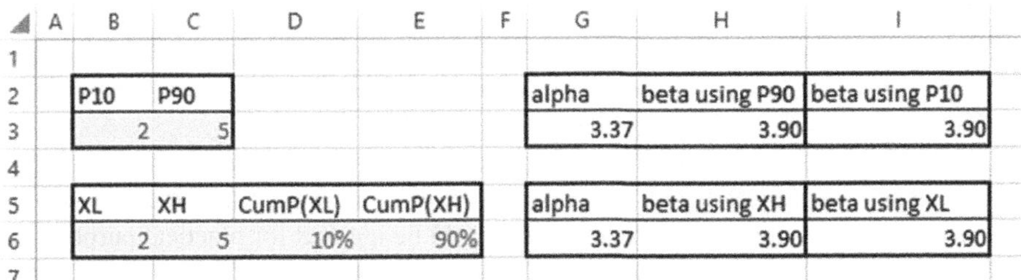

P10	P90
2	5

alpha	beta using P90	beta using P10
3.37	3.90	3.90

XL	XH	CumP(XL)	CumP(XH)
2	5	10%	90%

alpha	beta using XH	beta using XL
3.37	3.90	3.90

FIGURE 9.35 Excel Calculations of Weibull Parameters Given Percentile Information

and:

$$\beta = \frac{X_h}{\left(\mathbf{LN}\left(\frac{1}{1-P_h}\right)\right)^{\frac{1}{\alpha}}}$$

(alternatively, X_l and P_l could have been used in the equation for β).

One would also be able to use mixed parameter forms; for example, if β were known, and we needed to find α so that an x-value had a particular cumulative percentage, then this could be done using a similar approach.

The file Ch9.AltPs.Weibull.Excel.xlsx contains the above calculations, as shown in Figure 9.35.

In this sense, the Weibull distribution has a number of favourable properties:

- It is generally easy to handle analytically, especially to derive explicit expressions for its density and cumulative (and inverse cumulative) functions.
- It can be easily parameterised using percentiles, using the analytic formulae above.
- It has a minimum of zero and is unbounded to its right-hand side (and positively skewed).

Such a parameterisation is useful in many practical cases, including:

- When collecting estimates from experts, it may be easier to discuss (for example) the P10 and P90 cases, rather than the standard deviation.
- To avoid the potential underestimation of ranges; people may anchor themselves to observed events (which, since they have actually happened, cannot generally be the true maximum of the range of a continuous distribution, which has zero relative likelihood). The use of the P90 will extend the range (in 10% of cases) beyond the value of a "high" (P90) estimate. In practice, one may simply ask for an estimate of the maximum possible value, and then of the likelihood that this could be exceeded; although theoretically inconsistent (as the probability should be 0%), it often provides useful insights in practice.
- To be able to use a combination of parameter sets in pragmatic processes:
  - The minimum, most likely and P90. If one believes that a true minimum does exist (e.g. for the duration of a journey or the cost of an item), where one has a base case (corresponding to the most likely value), with the P90 value estimated using judgement.
  - The P10/most likely/P90. If one wishes to extend to the lower end of a range, whilst retaining the other benefits associated with the above point.

  - The P10/P50/P90. This is useful when the actual data are available, as the most likely value may be difficult to calculate accurately. On the other hand, for some combination of parameter values, distributions such as the PERT and lognormal (and normal) cannot be formed, and so can be inconvenient on occasion.
- It provides a consistent and robust way to approximate other processes. For example, although the theoretical length of a journey may be unbounded, it may be that very extreme outcomes are so unlikely that they could be ignored for practical purposes, and that a bounded (e.g. PERT) distribution would be used instead (with an appropriately large maximum figure). However, if two experts both have exactly the same view about the nature of the true unbounded process, but are required to state a fixed (bounded) figure for the maximum, each may provide a different value (one may give a figure that is implicitly the P99 [say], with the other giving the P95); for unbounded processes with long, thin tails, such estimates could be quite different to each other. On the other hand, if they are both asked to give a particular figure (say the P98), then each will provide the same estimate (as they have the same view of the process).
- In a sense, it allows for any distribution to be considered to be a pragmatic one, especially if it allows for inputs from experts to be made easily (even if data are not available).

For many distributions, the derivation of closed-form (exact analytic) solutions for the core parameters in terms of percentiles may be hard, or not possible. For example, since a beta (or PERT) distribution does not exist in closed form, such calculations are not possible. Therefore, when using Excel/VBA, the parameters may have to be found by iterative methods.

On the other hand, when using @RISK, the use of such approaches is available for almost all distributions, and is known as the "alternate parameter" form; its availability is one important advantage of using @RISK (especially as one may need to employ these pragmatic methods precisely in those contexts where one's mathematical or programming skills may not allow such approaches to be implemented). An example of the use of alternative parameters in @RISK is shown in Figure 9.36, in the context of a PERT distribution.

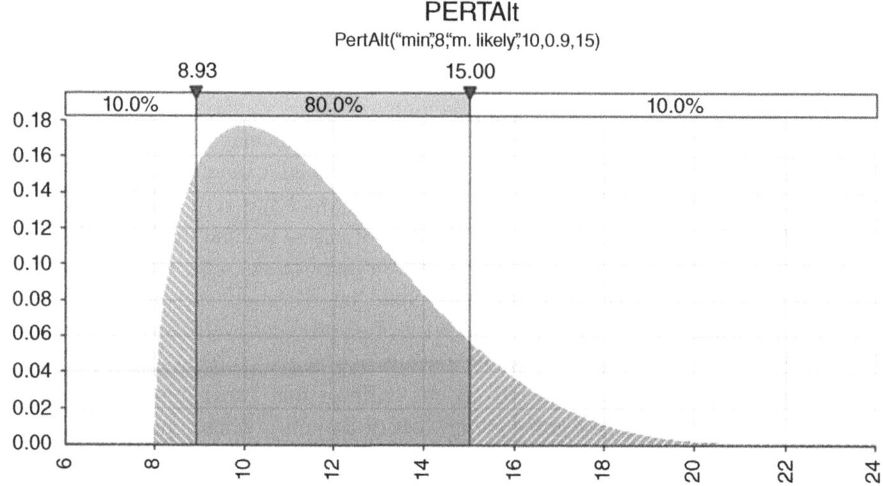

FIGURE 9.36 Example of a Percentile (Alternate) Parameter Form of the PERT Distribution

9.3 APPROXIMATION OF DISTRIBUTIONS WITH EACH OTHER

In Chapter 7, we discussed that models are both statements of hypotheses of relationships between variables (which can be used to generate insights about a situation, especially in the earlier stages of project evaluation), as well as having a calculatory purpose. In either case, a model is an approximation to reality. Thus, there is often no absolutely correct answer (or unique way) to address the issue of distribution selection. In addition, although risk assessment is used to improve the estimates (for example, of the mean outcome, of the likelihood of the base case and for providing reasonable information about the possible range), in most business decision-making contexts, there is generally not a requirement for extremely high levels of accuracy. Usually, there are other non-quantitative criteria, with quantitative analysis playing a valuable supporting role in an overall process. Thus, appropriate (and useful value-added models) of the same situation can often be built in a variety of ways. In principle, much value and insight can also be gained by comparing various modelling approaches to the same situation (however, for reasons of time such comparisons are rarely done in practice, except in certain selected areas or without formal consideration of the comparison process).

On the other hand, if the risks are mapped and quantified in a way that does not bear a reasonably close resemblance to the true nature of the risk, then clearly the model will be inaccurate and possibly misleading.

This section provides some examples of approaches that may be reasonable in many cases in general business risk modelling, and also points out some frequent pitfalls or mistakes that are made in risk mapping and model calibration.

9.3.1 Modelling Choices

In many cases, the use of one distribution over another is a modelling choice. Typical examples are discussed in the following (most of which have been mentioned at various places earlier in the text, so this discussion acts to consolidate these).

First, a distribution may be used to represent a variable that is, in reality, composed of more detailed processes. For example:

- An event risk (characterised by a probability) may be the result of many underlying factors:
  - The event of a person missing a train is a consequence of comparing the (uncertain) arrival time of the train at the station with the (uncertain) time taken for the person to travel to the station. The arrival time of the train at the station may itself depend on many uncertain factors, so that the backward-tracing process could continue indefinitely (as discussed in Chapter 7); hence most distributions are effectively aggregate representations of more detailed processes that are not explicitly modelled.
  - Whether a particular tennis player wins the Championship (as a yes/no event) depends on his/her winning each qualifying match (which are also yes/no events, each of which may be determined by other underlying uncertain factors, such as the state of fitness, injury or health of an opponent).
  - Whether a particular student is the one to win a class prize depends on their exam marks being above those of the next best student in a sufficient number of subjects (processes that themselves could be modelled individually).

  - Whether there is a delay of more than a week to the start-up of a manufacturing facility is the result of many aspects of the activities to build and test the facility.
- Non-symmetric continuous processes may be used in place of compound underlying processes:
  - A positively symmetric (e.g. PERT) distribution may be sufficient to capture a process that is made up of general (symmetric) uncertainty, as well as of several event risks that could increase the value of the outcome in some cases.
  - A lognormal distribution may be appropriate as a proxy for the existence of several underlying processes that act in a multiplicative manner.

Of course, in some cases, the separate explicit modelling of these more detailed processes is useful and necessary, whereas in others an aggregate approach may still suffice. For example, if one has historical data on the frequency of catching the train for the daily journey to work, such data could be used to populate a yes/no model, with the underlying nature of the train journey being irrelevant.

Second, the use of bounded distributions may be sufficiently accurate in some cases, even where the true distribution is unbounded (especially where the use of an unbounded distribution would create excess modelling complexity, compared to the benefit of additional accuracy, for example):

- A Bernoulli distribution may be a reasonable proxy (or pragmatic approximation) for a Poisson distribution where, although in theory an event could happen more than once (in a specific unit of time), it is very unlikely to do so. We showed earlier that a low-intensity Poisson process resembles a Bernoulli one and that, for example, when λ is less than approximately 0.15 (15%), the probability of having more than one occurrence of the process is less than 1% per unit time.
- One may generally use fixed probability parameters for binomial, Poisson or other distributions, even where there is (in theory) some uncertainty about the true values of the parameters.

Third, where continuous distributions are symmetric and single moded, there would be little difference between various distribution possibilities (as long as the parameter values are chosen appropriately):

- As shown earlier, a triangular distribution can provide a reasonable approximation to a normal distribution.
- In the case of symmetry, a PERT distribution will also provide a reasonable approximation to both.
- Other symmetric distributions (logistic, Student) would also provide fairly similar profiles.

Fourth, continuous processes may be sufficient to represent discrete ones, or vice versa:

- It is almost always sufficiently accurate to model financial quantities as continuous processes, rather than discrete ones (whose minimum unit is a cent, for example).
- Normal distributions may be sufficient to capture the (discrete) number of outcomes for high-intensity Poisson processes.

- Discrete scenarios may be more appropriate than continuous ranges in some cases. For example, one may have estimates of a low, most likely and high value for a process (such as a journey time), whereas in fact these figures could each be the most likely value that would apply in each of three scenarios, with a range of variation within each scenario around these. The use of continuous ranges within scenarios provides an example of a compound process.

9.3.2 Distribution Comparison and Parameter Matching

In the discussion earlier in the chapter we showed how distributions may be pragmatically approximated to each other using the visual overlay features in @RISK (such as finding that the P1 and P99 points of a normal distribution provided reasonable estimates of the minimum and maximum parameters of an approximating triangular distribution). We also showed how an approximation process can be formalised to create distributions whose parameters (or other statistical properties, such as percentiles) match each other.

In general, these more formal methods use statistical properties of the distribution functions, which may not always be easy to work with. In such cases, at least when using @RISK, one can often create such approximations by combining the use of the **RiskTheo** statistics functions with the alternative parameter form of distributions in appropriate ways. For example, the PERT distribution often provides a reasonable approximation of other continuous distributions, so that if one knew the mean and standard deviation (μ, σ) of a lognormal distribution (which, of course, is unbounded in the positive direction), then one could find a PERT distribution that had the same P10, most likely and P90 points as the lognormal distribution by:

- Creating the lognormal distribution with the given parameters.
- Using **RiskTheoPtoX** (or **RiskTheoPercentile**) to establish the P10 and P90 of this distribution, and **RiskTheoMode** to establish its most likely value.
- Creating the PERT distribution using the alternate parameter formulation, based on the P10, most likely and P90 values that have been established.

Figure 9.37 shows an overlay comparison of this for the case in which the lognormal distribution has a mean and standard deviation of 50 and 20, respectively.

The general discrete distribution can also be used to approximate continuous processes. One of the most well-known approaches is to use a three-point discrete distribution to approximate a normal distribution. For example, given a normal distribution, one could calculate its P10, P50 and P90, and then establish the required probabilities (or weightings) of each in such a way that the general discrete distribution formed with these values would have the same mean and standard deviation as the original normal distribution. Such a calculation can be performed by combining Excel's **GoalSeek** with the use of @RISK's **RiskTheo** functions and the alternate parameters by:

- Creating a normal distribution with the given parameters.
- Using the **RiskTheoPtoX** (**RiskTheoPercentile**) functions to calculate its P10, P50 and P90.
- Using these percentiles as the three x-values of a discrete process, in which the probability for each point is defined as p, $1 - 2p$, p, where p is a value to be found (the use of

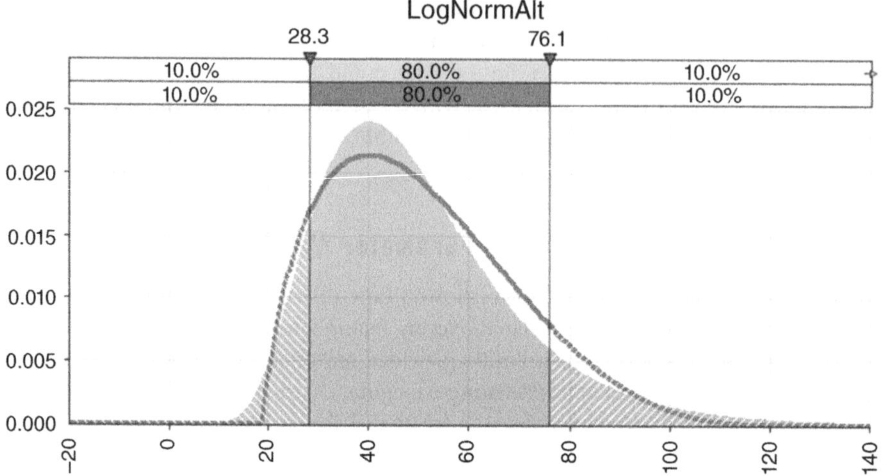

FIGURE 9.37 Comparison of Lognormal and PERT Distributions with the same P10, most Likely and P90 Values

these probabilities ensures that the resulting discrete distribution is symmetric and with probabilities that add to 100%; in other words, there is only a single variable to find, or one degree of freedom).

- Using the **RiskTheoStdDev** function to calculate the standard deviation of the discrete distribution.
- Creating a cell that calculates the difference between that and the standard deviation of the normal distribution.
- Running **GoalSeek** to set this cell (i.e. the difference between the standard deviations) to zero by changing the probability.

Figure 9.38 shows the results of this process, demonstrating that weightings of approximately 30%, 40% and 30% are required so that the two distributions have the same standard deviation; this is known as Swanson's rule. One important application is for the weights used in decision-tree models: the tree is a discrete process but often represents an underlying continuous one. Thus, for a given underlying assumed distribution, and with branch values assumed to be specific percentiles of this, one cannot choose the branch probabilities freely.

Note that, because the normal distribution is symmetric, the "30-40-30" weights apply to the P10, P50 and P90 points of any such distribution, irrespective of its parameters. If one applied the same process to a non-symmetric distribution (such as a lognormal), then one would need to solve for two weighting factors (with the third being the probability required to make the total 100%). In this case, as there is more than one item to be solved, one would need to use Excel's **Solver** (or alternative equivalent) in place of **GoalSeek**. Generally speaking, the required weights for the discrete process would depend on the parameters of the lognormal distribution. Thus, in some cases, one often uses the weights that apply for a normal distribution to other distributions, and accepts that the two distributions may not have parameters that match perfectly. Note that by using the same basic approaches, one could apply the (normal-derived) weights to the P10, P50 and P90 of any distribution, and then use

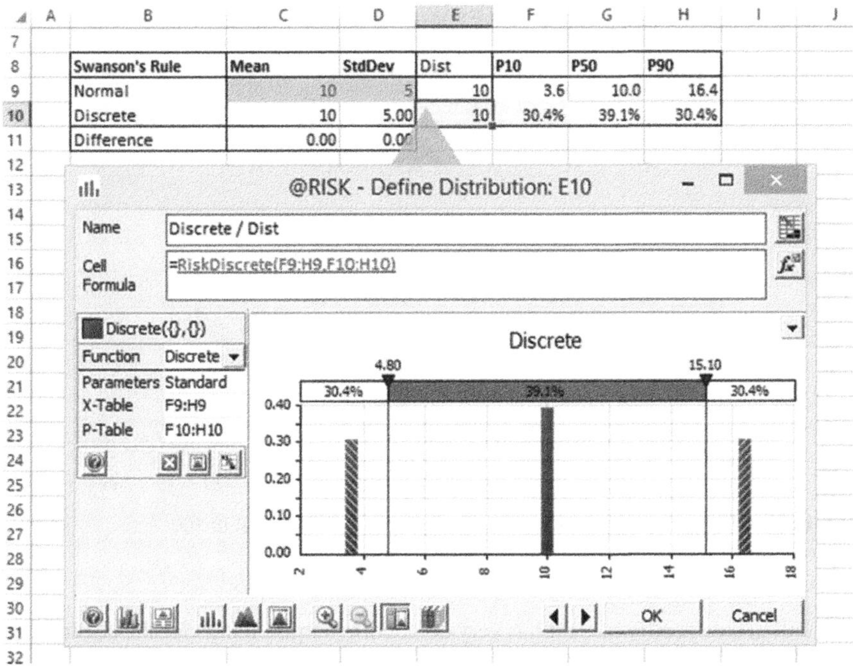

FIGURE 9.38 Derivation of Weights to Use at the P10, P50 and P90 Values, in Order to Approximate a Normal Distribution with a General Discrete Distribution

overlays, the alternative parameter form and statistics functions to compare the distributions. Figure 9.39 shows the corresponding approach that applies the weights derived above to the percentiles of the lognormal distribution, from which one sees that there would be a small difference between the means, and a slightly larger one between the standard deviation in this case.

Note that the parameter- and percentile-matching approaches shown here do not use the same criteria as those that apply in general distribution fitting (see Chapter 13); the latter approaches generally minimise the distance between the two by considering all points in the range.

9.3.3 Some Potential Pitfalls Associated with Distribution Approximations

In the above discussion, we aimed to show some examples of the types of approximations that may be necessary in practical business applications, and which generally may also be

Applying Weights	Mean	StdDev	Dist	P10	P50	P90
Lognormal	50.0	20.0	33.63	28.3	46.4	76.1
Discrete	49.94	18.83	46.42	30.4%	39.1%	30.4%
Difference	0.06	1.17				

FIGURE 9.39 Using 30-40-30 Weights for Non-normal Distributions will Provide Only an Approximation

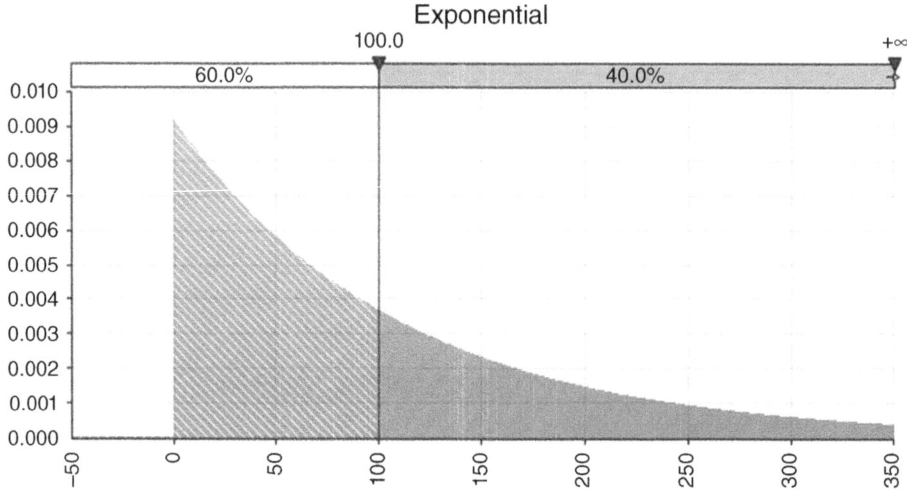

FIGURE 9.40 Using the Exponential Distribution with its P60 Equal to 100

sufficient, unless the specific context has very demanding requirements for the accuracy of the numerical results.

On the other hand, very often one observes that inappropriate approximation methods are used. In the following we provide a few examples of where caution may need to be exercised.

As mentioned in Chapter 3, and at various other places in this text, the use of probability-impact frameworks can be a very powerful one in some circumstances, and is a natural extension of the risk-register approach to (qualitative) risk management. We also described how the creation of full risk models by extending the results of risk-register approaches can have some associated issues; these tend to arise when the underlying process is, in fact, not of an event-risk nature, but the framework used to describe risks has guided one down this route. For example, a project team may have identified that there is a risk that additional costs may arise in the project. If the structure used to classify all risks is a probability-impact one, then (for example) such a risk may have been described as "having a 40% probability and an impact of $100". However (as for other cases in which one considers continuous uncertainties within such a framework), it may be that this "risk" will always materialise (so that the probability is essentially irrelevant, i.e. it is 100%), with the issue, in fact, being the extent (or uncertainty) of the additional costs. Thus, the data provided about this process (which may come from estimates or expert judgement) may really correspond to there being a 40% chance that the costs will be $100 or more (i.e. that $100 represents the P60 of the distribution). In other words, the probability is, in fact, that of a percentile of an impact distribution, rather than a probability-of-occurrence. Note that to create the actual distribution (and finalise the numerical calculations) for the additional cost, one would need to select the appropriate (continuous) uncertainty distribution, and generally make additional assumptions (or seek more information from the provider of the original data) on other parameter values:

- Figure 9.40 shows the consequence of using an exponential distribution, and using the additional assumption that the minimum cost is zero.

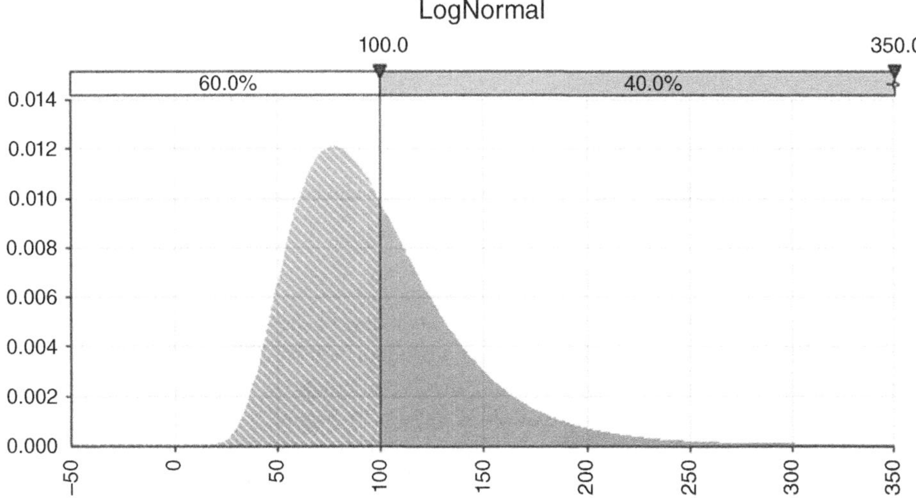

FIGURE 9.41 Using the Lognormal Distribution with its P60 Equal to 100

- Figure 9.41 shows the case of a lognormal distribution, and using the additional assumption that the minimum cost is zero and the P90 is 150.
- Figure 9.42 shows the case of a PERT distribution, and using the additional assumption that the minimum cost is zero and the maximum is 250.

Figure 9.43 shows the average (mean) values in each case, including for the implied base assumption that the extra cost of $100 occurs in 40% of cases. One can clearly see the large difference in consequences, and the potential that the base probability-impact framework misstates this risk, in these cases with a significant understatement of the averages (and worst cases).

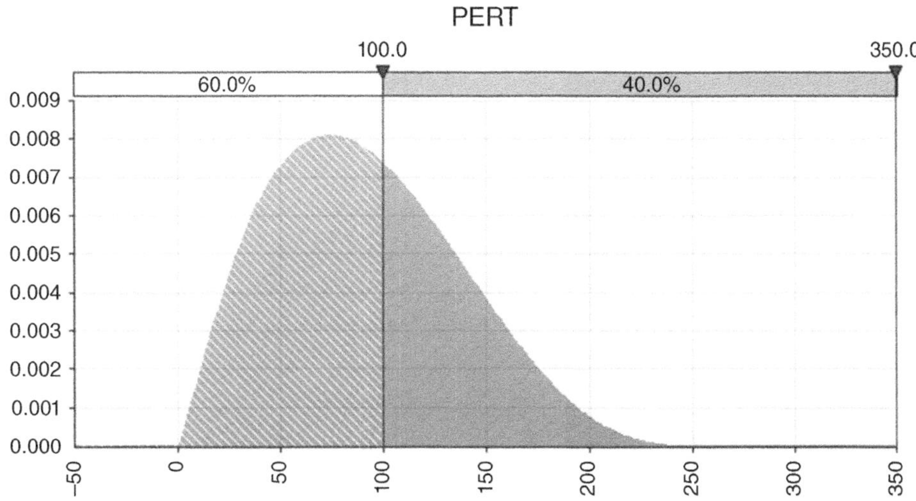

FIGURE 9.42 Using the PERT Distribution with its P60 Equal to 100

Distribution	Mean Value
Bernoulli, or using P*I multiplication	40
Exponential	109
LogNormal	98
PERT	91

FIGURE 9.43 Comparison of Mean Values for Various Distribution Assumptions

In some cases, the mean may be overstated by such approaches. For example, if a risk has been identified that the level of market prices of a product will be different to that which has been planned for, whereas the true process may involve fluctuations in both directions around a base value, then one may have a situation as shown in Figure 9.44. This uses a normal distribution with the same parameters as above (i.e. $100 as the P60), and the additional assumption that the mean is zero. In this case, the base assumption (of $40 for the mean) overstates the true figure (of $0), even if it does not capture the variability correctly.

Thus, the above issue may arise generally when the underlying process is a continuous uncertainty, but where a probability-impact framework is presented as a working tool to assist and facilitate group processes.

Another area where mistakes are sometimes made with probability-impact frameworks is not to attach a timeframe to the probability-of-occurrence. In some cases, such oversights may have little consequence in practice. For example, where a project is to be implemented over the course of the next 3 or 4 weeks, with each risk happening at most once, then the implicit timeframe is "over the course of the implementation phase of the project"; this may be sufficient for many purposes. However, where the timeframe of a project is significant (such as years), then an (apparently quantitative) phrase such as "there is a 20% chance of an incident happening" may have little meaning (from a quantitative perspective): clearly there

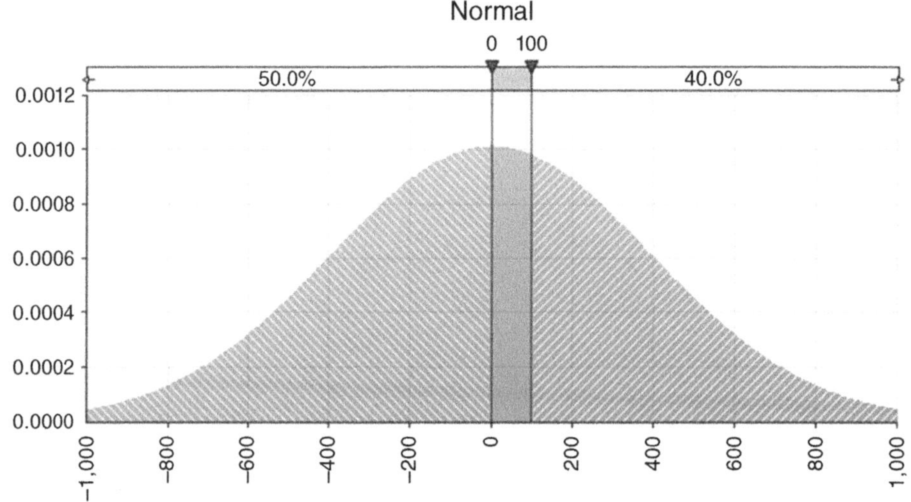

FIGURE 9.44 Using the Normal Distribution with its P60 Equal to 100

	A	B	C	D
1				
2		**From one-period to several**		
3		Probability (occurrence) per period	15.0%	
4		Number of periods	10	
5		Probability (non-occurrence) per period	85%	=1-C3
6		Probability (non-occurrence) over these periods	19.7%	=C5^C4
7		Probability (occurrence) over these periods	80.3%	=1-C6
8				
9		**From several periods to one**		
10		Probability (occurrence) over several periods	80.3%	
11		Number of periods	10	
12		Probability (non-occurrence) over several periods	20%	=1-C10
13		Probability (non-occurrence) over one period	85.0%	=C12^(1/C11)
14		Probability (non-occurrence) over one period	15.0%	=1-C13
15				
16		**Another way to collect pragmatic information**		
17		Periods to wait until X% sure that event has been observed	10	
18		X% confidence that event would be observed in this time	80%	
19		Probabilty per period	15%	=1-(1-C18)^(1/C17)

FIGURE 9.45 Cross-calibration of Probabilities of Occurrence for Time Periods

is a big difference between a 20% likelihood of occurrence per month versus 20% per year, for example. In addition, although it may be a reasonable approximation to assume that over a short timeframe an event can occur at most once (and use a Bernoulli distribution), over longer timeframes one may need to allow for multiple occurrences, which may change the distribution used, as well as the model approach and structure.

In the case of a process that can happen at most once, it is relatively straightforward to adjust probabilities that apply in one period to be suitable for longer periods: assuming that the occurrence of a risk is independent from one period to the next, then the probability of non-occurrence over several periods is the product of the non-occurrence in each period. Therefore, the probability of an occurrence in any period can be calculated from the probability of occurrence over a longer timeframe, and vice versa.

The file Ch9.Mapping.TimeToOccurrrence.Calibration.xlsx contains an example of the adjustment in probability required as one moves either from a one-period to a multi-period model, or the other way around. Figure 9.45 shows the calculations in each case. Note that the application of such procedures to clarify statements of probability estimates can, of course, lead to large changes to quantitative modelling results (roughly speaking, over a 5-year period, annual probabilities would be multiplied by five, for example, although the actual calculation is one of multiplication as shown in the file). When such large changes in values are made in a model's value as a result of such clarifications, it can be important to find alternative ways of cross-checking the assumptions. For example, one may ask a question such as "how long do you think one would have to wait so that the event would have happened in 90% of cases?" As shown in the file, such information can be used to cross-calibrate the process (if there are large differences in the estimates depending on the approach, then further exploration as to why this is so will be important and may generate additional insight).

	A	B	C	D	E
1					
2			P(occurrence)	P(Non-occurrence)	
3		Risk 1	10%	90%	=1-C3
4		Risk 2	5%	95%	=1-C4
5		Risk 3	5%	95%	=1-C5
6		Risk 4	10%	90%	=1-C6
7		Risk 5	5%	95%	=1-C7
8		Total	31%	69%	
9			=1-D8	=PRODUCT(D3:D7)	

FIGURE 9.46 Cross-calibration of Probabilities of Occurrence for Multiple Risks

More generally, some risk events may be able to happen more than once, depending on the timeframe under consideration, meaning that risks may be understated if they are allowed to occur only once: a probability-impact framework that allows only the yes/no question "is there an incident?" may be asking the wrong question (which is "how many incidents?"). In such cases, the use of a Poisson distribution is often more appropriate. In fact, this is often easier, as the Poisson (intensity) parameter scales linearly with time (unlike the binomial or Bernoulli probability), so that adjusting the intensities is a simple question of multiplication or division. On the other hand, in order to allow multiple occurrences within each period, one may be required to use compounding processes (as each occurrence may have a different impact, which needs to be captured separately); this can alter the structure of the model, and may require the use of compound distributions, such as @RISK's **RiskCompound** (see Chapter 13).

Related to the concept of multiple occurrences of the same risk items is the treatment of a number of "small" risks as a single item. For example, if each risk in a set has sufficiently low probability-of-occurrence, then it is unlikely that more than one risk would occur (the more risks that there are, the more likely it is that at least one would occur). Thus, one may consider substituting this set of individual risks for a single risk item, or a category representative. For example, Figure 9.46 shows a similar calculation to the above, in which the probability-of-occurrence (of one or more risks) can be seen by calculating the product of the probability of non-occurrence of each, and subtracting this from 100%. In other words, in the example shown, there is a 31% probability that at least one item of the five occurs, as there is a 69% chance that none of them occurs. Thus, one may consider replacing the set of event risks by a single event risk with a higher probability of occurrence (and ignoring that there may be a small chance of multiple occurrences when the full set is considered).

This technique may be simple as a concept, although it can be challenging to do if the impacts of each risk are very different to each other, because the impact (or its distribution) that should be associated with the occurrence of the single event risk is not well defined. In such cases, a more appropriate method would be to capture the individual risk impacts within the model, but to treat their aggregate impact as if it were a single risk item (for the purposes of the analysis and display of results). In the Excel/VBA approaches used in Chapter 12, this would be achieved by simply setting the cell(s) that contain the aggregate calculation as an output to be recorded during a simulation, whereas in @RISK, the cell would be marked with the **RiskMakeInput** function, as discussed in Chapter 13.

CHAPTER 10

Creating Samples from Distributions

This chapter describes the calculations required to create random samples from distributions. This is fundamental to modellers who wish to use the Excel/VBA approach, but relevant only as a background for those using @RISK (who may choose to skim or skip this chapter). In traditional statistics (and in Excel), distribution functions return a measure of relative or cumulative probability at a particular value of the variable (rather than a random sample), whereas in @RISK, distribution functions directly return samples (rather than probability information).

As described in Chapter 8 (see Figure 8.8), random samples can be created explicitly by inversion of the cumulative distribution function, involving two steps:

- The creation of a random sample from a (standard) uniform continuous distribution, i.e. of a random value between zero and one (0% and 100%). In Excel, this can be done using the **RAND**() function.
- The calculation of the associated percentile of the distribution.

Recall from Chapter 9 that a cumulative distribution is a function, F, that evaluates the cumulated probability, P, up to the point x:

$$P = F(\text{Par1}, \ldots, \text{ParN}, x)$$

where Par1, Par2... are the parameters of the distribution (e.g. μ, σ, α, β, λ, Min, ML, Max).

The inversion process involves finding, for any value of P, the corresponding x-value. Although one may conceive of this as requiring a search procedure, in many cases the mathematical formula for the inverse function is easy to find.

For example, in the case of a Weibull distribution, we noted in Chapter 9 that the cumulative function is:

$$F(x) = 1 - e^{-\left(\frac{x}{\beta}\right)^{\alpha}}$$

Thus, for a given cumulated probability, P, we would wish to find the x-value so that:

$$P = 1 - e^{-\left(\frac{x}{\beta}\right)^{\alpha}}$$

With a little mathematical manipulation, it is easy to see that this is:

$$x = \beta.\left(\mathbf{LN}\left(\frac{1}{1-P}\right)\right)^{1/\alpha}$$

Generally, the inverse function has P as an input (together with the parameters of the distribution) and x as the output:

$$x = FINV(\text{Par1}, \ldots, \text{ParN}, P)$$

Thus, random samples of P (such as those created using the **RAND**() function) will create random samples of the distribution. It is clear that the properties of the x-samples generated in this way (such as being truly accurate or representative of the distribution) will depend on the properties (or quality) of the random samples of the probability (assuming that the inversion calculations can be done exactly).

Note that, in some cases, this inversion process is so simple that its existence may be overlooked, as it is "hidden in plain sight". For example, the **RAND**() function directly generates a sample from a standard uniform continuous distribution without any apparent inversion: since the density curve is $f(x) = 1$, the cumulative curve is $F(x) = x$, so that one seeks the x-value that satisfies $P = x$, which, of course, is given by (the inverse function) $x = P$. Thus, the sampled value, P, directly provides a sampled value, x. Similarly, when the **RAND**() function is combined with an **IF** statement to sample the occurrence or not of an event-type risk, this is an inversion of the binomial (or Bernoulli) cumulative distribution.

More generally, the process to invert (or sample from) a distribution depends on the specific function, and can be considered to fall into several possible categories:

- Where inverse functions are in-built into Excel.
- Where the inverse function can be readily expressed as a (closed-form) formula (as in the example above for the Weibull distribution), and hence can be calculated directly.
- Where some form of search, lookup or iterative technique is required. Although applicable to all cases in theory, search techniques are generally less computationally efficient than direct calculations (or Excel functions) if they are available.

Depending on the function, one or other of these methods will be the most appropriate. These are discussed in the remainder of the chapter.

10.1 READILY AVAILABLE INVERSE FUNCTIONS

This section describes distributions whose inverse functions are readily available, either directly in Excel or by use of simple formulae that can be created explicitly.

10.1.1 Functions Provided Directly in Excel

A number of inverse functions are available in Excel. Fortunately, these often correspond to situations where closed-form formulae are not available. Note that one could choose to create one's own algorithms for inverse functions even where Excel provides an inverse function (for example, through simple internet searches one can find procedures to create samples from the normal distribution); however, generally it would seem logical to use the in-built approaches unless one has knowledge that a procedure is better than that which is built into Excel.

The inverse functions directly available in Excel are:

- **BINOM.INV** can be used to create a sample from a binomial distribution; the parameter **Alpha** of the function would refer to the random *P*. In versions prior to Excel 2007, there is no equivalent function (i.e. "**BINOMINV**" does not exist, so that search techniques could be used).
- **NORM.INV** (or **NORMINV**) can be used to sample from a normal distribution. One may also use **NORM.S.INV** or **NORMSINV** to sample from a standard normal distribution and rescale the results by multiplying by the standard deviation and adding the mean.
- **LOGNORM.INV** (or **LOGINV**) can be used to sample from a lognormal distribution. Note that this function uses the logarithmic parameters, not the natural ones (see Chapter 9).
- **BETA.INV** (or **BETAINV**) can be used to sample from a beta distribution. Note that these can be used to produce samples of the PERT distribution, due to the relationship described in Chapter 9.
- **GAMMA.INV** (or **GAMMAINV**) can be used to create samples from the gamma distribution.
- The **T.INV** (or **TINV**) function can be used to create samples from the *t* (Student) distribution, **CHISQ.INV** (or **CHIINV**) for the chi-squared distribution and **F.INV** (or **FINV**) for the *F*-distribution. Note that some of these inverse functions also exist in the two-tailed form (such as **CHISQ.INV.RT**, **F.INV.RT** and **T.INV.2T**), which are relevant for statistical calculations of confidence intervals, but not if one is inverting a distribution for simulation purposes; care therefore needs to be taken, as shown in the example in Chapter 9 for the *t*-distribution.

The file Ch10.InverseFunctions.Excel.xlsx contains an example of each of these, as shown in Figure 10.1. Note that the file also shows both forms of parameterisation of the

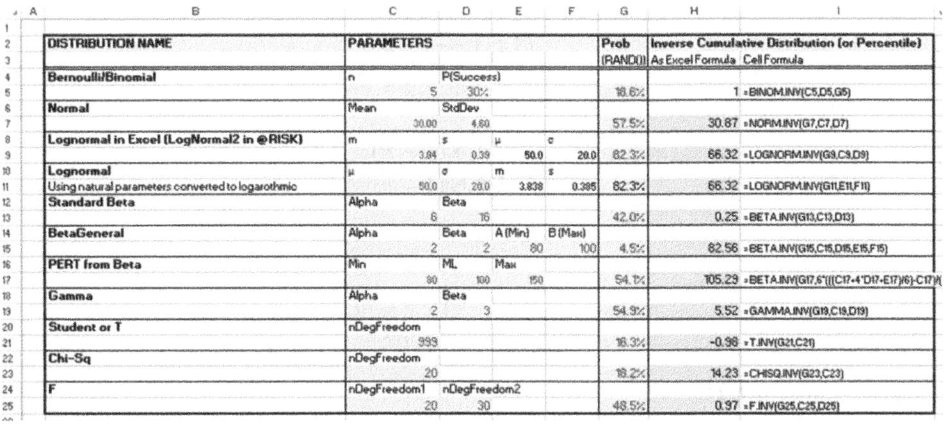

	A	B	C	D	E	F	G	H	I
1									
2		**DISTRIBUTION NAME**	**PARAMETERS**				**Prob**	**Inverse Cumulative Distribution (or Percentile)**	
3							(RAND())	As Excel Formula	Cell Formula
4		**Bernoulli/Binomial**	n	P(Success)					
5			5	30%			18.6%	1	=BINOM.INV(C5,D5,G5)
6		**Normal**	Mean	StdDev					
7			30.00	4.60			57.5%	30.87	=NORM.INV(G7,C7,D7)
8		**Lognormal in Excel (LogNormal2 in @RISK)**	m	s	μ	σ			
9			3.84	0.39	50.0	20.0	82.3%	66.32	=LOGNORM.INV(G9,C9,D9)
10		**Lognormal**	μ	σ	m	s			
11		Using natural parameters converted to logarothmic	50.0	20.0	3.838	0.385	82.3%	66.32	=LOGNORM.INV(G11,E11,F11)
12		**Standard Beta**	Alpha	Beta					
13			6	16			42.0%	0.25	=BETA.INV(G13,C13,D13)
14		**BetaGeneral**	Alpha	Beta	A (Min)	B (Max)			
15			2	2	80	100	4.5%	82.56	=BETA.INV(G15,C15,D15,E15,F15)
16		**PERT from Beta**	Min	ML	Max				
17			80	100	150		54.1%	105.29	=BETA.INV(G17,6*(((C17+4*D17+E17)/6)-C17)/(
18		**Gamma**	Alpha	Beta					
19			2	3			54.9%	5.52	=GAMMA.INV(G19,C19,D19)
20		**Student or T**	nDegFreedom						
21			999				16.3%	-0.98	=T.INV(G21,C21)
22		**Chi-Sq**	nDegFreedom						
23			20				18.2%	14.23	=CHISQ.INV(G23,C23)
24		**F**	nDegFreedom1	nDegFreedom2					
25			20	30			48.5%	0.97	=F.INV(G25,C25,D25)

FIGURE 10.1 Examples of Excel Inverse Functions

lognormal distribution (in which, in the second case, the natural parameters are first converted to logarithmic ones), as well as showing the PERT distribution using the parameter calculations described in Chapter 9. Column G contains various **RAND**() functions; the reader will see different figures by pressing **F9** (so that Excel recalculates) when using the file.

10.1.2 Functions Whose Formulae Can Easily Be Created

Several important and frequently occurring distributions do not (at the time of writing) have explicit inverse functions in Excel, but can be readily calculated by simple manipulation of the formula for the cumulative distribution function. These include (with their parameters shown in brackets):

Standard uniform continuous:

$$x = P$$

Uniform continuous(L, U):

$$x = L + P(U - L)$$

Bernoulli(p):

$$x = \mathbf{IF}\,(p \leq P, 1, 0)$$

or:

$$x = \mathbf{IF}\,(P > 1 - p, 1, 0)$$

Triangular(Min,ML,Max):

$$x = \text{Min} + \sqrt{P(\text{ML} - \text{Min})(\text{Max} - \text{Min})} \text{ if } P \leq \frac{\text{ML} - \text{Min}}{\text{Max} - \text{Min}}$$

$$x = \text{Max} - \sqrt{(1 - P)(\text{ML} - \text{Min})(\text{Max} - \text{Min})} \text{ if } P > \frac{\text{ML} - \text{Min}}{\text{Max} - \text{Min}}$$

Exponential(β):

$$x = \beta\mathbf{LN}\left(\frac{1}{1 - P}\right)$$

Geometric(p):

$$x = \mathbf{ROUNDUP}\left(\frac{\mathbf{LN}\,(1 - P)}{\mathbf{LN}\,(1 - p)}, 0\right) - 0$$

Weibull(α,β):

$$x = \beta.\left(\mathbf{LN}\left(\frac{1}{1 - P}\right)\right)^{1/\alpha}$$

Integer uniform(L,U):

$$x = L + \mathbf{INT}\,(P(U - L + 1))$$

Pareto(θ, α):

$$x = \frac{\alpha}{(1-P)^{\frac{1}{\theta}}}$$

Pareto2(B,Q):

$$x = -B + \frac{B}{(1-P)^{\frac{1}{Q}}}$$

ExtremeValueMax(a,b):

$$x = a - b\mathbf{LN}(-\mathbf{LN}(P))$$

ExtremeValueMin(a,b):

$$x = a + b\mathbf{LN}(-\mathbf{LN}(1-P))$$

Logistic(α,β):

$$x = \alpha + \beta\mathbf{LN}\left(\frac{P}{1-P}\right)$$

Log-logistic(γ,β,α):

$$x = \gamma + \beta\left(\frac{P}{1-P}\right)^{\frac{1}{\alpha}}$$

The file Ch10.InverseFunctions.Analytic.xlsx contains an example of each of these, as shown in Figure 10.2.

10.2 FUNCTIONS REQUIRING LOOKUP AND SEARCH METHODS

For certain distributions, especially discrete ones, it may be necessary to find a random sample in an incremental stepwise fashion in which one cumulates the probability from that of the lowest possible value upwards, until a value is found whose cumulated probability matches the random percentage. Examples include the general discrete, Poisson, negative binomial and hypergeometric distributions.

10.2.1 Lookup Tables

The general discrete distribution is parameterised by a table of values and probabilities, and hence the cumulative distribution cannot be expressed as a mathematical function in any true sense. On the other hand, with the set of x-values and their cumulative probabilities placed in ascending order, one can, for a given P, simply look within the table for the largest x-value whose cumulated probability is less than or equal to P (for example, using lookup functions such as **INDEX**, **MATCH**, etc.) One may also choose to adapt the table to ensure that the probability data automatically sum to 100%.

The file Ch10.InverseFunctions.Discrete.xlsx contains an example, shown in Figure 10.3, and covers the cases where the data are laid out either in a row or in a column. In the first

	A	B	C	D	E	F	G	H	I
1									
2		DISTRIBUTION NAME	PARAMETERS				Prob	Inverse Cumulative Distribution (or Percentile)	
3							(RAND())	As Excel Formula	Cell Formula
4		Uniform on [0,1]							
5							35.0%	0.35	=G5
6		Uniform between L and U	L	U					
7			3.20	7.90			67.2%	6.36	=C7+G7*(D7-C7)
8		Bernoulli	P(Success)						
9		Bernoulli using RAND() and IF	30%				5.9%	0	=IF(G9>1-C9,1,0)
10		Triangular	Min	ML	Max				
11			80	100	200		58.6%	129.51	=IF(G11<=(D11-C11)/(E11-C11),C11+SQRT(G11*(D11-C11)*(E11-
12		Geometric	P(Success)						
13			30%				99.3%	13	=ROUNDUP(LN(1-G13)/LN(1-C13),0)-1
14		Exponential	Lambda/Beta						
15			3.33				64.3%	3.43	=C15*(LN(1/(1-G15)))
16		Weibull	Alpha	Beta					
17			2	3			59.0%	2.83	=D17*(LN(1/(1-G17)))^(1/C17)
18		Integer Uniform between integers L and U	L	U					
19		Integer Uniform between L and U (both integers)	1994	2013			28.3%	1999	=C19+INT(G19*(D19-C19+1))
20		Pareto	Theta	a					
21			3.00	5.00			64.8%	7.08	=D21/((1-G21)^(1/C21))
22		Pareto2	B	Q					
23			1.00	3.00			13.5%	0.05	=-C23+C23/((1-G23)^(1/D23))
24		Extreme Value Max	a	b					
25			2.00	10.00			67.7%	-7.42	=C25+D25*LN(-LN(G25))
26		Extreme Value Min	a	b					
27			2.00	10.00			90.3%	-6.45	=C27-D27*LN(-LN(1-G27))
28		Logistic	Alpha	Beta					
29			30.0	2.0			21.1%	27.36	=C29+D29*LN(G29/(1-G29))
30		LogLogistic	Gamma	Beta	Alpha				
31			4.00	3.00	2.00		3.4%	4.56	=C31+D31*((G31/(1-G31))^(1/E31))

FIGURE 10.2 Inverse Functions Calculated Analytically

case, the input data to the function are contained in the cells D2:F3, with the other areas of the whole table C2:F5 used to cumulate and rescale the probabilities. On close inspection of the formulae in cells I3 and I8, one can see that the detailed syntax of the formulae depends on the layout of the data (which is one reason to create user-defined functions instead, as discussed later).

10.2.2 Search Methods

The Poisson distribution provides an example of where a search approach is necessary.

The density function is given by:

$$f(i) = e^{-\lambda}\lambda^i/i!$$

and the cumulative function by:

$$F(i) = e^{-\lambda}\sum_{j=0}^{j=i}\frac{\lambda^j}{j!}$$

Note that the density function is, in principle, simple to calculate analytically, although the cumulative distribution cannot be inverted analytically.

	A	B	C	D	E	F	G	H	I	J
1		Discrete Distribution								
2		X-Value	10	10	15	25		Prob (RAND())	X-Value	
3		Probabilities		25%	45%	55%		24.4%	15.0	=INDEX(C2:F2,1,IFERROR(MATCH(H3,C5:F5,0),MATCH(H3,C5:F5,1)+1))
4		Cumulative Probability	0%	25%	70%	125%				
5		Scaled Cum Prob	0%	20%	56%	100%				
6										
7			X-Value	Probab	Cumul	Scaled Cum Prob				
8			10		0%	0%		24.4%	15.0	=INDEX(C8:C11,IFERROR(MATCH(H8,F8:F11,0),MATCH(H8,F8:F11,1)+1),1)
9			10	25%	25%	20%				
10			15	45%	70%	56%				
11			25	55%	125%	100%				

FIGURE 10.3 Example of a Lookup Table to Calculate the Inverse

The inversion procedure, for a given probability, P, requires finding the largest integer (iEvents) such that:

$$F(\text{iEvents}) \leq P$$

Since the density and cumulative distributions are both available in Excel (**POISSON.DIST** or **POISSON** in earlier versions of Excel), this can be written (using the full parameter list of the function) as finding the largest integer (iEvents) such that:

$$\textbf{POISSON.DIST}(\text{iEvents}, \lambda, 1) \leq P$$

This would be cumbersome to set up in an Excel range, as the size of the required range would be potentially unlimited. However, a search procedure can be embedded within a user-defined function, as described later. Note also that the term $e^{-\lambda}$, although always positive, becomes small for large λ (and may evaluate either to zero or inaccurately when used in computational procedures), whereas in such cases, the distribution is essentially a normal one, albeit returning an integer, not a continuous, value. Thus, a sample from a normal distribution with mean λ and standard deviation $\sqrt{\lambda}$ can be used instead (see the example code later).

The creation of random samples by such iterative (search) methods also applies to any discrete process whose inverse cumulative function may not be available analytically, but where either the cumulative function is directly available in Excel, or the density function can be easily evaluated (if one is explicitly cumulating in a stepwise manner). In particular, the negative binomial and hypergeometric distributions fall into this category (the Excel distribution functions **NEGBINOM.DIST** and **HYPGEOM.DIST** can be used to evaluate the density and cumulative curves, whereas the earlier functions **NEGBINOMDIST** and **HYPGEOMDIST** provide only the density curves, so that an explicit process to cumulate the distribution is necessary).

10.3 COMPARING CALCULATED SAMPLES WITH THOSE IN @RISK

The interested reader may compare the values created by the above inversion processes (or others that they implement) with those produced by @RISK. However, since the @RISK distribution functions directly produce samples, one would not be able to perform an immediate comparison, because the random numbers used in Excel (created using **RAND**()) would not be the same as the ones implicitly being used by @RISK. For the purposes of the discussion at this point, we aim to focus only on the inversion process (and not the quality of the random numbers generated for the probabilities), and so we would wish to create samples of the @RISK distribution at the same probabilities. This can be done by using the **RiskTheoPercentile** (or **RiskTheoPtoX**) function applied to the @RISK distribution function, and linking its probability parameter to the same one used in the corresponding Excel inversion formula.

For example, one may check that:

$$\text{WeibullSample}(\alpha, \beta, P) = \text{RiskTheoPercentile}(\text{RiskWeibull}(a, \beta), P)$$

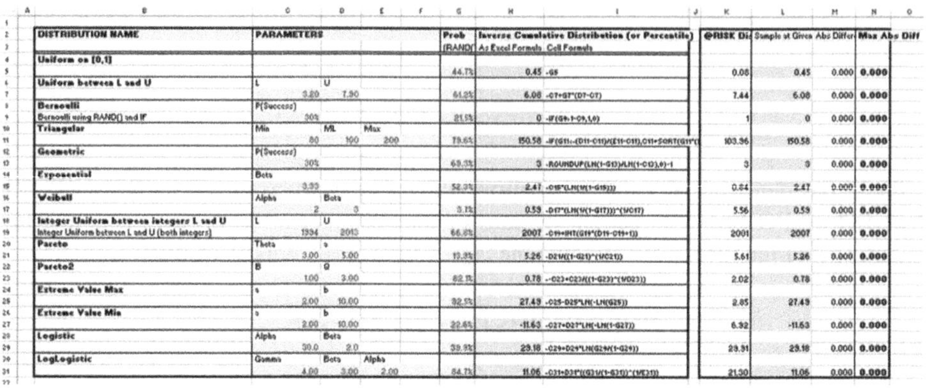

DISTRIBUTION NAME	PARAMETERS			Prob (RAND())	Inverse Cumulative Distribution (or Percentile) As Excel Formula	Cell Formula	@RISK Di	Sample at Given	Abs Differ	Max Abs Diff
Uniform on [0,1]				44.7%	0.45	=G5	0.08	0.45	0.000	0.000
Uniform between L and U	L: 3.20	U: 7.90		61.2%	6.08	=C7+G7*(D7-C7)	7.44	6.08	0.000	0.000
Bernoulli Bernoulli using RAND() and IF	P(Success): 30%			21.5%	0	=IF(G9>1-C9,1,0)	1	0	0.000	0.000
Triangular	Min: 80	ML: 100	Max: 200	79.6%	150.58	=IF(G11<(D11-C11)/(E11-C11),C11+SQRT(G11*(	103.36	150.58	0.000	0.000
Geometric	P(Success): 30%			69.3%	3	=ROUNDUP(LN(1-G13)/LN(1-C13),0)-1	3	3	0.000	0.000
Exponential	Beta: 3.33			52.3%	2.47	=C15*(LN(1/(1-G15)))	0.84	2.47	0.000	0.000
Weibull	Alpha: 2	Beta: 3		3.1%	0.53	=D17*(LN(1/(1-G17)))^(1/C17)	5.56	0.53	0.000	0.000
Integer Uniform between integers L and U Integer Uniform between L and U (both integers)	L: 1994	U: 2013		66.8%	2007	=C19+INT(G19*(D19-C19+1))	2001	2007	0.000	0.000
Pareto	Theta: 3.00	a: 5.00		13.3%	5.26	=D21/((1-G21)^(1/C21))	5.61	5.26	0.000	0.000
Pareto2	B: 1.00	Q: 3.00		82.1%	0.78	=-C23+C23/((1-G23)^(1/D23))	2.02	0.78	0.000	0.000
Extreme Value Max	a: 2.00	b: 10.00		92.5%	27.43	=C25-D25*LN(-LN(G25))	2.85	27.43	0.000	0.000
Extreme Value Min	a: 2.00	b: 10.00		22.6%	-11.63	=C27+D27*LN(-LN(1-G27))	6.32	-11.63	0.000	0.000
Logistic	Alpha: 30.0	Beta: 2.0		39.9%	29.18	=C29+D29*LN(G29/(1-G29))	29.31	29.18	0.000	0.000
LogLogistic	Gamma: 4.00	Beta: 3.00	Alpha: 2.00	84.7%	11.06	=C31+D31*((G31/(1-G31))^(1/E31))	21.30	11.06	0.000	0.000

FIGURE 10.4 Comparison of User-Defined Inverse Functions with Samples from @RISK

for all values of P, where WeibullSample is intended to represent the implemented inverse Weibull function, and so on for the other functions.

(Note that P can be varied automatically using **RAND**() or the **RiskUniform** distribution, and one may even choose to run a simulation to check that the difference between the two values is always equal to zero over a wide range of probability values.)

The file Ch10.InverseFunctions.AnalyticAnd@RISK.xlsx contains an example of this approach, implemented for the analytic inverse functions described above (one could, in principle, do this for all functions). Figure 10.4 shows a screen clip; in particular, column N of the file shows that the maximum of the absolute differences between the two approaches is zero (after running 5000 samples), indicating that the functions return the same values in all cases.

10.4 CREATING USER-DEFINED INVERSE FUNCTIONS

In most of this text, we use Excel formulae to calculate the inverse functions; this makes the screen clips readable. However, in practice (and in the files used in the later parts of Chapter 12), these are implemented as user-defined functions (in VBA). There are many advantages in doing so, including:

- Functions that require iterative procedures would be very cumbersome to evaluate in Excel, whereas they can be done easily within a calculation loop of VBA.
- Functions that are based on lookup tables can be built so that they work whether the data are provided in a row or in a column.
- VBA can detect which version of Excel is used, so that the latest function type available in that version of Excel can be used (e.g. **NORM.INV** if in Excel 2010 or later, and **NORMINV** in earlier versions). If functions were directly used in Excel, one may run into compatibility problems unless the older of the functions were always used.
- Each function can be given a name that corresponds to the distribution (e.g. `MRWeibullP` for a Weibull distribution); this can make the model easier to understand, as complex-looking formulae are replaced by named functions.

- The function's arguments only need to be listed once, even if the value is used in several places in the formula, so that cell references are not repeated.
- Any required parameter transformations can be done within the code, thus making the formulae smaller. For example, this is applicable when calculating the logarithmic parameters from the natural ones in order to sample the lognormal distribution, or when calculating the required parameters for a beta general distribution in order to sample the PERT distribution. Similarly, the more complex or involved multi-step formulae for a triangular distribution can be built as a single set of formulae within the function, rather than repeatedly in various Excel cells.
- The model will generally be visually smaller, especially in the cases where the inverse formula is a multi-step formula that may otherwise be broken into several calculation steps.
- Any changes or corrections to the formula need only be made with a single change to the VBA code, whereas a formula in Excel that has been used in several places would require each one to be changed. As well as the time lost in making such changes, in a large model, one may overlook some of the formulae that need correcting (since the numbers are random, it would not always be clear that the calculations may be incorrect).
- The functions are more readily embedded within other Excel formulae.
- The function is more easily transportable to other models, with reduced risk of making an error when reusing or copying it (especially if functions are linked to cells using absolute references).
- There is no "best practice" benefit in trying to avoid VBA in this context, as it will be needed in any case in order to run the simulation.

In the following text, we provide selected examples of the VBA code required to implement the user-defined functions for the sampling of the distributions covered in Chapter 9. We do not explicitly provide the code for every function, as the principles are essentially the same within each category (i.e. the ways to use Excel inverse functions, or exact inversion or search techniques can readily be extended from one distribution to another within the same category). Note that the actual VBA implementation of some of these functions is contained within the files provided with Chapter 12, rather than with the files associated with this chapter. Note also that, for reasons of space and focus, comment lines that would be included in the original code (and other aspects, such as some of the statements to declare variables) are generally not shown.

Readers who are not experienced in VBA may find it helpful to briefly read the relevant parts of Chapter 12 before proceeding; these are Sections 12.2.3 and 12.5.3.

In the following, the author has used his own naming conventions for functions; that is, a function name starts with the letters MR, so that it is easy to insert in an Excel cell by direct typing (and relying on Excel's autocomplete feature). Of course, readers may use their own naming convention if they prefer.

10.4.1 Normal Distribution

The code shown below for sampling from a normal distribution is designed to detect the Excel version used, and use the latest one available in that version of Excel. Such an approach would apply to the other in-built Excel inverse functions. Note that functions such as **NORM.INV** become NORM_INV in VBA (as the "." syntax is reserved in VBA to separate objects, methods and properties, and so on, and hence is not available to be used within a function's definition).

Note also that the user-defined function has been written to have the Prob as its last parameter. Thus, the order of the parameters is different to that within the Excel inverse function. By having an argument as a last parameter, it can, if desired, be made into an optional parameter (for example, if one wished to create a function in which the omission of the parameter would automatically result in a random number being drawn within the VBA code, rather than from the Excel worksheet).

```
Function MRNormalP(mu, sigma, Prob)
Set wsf = Application.WorksheetFunction
If Application.Version <= 12 Then
  xSample = wsf.NormSInv(Prob, mu, sigma)
 Else
  xSample = wsf.Norm_Inv(Prob, mu, sigma)
End If
MRNormalP = xSample
End Function
```

10.4.2 Beta and Beta General Distributions

The code for a (standard) beta distribution would be analogous to that for a normal distribution:

```
Function MRBetaP(alpha, beta, Prob)
Set wsf = Application.WorksheetFunction
If Application.Version <= 12 Then
  xSample = wsf.BetaInv(Prob, alpha, beta)
 Else
  xSample = wsf.Beta_Inv(Prob, alpha, beta)
End If
MRBetaP = xSample
End Function
```

For a beta general distribution, we simply use the additional optional parameters of the function:

```
Function MRBetaGenP(alpha, beta, Min, Max, Prob)
Set wsf = Application.WorksheetFunction
If Application.Version <= 12 Then
  xSample = wsf.BetaInv(Prob, alpha, beta, Min, Max)
 Else
  xSample = wsf.Beta_Inv(Prob, alpha, beta, Min, Max)
End If
MRBetaGenP = xSample
End Function
```

10.4.3 Binomial Distribution

The code for a binomial distribution reflects the availability of the inverse function in Excel 2010 onwards. In earlier versions of Excel, the procedure to cumulate probabilities iteratively is used.

```
Function MRBinomP(N, pSuccess, Prob)
Set wsf = Application.WorksheetFunction
CumProb = 0
iEvents = 0
If Application.Version <= 12 Then
  Do While CumProb <= Prob
   CumProb = CumProb + wsf.BinomDist(iEvents, N, pSuccess, 1)
   iEvents = iEvents + 1
  Loop
 Else
   iEvents = wsf.Binom_Inv(N, pSuccess, Prob)
   iEvents = iEvents + 1
 End If
 MRBinomP = iEvents - 1
End Function
```

10.4.4 Lognormal Distribution

The first function below is equivalent to Excel's lognormal distribution, which uses the logarithmic, rather than the natural, parameters.

```
Function MRLognorm2P(m, s, Prob)
Set wsf = Application.WorksheetFunction
If Application.Version <= 12 Then
  xSample = wsf.LogInv(Prob, m, s)
 Else
  xSample = wsf.LogNorm_Inv(Prob, m, s)
 End If
MRLognorm2P = xSample
End Function
```

The following function uses the natural parameters, which are transformed within the code into logarithmic ones, in order to create a distribution sample.

```
Function MRLognormP(mu, sigma, Prob)
m = Log((mu ^ 2) / Sqr(mu ^ 2 + sigma ^ 2))
s = Sqr(Log(1 + (sigma / mu) ^ 2))
MRLognormP = MRLognorm2P(m, s, Prob)
End Function
```

10.4.5 Bernoulli Distribution

```
Function MRBernoulliP(pSuccess, Prob)
 If Prob <=pSuccess Then
  MRBernoulliP = 1
 Else
  MRBernoulliP = 0
 End If
End Function
```

10.4.6 Triangular Distribution

```
Function MRTRIANGP(Xmin, xML, Xmax, Prob)
dTotRange = Xmax - Xmin
dLowRange = xML - Xmin
dHighRange = Xmax - xML
CumPML = dLowRange / dTotRange
If Prob <= CumPML Then
 xSample = Xmin + Sqr(Prob * dLowRange * dTotRange)
Else
 xSample = Xmax - Sqr((1 - Prob) * dHighRange * dTotRange)
End If
MRTRIANGP = xSample
End Function
```

Note that the Excel square root function **SQRT** is replaced by `Sqr` in VBA.

10.4.7 PERT Distribution

The code below creates the PERT distribution from a beta distribution, as described in Chapter 9.

```
Function MRPERTP(Min, ML, Max, Prob)
Set wsf = Application.WorksheetFunction
mu = (Min + 4 * ML + Max) / 6
 dScale = 6 / (Max - Min)
 alpha = dScale * (mu - Min)
 beta = dScale * (Max - mu)
If Application.Version <= 12 Then
  xSample = wsf.BetaInv(Prob, alpha, beta, Min, Max)
 Else
  xSample = wsf.Beta_Inv(Prob, alpha, beta, Min, Max)
End If
MRPERTP = xSample
End Function
```

10.4.8 Geometric Distribution

```
Function MRGeometricP(pSuccess, p)
Set wsf = WorksheetFunction
MRGeometricP = wsf.RoundUp(Log(1 - p) / Log(1 - pSuccess), 0) - 1
End Function
```

Note that the Excel natural logarithm function **LN** has the corresponding function `Log` in VBA.

10.4.9 Weibull Distribution

```
Function MRWEIBULLP(alpha, beta, Prob)
MRWEIBULLP = beta * ((Log(1 / (1 - Prob))) ^ (1 / alpha))
End Function
```

10.4.10 Weibull Distribution with Percentile Inputs

Using the formula in Chapter 9, one can create the alternate parameter form of the Weibull distribution by deriving its parameters from the values of given percentiles (e.g. P10 and P90).

```
Function MRWEIBULLALTP(XL, XH, PL, PH, Prob)
 alpha = Log(Log(1 - PH) / Log(1 - PL)) / Log(XH / XL)
 beta = XH / (Log(1 / (1 - PH)) ^ (1 / alpha))
MRWEIBULLALTP = MRWEIBULLP(alpha, beta, Prob)
End Function
```

10.4.11 Poisson Distribution

A user-defined function allows a search procedure to be embedded within a `Do While...Loop` to increment the trial integer until the appropriate result is found:

```
Function MRPoissonP(Lambda, Prob)
CumProb = 0
iEvents = 0
Do While CumProb <= Prob
 CumProb = Application.WorksheetFunction.Poisson_Dist(iEvents,
 Lambda, 1)
 iEvents = iEvents + 1
Loop
MRPoissonP = iEvents - 1
End Function
```

One may also wish to adapt the function so that the latest available function would be used, according to the Excel version:

```
Function MRPoissonP(Lambda, Prob)
Set wsf = Application.WorksheetFunction
CumProb = 0
 iEvents = 0
 If Application.Version <= 12 Then ' Excel 2007 or lower
  Do While CumProb <= Prob
   CumProb = wsf.Poisson(iEvents, Lambda, 1)
   iEvents = iEvents + 1
  Loop
 Else ' Excel 2010 or more: The "." in the func-
tion is replaced by "_" in VBA
  Do While CumProb <= Prob
   CumProb = wsf.Poisson_Dist(iEvents, Lambda, 1)
   iEvents = iEvents + 1
  Loop
 End If
 MRPoissonP = iEvents - 1
End Function
```

Note also that it may be computationally more efficient not to use the Excel cumulative distribution function, because – at each iteration of the `Do While Loop` – the call of the cumulative function (`Poisson_Dist(iEvents, Lambda, 1)` may itself require a looping process to sum the discrete densities up to the density of `iEvents`. On the other hand, when the cumulative function is calculated as the previous cumulated value plus the current value of the density function (i.e. as `CumProb = CumProb + dCumProb`), no further looping is required to evaluate that line. Thus, one could cumulate manually:

```
Function MRPoisson2P(Lambda, Prob)
ExpLambda = Exp(-Lambda)
CumProb = 0
dratio = 1
iEvents = 0
Do While CumProb <= Prob
dCumProb = ExpLambda * dratio
CumProb = CumProb + dCumProb
iEvents = iEvents + 1
dratio = dratio * Lambda / iEvents
Loop
MRPoisson2P = iEvents - 1
End Function
```

(A comparison of these approaches is beyond the scope of this text at this time, but interested readers may choose to experiment further themselves.)

Note that, in practice, one may include (at the beginning of the code) a check on the size of λ, so that when it is large, a function call is made to a sample from the normal distribution instead, as mentioned earlier. Bearing in mind that one needs to generate an integer from a continuous function, in order to avoid systematically only rounding downwards, a "continuity correction" of 0.5 needs to be applied before rounding down. Thus, the generic code in these cases would be:

$$\text{MRPoissonP}(\lambda, \text{P}) = \text{wsf.RoundDown}(\text{MRNormalP}(\lambda, \sqrt{\lambda}, \text{P}) + 0.5), 0)$$

10.4.12 General Discrete Distribution

A simple example of such code is:

```
Function MRDiscreteP(X As Range, P As Range, Prob)
Set wsf = Application.WorksheetFunction
PScale = wsf.Sum(P)
n = X.Count
icount = 0
CumP = 0
Do While CumP < Prob
 icount = icount + 1
 CumP = CumP + P(icount) / PScale
Loop
MRDiscreteP = X(icount)
End Function
```

10.5 OTHER GENERALISATIONS

This section describes some other areas that may be applicable in some situations, including enhanced iterative methods and the creation of Excel add-ins.

10.5.1 Iterative Methods using Specific Numerical Techniques

In theory, for any distribution whose cumulative distribution function can be evaluated analytically, one could always envision using a search procedure (such as **GoalSeek**) to find the x-value whose cumulative probability is equal to the given sample probability, P. That is, to find x, such that:

$$P = F(\text{Par1}, \ldots, \text{ParN}, x)$$

or:

$$F(\text{Par1}, \ldots, \text{ParN}, x) - \text{P} = 0$$

In principle, this approach could be applied to the sampling of any continuous distribution (for discrete distributions, one may consider using **Solver** to restrict the search space to valid trial values, such as integers).

In practice, iterative or lookup methods should be considered as a "last resort", as it will usually be much simpler, and more computationally efficient, to conduct the inversions if exact analytic methods or in-built functions are available. In addition, one generally has to ensure that, whilst the search procedure is running, the rest of the model is not updating (i.e. other distributions within it are not being resampled), both for considerations of speed and of the integrity of the calculations (especially if there are dependencies between the distribution in which the search procedure is operating and other distributions in the model).

If one nevertheless needed such iterative procedures (which are not required for the distributions covered in this chapter), one would ideally use a procedure that is specially adapted to reflect the nature of the distribution concerned (so that it returns a sample in a computationally efficient manner). For example, the Newton–Raphson method is a general iterative method to solve the equation:

$$g(x) = 0$$

by using iterations:

$$x_{i+1} = x_i - \frac{g(x_i)}{g'(x_i)}$$

where g' is the derivative of g.

This procedure requires that both the cumulative and density functions be calculated analytically, as they use the slope of the function at each iteration x_i to find the next value (so would solve perfectly with a single iteration if the cumulative function were a straight line); in contrast, **GoalSeek** cannot use information about the functional form, so would generally be less effective.

If the function G can be differentiated analytically twice (not just once, as above), then one can use Halley's method that also uses information about the change in slope of the function:

$$x_{i+1} = x_i - \frac{g(x_i)}{g'(x_i)}\left(\frac{1}{1 - \frac{g(x_i)g''(x_i)}{2\left(g'(x_i)^2\right)}}\right)$$

This recursive procedure can be implemented within a user-defined function and (using a `Do While ...Loop` construct) run until some tolerance level is reached (such as when the difference between the two latest x-values is less than some threshold), so that the iterations within the function code do not force the rest of the model to recalculate.

For illustration purposes, we show the application (using the Newton–Raphson method) to the case of the Weibull distribution (as covered earlier, for this distribution the inversion process is easy to implement directly analytically, and so, in reality, this procedure would not be used).

Although the iterative process can start with any x-value, as a general rule it would make sense to start it at a fairly central point (such as the mode), in the absence of other information.

The formulae for the density and cumulative functions were shown earlier (and by setting the derivative of the density function to zero) one can readily establish that the mode is given by:

$$\textbf{Mode} = \beta\left(1 - \frac{1}{\alpha}\right)^{\frac{1}{\alpha}}$$

Thus, the Newton-Raphson code could look like:

```
Function MRWEIBULLNRP(alpha, beta, Prob)
Tol = 0.00001
x = 0
x1 = beta * (1 - 1 / alpha) ^ (1 / alpha) ' initiate
at mode of the distribution
Do While Abs(x1 - x) >= Tol
 x = x1
 Smallfx = ((alpha * x ^ (alpha - 1)) / beta ^ alpha) * Exp(-
(x / beta) ^ alpha)
 BigFx = 1 - Exp(-(x / beta) ^ alpha)
 Numx = BigFx - Prob
 x1 = x - Numx / Smallfx
Loop
MRWEIBULLNRP = x1
End Function
```

10.5.2 Creating an Add-In

When planning to apply simulation to a number of different models, it can be inconvenient to copy functions from one workbook to the next. For this reason, one can create an add-in that contains a library of distribution functions, which are stored in a single (add-in) file and are accessible from Excel. The procedure depends slightly on the version of Office one has, but in principle the workbook containing the relevant functions would be saved (under the **File/Save As** options) as an add-in file (with a .xlam or .xla extension), and then would be loaded under **Excel Options/Add-Ins/Manage Excel-Add-Ins**. The disadvantage of this approach is that any other user of the model will also be able to access the add-in in order to work with the file.

The creation of an add-in is not an approach that is pursued specifically in this text; in Chapter 12, any user-defined functions that are required for the inverse distributions are placed directly within a VBA code module within the workbook, so that the file is self-contained.

CHAPTER 11

Modelling Dependencies between Sources of Risk

In this chapter, we concern ourselves with forms of dependency that specifically relate to risk modelling, in contrast to the general dependency relationships that were discussed in Chapter 7. In particular, we refer to cases where the distribution functions (or their sampling) are affected by the dependency; these fall into two main categories:

- Parameter dependencies. These are where the parameters of a distribution are determined from the samples of other distributions (either directly or through other calculations). Thus, the parameters may change at each iteration (recalculation) of the simulation. This type of relationship has a directionality of calculation (and hence an implied causality) inherent in it.
- Sampling dependencies. These are where the sampling of one distribution over the course of a simulation is aligned with the sampling of another. These relationships are of a joint nature, rather than a directional or causal one.

These are discussed in the remainder of this chapter in detail.

11.1 PARAMETER DEPENDENCY AND PARTIAL CAUSALITY

There are cases where one may wish to determine the parameters of a distribution at each iteration (recalculation) of a simulation; such parameters therefore depend (directly or indirectly) on samples of other distributions. A distribution whose parameters are determined in this way can be considered to be a dependent distribution, whereas a distribution with fixed parameters can be considered independent. The actual sampled outcome of the dependent distribution is still a random process, but its possible values are influenced by the sample(s) of the independent distribution(s). Thus, the (dependent) process can be described as one that is parameter dependent, or semi-dependent, or partially dependent, or conditionally dependent on the independent distribution(s).

There is an implied, directional (partial) causality, which will generally create a non-zero correlation between the samples of the independent and semi-dependent processes over the course of a simulation. (However, as discussed later, the implementation of this relationship will generally give different simulation results than if a correlated sampling relationship were implemented using the same measured correlation coefficient.)

There are several types of possible parameter-dependency relationships, which may be described with a different emphasis in different contexts. Some examples include:

- Conditional probability, where the occurrence of one risk changes the probability-of-occurrence of another. For example:
  - The probability of finding oil in a specific place is judged to be higher if oil has already been confirmed nearby in similar geological conditions.
  - The labour force of one company may be more likely to go on strike if workers in a competing company are granted a further pay rise and other benefits.
  - The probability of a project being delayed by more than 2 weeks may depend on whether the main project manager becomes ill during the project planning and execution phase.
- Scenario dependence, where the parameters depend on which scenario of another (random) process occurs. For example:
  - The parameters that determine the length of a journey or of the daily cost of construction activities may depend on which weather scenario occurs on a particular day.
  - There may be a set of ranges for the possible future value of the oil price: one range in the case that significant new advances are made in alternative energy sources (renewables, nuclear fusion), another range without such advances and a third range if such advances are not made and population growth is much higher than expected.
- Continuous dependencies. This is where the parameters of a continuous distribution depend on another risk item. For example:
  - The most likely figure for the market share of a company may depend on the number of competitors (which itself may depend on whether there are new entrants or product substitutes).
  - The most likely (or the mean) cost of each of a range of input materials may be determined from the oil price, or from an exchange rate, and so on.
  - Where the general level of house prices is affected by the unemployment rate.
  - Where the parameters that define the range for the volume sold of a product (e.g. minimum, most likely, maximum) are derived from the price level (which is independently sampled at each recalculation of the simulation).
  - In a sequence of projects, the cost of one may determine the most likely value for the cost of the next.
- Category-dependent parameters and contextual risks. This is where there are several categories of risks, with the range of variation of the items within each category being determined by the value of some "contextual" risk factor relevant to that category. The use of categories may form part of an approach that is combined with one of the above methods. For example, there could be several risk categories (e.g. macro-economic, operational, etc.), with each category containing several risk items. The probability-of-occurrence of the individual items and/or the ranges associated with their impacts would depend on the occurrence (or value) of the category-level risk items.

In the following, we provide some examples of each of these.

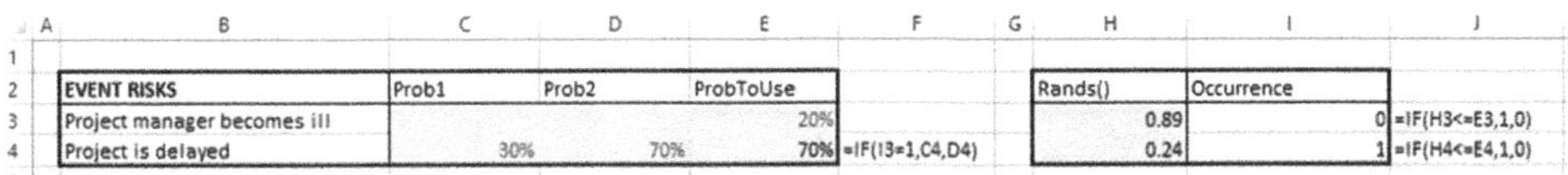

	A	B	C	D	E	F	G	H	I	J
1										
2		**EVENT RISKS**	Prob1	Prob2	ProbToUse			Rands()	Occurrence	
3		Project manager becomes ill			20%			0.89	0	=IF(H3<=E3,1,0)
4		Project is delayed	30%	70%	70%	=IF(I3=1,C4,D4)		0.24	1	=IF(H4<=E4,1,0)

FIGURE 11.1 An Example of the Use of Conditional Probabilities

11.1.1 Example: Conditional Probabilities

One simple example of a parameter dependency is that of a conditional probability-of-occurrence.

The file Ch11.ConditionalProbability.Excel.xlsx shows an implementation of this in Excel (see Figure 11.1), using the simple form of the distribution function (rather than, for example, the user-defined functions that were discussed in Chapter 10). It captures the case where there is a link between the project manager becoming ill during a project (for example, with a 20% probability of illness resulting in the manager being off work for several weeks), and a general risk that the project is delayed. The probability of delay is 30% if the manager does not fall ill, but 70% if he/she does. The occurrence of illness may be captured using the **IF/RAND()** combination to give a 1/0 (or yes/no) process that occurs in 20% of cases (cell I3). The occurrence of a delay would also use the **IF/RAND()** combination, with the probability used within the formula depending (through an **IF** statement) on whether (at each recalculation of the simulation) the manager is ill or not, i.e. on whether the first event has happened (i.e. cell I3 determining the value of cell E4).

Of course, one may also generalise this, so that the extent of delay (i.e. the impact or consequence of the risk) is determined from the duration of the illness, i.e. the dependency relationship is between the impacts of the risks, and is between continuous processes (some similar examples are shown later).

11.1.2 Example: Common Risk Drivers

The use of common risk drivers is where a single risk affects the parameters of a number of distributions (rather than just one, as in the example above). For example, one may have several areas (with similar geological characteristics) where one believes that oil may be present, with each having a probability of oil being found (based on current estimates and information). One may also believe that if oil is ultimately discovered in the main, central area (which will be the first to be drilled or explored further), then the likelihood of there being oil in the others should be considered to be higher. Thus, the model shown in Figure 11.1 would simply be modified to include multiple areas, with the probability of each being dependent on the outcome of the main area. Figure 11.2 shows an example using the Excel approach (which is also contained in the same example workbook as the above example with a single driver).

7	**OIL DISCOVERIES**	Prob1	Prob2	ProbToUse		Rands()	Occurrence	
8	Area 1: Main area			40%		[illegible]	1	=IF(H8<=E8,1,0)
9	Area 2	30%	70%	30%	=IF(I$8=1,C9,D9)	0.36	0	=IF(H9<=E9,1,0)
10	Area 3	30%	70%	30%	=IF(I$8=1,C10,D10)	0.18	1	=IF(H10<=E10,1,0)
11	Area 4	30%	70%	30%	=IF(I$8=1,C11,D11)	0.75	0	=IF(H11<=E11,1,0)
12	Area 5	30%	70%	30%	=IF(I$8=1,C12,D12)	0.65	0	=IF(H12<=E12,1,0)

FIGURE 11.2 Conditional Probabilities of Several Events with a Single Risk Driver

	A	B	C	D	E	F	G	H
1								
2		CONTEXTUAL RISKS	Prob	Occurrence				
3		CR-1	60%	1				
4		CR-2	50%	1				
5		CR-3	40%	0				
6								
7			Driver	Occurrence of driver	Prob1	Prob2	ProbToUse	Occurrence
8		Risk 1	CR-1	1	30%	80.0%	80.0%	1
9		Risk 2	CR-1	1	30%	80.0%	80.0%	1
10		Risk 3	CR-2	1	30%	80.0%	80.0%	1
11		Risk 4	CR-2	1	30%	80.0%	80.0%	0
12		Risk 5	CR-3	0	30%	80.0%	30.0%	0
13		Risk 6	CR-3	0	30%	80.0%	30.0%	0
14		Risk 7	CR-1	1	30%	80.0%	80.0%	1
15		Risk 8	CR-1	1	30%	80.0%	80.0%	0
16		Risk 9	CR-2	1	30%	80.0%	80.0%	1
17		Risk 10	CR-1	1	30%	80.0%	80.0%	1

FIGURE 11.3 Conditional Probabilities of Several Events with Several Categories of Risk Driver

11.1.3 Example: Category Risk Drivers

A further extension of the above approach is where there are several underlying risk drivers, with each impacting the probability of occurrence of one of each of a set of other risks, i.e. the occurrence of each underlying risk affects the probability used for the occurrence of the items within its category.

At the simplest level, such a model could be built by copying the structure in the above example, so that each risk driver had its own structure, and the probabilities of the risks that were dependent on it were directly linked to the occurrence cell for that driver. This would be computationally correct, but would be less flexible if more risk items needed to be added, or if some individual risks needed to be altered in terms of the driver that affected them. More flexibility will be achieved if each individual risk also has a category (the name of the risk driver) attached to it, so that lookup functions can be used to associate the individual items with a category.

The file Ch11.Contextual.ConditionalProbability.xlsx contains an example; a screen clip is shown in Figure 11.3. The cells D8:D17 use lookup functions (an **INDEX/MATCH** combination or a **VLOOKUP** could be used) to find out whether the contextual risk (CR-1, CR-2 or CR-3) that drives a particular item has occurred or not (contextual risks could be items such as general macro-economic circumstances, a specific regulatory or legal issue, the entry of a competitor, the successful development of a new technology or other issues that affect many individual risk items). The probability-of-occurrence for each risk is then adapted according to whether its contextual risk driver has occurred or not.

11.1.4 Example: Phased Projects

When projects occur in phases (say Phase 1 and Phase 2), the probability of success of Phase 2 may depend on the outcome in Phase 1. For example, Phase 1 may involve the conducting of tests that indicate the likelihood of Phase 2 (or overall) success. The implementation of this

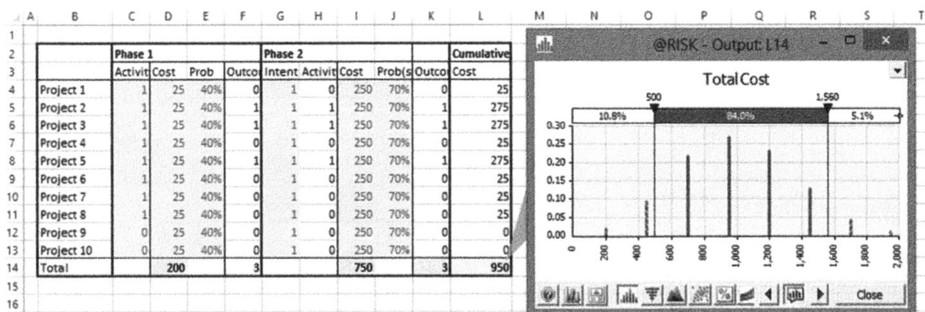

	Phase 1				Phase 2					Cumulative
	Activit	Cost	Prob	Outco	Intent	Activit	Cost	Prob(s	Outco	Cost
Project 1	1	25	40%	0	1	0	250	70%	0	25
Project 2	1	25	40%	1	1	1	250	70%	1	275
Project 3	1	25	40%	1	1	1	250	70%	1	275
Project 4	1	25	40%	0	1	0	250	70%	0	25
Project 5	1	25	40%	1	1	1	250	70%	1	275
Project 6	1	25	40%	0	1	0	250	70%	0	25
Project 7	1	25	40%	0	1	0	250	70%	0	25
Project 8	1	25	40%	0	1	0	250	70%	0	25
Project 9	0	25	40%	0	1	0	250	70%	0	0
Project 10	0	25	40%	0	1	0	250	70%	0	0
Total		200		3			750		3	950

FIGURE 11.4 Portfolios of Projects that Occur in Phases

approach would be similar to that of conditional probability. In other cases, one may wish to be able to explicitly decide whether to proceed with Phase 2 (thus one would have an intention to do so or not), but would only be able to do so if Phase 1 were successful.

The file Ch11.Project.TwoSteps.xlsx contains calculations intended to work out the total expenditure in a portfolio of projects, each of which may take place in two phases. Figure 11.4 shows a screen clip of the model and the distribution of total expenditure at the end of Phase 2. The user can decide which projects to proceed in Phase 1 (column C); each of these has a cost and probability of success. Each project has an intention parameter for Phase 2 (column G, set to 1 if a user would wish to proceed with Phase 2 whenever Phase 1 is successful). However, projects that are not successful in Phase 1 are not eligible for Phase 2; the logic of this is captured within the **IF** statements in column H.

Note that, in general, the choice variables (column C and column G) create a portfolio optimisation situation; if insufficient budget is available, one may not be able to proceed with some projects, even if it were desired to do so in principle. Thus, in the most general case, this model captures the issue of optimisation under uncertainty.

11.1.5 Example: Economic Scenarios for the Price of a Base Commodity

In Chapter 7, we showed an example of where the input values of a model's calculations vary according to the scenario used. One could generalise this so that within each scenario the value of a variable is uncertain. In other words, for each scenario there is a range of uncertainty associated with the variable.

The file Ch11.PriceScenarios1.xlsx contains an example. The distribution of the price of a base (or reference) product is assumed to follow a lognormal distribution, whose volatility is described as a percentage of its mean. However, the mean is scenario dependent, and is selected using a discrete distribution. (In general, the within-scenario volatility could also be scenario dependent, but we have used a single figure of 15% for ease of illustration.) Figure 11.5 shows a screen clip of the model, including the simulated distribution of prices in year 5. Note that the total price process has a volatility that is higher than that of the individual scenarios, as the total volatility is also driven by the random change of scenarios, as well as the (constant) within-scenario volatility.

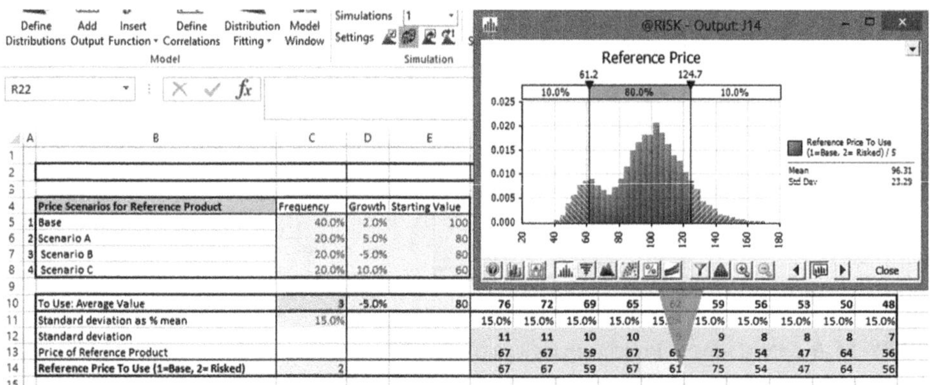

FIGURE 11.5 Distribution of Prices for a Reference Product with Uncertainty Ranges within Uncertain Scenarios

11.1.6 Example: Prices of a Derivative Product

The above example can be developed further, with the price of the reference product used to establish the average (mean) price of a derivative product, whose final price has its own independent variation around this.

The file Ch11.PriceScenarios2.xlsx shows an example, in which the derivative product has a volatility of 10% around its mean figure. Figure 11.6 shows a screen clip, including the simulated distribution of prices of the derivative in year 5, and a scatter plot of the prices of the reference and derivative (showing a close correlation, which will be explored later in the chapter).

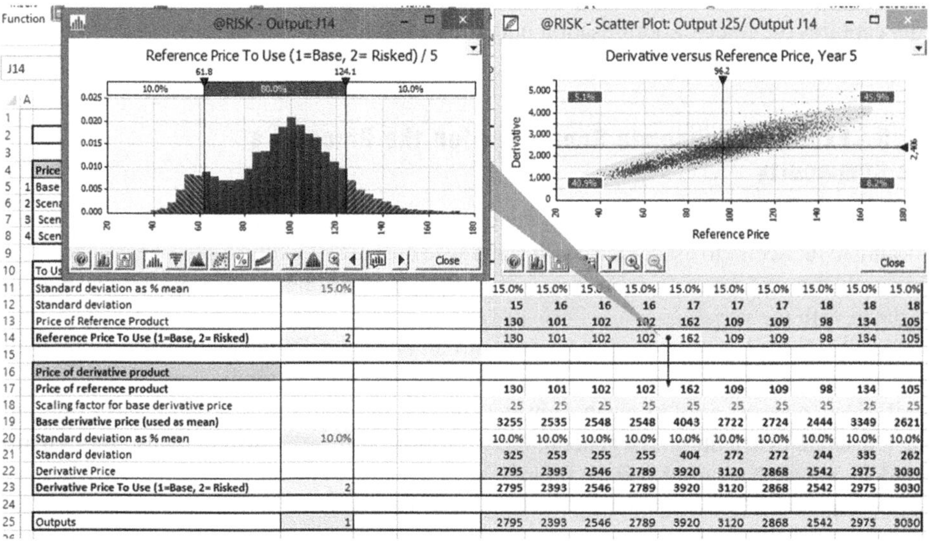

FIGURE 11.6 Distribution of Prices for a Derivative Product with Uncertain Ranges and Base Prices Depending on the Reference Product

	A	B	C	D	E	F	G	H	I	J
13		Price of Reference Product				99	47	66	64	76
14		Reference Price To Use (1=Base, 2= Risked)	2			99	47	66	64	76
15										
16		Calculations of Derivative Prices			FORMULAE IN COL F					
17		Scaling factors for base derivative price								
18		DP1				25	25	25	25	25
19		DP2				10	10	10	10	10
20		DP3				75	75	75	75	75
21		Base derivative price (used as mean)								
22		DP1			=F$14*F18	2485	1179	1644	1588	1911
23		DP2			=F$14*F19	994	472	657	635	764
24		DP3			=F$14*F20	7454	3538	4931	4764	5732
25		Standard deviation								
26		DP1	10.0%		=F22*$C26	248	118	164	159	191
27		DP2	12.0%		=F23*$C27	119	57	79	76	92
28		DP3	8.0%		=F24*$C28	596	283	394	381	459
29		Derivative Price								
30		DP1			=RiskLognorm(F22,F26)	2174	1243	1749	1700	1824
31		DP2			=RiskLognorm(F23,F27)	1023	674	580	780	656
32		DP3			=RiskLognorm(F24,F28)	6650	3653	4815	4736	6281
33		Derivative Price To Use (1=Base, 2= Risked)								
34		DP1	2		=CHOOSE($C34,F22,F30)	2174	1243	1749	1700	1824
35		DP2	2		=CHOOSE($C35,F23,F31)	1023	674	580	780	656
36		DP3	2		=CHOOSE($C36,F24,F32)	6650	3653	4815	4736	6281
37										

FIGURE 11.7 Distribution of Prices for Several Derivative Products

11.1.7 Example: Prices of Several Derivative Products

The above example can be extended to include several derivative products, essentially by copying the part of the model concerned with the derivative product several times. When doing so, one may instead alter the layout of the model to create tables of common items by product; this is done in the following example.

The file Ch11.PriceScenarios3.xlsx contains the required modifications to include several derivative products; Figure 11.7 shows a screen clip. Once again, it would be possible to show distributions of the prices of each derivative and various scatter plots (e.g. of one derivative against another); this is not done here as the principles are the same as earlier.

11.1.8 Example: Oil Price and Rig Cost

In some cases, one may wish to link variables that have non-linear behaviour. For example, one may believe that there is a relationship between the general oil price and the daily cost of renting an oil rig, as in Figure 11.8. That is, the cost per day of a rig is fixed for oil prices below $80 per barrel, and then increases linearly when the oil price is above this threshold.

In a risk model, one may wish not only to consider that the oil price is an uncertain variable, but also that the value calculated by the line may represent only the most likely daily cost of a rig, with the actual costs having a range of variation around that figure.

The file Ch11.OilPricetoRigCost.xlsx shows an example in which the oil price is regarded as a lognormally distributed variable, with each random sample being used to calculate the most likely rig cost, from which the range of rig cost is determined, and a random sample drawn. Figure 11.9 shows a screen clip, including a scatter plot of the rig cost and oil price, and the distribution of rig cost. (The model uses a range of –30% to +50% around the most likely figure for the rig cost.)

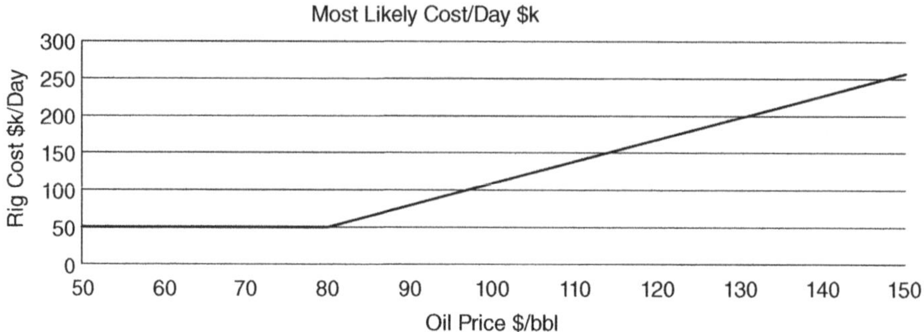

FIGURE 11.8 Base Case Values for Rig Cost as a Function of Oil Price

11.1.9 Example: Competitors and Market Share

Another example of a parameter dependency is where one wishes to determine market share that a company would achieve based on the number of competitors. In a simple case (where each company has the same share), one may write the relationship between market share and the number of competitors (N) as:

$$\text{Market share} = 1/(1+N)$$

When generalising this to risk modelling, there would be several possibilities:

- The market share has a range of variation (i.e. follows a distribution), with the formula calculating its most likely (or perhaps average) value.
- The number of competitors may be a figure that can be changed manually, or one that is represented by an uncertainty distribution or process.

The file Ch11.MS.Competitors.xlsx contains an example in which the number of competitors is the result of a Poisson process in which competitors may appear randomly in each

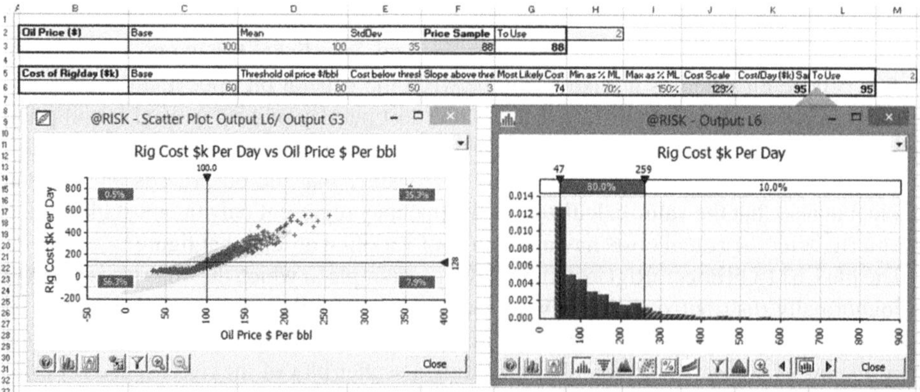

FIGURE 11.9 Simulated Distribution of Rig Cost and Scatter Plot of Rig Cost Against Oil Price

	B	C	D	E	F	G	H	J
1								
2			1	2	3	4	5	
3	**Number of Competitors**							
4	Number of Competitors: Starting		4	4	4	5	5	=G7
5	New Entrant Intensity	1.5	0.4	0.4	0.4	0.3	0.3	=$C5/H4
6	New Entrant?		0	0	1	0	1	=RiskPoisson(H5)
7	Number of Competitors: Ending	4	4	4	5	5	6	=H4+H6
8	**Number of Competitors: Average**		**4**	**4**	**4.5**	**5**	**5.5**	=(H4+H7)/2
9	**Market Share**							
10	Sampled Value		**19.6%**	**22.6%**	**16.7%**	**16.6%**	**17.0%**	=RiskPert(H12,H11,H13)
11	Most Likely	1	20.0%	20.0%	18.2%	16.7%	15.4%	=$C11/(1+H8)
12	Minimum	0.8	16.0%	16.0%	14.5%	13.3%	12.3%	=$C12*H$11
13	Maximum	1.2	24.0%	24.0%	21.8%	20.0%	18.5%	=$C13*H$11
14								
15	**Outputs**		1	2	3	4	5	
16	**Market Share**		**19.6%**	**22.6%**	**16.7%**	**16.6%**	**17.0%**	=RiskOutput(,B16,5)+H10
17	Average		19.3%	18.3%	17.3%	16.5%	15.8%	=RiskMean(H16)
18	P10		17.0%	15.0%	13.9%	12.9%	12.3%	=RiskPercentile(H16,10%)
19	P90		21.7%	21.3%	20.9%	20.3%	19.7%	=RiskPercentile(H16,90%)

FIGURE 11.10 Uncertainty Model for Market Share and Number of Competitors

period, but with an intensity-of-entry that is inversely proportional to their number at the beginning of the period. Thus, on average, the number of competitors will be increasing, even as the rate of entry declines over time. The number of competitors at the beginning of each period is used to determine the most likely market share, with the actual market share being drawn from a distribution with a ±20% variation around the most likely figure. The model calculates (through the simulation) the distribution of market share that could be observed in each period. (Once again, note that although this file is built with @RISK, it could also be built and run using Excel/VBA using the tools of Chapter 10 to create the distribution samples and those of Chapter 12 to run the simulation; the creation of the graphical displays would be possible but more cumbersome.)

Figure 11.10 shows the model and the (post-simulation) statistics that show the average and the range of market share as it develops over time (rows 17 to 19). Figure 11.11 shows the ranges of market share in each year over time, showing the average, the P25–P75 band and the P10–P90 band (this uses the **Summary Trend** plot in @RISK, but of course can also be created as an Excel chart if the relevant statistics are calculated in Excel). Figure 11.12 shows the overlay of the three distributions of market share in years 1, 3 and 5.

11.1.10 Example: Resampling or Data-Structure-Driven Dependence

In a resampling method, one generates input samples by sampling uniformly within a data set (of historic data). This is, in principle, equivalent to a scenario approach, in which there are many scenarios of equal likelihood, i.e. with each historic data point corresponding to a scenario. However, since the scenarios are many and equally likely, it is more convenient to create samples of the distribution using a uniform process, rather than using a general discrete distribution (which also requires the probabilities to be made explicit).

In principle, one could sample directly within a data set that consists of only one variable. For multiple variables, one would sample an integer that acts as an indexation number to the data set, and use this integer to look up the corresponding values within the data (at each recalculation). For example, when dealing with historic daily data (such as change in the prices

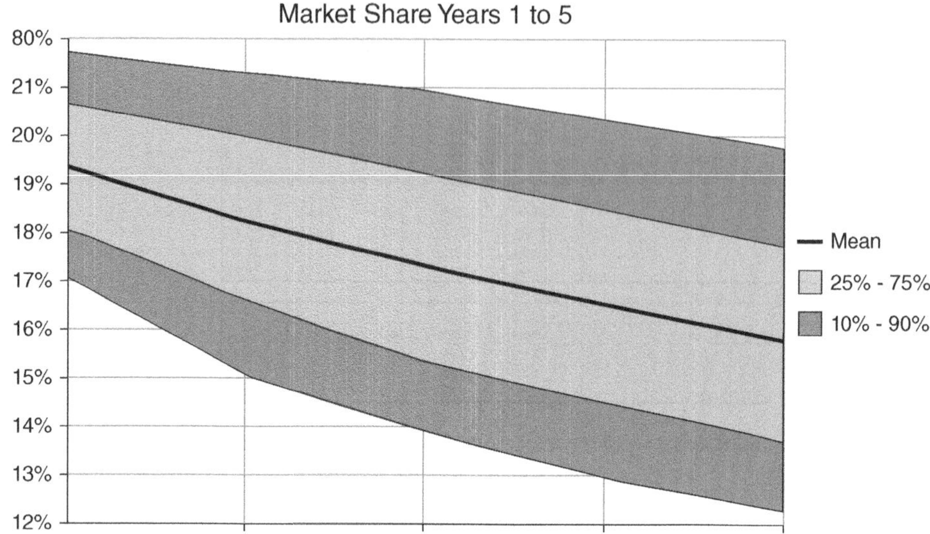

FIGURE 11.11 Time Development of Ranges for Market Share

of two assets), one may sample a random day and use a lookup function to see the changes in the value of both assets on that day. This would preserve any daily correlation patterns that are in the historic data (patterns that last over several days would have to be captured using sampling of historic blocks of data). Of course, such an approach can also be used for a single variable.

Thus, the implementation is essentially the same as the scenario approaches above, but uses an integer uniform distribution rather than a general discrete one.

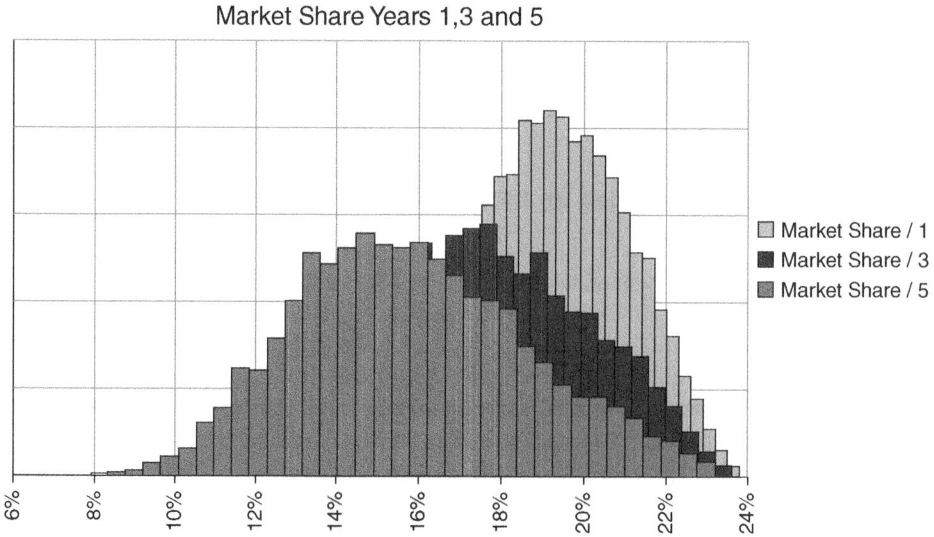

FIGURE 11.12 Time Development of Distribution of Market Share

DATE FIELDS		RETURNS DATA FOR THAT WEEK			
Week Start (M	WeekEnd (Fri)	Asset 1	Asset 2	Asset 3	Asset 4
31-Dec-14	04-Jan-15	5.40%	2.92%	2.95%	1.25%
07-Jan-15	11-Jan-15	-8.16%	-1.10%	-0.50%	0.59%
14-Jan-15	18-Jan-15	-2.42%	-1.17%	-2.04%	-1.57%
21-Jan-15	25-Jan-15	-1.00%	2.03%	3.51%	0.00%
28-Jan-15	01-Feb-15	2.09%	1.55%	1.88%	1.69%
04-Feb-15	08-Feb-15	0.80%	0.84%	0.60%	0.16%
11-Feb-15	15-Feb-15	0.16%	-0.70%	-0.64%	-0.44%
18-Feb-15	22-Feb-15	1.47%	0.33%	0.33%	2.09%
25-Feb-15	01-Mar-15	1.16%	1.16%	1.22%	0.15%
04-Mar-15	08-Mar-15	1.24%	2.27%	2.71%	0.38%

No. Data Points	200	=COUNT(D4:D203)
Random P	86%	=RAND()
Random Integer	172	=1+INT(J3*J2)

Multi-dimensional resampling as inputs (to a subseqent model)

	Asset 1	Asset 2	Asset 3	Asset 4	
Sampled Values	1.0%	-0.6%	0.5%	0.1%	=INDEX(G4:G203,$J4,1)

Correlation between Asset 1 and Asset 3	
Data	61.5%
Simulated	61.0%

FIGURE 11.13 Example of Resampling Method

The file Ch11.Resampling.xlsx provides an example (see Figure 11.13). The integer uniform distribution (between 1 and 200, i.e. the number of data points) is implemented in cell J4 (which uses the formula given in Chapter 10 for the inverse [percentile] function when working in Excel). The sampled integer drives a lookup function that provides the sampled values of the four processes simultaneously. The file also shows the correlation between the processes for Asset 1 and Asset 3, both for the historic data and for the simulation (cells J12 and J13).

The main advantages of resampling methods are:

- They do not make any assumptions about the nature of the distribution, other than that the past outcomes define the future possibilities. Thus, if one has limited knowledge of the process that has generated the data, or the data are not smooth, then a resampling method can be the most appropriate.
- Events will occur with the same frequency as in the historic data. In particular, for rarer (tail) outcomes, distributions that are parameterised through statistical measures (or are fitted to the historic data) would often reduce the frequency of such events.

There are also a number of disadvantages:

- There is an implicit assumption that the future will be essentially the same as the past (in a different order); this may be unrealistic and not reflect changes in context or one's knowledge of the situation.
- Historic data represent only one set of actual outcomes. However, there could be many other possible "realities" that could have happened, but did not, and so are not captured in the data (and therefore could never happen in the scenarios modelled for the future).
- Where data sets of historic data are small, the future would only capture a small number of possible outcomes. On the other hand, the larger the historic data set becomes (by using data from earlier time periods), the more likely it is that some of the data become invalid; processes are typically not stable over long periods of time, as business process definitions may have changed, or a production facility rationalised, or quality improvement initiatives implemented, and so on.
- Observed data may reflect the result of several effects, including the response of management to the underlying process outcomes, and so the underlying process may not be comparable to historic data.

Most resampling methods use sampling with replacement, meaning that a point that is sampled could be resampled. In @RISK, a specific **RiskResample** function exists that

Std/Mean	2.5%	5.0%	7.5%	10.0%	12.5%	15.0%
Correl Ref-DP	99.3%	97.3%	94.4%	91.0%	87.3%	83.6%

FIGURE 11.14 Declining Correlations as the Independent Range for a Semi-Dependent Variable Increases

allows for sampling with replacement, without replacement and in order (for example, to demonstrate the "reliving" of the past in sequence). Whereas a resampling using an integer uniform distribution is easy to implement in Excel/VBA, these other methods are more complex.

11.1.11 Implied Correlations within Parameter Dependency Relationships

The above examples of parameter dependency relationships of course result in a measurable coefficient of correlation between the samples produced for each process. For example, the scatter plot shown in Figure 11.6 clearly shows a correlation between the values of the derivative product and those of the reference product: a larger sampled value of the reference process means that the average value of the derivative is larger (and similarly for smaller sampled values), so that there will generally be a positive correlation between the two. Its strength is determined from the relative impact of the independent part of the variation of the partially dependent process.

Figure 11.14 shows the correlation between the reference and derivative prices in year 5, for various values of the extent of independent movement in the price of the derivative product (expressed as its standard deviation as a percentage of the mean, as in the original example). It clearly shows the reduction in the correlation as the extent of independent variation of the dependent process increases.

Similarly, Figure 11.15 shows the correlation matrix between each product (the reference and the derivatives) for the file shown in Figure 11.7

11.2 DEPENDENCIES BETWEEN SAMPLING PROCESSES

The other main category of dependency relationships between sources of risk is that which concerns the sampling processes for two or more distributions. For example, two distributions could be sampled in such a way that their higher values (percentiles) tend to occur together, and similarly for their low values. Correlation (correlated sampling) and copula relationships are of this type, with copulas allowing a more precise and explicit way to specify how the

Correlation in year 5	Ref	DP1	DP2	DP3
Ref	100%	92%	89%	95%
DP1	92%	100%	83%	87%
DP2	89%	83%	100%	84%
DP3	95%	87%	84%	100%

FIGURE 11.15 Cross-Correlations Between Simulated Product Prices

percentiles (samples) of distributions should occur. The focus of this text is on correlation procedures, as these are more widely known and accepted in general business contexts, and are fairly easy to implement in Excel/VBA. We briefly provide an introduction to copulas, as these are gradually becoming more widely used and available in add-in software.

11.2.1 Correlated Sampling

The creation of correlation relationships involves ensuring that distributions are jointly sampled, so that a desired correlation coefficient between the samples is achieved over the course of a simulation.

When using @RISK, it is the rank (Spearman) correlation of the samples that is used as the target measure (rather than the product or Pearson measure). Note that for small numbers of samples, it may not be possible to achieve a desired correlation with great accuracy, but one should be able to achieve one that is close to the desired figure as the number of samples increases. (As mentioned in Chapter 9, since rank correlation measures the correlation between sets of integers, for any given number of sampled points, there are only a finite number of achievable rank correlation figures that are possible, so achieving an exact preset figure may not be possible, even in theory.)

Sampling relationships govern the way that samples of each process are used together during the course of a simulation. In a sense, it is as if "behind the scenes", independent samples for each variable were first generated, before being reordered in order to pair larger values of one with larger values of the other (for positive correlation), and similarly for smaller values. The reordered sets would then be used during the actual simulation run.

Thus, sampling relationships have one key difference to parameter dependencies: the values of a process are determined only by its own parameters, and not by the values of another.

The file Ch11.Correl.ParChange.xlsx shows an example using @RISK. There are two processes, and the correlation coefficient between them is desired to be 70% (as expressed in the correlation matrix). Two simulations are run; during the second simulation, the values of the parameters of the first process are changed, whilst those of the second process are not. Figure 11.16 shows the value used for each process at each simulation (row 3 and row 4 for Process 1; row 7 and row 8 for Process 2). The sampled values generated for each during the course of the simulation are shown in the table of simulation data, starting at row 14. The key point is that whilst the values sampled for Process 1 do change as its parameters are altered, the values for Process 2 do not.

Thus, sampling relationships do not change the values sampled for a process, only the way that those samples are jointly used with the values of the other processes. In that sense, there is no notion of directionality or causality between the variables, whereas in parameter-dependency relationships, one variable can be considered to be independent and the other (partially) dependent.

In practical terms, sampling relationships are essentially implicit proxies for the existence of causality that arises due to variables that are not explicitly in the model. Thus:

- The prices of two products may be correlated because their prices are each strongly related to the price of a common raw material, but the price of this raw material is not an explicit line item in the model.

Values for Process 1	Min	ML	Max
Simulation 1	0	5	10
Simulation 2	10	18	30

Values for Process 2	Min	ML	Max
Simulation 1	20	50	80
Simulation 2	20	50	80

Values Use	Min	ML	Max	Dist
Process 1	0	5	10	3.81
Process 2	20	50	80	59.28

@RISK Corr	Process 1	Process 2
Process 1	100%	
Process 2	70%	100%

Simulation Data	Process 1		Process 2	
Iteration Number	Sim 1	Sim 2	Sim 1	Sim 2
1	2.2	14.0	34.6	34.6
2	4.9	18.9	48.8	48.8
3	4.7	18.5	31.8	31.8
4	5.8	20.8	66.9	66.9
5	6.1	21.5	54.2	54.2
6	4.0	17.2	58.1	58.1
7	7.2	23.9	64.8	64.8
8	5.7	20.6	32.8	32.8
9	8.7	27.1	71.8	71.8
10	3.0	15.4	51.1	51.1
11	4.8	18.7	60.1	60.1

FIGURE 11.16 Comparison of Effect of Parameter Changes on Samples Drawn for Correlated Variables

- The weekly level of sales of cameras and televisions in a retail store may be correlated, because each is driven by the general economic situation (as well as other factors), with such a situation not explicitly contained in the model.

11.2.2 Copulas

In a sense, copulas can be considered to be a generalisation of correlated sampling, in which one is able to more explicitly control (or specify) the way in which joint percentile (inverse) samples of distributions are to be drawn; in that sense, copulas represent an improvement over the use of correlation methods. However, copulas are still relationships of sampling dependency (i.e. they affect the sampling of distributions, and not their parameters), and therefore many of the features of correlated sampling in terms of their effects on the outputs of models are similar when copulas are used.

Some important types of copulas are:

- Archimedean copulas. These allow for sampling dependence to be stronger in selected parts of the joint distribution:
  - The Gumbel copula creates a stronger dependence in the upper tail of the joint distribution.

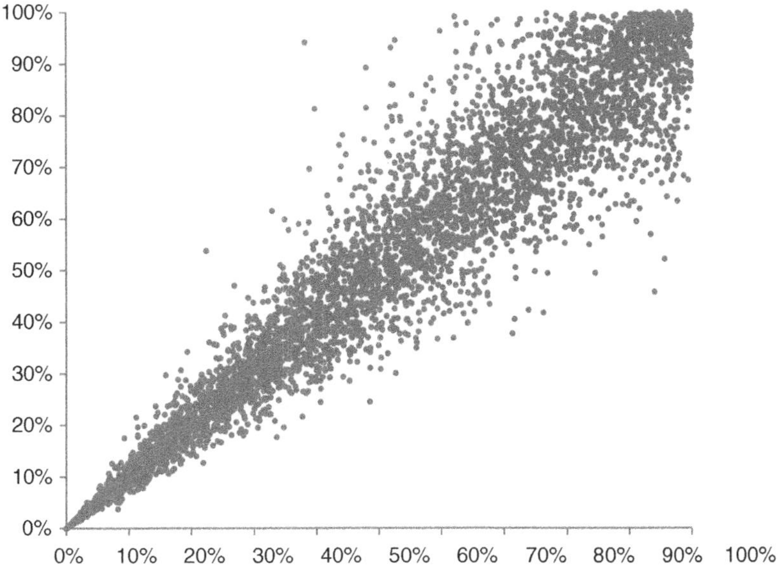

FIGURE 11.17 Example of Percentile Relationships for a Clayton Copula

  - The Clayton copula creates a stronger dependence in the lower tail of the joint distribution.
  - The Frank copula creates a stronger dependence in both the upper and lower tails equally (thus "pinching" each tail).
- Elliptical copulas. These resemble traditional correlation methods in some ways.
  - The Gaussian (normal) copula is similar to the use of a traditional correlation matrix, especially if applied to a model in which all distributions are normal, although its form is different when other distributions are involved.
  - The *t*-copula is also governed by a correlation matrix, and has an integer parameter that represents the number of degrees of freedom; as this parameter value is increased, the copula converges to a Gaussian copula (just as a Student (*t*) distribution becomes normal in similar circumstances).

Figure 11.17 provides an example of the percentile samples for two data series when using a Clayton copula (this graph was generated using another risk modelling add-in called ModelRisk, as such capability was not part of @RISK at the time of writing). The graph shows the stronger dependency for lower percentile values (i.e. due to there being less spread in the scatter plot at low percentiles, the sampled percentiles of one will be close to the sampled percentiles of the other, whereas for higher percentile values this is not the case). This is the type of situation that one may wish to use for modelling price movements in financial assets (e.g. equities), whose prices may tend to decrease together in situations of market distress, but show a lower level of relationship in normal and in positive conditions.

A detailed and complete discussion of copulas and their associated formulae is beyond this text, as there are many possibilities and variations that have been developed and implemented, and their Excel implementation is more complex than that of correlation coefficients.

11.2.3 Comparison and Selection of Parameter-Dependency and Sampling Relationships

Clearly, in principle, one would wish to use the relationship in the model that reflects the nature of the situation as far as possible.

From a practical perspective, one usually makes a choice to use either a parameter-dependency or a joint sampling relationship. However, in theory, these relationships do not exclude each other, and both could be used within the same processes. For example, a "high" value of one process may alter the parameter of another (say, causing it to be "high"), whilst simultaneously a correlated sampling of the processes would mean that – within the feasible range of the second process at that recalculation (or iteration) – a value is sampled that is to the higher end of this range due to the correlation (because the first distribution is being sampled at a high value). Thus, for the second process, a "high" sample would be drawn from a range that already has a "high" feasible range. Nevertheless, practically speaking, it is rare that one would use both approaches at the same time.

The use of parameter dependency is arguably more aligned with general modelling philosophy, which is based on capturing (or hypothesising) the relationships between variables. Such relationships express an explicit, directional causality from one variable to the parameter(s) of another, whereas there is no such directional causality within relationships of joint sampling. In particular, the existence of a non-zero correlation coefficient between two variables does not imply that the process that generated their values was one of correlation, as a partial causality also generates such a measured correlation.

On the other hand, the use of parameter-dependency relationships has some potential disadvantages:

- It represents a more fundamental intervention in a model; generally it requires several formulae to be changed, lines to be added and new formula links to be made.
- It may be open to criticism if the relationship between items is not understood sufficiently to justify the causality or directionality that has been modelled.
- It can be hard to calibrate the model (i.e. choose the distributions and their parameters, and the appropriate dependency formulae) so that the implied correlations between the variables match those that have been measured from historic data. For example, in the case of a single derivative product whose price is partly driven by that of a reference product, it may be possible to adjust the parameters of the processes (such as the standard deviation of each) in order to match historic correlations between the two processes. However, if there are several (or dozens) of derivative products, achieving not only the correlations with the reference product, but also the cross-correlations between the derivatives, would be much more challenging, and potentially very time-consuming, even if it were possible. (As a minimum, it would require several simulations to be run, with trial and error used, or it may be considered more formally as an optimisation problem.)

Sampling relationships have advantages that correspond to the above disadvantages of parameter-dependency approaches:

- The implementation of correlated sampling does not require any structural intervention in the model (apart from placing a correlation matrix within it); the model's formulae are not changed by the presence of this relationship, which only affects the way that random number samples are jointly used. Thus, correlations can be built in almost as an "after-thought" to the main build of the model.

- There is no requirement to understand the nature of the relationships, only that historic data are available (or estimates can be made) in order to calibrate the model (e.g. the correlation matrix). Thus, relationships contained within historic data sets may be replicated during a simulation, even where the true underlying causalities are not understood, or are excessively complex to capture in a model.
- A correlation coefficient between two variables is easy to measure; it is a simple mechanical calculation (such a measurement does not assess whether there is any partial causality, which can only be known or hypothesised from other information about the situation).

There can, therefore, be a temptation to use correlation as the default relationship in risk modelling situations. On the other hand, it is important to bear in mind that correlated sampling also has some disadvantages:

- It is generally a weaker relationship than parameter dependency. If it is used inappropriately, it may lead to incorrect assessment of ranges, or of the likelihood of extreme outcomes.
- One may not be able to change (or conduct sensitivity analysis to) the parameters of one process without also altering the parameters of the other; otherwise one may be led to incorrect conclusions (see the earlier Figure 11.16 and the associated file). For example:
  - In the earlier model relating the number of competitors to a company's market share, the use of a negative correlation between these variables would generally be an inappropriate relationship, or one that may be subject to unexpected error: if the range governing the number of competitors were doubled (or the intensity of the underlying processes and the number of competitors initially presented were significantly increased), this change would have no effect on the market share.
  - If one were to correlate the cost of a barrel of oil and that of a kilogram of oil-based plastics (or close derivate of oil), then an increase in the fundamental underlying assumed range for oil would have no effect on the sampled values for the cost of the plastics.
  - If advertising expenditure were correlated with sales volume, the addition of a fixed amount to the base advertising budget (say doubling it) would have no effect on the sales volume, because such a change in the values of the advertising expenditure would not affect the sampling of the distribution for sales volume.

In fact, although parameter dependency creates an implied correlation, an important but subtle point is that the use of this relationship in a multi-variable model will generally result in the distribution of outcomes that is different to that which would arise if a correlated sampling were implemented using the correlation coefficients that are implied by the parameter dependency. Thus, in multi-variable models, correlation is an insufficient proxy if causality relationships are known or could be reasonably assessed. This is shown in the following example.

The file Ch11.Correl.Dep.Comp.xlsx contains two worksheets (Correl and Causality). In each, there are five uncertain processes, each representing the cash flow of a project. These

Common Item	100	8	115.1

	Mean	StdDev	Sample
Project 1	115.1	2	115.3
Project 2	115.1	4	112.0
Project 3	115.1	6	128.2
Project 4	115.1	8	113.8
Project 5	115.1	10	104.3
Total			573.6

Simulation Results

Mean	StdDev
100.0	8.2
100.0	9.0
100.0	10.0
100.0	11.4
100.0	12.8
500.0	42.8

Correl with each other (simulated)

	Project 1	Project 2	Project 3	Project 4	Project 5
Project 1	100%	87%	78%	69%	60%
Project 2	87%	100%	72%	64%	56%
Project 3	78%	72%	100%	57%	50%
Project 4	69%	64%	57%	100%	44%
Project 5	60%	56%	50%	44%	100%

FIGURE 11.18 Simulation of Cross-correlations Implied by a Partial Dependency with a Common Risk Driver

are added up to give a total, which is then simulated to assess the distribution of its outcomes. In the worksheet Causality, there is an additional uncertain process, whose sampled value determines the parameter of the mean of the other five processes. After running a simulation, one can see the distribution of the output of the total, as well as the implied correlation between the five variables, as shown in Figure 11.18.

In the worksheet Correl, there is no common uncertainty, but the cash flows of the five processes are correlated using essentially the same values as those observed in the case of common causality, as shown in Figure 11.19.

Figure 11.20 shows an overlay of the simulation results. One can see that the process with the common partial causality is more spread (the simulation results show a standard deviation of 42.7 compared with 24.6 for the correlated case). In particular, the effect is noticeable in the tails of the distribution, where the effect on the likelihood of (apparently) rare events can be very significant. For example, in one case, a value of 575 or more would occur with a frequency of approximately 0.1% (which might be dismissed as a 1-in-1000 event), whereas in the other case (of causality), the corresponding frequency is approximately 4% (which might be considered significant, as a 1-in-25 event).

Thus, the results of the implementation of sampling relationships are different to those when using partial causality, even where the correlation coefficients used are cross-calibrated to be equal. Thus, where there is a common partial causality, it is important to attempt to capture it within a model (or at least to compare the effect of a hypothesised causality with that of a sampling relationship). Indeed, this may be a factor that (arguably) led to the incorrect estimation of the likelihood of defaults in mortgage portfolios, which itself may have been one of the causes of the Financial Crisis of the early 21st century.

	Mean	StdDev	Sample
Project 1	100	2	102.8
Project 2	100	4	102.7
Project 3	100	6	98.7
Project 4	100	8	107.7
Project 5	100	10	107.6
Total			519.4

Simulation Results

Mean	StdDev
100.0	2.0
100.0	4.0
100.0	6.0
100.0	8.0
100.0	10.0
500.0	24.5

@RISK Corre	Project 1 / S	Project 2 / S	Project 3 / S	Project 4 / S	Project 5 / Sam
Project 1 / S	100%				
Project 2 / S	87%	100%			
Project 3 / S	78%	72%	100%		
Project 4 / S	69%	64%	57%	100%	
Project 5 / S	60%	56%	50%	44%	100%

FIGURE 11.19 Model to Simulate Correlated Items Using Correlations Implied by a Common Risk Driver

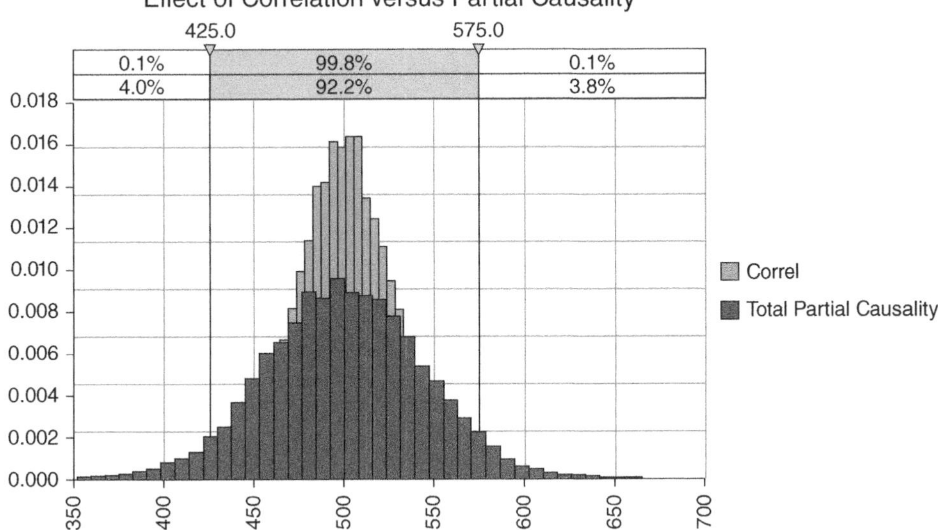

FIGURE 11.20 Overlay of Simulated Distributions of Project Totals that Result From Partial Causality and Correlation Relationships

11.2.4 Creating Correlated Samples in Excel using Cholesky Factorisation

When using @RISK, the creation of correlated sampling is an in-built procedure that is easy for a user to implement (by simply selecting the distributions and clicking the **Define Correlations** icon; also described briefly in Chapter 13).

When using Excel/VBA, correlated sampling can be created by using a procedure known as Cholesky factorisation (of the correlation matrix), as described below.

In the case where only two variables are to be correlated, one could initially draw two independent random numbers (r_1, r_2) and – for any given (or desired) correlation coefficient, ρ – generate a new set of random numbers (x_1, x_2) by defining:

$$x_1 = r_1$$

$$x_2 = \rho r_1 + \sqrt{\left(1 - \rho^2\right)} r_2$$

In this way, the data sets generated for x_1 and x_2 will be correlated with the coefficient ρ (at least for sufficiently large data sets created during the course of a simulation).

The file Ch11.Cholesky.CorrelTest.xlsx contains an implementation of this, as shown in Figure 11.21. Two data sets of 1000 independent points are randomly produced (using Excel's **RAND**() function) in column C and column D, from which the two other variables are calculated (column E and column F), using the above formulae. The desired correlation coefficient is placed in cell D3, with D4 working out the square root term. Finally, the **CORREL** function is used (cell F3) to measure the correlation between these latter two data sets; one can see a close match between the actual correlation and the desired value.

	Desired
Correlation	62.7%
Sqrt(1-Correl*Correl)	77.9%

Correl(X1, X2) in data samples
61.8%

Number	R1	R2	X1	X2
1	0.43	0.40	0.43	0.58
2	0.43	0.30	0.43	0.51
3	0.85	0.36	0.85	0.81
4	0.26	0.09	0.26	0.23
5	0.67	0.01	0.67	0.43
6	0.22	0.31	0.22	0.38
7	0.51	0.62	0.51	0.81
8	0.05	0.79	0.05	0.65
9	0.76	0.82	0.76	1.11
10	0.81	0.61	0.81	0.99
11	0.23	0.95	0.23	0.89
12	0.75	0.36	0.75	0.75
13	0.61	0.04	0.61	0.41
14	0.60	0.69	0.60	0.91
15	0.14	0.99	0.14	0.86
16	0.54	0.14	0.54	0.45
17	0.64	0.48	0.64	0.78
18	0.83	0.18	0.83	0.66
19	0.77	0.24	0.77	0.67
20	0.96	0.11	0.96	0.69

FIGURE 11.21 Testing the Formula to Generate Two Correlated Samples

The above formula can be written in matrix form as:

$$\begin{bmatrix} x_1 \\ x_2 \end{bmatrix} = \begin{bmatrix} 1 & 0 \\ \rho & \sqrt{(1-\rho^2)} \end{bmatrix} \begin{bmatrix} r_1 \\ r_2 \end{bmatrix}$$

which could be presented in matrix short form as:

$$\mathbf{X} = \mathbf{C}.\mathbf{R}$$

The matrix **C** has the property that (in the 2 × 2 case):

$$\mathbf{C}.\mathbf{C}^{\mathrm{T}} = \begin{bmatrix} 1 & \rho \\ \rho & 1 \end{bmatrix}$$

where $\mathbf{C}^{\mathrm{T}}$ is the transpose of the matrix **C**.

In other words, **C** can be thought of as the square root of the correlation matrix. When there are more than two variables, the matrix **C** can be calculated by a procedure known as the Cholesky factorisation of the correlation matrix. Once calculated, it can be used to

	A	B	C	D	E	F	G	H	I	J	K	L
1												
2		**Correlation Matrix**	**1**	**2**	**3**	**4**						
3		**1**	100%	63%	62%	58%						
4		**2**	63%	100%	73%	62%						
5		**3**	62%	73%	100%	58%						
6		**4**	58%	62%	58%	100%						
7												
8		**Cholesky as Excel Steps**	**1**	**2**	**3**	**4**						
9		**1**	100%	0%	0%	0%		=SQRT(C3)				
10		**2**	63%	78%	0%	0%		=C4/C9	=SQRT(D4-C10^2)			
11		**3**	62%	44%	65%	0%		=C5/C9	=(D5-C11*C10)/D10	=SQRT(E5-C11^2-D11^2)		
12		**4**	58%	33%	13%	74%		=C6/C9	=(D6-C12*C10)/D10	=(E6-C11*C12-D11*D12)/E11	=SQRT(F6-D12^2-E12^2-C12^2)	

FIGURE 11.22 Calculation of the Cholesky Matrix for Four Variables

create – from a (column) vector of independent random variables – a (column) vector of variables that will be correlated when repeated samples are drawn.

The file Ch11.Cholesky.ExcelSteps.xlsm contains examples of this procedure when applied to a two-by-two matrix, a three-by-three matrix and a four-by-four matrix (in the worksheets 2by2, 3by3 and 4by4, respectively). In the first two worksheets of the file, the calculations are performed by referring directly only to the values in the correlation matrix, as in the formula above for the two-by-two case. However, for larger matrices, this is not practical, as the elements of a Cholesky matrix are, in fact, made up of its other calculated elements. For example, Figure 11.22 shows the calculations in the four-by-four case, from which one sees that, although the first column of the Cholesky matrix (cells C9:C12, with their formulae shown in cells H9:H12) is directly calculated from the correlation matrix, the values in subsequent columns (e.g. column D with the formula shown in column I) require other values from the Cholesky matrix.

On close inspection of the formulae, one can see that the procedure is (for the Cholesky matrix being formed) to fix each column in turn, working down the rows of that column before moving to the next column. In doing so, one performs calculations that take the value of the correlation coefficient in the corresponding cell of the correlation matrix, and modify this using figures from those parts (of the Cholesky matrix) that have already been calculated at that point. For example, one can see that the diagonal elements of the Cholesky matrix are formed by subtracting the sum of the squares of the values of the previous row elements of the Cholesky matrix from the corresponding correlation coefficient, and taking the square root of this sum.

Since such formulae become large and cumbersome when there are several uncertain variables, any changes to a model (addition of variables, for example) would be very time-consuming and error prone. Thus, it is generally much more convenient to create the Cholesky decomposition as a user-defined array function (whose input is the correlation matrix), so that the above procedure of working down rows within fixed columns can be automated. In particular, as matrices change in size or become large, the creation of the explicit formulae would not be a very efficient way to work.

The following code has been used in some of the example models in this text (some comments and error-checking procedures have been left out of the code shown in the text), and this can be placed in a new code module within VBE (see Chapter 12) to make it available within the workbook.

```
Function MRCholesky(RCorrel As Range)
Dim rCholesky() As Double
```

```
N= RCorrel.Rows.Count
ReDim rCholesky(1 To N, 1 To N)
For j = 1 To N 'Fix a column and then work down rows for that column
For i = 1 To N
 If i < j Then
   rCholesky(i, j) = 0
 Else
  If i = j Then
    rsum = 0
    For k = 1 To i - 1
    rsum = rsum + rCholesky(i, k) * rCholesky(i, k)
    Next k
   rCholesky(i, j) = Sqr(RCorrel(i, i) - rsum) ' for i=j
  Else 'i>j
    rsum = 0
    For k = 1 To j - 1
    rsum = rsum + rCholesky(i, k) * rCholesky(j, k)
    Next k
   rCholesky(i, j) = (1 / rCholesky(j, j)) * (RCorrel(i, j) -
rsum) ' for i>j
  End If
  End If
 Next i
Next j
MRCholesky = rCholesky
Exit Function
End Function
```

The code has been used to calculate the function shown in the worksheet UDF4by4Ex. This is shown in Figure 11.23. The figure also shows the final required step of the process in practice, which uses the **MMULT** array function (entered using **CTRL+SHIFT+ENTER**) to multiply a column vector of independent random numbers by the Cholesky matrix. This would produce a set of random numbers that (over the course of repeated recalculation) were correlated according to the correlation matrix.

With regard to this final step, such matrix multiplications are only possible if the vector of random numbers is in a column. If such numbers form a row in the model, then the **TRANSPOSE** (array) function could be used within the **MMULT** function, and the results

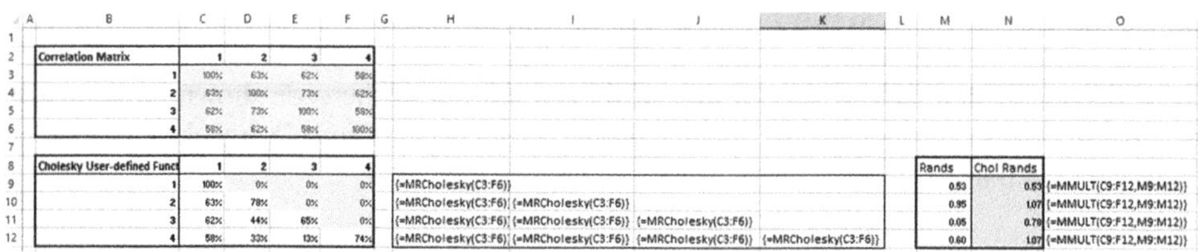

Correlation Matrix
1 2 3 4
1 100% 63% 62% 58%
2 63% 100% 73% 62%
3 62% 73% 100% 58%
4 58% 62% 58% 100%
Cholesky User-defined Funct
1 2 3 4
1 100% 0% 0% 0%
2 63% 78% 0% 0%
3 62% 44% 65% 0%
4 58% 33% 13% 74%
{=MRCholesky(C3:F6)}
Rands
Chol Rands
0.53 0.53 {=MMULT(C9:F12,M9:M12)}
0.95 1.07 {=MMULT(C9:F12,M9:M12)}
0.05 0.78 {=MMULT(C9:F12,M9:M12)}
0.60 1.07 {=MMULT(C9:F12,M9:M12)}

FIGURE 11.23 Creation of the Cholesky Matrix with a User-defined Array Function

	B	C	D	E	F	G	H	I	J
1									
2	**Correlation Matrix**	**1**	**2**	**3**	**4**				
3	**1**	100%	63%	62%	58%				
4	**2**	63%	100%	73%	62%				
5	**3**	62%	73%	100%	58%				
6	**4**	58%	62%	58%	100%				
7								**Correlated Numbers**	
8	**Cholesky as Excel Steps**	**1**	**2**	**3**	**4**		Rands	MMULT	MRMULT
9	**1**	100%	0%	0%	0%		0.07	0.07	0.07
10	**2**	63%	78%	0%	0%		0.26	0.25	0.25
11	**3**	62%	44%	65%	0%		0.23	0.31	0.31
12	**4**	58%	33%	13%	74%		0.47	0.50	0.50
13									
14	Rands	0.36	0.86	0.54	0.41				
15	MMULT	0.36	0.89	0.95	0.86	{=TRANSPOSE(MMULT(C9:F12,TRANSPOSE(C14:F14)))}			
16	MRMULT	0.36	0.89	0.95	0.86	{=MRMult(C9:F12,C14:F14)}			
17									

FIGURE 11.24 Creation of Random Samples as Row or Column Vectors with User-defined Functions

of that would need to be embedded within another **TRANSPOSE** function, in order for the correlated numbers to be aligned in a row with the original ones. The creation of a user-defined function for this final multiplication step can be more effective, as it will avoid having to transpose the ranges twice within Excel, which can be cumbersome. Figure 11.24 shows the use of such a function (MRMULT), and the code used is given subsequently. In row 15 (cells C15:F15), one sees the double-transpose formulae that would be required without such a function. Cells C16:F16 and J9:J12 show that the function works, whether the input random numbers are in a row or a column.

```
Function MRMult(Matrix As Range, Vector As Range)
'Array function to multiply matrices; Returns column vector if
Vector is a column; Returns row vector if Vector is a row
Set wsf = Application.WorksheetFunction
Dim CalcMatrix()
NRows = Vector.Rows.Count
NCols = Vector.Columns.Count
If NCols = 1 Then
 ReDim CalcMatrix(1 To NRows, 1 To 1)
 CalcMatrix = wsf.MMult(Matrix, Vector)
Else
 ReDim CalcMatrix(1 To 1, 1 To NRows)
 CalcMatrix = wsf.Transpose(wsf.MMult(Matrix, wsf.Transpose(Vector)))
End If
MRMult = CalcMatrix
End Function
```

Some further generalisations of this approach are discussed in Chapter 12, as here we aim to focus only on the principles.

11.2.5 Working with Valid Correlation Matrices

When correlating more than two variables, the choice of the elements of the desired correlation coefficient between them is not arbitrary. For example, if the first variable is correlated with the second at 90%, and the second with the third, also at 90%, then it would seem logical that there must be some reasonably strong relationship between the first and the third (as they are each closely correlated with the second). In fact, in this case, the correlation coefficient must be at least around 62% (see later).

The fact that some combinations of coefficients are not permissible can also be seen by recalling that many of the formulae in a Cholesky factorisation involve either taking the square root of the calculated arguments (which is only valid if such arguments are positive), or dividing by calculated quantities (which is only valid if the arguments are non-zero). From a mathematical perspective, a correlation matrix is valid only if it is positive semi-definite (equivalent to its eigenvalues all being non-negative). Intuitively, since the Cholesky matrix is the square root of the correlation matrix, it can be calculated only for particular (i.e. positive semi-definite) matrices, just as the square root of a real number only exists for non-negative numbers.

In principle, if a correlation matrix is created by taking actual historic data, then it should be a valid (or consistent) matrix. However, in practice, even actual data can result in inconsistent matrices:

- If there are insufficient data points compared to variables (e.g. 10 variables but only 8 data points for each), or if some variables are fully dependent on others.
- Due to statistical or measurement error if data are brought together from various sources. A common example concerns data on financial assets, where, due to time-zone differences or processes to manually report data on closing prices, one data source reports delayed data (such as that which actually occurred one or two periods earlier).
- If one is estimating values for the correlation coefficients, especially where there are more than three variables, so that the implied relationships between several of them is not easy to follow.

In @RISK, one can use the **RiskCorrectCorrmat** array function as an intermediate step in order to "correct" any inconsistencies in the desired correlation matrix, and then link this corrected matrix to the actual correlated matrix used for the simulation:

- The default correlation calculation involves modifying the correlation matrix to create one whose minimum eigenvalue is non-negative. This is done by subtracting the smallest eigenvalue from the diagonals of the correlation matrix (which then makes them larger than 100%, as the smallest one will be negative for an inconsistent matrix) and then rescaling the elements of the whole matrix so that the new diagonal elements are still equal to 100%, i.e. by creating the matrix $(\mathbf{C} - \lambda.\mathbf{I})/(1 - \lambda)$, where $\mathbf{C}$ is the original correlation matrix, λ is its smallest eigenvalue and $\mathbf{I}$ is the identity matrix.
- One can override the default correction factors and use an optional weighting matrix, so that some correlation figures could be unaffected by the correction process, which may make sense if some figures have been measured from data whereas others are only estimates.

The file Ch11.Correl.Corrected.xlsx contains an example. Figure 11.25 shows the worksheet Inconsistent, showing that (for the example described above) a correlation of 10% between the first and third variables would be invalid, with the Cholesky procedure producing an error. Figure 11.26 shows a similar case using @RISK (in the worksheet @RISK), in which (cells C8:E10) the **RiskCorrectCorrmat** function is used without specifying any weighting factors, whereas cells J8:L10 explicitly use the (otherwise optional) weighting factors so that

Correlation Matrix	1	2	3			
1	100%	90%	90%			
2	90%	100%	10%			
3	90%	10%	100%			
Cholesky as Excel Steps	**1**	**2**	**3**			
1	100%	0%	0%			
2	90%	44%	0%	=C4	=SQRT(1-C4^2)	
3	90%	-163%	#NUM!	=C5	=(D5-C5*C4)/SQRT(1-C4^2)	=SQRT(E5-C5^2-(D5-C5*C4)^2/(1-C4^2))

FIGURE 11.25 Example of an Invalid Correlation Matrix

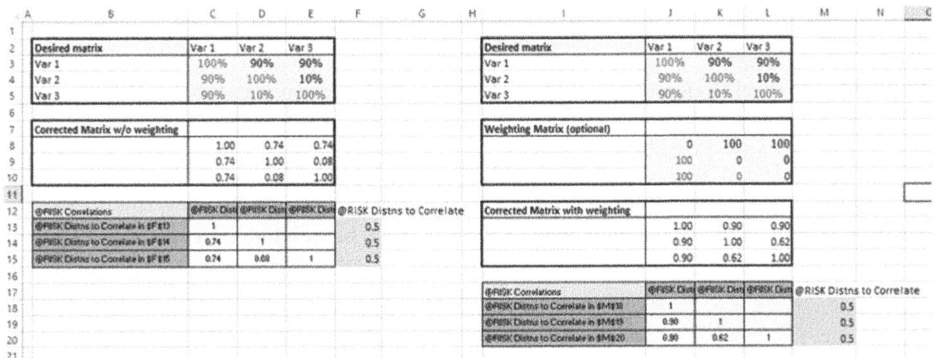

Desired matrix	Var 1	Var 2	Var 3
Var 1	100%	90%	90%
Var 2	90%	100%	10%
Var 3	90%	10%	100%

Corrected Matrix w/o weighting			
	1.00	0.74	0.74
	0.74	1.00	0.08
	0.74	0.08	1.00

@RISK Correlations	@RISK Dist	@RISK Dist	@RISK Dist	@RISK Distns to Correlate
@RISK Distns to Correlate in $F$13	1			0.5
@RISK Distns to Correlate in $F$14	0.74	1		0.5
@RISK Distns to Correlate in $F$15	0.74	0.08	1	0.5

Desired matrix	Var 1	Var 2	Var 3
Var 1	100%	90%	90%
Var 2	90%	100%	10%
Var 3	90%	10%	100%

Weighting Matrix (optional)			
	0	100	100
	100	0	0
	100	0	0

Corrected Matrix with weighting			
	1.00	0.90	0.90
	0.90	1.00	0.62
	0.90	0.62	1.00

@RISK Correlations	@RISK Dist	@RISK Dist	@RISK Dist	@RISK Distns to Correlate
@RISK Distns to Correlate in $M$18	1			0.5
@RISK Distns to Correlate in $M$19	0.90	1		0.5
@RISK Distns to Correlate in $M$20	0.90	0.62	1	0.5

FIGURE 11.26 Using @RISK's Functionality to Create an Adapted Correlation Matrix

the final matrix (J13:L15) is altered by only changing the value of the correlation between the first and third variable.

11.2.6 Correlation of Time Series

One may have two or more processes that develop over time, and it may be desired to implement correlations between them. Whilst the more general topic of time-series modelling is covered later in the chapter, in the simplest case, one may wish to correlate the changes between several time series within each period, whilst assuming no correlation between the changes in one period and the changes in the next. Such correlations can, in principle, be implemented using the above procedures, both in Excel/VBA and in @RISK. However, due to the assumption that there is no relationship between changes across periods, the correlation matrix would be large but mostly contain zeros, and be cumbersome to work with.

In @RISK, a special feature (**Create Correlated Time Series**) is available within the **Define Correlations** icon; this can be used to implement only a single correlation matrix that applies within each period, with this matrix reused across all periods (assuming the correlation coefficient is constant over time, otherwise multiple matrices or a large sparse matrix would need to be used). This is known (in @RISK) as using multiple **Instances** of the same correlation matrix.

The file Ch11.OpFlexRealOptions.TripleFuel.Correl.xlsx contains an implementation of this within the earlier example of a flexible production facility (see Chapter 4). Figure 11.27 shows that (in the case of positive correlation) the net benefit of the switching possibilities is reduced from approximately $400 to approximately $250 (as the frequency of, and the amount to be gained by, switching will be less).

O	P	Q	R	S	T	U	V	W	X
9	10		OptValue $/unit						
64	75	=O5*(1+P10)							
476	348	=O6*(1+P11)							
239	326	=O7*(1+P12)							
64	75	=MIN(P5:P7)	257						
					@RISK Corr	Oil / 1 in G	Gas / 1 in $G	Electricity / 1 in $G$12	
-5%	17%	=RiskNormal($E10,$F10,RiskCorrmat(NewMatrix2,1,1			Oil / 1 in G	1			
11%	-27%	=RiskNormal($E11,$F11,RiskCorrmat(NewMatrix2,2,1			Gas / 1 in $G	60%	1		
20%	36%	=RiskNormal($E12,$F12,RiskCorrmat(NewMatrix2,3,1			Electricity / 1	60%	60%	1	
0	0	=IF(MATCH(MIN(P5:P7),P5:P7,0)=MATCH(MIN(O5:O7),O5:O7,0),0,1)							

FIGURE 11.27 Real Options Value of Flexibility when Price Movements are Correlated

(Note that such correlations do not affect the trend in the prices, only their changes within each period; with other parameters, one series could be trending downward and another upward, even as the movements within each period around the trend are correlated.)

11.3 DEPENDENCIES WITHIN TIME SERIES

Many Excel models are of a forecasting nature, so that there is a time component to the development of variables (such as prices, volumes, revenues, cost, profit, and so on).

In many cases, one can use standard modelling techniques to forecast variables over time, even in the presence of uncertainty. For example, in some of the earlier models that involved forecasting over time (such as the valuation of the switching flexibility, and the price development of the reference and derivative products), we assumed a standard (discrete) model for the development of the prices over time, namely that the percentage change in each period is normally distributed. In fact, this is an approximation to a continuous-time process, in which instantaneous price changes are normally distributed (resulting in a lognormal process for the continuous-time price development), and is a special case of the general time-series models.

Within financial literature, there is a wide variety of time-series modelling approaches. In such contexts, in the first instance, the word "model" generally refers to the mathematical formulation (equation) that describes the instantaneous change (in continuous time) of a single variable, such as a stock price, or short-term interest rate (rather than referring to an implementation of such calculations). Similarly, there are equations (models) for multiple variables that may relate to each other, such as the instantaneous change in both short- and long-term interest rates. Some of these equations have exact (closed-form, analytic) solutions, whereas others require simulation or other numerical techniques. When working in Excel, generally speaking, one is also working with a discrete (not a continuous) time axis, a fact that may also need to be taken into account when calibrating the model by analysis of the historic data.

Some of the core relationships are described in this section, although the topic is extremely rich, with a complete coverage being beyond the scope of this text.

Note that some of the example files in this section are built in Excel only. Such files could also easily be built using @RISK. In addition, @RISK provides the possibility to fit time-series data to processes, which can be very powerful in practice, if one has data but does not know the appropriate series to use, or its parameters.

11.3.1 Geometric Brownian Motion

Brownian motion models are essentially the formal equivalent of growth formulae frequently used in Excel models, in which the change in a value of a quantity (prices, volumes, etc.) from one period to the next is given by a growth rate. Such a growth rate may be an uncertain or random process. Thus, in many corporate finance and other "corporate modelling" contexts, one implements equations in Excel (e.g. for the development of prices over time, with a growth rate g), such as:

$$P_{i+1} = P_i(1+g)$$

which can be written as:

$$P_{i+1} - P_i = P_i g$$

If g were considered to be an uncertain process, whose changes are independent from one period to the next, which follows a normal distribution (with parameters μ, σ), and if the time axis is regarded as continuous, then one could write an analogous equation for the instantaneous change in P for each instantaneous change in time as:

$$\mathrm{d}P = \mu P\mathrm{d}t + \sigma P N(0,1)\sqrt{\mathrm{d}t}$$

This equation describes a process of geometric Brownian motion (GBM); the square root term that multiplies the standard deviation is due to the fact that the variance of independent processes can be added (as covered earlier in the text), and hence scale linearly in time, so that the standard deviation scales as the square root of time.

The last term in the equation is sometimes called simple Brownian motion (or a Wiener process), and represents the random part of the movement, so that the GBM equation can be written as:

$$\mathrm{d}P = \mu P\mathrm{d}t + \sigma P\mathrm{d}W$$

where:

$$\mathrm{d}W = N(0,1)\sqrt{\mathrm{d}t}$$

The file Ch11.TimeSeries.PriceStochastics.xlsx shows an implementation of various approaches related to this, as shown in Figure 11.28. The model assumes that there is a set of historic data for the development of a price variable (over four periods), and uses these data to calibrate various time-series models, for which the starting value of the variable is the same as for the historic data (i.e. 100), but where, due to random fluctuation, the price

	A	B	C	D	E	F	G	H	I	J
1										
2		Historic Data	Mean	Volatility		Starting	1	2	3	4
3		Share Price				100.0	110.0	95.0	105.0	120.0
4		Simple Returns	4.66%	12.76%			10.00%	-13.64%	10.53%	14.29%
5		LN Returns	4.56%	12.92%			9.53%	-14.66%	10.01%	13.35%
6										
7		Model 1: Simple Returns using simple compounded average	Mean	Volatility		Starting				
8		Normally-D Simple Changes	4.66%	12.76%		100.0	105.3	108.5	114.3	113.8
9		Simple Returns					5.32%	3.05%	5.35%	-0.42%
10		Mean					5.32%	3.05%	5.35%	-0.42%
11		Volatilty					0.00%	0.00%	0.00%	0.00%
12										
13		Model 2: LN Returns using Average of LN Returns	Mean	Volatility		Starting				
14		Normally-D Ln Changes	4.56%	12.92%		100.0	116.9	117.3	122.0	103.1
15		Ln Returns					15.62%	0.36%	3.88%	-16.77%
16		Mean					15.62%	0.36%	3.88%	-16.77%
17		Volatility					0.00%	0.00%	0.00%	0.00%
18										
19		Model 3: LN Returns Forecast based on adjusted Average LN	Mean	Volatility	Adjusted Mean	Starting				
20		Normally-D Ln Changes adjusted drift	4.56%	12.92%	3.72%	100.0	112.1	109.2	99.3	126.4
21		Ln Returns					11.44%	-2.60%	-9.53%	24.10%
22		Mean					11.44%	-2.60%	-9.53%	24.10%
23		Volatility					0.00%	0.00%	0.00%	0.00%
24										
25		Model 4: Closed Form for any time	Mean	Volatility	Adjusted Mean		1	2	3	4
26		Ending Value	4.56%	12.92%	3.72%	100.0	96.4	103.7	96.1	87.1

FIGURE 11.28 Various Implementations of the Growth Formulae

development at any point in time would generally be different to that of the corresponding period. The ending value of the historic data is 120, thus one would wish that any model produces values that are equal to this on average.

The calculation tables shown for each model are as follows:

- Model 1 uses the traditional corporate modelling approach, for which the historic data are also used to calculate the simple percentage returns in each period.
- Model 2 uses the historic data to calculate the logarithmic returns (i.e. the natural logarithm of the ratio of prices from one period to the next), which is then used to create samples from a normal distribution in each period based directly on these data. These samples are then exponentiated and used to calculate the price in the next period:

$$P_{i+1} = P_i e^{N(\mu,\sigma)}$$

- Model 3 uses the same procedure as Model 2, but the average growth rate used is adjusted by a "convexity correction" factor:

$$P_{i+1} = P_i e^{N\left(\mu - \frac{\sigma^2}{2}, \sigma\right)}$$

- Model 4 calculates the equivalent to Model 3 over any time period T:

$$P_T = P_0 e^{N\left(\left(\mu - \frac{\sigma^2}{2}\right)T, \sigma\sqrt{T}\right)}$$

Figure 11.29 shows a screen clip of part of the same file, in particular the numerical figures in column M show the average of the ending value in period 4, calculated by simulation. Note that the values in Model 2 do not match the historic figure, whereas those in the other models do. In other words, when using the continuous-time compounding procedure base on logarithmic

J	K	L	M	N
4				
120.0				
14.29%	=J3/I3-1			
13.35%	=LN(J3/I3)			
			Mean at end	Difference
177.5	=I8*(1+RiskNormal($C8,$D8))		120.0	-0.001
17.66%	=J8/I8-1			
4.66%	=RiskMean(J9)			
12.76%	=RiskStdDev(J9)			
			Mean at end	Difference
84.6	=I14*EXP(RiskNormal($C$14,$D$14))		124.0	3.995
-23.04%	=LN(J14/I14)			
4.56%	=RiskMean(J15)			
12.92%	=RiskStdDev(J15)			
			Mean at end	Difference
101.8	=I20*EXP(RiskNormal($E20,$D20,RiskStatic($C20)))		120.0	-0.018
8.84%	=LN(J20/I20)			
3.72%	=RiskMean(J21)			
12.93%	=RiskStdDev(J21)			
4			Mean at end	Difference
105.7	=$F26*EXP(RiskNormal($E26*J25,$D26*SQRT(J25),RiskStat		120.0	0.002

FIGURE 11.29 Comparison of Simulated Means with Original Values for Various Growth Formulae

returns calculations (and the corresponding exponential process for forward calculations), the convexity adjustment of Model 3 (and 4) is required.

The file Ch11.TimeSeries.ConvexityAdj.xlsx provides further intuition to this (and is essentially a simplified form of the above Model 2); it calculates the average during a simulation of a process which exponentiates samples of a normal distribution with a closed-form calculation, as shown in Figure 11.30.

The convexity-adjustment factor will be seen in many time-series models, whether they are derived from fitting procedures (as they can be in @RISK) or implemented directly.

GBM methods are often extended to jump approaches, in which a Poisson-distributed number of shocks may happen in any period, each with an impact whose size is normally distributed, for example.

11.3.2 Mean-Reversion Models

Another important set of time-series models are those with mean-reverting properties. Processes that are sometimes considered to be mean reverting are:

- Interest rates. A high interest rate will slow the economy, leading to the possibility of an interest rate reduction, and a low rate will stimulate the economy, leading to interest rates needing to rise later.

	A	B	C	D
1				
2		Data		
3		Mean	10.0%	
4		StdDev	30.0%	
5				
6		Simulation:		
7		Normal	15.2%	=RiskNormal(C3,C4)
8		Exponential	116.4%	=EXP(C7)
9		Average	115.6%	=RiskMean(C8)
10				
11		Closed-Form	115.6%	=EXP(C3+C4*C4/2)

FIGURE 11.30 Example of Convexity Effect of Applying Non-linear Formulae to Uncertain Values

- Commodity prices. Higher commodity prices will reduce demand and slow the macroeconomy, leading to commodity price falls, whereas low prices would stimulate the economy, leading to price rises. Such trends may be overlaid within general inflation, so that the mean reversion is a short- or medium-term behaviour within a longer-term upward trend, for example.

Some examples of mean-reverting models (especially for interest rates) include:
Basic mean-reversion models:

$$dr = \alpha(\mu - r)\,dt + \sigma r\,dW$$

Cox–Ingersoll–Ross models:

$$dr = \alpha(\mu - r)\,dt + \sigma\,dW$$

Ornstein–Uhlenbeck (Vasicek) models:

$$dr = \alpha(\mu - r)\,dt + \sigma\sqrt{r}\,dW$$

The presence of the subtraction in the first term in each equation results in a negative term when r is greater than μ, and a positive term when r is less than μ, thus creating a process that reverts to μ on average, but is subject to random variation as it does so.

Mean-reverting models can also be implemented in which multiple variables relate to each other. For example, one may have a model for short- and long-term oil price forecasts (or short- and long-term interest rates), with the long-term price of oil being regarded as growing (perhaps according to a geometric Brownian motion model), and the short-term price following a mean-reverting process whose mean-reversion target is the long-term price. In such cases, the random part of the changes in each period can be correlated with each other, as mentioned earlier in this chapter.

The reader can find more about such models and other examples through simple internet or literature searches.

11.3.3 Moving Average Models

There are a variety of moving average models, meaning that there is a variation around a long-term average (and not that prior values of the variable are explicitly taken into account). For example, a first-order moving average process is equal to its mean, plus a random "error" term, plus a scaling factor applied to the error term in the prior period:

$$\varepsilon_t = \sigma N(0, 1)$$

$$S_t = \mu + \varepsilon_t + B\varepsilon_{t-1}$$

A second-order model would include scaling factors for the error term two periods earlier.

The file Ch11.TimeSeries.MA1.xlsx contains the implementation of this in Excel, as shown in Figure 11.31.

11.3.4 Autoregressive Models

Another category of time-series models is those with autoregressive processes. For example, a first-order autoregressive model in discrete time is a process (here called *S*), where:

$$S_t = \mu + \alpha\left(S_{t-1} - \mu\right) + \sigma N(0, 1)$$

or:

$$S_t - \mu = \alpha\left(S_{t-1} - \mu\right) + \sigma N(0, 1)$$

Thus, at the current time, the distance of the variable from the long-term average, μ, is related (by a scaling factor α, the autoregression coefficient) to the distance at the previous time period, as well as having a random variation around that (governed by the volatility, σ). The process needs a starting value, S_0, and thus there are four parameters.

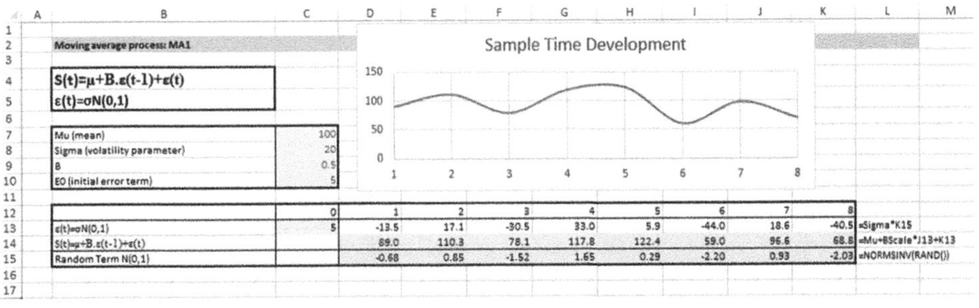

FIGURE 11.31 Example of Moving Average Time Series

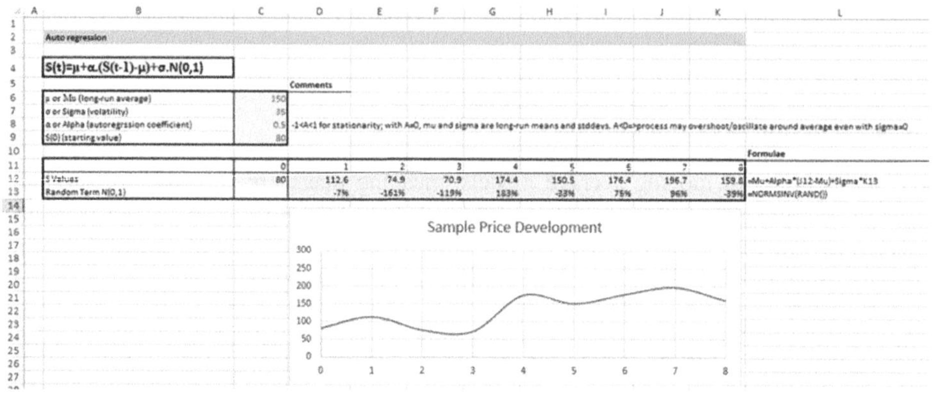

FIGURE 11.32 Example of Autoregressive Time Series

Second-order (and third-order) processes are similar, with the formulae adapted to reflect that the values of two prior periods are also straightforward:

$$S_t - \mu = \alpha_1 \left(S_{t-1} - \mu\right) + \alpha_2 \left(S_{t-2} - \mu\right) + \sigma N(0, 1)$$

The file Ch11.TimeSeries.AR1.xlsx contains an implementation of the first-order process in Excel, where the random terms are captured using the direct Excel inverse function; the @RISK equivalent would, of course, also be easy to implement. A sample is shown in Figure 11.32.

More complex examples of autoregressive processes include where two time series interact, such as in generalised autoregressive conditional heteroskedasticity (GARCH) models; in these, the volatility parameter is not constant, but forms a second time series that is related to the process S:

$$\sigma_t^2 = \gamma + \beta \left(S_{t-1} - \mu\right)^2 + \alpha\sigma_{t-1}^2$$
$$S_t = \mu + \sigma_t N(0, 1)$$

The file Ch11.TimeSeries.GARCH.xlsx contains an implementation of the first-order process in Excel (Figure 11.33), where the random terms are captured using the direct Excel inverse function; the @RISK equivalent would, of course, also be easy to implement.

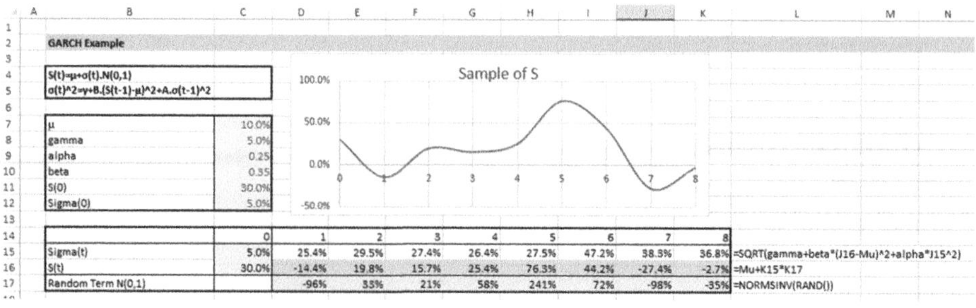

FIGURE 11.33 Example of GARCH Time Series

11.3.5 Co-Directional (Integrated) Processes

As noted earlier, when dealing with time series for several variables, the creation of time series whose random changes are correlated with each other does not necessarily mean that they move in the same direction: correlation affects only the sampling of each distribution relative to its own average, so that the series may develop in different senses, depending on the nature of each time series and its parameters. Of course, sometimes one wishes for two series to have a co-directionality between their long-term development, and this can be achieved by ensuring a tighter relationship between the series (directly between either their values or their parameters). For example, if an "independent" process develops randomly, whereas another is scaled from this but has its own error term, then the process will have a directionality between them. This is similar to several of the examples given earlier, such as that relating the price of a derivative product to the price of a reference product, so is not covered further.

11.3.6 Random State Switching and Markov Chains

Earlier in the text we gave examples of where a scenario chosen randomly at each recalculation (iteration) affected the parameters to be used for a process for all future time periods; in other words, at each recalculation, a single scenario applied across all time periods. More generally, one could create a model in which the scenario used changed from one time period to the next in a random fashion. Further, one could allow the probability that a particular scenario would occur at a specific point in time to depend on which scenario applied at the prior time point, and thus use a matrix of probabilities for the switching of one state (scenario) to another, as in a Markov chain. This is simple to implement by using the general discrete function, in which (using a lookup function) the probabilities that apply for the state that will apply within the period are looked up within the transition probability matrix depending on the prior period (ending) state. The modelling aspects of this should be fairly simple to implement for any reader who has followed the discussion to this point; the challenge is often to calibrate the transition matrix, as historic data need to be allocated to states (which may be arbitrary to some extent), and some state-switching scenarios may never have arisen historically, whereas the matrix demands that a full range of switching possibilities be defined.

PART III

Getting Started with Simulation in Practice

CHAPTER 12

Using Excel/VBA for Simulation Modelling

In this chapter, we use a simple example model to show the basic elements required to create and run simulation models using Excel and VBA. We assume that the reader has no prior experience with VBA, and intend to provide a step-by-step description in sufficient detail for the beginner to be able to replicate.

Most of the chapter focuses on the mechanical aspects necessary to automate the process of repeatedly calculating a model and storing the results. The aim is to focus on such issues in a simple context, separate to the detailed discussions concerning the design of risk models, distribution selection and sampling, dependency relationships and other issues discussed earlier in the text. Indeed, this chapter aims to be accessible as an introduction to the pure simulation aspects if it were to be read on a stand-alone basis, i.e. without reference to the rest of the text.

In the latter part of the chapter, we describe how the specific techniques of risk modelling may be integrated with the simulation approach (especially the inclusion of the richer set of distributions discussed in Chapter 9 and Chapter 10, and the use of correlated sampling techniques, as covered in Chapter 11). We also mention some areas of further possible generalisation and sophistication that may be considered.

12.1 DESCRIPTION OF EXAMPLE MODEL AND UNCERTAINTY RANGES

The file Ch12.CostEstimation.Basic.Core.xlsx contains the simple model that we use as a starting point for the discussion. It aims to estimate the possible required budget for a family vacation. As shown in Figure 12.1, the initial model indicates a total estimated cost of $10,000.

For the purposes here, we do not make any genuine attempt to capture the real nature of the uncertainty distribution for each item (as discussed in Chapter 9). We also make the (not-insignificant) assumption that the line items in the model correspond to the drivers of risk (see Chapter 7). This is in order to retain the focus on the core aspects relevant for this chapter.

In particular, we shall assume that:

	A	B	C
1		BUDGET FOR FAMILY VACATION	
2			
3		CORE ITEMS	
4			BASE ($)
5		Flight	1000
6		Hotel	3000
7		Taxis/transfers etc	1000
8		Food and drink	2000
9		Insurance	1000
10		Tourist attractions	1000
11		Presents, misc items	1000
12		Total ($)	10000

FIGURE 12.1 Base Cost Model

- Each item can take any (random) value within a uniform range (of equally likely values).
- There are some event risks that may occur with a given probability, having an impact (in terms of additional costs) when they do so. In this example, these risks are assumed to be associated with changes in the availability of flights or of hotels compared to the base plan. The event risks are shown separately to the base model (in the form of a small risk register). For consistency of presentation, we have adapted the original model to include these event risks, with their value being zero in the base case. The range of additional costs when an event occurs is assumed to be uniform (and, for the hotel, includes the possibility that it may be possible to find a slightly cheaper one, as the lower end of the range extends to negative values).

The file Ch12.CostEstimation.Basic.RiskRanges.xlsx contains the values used for the probabilities and ranges, as shown in Figure 12.2.

12.2 CREATING AND RUNNING A SIMULATION: CORE STEPS

This section describes the core steps required to create and run a simulation using Excel/VBA approaches, including the generation of basic random samples, the repeated calculation of the model and simple ways to store results. Later in the chapter, we discuss more general techniques that may be used in many real-life modelling situations in order to create more flexibility in some areas.

12.2.1 Using Random Values

The file Ch12.CostEstimationBasic.RiskRanges.WithRANDS.xlsx contains the next stage, in which the Excel **RAND**() function is used to generate uniformly distributed random numbers between zero and one; these are used to create random values within the uncertainty ranges:

	B	C	D	E	F
1	**BUDGET FOR FAMILY VACATION**				
2					
3	**CORE ITEMS**		Risk (Uncertainty) Ranges		
4		BASE ($)	Min	Max	
5	Flight	1000	900	1300	
6	Hotel	3000	2500	4500	
7	Taxis/transfers etc	1000	900	1500	
8	Food and drink	2000	1800	2400	
9	Insurance	1000	900	1100	
10	Tourist attractions	1000	600	2500	
11	Presents, misc items	1000	800	1500	
12	**Total ($)**	**10000**			
13					
14	**EVENT RISKS**				
15		BASE ($)	Prob	Min	Max
16	Extra cost due to planned flight being unavailable	0	20%	500	2000
17	Extra cost due to planned hotel being unavailable	0	15%	-200	1500
18	**Total ($)**	**0**			
19					
20	**TOTAL ($)**	**10000**			

FIGURE 12.2 Cost Model with Values Defining the Uncertainty Ranges

- For the uniform continuous ranges:

$$\text{Value or Impact} = \text{Min} + (\text{Max} - \text{Min}) * \textbf{RAND}()$$

- For the occurrence of the risk events:

$$\text{Occurrence or Not} = \textbf{IF}(\textbf{RAND}() \leq \text{Prob}, 1, 0)$$

The final impact of the event risks is calculated by multiplying the occurrence figure by the impact (so that the result will be a value of zero for the case of non-occurrence and equal to the impact in the case of occurrence), as shown in Figure 12.3.

This example is sufficiently simple that some important points about more general cases may be overlooked:

	B	C	D	E	F	H	I	J	K	L	N	O	P
1	BUDGET FOR FAMILY VACATION												
2											Column J	Column K	Column L
3	CORE ITEMS		Risk (Uncertainty) Ranges										
4		BASE ($)	Min	Max					Rands()	Values			
5	Flight	1000	900	1300					0.32	1030		=RAND()	=D5+(E5-D5)*K5
6	Hotel	3000	2500	4500					0.18	2854		=RAND()	=D6+(E6-D6)*K6
7	Taxis/transfers etc	1000	900	1500					0.39	1133		=RAND()	=D7+(E7-D7)*K7
8	Food and drink	2000	1800	2400					0.98	2385		=RAND()	=D8+(E8-D8)*K8
9	Insurance	1000	900	1100					0.19	937		=RAND()	=D9+(E9-D9)*K9
10	Tourist attractions	1000	600	2500					0.12	829		=RAND()	=D10+(E10-D10)*K10
11	Presents, misc items	1000	800	1500					0.20	940		=RAND()	=D11+(E11-D11)*K11
12	Total ($)	10000								10108			=SUM(L5:L11)
13													
14	EVENT RISKS							Values					
15		BASE ($)	Prob	Min	Max	Rands()	Rands()	Occurrenc	Impact or	Impact			
16	Extra cost due to planned flight being unavailable	0	20%	500	2000	0.23	0.57	0	1359	0	=IF(H16<=D16,1,0)	=E16+(F16-E16)*I16	=J16*K16
17	Extra cost due to planned hotel being unavailable	0	15%	-200	1500	0.81	0.68	0	962	0	=IF(H17<=D17,1,0)	=E17+(F17-E17)*I17	=J17*K17
18	Total ($)	0								0			=SUM(L16:L17)
19													
20	TOTAL ($)	10000								10108			

FIGURE 12.3 Cost Model with Uncertainty Distributions

- For clarity of presentation of the core concept at this stage, the uncertain values generated are used as inputs to a repeated (parallel) model (i.e. that in column L, rather than in the original column C). Of course, most models are too complex to be built and maintained twice in this way: generally, the uncertain values would instead be integrated within the original model, for example by using an **IF** statement or a **CHOOSE** function to act as a switch that determines whether the input area to the original model (i.e. column C) would use the base values or uncertain values (so that the base values would need to be stored elsewhere and column C replaced with formulae).
- Where other distributions are required, as discussed in Chapter 10, the **RAND**() function would be used as an input into the calculation of the inverse cumulative distribution function.

12.2.2 Using a Macro to Perform Repeated Recalculations and Store the Results

With the model as built so far, the user can press the **F9** key (which instructs Excel to recalculate), so that the **RAND**() functions will be resampled, and the model's values will update. In other words, each use of **F9** will create a new scenario for the uncertain inputs and for the total cost. The automation of this step (so that it can be repeated many times) can be done using a looping procedure within a VBA macro.

The file Ch12.CostEstimation.Basic1.Macro.xlsm contains the VBA code (macros) for the simulation, so that the macros within it will need to be enabled.

(Alternatively, the file Ch12.CostEstimation.Basic.RiskRanges.xlsx may be used as a starting point for readers wishing to build the model from scratch by following the steps described below; in that case, the workbook would have to be resaved as a macro-enabled one, with the .xlsm extension, when using Excel 2007 onwards.)

12.2.3 Working with the VBE and Inserting a VBA Code Module

The **Visual Basic Editor** (VBE) can be accessed either using the **Alt+F11** shortcut or (from Excel 2007 onwards) from the **Developer** tab. (The **Developer** tab is usually hidden by default and can be shown using the Excel Options, e.g. in Excel 2013 choosing **Customize Ribbon** under the [Excel] **Options** and checking the box for the **Developer** tab; the procedures for Excel 2007 and 2010 are similar but slightly different, but the reader should be able to find this without difficulty.)

Once in the VBE, one needs to insert a new module (**Insert/Module**) into the workbook (**Project**) that is being used (not into another workbook that also may be open); this operation is shown in Figure 12.4. A code window should also appear once the module is inserted; if not, **View/Code** can be used to display it.

One can then start typing the macro (called a `Sub`, for subroutine) giving it an appropriate name, for example `MRRunSim` (spaces and words reserved by Excel/VBA are not allowed).

(The same basic procedure applies to user-defined functions, with the word `Function` used in place of `Sub`; functions also require a return statement. Section 12.5.3 provides more information.)

FIGURE 12.4 The Visual Basic Editor (VBE)

12.2.4 Automating Model Recalculation

The VBA statement `Application.Calculate` recalculates the model (`Application` refers to the Excel application). This is analogous to pressing **F9** in Excel, and the required syntax could also be established by recording a macro during which one presses **F9** (i.e. selecting **Developer/Record Macro**, pressing **F9** and then using **Developer/Stop Recording**), and viewing the code that would have been inserted into a new module within the VBE.

At this stage the code would read:

```
Sub MRRunSim()
Application.Calculate
End Sub
```

It is often convenient to resize the VBE and Excel windows so that they are shown side by side, with each taking a half-screen. This will allow more transparent testing of the code by observing the worksheet updating as the code is run or tested.

Generally, rather than running the code all at once (see later), one may first run through it step by step using **F8** repeatedly from within the VBE window (placing the cursor at the beginning of the `Sub`), as shown in Figure 12.5. The code line that is about to execute will be shaded yellow, and on execution those values that are affected by the **RAND()** functions will change.

12.2.5 Creating a Loop to Recalculate Many Times

The next stage in the process would be to put the code within a loop, so that it could be run several times automatically. When initially developing and testing code, one would create a

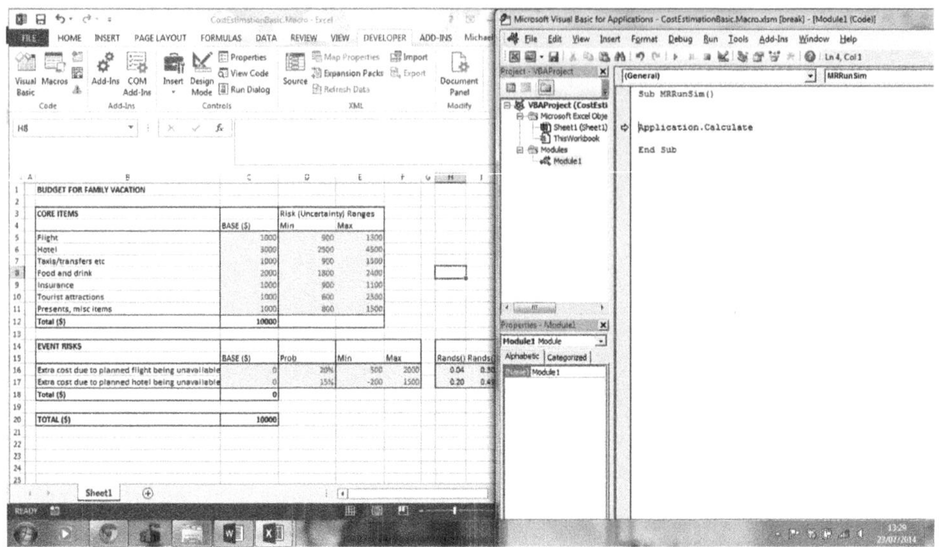

FIGURE 12.5 Split Screen of Uncertainty Model and VBE with Code Window

loop that would run only a few times (such as 10); once the code is working one would, of course, increase this (typically) to several thousand.

The core looping structure is a `For` loop (which is closed with the `Next` statement, so that the code knows to return to the beginning of the loop and increment the indexation number `i` by one):

```
Sub MRRunSim()
For i = 1 to 10
Application.Calculate
Next i
End Sub
```

Once again, one may step through the macro using **F8** (one can escape from the step-through procedure using the `Reset` button [■] in VBE, to avoid having to run all 10 loops if one feels that the code is working).

Of course, at this point, the model is recalculating new values at each pass through the loop, but the results are not yet being stored.

12.2.6 Adding Comments, Indentation and Line Breaks

As the code starts to become longer and a little more complex, one would ideally add comment lines to document what it is trying to achieve. A comment line is one that starts with an apostrophe and (automatically) appears in green text. It will not be executed when the code is run, but rather will be skipped over. For very simple code, comments may be regarded as unnecessary. However, it is usually preferable to create comments as the code is being written (and not afterwards), as it is otherwise easy to overlook the documentation of important items or the limitations of applicability of the code. Therefore, generally, comments should ideally be used even in simple situations, in order to avoid cases arising where code that has been gradually developed without comments becomes extremely complex to audit.

Another use of comment lines is to retain alternative functionality that can be flexibly used (i.e. turned on or off) without have to keep rewriting (and testing) the code: by simply adding or deleting an apostrophe before the relevant code, the line will be treated as a comment or as executable code respectively (this method is also useful when testing code).

Indenting the code lines can improve visual transparency. For example, the code within a `For...Next` loop can be indented. This can be done with the tab key (the tab width of indenting can be reduced from [the default of] four to one or two using VBE's **Tools/Options** menu); this is often preferable when multiple indentation is required (e.g. for loops within loops).

The use of " _" (**SPACE UNDERSCORE** followed by pressing **ENTER**) continues the code on a new line, and will often help to make long lines of code easier to read.

(These techniques are used selectively in the files provided, although when showing code in the text we often delete the comments to aid the focus on the code lines.)

12.2.7 Defining Outputs, Storing Results, Named Ranges and Assignment Statements

Simulation outputs are simply those items that are to be recorded at each recalculation of the simulation so that they can be analysed later. As a minimum, this would include at least one traditional model output (i.e. the results of calculations) but generally may also include the values of some inputs or intermediate quantities, so that other forms of results analysis can be undertaken.

The most robust way to define outputs is to name the Excel cell containing that output. For example, the statement `Range("O20")` would always refer to cell O20, and thus may no longer refer to the desired output cell if a row were added in the Excel worksheet before the existing row 20 (which contains the output in the original model).

Similarly, if the results are to be stored directly into the model worksheet (as in our simple example), then it would also make sense to name not only the output cell(s) but also the beginning (or header) of the cell into which results are to be placed, so that this can act as a reference point for the storage operations, whose position would change by one row or column at each pass through the simulation loop.

Thus, generally, when using VBA, it is preferable to refer to Excel cells (or ranges) as named ranges, rather than cell references (using **Formulas/NameManager**). When doing so, it is often useful, more flexible and robust to ensure that the names have a workbook (not a sheet) scope, although some exceptions exist. This allows for the cell to be referred to in another worksheet (and from the VBA code) using its named range without having to change the code (for example, if part of the model were moved into another worksheet), and without requiring an explicit reference to a particular worksheet.

Of course, where named ranges are used in Excel, it is fundamental that they are spelt in the same way when used within the VBA code. In this respect, it can be helpful to use the **F3** key in Excel to paste a list of the named ranges, and then to copy these into the VBA code when needed.

In our example:

- Cell L20 has been given the name SimOutput, which can be referred to within VBA as `Range("SimOutput").Value`.
- Cell O20 has been given the name NCalcs, so that `NCalcs=Range("NCalcs").Value` can be used to define within Excel the number of recalculations, which is then read into VBA. Although the same name has been used for the Excel named range and the VBA code variable, their underlying definitions are different: one is a range in Excel and the other a VBA variable (one could give them different names if this were considered to be confusing).

There are also many options for where results data could be stored. Generally, it would normally be best to place them in a separate results worksheet, which will be done later in the chapter. For now, we use the simplest approach, which is to place them directly in the model worksheet, for example in some blank area underneath, or to the side of, the calculations. This is done:

- In Excel, by naming the cell L22 as SimResultsHeader.
- In VBA, by using the `offset` property of a range to ensure that the values of the simulation outputs are placed sequentially one row below the previous value when the `For` loop is executing (as the `i` value is incrementing by 1 at each pass through the loop).

The code (excluding comments) at this point reads:

```
Sub MRRunSim()
NCalcs = Range("NCalcs").Value
For i = 1 To NCalcs
 Application.Calculate
 Range("SimResultsHeader").Offset(i, 0).Value = Range("SimOutput").
Value
Next i
End Sub
```

Note that the "=" sign is used to assign the value from the right-hand side to the left-hand side, i.e. it is an assignment operator, not a statement of equality. This can be confusing at first to some people, but in fact is the same as in Excel: one writes "=B2" in cell C2, in order to assign the value of cell B2 to the value in cell C2. Assignment statements will execute significantly more quickly than corresponding **Copy/Paste** operations (which initially may appear to be more intuitive); **Copy/Paste** procedures are not generally recommended, and are not used in this text.

12.2.8 Running the Simulation

One can step through the code (using **F8** within VBE), and the results will start to appear in the model worksheet. Of course, in practice, one would generally wish to run the whole code once the testing phase is complete.

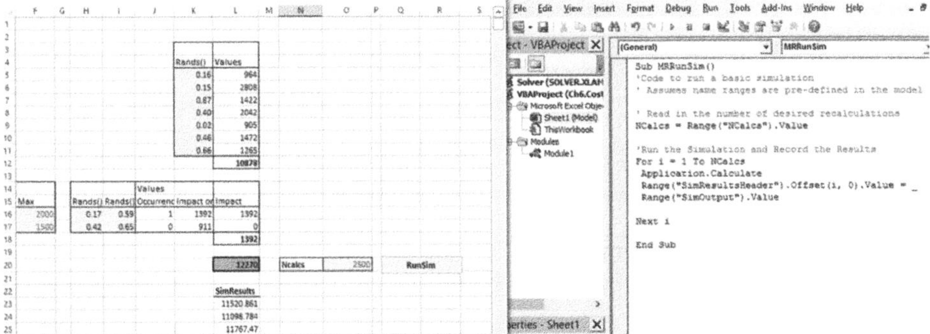

FIGURE 12.6 Basic Simulation Code and First Results

This can be done in several ways, although often the easiest route is to create a button (or other object in Excel) to which one assigns a macro. For example, one may insert a text box (**Insert/Text/Text Box** in Excel) and label it Run Simulation (for example) and then right click on the box to select **Assign Macro** from the drop-down menu; once the macro is assigned, clicking on the text box will run the macro. Alternatively, **Form Controls** can be inserted from the **Developer** tab using **Insert/Form Controls**, and the macro assigned to the inserted control (such as a button).

Other ways to run the code include:

- From within the VBE window, using **F5** (the cursor can be placed anywhere in the subroutine when doing this).
- From Excel, using **Alt+F8**, or **Macros/Run** on the **Developer** tab.

As the code becomes larger, one may wish to run it to a certain point before stepping through line by line; this can be accomplished by using **CTRL+F8** to run the code to the position of the cursor, from which point one can step through using **F8**. Alternatively, one can set a break point by clicking in the margin of the code and using **F5** to run the code up until the break point, and step through using **F8** afterward (one can click in the margin to remove the break point).

Figure 12.6 shows the results of running the simulation.

12.3 BASIC RESULTS ANALYSIS

The file Ch12.CostEstimation.Basic1.Macro.xlsm contains the implementation up to this point in the text.

The file Ch12.CostEstimation.Basic2.Macro.xlsm contains the implementation of the additional features that will be discussed in the remainder of this section.

12.3.1 Building Key Statistical Measures and Graphs of the Results

In the simplest case, one may choose to build key statistical measures directly in the model worksheet. By using the value in the named cell NCalcs, the statistics functions can be given

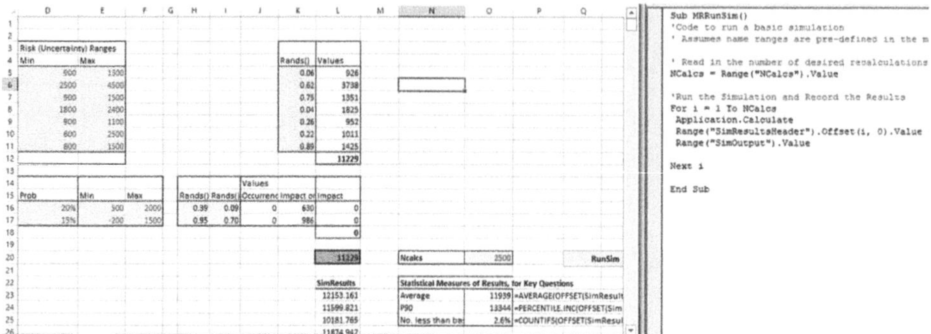

FIGURE 12.7 Basic Simulation Results and Statistics

arguments that are dynamic and refer to the specific range in which the results data are contained (in this way, results of previous simulations do not need to be cleared). For example, one could find the average, the P90 and the frequency of simulated costs being lower than the base case with the formulae:

=**AVERAGE**(**OFFSET**(SimResultsHeader,1,0,Ncalcs,1))
=**PERCENTILE.INC**(**OFFSET**(SimResultsHeader,1,0,Ncalcs,1),9/10)
=**COUNTIFS**(**OFFSET**(SimResultsHeader,1,0,Ncalcs,1),"<="&BaseCaseOutput) /Ncalcs)

(where, to create the last formula, the cell C20 was given the name BaseCaseOutput).

In this model, the average cost is around \$12,000, the P90 is around \$13,300 and the probability of costs being less than the original base figure is around 2%, as shown in Figure 12.7.

One can also build graphs of distribution curves (although the Excel options to do so are generally significantly less flexible than those in @RISK, which are specifically designed for the purpose of displaying probabilistic data). To do so, one would need to define "bins" on the x-axis and count the number of outcomes within each one (using **COUNTIFS** or the **FREQUENCY** array function).

In the example file, we created 12 bins by dividing the x-axis into equally spaced regions between the lowest and highest values resulting during the simulation (calculated using the **MIN** and **MAX** functions). From these data, a line graph or a histogram is produced, as shown in Figure 12.8.

Of course, in practice, one may wish to add more granularity (bins) to the x-axis, which can be done by adapting the bin range and formulae appropriately (this should be straightforward to implement for the interested reader). In addition, other preferred graph options can be applied to the generated data sets.

12.3.2 Clearing Previous Results

When running a new simulation it may be preferable to clear the previous results each time a new simulation is run (especially to cover the case where a new simulation has been run with fewer recalculations than the previous one, so that previous results do not get overwritten).

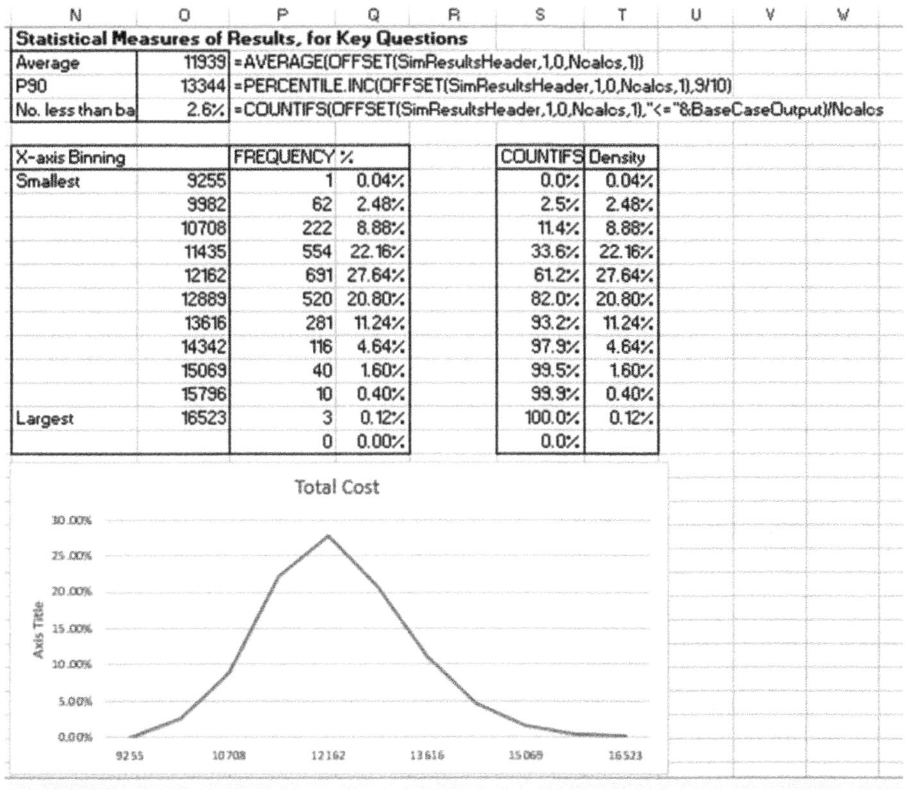

Statistical Measures of Results, for Key Questions		
Average	11939	=AVERAGE(OFFSET(SimResultsHeader,1,0,Ncalcs,1))
P90	13344	=PERCENTILE.INC(OFFSET(SimResultsHeader,1,0,Ncalcs,1),9/10)
No. less than ba	2.6%	=COUNTIFS(OFFSET(SimResultsHeader,1,0,Ncalcs,1),"<="&BaseCaseOutput)/Ncalcs

X-axis Binning		FREQUENCY	%	COUNTIFS	Density
Smallest	9255	1	0.04%	0.0%	0.04%
	9982	62	2.48%	2.5%	2.48%
	10708	222	8.88%	11.4%	8.88%
	11435	554	22.16%	33.6%	22.16%
	12162	691	27.64%	61.2%	27.64%
	12889	520	20.80%	82.0%	20.80%
	13616	281	11.24%	93.2%	11.24%
	14342	116	4.64%	97.9%	4.64%
	15069	40	1.60%	99.5%	1.60%
	15796	10	0.40%	99.9%	0.40%
Largest	16523	3	0.12%	100.0%	0.12%
		0	0.00%	0.0%	

FIGURE 12.8 Basic Simulation Results, Statistics and Graph

One can clear an Excel range (using VBA) by applying the `ClearContents` method. To automatically detect the range to be cleared, it is useful if the results range is not contiguous with any other range in the worksheet (apart from the title field SimResults); the `CurrentRegion` property of a range can be used to find the range consisting of all contiguous cells, which (once the header is excluded) defines the range to be cleared. The code would be:

```
With Range("SimResultsHeader")
NResRows = .CurrentRegion.Rows.Count
If NResRows > 1 Then
Range(.Offset(1, 0), .Offset(NResRows - 1, 0)).ClearContents
Else
'Do Nothing
End If
End With
```

Several points are worthy of note:

- The `With ... End With` construct ensures that one uses the range SimResultsHeader as a reference point for all the operations contained within the construct.

- The number of rows to be cleared depends on the number of data points in the current results range, not on the desired number of calculations (NCalcs) that is planned for the next run.
- The `If ...Then` statement ensures that the header text is not cleared: if there are no results currently stored then the number of rows in the current region of the header will be one (i.e. not greater than one) and so the code will move to the `Else` line (which results in no operations being performed).
- If one were not aware of this syntax for the `CurrentRegion` property of a range, one could record a macro whilst the Excel shortcut for the equivalent procedure was performed (i.e. **CTRL+SHIFT+***).
- As the code becomes more complex, one could think of dividing the current code for the `Sub` into two separate subroutines: one to clear the contents and the other to run the simulation, and then to call each in turn from a master macro (this is done in some examples later in this chapter).

12.3.3 Modularising the Code

As code becomes larger, it is usually preferable to structure it in a modular fashion, in which tasks that are logically distinct are performed in separate subroutines, which are developed and tested separately. A master subroutine is then used to call individual procedures in the appropriate order. When doing so, one can use the **Name** box in the VBE **Properties Window** to name the modules to make it clear where modularised code is to be found, as shown in Figure 12.9. This is done in many of the examples later in the text.

For some procedures contained in separate modules, one may wish to run them independently by creating a separate button in Excel for them. When the procedures are used from another procedure within the VBA code, one can use the `Call` statement to invoke this, as shown in the example file.

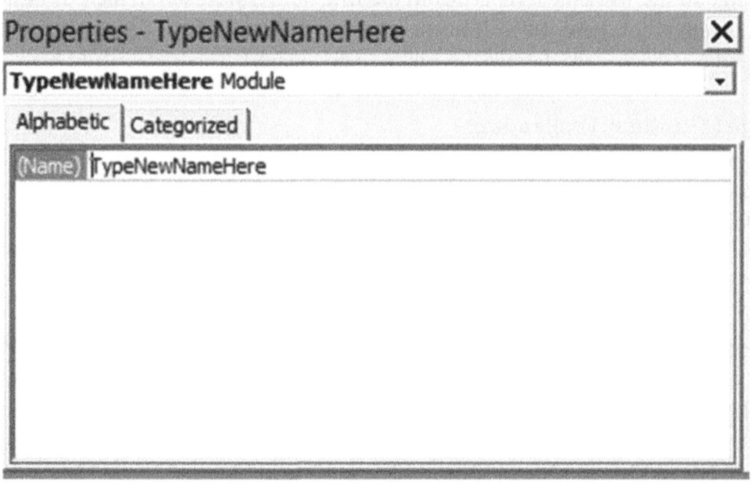

FIGURE 12.9 The VBE Properties Window

12.3.4 Timing and Progress Monitoring

The `Timer` function in VBA can be used in two places of the code in order to record the run time. For example, one could record the time using `StartTime=Timer()` toward the beginning of the code, and towards the end use `EndTime=Timer()`, so that the run time (in seconds) is the difference between these two. One can, of course, also use such techniques to measure the run time of only parts of the code. (These measures are, in fact, not very precise, in the sense that the simulation run time will depend on whether other applications are running in the background on the computer processor at the same time, but nevertheless often provide a useful general indication, especially if one is testing options that may have a major impact on the run time.)

At the completion of the simulation, one can display the total run time to Excel's **StatusBar** by inserting (toward the end of the code):

```
Application.StatusBar = "RunTime " & Round(SimRunTime, 2) &
"Seconds "
```

Similarly, the average number of recalculations per second could be calculated and displayed at the end of a simulation.

It can be useful to provide feedback during the course of a simulation as to the percentage completion, especially when using large numbers of recalculations (or where screen updating is switched off, as discussed below). This can be done by adding within the loop:

```
Application.StatusBar = Round((i / NCalcs) * 100) & "% Complete"
```

12.4 OTHER SIMPLE FEATURES

Other simple features are possible to implement, and are briefly discussed in this section, although they are not implemented in the example files provided.

12.4.1 Taking Inputs from the User at Run Time

An alternative to using an Excel named cell to define the number of recalculations is to ask the user for this when the code is run. For example:

```
NCalcs = Application.InputBox("Please type in the number of recalculations required, as an Integer")
```

would create a variable `NCalcs` within the VBA code. The value of this would need to be placed in the model instead of any legacy value within the Excel range NCalcs, by using:

```
Range(NCalcs).Value = NCalcs
```

The latter feature of taking user input at run time is commented out in the example file, but may be implemented by deleting the apostrophes before the two appropriate code lines.

One may also allow the identification of the output cell to be set at run time (instead of having it as a predefined cell in Excel) by:

```
Set SimOutput = Application.InputBox("Select Output Cell", Type: = 8)
```

The `Set` statement on the left-hand side is required to indicate that we are working with objects (cells) rather than simple values. The `Type:=8` statement on the right-hand side defines that the nature of the input is a cell reference.

The taking of user input at run time may appear flexible, but has the disadvantage that often one wishes to be able to repeatedly run several simulations without changing any aspects of them (e.g. definitions of output cells, or number of recalculations); in such cases, it can be inconvenient to have to provide such input at each simulation run. Therefore, these approaches are not implemented in this text.

12.4.2 Storing Multiple Outputs

One may wish to analyse relationships between the values of variables in the model. For example, one may wish to create a scatter plot of the values and an input and an output, or of two outputs, or to calculate the correlation coefficient between an input and output or between an intermediate quantity and one of these, and so on. Of course, in such cases, one needs to store the data for each relevant variable, and then apply the required statistical or graphical process to these data.

In order to create the maximum flexibility in defining which items are to be stored during the simulation (which we shall refer to as outputs), it is often easiest to have a preset area designated as the output area (with the range given an appropriate name so that it can be referred to from VBA). In this way, the defining of a new output simply involves the creation of a formula reference from the cell in the output area to the cell in the model that contains the relevant calculation. Thus, if one needs to alter which output(s) are recorded, one can do this with a simple change of the cell being referred to, rather than having to rename the calculated cell.

This approach is used later in the chapter, and is combined with the placement of the output definition in a separate worksheet of the workbook.

12.5 GENERALISING THE CORE CAPABILITIES

It is possible to generalise many of the aspects of the above approaches. The features discussed in this section are those that are implemented within the example files shown later, and so are not shown separately in their own files, despite their importance.

12.5.1 Using Selected VBA Best Practices

A number of other simple steps can be taken to enhance the transparency and robustness of the VBA code, especially as it becomes larger and contains more complex procedures or analyses.

- Requiring variable declaration. This can be done by placing the `Option Explicit` statement at the top of the code module, or under **Tools/Options** checking the **Require**

Variable Declaration box. The main advantage of doing so is that one is alerted if a variable is used that has not been declared. In particular, typing errors in more complex code can be picked up (there may be many variables with fairly long but similar names, for example). In addition, it is computationally more efficient, as memory is allocated in advance of the variable being used. Declaration of a variable is done using the `Dim` statement, and key data types are `Integer` (values from $-r^{15}$to $2^{15} - 5$, or to +32,767), `Long` (integers from $-r^{63}$to $2^{63} - 3$) and `Double` (any decimal values from approximately 10^{-0pp} to 10^{308}). `Range` may also be required when a range variable is created. Examples of this are used in the subsequent models in this text.

- Referring to ranges using full referencing, so that it is explicitly clear on which worksheet (and possibly which workbook) the ranges are to be found. This has not been implemented in the simple examples so far, but would be potentially important in more complex cases. In the examples in the text, the workbooks are all self-contained and generally use named ranges of workbook scope, and hence full referencing is generally not required in our particular examples.

12.5.2 Improving Speed

The issue of speed improvement in simulation models is generally complex and multifaceted. There are issues concerning individual process steps, such as the creation of samples of random numbers, the recalculation of the model, the processes to store results and processes to analyse results (such as sorting and binning processes, and statistical calculations), as well as issues of a more structural nature, such as the layout of the workbook.

Some core aspects of ensuring a reasonably efficient approach include:

- Using assignment statements, rather than **Copy/Paste** operations (as covered earlier).
- Declaring variables within the VBA code (as covered earlier).
- Switching off the updating of the Excel screen when the simulation is running, and switching it back on at the end. To do this, one would place the following statements towards the beginning and end of the code (to ensure that, as a minimum, during the execution of the `For` loop, updating is switched off):

```
Application.ScreenUpdating = False
Application.ScreenUpdating = True
```

- One could remove or switch off the use of the `Status Bar` discussed earlier to avoid any unnecessary calculations and communication overhead.
- Separate the process of performing calculations on the results data from the simulation. For example, in the case of the model used so far, the results statistics functions are re-evaluated at each recalculation, whereas this is only needed once the simulation is complete. One could implement various approaches to ensure that such functions are not calculated at each recalculation of the simulation:
  - Clear the formulae at the start of any simulation, and then reinstate them at the end (automatically). This is possible, but the syntax required to write formulae into Excel using VBA code can be complex (for example, within the **COUNTIFS** function, double quotation marks are required to avoid the single quotation mark around the

"<=" from creating an error) and the array function for the frequency would be even more cumbersome.
  - Place the results in a separate worksheet(s), which is referred to only when needed and whose recalculation is switched off during a simulation. This is the method that we shall use in the later examples.
- One may have to conduct a more thorough investigation of the time taken by different process stages and trying to find methods to improve the performance of each.
- In general, a major improvement in speed can be achieved by using VBA arrays to generate random numbers and store results as far as possible. Examples of this are given later in the chapter, but we do not pursue this here (despite its potential significance) in order to keep the focus on the main concepts, and to work first with simpler approaches that are initially easier to implement.

12.5.3 Creating User-Defined Functions

There is an important role for the use of user-defined functions when building simulation models in Excel/VBA. These include:

- To perform bespoke statistical calculations on a data set or on the output, such as calculating the semi-deviation of the output data (as described in Chapter 8).
- To calculate inverse (percentile) functions in order to sample from distributions (see Chapter 10).
- To create correlations between random samples (see Chapter 11).

As mentioned in Chapter 10, some readers may also wish to store their functions as a separate add-in, rather than in each individual workbook.

Examples of user-defined functions have been provided earlier in the text. For the purposes of completion of presentation, and for those using such functions for the first time, we note some core points:

- A function would be placed in a code module of the workbook, just like a subroutine.
- A function's name can be chosen from a wide set of possibilities, but there are some restricted words that are not allowed; largely the same principles apply as for subroutines.
- A function must have a return statement at the appropriate point (usually almost at the end), which defines its result to be shown to Excel.
- Functions can be entered in Excel either by direct typing or under the **Insert/Function** menu, where they are found within the user-defined function category.
- A function may need to be defined as `Volatile` if it is required to be recalculated (at every Excel recalculation) even where its parameters are unchanged (as is the case with the Excel **RAND**() function, for example). Where necessary, this can be done by using the `Application.Volatile` statement at the beginning of a function; see elsewhere for examples.
- Array functions can be created, and are entered as for other Excel array functions, i.e. by using **CTRL+SHIFT+ENTER**. The VBA code also generally needs to have an array to store these values; such arrays need to be declared (using the `Dim` statement), and are usually required to be resized at run time (using `ReDim`). An example that illustrates these points is the function to perform the Cholesky decomposition (Chapter 11).

12.6 OPTIMISING MODEL STRUCTURE AND LAYOUT

Although there are many advantages to having most aspects of models in a single worksheet, there can be advantages to having multiple worksheets in some cases. In the context of a simulation model, it may be useful and most flexible to have specific functionality on separate worksheets:

- A "model" worksheet may contain (often ideally in a single worksheet) the main calculations (including inputs in many cases).
- A "simulation control" worksheet may contain a cell that defines the number of recalculations to run and a button to run the code, govern other user options, such as whether previous results are to be cleared or saved when a new simulation is run, and to aid navigation around the workbook, for example. (If such navigation tools are included, then it can be convenient for this worksheet to be automatically activated at the end of the simulation.)
- An "output links" worksheet that is used to link to the calculations in the model that are desired to be stored in a particular simulation run.
- A "results" worksheet that stores simulation results and may be either cleared out or overwritten as a new simulation is run, or new results may be inserted automatically at each run (with or without deletion of the older results).
- An "analysis" worksheet that links into the results sheets (as described later; this is done in such a way that the model becomes robust and flexible as results worksheets are deleted and added, by using indirect links rather than direct ones).

The file Ch12.CostEstimation.Basic3.Macro.xlsm uses this structure, and is described in more detail below.

12.6.1 Simulation Control Sheet

This contains the data on the number of recalculations that are desired to be run (the named range NCalcs was created having a global scope). It also contains buttons to run a simulation (which would automatically mean that a new results sheet is inserted), as well as a button to delete all existing results sheets. Note that we have given each worksheet a name using the Properties box within the VBE window, and these are the names that are used in the code.

There are also some buttons to aid navigation around the workbook, such as going to the model or analysis worksheets, for example:

```
Sub MRGoToModel()
With ThisWorkbook
 ModelSheet.Activate
End With
End Sub
```

Within the code modules, there is also a procedure to return one to this simulation control sheet; this is run automatically at the end of the simulation.

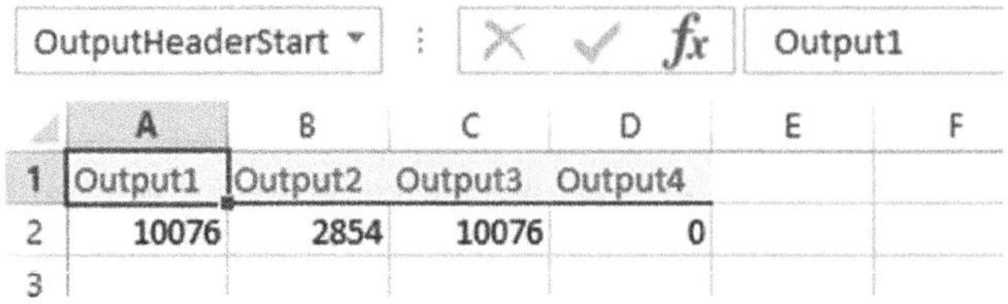

OutputHeaderStart | fx | Output1

	A	B	C	D	E	F
1	Output1	Output2	Output3	Output4		
2	10076	2854	10076	0		
3						

FIGURE 12.10 Use of Separate Worksheet to Reference Output Cells

```
Sub MRGoToSimControl()
With ThisWorkbook
 SimControlSheet.Activate
End With
End Sub
```

12.6.2 Output Links Sheet

The use of a separate worksheet to link to the items calculated in the model creates a high degree of flexibility to change the outputs that are being stored during a simulation run. For example, one may wish to add new outputs, or decide that some previously captured outputs are no longer necessary.

In the example file, cell A1 of the corresponding worksheet has been given the Excel named range OutputHeaderStart. The user should type the name of the outputs along the first row (in a contiguous range), and place the cell links to the model in the second row, as shown in Figure 12.10.

Although only the first cell of the header range is defined, as the number of outputs may change, one can refer to the full header range (in this case A1:D1) using:

```
Set outrngHeader = Range("OutputHeaderStart").CurrentRegion.Rows(1)
```

The right-hand side returns the first row of the current region of cell A1 (i.e. cells A1:D1 in this case) and assigns this to the variable `outrngHeader`. Therefore, if more outputs are added, this range will adjust automatically.

The `Set` statement is required as the variables concerned are both objects (i.e. ranges in this case) rather than values.

12.6.3 Results Sheets

In general, it would be most flexible and robust for the simulation results to be placed in a new worksheet, rather than in the model worksheet. Although one could work with a single predefined results worksheet, it is usually more convenient to have several possible ones, which are automatically inserted each time a simulation is run. Of course, after several simulation runs, one may wish to manually delete those that are not needed any more. However, in general, it can be convenient to have a mechanism to automatically delete them all on request.

The automatic insertion of results worksheets at each simulation run is easy to perform; the deletion of worksheets is also straightforward, providing one has a mechanism to distinguish those that are desired not to be deleted from those that are.

In the following code example, we automatically name the results worksheets as Results1, Results2, Results3, and so on. At the start of a simulation, the code counts the number of such worksheets in the workbook, and then adds a new one to the workbook, including the appropriate number in its name, i.e. if the workbook already contains Results1 and Results2, then the added worksheet will be Results3. (This part of the code would need to execute before the running of the simulation loop, so it can be placed either directly in the code or (as below) used as a separate subroutine that is called at that point.)

Note that the function loops through all worksheets (worksheet objects) in the workbook using the `For Each ... Next` construct. The VBA `Left` function finds the first seven characters of the name, and these are converted to uppercase using the `UCase` function. If the resulting text equals "RESULTS" then the variable `iCount` is incremented by one, otherwise one moves to the next sheet.

```
Function MRCountResSheets()
Dim wksSheet As Worksheet
Dim iCount As Integer
iCount = 0
With ThisWorkbook
 For Each wksht In Worksheets
  If UCase(Left(wksht.Name, 7)) = "RESULTS" Then
  iCount = iCount + 1
  Else
  'Do nothing
  End If
 Next wksht
End With
MRCountResSheets = iCount
End Function
```

The code to add the sheet is then:

```
With ThisWorkbook
 isheetCount = MRCountResSheets   ' count number of results
sheets in model
 isheetNo = isheetCount + 1 'number of sheet to be inserted
 .Worksheets.Add.Name = "Results" & isheetNo ' insert sheet
End With
```

The code to run the simulation must, of course, write the data from row 2 of the output links worksheet into the newly created results worksheet (at each recalculation). The results data are written into the sequential rows of the results sheet (starting at row 2), and finally the output header names are placed in row 1 of the results sheet:

```
'Define output ranges and where results are to be written to
Set outrngHeader = Range("OutputHeaderStart").CurrentRegion.Rows(1)
icolcount = outrngHeader.Columns.Count
```

```
Set outrng = outrngHeader.Offset(1, 0) 'range of actual output
values
Set resrng1 = Worksheets("Results" & isheetNo).Range("A1")
With resrng1
 Set resrng2 = Range(.Offset(0, 0), .Offset(0, icolcount - 1))
End With
'Run the Simulation and Record the Results to the new sheet
NCalcs = Range("NCalcs")
For i = 1 To NCalcs
 Application.Calculate
 resrng2.Offset(i, 0).Value = outrng.Value
Next i
'Place headers
resrng2.Value = outrngHeader.Value
```

One will generally wish to have code that deletes all the results worksheets at the click of a button. In a similar way to earlier, the following code uses a `For Each ... Next` construct to loop through all worksheets in a workbook and delete those that start with the word "RESULTS" when converted to uppercase.

Note also that the use of `Application.DisplayAlerts=False` in the early part of the code ensures that code execution is not halted; Excel's default would be to ask (and wait) for user input before deleting a worksheet; the code switches back the defaults after it is run, using the `Application.DisplayAlerts=True` statement:

```
Sub MRDeleteResultsSheets()
Dim ResSheet As Worksheet
Application.DisplayAlerts = False
For Each ResSheet In ActiveWorkbook.Worksheets
 If UCase(Left(ResSheet.Name, 7)) = "RESULTS" Then
  ResSheet.Delete
 Else
 ' Do nothing
 End If
Next ResSheet
Application.DisplayAlerts = True
End Sub
```

12.6.4 Use of Analysis Sheets

There are several advantages to the structuring of the analysis of results in a separate worksheet(s) to those containing the results data:

- It allows (as above) the deletion of results worksheets without deleting any of the formula required for the analysis.
- A single analysis worksheet with standardised analysis can be created, with the formulae built so that the results data referred to can be chosen by the user in a flexible manner, and without having to rebuild formula links. This is done by using an **INDIRECT** function

	A	B	C	D	E
1					
2		Result Sheet To Analyse (type name of sheet)	Results1		
3					
4		Output Variable: For individual analysis	Output1		
5		Average	11950		
6		Standard Deviation	1075		
7	10%	P10	10611		
8	50%	P50	13407		
9	90%	P90	13407		
10		Prob(<=base)	2.6%		
11					
12		Correlation of Output Variables	Output1	Output2	55.2%

FIGURE 12.11 Use of Analysis Sheet that Links Indirectly to Results Sheets

(rather than [say] a **CHOOSE** function), so that there are no direct formulae links to the results worksheets (which can be inserted or deleted independently of the analysis worksheet).

- To speed up the simulation, one can switch off the calculation of the analysis worksheet so that the analysis is only done after the simulation is complete (when the analysis worksheet's calculation is switched back on), rather than being performed at each recalculation of the simulation. (Note that this will only be fully effective if other workbooks are closed when the simulation is run, or their recalculation is also switched off.) To switch the recalculation in the specific analysis worksheet on and off, one would include code such as the following (at the beginning and at the end of the simulation, respectively):

```
Sub MRSwitchOffCalcAnalysis()
With AnalysisSheet
.EnableCalculation = False
End With
End Sub

Sub MRSwitchOnCalcAnalysis()
With AnalysisSheet
.EnableCalculation = True
End With
End Sub
```

Figure 12.11 shows the Analysis worksheet in the example file, after a simulation has been run, with some core output statistics built in. The linkages to the particular results worksheet that one wishes to consider are established by typing the name of the desired results worksheet in cell C2. The statistics immediately underneath are established using the regular Excel functions (as well as the semi-deviation function mentioned earlier), with the range that the function refers to be adapted automatically using the indirect reference provided by the name of the results worksheet. For example, the range used within each function:

OFFSET(**INDIRECT**($C$2&"!A1"), 1, **MATCH**($C$4, **INDIRECT**($C$2&"!"&"1 : 1"), 0)
−1, Ncalcs, 1)

This complex-looking formula simply states that the range is the one that is defined by referring to cell A1 of the worksheet specified in cell C2, and from that point, creating a range that starts one row below it (i.e. in row 2), but where the column position to start the range determined (using the **MATCH** function) as the column whose title (in row 1 of the results worksheet being referred to) matches the name of the output that one has entered in cell C4 of the analysis worksheet. From this starting point, a range of height NCalcs is created, and acts as the inputs to the functions.

(These formulae assume that each set of results has the same number of data points, equal to NCalcs; one could generalise the above, but the simulation code would also need to be adapted to record the value of NCalcs for each simulation within its own results worksheet.)

There are many further generalisations possible from this point:

- One could also generate a **DataTable** of results for a particular statistic. For example:
  - One could create a one-way table that shows the average for all the outputs in a particular worksheet (this is done in a later example).
  - One could create a one-way table that shows the correlation of each of many outputs with one single, particular output. If this latter output is a genuine model output (i.e. a calculated figure), whereas the others refer to the values of model input cells, then such figures can be used to produce basic correlation tables, as used in risk-tornado diagrams, for example.
- One could also generate graphs. However, chart data ranges in Excel do not permit the indirect form of reference used above (at the time of writing); therefore, chart data would generally have to refer directly to the results data. Alternatively, one could write a separate macro to retrieve the specific results data required and place this into a predefined column to which preset chart(s) may be linked.

Figure 12.12 shows a screen clip of the Analysis worksheet, showing two **DataTables**; the one shown in rows 14 to 18 is the correlation matrix between all outputs (calculated for the data from the Results1 worksheet defined in cell C2), and the one shown in rows 20 to 24 is the average value of several outputs for different simulation runs or results data sets.

12.6.5 Multiple Simulations

It can often be necessary to run a simulation if formulae in the model change, corrections are made, other outputs wish to be captured or if parameter values have been changed. In many such cases, there is no particular reason to need to compare the updated simulation results with those of prior simulations. However, in other circumstances, one may wish to be able to store and compare the results of one simulation run with those of another. For example, one may wish to see the effect of mitigation measures or of other decisions on a project, such as to judge whether to implement a risk-mitigation measure (at some cost) by comparing the results

14		55.2%	Output1	Output2	Output3	Output4
15	Output1		100.0%	55.2%	81.2%	52.3%
16	Output2		55.2%	100.0%	67.5%	2.5%
17	Output3		81.2%	67.5%	100.0%	2.2%
18	Output4		52.3%	2.5%	2.2%	100.0%
19						
20		11950	Output1	Output2	Output3	Output4
21	Results1		11950	3509	11596	250
22	Results2		11888	3462	11570	213
23	Results3					
24	Results4					

FIGURE 12.12 Additional Example of Output Analysis: Cross-Correlations of Outputs for a Selected Results Data Set, and Average Values for Each Output for Several Data Sets

pre- and post-mitigation. More generally, the effect of other decisions may be captured in a model (such as the "decision risk" associated with whether internal management authorise a particular suggested technical solution, as discussed in Chapters 2 and 7), and one may wish to see the distribution of results depending on which decision is taken.

In principle, when using the above approach (in which a separate results worksheet is inserted automatically for each simulation), the running of multiple simulations poses no particular problem: one can simply change the model as required, rerun the simulation and compare the results, which will be recorded in separate worksheets.

One could also automate the process of changing the data in the model by embedding the basic simulation run within a second (outside) loop within the VBA code, so that a simulation is run at each pass through this outer loop. The index number of this loop (1 for the first simulation, 2 for the second, and so on) would then be assigned to the value of an Excel cell, and this cell would cause an Excel lookup function to return the required parameter values for that particular simulation run. For example, the outer simulation loop would be of the form `For j = 1 to 5...Next j` (where five simulations are to be run), and one would then name a cell in the Excel model (say) jIndex, so that, with the outer loop of the code, one includes a line such as:

```
Range("jIndex")=j
```

so that the value of jIndex is changing for each simulation, and this value is used to determine the value of the model parameters for that simulation run (by using it as the argument of an Excel lookup function).

The file Ch12.CostEstimation.Basic4.Macro.xlsm contains an implementation of multiple simulations. The main adaptations to the previous example file are:

- Inclusion in the model worksheet of the data required for each simulation. In this case, we have assumed that we are testing the effect of the maximum values of all base items being different, using three possible values for each (of which the first is the original base case).
- Inclusion of a cell named jIndex in the model sheet, and the use of this cell to drive the **CHOOSE** function, which is then linked to the original values for the maximum of each variable.

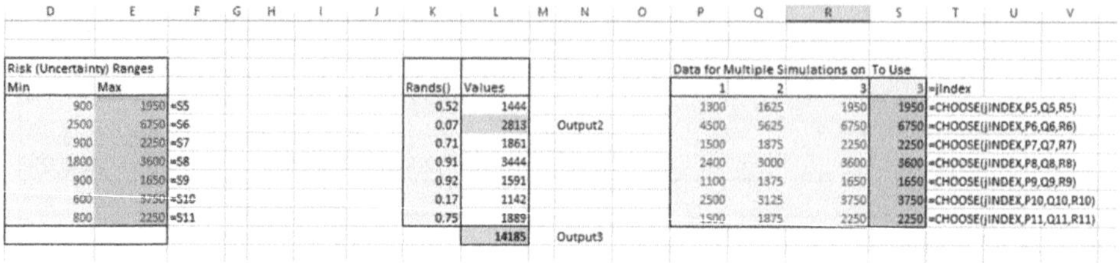

Risk (Uncertainty) Ranges		
Min	Max	
900	1950	=S5
2500	6750	=S6
900	2250	=S7
1800	3600	=S8
900	1650	=S9
600	3750	=S10
800	2250	=S11

Rands()	Values	
0.52	1444	
0.07	2813	Output2
0.71	1861	
0.91	3444	
0.92	1591	
0.17	1142	
0.75	1889	
	14185	Output3

Data for Multiple Simulations on			To Use	
1	2	3	3	=jIndex
1300	1625	1950	1950	=CHOOSE(jINDEX,P5,Q5,R5)
4500	5625	6750	6750	=CHOOSE(jINDEX,P6,Q6,R6)
1500	1875	2250	2250	=CHOOSE(jINDEX,P7,Q7,R7)
2400	3000	3600	3600	=CHOOSE(jINDEX,P8,Q8,R8)
1100	1375	1650	1650	=CHOOSE(jINDEX,P9,Q9,R9)
2500	3125	3750	3750	=CHOOSE(jINDEX,P10,Q10,R10)
1500	1875	2250	2250	=CHOOSE(jINDEX,P11,Q11,R11)

FIGURE 12.13 Adapted Model to Run Multiple Simulations in an Automated Sequence

- Inclusion of a cell named NSims in the simulation control worksheet.
- Addition of an outer loop to the VBA code.

Figure 12.13 shows the changes in the model worksheet, and the code shown below highlights the key changes to the VBA part.

```
Sub MRRunSim()
...
'Switch off calculation in analysis sheet
Call MRSwitchOffCalcAnalysis
NSims = Range("NSims")
For j = 1 To NSims
Range("jIndex") = j
  'Add a new results sheet
   AS PREVIOUS INCLUDING RUNNING SIMULATION AND WRITING RESULTS
TO RESULTS SHEET
Next j
'Switch on calculation in analysis sheet
Call MRSwitchOnCalcAnalysis
End Sub
```

In each of the above cases, one issue that may be of relevance (depending on the number of recalculations run and the accuracy requirements) is that one will not have control over the random numbers produced by the **RAND**() function; thus, some of the differences in the results of the various simulations will be driven by the different random numbers used in each, rather than by changes that occurred within the model. Overcoming this requires controlling the generation of random numbers, and is covered later in the chapter.

12.7 BRINGING IT ALL TOGETHER: EXAMPLES USING THE SIMULATION TEMPLATE

The mechanical techniques used so far in this chapter would, of course, in practice be combined with other tools discussed in this text, including the appropriate model design (Chapter 7), the use of distributions (Chapter 9), the creation of their samples (Chapter 10) and of correlations or dependencies between them (Chapter 11). This section presents some simple examples to show how this may be done in practice.

The file Ch12.TemplateExamplesMacro.xlsm contains various models that, for ease of presentation, are all contained in the single Models worksheet.

The template file has the following features:

- Its core structure and simulation component are based on the capability shown earlier in the chapter (except that we have not included the multiple simulation functionality).
- There are a number of distributions built in as user-defined functions:
  - Bernoulli.
  - Beta, beta general, PERT.
  - Normal and lognormal (with both the natural and logarithmic parameters).
  - Weibull, with both standard and percentile (alternative) parameter forms.
- The code to perform the Cholesky decomposition is included, as is the user-defined function mentioned in Chapter 11 (`MRMult`), which performs the required matrix multiplication for both row and column vectors.

The five models that are included within the single Models worksheet (and whose outputs are captured in the OutputLinks worksheet) are each described below. Most of these issues should be self-explanatory for readers who have read the remainder of this text, so the descriptions are brief.

12.7.1 Model 1: Aggregation of a Risk Register using Bernoulli and PERT Distributions

Model 1 contains a typical risk register in which a risk occurrence is associated with an impact that is drawn from a PERT distribution, as shown in Figure 12.14.

MODEL 1: Risk Register using Bernoulli and PERT Distributions

Risk Item	Prob	Rands	Occur	Min	ML	Max	Rands	PERT	Impact
Risk 1	35%	0.46	0	8	10	15	0.64	10.9	0.00
Risk 2	35%	0.77	0	8	10	15	0.06	8.7	0.00
Risk 3	35%	0.23	1	8	10	15	0.99	13.6	13.59
Risk 4	35%	0.22	1	8	10	15	0.62	10.8	10.81
Risk 5	35%	0.31	1	8	10	15	0.94	12.7	12.70
Risk 6	35%	0.89	0	8	10	15	0.06	8.7	0.00
Risk 7	35%	0.19	1	8	10	15	0.38	10.0	9.98
Risk 8	35%	0.84	0	8	10	15	0.68	11.1	0.00
Risk 9	35%	0.25	1	8	10	15	0.41	10.1	10.07
Risk 10	35%	0.99	0	8	10	15	0.76	11.4	0.00
Total									57.1

FIGURE 12.14 Using the Simulation Template Model: Example 1

	A	B	C	D	E	F	G
17		MODEL 2: Cost Budget using Lognormal					
18							
19			Mean	StdDev	Rands	Lognormal	
20		Cost 1	100	25	0.50	97	
21		Cost 2	100	25	0.93	139	
22		Cost 3	100	25	0.34	88	
23		Cost 4	100	25	0.59	103	
24		Cost 5	100	25	0.87	128	
25		Cost 6	100	25	0.18	77	
26		Cost 7	100	25	0.26	83	
27		Cost 8	100	25	0.34	87	
28		Cost 9	100	25	0.54	99	
29		Cost 10	100	25	0.79	118	
30		Total				1019.9	

FIGURE 12.15 Using the Simulation Template Model: Example 2

12.7.2 Model 2: Cost Estimation using Lognormal Distributions

Model 2 contains a cost estimation, in which the items are assumed to follow lognormal distributions, and is shown in Figure 12.15.

12.7.3 Model 3: Cost Estimation using Weibull Percentile Parameters

Model 3 contains a cost estimation, in which the items are assumed to follow Weibull distributions, parameterised with their P10 and P90 values (as discussed in Chapter 9), and is shown in Figure 12.16.

	A	B	C	D	E	F	G	H	I
32		MODEL 3: Cost Budget using alternate parameter form of Weibull							
33									
34			XL	XH	PL	PH	Rands	WeibullAlt	
35		Cost 1	80	150	10%	90%	0.94	157	
36		Cost 2	80	150	10%	90%	0.68	130	
37		Cost 3	80	150	10%	90%	0.75	135	
38		Cost 4	80	150	10%	90%	0.43	112	
39		Cost 5	80	150	10%	90%	0.70	131	
40		Cost 6	80	150	10%	90%	0.36	108	
41		Cost 7	80	150	10%	90%	0.30	103	
42		Cost 8	80	150	10%	90%	0.31	104	
43		Cost 9	80	150	10%	90%	0.74	134	
44		Cost 10	80	150	10%	90%	0.09	78	
45		Total						1192.2	

FIGURE 12.16 Using the Simulation Template Model: Example 3

MODEL 4: Correlated Items													
CORRELATION	Cost 1	Cost 2	Cost 3	Cost 4	Cost 5		CHOLESKY	Cost 1	Cost 2	Cost 3	Cost 4	Cost 5
Cost 1	100%	50%	50%	50%	50%		Cost 1	100%	0%	0%	0%	0%
Cost 2	50%	100%	50%	50%	50%		Cost 2	50%	87%	0%	0%	0%
Cost 3	50%	50%	100%	50%	50%		Cost 3	50%	29%	82%	0%	0%
Cost 4	50%	50%	50%	100%	50%		Cost 4	50%	29%	20%	79%	0%
Cost 5	50%	50%	50%	50%	100%		Cost 5	50%	29%	20%	16%	77%

	XL	XH	PL	PH	Rands	Correl Rands	WeibullAlt
Cost 1	80	150	10%	90%	0.26	26%	99
Cost 2	80	150	10%	90%	0.58	63%	99
Cost 3	80	150	10%	90%	0.84	98%	99
Cost 4	80	150	10%	90%	0.58	92%	99
Cost 5	80	150	10%	90%	0.52	96%	99
Total							494.1

FIGURE 12.17 Using the Simulation Template Model: Example 4

12.7.4 Model 4: Cost Estimation using Correlated Distributions

Model 4 contains a cost estimation, in which the items are assumed to follow Weibull distributions parameterised with their P10 and P90 values (as in Model 3), in which these distributions are correlated using a correlation matrix that has been defined. The Cholesky matrix is produced using a user-defined function and multiplied by the array of random numbers (also the user-defined array function MRMULT that was discussed in Chapter 11) to create the final random samples, and is shown in Figure 12.17.

12.7.5 Model 5: Valuing Operational Flexibility

Model 5 is similar to the model discussed in Chapter 4 to value operational flexibility (not in the presence of correlations). The price movement of each energy source is normally distributed. After the simulation is run, the relevant output results (in this case the average expenditure associated with each possibility using the values shown for Output5, Output6, Output7 and Output8 from the **DataTable** in the Analysis worksheet) are pasted into the appropriate area of the model (cells D68:D71) in order to calculate the value of the switching option. The model and option value (cell R71) are shown in Figure 12.18.

Model 5: Valuing a Switching option																
				0	1	2	3	4	5	6	7	8	9	10		OptValue $/unit
Values, $/unit	Total $/unit	PASTED VALUES Sim Average $/unit														
Oil	1,626	1,242		100	117	173	254	131	147	180	173	199	134	116	=O68*(1+P77)	
Gas	1,233	1,318		90	85	97	105	106	111	152	144	127	142	166	=O69*(1+P78)	
Electricity	1,292	1,463		110	128	87	110	108	106	131	147	145	154	175	=O70*(1+P79)	
Expenditure with a sw	1,140	846		90	85	87	105	106	106	131	144	127	134	116	=MIN(P68:P70)	395
RANDS																
Oil					0.71	0.96	0.96	0.02	0.63	0.77	0.38	0.67	0.07	0.24		
Gas					0.26	0.64	0.54	0.37	0.46	0.93	0.27	0.17	0.59	0.70		
Electricity					0.78	0.01	0.93	0.32	0.32	0.90	0.69	0.32	0.53	0.72		
% Changes			Mean	StdDev												
Oil			4.0%	25%	17%	47%	47%	-48%	12%	23%	-4%	15%	-33%	-13%	=MRNormalP($E77,$F77,P73)	
Gas			7.0%	20%	-6%	14%	9%	0%	5%	37%	-5%	-12%	12%	18%	=MRNormalP($E78,$F78,P74)	
Electricity			5.0%	15%	17%	-32%	27%	-2%	-2%	24%	12%	-2%	6%	14%	=MRNormalP($E79,$F79,P75)	

FIGURE 12.18 Using the Simulation Template Model: Example 5

12.8 FURTHER POSSIBLE USES OF VBA

The text so far within this chapter has focused on aspects of the use of Excel/VBA that are the easiest to implement within a simulation modelling context. Indeed – arguably with the exception of the Cholesky factorisation and the creation of correlated samples – all aspects covered so far have been relatively straightforward.

This section introduces some areas where one could develop the use of VBA further. Most of the topics relate to the use of the generation of random numbers within VBA, rather than directly in Excel. Once again, we aim to highlight those features of simulation modelling that can be fairly readily implemented in Excel/VBA without undue complexity, and without the requirement to have genuine application-programming skills.

12.8.1 Creating Percentile Parameters

In some cases it can be relatively straightforward to derive the parameters of a distribution given information about its percentiles; the Weibull distribution provides an example (as discussed in Chapter 9). However, in many cases, this is not easy or possible to do analytically (this applies both to distributions whose cumulative function has no closed-form solution, and to those where it has, but this function does not easily allow the derivation of the parameters in terms of percentiles, due to the specific nature of the formulae). In principle, one could always find the required parameters of a distribution from its percentiles by using iterative techniques. In particular, techniques such as Newton–Raphson iterations or Halley's method (see Chapter 11) could be implemented within many functions. These are usually highly effective as quantitative methods, as their precise implementation depends on the specific functions (so that few iterations are required to find the appropriate parameter values). On the other hand, such methods require a separate implementation within each function, which would be time-consuming to do for a wide set of functions.

12.8.2 Distribution Samples as User-Defined Functions

In the text so far, we generated random samples (for a probability value) in Excel using **RAND**(), and then used formulae for the inverse cumulative distribution to generate samples. One could consider an alternative in which the equivalent probability values are generated directly in VBA using the equivalent `Rnd` function. In such a case, the probability value would, of course, no longer be an input parameter to the function, for example code such as (where `Prob` is linked to the Excel cell containing the **RAND**() function):

```
Function MRWEIBULLP(alpha, beta, Prob)
MRWEIBULLP = beta * ((Log(1 / (1 - Prob))) ^ (1 / alpha))
End Function
```

would instead read:

```
Function MRWEIBULL(alpha, beta)
Application.Volatile
Prob=Rnd
MRWEIBULL = beta * ((Log(1 / (1 - Prob))) ^ (1 / alpha))
End Function
```

This approach would create a function that – when placed in an Excel cell – directly provided distribution samples (analogous to @RISK's distribution functions). However, it would not be a convenient approach if one desired to create a set of correlated random numbers (note that the correlation procedure we have implemented is one in which the probabilities are correlated, and so, by implication, the rank correlation of the samples has the same correlation coefficient, whereas in general the application of a Cholesky matrix after samples from the distributions have been created would not be a valid approach).

12.8.3 Probability Samples as User-Defined Array Functions

One possibility to be able to rapidly enter random numbers (to represent probability samples) in a multi-cell range is to use an array function.

The file Ch12.RandsinArray.VBA.xlsm contains the user-defined array function `MRRandArray1()`. The function has no arguments and can be used to simply select any (contiguous) range of cells in Excel and enter the function as an array function (i.e. using **CTRL+SHIFT+ENTER**). The function counts the number of rows and columns in the selected range and places a random number in each cell. Figure 12.19 shows an example of this being done in three cases: a column range, a row range and a range with multiple rows and columns:

```
Function MRRandArray1()
Application.Volatile
Dim Storage() As Double
NCols = Application.Caller.Columns.Count
NRows = Application.Caller.Rows.Count
ReDim Storage(1 To NRows, 1 To NCols)
For i = 1 To NRows
```

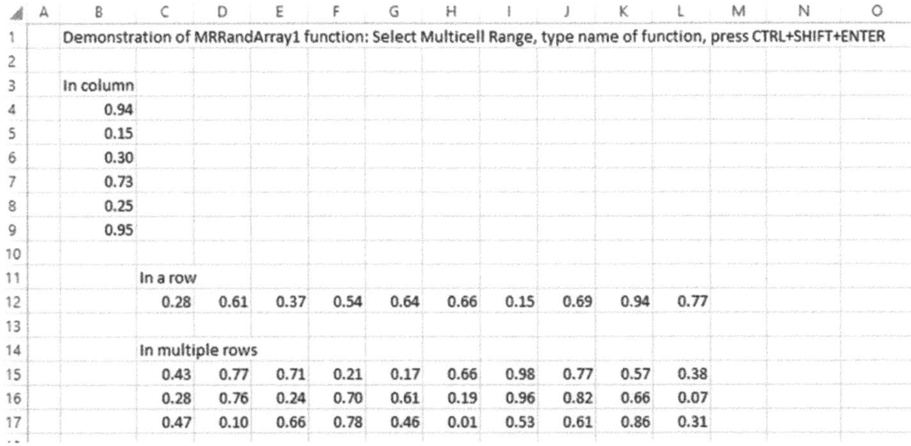

	A	B	C	D	E	F	G	H	I	J	K	L	M	N	O
1		Demonstration of MRRandArray1 function: Select Multicell Range, type name of function, press CTRL+SHIFT+ENTER													
2															
3		In column													
4		0.94													
5		0.15													
6		0.30													
7		0.73													
8		0.25													
9		0.95													
10															
11			In a row												
12			0.28	0.61	0.37	0.54	0.64	0.66	0.15	0.69	0.94	0.77			
13															
14			In multiple rows												
15			0.43	0.77	0.71	0.21	0.17	0.66	0.98	0.77	0.57	0.38			
16			0.28	0.76	0.24	0.70	0.61	0.19	0.96	0.82	0.66	0.07			
17			0.47	0.10	0.66	0.78	0.46	0.01	0.53	0.61	0.86	0.31			

FIGURE 12.19 Creating a User-defined Array Function to Generate Random Numbers in Rows or Columns

```
 For j = 1 To NCols
 Storage(i, j) = Rnd()
 Next j
Next i
MRRandArray1 = Storage
End Function
```

12.8.4 Correlated Probability Samples as User-Defined Array Functions

So far in this text, the Cholesky matrix that is required to create correlated probability samples has been placed explicitly in Excel, and the necessary matrix multiplication has also been performed in Excel. Since both steps can be written as user-defined functions, they could be combined (in various ways), in particular so that:

- The correlation matrix would be shown in Excel (but not the Cholesky matrix).
- The raw random number generation, the Cholesky factorisation and their final matrix multiplication would be conducted within the VBA code.
- A user-defined array function would be used in Excel to produce a set of correlated random numbers in either a single row or a single column range, based on the steps above.
- The function would use the correlation matrix as an optional argument: if no matrix was present, a set of random numbers could be placed in a range of any size (as in the above example), whereas if a correlation matrix was present, then the number of elements in the range would need to be the same as the number of variables (either rows or columns) in the correlation matrix.

The file Ch12.RandsinArray.DirectCorrel.xlsm contains the user-defined array function `MRRandArray2()`. The function has no required arguments; the correlation matrix is optional, a described above. Figure 12.20 shows a screen clip of the various possibilities, including its

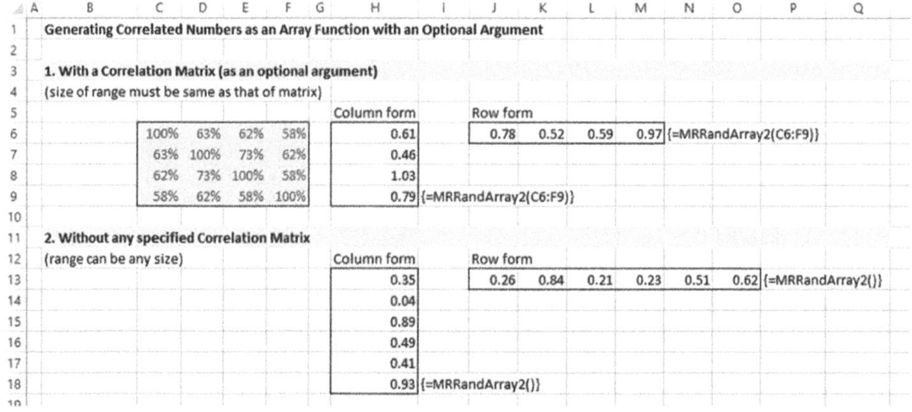

FIGURE 12.20 Creating a User-defined Array Function to Generate Correlated or Uncorrelated Samples in Rows or Columns

use in row and column form (of the appropriate size) when a correlation matrix is present, and in row and column form (of any size) when no correlation matrix is present.

The code is shown below. The main function makes a separate call to a function `MRRands`, which produces a set of uncorrelated numbers, and is deemed `Private` so that it can only be accessed from this code module (and not from the Excel workbook, for example); this is done for reasons of robustness of use.

Note that, in practice, one may want to build in some error-checking procedures (for example, in terms of the size of the ranges, or whether the Cholesky procedure can be performed without producing an error, and so on). This is not done here in order to retain the focus on the core computational and algorithmic aspects.

```
Function MRRandArray2(Optional ByVal RCorrel As Range = Nothing)
Dim Storage1() As Double
Dim Storage2() As Double
Set wsf = Application.WorksheetFunction
With Application.Caller ' find size of input range
 NRangeTypeCols = .Columns.Count
 NRangeTypeRows = .Rows.Count
End With
If RCorrel Is Nothing Then
' no correlation matrix given; Generate random numbers only
  If NRangeTypeCols = 1 Then
   ReDim Storage1(1 To NRangeTypeRows)
   Storage1 = MRRands(NRangeTypeRows)
   MRRandArray2 = wsf.Transpose(Storage1)
  Else 'NRangeTypeRows = 1
   ReDim Storage1(1 To NRangeTypeCols)
   Storage1 = MRRands(NRangeTypeCols)
   MRRandArray2 = Storage1
 End If
 Exit Function
Else ' Do Cholesky factorisation and generate random numbers
  NCols = RCorrel.Columns.Count
   ReDim Storage1(1 To NCols)
   ReDim Storage2(1 To NCols, 1 To NCols)
   Storage1 = MRRands(NCols)
   Storage2 = MRCholesky(RCorrel)

   If NRangeTypeCols = 1 Then
     MRRandArray2 = wsf.MMult(Storage2, wsf.Transpose(Storage1))
    Else ' NRangeTypeRows = 1
     MRRandArray2 = wsf.Transpose(wsf.MMult(Storage2, wsf.Transpose
(Storage1)))
    End If
  End If
End Function
```

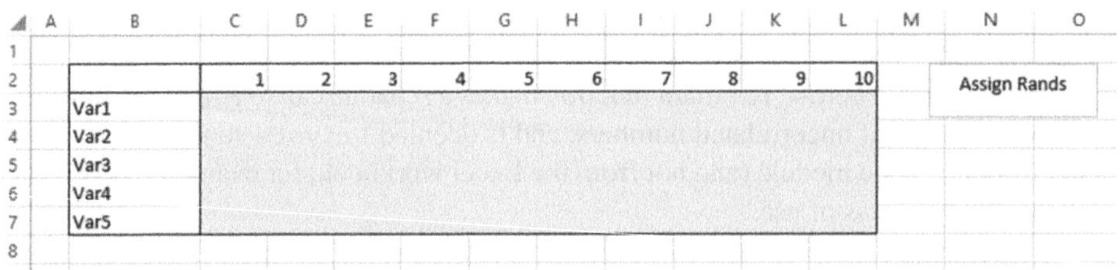

FIGURE 12.21 Named Range into Which Random Numbers are to be Assigned

```
Private Function MRRands(ByVal NCols)
Application.Volatile
'Provides an array of random numbers
Dim Storage() As Double
ReDim Storage(1 To NCols)
 For i = 1 To NCols
 Storage(i) = Rnd()
 Next i
MRRands = Storage
End Function
```

12.8.5 Assigning Values from VBA into Excel

When creating random samples for probabilities within VBA, instead of linking these into the worksheet by using a function, one could instead assign values to the corresponding cells.

The file Ch12.RandsAssignedFromVBA.xlsm contains an example in which a macro is used to assign random numbers into a predefined range (given the name RangetoAssignRands in Excel, and shown as shaded in the screen clip in Figure 12.21). Once the macro is run (the button can be used), the range is filled with random values that are assigned from VBA, as shown in Figure 12.22. The code used is also shown.

```
Sub MRAssignRandstoRange()
Dim Storage() As Double
With Range("RangetoAssignRands")
  NCols = .Columns.Count
  NRows = .Rows.Count
```

	1	2	3	4	5	6	7	8	9	10
Var1	0.85	0.17	0.66	0.28	0.87	0.73	0.39	0.10	0.62	0.11
Var2	0.67	0.31	0.09	0.63	0.55	0.58	0.84	0.93	0.21	0.15
Var3	0.72	0.81	0.32	0.85	0.78	0.38	0.58	0.37	0.52	0.47
Var4	0.59	0.77	0.33	0.26	0.87	0.26	0.16	0.16	0.24	0.18
Var5	0.52	0.96	0.39	0.30	0.67	0.23	0.69	0.33	0.05	0.94

Assign Rands

FIGURE 12.22 Completed Range after Assignment of Random Numbers

```
End With
ReDim Storage(1 To NRows, 1 To NCols)
For i = 1 To NRows
 For j = 1 To NCols
  Storage(i, j) = Rnd()
 Next j
Next i
Range("RangetoAssignRands").Value = Storage
End Sub
```

12.8.6 Controlling the Random Number Sequence

One can control the random seed that is used to generate the random numbers in VBA, so that the random number sequence could be repeated. This involves using `Rnd` with a negative argument (such as `Rnd(-1)`) to repeat the sequence followed by `Randomize` with a positive argument (such as `Randomize(314159)`), where a different value for the argument could be used to give a different, but repeatable, sequence.

The file Ch12.RandsinVBA.Seed.xlsm contains an example of this. It generates a set of random samples in VBA using a fixed seed that the user inputs into the model. For reasons of clarity and flexibility when the procedure is repeatedly used, any previously generated sequences are cleared, and the number of items to be generated is defined by the user within the Excel worksheet. (In practice, within a larger model and when using the multi-worksheet approach discussed earlier in the chapter, both of these user inputs would be placed on a worksheet that was dedicated to simulation control issues.) Figure 12.23 shows an example of running the procedure to generate 20 random numbers, using the fixed seed 314159. A reader working with the file can verify that the set of generated numbers is unchanged if the procedure is rerun at the same seed value.

The following is the code used within the file (including the subroutine call to clear out any previous numbers); it assumes that the required cells have been prenamed in Excel (which essentially should be self-explanatory here), i.e. SeedNo, NSizeofSet and RandsList, with the latter referring to the header cell of the range in which results are stored:

```
Sub MRGenRands()
Rnd (-1)
N = Range("SeedNo").Value
Randomize (N)
Call MRClearPreviousRands
With Range("RandsList")
 For i = 1 To Range("NSizeofSet")
 .Offset(i, 0) = Rnd()
 Next i
End With
End Sub

Sub MRClearPreviousRands()
With Range("RandsList")
 NRows = .CurrentRegion.Rows.Count
```

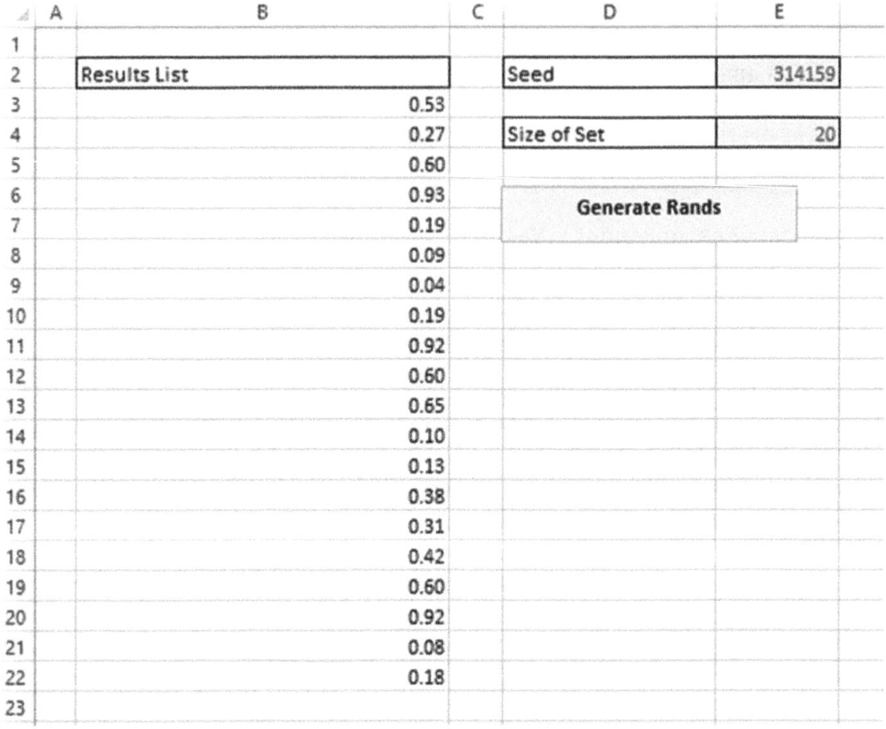

	A	B	C	D	E
1					
2		Results List		Seed	314159
3		0.53			
4		0.27		Size of Set	20
5		0.60			
6		0.93		Generate Rands	
7		0.19			
8		0.09			
9		0.04			
10		0.19			
11		0.92			
12		0.60			
13		0.65			
14		0.10			
15		0.13			
16		0.38			
17		0.31			
18		0.42			
19		0.60			
20		0.92			
21		0.08			
22		0.18			
23					

FIGURE 12.23 Generation of a Set of Random Numbers Using a Fixed Seed

```
  If NRows <> 1 Then ' use this to avoid clearing out header when
data range is empty
    Set RngToClear = Range(.Offset(1, 0), .Offset(NRows - 1, 0))
    RngToClear.ClearContents
  Else ' Do Nothing
  End If
End With
End Sub
```

This procedure to generate a repeatable sequence of numbers could be combined with the earlier approach to generate numbers in VBA and then assign them into Excel. From a simulation perspective, one could generate all the required numbers before a simulation starts and assign (some of) them into the model at each recalculation of the simulation.

The file Ch12.RandsAssignedFromVBA.FixedSeed.xlsm contains an example of this, based on a generalisation of the earlier example. Figure 12.24 contains a screen clip in which the user fixes the seed and also defines the number of sequences required. In a simulation context, each sequence would correspond to a recalculation (iteration) of the simulation, so that one may set this figure to several thousand, for example; a reader working with the file will be able to do so, and to see that different sequences are generated. As mentioned earlier, one would also see that this method to generate the random numbers results in a simulation speed that would be significantly improved compared to the earlier methods.

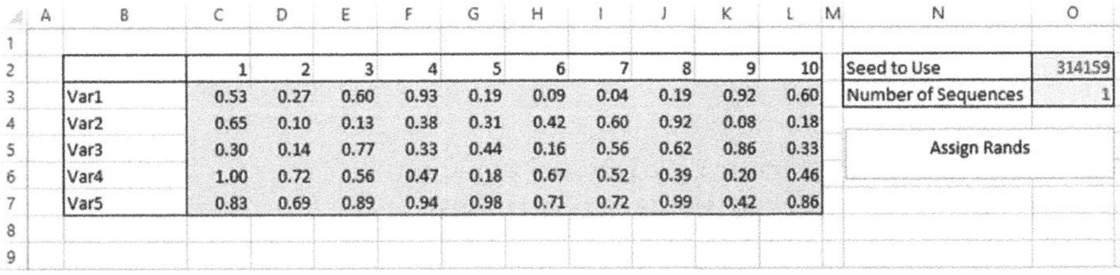

	1	2	3	4	5	6	7	8	9	10
Var1	0.53	0.27	0.60	0.93	0.19	0.09	0.04	0.19	0.92	0.60
Var2	0.65	0.10	0.13	0.38	0.31	0.42	0.60	0.92	0.08	0.18
Var3	0.30	0.14	0.77	0.33	0.44	0.16	0.56	0.62	0.86	0.33
Var4	1.00	0.72	0.56	0.47	0.18	0.67	0.52	0.39	0.20	0.46
Var5	0.83	0.69	0.89	0.94	0.98	0.71	0.72	0.99	0.42	0.86

Seed to Use	314159
Number of Sequences	1

Assign Rands

FIGURE 12.24 Generation of Sequences of Random Number Sets Using a Fixed Seed

The code used is as follows (once again, this assumes that the cells containing the seed and the number of sequences have been given predefined named ranges in Excel; and in practice these items may instead be placed within a separate worksheet dedicated to simulation control issues):

```
Sub MRGenRandsinArraySequence()
Dim Storage1() As Double
Dim Storage2() As Double
'Find size of array to generate, and create its storage space
 With Range("RangetoAssignRands")
   NCols = .Columns.Count
   NRows = .Rows.Count
 End With
 NSeq = Range("NSequences").Value

 ReDim Storage1(1 To NRows, 1 To NCols, 1 To NSeq)
 ReDim Storage2(1 To NRows, 1 To NCols)

'Fix the Seed, taking it from the sheet
Rnd (-1)
N = Range("SeedNo").Value
Randomize (N)

'Generate the numbers within the VBA array
For k = 1 To NSeq
 For i = 1 To NRows
  For j = 1 To NCols
    Storage1(i, j, k) = Rnd()
  Next j
 Next i
Next k

'Place Numbers sequentially in Excel i.e. as if doing a simulation
with repeated sets of rands
For k = 1 To NSeq ' This would be an outer simulation loop
 For i = 1 To NRows
```

```
  For j = 1 To NCols
    Storage2(i, j) = Storage1(i, j, k)
  Next j
 Next i
 Range("RangetoAssignRands").Value = Storage2
 'SIMULATION RECALCULATION WOULD GO IN HERE
Next k
End Sub
```

Note that:

- The code first generates all random numbers required in a three-dimensional array, before using only part of that array at each assignment to Excel, corresponding to a simulation recalculation (where the indexation number *k* defines the iteration [or recalculation] of the simulation loop).
- This procedure could also be generalised further by the inclusion of correlations between the random numbers. That is, given a correlation matrix defined within a model, its Cholesky decomposition would be performed purely in VBA and those factors used to create an array in VBA that creates correlated numbers. That is, in the above code, the array `Storage1` would be combined with a Cholesky procedure to produce a new array of correlated numbers, which would then be those that are assigned into Excel at each simulation recalculation. The principles of doing so are a direct extension of the above approaches and so are not covered further here.

In terms of comparing speed of the various approaches, the following files each contain the same simple model, which generates the required probabilities in the corresponding ways:

- The file Ch12.TemplateForAssignmentComp.xlsm is based on generating the probabilities directly in Excel using the **RAND**() function.
- The file Ch12.RandsAssignedFromVBA.CompTemplate.xlsm uses the assignment method, in which all random numbers are generated within the VBA code and then used sequentially as the simulation is run. The code used has been adapted by using components from the above examples, and is not shown within the text to avoid repetition (the interested reader can inspect the code in the files directly).

Figure 12.25 shows the standard model used in each case. The model has been created in order that calculations within it represent the types of operations that generally occur in typical risk models, i.e. it uses distribution sampling, arithmetic operations and lookup functions. The probabilities generated are used to sample Weibull distributions using the percentile parameter form, the column sums are formed, the maximum value of these sums is determined and the position of this maximum within the range of sums is found. The simulation output is set to be equal to this maximum and its position.

The reader may test the run speed of the two approaches (the run time is reported in each case at the end of the simulation); in the author's testing of these approaches, the assignment method runs approximately twice as fast as the within-worksheet generation method.

Note that in this comparison we have only altered the way that random numbers are generated; we did not alter the way that results are stored; in principle, the output calculations

	A	B	C	D	E	F	G	H	I	J	K	L	M
1													
2		Probabilities	1	2	3	4	5	6	7	8	9	10	
3		Var1	0.94	0.95	0.20	1.00	0.68	0.40	0.15	0.59	0.84	0.32	
4		Var2	0.40	0.06	0.03	0.24	0.45	0.72	0.84	0.65	0.89	0.66	
5		Var3	0.60	0.92	0.68	0.73	0.29	0.41	0.80	0.83	0.76	0.87	
6		Var4	0.05	0.44	0.18	0.11	0.08	0.34	0.75	0.85	0.79	0.67	
7		Var5	0.64	0.88	0.88	0.14	0.21	0.44	0.67	0.63	0.44	0.88	
8													
9													
10		**Model Calculations**											
11													
12		P10	80										
13		P90	150										
14													
15		Values	1	2	3	4	5	6	7	8	9	10	
16		Var1	156.0	159.3	93.7	182.7	129.8	110.1	87.6	123.7	143.4	103.9	
17		Var2	110.5	71.6	61.7	96.8	114.3	132.9	143.6	127.8	148.1	128.2	
18		Var3	124.6	152.7	129.9	133.3	102.0	110.8	139.9	142.6	136.2	146.6	
19		Var4	67.8	113.5	91.1	82.1	75.6	106.2	135.1	144.2	138.7	128.9	
20		Var5	127.0	146.9	147.9	86.3	93.8	112.9	129.2	126.5	113.1	147.2	
21		**Total**	**585.9**	**644.0**	**524.3**	**581.2**	**515.4**	**572.9**	**635.4**	**664.8**	**679.5**	**654.8**	
22													
23		Maximum	**679.5**										
24		Position of Maximum	9										
25													

FIGURE 12.25 Model Used to Compare Speed of Assignment with Use of Functions

could be written (at each loop of the simulation) into a VBA array, with the results worksheet populated from this array at the end of the simulation run; interested readers can experiment with the effect of such issues on run time.

12.8.7 Sequencing and Freezing Distribution Samples

As mentioned in Chapter 7, when a simulation model requires a macro (or other procedure) to be run at each recalculation of a simulation, the input random numbers generally need to be "frozen" at each iteration; this is especially the case when using iterative procedures that themselves refer to values in the model (such as **GoalSeek**, **Solver** or the resolution of circular references), as such procedures may never converge if the values in the model are changing, as the procedure would generally cause the workbook to recalculate as the procedure iterated.

Thus, the approach of generating the probabilities within the worksheet would require an additional input range containing values that are assigned to each at each iteration/recalculation of the simulation, using a simple assignment statement. This is straightforward to do in principle. However, it would have the disadvantage that the ranges containing the **RAND()** functions were being resampled during such iterative procedures, even if such sampled values were not used in the calculations. This will slow down the calculation, and may create integrity problems in terms of knowing which input values actually created each output value.

Hence, the use of assignment statements using values generated from VBA code can be one way to implement the freezing procedure (i.e. no formal separate freezing procedure is necessary, rather at each recalculation of the simulation, the values created in VBA are assigned into the model, which is then recalculated and the additional procedure run, before proceeding to the next simulation step).

12.8.8 Practical Challenges in using Arrays and Assignment Operations

The generation of probability samples in VBA does have a number of advantages highlighted above, namely:

- Improved speed.
- Ability to control the random number sequencing, and hence to repeat a simulation exactly.
- Easier integration within the simulation loop of other procedures that require distribution samples to be frozen.

However, the main disadvantage of such methods in practice is where the set of probability values (i.e. the **RAND**() functions or assigned values) is not in contiguous ranges, and/or have different subsequent roles. For example, if some are required to be correlated together, and others are not, or separate random processes are calculated with probability values that are not in a single contiguous range (e.g. the occurrence and impact in the risk-register example), then such assignment approaches become harder to implement: one needs to develop a mechanism to count the number of random variables in the model (in order to size the VBA array), and also a mechanism to assign the values from the array to the relevant places in the model.

12.8.9 Bespoke Random Number Algorithms

To the extent that one decides to generate random numbers in VBA, one could also consider developing one's own algorithm to so do (such as using the well-known Mersenne Twister method in place of the VBA function `Rnd()`). Such endeavours are generally not trivial; of course, many such algorithms are available in @RISK, and so this is not discussed further here.

12.8.10 Other Aspects

Of course, with sufficient time, and the appropriate development of expertise, one could, in principle, develop the Excel/VBA application further, and eventually create a very wide range of functionality. Clearly, the more sophistication one develops, the more one may ask whether an equivalent functionality is already available in an add-in, and if so, whether the use of an add-in would be more time and cost effective. In particular, issues such as the speed of creation of a wide variety of quality graphical output, the use of a wide set of distributions (especially in the alternate parameter form) and a range of issues concerning simulation control represent significant advantages in the use of @RISK (others are mentioned in Chapter 13). In practice, perhaps after some initial exploratory activity has taken place using Excel/VBA approaches, it is often more effective to work with an add-in such as @RISK, especially in contexts in which quantitative risk assessment is aimed at achieving a wide organisational acceptance and implementation within standardised risk assessment processes.

CHAPTER 13

Using @RISK for Simulation Modelling

This chapter covers the core aspects of using @RISK to design and build simulation models. We assume that the reader is a beginner with the software, and have designed this chapter so that it is self-contained from the point of view of the basic mechanics and features. However, the reading of this chapter alone would not be sufficient to build value-added risk models; the required concepts to do so are covered earlier in the text. The chapter aims to provide a basis to learn the core features of the software, rather than to cover the associated modelling and organisational alignment issues dealt with elsewhere. We do not aim to cover all aspects of the software; rather, we emphasise those topics that are required to work with the models in this text, as well as those features that are generally important from a modelling perspective. Thus, we do not cover the full set of graphics options, the detailed mechanics of formatting them, nor do we cover all of the results analysis possibilities, functions or other features; a reader wishing for more complete coverage can refer to the manual that is provided within the software, as well as to the **Help** features, other documentation and examples provided with the software (including its trial versions), and the Palisade website. As described at the beginning of the text (see Preface), readers who are working with a trial version of the software (which is time limited) may choose to skim-read this chapter (and the rest of the book) before downloading the software to work more specifically with some of the examples.

We start the chapter with a simple example that shows basic elements required to create and run a simulation using @RISK; the example is the same as that used in Chapter 12 for readers using Excel/VBA approaches. We then introduce some additional example models in order to show other key aspects of the software, many of which are used (or mentioned) in the examples earlier in the text. In the latter part of the chapter, we cover some additional features, including the use of VBA macros with @RISK.

13.1 DESCRIPTION OF EXAMPLE MODEL AND UNCERTAINTY RANGES

The file Ch13.CostEstimation.Basic.Core.xlsx contains the simple model that we will use as a starting point for the discussion. It aims to estimate the possible required budget for a family vacation. As shown in Figure 13.1, the initial model indicates a total estimated cost of $10,000.

For the purposes here, we do not make any genuine attempt to capture the real nature of the uncertainty distribution for each item (as discussed in Chapter 9). We also make the

	A	B	C
1		BUDGET FOR FAMILY VACATION	
2			
3		CORE ITEMS	
4			BASE ($)
5		Flight	1000
6		Hotel	3000
7		Taxis/transfers etc	1000
8		Food and drink	2000
9		Insurance	1000
10		Tourist attractions	1000
11		Presents, misc items	1000
12		Total ($)	10000

FIGURE 13.1 Base Cost Model

(not-insignificant) assumption that the line items correspond to the risk drivers (see Chapter 7). This is in order to retain the focus on the core aspects relevant for this chapter.

In particular, we shall assume that:

- Each item can take any (random) value within a uniform range (of equally likely values).
- There are some event risks that may occur with a given probability, each having an impact (in terms of additional costs) when it does so. In this example, these risks are assumed to be associated with changes in the availability of flights or of hotels compared to the base plan. The event risks are shown separately to the base model (in the form of a small risk register). For consistency of presentation, we have adapted the original model to include these event risks, with their value being zero in the base case. The range of additional costs when an event occurs is assumed to be uniform (and for the hotel, includes the possibility that it may be possible to find a slightly cheaper one, as the lower end of the range extends to negative values).

The (modified) file Ch13.CostEstimation.Basic.RiskRanges.xlsx shows the values used for the probabilities and ranges, as shown in Figure 13.2.

13.2 CREATING AND RUNNING A SIMULATION: CORE STEPS AND BASIC ICONS

The screenshot in Figure 13.3 shows (part of) the @RISK toolbar (in version 6.3) that contains the key icons for getting started.

Recalling the discussion earlier in the text that the core of simulation is the repeated recalculation of a model as its inputs are simultaneously varied (by drawing random samples from probability distributions, which may also be correlated with each other), one can see the absolutely fundamental icons required for the purposes of getting started with @RISK (in the sense of implementing these core steps) are only a few:

	A	B	C	D	E	F
1		**BUDGET FOR FAMILY VACATION**				
2						
3		**CORE ITEMS**		Risk (Uncertainty) Ranges		
4			BASE ($)	Min	Max	
5		Flight	1000	900	1300	
6		Hotel	3000	2500	4500	
7		Taxis/transfers etc	1000	900	1500	
8		Food and drink	2000	1800	2400	
9		Insurance	1000	900	1100	
10		Tourist attractions	1000	600	2500	
11		Presents, misc items	1000	800	1500	
12		**Total ($)**	**10000**			
13						
14		**EVENT RISKS**				
15			BASE ($)	Prob	Min	Max
16		Extra cost due to planned flight being unavailable	0	20%	500	2000
17		Extra cost due to planned hotel being unavailable	0	15%	-200	1500
18		**Total ($)**	**0**			
19						
20		**TOTAL ($)**	**10000**			

FIGURE 13.2 Cost Model with Values Defining the Uncertainty Ranges

- **Define Distribution**. This can be used to place a distribution in a cell (for transparency reasons, the parameters of the distributions would generally be cell references rather than hard-coded numbers).
- **Add Output**. This icon is used to define a cell (or a range of cells) as an output; such values are recorded at every iteration during the simulation, and are available for post-simulation analysis and graphical display.
- **Insert Function**. This @RISK icon can be used to enter distributions as well as statistics and other functions; such functions can also be entered using Excel's Insert Function icon (although one would then have to search for the applicable @RISK function category within the full function list). As in Excel, @RISK functions can also be entered by direct typing, but often the syntax is too complex for this to be practical except in special cases.
- **Random/Static Recalculation**. This icon ( ) can be used to switch (toggle) the values shown in the distribution functions between fixed (static) values and random values. When random values are shown, the repeated pressing of **F9** can be used to gain a crude idea of the range of values that would be produced during a simulation, and to test the model.
- **Iterations**. In the terminology used in @RISK, an iteration represents a single sampling of all distributions in the model and a recalculation of the model, whereas a (single) simulation consists of conducting several (many) iterations (or recalculations).
- **Start Simulation**. This button will run the simulation with the chosen number of iterations.

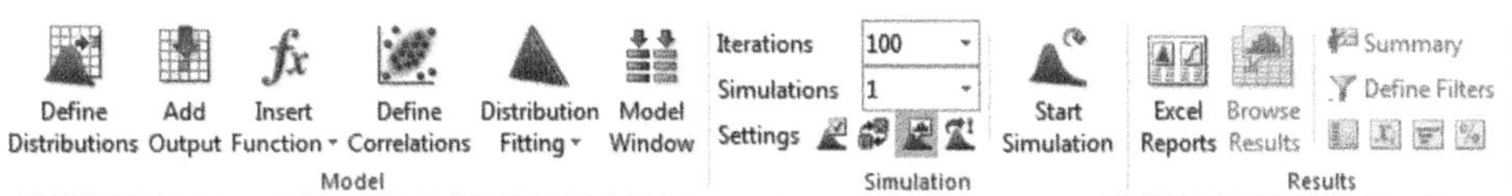

FIGURE 13.3 Core Icons to Build and Run a Simulation Model with @RISK

- **Browse Results**. If a results graph does not appear automatically then one can use the **Browse Results** icon (which would usually appear as the default setting if the **Automatically Show Results Graph** toggle icon (icon) is selected). The **Tab** key can be used to move between outputs if there are several.

13.2.1 Using Distributions to Create Random Samples

The file Ch13.CostEstimationBasic.RiskRanges.With@RISK.xlsx contains a model in which we have used the **Define Distribution** icon to capture the uncertainty ranges both for the core cost items and for the impacts of the event risks (using the **RiskUniform** distribution), and the occurrence of the risk event uses the **RiskBernoulli** distribution (see Chapter 9 for a detailed discussion of the distributions). Note that one can use cell references as parameters of the distributions using the icon (icon).The results of this process are shown in Figure 13.4.

This example is sufficiently simple that some important points about more general cases may be easy to overlook:

- For clarity of presentation of the core concept at this stage, the uncertain values generated are used as inputs to a repeated (parallel) model (i.e. that in column L, rather than in the original column C). Of course, most models are too complex to be built and maintained twice in this way: generally, the uncertain values would instead be integrated within the original model.

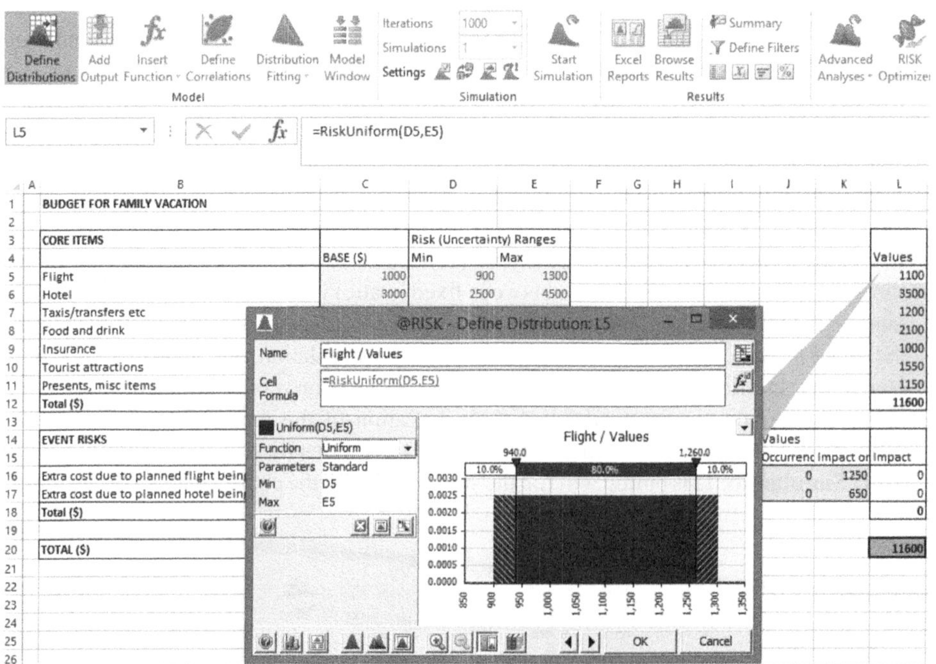

FIGURE 13.4 Cost Model with Uncertainty Distributions

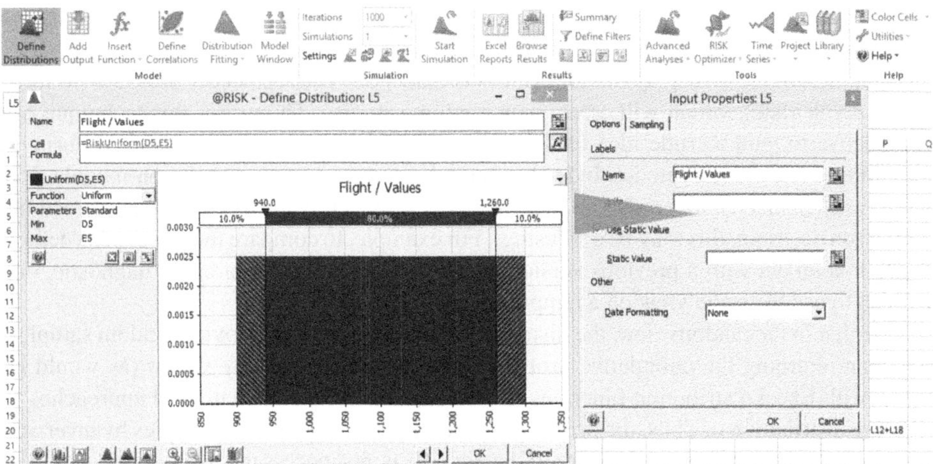

FIGURE 13.5 Defining Properties of an Input Distribution

- When using @RISK to overwrite the value of an input cell in an existing model, several approaches are possible:
  - Copying the original (base case) values to a separate range of the model, so that the values are shown explicitly, and replacing the contents of the original input cells with an **IF** statement (or, more generally, a **CHOOSE** function) driven by a model switch that directs the model's values (e.g. 1 = base case, 2 = risked values). This is the approach that the author generally prefers as it is often the most transparent, flexible and robust, and will often be used in many of the examples in the text (especially those where base cases are explicitly defined; in some cases, only the risk aspect is highlighted).
  - Delete the cell contents before placing a distribution in it. This would not be ideal in general, as one would lose the original (or base case) value of the input.
  - Insert the distribution directly in the cell (i.e. without first deleting the cell content). In this case (on the default settings), @RISK will automatically insert a **RiskStatic** function within the distribution function's argument list. For example, if this were done in cell C5, its content would then read =**RiskUniform(D5,E5,RiskStatic(1000)**). One can also insert a **RiskStatic** function (and link its value to a cell) into a distribution that initially does not contain one by using the **Input Properties** accessible using the icon, as shown in Figure 13.5. There are a number of advantages and disadvantages of this approach, but in general it is not an approach that we use in this text, which relies mostly on switches.

13.2.2 Reviewing the Effect of Random Samples

When a distribution is placed in a cell, the value shown can be chosen to be either static or random. The choice can be set by using the **Random/Static** toggle. When using the static option, the values shown are either those defined through the **RiskStatic** argument (if it is present as an argument of the distribution) or as one of the options defined through the **Simulation Settings** icon ( ), and are discussed in more detail later. A simulation can be run even when the model is displayed in static view, as this is simply a viewing choice; when a simulation is run, random values are automatically used (by default).

When the choice to display random values is made, one can repeatedly press **F9** (to force Excel to recalculate), which will create new random samples. The use of this technique can be instructive to gain a crude idea of the range of values that would be produced during a simulation, and to test the model. Indeed, often when working with simulation models, it is better to work in this random mode, so that the model is reflecting the true random nature of the situation (on occasion, this may be confusing). For example, to compare the effect of structural changes in a model with a previous version, or for some other types of error diagnostic, one may wish to use the static view on a temporary basis.

Note that in the random view, the distribution functions directly provide random samples, rather than returning the cumulative probability or probability density values (as would be the case with Excel distribution functions and most other traditional statistical approaches to presenting distributions). Thus, the process of explicitly creating random samples by inversion of the cumulative distribution function (Chapter 10) is not necessary when using @RISK. Such an inversion process is generally used "behind the scenes" in @RISK, and is not explicit to the user.

13.2.3 Adding an Output

Once one has pressed **F9** a few times (for example, to check that the calculations seem to be working), one would typically set the output(s) for the simulation. These are cells whose values will be recorded at each recalculation (iteration) of the simulation. The main purpose of setting an output is to ensure that the set of data is fully available for post-simulation analysis (such as the creation of graphs); the simulation statistics functions, such as **RiskMean** (see later), do not require their data source to be defined as an output.

In the example model, cell L20 has been set as an output by selecting the cell and using the **Add Output** icon, as shown in Figure 13.6. One can set the desired name of the output, or simply leave the software default names (in this latter case the **RiskOutput()** property function that appears in the cell will contain no explicit arguments; otherwise, its argument is a text field of the chosen name).

13.2.4 Running the Simulation

One can run a simulation by simply pressing the **Start Simulation** icon. For the initial runs of a model (and when developing a large or complex model), one may choose to run only a small number of recalculations (which are called **Iterations** in @RISK), and to run more iterations once the model is closer to being finalised, or decisions are to be made with it. The drop-down menu can be used to set the number of iterations, or an alternative number (such as 2500) can be entered directly.

13.2.5 Viewing the Results

By default, @RISK has the **Automatically Show Results Graph** icon ( ) selected, so that a graph of the simulation output will be shown automatically (where there are several outputs, the **Tab** key can be used to move between them). If the icon is not selected, or a graph does not appear, then the **Browse Results** icon can be used (if no outputs are available to view, one

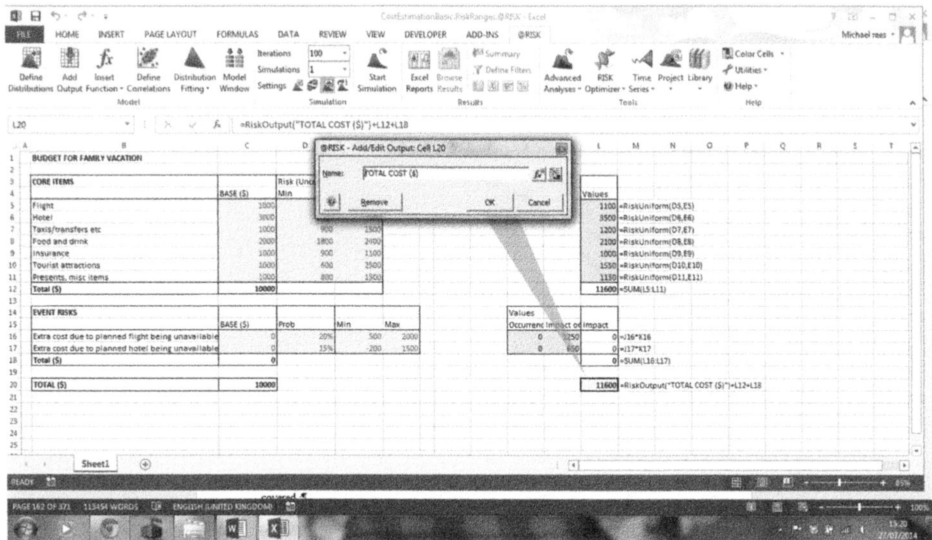

FIGURE 13.6 Adding an Output

may have forgotten to define any outputs!). The **Tab** key can be used to cycle through several output cells.

Figure 13.7 shows the results of running 2500 iterations with the example model.

As mentioned earlier in the text, the analysis of results would normally revolve around answering, in a statistical manner, the key questions that have been posed in relation to the situation, such as:

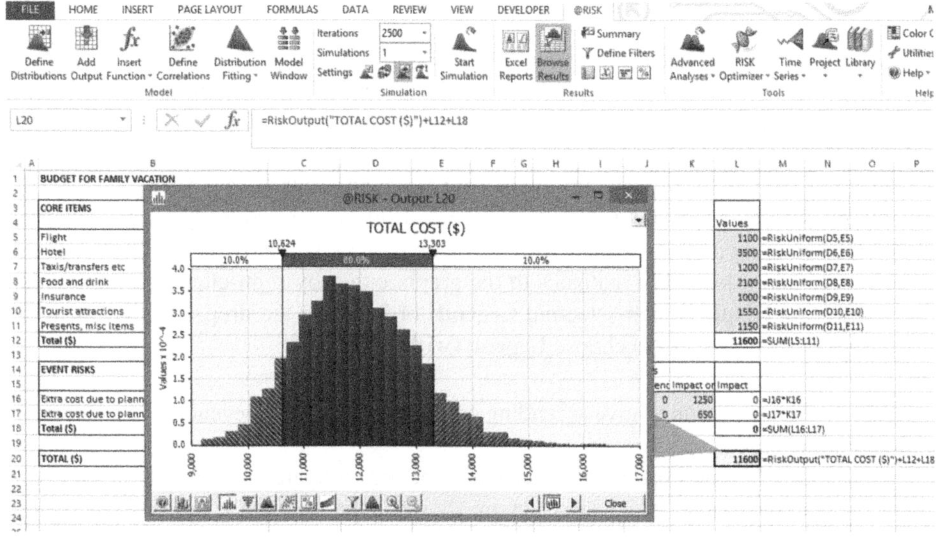

FIGURE 13.7 Simulated Distribution of Total Cost

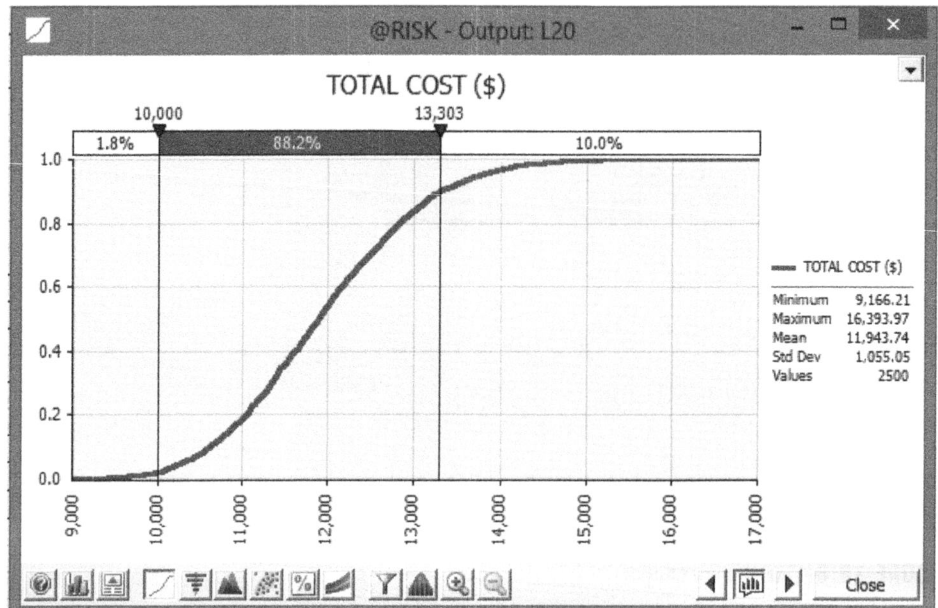

FIGURE 13.8 Cumulative Ascending Curve for Simulated Total Cost

- What would the costs be in the worst 10% of cases, or the best 10% of cases?
- With what likelihood will the vacation cost less than or equal to the original plan?
- What would be the average cost?

Some of these answers can be seen from the graph (i.e. the P10 budget is about $10,600, and the P90 is about $13,300), whereas others would require additional information or displays:

- The delimiter lines on the graph can be moved to any desired place by selecting and moving them with the cursor; they provide information about the results distribution, without changing it. For example, one may wish to place the line at the base case value ($10,000) to see the probability of being below the base figure is about 2%.
- One could instead display the curve as a cumulative one instead of a density curve. This could be done by right-clicking on the graph and selecting **Graph Options** to bring up the corresponding dialog, or using the equivalent icon (▦) directly on the graph.
- One could add a legend of statistics to the graph, either by right-clicking on the graph and selecting **Display** (then selecting **Legend**) or by using the drop-down arrow at the top right of the graph (▾) to choose **Legend (with Statistics)**.

Figure 13.8 shows a cumulative ascending graph with a statistics legend and the delimiter line placed at the base case value.

The use of the **Graph Options** is fairly intuitive, and there are a number of tabs that can be used, for example to alter which statistics are shown in the legend, the colour of the graph, and so on. These are mostly very user-friendly and intuitive, and so although used at various points in the later text are generally not discussed in great detail here.

For readers who have worked through Chapter 12, one can note that the basic statistical results are similar (although not identical) to those shown in the Excel/VBA context. However, the overall visual interface, and the ease and speed of viewing and analysing inputs and results graphically is much quicker, richer and more flexible; this represents one key advantage of using @RISK.

13.2.6 Results Storage

There are a number of possibilities to store the results data that are, by default, presented when one first saves the model (the defaults can be changed under **Utilities/Application Settings/General/Save Results**). Possibilities include:

- Not saving the results (so that one would rerun a simulation the next time it was required).
- Saving the results within the workbook (the results data set is not visible, but is behind the scenes).
- Using an external (.rsk extension) data file that (apart from the extension) has the same name as the model's file, and is contained within the same folder.
- Within the @RISK **Library**. This feature is not covered within this text, as it is a separate database application using SQL Server, and although powerful, is beyond the scope of the modelling focus of this text.

For many day-to-day purposes, it is often simply easiest to save the results within the workbook. With large numbers of iterations, the amount of data saved can make the workbook file very large, in which case one of the other options may be considered. One can entirely clear saved results (in order to minimise the file size if e-mailing it, for example) under **Utilities/Clear @RISK Data/Simulation Results**.

13.2.7 Multiple Simulations

It can often be necessary to run a simulation if formulae in the model change, corrections are made, one wishes to capture other outputs or if parameter values have been changed. In many such cases, there is no particular reason to compare the updated simulation results with those of prior simulations. However, in other circumstances, one may wish to be able to store and compare the results of one simulation run with those of another. For example, one may wish to see the effect of mitigation measures or of other decisions on a project, such as to judge whether to implement a risk-mitigation measure (at some cost) by comparing the results pre- and post-mitigation. More generally, the effect of other decisions may be captured in a model (such as the "decision risk" associated with whether internal management authorise a particular suggested technical solution, as discussed in Chapters 2 and 7), and one may wish to see the distribution of results depending on which decision is taken.

In @RISK, one can run multiple simulations using the **RiskSimtable** function (each simulation uses the same number of iterations). The function requires a list of values as its arguments, and these are used in order within sequential simulations. Thus, the most flexible approach is usually to use the function with integer arguments (from one upwards); therefore, it simply shows the number of the particular simulation being run, and can act as an indexation number for an Excel lookup function that provides the actual parameter values for that particular simulation. When a simulation is not running, the **RiskSimtable** function returns the value of its first argument, so that for convenience it usually makes sense for the first element of a range whose values are looked up to be the base case (i.e. the values that one would most frequently desire to work with).

The file Ch13.CostEstimationBasic.RiskRanges.With@RISK.MultiSim.xlsm contains an example of the implementation of this, in which the main adaptations required were:

- Inclusion in the model worksheet of the data required for each simulation. In this case, we have assumed that we are testing the effect of changing the maximum values of all base items, using three possible values for each (of which the first is the original base case).
- Inclusion of a cell containing the **RiskSimtable** in the model, and the use of this cell to drive the **CHOOSE** function, which is then linked to the original values for the maximum of each variable (the cell containing the **RiskSimtable** function has also been given the range name jIndex for consistency with the presentation in Chapter 12, although this is not necessary).
- Changing the number of simulations to three in the drop-down menu on the main @RISK toolbar.

Figure 13.9 shows the changes in the model sheet.

By default, each simulation in @RISK will use the same set of random numbers, in order to ensure that differences in the results of the various simulations will be driven only by the changes that occurred within the model from one simulation to the next (one can alter the defaults for a particular model on **Simulation Settings/Sampling** and on the **Multiple Simulation** drop-down, selecting **All Use Same Seed**).

Figure 13.10 shows the results of running the model for the three simulations and using the overlay feature to overlay their results. (The overlay icon can be accessed by creating a graph of the simulation results as shown earlier, and then using the icon .)

13.2.8 Results Statistics Functions

@RISK allows statistics of simulation results to be written directly into cells of Excel, using the @RISK Statistics functions (such as **RiskMean**); these can be accessed through @RISK's **Insert Function** icon, as shown in Figure 13.11.

Some key points relating to these functions are:

- The data source that each function requires is simply a reference to an Excel cell. This data source would often already have been defined as a simulation output. However, there is no requirement for this to be so in order for simulation statistics to be displayed, but the simulation must, of course, be run.
- There is some repetition between the functions. For example, **RiskPtoX** is the same as **RiskPercentile**, and **RiskXtoP** is the same as **RiskTarget**. In addition, functions with **Q** in place of **P** (such as **RiskQtoX**) work with descending percentiles (where **P+Q**=1).
- Each function has an optional parameter corresponding to the simulation number (where multiple simulations have been used):
  - If the parameter is not included, the results of the first simulation are shown.
  - If one uses the **RiskSimtable** feature in the way shown above (i.e. its arguments are the integers from one upwards that are placed in an Excel range), then the simulation number within a statistics function can be linked into the cells of that range (so that the

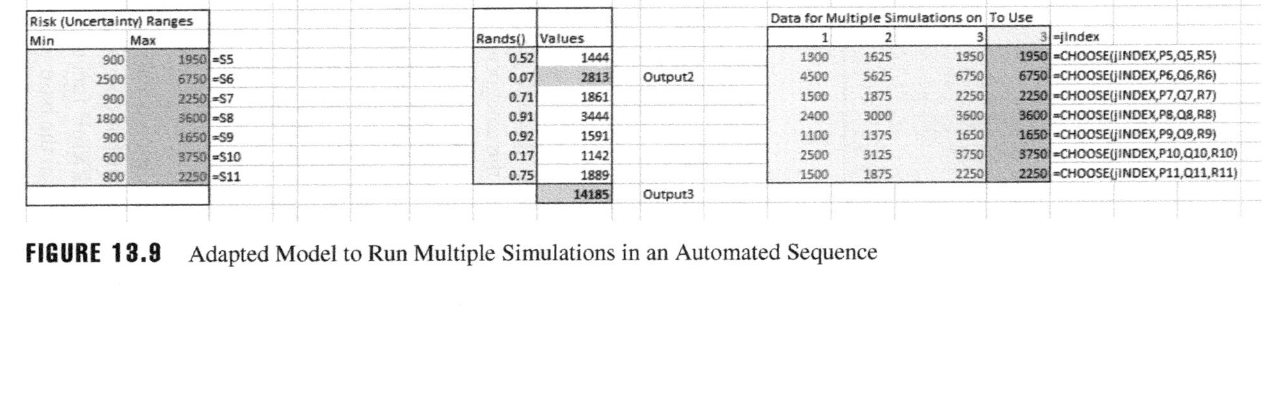

D	E	F	G	H	I	J	K	L	M	N	O	P	Q	R	S	T	U	V
Risk (Uncertainty) Ranges												Data for Multiple Simulations on			To Use			
Min	Max						Rands()	Values				1	2	3	3	=jIndex		
900	1950	=S5					0.52	1444				1300	1625	1950	1950	=CHOOSE(jINDEX,P5,Q5,R5)		
2500	6750	=S6					0.07	2813		Output2		4500	5625	6750	6750	=CHOOSE(jINDEX,P6,Q6,R6)		
900	2250	=S7					0.71	1861				1500	1875	2250	2250	=CHOOSE(jINDEX,P7,Q7,R7)		
1800	3600	=S8					0.91	3444				2400	3000	3600	3600	=CHOOSE(jINDEX,P8,Q8,R8)		
900	1650	=S9					0.92	1591				1100	1375	1650	1650	=CHOOSE(jINDEX,P9,Q9,R9)		
600	3750	=S10					0.17	1142				2500	3125	3750	3750	=CHOOSE(jINDEX,P10,Q10,R10)		
800	2250	=S11					0.75	1889				1500	1875	2250	2250	=CHOOSE(jINDEX,P11,Q11,R11)		
								14185		Output3								

FIGURE 13.9 Adapted Model to Run Multiple Simulations in an Automated Sequence

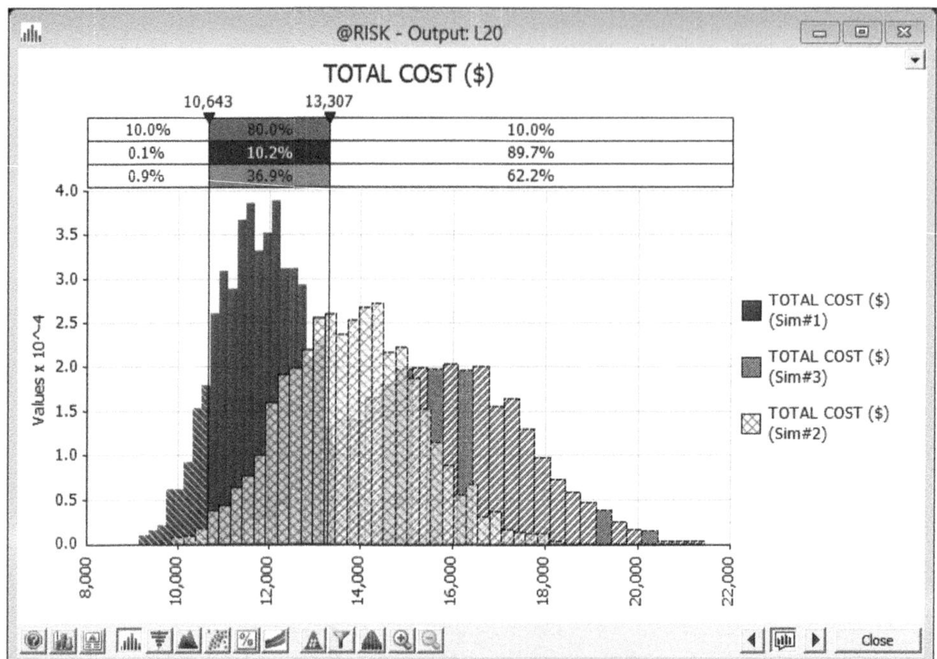

FIGURE 13.10 Overlaying the Results of Three Simulations

statistics functions can more easily be copied to show the results of that statistic for each simulation).

The functions can also be accessed through Excel's **Formula Bar** using the **Insert Function** icon, and are contained within the category @RISK Statistics. Within this category one also finds the legacy **RiskResultsGraph** function, which pastes a graph of the simulation results into the workbook at the end of each simulation.

The statistic functions (most importantly **RiskStdDev**) do not include the correction term that is often needed in order for the statistics of a sample to provide a non-biased estimate. Thus, the functions effectively assume that the sample is the population, which, for large sample sizes (numbers of iterations), is generally an acceptable approximation (see Chapters 8 and 9).

By default, the functions calculate only at the end of a simulation; they can be set to recalculate at each iteration of a simulation under the options within **Settings/Sampling**, although this would rarely be required.

The function syntax can be confusing on occasion, because the "Data source" is a cell reference, but the statistics relate to the distribution of the value of that cell during a simulation. For example, if one were to use the **RiskXtoP** function to calculate the probability that the actual outcomes of a project were less than the base value, one may have a formula such as:

= **RiskXtoP**(BaseCaseCellRef, BaseCaseCellRef, SimulationNumber)

Such a formula would only be valid in a static (or base case) view; whilst the first function argument identifies a cell whose post-simulation distribution is to be queried, the second

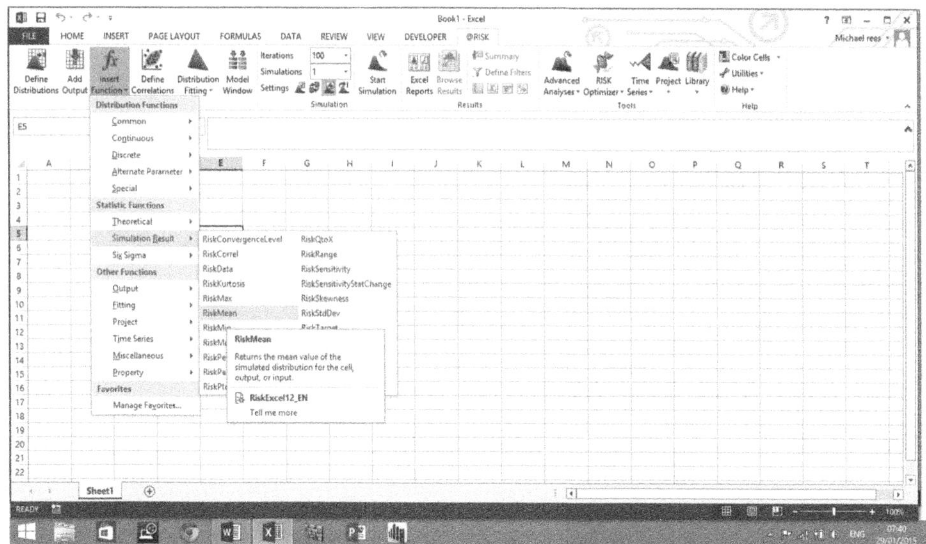

FIGURE 13.11 Use of @RISK's Insert Function Icon

argument needs to refer to a fixed value. In addition, in the static (or base case) view, one may think that such a formula should evaluate to 0% (or perhaps 100%) but in fact (after a simulation and when in static view) it will show the frequency with which the calculation in the cell is below the value of that cell in the base case.

The file Ch13.CostEstimationBasic.RiskRanges.With@RISK.MultiSim.Stats has three statistics functions built in for each simulation. Figure 13.12 shows the results of these as well as the corresponding formulae.

13.3 SIMULATION CONTROL: AN INTRODUCTION

One of the important advantages of @RISK over Excel/VBA is the ability to easily control many aspects of the simulation and the model environment. The **Simulation Settings** (or **Settings**) icon () provides an entry point into a set of features in this regard, some of which, such as the number of iterations or the number of simulations, are also displayed on the toolbar.

13.3.1 Simulation Settings: An Overview

When one has selected the **Settings** icon, a multi-tab dialog box will appear, as shown in Figure 13.13. Some of the points within this dialog are self-explanatory; for others, we provide a brief description either below or in later parts of the text.

13.3.2 Static View

Earlier in the chapter, we noted how a model using @RISK can be placed either in a random view or in a static view, by use of the toggle icon ; in random view one can press **F9** to see

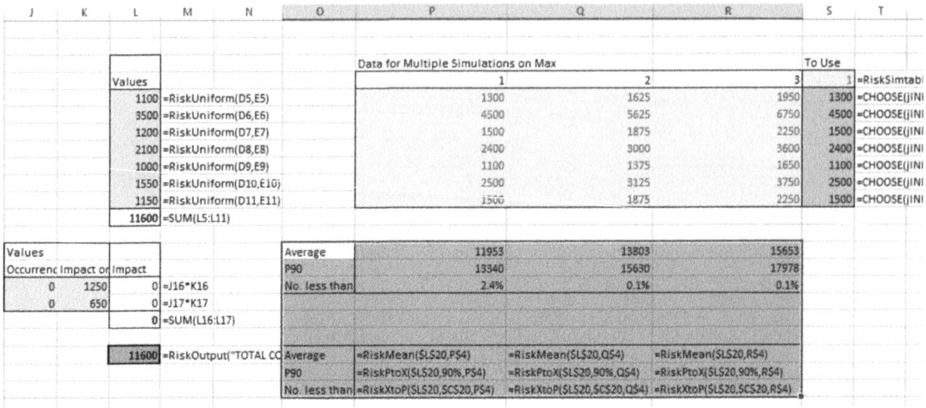

FIGURE 13.12 Use of RiskStatistics Functions with Multiple Simulations

resampled values. The use of this icon would be the same as switching between the options for **Random Values** and **Static Values** in the dialog below (Figure 13.13).

We also noted that if a risk distribution contains the **RiskStatic** function as one of its arguments, then in the static view, the distribution will return the value shown by the argument of the **RiskStatic** function. For example, **RiskTriang(D2,E2,F2,RiskStatic(B2))** would – when in the random view – create random samples from a triangular distribution (with minimum, most likely and maximum parameters equal to the values of the cells D2,

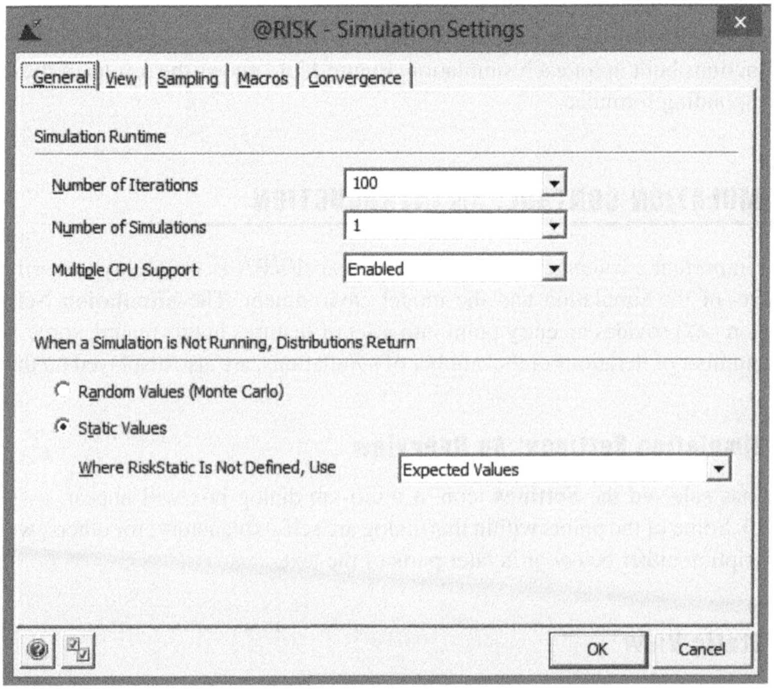

FIGURE 13.13 The Simulation Settings Dialog

E2 and F2), whereas in the static view it would show the value of B2. (Typically, B2 may be a base case value, for example.) The **RiskStatic** function will appear by default when one tries to place an @RISK distribution in a cell containing a number; this is both a protection mechanism to ensure that the number is not lost, and also a practical measure to allow (for example) a base case to be displayed.

However, in this text, we do not use the **RiskStatic** function in most of the examples provided. Instead, we prefer to use a switch in the model (generally an **IF** or **CHOOSE** function) to explicitly control whether the model uses random samples from distributions as its inputs, or uses the base case (or other fixed) values for the inputs. When this approach is used, if one selects the static view, then under **Static Values**, there are several options as to what a distribution may display (i.e. when the **RiskStatic** function is not present). These are available on the drop-down menu, and provide some additional viewing options that would not be present if the **RiskStatic** function were used:

- Mode. The modal value would often correspond to a base case.
- True Expected Values. Displaying average values is useful when all inputs are continuous distributions and the model is of a linear nature, as the calculations will then show the (theoretical) average of the calculations that would arise during the simulation.
- Percentiles. One could quickly see the effect of any systematic bias in the input assumptions, such as the effect of placing all inputs as their P30 values or their P70 values, for example.
- "Expected" Value. This is the default setting, and shows the value that is closest to the mean, but still valid. For continuous distributions, it will be the same as the mean; for discrete distributions it will be the closest valid outcome to the mean. The use of this as a default is a legacy feature, as in versions of @RISK prior to version 5 (i.e. approximately prior to late 2008), the other above options did not exist; arguably, a more appropriate default for later versions would be to use the modal values (if desired, this can be changed under **Utilities/Application Settings/Default Simulation Settings**).

The **RiskStatic** argument (if it is present) also governs the value that would be placed in a cell if the swap feature was used to swap out functions (**Utilities/Swap Out Functions**). If **RiskStatic** is not present, functions are swapped according to the setting within **Utilities/Application Settings/Swap Functions**. (Swapping could be used if the model were to be sent to someone who does not have @RISK; on the other hand, with the approach taken in most of this text [i.e. using a model switch], such swapping would not be necessary.)

13.3.3 Random Number Generator and Sampling Methods

As covered extensively in the text, in order to create samples of distributions (both in Excel/VBA and in @RISK) it is generally necessary to invert cumulative distribution functions, a process that requires random samples from a standard uniform continuous distribution. Thus, the quality of the samples generated ultimately depends on the quality of the methods to generate samples from a standard uniform continuous distribution. The generation of such numbers is not trivial; many algorithms have been developed by researchers in statistics (and related fields) that aim to generate "random" numbers. Such algorithms are (generally) fully deterministic, in the sense that once a starting point (or "seed") is known, then other numbers in the sequence follow. One complexity in such algorithms is that the numbers generated

Sample	Monte Carlo	Latin Hypercube
1	0.931	0.931
2	0.523	0.523
3	0.078	0.078
4	0.928 →	0.828
5	0.374	0.374
6	0.625	0.625
7	0.838 →	0.738
8	0.088 →	0.188
9	0.091 →	0.291
10	0.953 →	0.453

FIGURE 13.14 Adaptation of Random Numbers in Latin Hypercube Sampling

should be truly representative of the process, but also not systematically biased. For example, if one is asked to choose five numbers that best represent a uniform continuous distribution between zero and one, possibly one would think of choosing 0.1, 0.3, 0.5, 0.7, 0.9; similarly for 10 numbers one might think of 0.05, 0.15, 0.25, …., 0.85, 0.95. We can see, however, that (the implied generalisation of) this algorithm is biased (and hence not truly representative), as certain parts of the range (for example, the number 0.43728) would only ever be chosen if the number of samples (iterations) used were very large. In addition to creating samples that are non-biased and representative, further criteria in the design of such algorithms are the cycle length before the numbers repeat (since a computer is a finite instrument, repetition will eventually happen in theory for any algorithm), as well as the computational speed.

Within @RISK, there are many possible ways to control the generation of random numbers (**Simulation Settings/Sampling**); these include the default Mersenne Twister algorithm (used from version 5) and the legacy RAN3I (used prior to version 5). The Mersenne Twister is widely regarded as being effective, and is essentially superior to the other algorithms within the software (at the time of writing); there is generally no reason to use any other generation method.

The software also contains two possible "sampling types", known as Monte Carlo (MC) and Latin Hypercube (LH). The latter performs a "stratification" of the random numbers, so that they are equally distributed within each probability interval. Figure 13.14 shows a sample of 10 random numbers drawn from a uniform continuous distribution between zero and one, using both MC and LH sampling. One would generically expect to find one random sample in each interval of length 0.1, i.e. one number between 0 and 0.1, one between 0.1 and 0.2, and so on. One can see that with MC sampling, this is not necessarily the case: the numbers drawn for the 4th, 7th, 8th, 9th and 10th samples are in intervals in which a number already exists. In the LH approach, these samples have been replaced with different figures, ensuring that there is one sample in each (equal probability) interval.

Generically, one may therefore consider LH to be a superior method. Unfortunately, the comparison is not as simple as one might wish to believe.

The general arguments used in favour of using LH are:

- It would require fewer iterations to achieve a given accuracy.
- It is worthwhile to spend a small amount of extra time to generate better random samples, because the time taken to generate random samples is a relatively small part of the overall time considerations. First, the time taken to run a simulation is a very small proportion of the total time taken to build, test and work with the model. Second, the computational time of running a simulation is also affected by the nature of the model and its recalculations, and by post-simulation data sorting and results processing. Especially if a model is large, but has only a few sources of risk, much time will be taken up by calculations, rather than sampling, so that for models with a large number of calculations (relative to the number of risk items), superior sampling methods should be preferred.

On the other hand, some key points that argue against LH are:

- The accuracy achieved after running a given number of iterations is not a relevant measure to compare the two methods; what is relevant is the total computational time (and perhaps also computer memory requirements). Measures of total computation time should include any set-up time after one initiates a simulation but before it actually starts to recalculate the model (this is often not included in some basic measures of simulation run time or simulation speed). These factors are harder for a user to estimate than simply comparing the number of iterations (although it is intuitively clear that, in order to perform stratification, LH sampling is more computationally and memory intensive than MC).
- In @RISK, LH performs the stratification only in a univariate sense, so that as soon as there are multiple risks, the effect of stratification starts to be lost: however, such multi-variation situations are precisely the situations when simulation modelling is most likely to be required. Thus, the benefits of LH are diluted in many real-life models.

One complexity in designing robust tests to compare the methods is that in most simulation models, one does not know what the exact value (or distribution) of the output is; this is usually why a simulation is being run in the first place!

However, a special case in which the correct value is known is when one uses simulation to estimate the value of π (3.14159...). An example is shown later in the text within the context of the @RISK Macro Language (XDK Developer Kit); these appear to show that LH is marginally preferable for models with small numbers of variables (say less than 10), beyond which there is little to choose between them.

13.3.4 Comparison of Excel and @RISK Samples

The existence of an effective random number generation method is one of the benefits of using @RISK in place of Excel/VBA. One can crudely compare the relative effectiveness of the random number methods using each approach by comparing the results of repeatedly sampling Excel's **RAND()** function with those of a **RiskUniform** distribution between zero and one. The effectiveness of such sampling is important, because in both Excel/VBA and @RISK, such samples are required to create (by inversion) samples of other distributions.

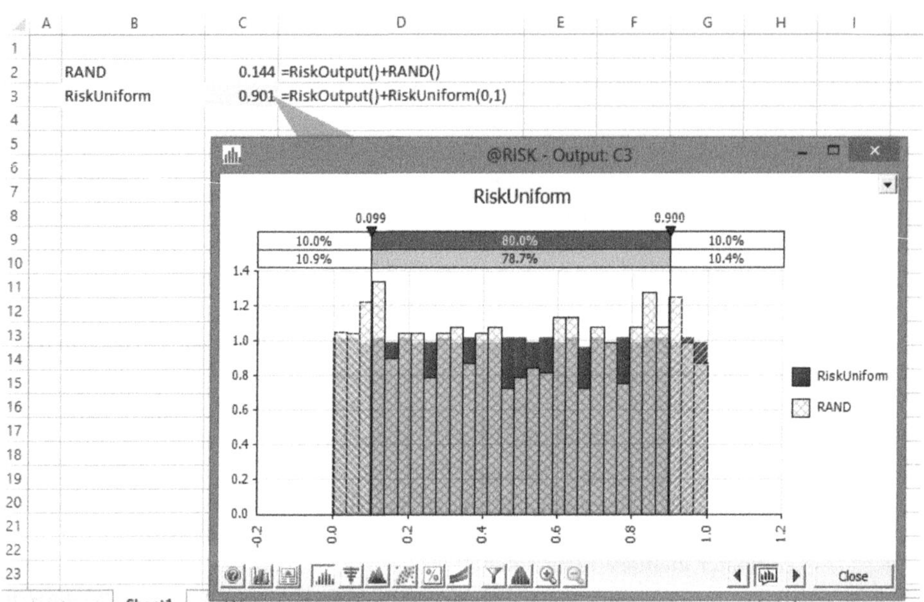

FIGURE 13.15 Overlay of Excel and @RISK Samples from a Standard Uniform Continuous Distribution

The file Ch13.RANDvsRiskUniform.xlsx contains an example in which this has been implemented; a sample of the results is shown in Figure 13.15 as a graphical overlay (after running a simulation of the model – each function is also defined as an @RISK output to aid in producing the overlay graphs); the @RISK settings are using Mersenne Twister generation and Latin Hypercube sampling (using a seed that was randomly chosen at run time). One can visually see the more even distribution of the numbers generated by @RISK.

More formal methods to quantify the efficacy or random number generation methods are available but are generally highly mathematical and beyond the scope of this text.

13.3.5 Number of Iterations

Of course, all other things being equal, running more iterations will give a more accurate result. If one needs to justify or estimate the number of iterations required, one can use the **Settings/Convergence** options within @RISK, and set the number of iterations to **Auto** on the main toolbar.

13.3.6 Repeating a Simulation and Fixing the Seed

A simulation can be repeated exactly, if that is desired. One may wish to do this if results have not been saved or accidentally overwritten. In principle, the repetition of a simulation is a purely cosmetic exercise (for example, to avoid low-value-added discussions about why a P90 figure has changed very slightly, when that is only a result of statistical randomness, which may have no practical bearing on a decision, but can be inconvenient to have to deal with in a discussion with management!).

A simulation can be repeated if all of the following conditions hold:

- The sampling type and generator methods are the same.
- The number of iterations is the same.
- The seed used to run a simulation is the same. To repeat a simulation, the seed need not be fixed as such; rather, the seed of the previous simulation needs to be known and used again. However, in practice, it is often necessary to fix the seed at some preferred number and use this for all model runs. The seed can be fixed under **Simulation Settings/Sampling**.
- The model (and modelling environment) is the same. The notion of having the same model may seem obvious, but it is a subtle requirement in many ways, and really refers to the modelling environment as well as the model, for example:
  - If the position of distributions were altered in a model (such as their rows being swapped), the model would have changed, as each distribution may use the random numbers that were previously used for others.
  - If a distribution is added to a model, then the model has changed; even if the distribution is not linked to any formula in the model, the random number sequencing will be different.
  - If another workbook containing @RISK is open when a simulation is run on a model, the results will generally be different than if this other workbook was closed. Even if this other workbook is not linked to the model in any calculatory sense, when they are both open, they will share the random number sequences used.

The data required for the repetition of a simulation (providing the model and its context do not change) are also contained as part of the information in a **Quick Report** that can be produced by clicking on the **Edit and Export** options icon () of an output graph, or using the **Excel Reports** icon on the main toolbar.

13.3.7 Simulation Speed

The speed of an @RISK simulation is largely determined by the computer used, and the structure, size and logic of the model. A number of simple ideas can be used to minimise the run time, but of course they typically will not have order of magnitude effects. These include (listed approximately in order of the easiest to the more complex to implement in general):

- Close workbooks that are not used in the simulation, as well as other applications.
- Within the **Simulation Settings**:
  - Turn off the **Update Windows (Display)** and the **Show Excel Recalculation** options, and any other real-time (within simulation) update options, including convergence monitoring and the updating of statistics functions during a simulation (unless the intermediate values are required during a simulation, which is rare).
  - Change the **Collect Distributions Samples** option to **None**; alternatively, mark specific inputs with the **RiskCollect**() function and change the setting to **Inputs Marked with Collect**, so that the input data for these samples will be available for tornado and related analyses.
- Remove unnecessary graphs, graphics and tables from the model, as these may take significant time to calculate and update, especially Excel **DataTables**. As mentioned in

Chapter 7, an alternative is to place these items on a separate worksheet whose recalculation is switched off for the duration of the simulation and switched back on at the end (demonstrated in detail in Chapter 12).
- Work on items that generally improve the speed of single recalculation of a model. For example, ensure that any macros use assignment statements, rather than **Copy/Paste**, and that any lookup functions are appropriately chosen and most efficiently used, as well as considering whether circular references can be removed through model reformulation or simplification.
- Install both Excel and @RISK locally, instead of running over a network.
- Increase the system's physical (i.e. RAM) memory.

(Palisade's website and its associated resources [or its technical support function] may be able to provide more information when needed.)

13.4 FURTHER CORE FEATURES

This section briefly describes further core features of @RISK. Many of them are used in the examples shown earlier in the text. Some of these features can also be implemented in Excel/VBA approaches, although doing so is often quite cumbersome and time-consuming.

13.4.1 Alternate Parameters

Most @RISK distributions can be used in the alternate parameter form; that is where some or all of the distribution parameters are percentiles of the distribution, rather than standard parameters. In Chapter 9, we discussed the benefits of doing so, and also provided some examples; readers are referred to that discussion for more information.

13.4.2 Input Statistics Functions

As well as providing statistics for simulation results, @RISK has in-built functions that provide the statistics of input distributions. Such functions return the "theoretical" values of their input distribution functions, as no simulation is required to calculate them. The parameters of the functions are analogous to those for outputs, except that the data source is a cell containing a distribution function (not an output calculation), and the name is appropriately altered, i.e. **RiskTheoMean, RiskTheoStddev, RiskTheoPtoX, RiskTheoXtoP**, and so on.

The functions are particularly powerful when used in conjunction with alternative parameter formulations, for example:

- One could use **RiskTheoMax** to find the maximum value of a bounded distribution that was created using the P90 figure in the alternate parameter form.
- One could use **RiskTheoPtoX** to find out the percentile values for distributions created with standard parameters, or **RiskTheoMode** to find the mode of such a distribution.

These techniques can be combined to approximate one distribution with another by matching percentile or other parameter figures, as shown in Chapter 9.

13.4.3 Creating Dependencies and Correlations

Earlier in the text, we discussed the topic of dependency modelling, including techniques to capture general dependencies (Chapter 7) and those between risk sources (Chapter 11); in this latter case, we noted that such dependencies are either of a parameter-dependent form (which is implemented through Excel formulae) or of a sampling form (which is implemented through the algorithms used to generate random numbers, and includes the generation of correlated samples or of those linked through copula functions).

In @RISK, the creation of correlated sampling is straightforward using the **Define Correlations** icon to create a correlation matrix in Excel, which is then populated with data or estimates. As mentioned in Chapter 11, the values used in this (final) matrix can also be taken from values calculated in other matrices (such as that which results from using the **RiskCorrectCorrmat** array function to modify any [original] inconsistent or invalid matrices).

In Chapter 11, we also mentioned that time series that are correlated only within periods can be created using this icon. Correlated series also often arise when explicitly using the **Time Series** features (such as **Time Series/Fit**), which are briefly mentioned later.

13.4.4 Scatter Plots and Tornado Graphs

One significant advantage of the use of @RISK over Excel/VBA is the ease and flexibility of creating visual displays of results data. Of course, when using such displays, it is important not to forget the key messages that such displays may show. As discussed in Chapter 7, in some cases one generally needs to design a model so that the appropriate graphs can be shown to decision-makers, and so that the model is correctly aligned with the general risk assessment process.

There is a large (an ever-increasing) set of graphical options within @RISK, so that it is beyond the scope of this text to cover these comprehensively. In this section, we briefly mention scatter plots and some aspects of tornado graphs, bearing in mind that some of the underlying concepts have been covered in Chapter 8, and some results using scatter plots have been presented at various other places in the text (Chapters 4 and 11). Those readers interested in a wider presentation of the options within @RISK can, of course, explore the possible displays by referring to the @RISK **Help** and other resources.

It is important to bear in mind that the relationships shown through a scatter plot also reflect the effect of dependency relationships. For example, if the X-variable of the scatter plot is highly related to other variables (such as positively correlated with them), then any change in an X-value will be associated with changes in the other variables, so that the Y-variable may change significantly, even if the apparent direct relationship between X and Y is not as strong.

By default, @RISK scatter plots show an output on the y-axis and an input on the x-axis. However, it is also often useful to show the values of outputs on each axis (for example, revenues and cost, where each is the result of several uncertain processes). In addition, one may also be interested in the equivalent display in which the X-values are those associated with some item that has not been originally included in the model (such as the total cost of hotels, i.e. that of the base uncertainty and the event risk together). One way to display such items is simply to create a new model cell containing this calculation, and to set this cell as a simulation output, so that its values are recorded and a scatter plot can be produced.

The file Ch13.MultiItem.Drivers.Tornado1.xlsx contains an example to illustrate some of the display options. The model is an extension of the one shown in Chapter 7 (containing common drivers of uncertainty), with the extension to create parameter dependencies (as discussed in Chapter 11); that is, the unit labour cost (cell G3) is an uncertain value that determines the most likely values for each of the other cost elements, which are themselves uncertain. The total project cost is the sum of these uncertain cost elements, but of course the unit labour cost is not contained within the calculation of the total cost.

Figure 13.16 contains a screen clip of the file, in which all uncertainties are modelled as PERT distributions.

Following a simulation, one could produce a scatter plot of the output against any other cell (as long as this latter cell has been defined as an output, or is an input distribution, including those that may have been defined using the **RiskMakeInput** function; see later). Figure 13.17 shows a scatter plot of the total project cost against the unit labour cost.

One can see that there is a probability of around 80% that the project would cost more than the original base of $50,000; to see this, one can sum the two percentages that are above this point on this *y*-axis (as in Chapter 7, the base values are those when each input is set to its most likely value).

One can also see that there is an approximately 80% correlation between the items.

With regard to tornado charts, there are many possible variations of the displays of tornado graphs, which are briefly discussed below.

The classical tornado graph (i.e. those produced in the older versions of the software, such as prior to version 5, released in 2008) provided two main viewing possibilities:

- Correlation form.
- Regression form.

The correlation form shows the correlation coefficient between the selected output and the inputs. Some specific points are worth noting:

- The calculation of correlation coefficients usually requires large data sets in order to be very reliable (i.e. have a reasonably narrow confidence interval); small differences between coefficients are usually immaterial.
- As for scatter plots, such measures would, by default, implicitly include the effect of any dependency relationships in the model, and are valid measures when such dependencies exist.

These points can be illustrated with the same example as above. Figure 13.18 shows a tornado diagram of the correlation coefficients using the default settings (in @RISK 6.3, with **Smart Sensitivity Analysis** enabled) and running 1000 iterations. We see that the correlation coefficients are not all identical, even though every distribution has the same role and parameter values. (Note that the tornado bars can be given an appropriate name by using the **Properties** icon [ ] within the **Define Distribution** window to type the desired name [or take it from a cell reference], which results in the **RiskName** property function appearing with the main distribution function argument list.)

A similar chart when 10,000 iterations are run is shown in Figure 13.19, showing that the coefficients are more nearly equal to each other in value.

Note that the graphs do not show the unit labour cost as an item; this is because the default setting has screened out this item. By disabling the **Smart Sensitivity Analysis** (using the **Sampling** tab under **Simulation Settings**, for example), one can produce a chart as in

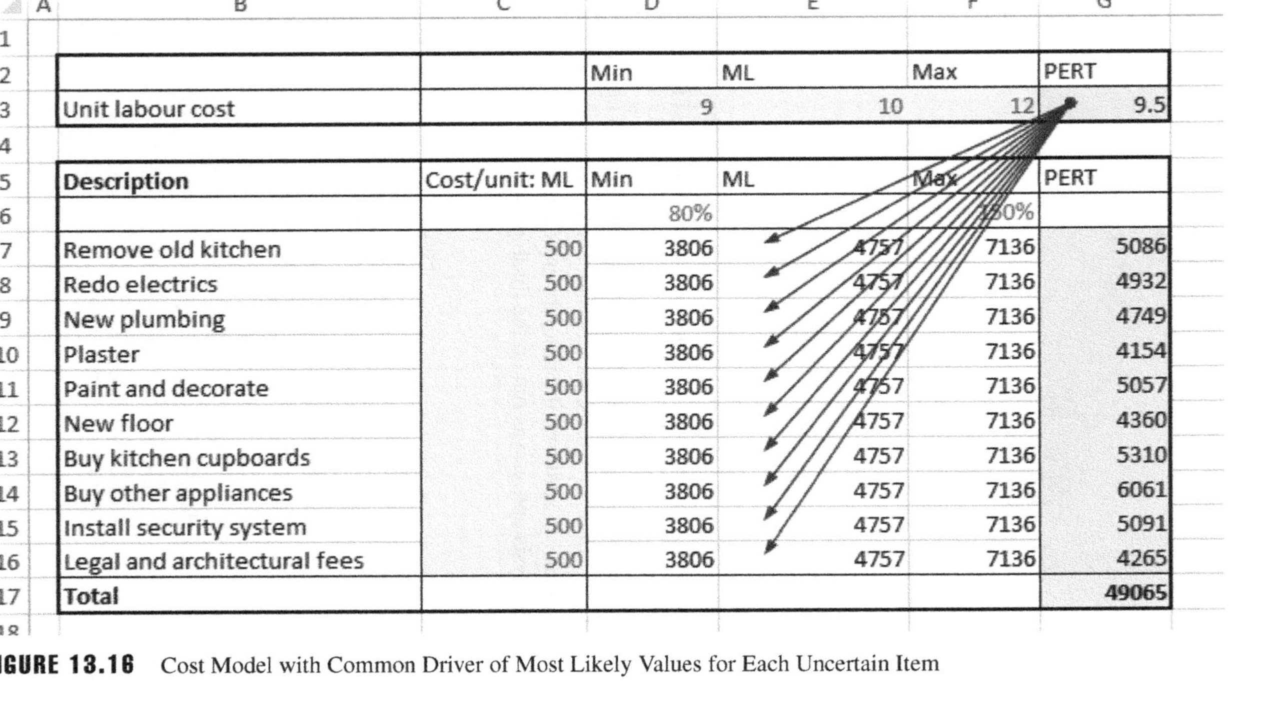

	A	B	C	D	E	F	G
1							
2				Min	ML	Max	PERT
3		Unit labour cost		9	10	12	9.5
4							
5		**Description**	Cost/unit: ML	Min	ML	Max	PERT
6				80%		150%	
7		Remove old kitchen	500	3806	4757	7136	5086
8		Redo electrics	500	3806	4757	7136	4932
9		New plumbing	500	3806	4757	7136	4749
10		Plaster	500	3806	4757	7136	4154
11		Paint and decorate	500	3806	4757	7136	5057
12		New floor	500	3806	4757	7136	4360
13		Buy kitchen cupboards	500	3806	4757	7136	5310
14		Buy other appliances	500	3806	4757	7136	6061
15		Install security system	500	3806	4757	7136	5091
16		Legal and architectural fees	500	3806	4757	7136	4265
17		**Total**					**49065**

FIGURE 13.16 Cost Model with Common Driver of Most Likely Values for Each Uncertain Item

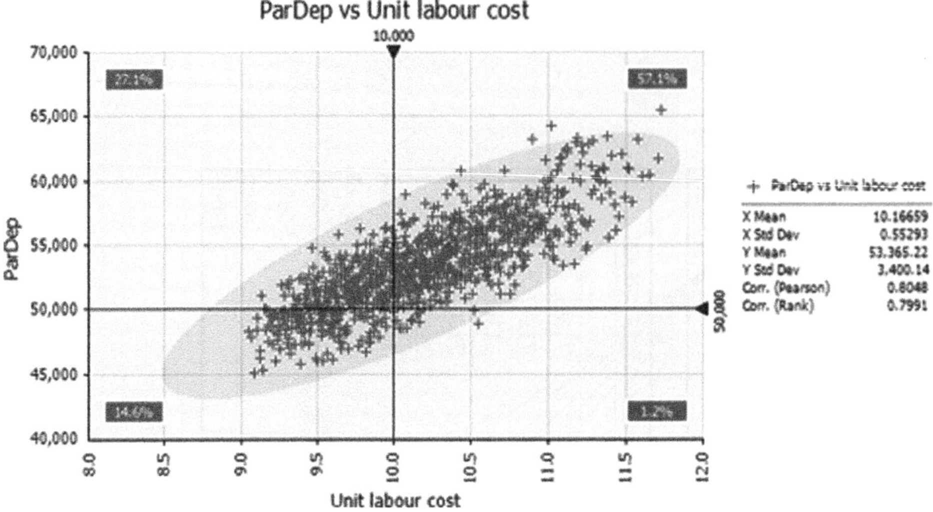

FIGURE 13.17 Scatter Plot of Total Cost Against Unit Labour Cost

Figure 13.20, in which this item is in first place. (A user deciding that the bar should not be shown after all can right click on the bar to hide it, and does not need to alter the setting and rerun the simulation.)

Note that in this model, the use of the **Regression Coefficients** option would produce a graph as in Figure 13.21. In other words, the coefficients are of equal size, but do not match the correlation coefficients. In addition, the unit labour cost item is excluded even though the **Smart Sensitivity Analysis** option was run on the disabled setting.

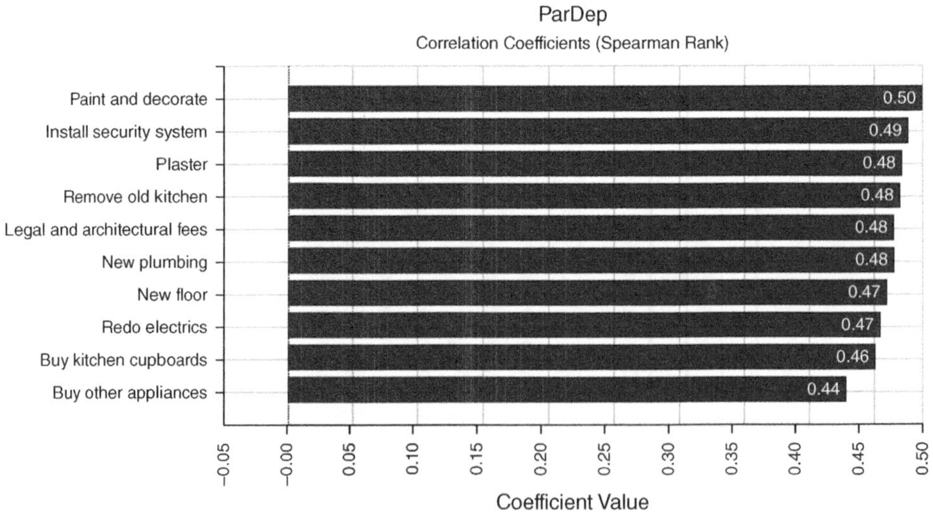

FIGURE 13.18 Tornado Chart of Correlation Coefficients with Smart Sensitivity Analysis Enabled (1000 Iterations)

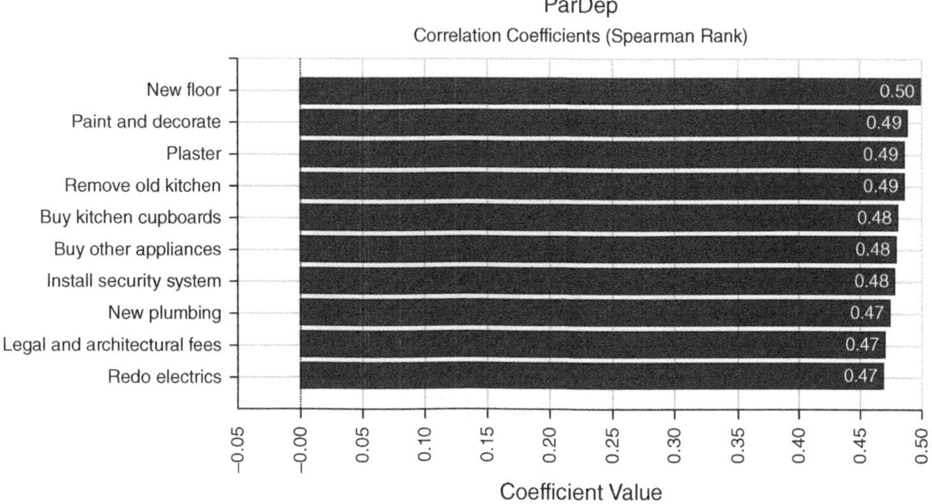

FIGURE 13.19 Tornado Chart of Correlation Coefficients with Smart Sensitivity Analysis Enabled (10,000 Iterations)

We can recall from the discussion in Chapter 8 that the slope of a (traditional, least-squares) regression line that is derived from the data in a scatter plot is closely related to the correlation coefficient between the *X*- and *Y*-values, and to the standard deviations of each. However, such regression analyses are typically valid only when the inputs are independent, which in this case is not so.

The file Ch13.MultiItem.Drivers.Tornado2.xlsx contains an example in which the uncertain items are all independent. From Figure 13.22, one can see that the **Regression Coefficients**

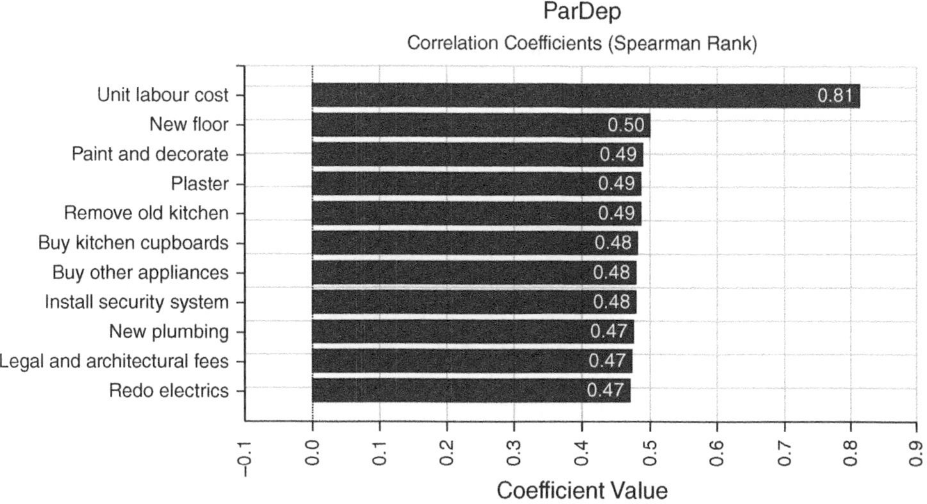

FIGURE 13.20 Tornado Chart of Correlation Coefficients with Smart Sensitivity Analysis Disabled

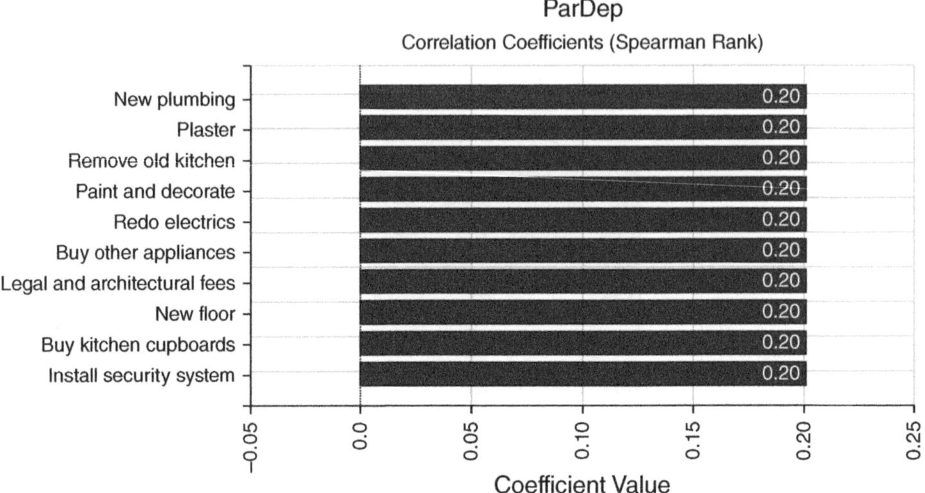

FIGURE 13.21 Tornado Chart of Regression Coefficients

option in this case has coefficients that are similar to those that would be produced by the **Correlation Coefficients** option, which is shown in Figure 13.23.

In cases where the items are independent, the sum of the squares of the regression coefficients will add to one, and hence these squared figures represent the contribution to the variance of the total output.

An option for the display of tornado graphs is the **Regression-Mapped Values**. As covered in Chapter 8, the slope of a regression line placed through a scatter plot is related to the correlation coefficient and the standard deviations of each:

$$\text{Slope} = \frac{\rho_{xy}\sigma_y}{\sigma_x}$$

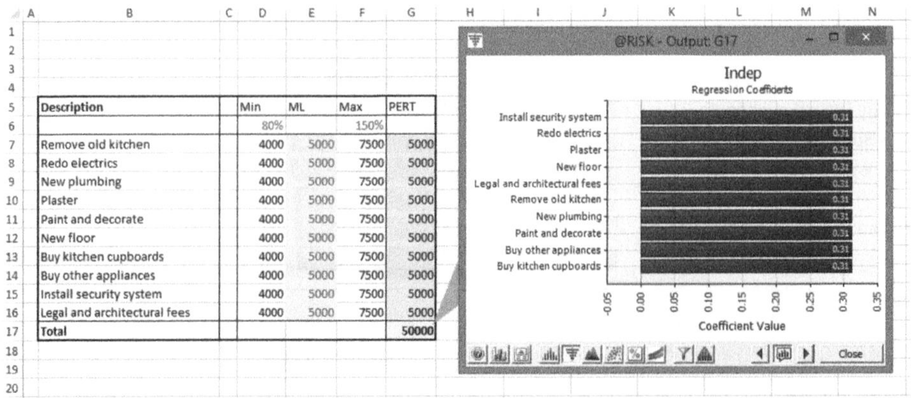

Description	Min	ML	Max	PERT
	80%		150%	
Remove old kitchen	4000	5000	7500	5000
Redo electrics	4000	5000	7500	5000
New plumbing	4000	5000	7500	5000
Plaster	4000	5000	7500	5000
Paint and decorate	4000	5000	7500	5000
New floor	4000	5000	7500	5000
Buy kitchen cupboards	4000	5000	7500	5000
Buy other appliances	4000	5000	7500	5000
Install security system	4000	5000	7500	5000
Legal and architectural fees	4000	5000	7500	5000
Total				50000

FIGURE 13.22 Tornado Chart of Regression Coefficients for Independent Items

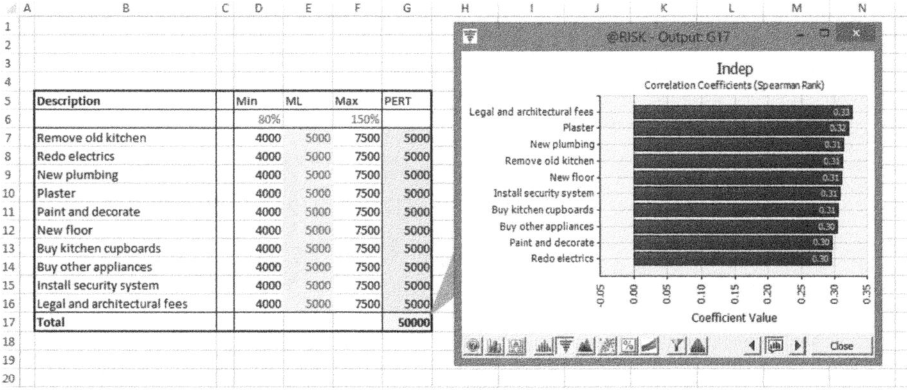

Description	Min	ML	Max	PERT
	80%		150%	
Remove old kitchen	4000	5000	7500	5000
Redo electrics	4000	5000	7500	5000
New plumbing	4000	5000	7500	5000
Plaster	4000	5000	7500	5000
Paint and decorate	4000	5000	7500	5000
New floor	4000	5000	7500	5000
Buy kitchen cupboards	4000	5000	7500	5000
Buy other appliances	4000	5000	7500	5000
Install security system	4000	5000	7500	5000
Legal and architectural fees	4000	5000	7500	5000
Total				50000

FIGURE 13.23 Tornado Chart of Correlation Coefficients for Independent Items

Since the slope describes the amount by which the y-value would move if the x-value changed by one unit, it is clear that if the x-value is changed by σ_x then the y-value would change by an amount equal to $\rho_{xy}\sigma_y$. Thus, the mapped values can be directly derived from the regression coefficient values (i.e. the correlation coefficients that are derived through regression) by multiplying each by the output's standard deviation. Once again, such calculations only really make sense where the input distributions are independent of each other, because in the presence of dependencies, a movement of one variable would be associated with that of another, so the output would be affected by more than that implied through the change of a single variable only.

Another form of tornado graph is the **Change in Output Mean**. This is fundamentally different to the tornado graphs discussed above, as it is not based on correlation coefficients. Rather, the (conditional) mean value of the output is calculated for "low" values of an input and also for "high" values of an input. Figure 13.24 shows an example (using the model in which the items are independent).

With respect to such charts, the following are worth noting:

- There is some statistical error in them, in the sense that the bars are not of identical size, even where the variables have identical roles and values.

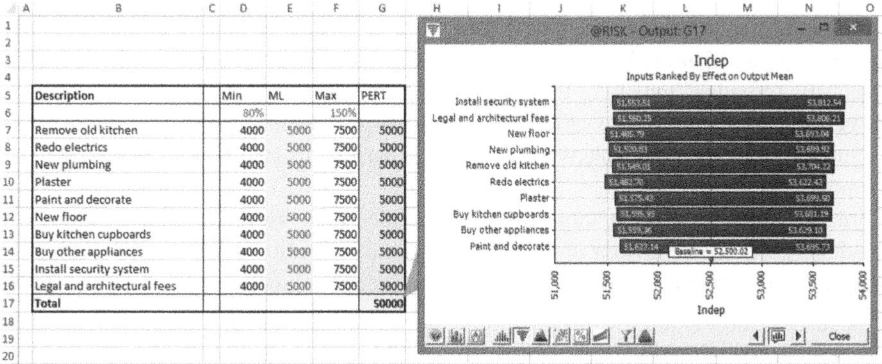

Description	Min	ML	Max	PERT
	80%		150%	
Remove old kitchen	4000	5000	7500	5000
Redo electrics	4000	5000	7500	5000
New plumbing	4000	5000	7500	5000
Plaster	4000	5000	7500	5000
Paint and decorate	4000	5000	7500	5000
New floor	4000	5000	7500	5000
Buy kitchen cupboards	4000	5000	7500	5000
Buy other appliances	4000	5000	7500	5000
Install security system	4000	5000	7500	5000
Legal and architectural fees	4000	5000	7500	5000
Total				50000

FIGURE 13.24 Use of Change in Output Mean Tornado Graphs: Independent Items

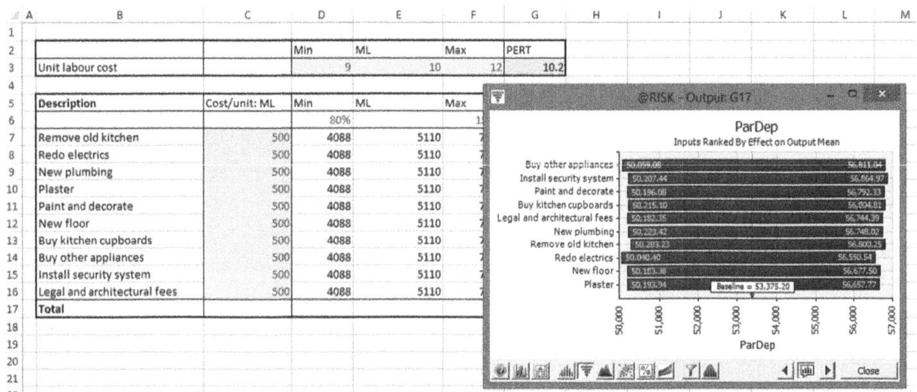

FIGURE 13.25 Use of Change in Output Mean Tornado Graphs: Items with Common Risk Driver

- Dependencies between items will be reflected in the graphs. Figure 13.25 shows the equivalent chart for the model in which there is a common (partial) causality, as described earlier.
- There is no clear directionality of the effect of an increase in the value of a variable (unlike for correlation-driven charts); see Figures 13.26 and 13.27.

The file Ch13.MultiItem.Drivers.Tornado3.xlsx contains an example in which the margin generated by a company is calculated as the difference between the total sales of five products and the cost of producing the products, on the assumption that all items are independent. Figure 13.26 shows the model using the **Change in Output Mean** tornado chart, and Figure 13.27 shows the **Regression-Mapped Values** one.

From the above discussion, and also relating this to the more general points made earlier in the text, a number of points are often worth bearing in mind when using tornado charts in practice:

- The charts show the effect of the variability of the uncertain items, whereas (as discussed in Chapter 7), in many cases, it is the effect of decisions that are often equally or more important from a decision-making perspective; thus, one should not overlook that "decision tornados" may need to be produced by a separate explicit process.
- In general, as there is a large variety of possible displays, and some of them are non-trivial to interpret properly, one needs to maintain a sharp focus on the objectives and general communication aspects.
- Tornado graphs can often quite quickly provide some useful general insight (to the modeller) into the behaviour of a model, and the contribution of various model inputs to the overall risk profile, even if they are not used for subsequent communication or process stages.
- The graphs may have different roles at the various stages of a risk assessment process:
    - Early on, they may provide some idea of where to look for mitigation possibilities. That said, one should not overlook that the graphs will provide no insight into factors

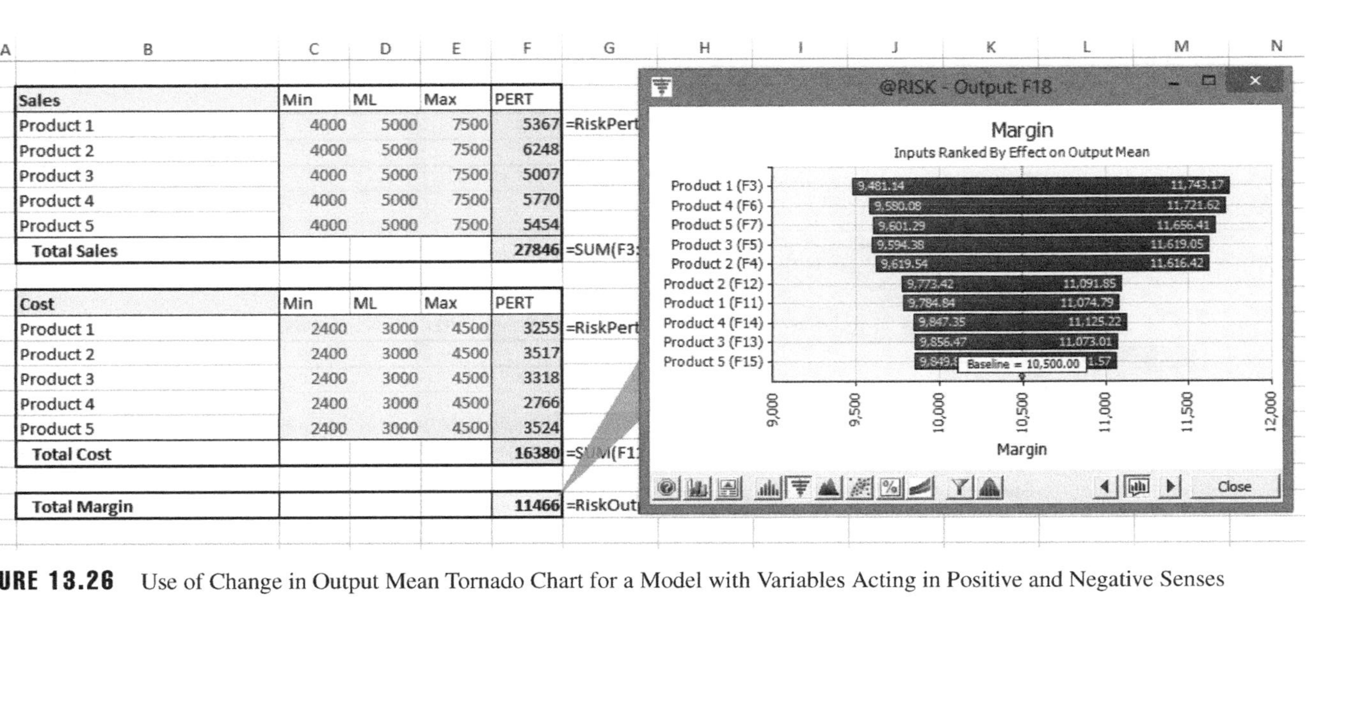

A B C D E F G H I J K L M N
Sales | Min | ML | Max | PERT
Product 1 | 4000 | 5000 | 7500 | 5367 | =RiskPert
Product 2 | 4000 | 5000 | 7500 | 6248
Product 3 | 4000 | 5000 | 7500 | 5007
Product 4 | 4000 | 5000 | 7500 | 5770
Product 5 | 4000 | 5000 | 7500 | 5454
Total Sales | 27846 | =SUM(F3:
Cost | Min | ML | Max | PERT
Product 1 | 2400 | 3000 | 4500 | 3255 | =RiskPert
Product 2 | 2400 | 3000 | 4500 | 3517
Product 3 | 2400 | 3000 | 4500 | 3318
Product 4 | 2400 | 3000 | 4500 | 2766
Product 5 | 2400 | 3000 | 4500 | 3524
Total Cost | 16380
Total Margin | 11466 | =RiskOut
@RISK - Output: F18
Margin
Inputs Ranked By Effect on Output Mean
Product 1 (F3) 9,481.14 11,743.17
Product 4 (F6) 9,580.08 11,721.62
Product 5 (F7) 9,601.29 11,656.41
Product 3 (F5) 9,594.38 11,619.05
Product 2 (F4) 9,619.54 11,616.42
Product 2 (F12) 9,773.42 11,091.85
Product 1 (F11) 9,784.84 11,074.79
Product 4 (F14) 9,847.35 11,125.22
Product 3 (F13) 9,856.47 11,073.01
Product 5 (F15)
Baseline = 10,500.00
9,000 9,500 10,000 10,500 11,000 11,500 12,000
Margin
Close

FIGURE 13.26 Use of Change in Output Mean Tornado Chart for a Model with Variables Acting in Positive and Negative Senses

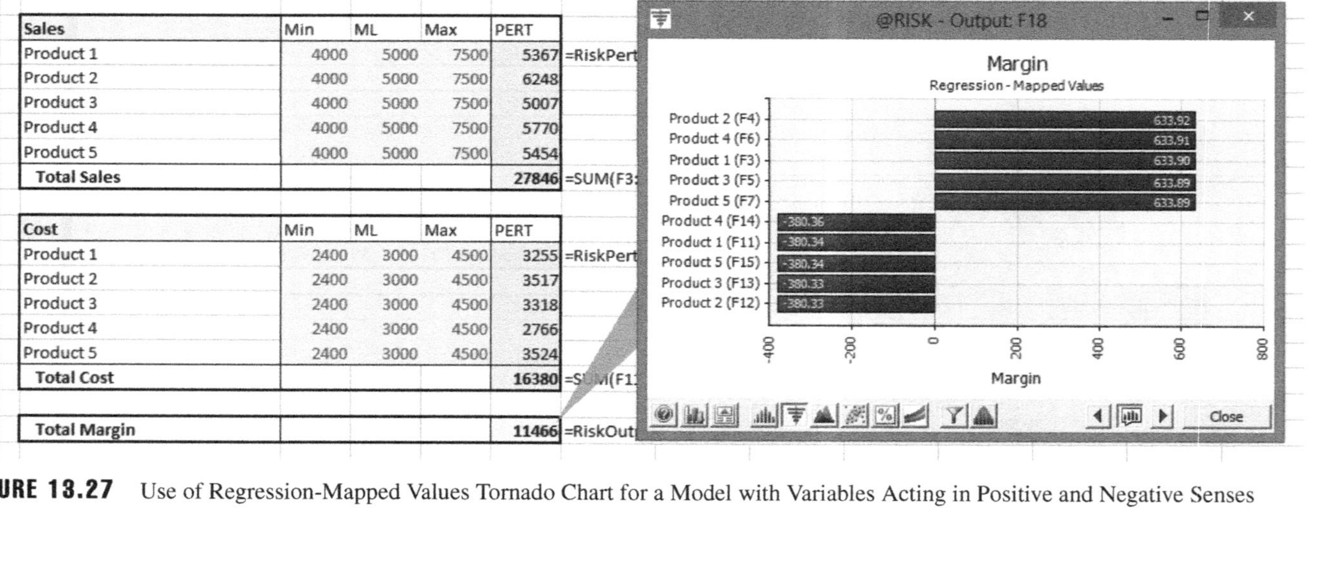

FIGURE 13.27 Use of Regression-Mapped Values Tornado Chart for a Model with Variables Acting in Positive and Negative Senses

that are exogenous to the model, including which project decisions may be available, or whether a particular risk item can be mitigated at all, or at what cost.

- Later in the process (such as when all project decisions have been taken, and all mitigation actions planned for), such graphs may provide insight into the sources of residual risk, which, by definition, are those that one has concluded are not controllable in an economically efficient manner.
- Thus, in either case, the charts may be more relevant for project participants than for senior management (whereas decision tornados are of much more relevance to such a group).

13.4.5 Special Applications of Distributions

@RISK contains several distributions that are not easily available in Excel/VBA approaches, or which are frequently useful for other reasons. This section briefly describes some of these.

The **RiskMakeInput** function can be used to mark a calculated Excel cell so that @RISK treats it (for results analysis purposes) as if it were a distribution; that is, during the course of a simulation (as the cell's value is changing if it has other distributions as precedents) the value in the cell is recorded, whereas its precedents are ignored. The recorded values form a set of points that for analysis purposes (such as the production of a scatter plot or tornado chart) are treated as if they were the recorded values of any other "pure" input distribution; the key difference being that the values of the precedent distributions are no longer used in the analysis.

(For readers who have studied Chapter 12, using this function would be equivalent to capturing the value in the cell as if it were any other simulation output, and then simply ignoring precedent distributions in any analysis; thus, the equivalent procedure readily exists in Excel.)

There are several important potential uses of the function in practice:

- To combine smaller risks together into a single larger risk.
- To treat category-level summary data as if it were an input.
- In a risk register, to combine the occurrence and the impact process, so that they are presented as a single risk.

The following shows examples of these.

The file Ch13.MakeInput.RevenueForecast1.xlsx shows a model in which a revenue forecast for a company is established by forecasting future revenues for each country, with regional totals also shown; there is a switch cell to allow the use of the base case or the risk case. Figure 13.28 shows the regression tornado that results from running the risk model.

In practice, it might be desired to see such a tornado graph by regional breakdown; however, the regional totals are not model inputs.

The file Ch13.MakeInput.RevenueForecast2.xlsx contains the use of the **RiskMakeInput** function, which has been placed around the calculations of the regional totals. Figure 13.29 shows the model and the resulting tornado graph (note also the use of the **RiskName** function used within the **RiskMakeInput**).

Note that, in practice, the placement of such functions around other formulae (i.e. the parameter of the **RiskMakeInput** function) may be cumbersome to do and prone to error; an alternative procedure is to create "dummy" cells, which have no role in the actual calculations

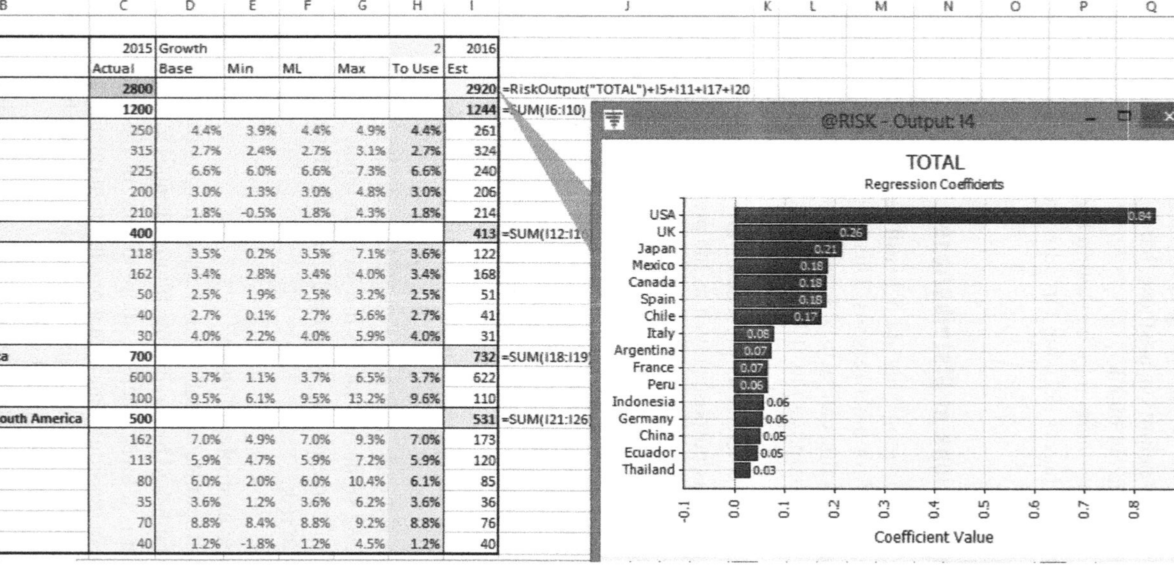

2015 Growth 2 2016
Actual Base Min ML Max To Use Est
TOTAL 2800 2920 =RiskOutput("TOTAL")+I5+I11+I17+I20
Europe 1200 1244 =SUM(I6:I10)
France 250 4.4% 3.9% 4.4% 4.9% 4.4% 261
Germany 315 2.7% 2.4% 2.7% 3.1% 2.7% 324
Italy 225 6.6% 6.0% 6.6% 7.3% 6.6% 240
Spain 200 3.0% 1.3% 3.0% 4.8% 3.0% 206
UK 210 1.8% -0.5% 1.8% 4.3% 1.8% 214
Asia 400 413 =SUM(I12:I1
Japan 118 3.5% 0.2% 3.5% 7.1% 3.6% 122
China 162 3.4% 2.8% 3.4% 4.0% 3.4% 168
Malaysia 50 2.5% 1.9% 2.5% 3.2% 2.5% 51
Indonesia 40 2.7% 0.1% 2.7% 5.6% 2.7% 41
Thailand 30 4.0% 2.2% 4.0% 5.9% 4.0% 31
North America 700 732 =SUM(I18:I19)
USA 600 3.7% 1.1% 3.7% 6.5% 3.7% 622
Canada 100 9.5% 6.1% 9.5% 13.2% 9.6% 110
Central and South America 500 531 =SUM(I21:I26)
Mexico 162 7.0% 4.9% 7.0% 9.3% 7.0% 173
Argentina 113 5.9% 4.7% 5.9% 7.2% 5.9% 120
Chile 80 6.0% 2.0% 6.0% 10.4% 6.1% 85
Ecuador 35 3.6% 1.2% 3.6% 6.2% 3.6% 36
Colombia 70 8.8% 8.4% 8.8% 9.2% 8.8% 76
Peru 40 1.2% -1.8% 1.2% 4.5% 1.2% 40
@RISK - Output I4
TOTAL
Regression Coefficients
USA 0.84
UK 0.26
Japan 0.21
Mexico 0.18
Canada 0.18
Spain 0.18
Chile 0.17
Italy 0.08
Argentina 0.07
France 0.07
Peru 0.06
Indonesia 0.06
Germany 0.06
China 0.05
Ecuador 0.05
Thailand 0.03
-0.1 0.0 0.1 0.2 0.3 0.4 0.5 0.6 0.7 0.8 0.9
Coefficient Value

FIGURE 13.28 Tornado Chart for a Model with Many Line Items

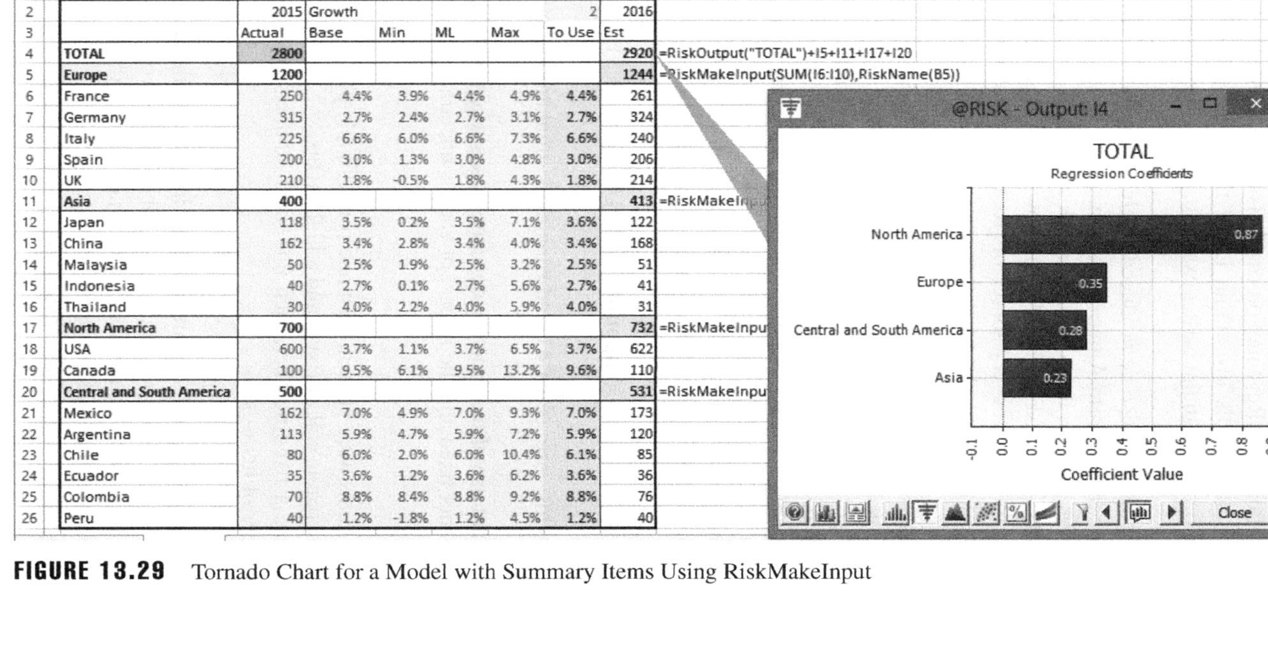

	2015	Growth				2	2016
	Actual	Base	Min	ML	Max	To Use	Est
TOTAL	**2800**						**2920**
Europe	**1200**						**1244**
France	250	4.4%	3.9%	4.4%	4.9%	4.4%	261
Germany	315	2.7%	2.4%	2.7%	3.1%	2.7%	324
Italy	225	6.6%	6.0%	6.6%	7.3%	6.6%	240
Spain	200	3.0%	1.3%	3.0%	4.8%	3.0%	206
UK	210	1.8%	-0.5%	1.8%	4.3%	1.8%	214
Asia	**400**						**413**
Japan	118	3.5%	0.2%	3.5%	7.1%	3.6%	122
China	162	3.4%	2.8%	3.4%	4.0%	3.4%	168
Malaysia	50	2.5%	1.9%	2.5%	3.2%	2.5%	51
Indonesia	40	2.7%	0.1%	2.7%	5.6%	2.7%	41
Thailand	30	4.0%	2.2%	4.0%	5.9%	4.0%	31
North America	**700**						**732**
USA	600	3.7%	1.1%	3.7%	6.5%	3.7%	622
Canada	100	9.5%	6.1%	9.5%	13.2%	9.6%	110
Central and South America	**500**						**531**
Mexico	162	7.0%	4.9%	7.0%	9.3%	7.0%	173
Argentina	113	5.9%	4.7%	5.9%	7.2%	5.9%	120
Chile	80	6.0%	2.0%	6.0%	10.4%	6.1%	85
Ecuador	35	3.6%	1.2%	3.6%	6.2%	3.6%	36
Colombia	70	8.8%	8.4%	8.8%	9.2%	8.8%	76
Peru	40	1.2%	-1.8%	1.2%	4.5%	1.2%	40

FIGURE 13.29 Tornado Chart for a Model with Summary Items Using RiskMakeInput

of the model, but which are cells (placed anywhere in the model) containing **RiskMakeInput** functions whose parameters are simply references to the original model calculations that are desired to be treated as inputs. This approach produces the same result simply because all precedents to the actual calculation are ignored, with the cells that are turned into inputs providing the post-simulation data that are used to produce the chart.

The file Ch13.MakeInput.RevenueForecast3.xlsx contains an example, shown in Figure 13.30 (the populated cells in column L are the dummy cells); the tornado graph has the same resulting profile as in the earlier example, but no intervention in the model itself is required.

Note that scatter plots can also be produced, such as that shown in Figure 13.31 for the total sales against those in the North American region.

The same principles apply in the context of a risk register, as shown below.

The file Ch13.MakeInput.RiskRegister1.xlsx shows a risk register with the tornado graph of the simulated total; by default, every source of risk (i.e. a distribution) is an input, so that the occurrence and the impact are shown with separate bars on the tornado (bar) chart; see Figure 13.32.

The file Ch13.MakeInput.RiskRegister2.xlsx contains essentially the same model, but additional cells (column M) are included, which are simple cell references to the calculated column K, and these cells are the arguments to the **RiskMakeInput** function. Figure 13.33 shows the resulting model and tornado graph.

Another useful function is **RiskCompound**. Its basic property is to directly provide the result of adding a number of random samples together. For example, one can test the effect of the addition of two uniform continuous distributions (which we know from Chapter 9 results in a triangular distribution), by simply placing the single formula

$$C4 = \textbf{RiskCompound(2, RiskUniform(0, 1))}$$

in a cell of Excel (in this case, cell C4), and running a simulation. Figure 13.34 shows the result of doing this.

Of course, the main use of the function concerns cases where both the number of distributions to be added is not fixed and the impact of each is uncertain (and independent of each other):

- If the number of items were known, then one could simply place each underlying impact distribution in a separate cell of Excel and add them up.
- If the impact were a fixed number, then this fixed number could be multiplied by the (uncertain) number of items.

The function adds up independent samples of the impact distributions; one cannot simply multiply the number of items with a single impact number, as this would imply that the impacts of all processes were fully dependent on each other (i.e. all high or all low together), and so would create a wider (typically not appropriate) range.

Applications include operations and insurance:

- The number of customer service calls arriving per minute may be uncertain, as is the time (or resource) required to service them.

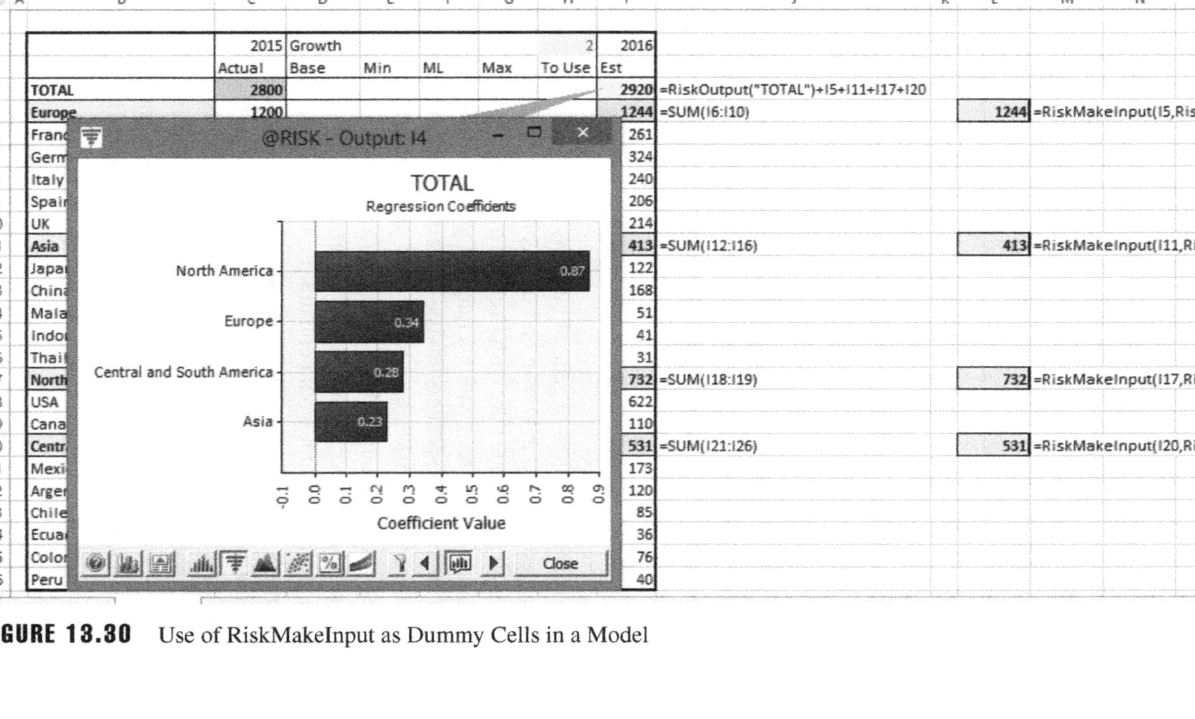

2015 Growth 2 2016
Actual Base Min ML Max To Use Est
TOTAL 2800 2920 =RiskOutput("TOTAL")+I5+I11+I17+I20
Europe 1200 1244 =SUM(I6:I10) 1244 =RiskMakeInput(I5,RiskName(B5))
261
324
240
206
214
Asia 413 =SUM(I12:I16) 413 =RiskMakeInput(I11,RiskName(B11))
122
168
51
41
31
North 732 =SUM(I18:I19) 732 =RiskMakeInput(I17,RiskName(B17))
USA 622
110
531 =SUM(I21:I26) 531 =RiskMakeInput(I20,RiskName(B20))
173
120
85
36
76
Peru 40
@RISK - Output: I4
TOTAL
Regression Coefficients
North America 0.87
Europe 0.34
Central and South America 0.28
Asia 0.23
Coefficient Value
Close

FIGURE 13.30 Use of RiskMakeInput as Dummy Cells in a Model

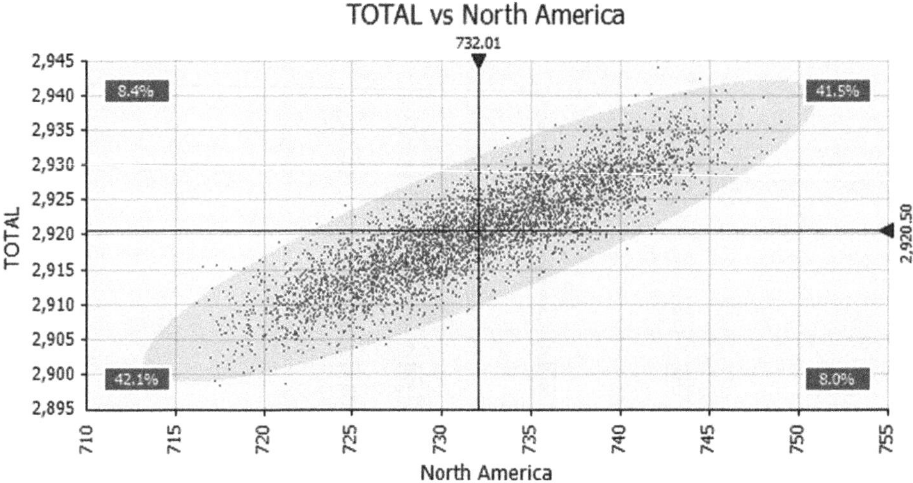

FIGURE 13.31 Scatter Plot of Total Revenues Against those of North America

- The number of car accidents in a region per month may be uncertain, as is the impact (or insurance loss) for each one.
- Generalised risk registers, in which risks may occur more than once, but each has a separate impact.

The function can also be applied in general business forecasting, where generic items are used. For example, a generic (i.e. unknown and unspecific) new customer may purchase an uncertain amount next year, and one may wish to create a forecast in which the number of new customers is an uncertain figure from within a range of general prospects.

The file Ch13.Compound.RiskRegister.xlsx contains an example in which there is a register of items, where each "risk" may occur more than once (such items could be the number of customers with a certain type of query who call into a customer service centre, for example). The intensity of occurrence is the parameter that is used in the Poisson distributions in column D (this column would contain the Bernoulli distribution in a traditional risk register). Column K contains the **RiskCompound** function, which adds up a number of independent samples of the impact distributions, with this number being that which is sampled by the Poisson process. Figure 13.35 shows a screen clip of the model and the simulation results. Although it is not shown here, the reader will be able to verify that the tornado diagram of the output treats the items in column K (i.e. the compound distributions) as inputs, so that there is no need to explicitly also use the **RiskMakeInput** function in order to do so.

13.4.6 Additional Graphical Outputs and Analysis Tools

There is a large variety of other graphical display and reporting possibilities with @RISK. Some of these are:

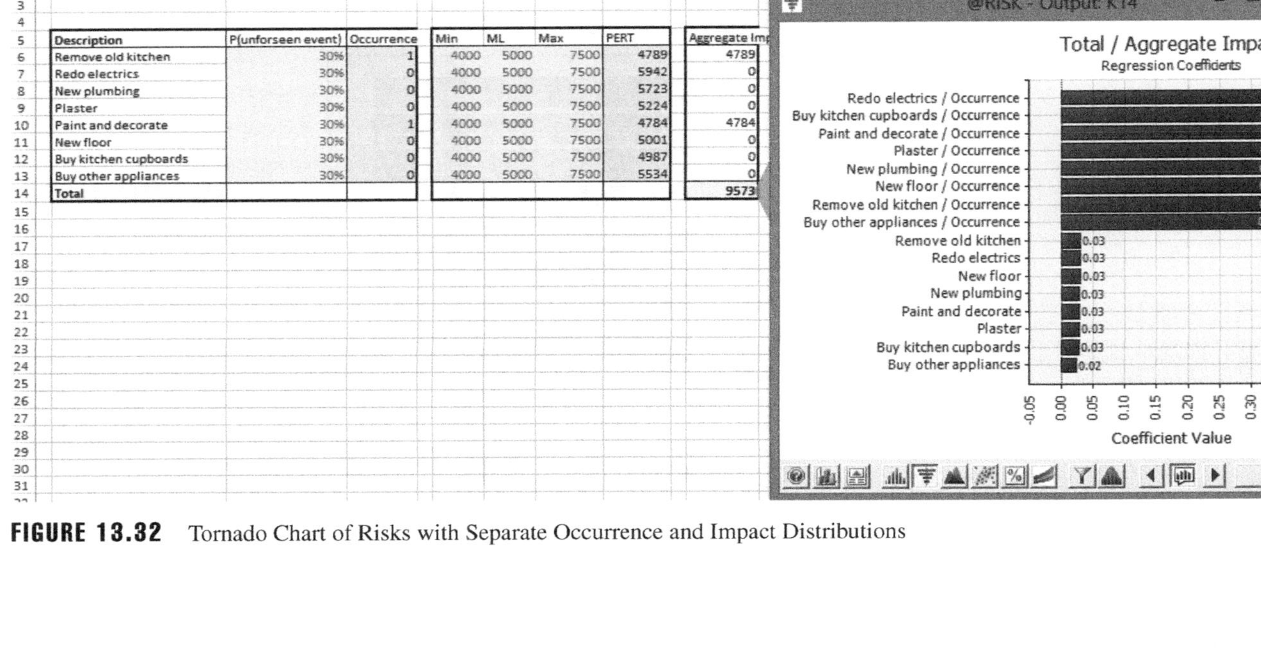

Description	P(unforseen event)	Occurrence	Min	ML	Max	PERT	Aggregate Imp
Remove old kitchen	30%	1	4000	5000	7500	4789	4789
Redo electrics	30%	0	4000	5000	7500	5942	0
New plumbing	30%	0	4000	5000	7500	5723	0
Plaster	30%	0	4000	5000	7500	5224	0
Paint and decorate	30%	1	4000	5000	7500	4784	4784
New floor	30%	0	4000	5000	7500	5001	0
Buy kitchen cupboards	30%	0	4000	5000	7500	4987	0
Buy other appliances	30%	0	4000	5000	7500	5534	0
Total							9573

FIGURE 13.32 Tornado Chart of Risks with Separate Occurrence and Impact Distributions

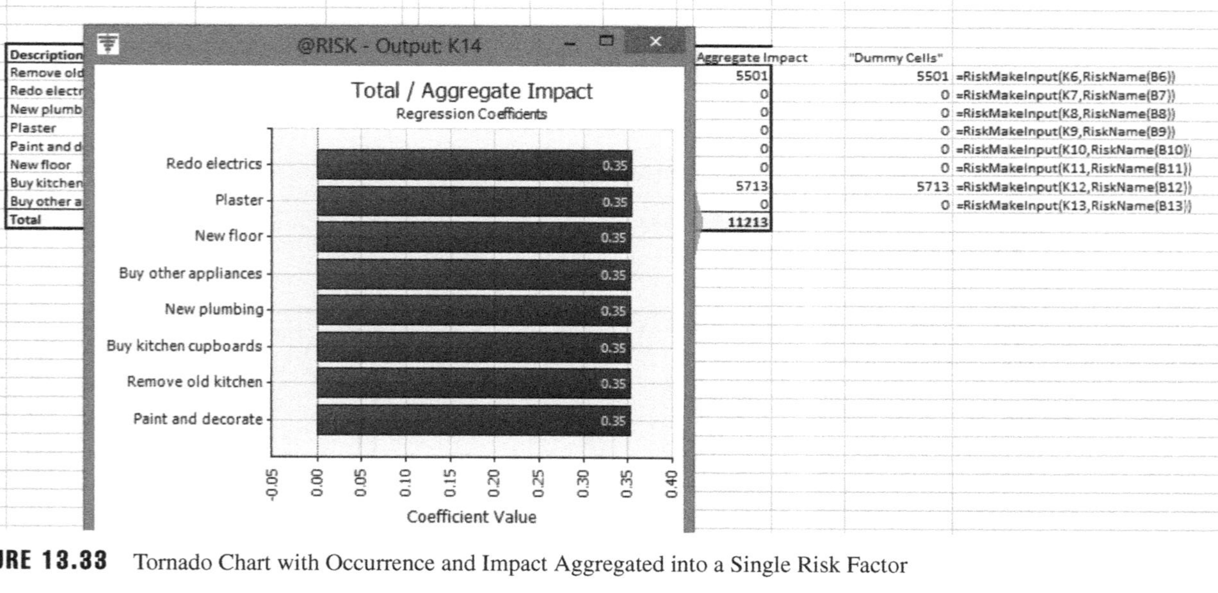

FIGURE 13.33 Tornado Chart with Occurrence and Impact Aggregated into a Single Risk Factor

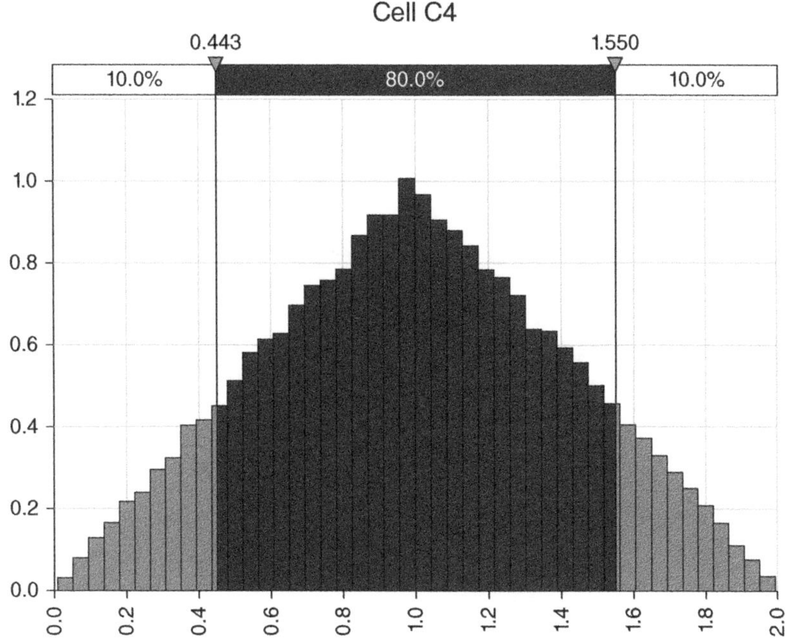

FIGURE 13.34 A Triangular Process as a Compound Distribution

- **Quick Report**. This is a useful one-page summary containing key graphs and statistics for any output, including recording the data required to repeat the simulation in principle (i.e. if the model or the modelling environment has not changed).
- **Summary Trend** plots for time series of data ("fan" charts); an example was used in Chapter 11 in the model concerning the development of market share over time.
- **Excel Reports**. This toolbar icon allows one to generate a number of reports in Excel.

Additional analysis features (under the **Advanced Analyses** icon) include:

- **Goal Seek**. This is analogous to Excel's **GoalSeek**, and could be used, for example, to find the value required of an input variable so that some target is met in (say) 90% of cases.
- **Stress Analysis**. This allows one to run simulations to see the effect on an output if the input distributions are restricted to part of the range (such as all being at their P90 point or more).
- **Advanced Sensitivity Analysis**. This runs several simulations, one for each of a set of values that are input, where such an input can be selected values from a distribution (such as specified percentiles) or static input values.

Each of these procedures generally needs to run several simulations in order to perform the analysis.

The interested reader can explore these further using the manual, in-built examples and **Help** features within the software.

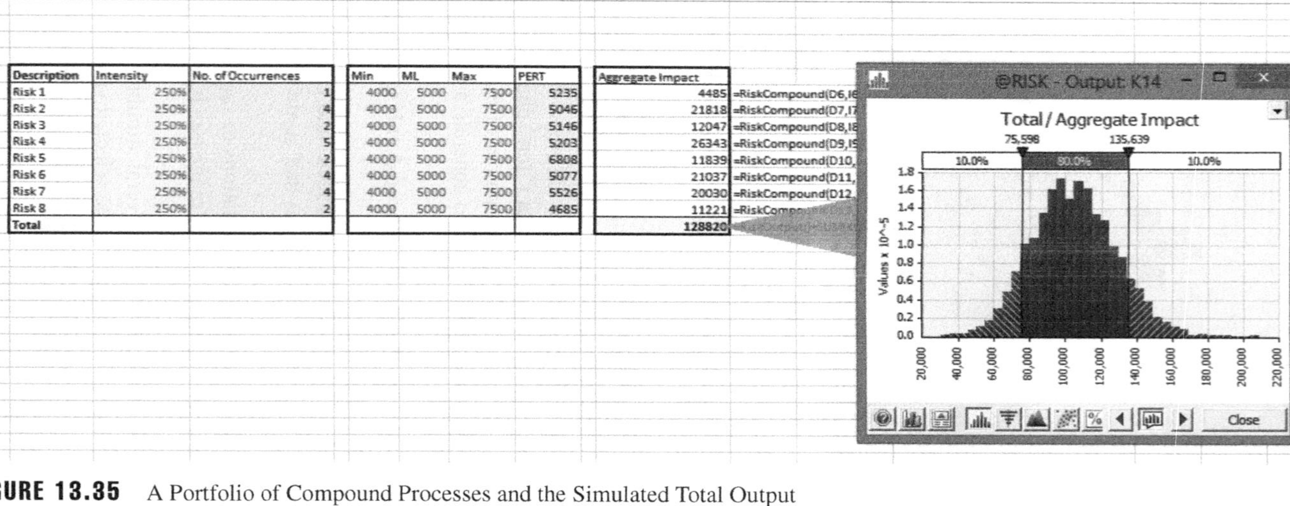

Description | Intensity | No. of Occurrences | Min | ML | Max | PERT | Aggregate Impact
Risk 1 | 250% | 1 | 4000 | 5000 | 7500 | 5235 | 4485
Risk 2 | 250% | 4 | 4000 | 5000 | 7500 | 5046 | 21818
Risk 3 | 250% | 2 | 4000 | 5000 | 7500 | 5146 | 12047
Risk 4 | 250% | 5 | 4000 | 5000 | 7500 | 5203 | 26343
Risk 5 | 250% | 2 | 4000 | 5000 | 7500 | 6808 | 11839
Risk 6 | 250% | 4 | 4000 | 5000 | 7500 | 5077 | 21037
Risk 7 | 250% | 4 | 4000 | 5000 | 7500 | 5526 | 20030
Risk 8 | 250% | 2 | 4000 | 5000 | 7500 | 4685 | 11221
Total | 128820
@RISK - Output: K14
Total / Aggregate Impact
75,598
135,639
10.0%
80.0%
10.0%
Values x 10^-5
Close

FIGURE 13.35 A Portfolio of Compound Processes and the Simulated Total Output

13.4.7 Model Auditing and Sense Checking

Of course, risk models can become quite complex due to the larger input data areas compared to static models, the potential for more detail to be required on some line items and the need for formulae that work flexibly across a wider variety of input scenarios.

As discussed in Chapter 7, when faced with a model that produces non-intuitive results, the model may be wrong, or one's intuition may be so; in the latter case, the model will often prove to be a valuable tool to develop one's intuition and understanding further.

@RISK has a number of techniques to help gain an overview of a model, consider its integrity and search for errors. Some of the core features include:

- The **Model Window** icon on the toolbar provides an overview of the distributions in the model. It is instructive to look at the general type of distributions used (discrete, continuous), as this often gives some reasonable indication of the general model context (e.g. risk registers versus continuous uncertainties). One can also see whether there are any correlated items, and which cells are defined as outputs. The knowledge of the desired output (for a model that one has not built oneself) is a very important piece of information; a traditional Excel model does not directly inform one of what the output cell is, whereas this knowledge is fundamental in order to know the objectives of the model.
- Using tornado graphs and scatter plots to gain a quick overview of key risk factors within a model.
- **Simulation Data**. The toolbar icon allows one access to the simulation data (). One can use this to sort or filter the data (e.g. to find those iterations that generated error values, or other unusual outcomes, and to see the corresponding input values that applied). One can also step through these data, whilst the values in the Excel worksheet update at each step. As an example, in a model with a parameter dependency, if the most likely value of a PERT distribution is varying throughout a simulation (as it is determined from samples of other distributions), but its minimum and maximum values are hard coded and not linked to the most likely value, then cases may arise where the most likely is less than the minimum, so that the distribution cannot be formed and an error arises. These types of errors are made transparent by reviewing the individual iterations that caused errors to arise.
- On the **Simulation Settings/View** tab, one can check the boxes corresponding to **Show Excel Recalculations** or **Pause on Output Errors**. The first option will slow down the simulation, so should generally not be used as a default setting.

13.5 WORKING WITH MACROS AND THE @RISK MACRO LANGUAGE

This section describes some key elements of working with VBA macros when using @RISK, including an introduction to @RISK's own macro language.

13.5.1 Using Macros with @RISK

In principle, the use of macros with @RISK is straightforward. Of course, for many people, one of the reasons to use @RISK is to avoid having to use macros! Nevertheless, on occasion the use of fairly simple macros is helpful or necessary.

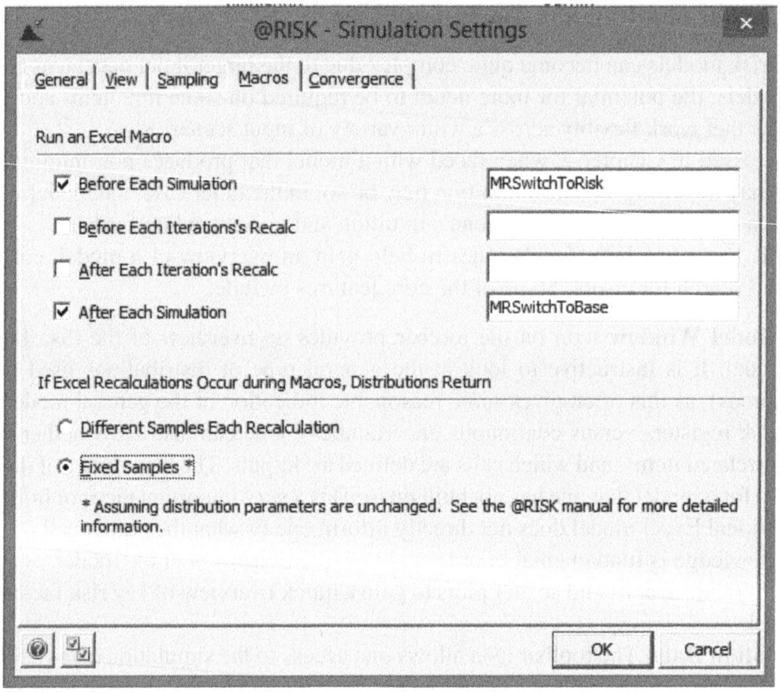

FIGURE 13.36 The Macros Tab of the SimulationSettings Dialog

In Chapter 7, we mentioned typical cases where macros may be required, such as:

- Before or after a simulation, to toggle the value of a switch, so that risk values are used during the simulation, but that the base case is shown as soon as the simulation has finished running. Similarly, one may need to remove Excel **Data/Filters** before a simulation, or to run **GoalSeek** or **Solver** before or after a simulation, and so on.
- At each iteration of a simulation, to run procedures such as the resolution of circular references, or use **GoalSeek** or **Solver**.

In principle, the macros associated with such procedures can be placed at the appropriate place within the **SimulationSettings/Macros** tab. Figure 13.36 shows an example, in which the procedures used in Chapter 7 to toggle the switch are placed in the tab; when a user runs the simulation (using the **Start Simulation** icon), the model switch will first be toggled to ensure that the risk values are used, and after the simulation the procedure to toggle to base values will be run.

Where macros need to be run at each iteration, there is more potential complexity; as discussed in Chapter 7, in general one would wish for the distribution samples to be frozen when such procedures are running. Fortunately, this is easy to achieve in @RISK (versions 6.3 onwards), as one can simply select the **Fixed Samples** option in the dialog box. (As the dialog box indicates, this would not be a valid procedure if the macro changed the value of distribution parameters, which would be a very unusual situation; even where there are parameter dependencies in the model, since distribution samples are fixed, the parameters of dependent distributions would not change during such recalculations unless the parameters of the independent distributions were changed by the macro.)

In versions prior to 6.3, although a dialog box existed that was superficially similar to the one above, the **Fixed Samples** option did not exist. In those cases, one generally needed to fix distribution samples using a separate macro to assign values from distributions to fixed cells (analogous to that discussed in Chapter 12), and also would frequently have then created cells that referred directly to these fixed values, which would have been defined as inputs using the **RiskMakeInput** function, in order to record the sampled values actually used and for purposes of producing graphical output. Fortunately, such procedures are no longer necessary. (An exception to this requirement was when models used Excel iterations to resolve circularities, in which case the fixing procedure was built into @RISK, but not explicit to the user. Note that this process can, however, not be readily observed: whilst Excel's iterative method will resolve in **Static** view, in the **Random** view, as Excel iterates to try to resolve the circularity, new samples from the distributions are drawn from each iteration, and hence the target for the iterative process is constantly moving.)

Note also that if one tests models that contain macros by using **F8** in VBA to step through it, one may observe results that are not the same as those that would occur when the simulation is actually run: stepping through may cause the worksheet to update, which would often lead to the distributions being resampled, whereas during the simulation, the values would be fixed when using the **Fixed Samples** option.

13.5.2 The @RISK Macro Language or Developer Kit: An Introduction

In the above, we discussed the use of @RISK functionality to manage the sequencing of general VBA macros. In addition, @RISK has its own macro language, known as the VBA Macro Language or the @RISK for Excel Developer Kit (XDK). Information about this can be found under the general **Help** menu within @RISK, as shown in Figure 13.37.

Some general uses of these tools could be:

- To create a "black-box" interface in which the user needs only to press a button in Excel to launch a macro to run the simulation. Such a macro could also ask the user for information (such as the desired number of iterations, or the sampling type desired to be used, etc.), so that the user does not have to directly interface with (or learn) the @RISK toolbar.
- To change **Simulation Settings** at run time, so that the same defaults are used, irrespective of what is currently set on the toolbar.
- To generate output statistics and reports.
- To automate other procedures that would be time-consuming to implement.

In the following, we provide examples of the use of these tools to repeatedly run simulations, to change aspects of the random number sampling and generator methods and to generate reports of the simulation data.

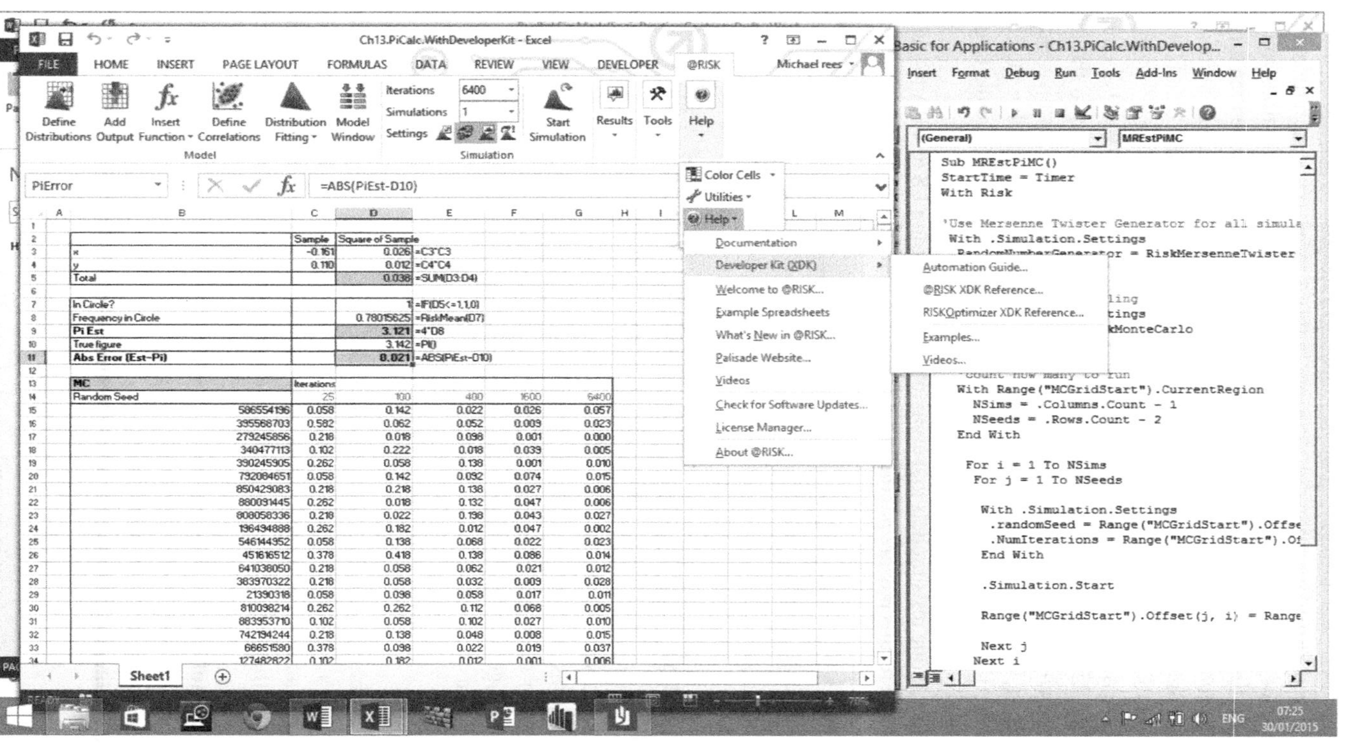

FIGURE 13.37 Accessing the XDK Help Menu

	A	B	C	D	E
1					
2			Sample	Square of Sample	
3		x	-0.193	0.037	=C3*C3
4		y	-0.225	0.051	=C4*C4
5		Total		0.088	=SUM(D3:D4)
6					
7		In Circle?		1	=IF(D5<=1,1,0)
8		Frequency in Circle		0.7794	=RiskMean(D7)
9		**Pi Est**		**3.118**	=4*D8
10		True figure		3.142	=PI()
11		**Abs Error (Est-Pi)**		**0.024**	=ABS(PiEst-D10)

FIGURE 13.38 Model to Calculate π Using the Dartboard Method

13.5.3 Using the XDK to Analyse Random Number Generator and Sampling Methods

In this section, we use the XDK to show how one may compare the effectiveness of the random number generation methods in @RISK.

We start by noting that a particular case of a simulation model in which the true value of the output is known is that in which one estimates the value of π (3.14159...) by the "dartboard" method:

- Draw random samples of x and y from uniform continuous distributions between minus one and plus one (these represent the final position that the dart lands within a square).
- For each draw, test whether the sum of the squares of the two variables is less than one: when centred at the origin, the circle is defined by x and y points, which satisfy $x^2 + y^2 = 1$, so this can be used to test whether the dart lands within the circular dartboard.
- Use the **RiskMean** function to report the frequency with which the test shows that the sum is within the circle, and multiply this by four. At the end of the simulation the frequency with which this is the case will be approximately $\pi/4$ (because a circle of radius one has an area equal to π, whereas the square drawn around that circle has area four).

The file Ch13.PiCalc.xlsx contains these calculations, with an example post-simulation shown in Figure 13.38.

In order to test the effectiveness of each sampling type (MC or LH, discussed earlier in the chapter), one could perform the same calculations several times with each, and measure the run time and accuracy:

- Run a simulation using each type, where each simulation uses the same seed value.
- Measure the run time of each simulation.
- Calculate the error compared with the true value.
- Repeat the above in an automatic fashion many times over, using a new random number seed each time, and compare the accuracy of the results against the time taken.

The file Ch13.PiCalc.2DResultsTable.xlsx contains the results of running 30 simulations for each method, and for various numbers of iterations. The summary results are shown in

Figure 13.39. (The same set of randomly chosen seeds was used for each sampling method, shown in the results tables in column B.) The summary table shows the average (over 30 simulations) of the error (in absolute terms) for the MC and the LH sampling types, for various numbers of iterations, as well as the total run time. (Such a comparison is, of course, still imperfect, as run time may be affected by other processes that were occurring on the computer at the same time.)

As mentioned in Chapter 6, as the number of iterations increases by multiples of four (i.e. from 25 to 100 to 400, and so on), the error should generally be half (the inverse square root law). This is broadly confirmed in this case: if one considers the error values of the LH method, comparing column G (6400 iterations) with column C (25 iterations), the error ratio is 0.012/0.184 (around 6.6%); this corresponds to halving the original error (0.184) four times over, i.e. to one-sixteenth of the original value.

From this particular experiment, one would conclude that LH generally reduces the statistical error by about 20% compared to MC at the expense of approximately 10% more computational time (the computational time in this case is dominated by the cases in which 6400 iterations were run). Note that one may state this in an alternative way: to reduce the error to 80% of the original value would generally require (using the inverse square root law) that the number of iterations be increased by approximately 56% (as $80\% = \frac{1}{\sqrt{1.5625}}$). Thus, one would conclude that it would be more efficient (from a time perspective) to use an LH method (requiring 10% extra time) than additional iterations of the MC method (requiring 56% extra time).

The above experiment involves repeated running of simulations in which each one required changing (compared to the immediately prior one) at least one of the seed values, or the number of iterations, or the sampling type. Of course, this could be done manually, but clearly it would be very cumbersome (and one would also have to measure the run time precisely). The XDK is therefore ideal for such an experiment.

The file Ch13.PiCalc.2D.WithDeveloperKit.xlsm contains the implementation of the above procedure using the XDK. (When using the XDK, one needs to create a reference to the @RISK add-in [under **Tools/References** within the Visual Basic Editor], in order to access the @RISK object model; this step is not shown here.) Figure 13.40 shows a screen clip of the file, from which one can see that buttons have been created so that the user can run subroutines for both the MC and LH sampling types, or run them individually.

The code used in the file is split across two (essentially identical) subroutines, one that runs the simulations in the case that Monte Carlo sampling was used and the other for Latin Hypercube.

Thus, the master routine to run both is:

```
Sub MRRunBoth()
 Call MREstPiMC
 Call MREstPiLH
End Sub
```

with the full code for the MC-related simulations being:

```
Sub MREstPiMC()
StartTime = Timer
```

```
With Risk
'Use Mersenne Twister Generator for all simulations
 With .Simulation.Settings
 .RandomNumberGenerator = RiskMersenneTwister
 End With
'Run Monte Carlo Sampling
 With .Simulation.Settings
  .SamplingType = RiskMonteCarlo
  End With
  'count how many to run
  With Range("MCGridStart").CurrentRegion
    NSims = .Columns.Count - 1
    NSeeds = .Rows.Count - 2
  End With
   For i = 1 To NSims
    For j = 1 To NSeeds
     With .Simulation.Settings
      .randomSeed = Range("MCGridStart").Offset(j, 0)
      .NumIterations = Range("MCGridStart").Offset(0, i)
     End With
     .Simulation.Start
     Range("MCGridStart").Offset(j, i) = Range("PiError")
     Next j
    Next i
End With 'end Risk
EndTime = Timer
Range("RunTimeMC") = EndTime - StartTime
End Sub
```

Analogous code applies for the LH-related simulations, with a simple adaptation of the line referring to the sampling type, from RiskMonteCarlo to RiskLatinHypecube, as well as adapting the ranges referred to for the data requirements and storage, i.e. the predefined Excel-named ranges MCGridStart (cell B13) and LHGridStart (cell B48).

From this example, some key syntax within the XDK should be visible, such as how to set the random number generator method, the sampling type, the number of iterations and how to run (start) a simulation. The VBA Timer function is used to measure the total elapsed time for the run of all simulations and all iterations for each method.

With respect to the comparison of MC with LH methods, one may argue that the above test unfairly favours LH sampling, as it is only conducted with respect to two uncertain variables (or dimensions): as stated earlier, the stratification process used by @RISK's LH sampling type is done as a one-dimensional process for each variable, so that its effect would be diminished in multi-variable models. In fact, it is possible to generalise the experiment to have more variables, so that the comparison would be fairer in more general cases where there are multiple sources of uncertainty. For example, instead of referring to a circular "dartboard" (in two dimensions), one could refer to a sphere (in three dimensions), whose volume is $VU_3 = \frac{4\pi}{3}$, where VU_3 refers to the volume of the unit sphere in three dimensions; the box

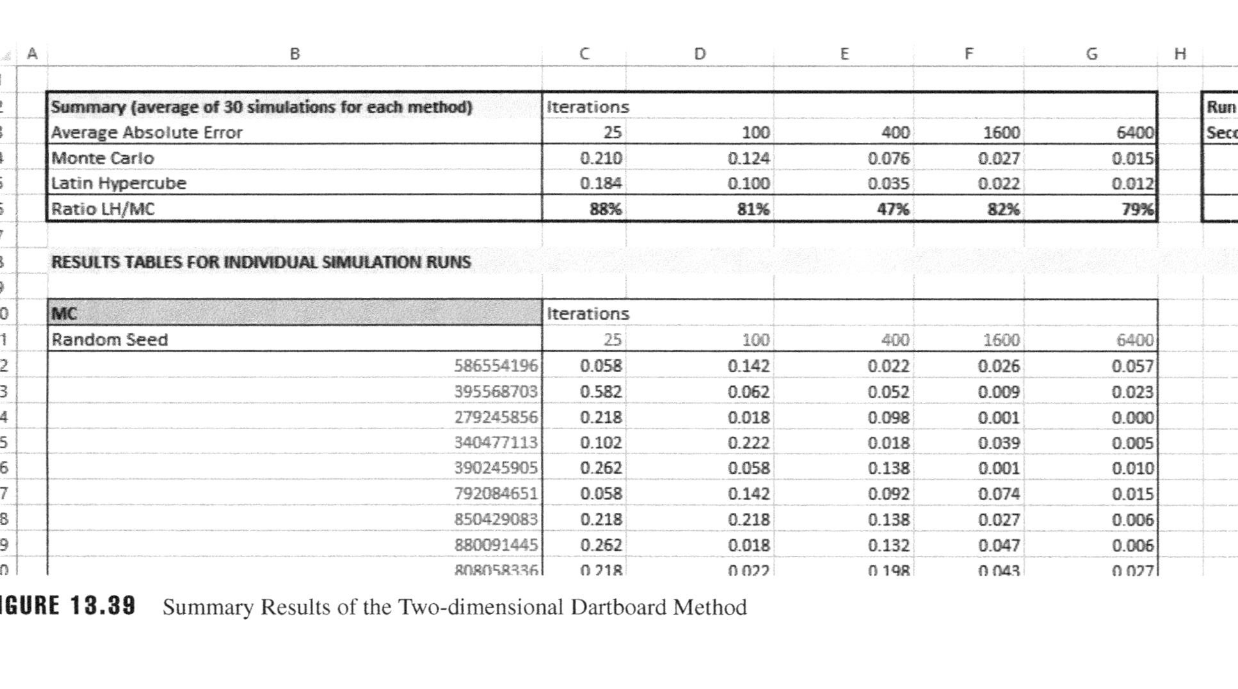

	A	B	C	D	E	F	G	H	I
1									
2		**Summary (average of 30 simulations for each method)**	Iterations						**Run Time**
3		Average Absolute Error	25	100	400	1600	6400		**Seconds**
4		Monte Carlo	0.210	0.124	0.076	0.027	0.015		474
5		Latin Hypercube	0.184	0.100	0.035	0.022	0.012		527
6		Ratio LH/MC	**88%**	**81%**	**47%**	**82%**	**79%**		**111%**
7									
8		**RESULTS TABLES FOR INDIVIDUAL SIMULATION RUNS**							
9									
10		**MC**	Iterations						
11		Random Seed	25	100	400	1600	6400		
12		586554196	0.058	0.142	0.022	0.026	0.057		
13		395568703	0.582	0.062	0.052	0.009	0.023		
14		279245856	0.218	0.018	0.098	0.001	0.000		
15		340477113	0.102	0.222	0.018	0.039	0.005		
16		390245905	0.262	0.058	0.138	0.001	0.010		
17		792084651	0.058	0.142	0.092	0.074	0.015		
18		850429083	0.218	0.218	0.138	0.027	0.006		
19		880091445	0.262	0.018	0.132	0.047	0.006		
20		808058336	0.218	0.022	0.198	0.043	0.027		

FIGURE 13.39 Summary Results of the Two-dimensional Dartboard Method

	A	B	C	D	E	F	G	H	I	J	K	L	M
1													
2			Sample	Square of Sample									
3		x1	-0.187	0.035	=C3*C3								
4		x2	-0.010	0.000	=C4*C4								
5		Total		0.035	=SUM(D3:D4)								
6													
7		In Hypersphere?		1	=IF(D5<=1,1,0)								
8		Frequency in Hypersphere		1	=RiskMean(D7)								
9		**Pi Est**		**4.000**	=4*(1*D8)*(1/1)								
10		True figure		3.142	=PI()								
11		**Abs Error (Est–Pi)**		**0.858**	=ABS(PiEst–D10)					Run PiEstMC and PiEstLH			
12													
13		**MC**	Iterations										
14		Random Seed	25	100	400	1600	6400						
15		586554196	0.058	0.142	0.022	0.026	0.057			Run PiEstMC			
16		395568703	0.582	0.062	0.052	0.009	0.023						
17		279245856	0.218	0.018	0.098	0.001	0.000						
18		340477113	0.102	0.222	0.018	0.039	0.005						
19		390245905	0.262	0.058	0.138	0.001	0.010						
20		792084651	0.058	0.142	0.092	0.074	0.015						
21		850429083	0.218	0.218	0.138	0.027	0.006						
22		880091445	0.262	0.018	0.132	0.047	0.006						
23		808058336	0.218	0.022	0.198	0.043	0.027						
24		196494888	0.262	0.182	0.012	0.047	0.002						
25		546144952	0.058	0.138	0.068	0.022	0.023						
26		451616512	0.378	0.418	0.138	0.086	0.014						
27		641038050	0.218	0.058	0.062	0.021	0.012						
28		383970322	0.218	0.058	0.032	0.009	0.028						
29		21390318	0.058	0.098	0.058	0.017	0.011						

FIGURE 13.40 Model Used to Run the Two-dimensional Dartboard Method

Number of Dimensions, *N*	Frequency that Dart is Within Sphere	Avg. Throws Needed Per Hit
2	78.5%	1.27
4	30.8%	3.24
6	8.1%	12.38
8	1.6%	63.07
10	0.2%	401.54

FIGURE 13.41 Expected Frequency of Hits with the Multi-dimensional Dartboard Method

surrounding this sphere would have volume 8 (i.e. 2^3), so that the "dart" should land within the sphere with a frequency of $f_3 = \frac{4\pi}{3.8}$, or $\frac{\pi}{6}$.

In fact, one can generalise this further. In four dimensions the volume of the unit sphere is given by $VU_4 = \frac{\pi^2}{6}$, whereas that of the surrounding box is 16, and in five dimensions, $VU_5 = \frac{8\pi^2}{15}$ (thus, the power term relating to π increases by one for every two increases in dimension). Thus, to test the effect of MC versus LH in multi-variable models, we shall work in even dimensions only, using the formula:

$$VU_N = \frac{\pi^n}{n!}$$

where N is the (even) number of variables (dimensions), $n = N/2$ (or $N = 2n$) and ! denotes the factorial.

The volume of the surrounding box is 2^N. Thus, the frequency, f, with which the dart lands within the hypersphere is given by:

$$f = \frac{\pi^n}{2^N n!}$$

Thus, where f_{est} is the estimated frequency (i.e. as measured in the simulation), the estimated value of π (π_{est}) would be given by $\pi_{\text{est}} = 4\left(f_{\text{est}} n!\right)^{\frac{1}{n}}$.

In principle, therefore, a multi-dimensional test is straightforward to conduct. In fact, the practical challenge is that the value of f rapidly becomes small as N ($2n$) becomes large, as shown in Figure 13.41. Thus, the number of iterations needed would become large.

The file Ch13.PiCalc.10D.WithDeveloperKit.2.xlsm contains the model necessary to test the above with 10 input variables (i.e. where the "dartboard" is a 10-dimensional hypersphere). Due to the low frequency of hitting the target (i.e. approximately 0.2%), the model has been run with 102,400 iterations (i.e. 6400 times 16), and for the same 30 seeds as in the above example. In addition, the summary statistic (absolute error and run time) is recorded for each simulation. Figure 13.42 shows a screen clip of the model, which is laid out slightly differently to the earlier example. To minimise the effect of any cases where the computer processor is tied up with some other activity, the simulation runs alternately between the MC and LH sampling type (rather than doing all the MC simulations followed by all the LH ones, as done above). Row 35 contains the header fields that are used to predefine most of the named ranges that are used within the code (which is shown below).

	A	B	C	D	E	F	G
1							
2			Sample	Square of Sample			
3		x1	-0.683	0.467	=C3*C3		
4		x2	0.593	0.352	=C4*C4		
5		x3	-0.772	0.595	=C5*C5		
6		x4	0.325	0.106	=C6*C6		
7		x5	0.671	0.450	=C7*C7		
8		x6	0.114	0.013	=C8*C8		
9		x7	-0.255	0.065	=C9*C9		
10		x8	-0.009	0.000	=C10*C10		
11		x9	-0.408	0.166	=C11*C11		
12		x10	-0.062	0.004	=C12*C12		
13		Total		2.218	=SUM(D3:D12)		
14							
15		In Hypersphere?		0	=IF(D13<=1,1,0)		
16		Frequency in Hypersphere		0	=RiskMean(D15)		
17		**Pi Est**		**0.000**	=4*(120*D16)^(1/5)		
18		True figure		3.142	=PI()		
19		**Abs Error (Est-Pi)**		**3.142**	=ABS(PiEst-D18)		
20							
21		Iterations	102400				
22							
23		**RESULTS SUMMARY**					
24		Average	0.0363	0.0362	68.36	68.67	
25		LH/MC		99.65%		100.45%	
26							
27		**Conditional Averages**					
28		Cut Off points for times			60	60	
29		No. of sets			22	23	
30		Averages	0.0383	0.0373	51.011	51.323	
31		LH/MC		97.26%		100.61%	
32							
33							
34		**RESULTS DETAIL**	**Error**		**Run Time**		
35		Random Seed Header	**MC**	**LH**	**MC**	**LH**	
36		586554136	0.054	0.043	50.2	50.2	
37		395568703	0.025	0.007	50.7	51.3	
38		279245856	0.012	0.000	52.0	51.5	
39		340477113	0.033	0.023	51.5	51.9	

FIGURE 13.42 Summary Results of the 10-dimensional Dartboard Method

```
Sub MRRunBoth()
With Risk
 'Use Mersenne Twister Generator for all simulations, and fix num-
ber of iterations
  With .Simulation.Settings
  .RandomNumberGenerator = RiskMersenneTwister
  .NumIterations = Range("NIterations").Value
  End With
 'Initiate runtime tracking variable
  RunTime = 0
 'count how many simulations to run, according to seed list
  With Range("SeedListHeader").CurrentRegion
   NSeeds = .Rows.Count - 2
  End With
```

```
 For i = 1 To NSeeds ' Run simulation for each sampling type
  With .Simulation.Settings
    .randomSeed = Range("SeedListHeader").Offset(i, 0)
  End With
 '############# DO MC SAMPLING METHOD
 'Set sampling to Monte Carlo
  With .Simulation.Settings
   .SamplingType = RiskMonteCarlo
  End With
 ' Measure time and run simulation, and record error
  StartTime = Timer
  .Simulation.Start
  EndTime = Timer
  RunTime = EndTime - StartTime
  Range("ErrorHeaderMC").Offset(i, 0) = Range("PiError")
  Range("RunTimeHeaderMC").Offset(i, 0) = RunTime
 '############# DO LH SAMPLING METHOD
  With .Simulation.Settings
   .SamplingType = RiskLatinHypercube
  End With
 ' Measure time and run simulation, and record error
  StartTime = Timer
  .Simulation.Start
  EndTime = Timer
  RunTime = EndTime - StartTime
  Range("ErrorHeaderLH").Offset(i, 0) = Range("PiError")
  Range("RunTimeHeaderLH").Offset(i, 0) = RunTime
 Next i 'next seed value
End With 'Risk
End Sub
```

In terms of aggregate results, we can note (row 24 and row 25) that there is essentially no difference in accuracy, or average run time requirements, between the approaches. A closer inspection of the data sets reveals that most run times are around 50 seconds, but some are significantly higher; row 30 and row 31 contain the averages that apply when run times above 60 seconds are excluded (perhaps other processes were running in the background during such runs); however, doing so does not change the general picture.

The results would seem to suggest that there is little to choose between the sampling types, with one being as good as the other. Note that the structure of this test arguably favours MC methods slightly, as the model used is small (in terms of the number of calculations that are performed once the random samples are generated); in a larger model, the proportion of time spent generating random numbers (compared to the total run time including recalculating the model) would be less than in a small model, and so the total MC computational time would be closer to that of LH, even as the LH accuracy may be marginally better.

As a conclusion, it would seem that LH is a marginally superior method when there are small numbers of model variables (fewer than about 10), whereas for larger numbers of variables, there is little difference between the methods. Interested readers (with sufficient time) can, of course, test these issues for themselves, as the basic infrastructure to do so is provided within the model (for example, more iterations and simulations with different seed values could be run, or the number of dimensions increased).

13.5.4 Using the XDK to Generate Reports of Simulation Data

Another powerful use of the XDK is to generate reports or other aspects of simulation data, as shown in the following example.

The file Ch13.XDK.PreGenerateCorrelRands.xlsm contains code that would allow one to generate a set of correlated random numbers and store their values in a data worksheet. One application of this may be if one needs to work with "frozen" random numbers (as covered earlier in the chapter and in the text), if other procedures need to be run at each iteration. In such cases, one could pregenerate all the numbers and then use them in sequence as fixed numbers in a subsequent simulation. Figure 13.43 shows an example. Row 4 contains five random variables (PERT distributions) that are correlated in accordance with the correlation matrix shown. The button runs the macro GenerateData that instructs the XDK to run a simulation (which generates the correlated samples) and then to generate a report of the data in Excel (in order to set the required sample size, the user inputs the value in the cell named NSamples, containing the value 20 in the screen clip); the code is shown below.

```
Sub GenerateData()
With Risk
'Ensure that sheet containing the data gets writ-
ten into the same workbook
 With .ApplicationSettings
  .ReportPlacement = RiskActiveWorkbook
  .ReportOverwriteExisting = True
 End With
 With .Simulation.Settings
  .NumIterations = Range("NSamples").Value
 End With
 .Simulation.Start
 .GenerateExcelReports RiskSimulationReportData
End With
End Sub
```

The XDK has many other options that the interested reader can further explore by referring to the **Help** menu and the manual associated with it.

13.6 ADDITIONAL IN-BUILT APPLICATIONS AND FEATURES: AN INTRODUCTION

This section provides an overview of some other application areas and features that are built into the @RISK software.

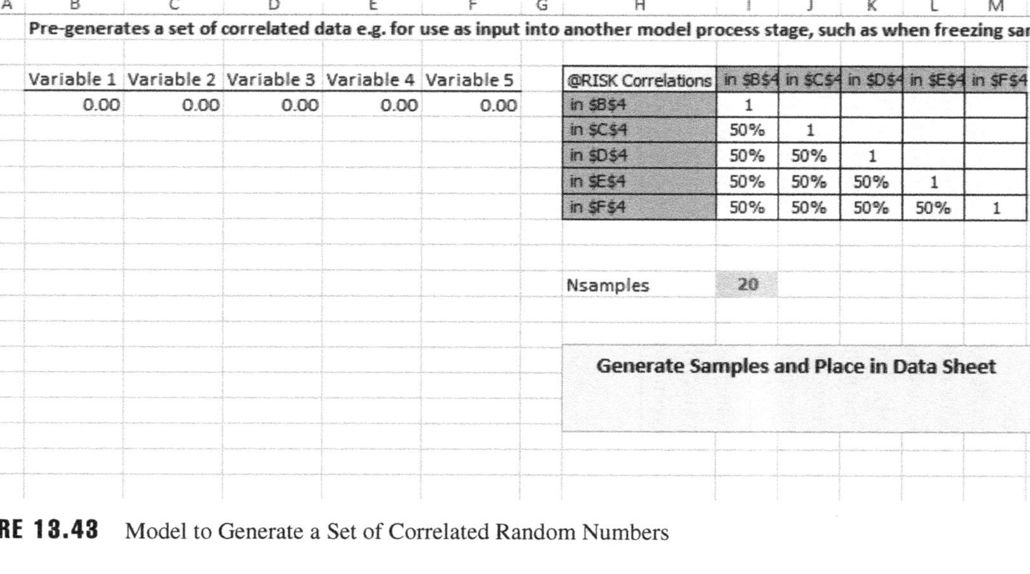

FIGURE 13.43 Model to Generate a Set of Correlated Random Numbers

13.6.1 Optimisation

As mentioned in various places in this text, there is a close link between optimisation and risk modelling:

- Optimisation modelling arises in the case where some of a model's inputs are choice variables (such as the launch dates that one may choose to launch a project, or the percentage participation that one may wish to take in an asset or business project).
- Risk modelling arises when a model has inputs whose values are uncertain (and may be controllable only by adjusting the context in which one operates), as discussed throughout this book.

Many real-life situations may contain both optimisation and uncertainty characteristics. In many cases, it can be challenging to create a single model that is valid for all possible cases; for example, so that the uncertainty profile is correctly captured for whatever selection of choice variables (decisions) is made. For this reason, heuristic (pragmatic) techniques are often used, and they can be reasonably accurate (partly due to the flat nature of any optimisation curve around its optimal point, as mentioned in Chapter 6).

Nevertheless, on occasion, one can build models whose inputs consist of both choice and uncertain variables, and where the uncertainty profile is accurately captured for all combinations of choice variables. This is particularly applicable when a model consists of summing a set of independent items or projects, as is the case in many portfolio situations (where the total portfolio output is simply the sum of the elements). Thus, if each project in the portfolio is independent, aspects of the portfolio construction can be considered to be an optimisation problem.

An example was provided in Chapter 4, where we presented a set of independent projects and considered the optimisation of their launch dates (using **Solver**). Such a solution could also have been searched for using Palisade's **Evolver** tool, which is part of the **DecisionTools Suite**, of which @RISK is also a part.

On the other hand, when aspects of each project are uncertain (such as the initial investment required or the future cash flow profile), then the optimisation has to take this into account. In standard financial portfolio theory, many of the associated optimisation algorithms make use of the underlying mathematics embedded in a situation. However, in the most general case, one may have to repeatedly create a set of trial values to act as a test of the optimal solution, run a simulation to see the uncertainty profile that would result for this set of trial assumptions and repeat this for other sets of trial values. Of course, the choice of which solution is optimal will depend on the user defining appropriate criteria, which relate to statistics of the distribution of output; for example, one may wish to find the solution that maximises the average or minimises the variability (standard deviation) of some project metric (such as cash flow in a particular year, or net present value).

The process of generating sets of trial values in an automated way, and of running a simulation for each set of trial values, is facilitated by the use of the **RiskOptimizer** tool that is embedded within @RISK Industrial. The trial values generated are not totally random, but partly use information about previous trial solutions to generate others, and therefore are more efficient than simply running many simulations to do so (i.e. in theory, one could generate trial values by one random sampling process, fix them and then run a full simulation, before moving to a new set of randomly generated trial values).

The tool is fairly straightforward to use, once the model has been created in a valid way (for example, so that project launch dates can be changed, if these items are to be optimised, as discussed in the example in Chapter 4), the optimisation criteria are set and constraints defined. In this context, as mentioned earlier in the text, it can be important to try to understand (at an intuitive level) what effect any uncertainty would have on the final optimal solution, as there is a potential to create unnecessary complexity otherwise. For example, the optimal route to travel across a town may be the same independently of whether one considers the travel time on each segment to be fixed or whether one considers it to be uncertain. On the other hand, this conclusion can be changed by risk tolerances and/or non-symmetry of the uncertainties, as well as non-linearities in the modelling situation: for example, for the sake of always arriving on time, one may decide to cycle to work, even though, on average, it takes longer than taking the train, because in some cases the train journey is subject to severe disruption. In these cases, optimisation tools are powerful methods, as pragmatic techniques may be insufficient.

13.6.2 Fitting Distributions and Time Series to Data

@RISK has two main categories of fitting capabilities:

- Distribution fitting.
- Time series fitting.

Each of these is fairly straightforward from the perspective of the software mechanics, although the underlying theory and concepts concerning the various fitting procedures and criteria are more complex, and are beyond the scope of this text. Note that fitting procedures take into account the full set of data, unlike some of the approaches to parameter matching that were discussed in Chapter 9.

In the following, we simply make several remarks that relate most directly to modelling issues.

When using distribution fitting, one (implicitly) assumes that data points are independent of each other, and are all random samples drawn from the same distribution with the same parameters. The procedure then finds, for each distribution tried, the parameters of that distribution that would best fit the data, before ranking the fits (of the best fitting) of these distributions. As mentioned in Chapter 9, when using fitting as a distribution selection tool, in practice one may sometimes simply use the best fitting distribution, whereas for others, one may believe that it is appropriate to combine the fitting process with other aspects of distribution selection (such as the use of scientific or conceptual methods). One is also implicitly assuming that the underlying distribution that generates the data set is one of those available in the fitting procedure (so, for example, one would not directly find a reasonable fit to compound processes). Finally, as noted in Chapter 9, any procedure based on data implicitly assumes the integrity and validity of the data.

The **Time Series** fitting procedures apply to a set of data points that have occurred in time (and that are not independent of each other, in the sense that the order in which they occurred is necessary to take into account the fit, unlike for simple distribution fitting). One can then find the best fitting times series, for a single series, or use the **Batch Fit** when data from several series are available; if a correlation is found between them, the fitting tool can also generate correlated time series.

Note that, in general, the creation of many time series processes does not explicitly require @RISK's time series functionality, as the examples discussed in Chapter 11 show. However, the ability to find (through fitting) the appropriate time series to create is an important feature of the software.

In the case that one wishes to create a time series directly, this can be done in a similar way to Chapter 11, as discussed below.

The file Ch13.TimeSeries.MA1.xlsx contains an example of the first-order moving average function that was also implemented using Excel in Chapter 11. These functions are array functions; at the time of writing they are not allowed to be set directly as simulation outputs; one can instead create a cell reference to them, and set this cell as an output; see Figure 13.44.

13.6.3 MS Project Integration

As discussed earlier in the text, project schedules (and integrated cost analysis) can be built in Excel, provided that the project structure is sufficiently simple; indeed, a simulation of the schedule can be done in such a case (see the example in Chapter 4).

However, very often, project structures are such that a change in an input assumption (such as the length of a task duration) would alter the critical path in the project, perhaps by changing the branching structure. For example, a failure at the product testing stage may mean that one needs to branch to a product redesign task. In such cases, tools such as Microsoft Project can be very useful, as they are specifically designed to capture such linkages.

@RISK's **Project** capability allows a user who has both **MS Project** and @RISK to work with files that are essentially linked; the .mpp file can be "imported" so that it appears in Excel and the task durations can be changed (in Excel), with the project schedule recalculating in MS Project and then updating in Excel as well; both applications are open simultaneously.

Note that this tool could be used to create an integrated cost-schedule model in Excel, so that task durations (or costs) could be changed, or sensitivity analysis of the items run, even where none of @RISK's risk or simulation capability was used. A simulation can, of course, also be run; typically the end date of a project or a subtask (as well as some cost estimates) would be set as outputs and simulated, distributions of each calculated and scatter plots (e.g. of cost and schedule) shown, as demonstrated in Chapter 4.

13.6.4 Other Features

As stated earlier, this text has not tried to cover all aspects of @RISK comprehensively. Readers wishing to know more can refer to the **Help** menu within the software, and the various files, other utilities and resources that are provided with it, as well as the Palisade website and its associated resources.

13.7 BENEFITS OF @RISK OVER EXCEL/VBA APPROACHES: A BRIEF SUMMARY

The following is a brief summary of some key points relating to the benefits of using @RISK versus (the cost-free and ubiquitous) Excel/VBA. The list is not intended to be totally exhaustive, but to highlight many of the key points made at various places in the text:

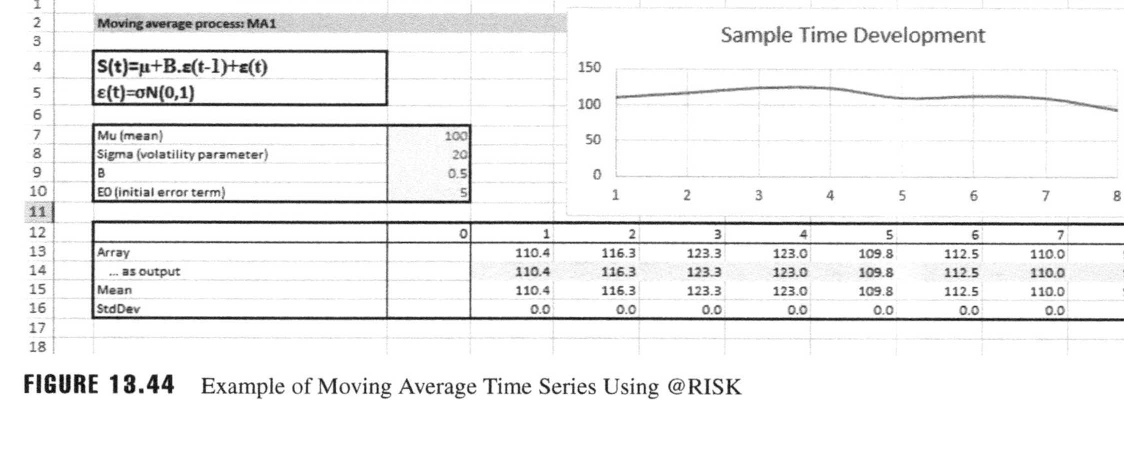

Moving average process: MA1
S(t)=μ+B.ε(t-1)+ε(t)
ε(t)=σN(0,1)
Mu (mean) 100
Sigma (volatility parameter) 20
B 0.5
E0 (initial error term) 5
Sample Time Development
150
100
50
0
1 2 3 4 5 6 7 8
0 1 2 3 4 5 6 7 8
Array 110.4 116.3 123.3 123.0 109.8 112.5 110.0 94.5 {=RiskMA1(C7,C8,C9,C10)}
... as output 110.4 116.3 123.3 123.0 109.8 112.5 110.0 94.5 =RiskOutput(,B14,8)+K13
Mean 110.4 116.3 123.3 123.0 109.8 112.5 110.0 94.5 =RiskMean(K13)
StdDev 0.0 0.0 0.0 0.0 0.0 0.0 0.0 0.0 =RiskStdDev(K13)

FIGURE 13.44 Example of Moving Average Time Series Using @RISK

- The use of @RISK facilitates many aspects of the processes of building risk models and communicating their content, concepts and results. It generally makes key steps easier, quicker, more transparent and more robust, especially due to the graphics capabilities and statistical tools, as well as the ease of creating relationships of sampling dependencies.
- There is a large set of distributions and parameters available, and the percentile (alternate) parameter form is available for most distributions. Some special distributions would also be cumbersome to replicate with Excel/VBA approaches.
- Many aspects of the simulation and random number selection are easy to control, including the ability to repeat a simulation exactly, to conduct multiple simulations, to select the random number generation algorithms and the sampling type. In addition, it is straightforward to embed within the simulation procedures that need to be run at each iteration.
- There are tools to assist in the auditing of models, and to conduct enhanced results analysis.
- Additional functionality includes the ability to fit distributions and time series to data, to conduct optimisation under uncertainty and to integrate Microsoft Project with Excel. Clearly, much of this functionality would (at best) be extremely complex and time-consuming to implement in Excel/VBA, and attempting to do so would likely detract from the core task of providing value-added decision support.
- Models can generally be structured without particular consideration given to where risk distributions are placed within them, or to whether their ranges need to be contiguous to each other.
- There is generally no VBA coding required (although basic VBA can be useful on occasion, even where not strictly necessary).
- It is a tried and tested application, whereas bespoke-written VBA code is more likely to contain coding errors or not be robust.

In summary, more time can be focused on generation of insights, solutions and recommendations, and creating value-added in a business and organisational context.

Index

Printed and bound by CPI Group (UK) Ltd, Croydon, CR0 4YY

23/04/2025

14660969-0003